THE
METHODIST HYMNAL

THE METHODIST HYMNAL

OFFICIAL HYMNAL OF THE METHODIST CHURCH

THE METHODIST PUBLISHING HOUSE
NASHVILLE, TENNESSEE

SET UP, PRINTED, AND BOUND BY THE PARTHENON PRESS, AT NASHVILLE, TENNESSEE, UNITED STATES OF AMERICA.

Scripture quotations unless otherwise noted are from the Revised Standard Version of the Bible, copyright 1946 and 1952 by the Division of Christian Education, National Council of Churches, and are used by permission.

Acknowledgment is made to the following who have granted permission for the use of copyrighted material in the Aids to Worship:

The Committee on Public Worship and Aids to Devotion of the General Assembly of the Church of Scotland for prayers from *Prayers for the Christian Year* (No. 678) and *The Book of Common Order* (Nos. 746, 754).

Epworth Press for prayers from *Divine Worship* (Nos. 726, 756).

The Pilgrim Press for prayer from *Prayers of the Social Awakening* by Walter Rauschenbusch (No. 743).

Westminster Press for prayer by Henry van Dyke from *The Book of Common Worship;* revised; copyright 1932, The Board of Christian Education of the Presbyterian Church, U.S.A.; copyright 1960; used by permission (No. 745).

Acknowledgment is also made to Dr. Fred Gealy for permission to reprint his prayers (Nos. 719-722).

Preface

John Wesley's *A Collection of Psalms and Hymns,* published at Charlestown, South Carolina, in 1737, was one of the first hymnals in the English language prepared for use in public worship. Wesley's own concern for the publishing and singing of hymns continued until his death. American Methodists have perpetuated the Wesleyan concern by compiling new hymnals in each succeeding generation.

In 1960 the General Conference of The Methodist Church authorized the Commission on Worship to appoint a committee to prepare a revised edition of the hymnal. The Hymnal Committee was duly appointed and in cooperation with laymen, pastors, musicians, hymnologists, bishops, and staff members of various boards and agencies of our church prepared its report for the General Conference of 1964, meeting in Pittsburgh. The conference unanimously adopted the report. The hymnal is respectfully submitted to Methodism.

In the present hymnal, the Hymnal Committee desires to provide all Methodists with adequate aids to the worship of almighty God. In brief, this revision attempts to do three things: (1) to draw upon the rich heritage of ecumenical hymnody, including our own Wesleyan traditions; (2) to bring to our people for use in worship a hymnal of sufficient diversity to allow for the variety of religious experiences, thus meeting the needs of the present age; and (3) to reach into the future with a hymnal that will serve the religious needs of the next generation. We attempt to do for our generation what our predecessors sought to do for theirs: *to provide a hymnal that makes it possible for us to sing our common faith in Christ as Lord and Savior.*

John Wesley, in his preface to *A Collection of Hymns for the Use of the People Called Methodists,* 1780, expressed a concern that a hymnal should "contain all the important truths of our most holy religion, whether speculative or practical," that the hymns should not be "carelessly jumbled together," but that they should be "carefully ranged under proper heads, according to the experience of real Christians."

The Hymnal Committee believes (1) that each hymn in this new hymnal expresses some facet of essential truth of the Christian faith; (2) that the classification and indexing of hymns have simplified the hymnal for ready use in any church and for a wide variety of circumstances; (3) that "real Christians" (to use Wesley's words) will find hymns and psalms with which they can sing of their Christian experience, recalling whence they came, how they have been lifted up, and whither they are tending.

A modern hymnal, in addition to hymns, properly includes a psalter, other acts of praise, prayers and other aids to worship, the ritual of the church, and service music. The committee commends these materials for both private and corporate use.

Finally, this hymnal is dedicated to all who earnestly desire redemption and who long for life in Christ. It is the committee's prayer that the hymnal will find joyful and extensive use throughout all Methodism as together we unite in the worship and service of God through Jesus Christ our Lord.

THE HYMNAL COMMITTEE

Edwin E. Voigt, Chairman
Paul Burt, Secretary
Nolan B. Harmon, Chairman, subcommittee on Texts
Earl E. Harper, Chairman, Executive-editorial subcommittee
Will Hildebrand, Chairman, subcommittee on Psalter and Ritual
Austin C. Lovelace, Chairman, subcommittee on Tunes
Emory Stevens Bucke, Book Editor
Lovick Pierce, Publisher
Carlton R. Young, Editor

Leon M. Adkins
Warren A. Bugbee
Henry M. Bullock
William R. Cannon
Virgil Y. C. Eady
Eugene M. Frank
Marvin A. Franklin
John O. Gross
J. Robert Hammond
Charles S. Hempstead
James R. Houghton
Gerald H. Kennedy
J. deKoven Killingsworth
John Wesley Lord
Noah W. Moore, Jr.
Joseph D. Quillian, Jr.
Richard C. Raines
Daniel L. Ridout
Mrs. Floyd W. Rigg
Amos A. Thornburg

Consultants to the Hymnal Committee

Pat Beaird
V. Earle Copes
Philip R. Dietterich
William F. Dunkle, Jr.
Fred D. Gealy
Alfred B. Haas
Cecil D. Jones
Cecil E. Lapo
Gerald O. McCulloh
J. Edward Moyer
William C. Rice
Bliss Wiant

Directions for Singing

I. Learn these tunes before you learn any others; afterwards learn as many as you please.

II. Sing them exactly as they are printed here, without altering or mending them at all; and if you have learned to sing them otherwise, unlearn it as soon as you can.

III. Sing all. See that you join with the congregation as frequently as you can. Let not a slight degree of weakness or weariness hinder you. If it is a cross to you, take it up, and you will find it a blessing.

IV. Sing lustily and with a good courage. Beware of singing as if you were half dead, or half asleep; but lift up your voice with strength. Be no more afraid of your voice now, nor more ashamed of its being heard, than when you sung the songs of Satan.

V. Sing modestly. Do not bawl, so as to be heard above or distinct from the rest of the congregation, that you may not destroy the harmony; but strive to unite your voices together, so as to make one clear melodious sound.

VI. Sing in time. Whatever time is sung be sure to keep with it. Do not run before nor stay behind it; but attend close to the leading voices, and move therewith as exactly as you can; and take care not to sing too slow. This drawling way naturally steals on all who are lazy; and it is high time to drive it out from us, and sing all our tunes just as quick as we did at first.

VII. Above all sing spiritually. Have an eye to God in every word you sing. Aim at pleasing him more than yourself, or any other creature. In order to do this attend strictly to the sense of what you sing, and see that your heart is not carried away with the sound, but offered to God continually; so shall your singing be such as the Lord will approve here, and reward you when he cometh in the clouds of heaven.

From John Wesley's preface to *Sacred Melody,* 1761

The Order of Worship

COMPLETE FORM

† *Let the people be in silent meditation and prayer upon entering the sanctuary. Let the service of worship begin at the time appointed.*

† *Scripture sentences, alternate prayers, affirmations of faith, and benedictions may be found in* The Book of Worship *and* The Methodist Hymnal.

† *At the end of all prayers the people shall say Amen.*

PRELUDE

SCRIPTURE SENTENCES, OR CALL TO WORSHIP † *To be said or sung.*

HYMN † *The people standing.*

† *If a processional, the hymn may precede the Scripture sentences.*

INVOCATION † *By the minister, the people standing.*

Almighty God, from whom every good prayer cometh, and who pourest out on all who desire it, the spirit of grace and supplication: Deliver us, when we draw nigh to thee, from coldness of heart and wanderings of mind, that with steadfast thoughts and kindled affections, we may worship thee in spirit and in truth; through Jesus Christ our Lord. **Amen.**

CALL TO CONFESSION † *By the minister, the people standing.*

Dearly beloved, the Scriptures move us to acknowledge and confess our sins before almighty God, our heavenly Father, with a humble, lowly, penitent, and obedient heart, to the end that we may obtain forgiveness by his infinite goodness and mercy. Wherefore I pray and beseech you, as many as are here present, to accompany me with a pure heart and humble voice, unto the throne of heavenly grace.

† *Or the minister may say,*

Let us confess our sins to almighty God.

GENERAL CONFESSION † *To be said by all, the people seated and bowed, or kneeling.*

Almighty and most merciful Father, we have erred and strayed from thy ways like lost sheep. We have followed too much the devices and desires of our own hearts. We have offended against thy holy

laws. We have left undone those things which we ought to have done, and we have done those things which we ought not to have done. But thou, O Lord, have mercy upon us. Spare thou those, O God, who confess their faults. Restore thou those who are penitent, according to thy promises declared unto mankind in Christ Jesus our Lord. And grant, O most merciful Father, for his sake, that we may hereafter live a godly, righteous, and sober life, to the glory of thy holy name. Amen.

PRAYER FOR PARDON OR WORDS OF ASSURANCE † *By the minister.*

O Lord, we beseech thee, absolve thy people from their offenses, that through thy bountiful goodness, we may be delivered from the bonds of those sins which by our frailty we have committed. Grant this, O heavenly Father, for the sake of Jesus Christ, our blessed Lord and Savior. **Amen.**

THE LORD'S PRAYER † *To be said by all.*

Our Father, who art in heaven, hallowed be thy name. Thy kingdom come, thy will be done on earth as it is in heaven. Give us this day our daily bread. And forgive us our trespasses, as we forgive those who trespass against us. And lead us not into temptation, but deliver us from evil. For thine is the kingdom, and the power, and the glory, forever. Amen.

Minister: O Lord, open thou our lips.

People: **And our mouth shall show forth thy praise.**

Minister: Praise ye the Lord.

People: **The Lord's name be praised.**

PSALTER OR OTHER ACT OF PRAISE † *To be read responsively or in unison, the people standing; then shall be said or sung,*

Glory be to the Father, and to the Son, and to the Holy Ghost; as it was in the beginning, is now and ever shall be, world without end. Amen.

ANTHEM

THE SCRIPTURE LESSONS † *Here shall be read two lessons, one from the Old Testament, and one from the Epistles or Gospels.*

AFFIRMATION OF FAITH † *The people standing; then may be sung a doxology.*

Minister: The Lord be with you.

People: **And with thy spirit.**

Minister: Let us pray.

COLLECT † *By the minister, or the minister and people, the people seated and bowed, or kneeling.*

O Lord, our heavenly Father, almighty and everlasting God, who hast safely brought us to the beginning of this day: Defend us in the same with thy mighty power; and grant that this day we fall into no sin, neither run into any kind of danger, but that all our doings may be ordered by thy governance, to do always that which is righteous in thy sight; through Jesus Christ our Lord. **Amen.**

PASTORAL PRAYER

OFFERTORY

† *Here parish notices may be given.*

† *The minister may read Scripture sentences before the offering is received. An anthem may be sung during the receiving of the offering. Following the presentation of the offering a prayer of dedication may be said or sung.*

† *At the discretion of the minister the offertory and prayers may follow the sermon.*

HYMN † *The people standing.*

THE SERMON

INVITATION TO CHRISTIAN DISCIPLESHIP

HYMN † *The people standing. This may be a recessional hymn.*

BENEDICTION † *The people may be seated for silent prayer.*

POSTLUDE

The Order of Worship

BRIEF FORM

† *Let the people be in silent meditation and prayer upon entering the sanctuary. Let the service of worship begin at the time appointed.*

† *At the end of all prayers the people shall say Amen.*

PRELUDE

SCRIPTURE SENTENCES, OR CALL TO WORSHIP † *To be said or sung.*

HYMN † *The people standing.*

PRAYERS † *Here the minister may use an invocation or collect and prayers of confession and the Lord's Prayer.*

PSALTER OR OTHER ACT OF PRAISE † *To be read responsively or in unison, the people standing; then shall be said or sung the* Gloria Patri.

ANTHEM

THE SCRIPTURE LESSONS

AFFIRMATION OF FAITH † *The people standing; then may be sung a doxology.*

PASTORAL PRAYER

OFFERTORY

† *Here parish notices may be given.*

† *The minister may read Scripture sentences before the offering is received. An anthem may be sung during the receiving of the offering. Following the presentation of the offering a prayer of dedication may be said or sung.*

† *At the discretion of the minister the offertory and prayers may follow the sermon.*

HYMN † *The people standing.*

THE SERMON

INVITATION TO CHRISTIAN DISCIPLESHIP

HYMN † *The people standing.*

BENEDICTION † *The people may be seated for silent prayer.*

POSTLUDE

Contents

HYMNS

The Gospel and Christian Experience 1-291
- The Praise of God 1-70
- The Gospel of Jesus Christ 71-130
- The Holy Spirit 131-138
- The Christian Life 139-291

The Church 292-352
- Nature and Mission 292-299
- Unity and Fellowship 300-311
- Baptism 312
- The Lord's Supper 313-332
- Marriage 333-334
- The Ministry 335-342
- Dedications 343-352

The Christian Year 353-486
- Advent Season 353-372
- Christmastide 373-396
- Epiphany Season 397-411
- Lenten Season 412-436
- Eastertide 437-458
- Pentecost Season 459-467
- Kingdomtide 468-486

Times, Seasons, Occasions 487-552
- The Lord's Day 487-489
- Morning and Evening 490-506
- Seasonal Hymns 507-525
- Anniversaries 526-537
- Travel 538-541
- City, Nation, World 542-552

ACTS OF PRAISE

The Psalter 554-606

Canticles and Other Acts of Praise 607-661

Canticles with Music 662-673
Instructions on Chanting 662

AIDS FOR THE ORDERING OF WORSHIP
The Christian Year 674-714
A Lectionary for Public Worship 674
A Table for Easter Day 675
Advent Season 676-681
Christmastide 682-685
Epiphany Season 686-690
Lenten Season 691-694
Eastertide 695-701
Pentecost Season 702-707
Kingdomtide 708-714

General Aids to Worship 715-772
Prayers for Use on Entering the Church 715-718
Prayers with the Choir 719-722
Prayers of Confession 723-727
Words of Assurance 728-734
Prayers for Pardon and Forgiveness 735-737
Affirmations of Faith 738-741
Prayers of Petition and Intercession 742-746
Offertory Sentences and Prayers 747-757
Ascriptions of Glory 758-762
Benedictions 763-767
Prayers for Use Before Leaving the Church 768-772

Service Music for the Order of Worship 773-827
Opening Sentences 773-791
Glory Be to the Father 792-794
Before Scripture 795-798
After Scripture 799-801
Before Prayer 802-804
Versicles Before Prayer 805-806
Offering 807-808
Doxologies 809-812
Closing 813-815
Amens 816-825
Other Service Music 826-827

THE RITUAL

The Order of Worship, Complete Form ix
The Order of Worship, Brief Form xii
The Order for the Administration of the Sacrament of Baptism 828
The Order for Confirmation and Reception into the Church 829
The Order for the Administration of the Sacrament of the Lord's Supper or Holy Communion 830
Proper Prefaces 831
A Brief Form of the Order for the Administration of the Sacrament of the Lord's Supper or Holy Communion 832
Other Music for Holy Communion 833-843

INDEXES

Index of First Lines and Titles of Acts of Praise and Aids to Worship 844
Index of Canticles with Music, Service Music, and Communion Music 845
Index of Scripture of the Psalter, Canticles, and Other Aids to Worship 846
Index of Scripture References of Hymns 847
Index of Composers, Authors, and Sources 848
Index of Tune Names 849
Metrical Index 850
Topical Index 851
Index of Hymns by Classification 852
Index of First Lines and Common Titles of Hymns 853

HYMNS

THE GOSPEL AND CHRISTIAN EXPERIENCE

1

O For a Thousand Tongues to Sing

AZMON CM
CARL G. GLÄSER, 1784-1829
Arr. by LOWELL MASON, 1792-1872

CHARLES WESLEY, 1707-1788

1. O for a thou - sand tongues to sing My
2. My gra - cious Mas - ter and my God, As -
3. Je - sus! the name that charms our fears, That
4. He breaks the power of can - celed sin, He
5. He speaks, and listen - ing to his voice, New
6. Hear him, ye deaf; his praise, ye dumb, Your
great Re - deem - er's praise, The glo - ries of my
sist me to pro - claim, To spread thro' all the
bids our sor - rows cease, 'Tis mu - sic in the
sets the pris - oner free; His blood can make the
life the dead re - ceive; The mourn - ful, bro - ken
loos-ened tongues em - ploy; Ye blind, be - hold your
God and King, The tri-umphs of his grace!
earth a - broad The hon - ors of thy name.
sin - ners' ears, 'Tis life, and health, and peace.
foul - est clean; His blood a - vailed for me.
hearts re - joice; The hum - ble poor, be - lieve.
Sav - ior come; And leap, ye lame, for joy. A - men.

Alternate tune: RICHMOND

Angel Voices, Ever Singing

ANGEL VOICES 85.85.843.
ARTHUR S. SULLIVAN, 1842-1900
Adapt. by A. C. L.

FRANCIS POTT, 1832-1909

Unison
1. An - gel voic - es, ev - er sing - ing Round thy throne of light,
2. Thou who art be - yond the far - thest Mor - tal eye can scan,
3. Yea, we know that thou re - joic - est O'er each work of thine;
4. Here, great God, to - day we of - fer Of thine own to thee;
5. Hon - or, glo - ry, might, and mer - it Thine shall ev - er be,
An - gel harps for - ev - er ring - ing, Rest not day nor night;
Can it be that thou re - gard - est Songs of sin - ful man?
Thou didst ears and hands and voic - es For thy praise de - sign;
And for thine ac - cept - ance prof - fer, All un - wor - thi - ly,
Fa - ther, Son, and Ho - ly Spir - it, Bless - ed Trin - i - ty:
Thou - sands on - ly live to bless thee, And con - fess thee Lord of might.
Can we feel that thou art near us And wilt hear us? Yea, we can.
Crafts - man's art and mu - sic's mea - sure For thy plea - sure All com - bine.
Hearts and minds, and hands and voic - es, In our choic - est Mel - o - dy.
Of the best that thou hast giv - en, Earth and heav - en Ren - der thee. A - men.

Come, Thou Almighty King

ANONYMOUS

ITALIAN HYMN 664.6664.
FELICE DE GIARDINI, 1716-1796

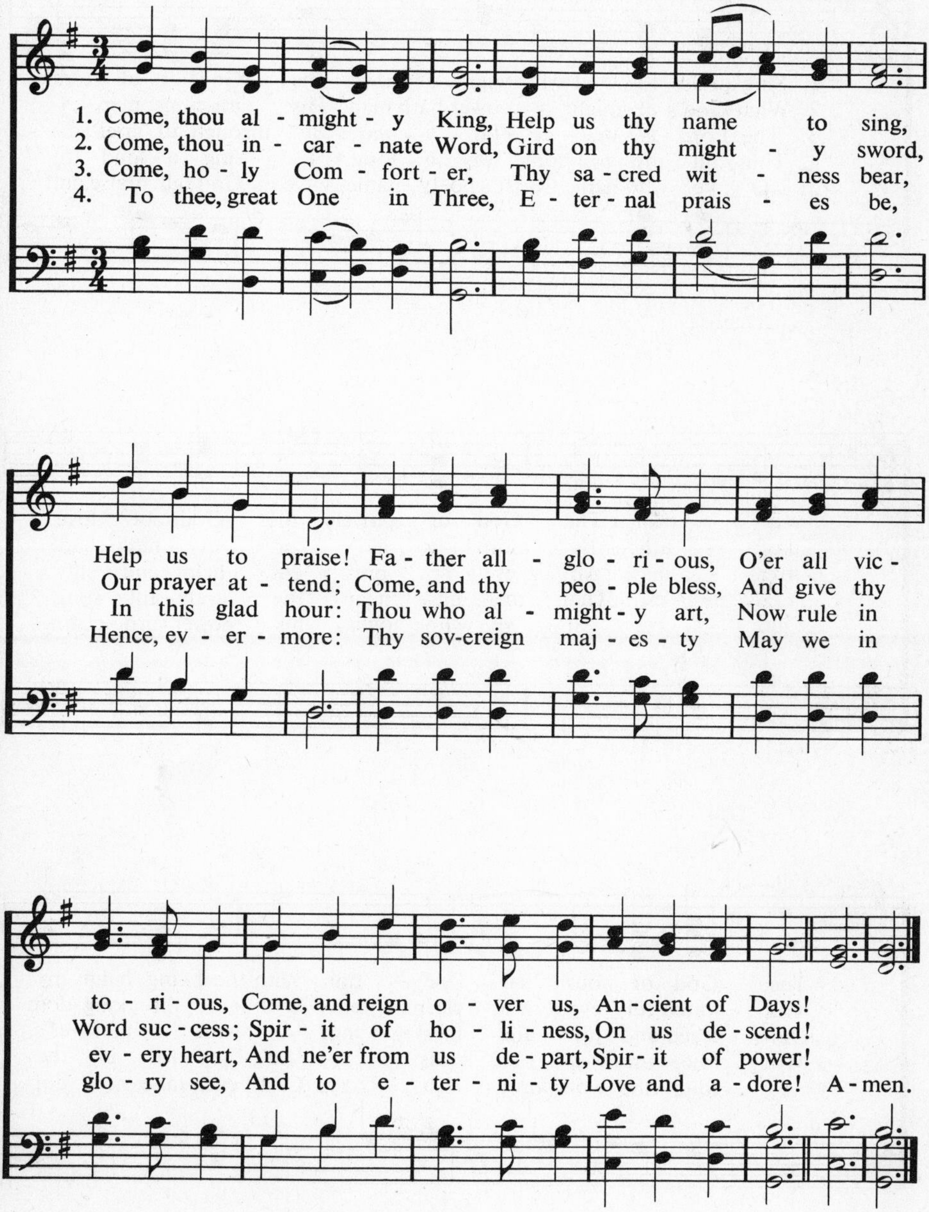
1. Come, thou al - might - y King, Help us thy name to sing,
2. Come, thou in - car - nate Word, Gird on thy might - y sword,
3. Come, ho - ly Com - fort - er, Thy sa - cred wit - ness bear,
4. To thee, great One in Three, E - ter - nal prais - es be,
Help us to praise! Fa - ther all - glo - ri - ous, O'er all vic -
Our prayer at - tend; Come, and thy peo - ple bless, And give thy
In this glad hour: Thou who al - might - y art, Now rule in
Hence, ev - er - more: Thy sov-ereign maj - es - ty May we in
to - ri - ous, Come, and reign o - ver us, An - cient of Days!
Word suc - cess; Spir - it of ho - li - ness, On us de - scend!
ev - ery heart, And ne'er from us de - part, Spir - it of power!
glo - ry see, And to e - ter - ni - ty Love and a - dore! A - men.

ADORATION

Sing Praise to God Who Reigns Above

DEUTERONOMY 32:3
JOHANN J. SCHÜTZ, 1640-1690
Trans. by FRANCES E. COX, 1812-1897

MIT FREUDEN ZART 87.87.887.
Bohemian Brethren's *Kirchengesänge . . .*, 1566

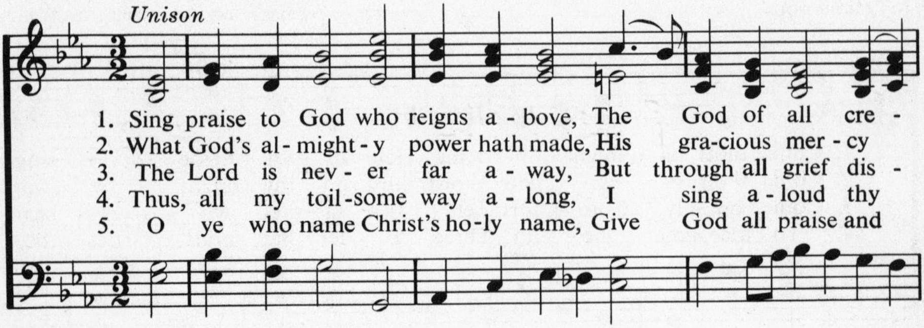
Unison
1. Sing praise to God who reigns a - bove, The God of all cre -
2. What God's al - might - y power hath made, His gra-cious mer - cy
3. The Lord is nev - er far a - way, But through all grief dis -
4. Thus, all my toil-some way a - long, I sing a - loud thy
5. O ye who name Christ's ho-ly name, Give God all praise and

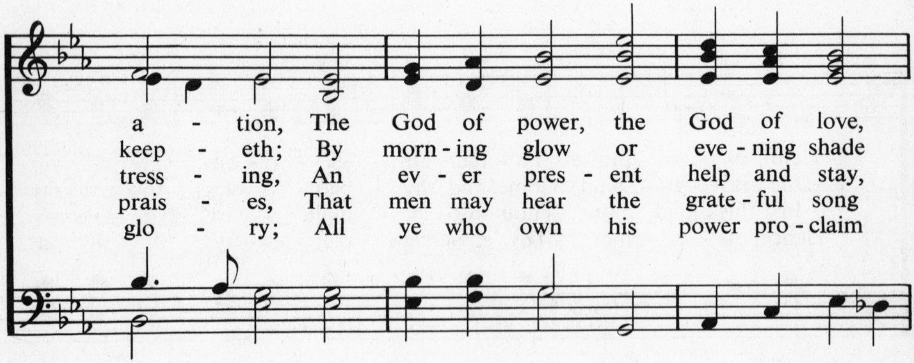
a - tion, The God of power, the God of love,
keep - eth; By morn - ing glow or eve - ning shade
tress - ing, An ev - er pres - ent help and stay,
prais - es, That men may hear the grate - ful song
glo - ry; All ye who own his power pro - claim

The God of our sal - va - tion; With heal - ing balm my
His watch-ful eye ne'er sleep - eth; With - in the king-dom
Our peace and joy and bless - ing; As with a moth-er's
My voice un - wea - ried rais - es; Be joy - ful in the
A - loud the won - drous sto - ry! Cast each false i - dol

Alternate tune: KIRKEN DEN ER ET GAMMELT HUS

soul he fills, And ev - ery faith - less mur - mur stills:
of his might, Lo! all is just and all is right:
ten - der hand, He leads his own, his cho - sen band:
Lord, my heart, Both soul and bod - y bear your part:
from his throne, The Lord is God, and he a - lone:

To God all praise and glo - ry. A - men.

Come, Ye That Love the Lord 5

ST. THOMAS SM

ISAAC WATTS, 1674-1748 AARON WILLIAMS, *The New Universal Psalmodist,* 1770

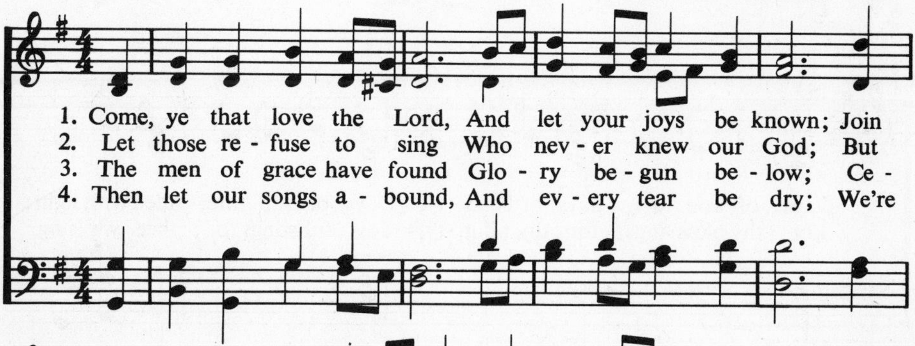
1. Come, ye that love the Lord, And let your joys be known; Join
2. Let those re - fuse to sing Who nev - er knew our God; But
3. The men of grace have found Glo - ry be - gun be - low; Ce -
4. Then let our songs a - bound, And ev - ery tear be dry; We're

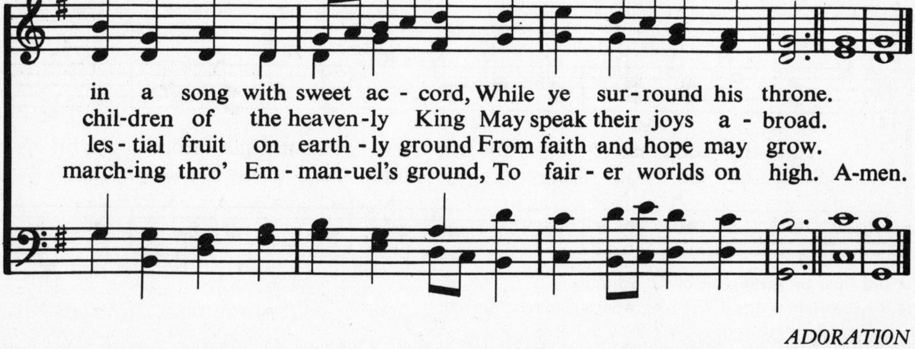
in a song with sweet ac - cord, While ye sur - round his throne.
chil - dren of the heaven - ly King May speak their joys a - broad.
les - tial fruit on earth - ly ground From faith and hope may grow.
march - ing thro' Em - man - uel's ground, To fair - er worlds on high. A - men.

6

We, Thy People, Praise Thee

ST. ANTHONY'S CHORALE Irregular
FRANZ JOSEPH HAYDN, 1732-1809
KATE STEARNS PAGE, 1873-1963 Arr. by EDITH LOVELL THOMAS, 1878-

Unison
1. We, thy peo-ple, praise thee, praise thee, God of ev-ery na-tion!
2. We, thy peo-ple, praise thee, praise thee, God of ev-ery na-tion!
We, thy peo-ple, praise thee, praise thee, Lord of hosts e-ter-nal!
We, thy peo-ple, praise thee, praise thee, Lord of hosts e-ter-nal!
Days of won-der, days of beau-ty, Days of rap-ture, filled with light;
For thy bless-ings, for thy boun-ty, Joy-ful songs to thee we sing,
Tell thy good-ness, tell thy mer-cies, Tell thy glo-rious might.
Songs of glo-ry, songs of tri-umph To our God and King.

We, thy peo-ple, praise thee, praise thee, Praise thee ev - er - more!
We, thy peo-ple, praise thee, praise thee, Praise thee ev - er - more! A-men.

See the Morning Sun Ascending 7

UNSER HERRSCHER 87.87.87.

CHARLES PARKIN, 1894-

JOACHIM NEANDER, 1650-1680

1. See the morn-ing sun as-cend-ing, Ra-diant in the east-ern sky;
2. So may we, in low-ly sta-tion, Join the cho-ris-ters a-bove;
3. For his lov-ing-kind-ness ev-er Shed up-on our earth-ly way;
4. "Wis-dom, hon-or, power, and bless-ing!" With the an-gel-ic host we cry;
Hear the an-gel voic-es blend-ing In their praise to God on high!
Sing-ing with the whole cre-a-tion, Prais-ing God for his great love.
For his mer-cy, ceas-ing nev-er, For his bless-ing day by day.
Round thy throne, thy name con-fess-ing, Lord, we would to thee draw nigh.
Al-le-lu-ia! Al-le-lu-ia! Glo-ry be to God on high!
Al-le-lu-ia! Al-le-lu-ia! Glo-ry be to God a-bove!
Al-le-lu-ia! Al-le-lu-ia! Glo-ry be to God al-way!
Al-le-lu-ia! Al-le-lu-ia! Glo-ry be to God on high! A-men.

Holy God, We Praise Thy Name

Attr. to Ignaz Franz, 1719-1790 — GROSSER GOTT 78.78.77.
Trans. by Clarence Walworth, 1820-1900 — *Katholisches Gesangbuch*, Vienna, c. 1774

1. Ho - ly God, we praise thy name; Lord of all, we
2. Hark, the glad ce - les - tial hymn, An - gel choirs a -
3. Lo! the ap - os - tol - ic train Joins thy sa - cred
4. Ho - ly Fa - ther, ho - ly Son, Ho - ly Spir - it:

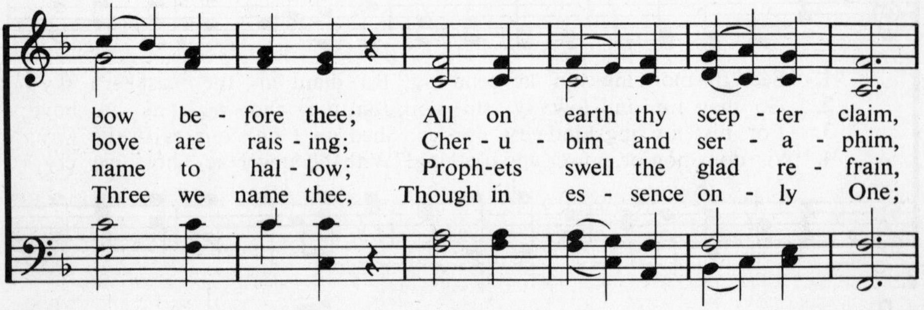
bow be - fore thee; All on earth thy scep - ter claim,
bove are rais - ing; Cher - u - bim and ser - a - phim,
name to hal - low; Proph-ets swell the glad re - frain,
Three we name thee, Though in es - sence on - ly One;

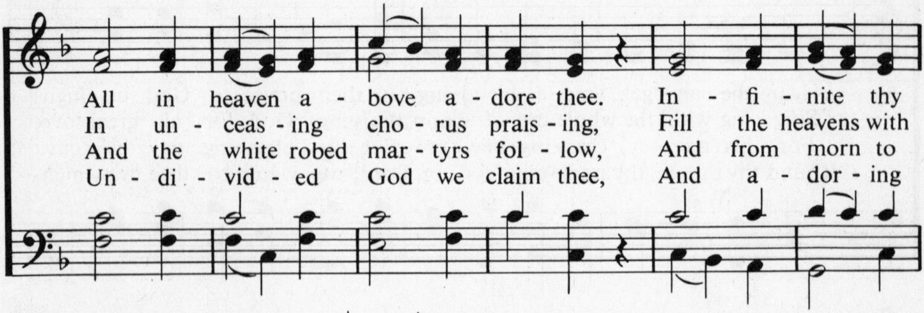
All in heaven a - bove a - dore thee. In - fi - nite thy
In un - ceas - ing cho - rus prais - ing, Fill the heavens with
And the white robed mar - tyrs fol - low, And from morn to
Un - di - vid - ed God we claim thee, And a - dor - ing

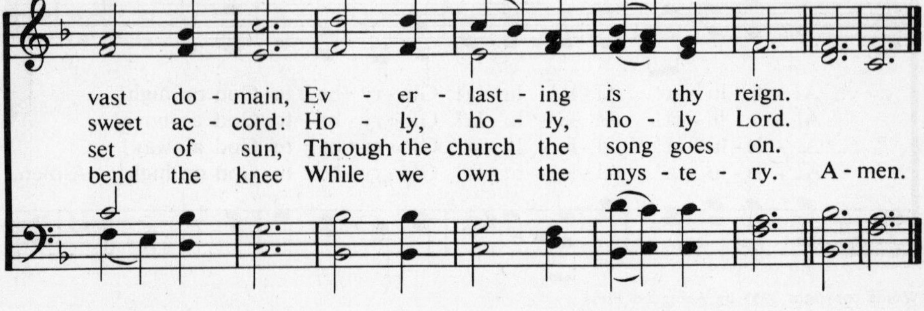
vast do - main, Ev - er - last - ing is thy reign.
sweet ac - cord: Ho - ly, ho - ly, ho - ly Lord.
set of sun, Through the church the song goes on.
bend the knee While we own the mys - te - ry. A - men.

I'll Praise My Maker While I've Breath

PSALM 146
ISAAC WATTS, 1674-1748
Alt. by JOHN WESLEY, 1703-1791

OLD 113TH 888.888.
Strassburger Kirchenamt, 1525
Probably by MATTHÄUS GREITER, c. 1500-1552
Harm. by V. E. C.

Unison
1. I'll praise my Mak - er while I've breath; And when my voice
2. Hap - py the man whose hopes re - ly On Is - rael's God;
3. The Lord pours eye - sight on the blind; The Lord sup - ports
4. I'll praise him while he lends me breath; And when my voice
is lost in death, Praise shall em - ploy my no - bler powers.
he made the sky And earth and seas, with all their train.
the faint - ing mind; He sends the la - boring con - science peace.
is lost in death, Praise shall em - ploy my no - bler powers.
My days of praise shall ne'er be past, While life, and thought,
His truth for - ev - er stands se - cure, He saves th'op - pressed,
He helps the stran - ger in dis - tress, The wid - ow and
My days of praise shall ne'er be past, While life, and thought,
and be - ing last, Or im - mor - tal - i - ty en - dures.
he feeds the poor, And none shall find his prom - ise vain.
the fa - ther - less, And grants the pris - oner sweet re - lease.
and be - ing last, Or im - mor - tal - i - ty en - dures. A - men.

10

Let All the World in Every Corner Sing

ALL THE WORLD 10 4.66.66.10 4.

GEORGE HERBERT, 1593-1632 — ROBERT G. MCCUTCHAN, 1877-1958

Unison
1. Let all the world in ev-ery cor-ner sing: My God and King!
2. Let all the world in ev-ery cor-ner sing: My God and King!
The heavens are not too high, His praise may thith-er fly; The
The church with psalms must shout, No door can keep them out; But,
earth is not too low, His prais-es there may grow. Let
more than all, the heart Must bear the long-est part. Let
all the world in ev-ery cor-ner sing: My God and King!
all the world in ev-ery cor-ner sing: My God and King! A - men.

11

Men and Children Everywhere

ROCK OF AGES 77.77.57. with Refrain

JOHN J. MOMENT, 1875-1959

Trad. Hebrew Melody

1. Men and chil-dren ev-ery-where, With sweet mu-sic fill the air!
2. Morn-ing, eve-ning, bless his name, Skies with crim-son clouds a-flame,
3. Storm and flood and o-cean's roar, Break-ers crash-ing on the shore,
Na-tions, come, your voic-es raise To the Lord in hymns of praise!
Rain-bow arch, his cov-enant sign, Count-less stars by night that shine!
Wa-ter-falls that nev-er sleep, Tower-ing moun-tain, can-yon deep,
Join the an-gel song, All the worlds to him be-long!
Through his far do-main, Love is king where he doth reign!
Tell ye forth his might, Lord of life and truth and right!
Refrain
Ho-ly, ho-ly, To our God all glo-ry be!
Ho-ly, ho-ly, To our God all glo-ry be!
Ho-ly, ho-ly, To our God all glo-ry be! A-men.

12

O Thou in All Thy Might So Far

RICHMOND CM

Frederick Lucian Hosmer, 1840-1929 | Thomas Haweis, 1734-1820

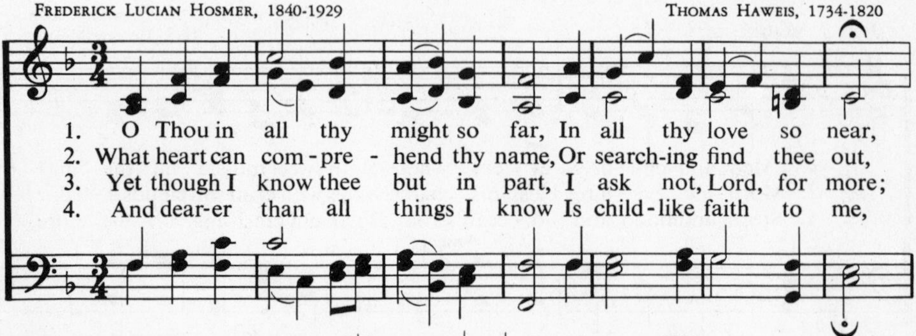
1. O Thou in all thy might so far, In all thy love so near,
2. What heart can com-pre-hend thy name, Or search-ing find thee out,
3. Yet though I know thee but in part, I ask not, Lord, for more;
4. And dear-er than all things I know Is child-like faith to me,

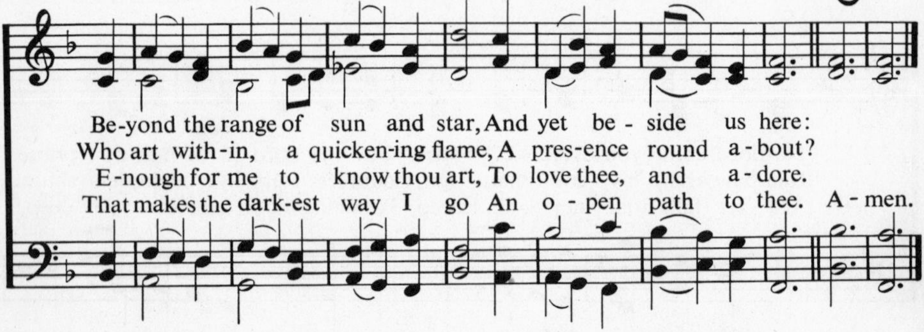
Be-yond the range of sun and star, And yet be-side us here:
Who art with-in, a quicken-ing flame, A pres-ence round a-bout?
E-nough for me to know thou art, To love thee, and a-dore.
That makes the dark-est way I go An o-pen path to thee. A-men.

13

Open Now Thy Gates of Beauty

UNSER HERRSCHER 87.87.77.

Benjamin Schmolck, 1672-1737
Trans. by Catherine Winkworth, 1827-1878

Joachim Neander, 1650-1680

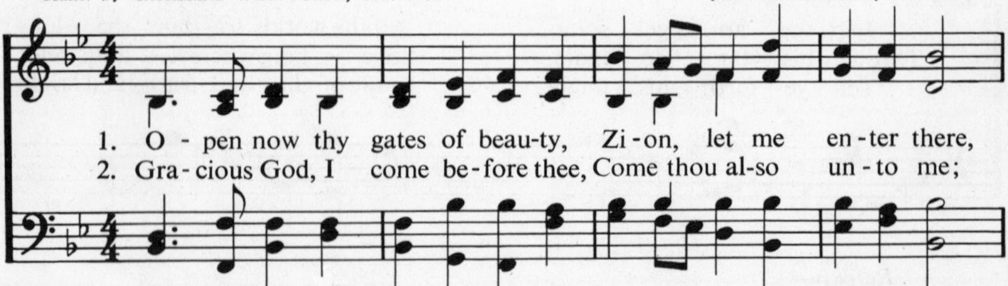
1. O-pen now thy gates of beau-ty, Zi-on, let me en-ter there,
2. Gra-cious God, I come be-fore thee, Come thou al-so un-to me;

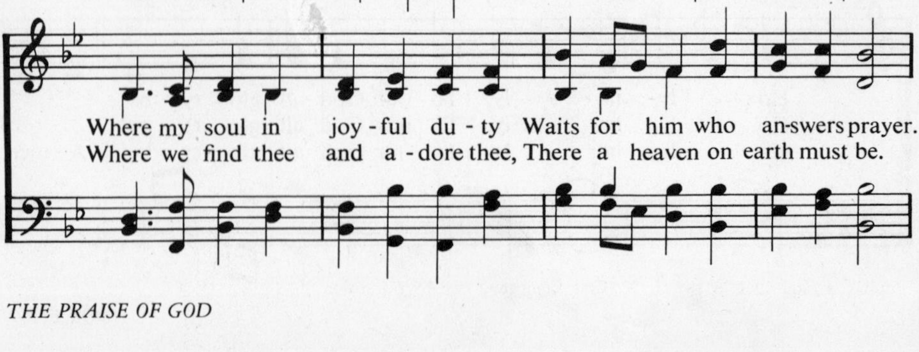
Where my soul in joy-ful du-ty Waits for him who an-swers prayer.
Where we find thee and a-dore thee, There a heaven on earth must be.

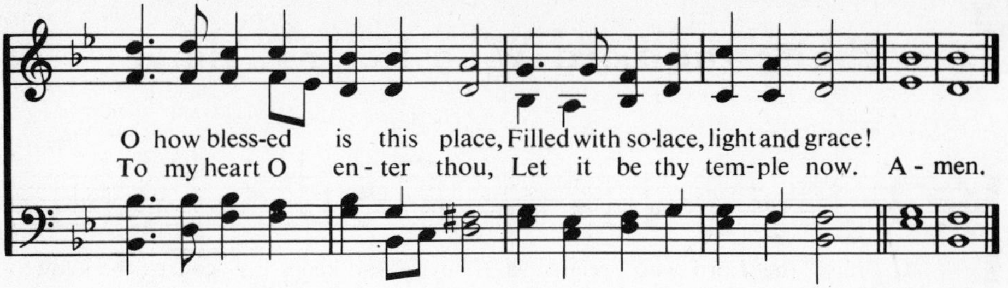
O how bless-ed is this place, Filled with so-lace, light and grace!
To my heart O en-ter thou, Let it be thy tem-ple now. A-men.

From All That Dwell Below the Skies 14

PSALM 117
Stanzas 1, 2, ISAAC WATTS, 1674-1748
Stanzas 3, 4, ANONYMOUS

DUKE STREET LM
JOHN HATTON, d. 1793

1. From all that dwell be-low the skies, Let the Cre-a-tor's
2. E-ter-nal are thy mer-cies, Lord; E-ter-nal truth at-
3. Your loft-y themes, ye mor-tals, bring; In songs of praise di-
4. In ev-ery land be-gin the song; To ev-ery land the
praise a-rise; Let the Re-deem-er's name be sung,
tends thy word: Thy praise shall sound from shore to shore,
vine-ly sing; The great sal-va-tion loud pro-claim,
strains be-long; In cheer-ful sounds all voic-es raise,
Through ev-ery land by ev-ery tongue.
Till suns shall rise and set no more.
And shout for joy the Sav-ior's name.
And fill the world with loud-est praise. A-men.

Praise the Lord Who Reigns Above

Psalm 150
Charles Wesley, 1707-1788

AMSTERDAM 76.76.77.76.
Foundery Collection, 1742

1. Praise the Lord who reigns a - bove, And keeps his court be - low;
2. Cel - e - brate th'e - ter - nal God With harp and psal - ter - y,
3. Him, in whom they move and live, Let ev - ery crea - ture sing,
Praise the ho - ly God of love, And all his great - ness show;
Tim - brels soft and cym - bals loud In his high praise a - gree;
Glo - ry to their Mak - er give, And hom - age to their King.
Praise him for his no - ble deeds, Praise him for his match - less power;
Praise him ev - ery tune - ful string; All the reach of heaven - ly art,
Hallow - ed be his name be - neath, As in heaven on earth a - dored;
Him from whom all good pro - ceeds Let earth and heaven a - dore.
All the powers of mu - sic bring, The mu - sic of the heart.
Praise the Lord in ev - ery breath, Let all things praise the Lord. A - men.

Stand Up and Bless the Lord

ST. MICHAEL SM

NEHEMIAH 9:5
JAMES MONTGOMERY, 1771-1854

Genevan Psalter, 1551
Adapt. by WILLIAM CROTCH, 1775-1847

1. Stand up and bless the Lord, Ye peo - ple of his
2. Though high a - bove all praise, A - bove all bless - ing
3. O for the liv - ing flame From his own al - tar
4. God is our strength and song, And his sal - va - tion
5. Stand up and bless the Lord; The Lord your God a -
choice; Stand up and bless the Lord your God
high, Who would not fear his ho - ly name,
brought, To touch our lips, our minds in - spire,
ours; Then be his love in Christ pro - claimed
dore; Stand up and bless his glo - rious name,
With heart and soul and voice.
And laud and mag - ni - fy?
And wing to heaven our thought!
With all our ran - somed powers.
Hence - forth for - ev - er - more. A - men.

Alternate tune: ST. THOMAS

ADORATION

How Great Thou Art

O STORE GUD Irregular with Refrain

CARL BOBERG, 1859-1940 | Swedish Folk Melody

Trans. by STUART K. HINE, 1899- | Arr. by MANNA MUSIC, INC.

1. O Lord my God! When I in awe-some won - der Con - sid - er
2. When through the woods and for - est glades I wan - der And hear the
3. And when I think that God, his Son not spar - ing, Sent him to
4. When Christ shall come with shout of ac - cla - ma - tion And take me
all the worlds thy hands have made, I see the stars, I hear the roll - ing
birds sing sweet - ly in the trees; When I look down from loft - y moun - tain
die, I scarce can take it in; That on the cross, my bur - den glad - ly
home, what joy shall fill my heart! Then I shall bow in hum - ble ad - o -
thun - der, thy pow'r through-out the un - i - verse dis - played,
gran - deur And hear the brook and feel the gen - tle breeze;
bear - ing, He bled and died to take a - way my sin;
ra - tion And there pro - claim, my God, how great thou art!
Refrain
Then sings my
soul, my Sav-ior God to thee; How great thou art, how great thou art! Then sings my
soul, my Sav-ior God to thee; How great thou art, how great thou art!

*Translator's original words are "works" and "mighty."

Thanks to God Whose Word Was Spoken

LAUDA ANIMA 87.87.87.

R. T. BROOKS, 1918- JOHN GOSS, 1800-1880

1. Thanks to God whose Word was spo - ken In the deed that
2. Thanks to God whose Word in - car - nate Glo - ri - fied the
3. Thanks to God whose Word is an - swered By the Spir - it's
made the earth. His the voice that called a na - tion;
flesh of man. Deeds and words and death and ris - ing
voice with - in. Here we drink of joy un - mea - sured,
His the fires that tried her worth. God has spo - ken;
Tell the grace in heav - en's plan. God has spo - ken;
Life re - deemed from death and sin. God is speak - ing;
God has spo - ken; Praise him for his o - pen Word.
God has spo - ken; Praise him for his o - pen Word.
God is speak - ing; Praise him for his o - pen Word. A-men.

Alternate tune: REGENT SQUARE

Ye Watchers and Ye Holy Ones

LASST UNS ERFREUEN 88.44.88. with Alleluias

ATHELSTAN RILEY, 1858-1945

Geistliche Kirchengesänge, 1623, Harm. by C. R. Y.

Unison
1. Ye watch-ers and ye ho - ly ones, Bright ser-aphs, cher-u-bim and thrones,
2. O high-er than the cher - u - bim, More glo-rious than the ser - a - phim,
3. Re-spond, ye souls in end-less rest, Ye pa-tri-archs and proph-ets blest,
4. O friends, in glad-ness let us sing, Su - per-nal an-thems ech-o - ing,
Raise the glad strain, Al - le - lu - ia! Cry out, do-min-ions, prince-doms, powers,
Lead their prais-es, Al - le - lu - ia! Thou bear-er of th'e-ter-nal Word,
Al - le - lu - ia! Al - le - lu - ia! Ye ho-ly twelve, ye mar-tyrs strong,
Al - le - lu - ia! Al - le - lu - ia! To God the Fa-ther, God the Son,
Vir - tues, arch-an-gels, an-gels' choirs, Al - le - lu - ia, Al - le - lu - ia,
Most gra-cious, mag-ni-fy the Lord, Al - le - lu - ia, Al - le - lu - ia,
All saints tri-um-phant, raise the song, Al - le - lu - ia, Al - le - lu - ia,
And God the Spir-it, Three in One, Al - le - lu - ia, Al - le - lu - ia,
Al - le - lu - ia, Al - le - lu - ia, Al - le - lu - ia! A - men.

Words from *The English Hymnal* by permission of Oxford University Press.

A Mighty Fortress Is Our God

Psalm 46
Martin Luther, 1483-1546
Trans. by Frederick H. Hedge, 1805-1890

EIN' FESTE BURG 87.87.66.667.
Melody by Martin Luther, 1483-1546

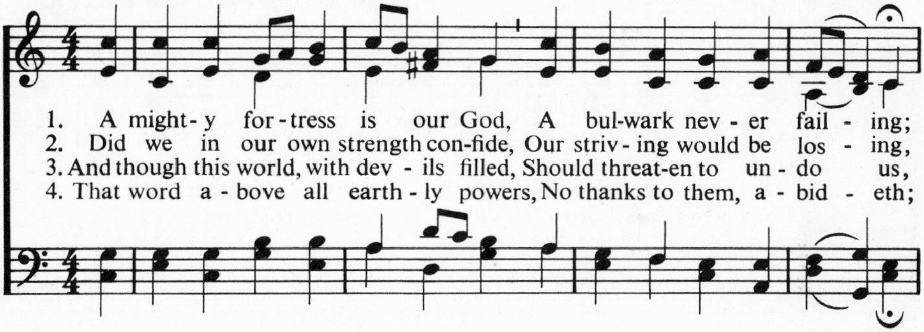
1. A might-y for-tress is our God, A bul-wark nev - er fail - ing;
2. Did we in our own strength con-fide, Our striv-ing would be los - ing,
3. And though this world, with dev - ils filled, Should threat-en to un - do us,
4. That word a - bove all earth - ly powers, No thanks to them, a - bid - eth;

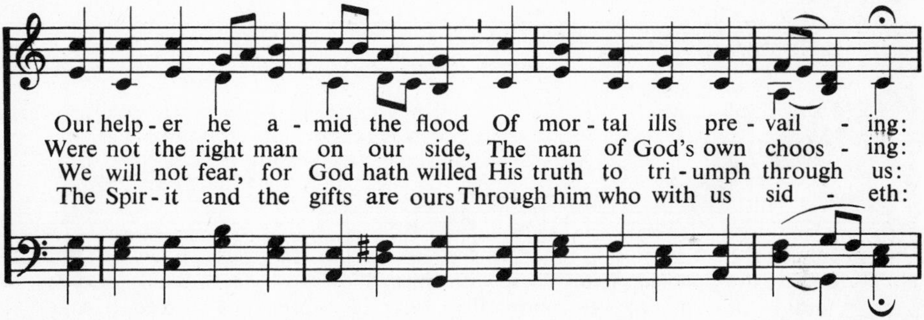
Our help - er he a - mid the flood Of mor - tal ills pre - vail - ing:
Were not the right man on our side, The man of God's own choos - ing:
We will not fear, for God hath willed His truth to tri - umph through us:
The Spir - it and the gifts are ours Through him who with us sid - eth:

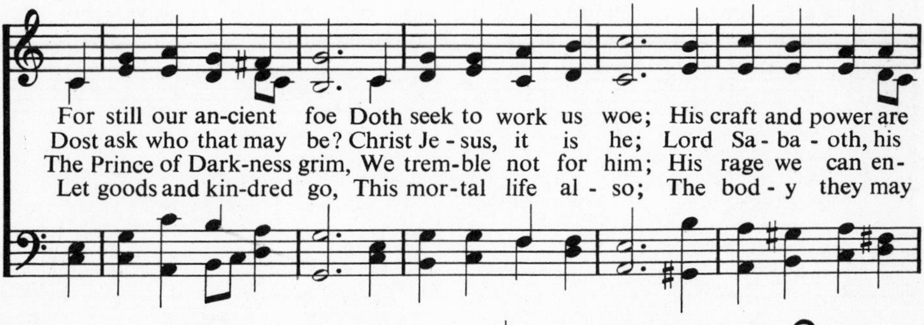
For still our an-cient foe Doth seek to work us woe; His craft and power are
Dost ask who that may be? Christ Je - sus, it is he; Lord Sa - ba - oth, his
The Prince of Dark-ness grim, We trem-ble not for him; His rage we can en-
Let goods and kin-dred go, This mor-tal life al - so; The bod - y they may

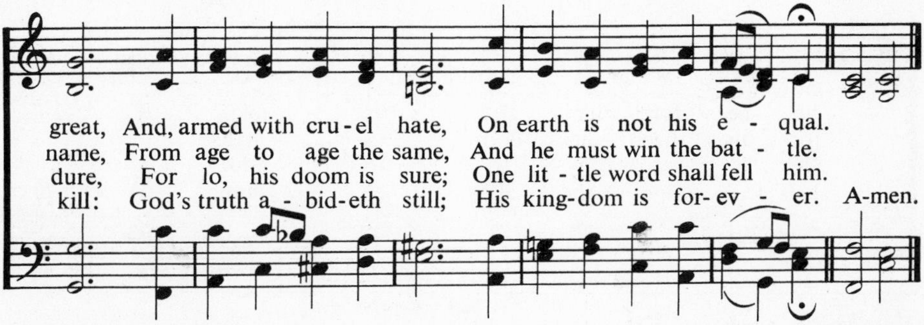
great, And, armed with cru - el hate, On earth is not his e - qual.
name, From age to age the same, And he must win the bat - tle.
dure, For lo, his doom is sure; One lit - tle word shall fell him.
kill: God's truth a - bid-eth still; His king-dom is for-ev - er. A-men.

21

All People That on Earth Do Dwell

OLD 100TH LM

PSALM 100 — *Genevan Psalter*, 1551

Attr. to WILLIAM KETHE, d. 1593 — Attr. to LOUIS BOURGEOIS, c. 1510-c. 1561

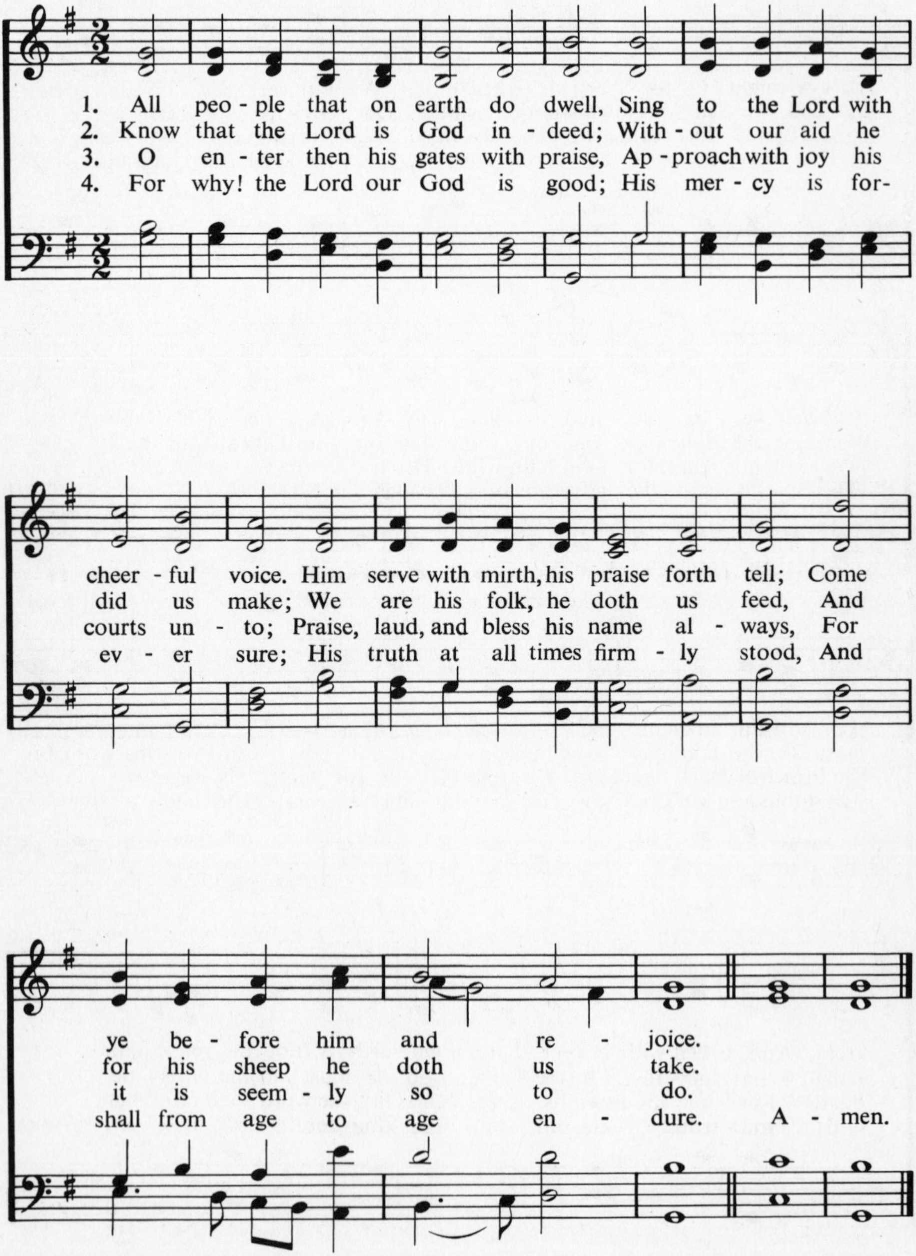

1. All peo - ple that on earth do dwell, Sing to the Lord with
2. Know that the Lord is God in - deed; With - out our aid he
3. O en - ter then his gates with praise, Ap - proach with joy his
4. For why! the Lord our God is good; His mer - cy is for-
cheer - ful voice. Him serve with mirth, his praise forth tell; Come
did us make; We are his folk, he doth us feed, And
courts un - to; Praise, laud, and bless his name al - ways, For
ev - er sure; His truth at all times firm - ly stood, And
ye be - fore him and re - joice.
for his sheep he doth us take.
it is seem - ly so to do.
shall from age to age en - dure. A - men.

Before Jehovah's Awful Throne

PSALM 100
ISAAC WATTS, 1674-1748
Altered by JOHN WESLEY, 1703-1791

OLD 100TH LM
Genevan Psalter, 1551
Attr. to LOUIS BOURGEOIS, c. 1510-c. 1561

1. Be - fore Je - ho - vah's aw - ful throne, Ye
2. His sov - ereign power, with - out our aid, Made
3. We'll crowd thy gates with thank - ful songs, High
4. Wide as the world is thy com - mand; Vast

na - tions, bow with sa - cred joy; Know that the Lord is
us of clay, and formed us men; And, when like wand - ering
as the heavens our voic - es raise; And earth, with her ten
as e - ter - ni - ty thy love; Firm as a rock thy

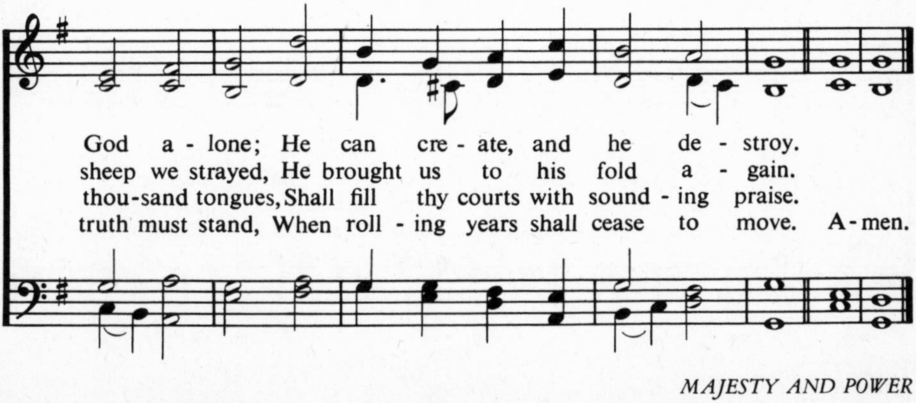
God a - lone; He can cre - ate, and he de - stroy.
sheep we strayed, He brought us to his fold a - gain.
thou-sand tongues, Shall fill thy courts with sound - ing praise.
truth must stand, When roll - ing years shall cease to move. A - men.

Come, Let Us Tune Our Loftiest Song

DUKE STREET LM

ROBERT A. WEST, 1809-1865 — JOHN HATTON, d. 1793

1. Come, let us tune our loft - iest song And raise to
2. His sov-ereign power our bod - ies made; Our souls are
3. Burn ev - ery breast with Je - sus' love; Bound ev - ery
4. Ex - tol the Lamb with loft - iest song; As - cend for
Christ our joy - ful strain; Wor-ship and thanks to him be -
his im - mor - tal breath; And when his crea - tures sinned, he
heart with rap - turous joy; And saints on earth, with saints a -
him our cheer - ful strain; Wor-ship and thanks to him be -
long, Who reigns, and shall for - ev - er reign.
bled, To save us from e - ter - nal death.
bove, Your voic - es in his praise em - ploy.
long, Who reigns and shall for - ev - er reign. A - men.

Come, Sound His Praise Abroad

CAMBRIDGE SM

PSALM 95
ISAAC WATTS, 1674-1748

Arr. from RALPH HARRISON, 1748-1810
by SAMUEL S. WESLEY, 1810-1876

1. Come, sound his praise a - broad And hymns of glo - ry sing: Je - ho - vah is the sov - ereign God, The u - ni - ver - sal King.
2. He formed the deeps un - known; He gave the seas their bound; The wa - tery worlds are all his own, And all the sol - id ground.
3. Come, wor - ship at his throne; Come, bow be - fore the Lord: We are his works and not our own; He formed us by his Word.
4. To - day at - tend his voice, Nor dare pro - voke his rod; Come, like the peo - ple of his choice, And own your gra-cious God. A - men.

25

Great God, Attend, While Zion Sings

PSALM 84
ISAAC WATTS, 1674-1748

PARK STREET LM
FREDERICK M. A. VENUA, 1788-1872

1. Great God, at - tend, while Zi - on sings The joy that
2. Might I en - joy the mean - est place With - in thy
3. God is our sun, he makes our day; God is our
4. O God, our King, whose sov - ereign sway The glo - rious
from thy pres - ence springs; To spend one day with
house, O God of grace, Nor tents of ease, nor
shield, he guards our way From all th'as-saults of
hosts of heaven o - bey, And dev - ils at thy
thee on earth Ex - ceeds a thou - sand days of mirth,
thrones of power, Should tempt my feet to leave thy door,
hell and sin, From foes with - out and foes with - in,
pres - ence flee; Blest is the man that trusts in thee,
Ex - ceeds a thou - sand days of mirth.
Should tempt my feet to leave thy door.
From foes with - out and foes with - in.
Blest is the man that trusts in thee. A - men.

Holy, Holy, Holy! Lord God Almighty

REVELATION 4:8-11
REGINALD HEBER, 1783-1826

NICAEA 11 12.12 10.
JOHN B. DYKES, 1823-1876

1. Ho - ly, ho - ly, ho - ly! Lord God Al - might - y!
2. Ho - ly, ho - ly, ho - ly! All the saints a - dore thee,
3. Ho - ly, ho - ly, ho - ly! Though the dark - ness hide thee,
4. Ho - ly, ho - ly, ho - ly! Lord God Al - might - y!
Ear - ly in the morn - ing our song shall rise to thee;
Cast - ing down their gold - en crowns a - round the glass - y sea;
Though the eye of sin - ful man thy glo - ry may not see;
All thy works shall praise thy name in earth and sky and sea;
Ho - ly, ho - ly, ho - ly! mer - ci - ful and might - y;
Cher - u - bim and ser - a - phim fall - ing down be - fore thee,
On - ly thou art ho - ly; there is none be - side thee,
Ho - ly, ho - ly, ho - ly! mer - ci - ful and might - y;
God in three per - sons, bless - ed Trin - i - ty!
Which wert, and art, and ev - er - more shalt be.
Per - fect in power, in love, and pur - i - ty.
God in three per - sons, bless - ed Trin - i - ty! A - men.

Immortal, Invisible, God Only Wise

ST. DENIO 11 11.11 11.

I TIMOTHY 1:17
WALTER CHALMERS SMITH, 1824-1908

Welsh Melody
JOHN ROBERTS' *Canaidau y Cyssegr*, 1839

1. Im - mor - tal, in - vis - i - ble, God on - ly wise,
2. Un - rest - ing, un - hast - ing, and si - lent as light,
3. To all, life thou giv - est, to both great and small;
4. Great Fa - ther of glo - ry, pure Fa - ther of light,
In light in - ac - ces - si - ble hid from our eyes,
Nor want - ing, nor wast - ing, thou rul - est in might;
In all life thou liv - est, the true life of all;
Thine an - gels a - dore thee, all veil - ing their sight;
Most bless - ed, most glo - rious, the An - cient of Days,
Thy jus - tice like moun - tains high soar - ing a - bove
We blos - som and flour - ish as leaves on the tree,
All praise we would ren - der: O help us to see
Al - might - y, vic - to - rious, thy great name we praise.
Thy clouds which are foun - tains of good - ness and love.
And with - er and per - ish, but naught chang - eth thee.
'Tis on - ly the splen - dor of light hid - eth thee. A - men.

O God, Our Help in Ages Past

PSALM 90
ISAAC WATTS, 1674-1748

ST. ANNE CM
Probably by WILLIAM CROFT, 1678-1727

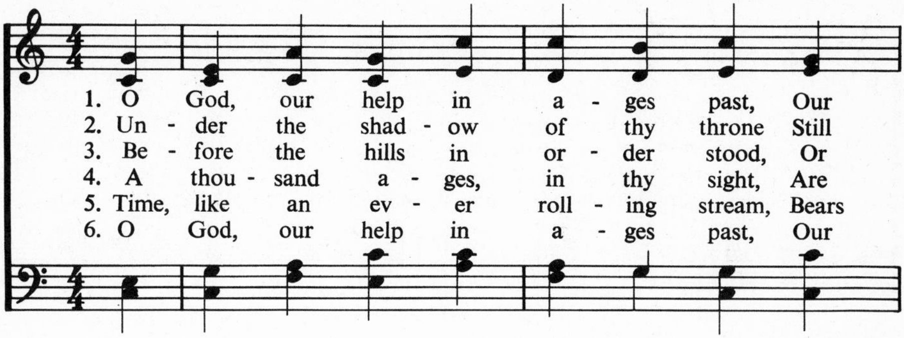
1. O God, our help in a - ges past, Our
2. Un - der the shad - ow of thy throne Still
3. Be - fore the hills in or - der stood, Or
4. A thou - sand a - ges, in thy sight, Are
5. Time, like an ev - er roll - ing stream, Bears
6. O God, our help in a - ges past, Our

hope for years to come, Our shel - ter from the
may we dwell se - cure; Suf - fi - cient is thine
earth re - ceived her frame, From ev - er - last - ing
like an eve - ning gone; Short as the watch that
all its sons a - way; They fly for - got - ten,
hope for years to come; Be thou our guide while

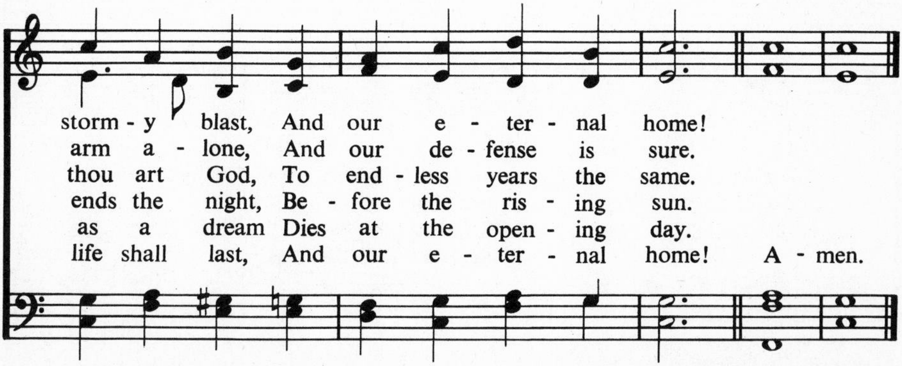
storm - y blast, And our e - ter - nal home!
arm a - lone, And our de - fense is sure.
thou art God, To end - less years the same.
ends the night, Be - fore the ris - ing sun.
as a dream Dies at the open - ing day.
life shall last, And our e - ter - nal home! A - men.

O Splendor of God's Glory Bright

AMBROSE OF MILAN, 340-397
Trans. by ROBERT S. BRIDGES, 1844-1930

WAREHAM LM
WILLIAM KNAPP, 1698-1768

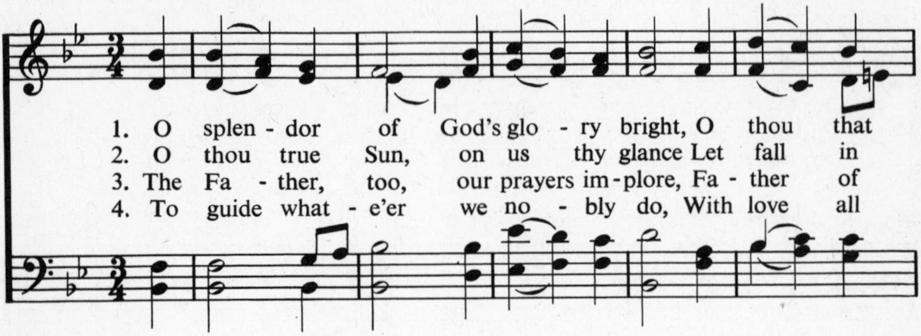
1. O splen - dor of God's glo - ry bright, O thou that
2. O thou true Sun, on us thy glance Let fall in
3. The Fa - ther, too, our prayers im - plore, Fa - ther of
4. To guide what - e'er we no - bly do, With love all

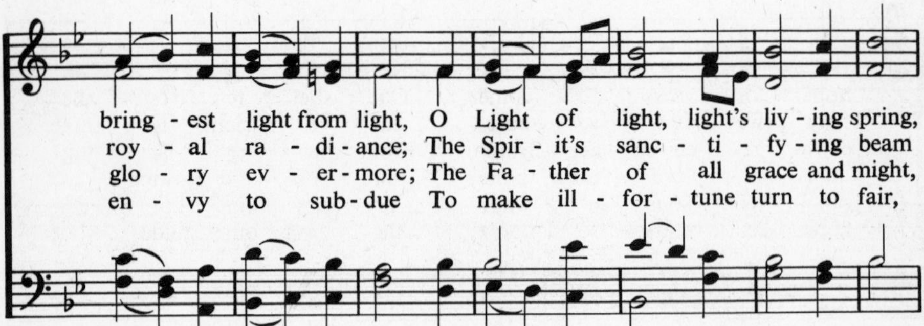
bring - est light from light, O Light of light, light's liv - ing spring,
roy - al ra - di - ance; The Spir - it's sanc - ti - fy - ing beam
glo - ry ev - er - more; The Fa - ther of all grace and might,
en - vy to sub - due To make ill - for - tune turn to fair,

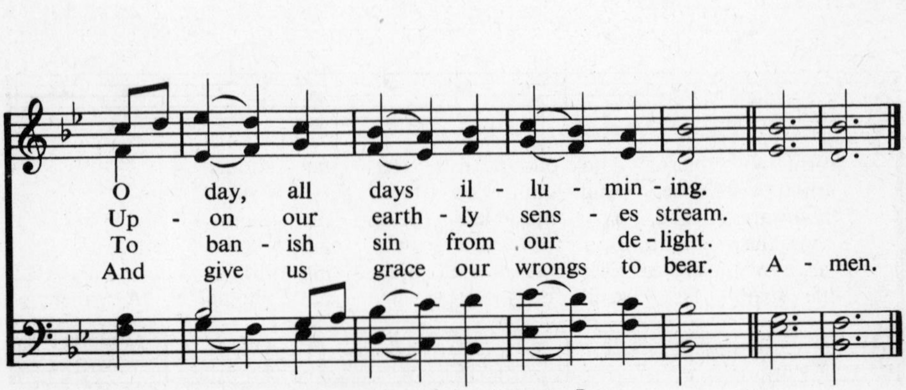
O day, all days il - lu - min - ing.
Up - on our earth - ly sens - es stream.
To ban - ish sin from our de - light.
And give us grace our wrongs to bear. A - men.

Words from *The Yattendon Hymnal* by permission of Oxford University Press.

THE PRAISE OF GOD

Praise to the Living God

Based on the Yigdal of DANIEL BEN JUDAH, 14th Century
Trans. by NEWTON MANN, 1836-1926
and MAX LANDSBERG, 1845-1928

LEONI 66.84.D.
Arr. from a Hebrew Melody
by MEYER LYON (LEONI), 1751-1797

1. Praise to the liv - ing God! All prais - ed be his name,
2. His spir - it flow - eth free, High surg - ing where it will;
3. He hath e - ter - nal life Im - plant - ed in the soul;
Who was, and is, and is to be, And still the same!
In proph - et's word he spoke of old; He speak - eth still.
His love shall be our strength and stay, While a - ges roll.
The one e - ter - nal God, Ere aught that now ap - pears;
Es - tab - lished is his law, And change - less it shall stand,
Praise to the liv - ing God! All prais - ed be his name,
The first, the last: be - yond all thought His time - less years!
Deep writ up - on the hu - man heart, On sea or land.
Who was, and is, and is to be, And still the same! A - men.

31

The Lord Jehovah Reigns

Psalm 148
Isaac Watts, 1674-1748

MILLENNIUM 66.66.88.
Plymouth Collection, 1855

1. The Lord Je - ho - vah reigns, His throne is built on
2. The thun-ders of his hand Keep the wide world in
3. Through all his might - y works A - maz - ing wis - dom
4. And will this sov - ereign King Of glo - ry con - de -
high; The gar-ments he as-sumes Are light and maj - es -
awe; His wrath and jus - tice stand To guard his ho - ly
shines; Sub - dues the powers of hell, Con-founds their dark de -
scend; And will he write his name, My Fa - ther and my
ty; His glo - ries shine with beams so bright, No
law; And where his love re - solves to bless, His
signs; Strong is his arm, and shall ful - fill His
friend? I love his name, I love his word; Join
mor - tal eye can bear the sight.
truth con - firms and seals the grace.
great de - crees and sov - ereign will.
all my powers to praise the Lord! A - men.

Alternate tune: DARWALL'S 148TH

The Lord Our God Is Clothed with Might

DETROIT CM

Supplement to Kentucky Harmony, 1820

Harm. by A. C. L.

H. KIRKE WHITE, 1785-1806

1. The Lord our God is clothed with might, The
2. Re - bel, ye waves, and o'er the land With
3. Ye winds of night, your force com - bine; With -
4. His voice sub - lime is heard a - far; In
5. Ye na - tions bend, in rev - erence bend; Ye

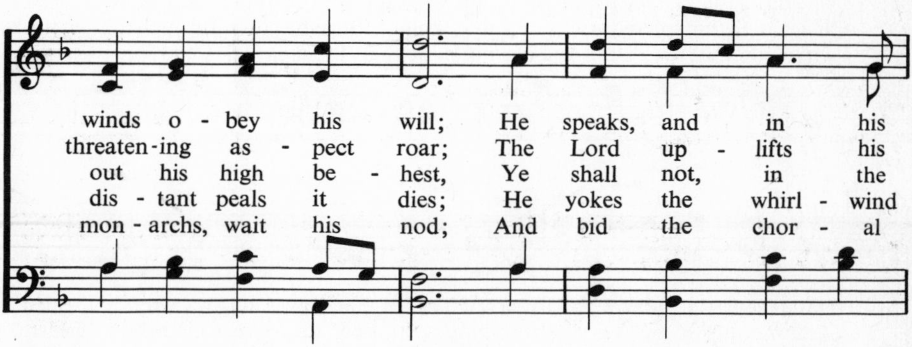
winds o - bey his will; He speaks, and in his
threaten-ing as - pect roar; The Lord up - lifts his
out his high be - hest, Ye shall not, in the
dis - tant peals it dies; He yokes the whirl - wind
mon - archs, wait his nod; And bid the chor - al

heaven-ly height The roll - ing sun stands still.
aw - ful hand And chains you to the shore.
moun - tain pine, Dis - turb the spar - row's nest.
to his car And sweeps the howl - ing skies.
song as - cend To cel - e - brate our God. A - men.

All Beautiful the March of Days

FOREST GREEN CMD
Trad. English Melody

FRANCES W. WILE, 1878-1939
Arr. by R. VAUGHAN WILLIAMS, 1872-1958

1. All beau-ti-ful the march of days, As sea-sons come and go;
2. O'er white ex-pan-ses spark-ling pure The ra-diant morns un-fold;
3. O thou from whose un-fath-omed law The year in beau-ty flows,
The hand that shaped the rose hath wrought The crys-tal of the snow,
The sol-emn splen-dors of the night Burn bright-er through the cold.
Thy-self the vi-sion pass-ing by In crys-tal and in rose,
Hath sent the hoar-y frost of heaven, The flow-ing wa-ters sealed,
Life mounts in ev-ery throb-bing vein, Love deep-ens round the hearth,
Day un-to day doth ut-ter speech, And night to night pro-claim,
And laid a si-lent love-li-ness On hill and wood and field.
And clear-er sounds the an-gel hymn, "Good will to men on earth."
In ev-er-chang-ing words of light, The won-der of thy name. A-men.

Words used by permission of Mrs. Dorothy M. W. Bean. Music from *The English Hymnal* by permission of Oxford University Press.

All Things Bright and Beautiful

ROYAL OAK 76.76. with Refrain
17th Century English Melody
Harm. by V. E. C.

GENESIS 1:31
CECIL FRANCES ALEXANDER, 1818-1895

Unison Refrain
All things bright and beau-ti - ful, All crea-tures great and small,
All things wise and won - der - ful: The Lord God made them all.
Fine
1. Each lit - tle flower that o - pens, Each lit - tle bird that sings,
2. The pur - ple-head- ed moun-tain, The riv - er run-ning by,
3. The cold wind in the win - ter, The pleas - ant sum- mer sun,
4. He gave us eyes to see them, And lips that we might tell
He made their glow - ing col - ors, He made their ti - ny wings.
The sun - set, and the morn - ing That bright-ens up the sky,
The ripe fruits in the gar - den: He made them ev - ery - one.
How great is God Al - might - y, Who has made all things well.
Repeat Refrain

For the Beauty of the Earth

DIX 77.77.77.
Arr. from CONRAD KOCHER, 1786-1872
by W. H. MONK, 1823-1889

FOLLIOT S. PIERPOINT, 1835-1917

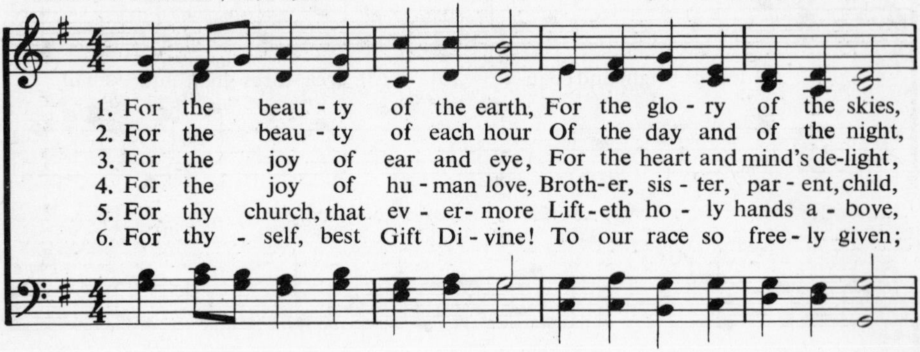
1. For the beau - ty of the earth, For the glo - ry of the skies,
2. For the beau - ty of each hour Of the day and of the night,
3. For the joy of ear and eye, For the heart and mind's de-light,
4. For the joy of hu - man love, Broth-er, sis - ter, par - ent, child,
5. For thy church, that ev - er- more Lift-eth ho - ly hands a - bove,
6. For thy - self, best Gift Di - vine! To our race so free - ly given;

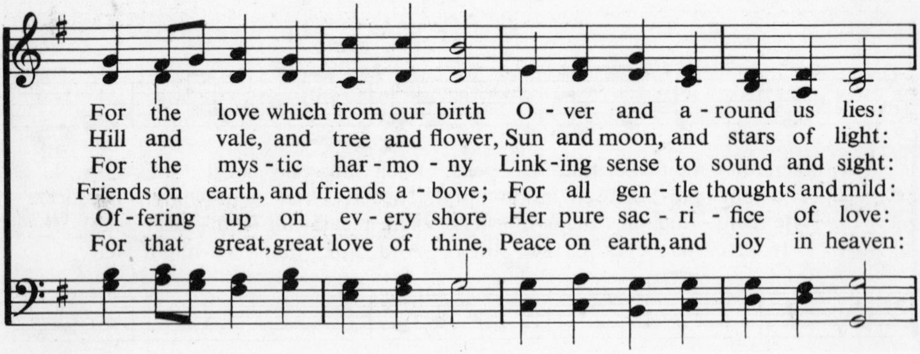
For the love which from our birth O - ver and a - round us lies:
Hill and vale, and tree and flower, Sun and moon, and stars of light:
For the mys - tic har - mo - ny Link-ing sense to sound and sight:
Friends on earth, and friends a - bove; For all gen - tle thoughts and mild:
Of - fering up on ev - ery shore Her pure sac - ri - fice of love:
For that great, great love of thine, Peace on earth, and joy in heaven:

Lord of all, to thee we raise This our hymn of grate-ful praise. A-men.

God of the Earth, the Sky, the Sea

GERMANY LM
From WILLIAM GARDINER'S
SAMUEL LONGFELLOW, 1819-1892
Sacred Melodies, 1815

1. God of the earth, the sky, the sea, Mak - er of
2. Thy love is in the sun - shine's glow, Thy life is
3. We feel thy calm at eve - ning's hour, Thy gran - deur
4. But high - er far, and far more clear, Thee in man's

all a - bove, be - low, Cre - a - tion lives and
in the quick - ening air; When light - nings flash and
in the march of night; And when the morn - ing
spir - it we be - hold; Thine im - age and thy -

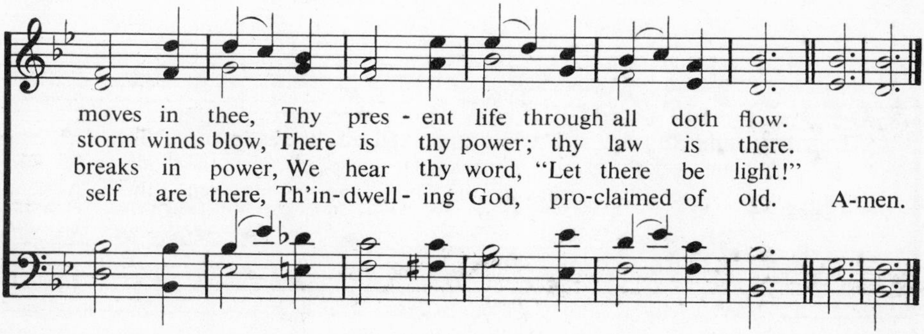
moves in thee, Thy pres - ent life through all doth flow.
storm winds blow, There is thy power; thy law is there.
breaks in power, We hear thy word, "Let there be light!"
self are there, Th'in-dwell - ing God, pro-claimed of old. A-men.

I Sing the Almighty Power of God

FOREST GREEN CMD
Trad. English Melody
Arr. by R. VAUGHAN WILLIAMS, 1872-1958

ISAAC WATTS, 1674-1748

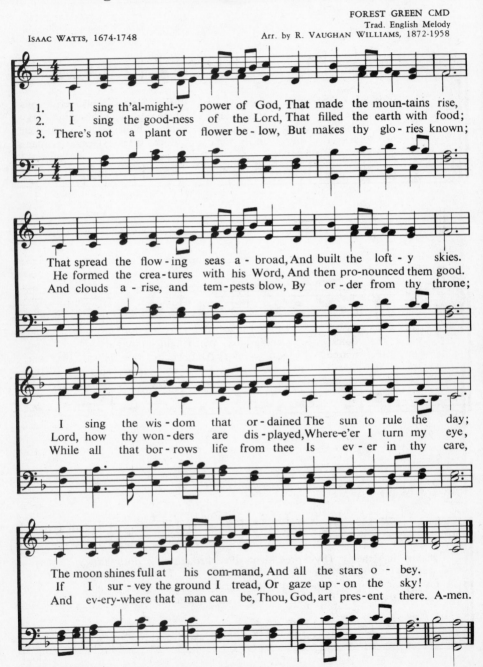

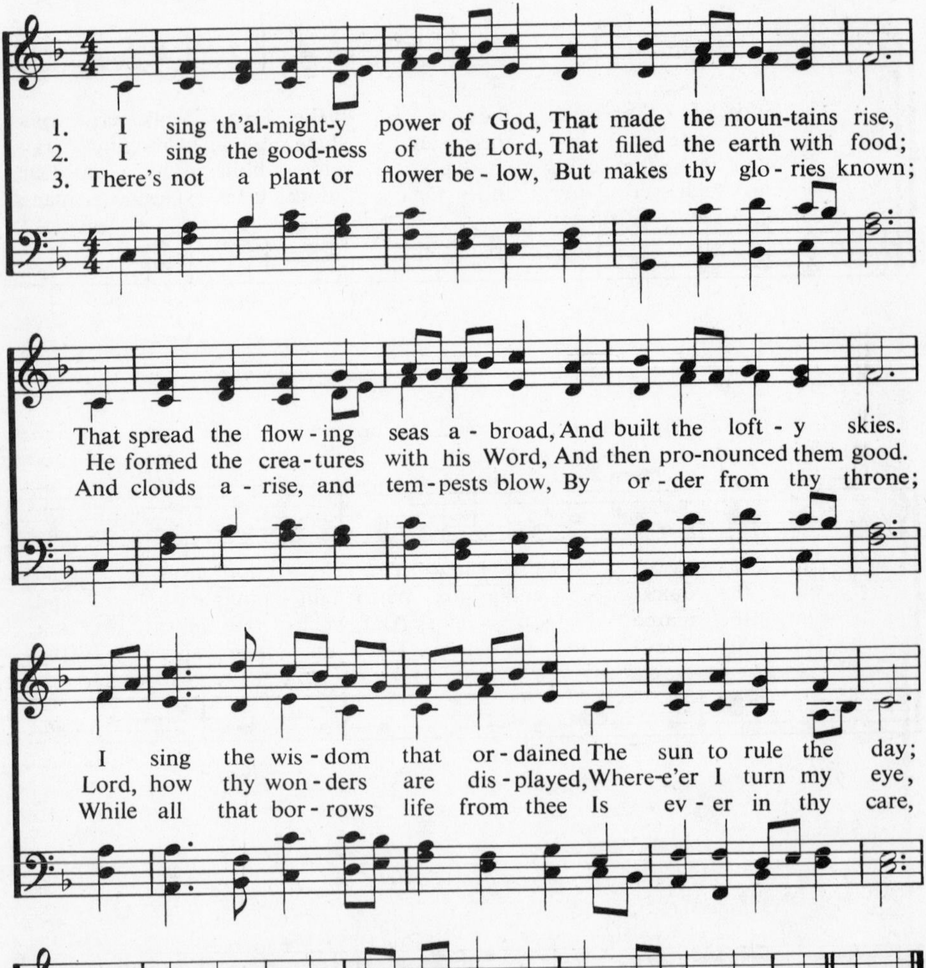
1. I sing th'al-might-y power of God, That made the moun-tains rise,
2. I sing the good-ness of the Lord, That filled the earth with food;
3. There's not a plant or flower be - low, But makes thy glo - ries known;
That spread the flow - ing seas a - broad, And built the loft - y skies.
He formed the crea - tures with his Word, And then pro-nounced them good.
And clouds a - rise, and tem - pests blow, By or - der from thy throne;
I sing the wis - dom that or - dained The sun to rule the day;
Lord, how thy won - ders are dis - played, Where-e'er I turn my eye,
While all that bor - rows life from thee Is ev - er in thy care,
The moon shines full at his com-mand, And all the stars o - bey.
If I sur - vey the ground I tread, Or gaze up - on the sky!
And ev-ery-where that man can be, Thou, God, art pres - ent there. A-men.

Joyful, Joyful, We Adore Thee

HENRY VAN DYKE, 1852-1933

HYMN TO JOY 87.87.D.
Arr. from LUDWIG VAN BEETHOVEN, 1770-1827
by EDWARD HODGES, 1796-1867

1. Joy-ful, joy-ful, we a-dore thee, God of glo-ry, Lord of love;
2. All thy works with joy sur-round thee, Earth and heav'n re-flect thy rays,
3. Thou art giv-ing and for-giv-ing, Ev-er bless-ing, ev-er blest,
4. Mor-tals join the might-y cho-rus, Which the morn-ing stars be-gan;
Hearts un-fold like flowers be-fore thee, Open-ing to the sun a-bove.
Stars and an-gels sing a-round thee, Cen-ter of un-bro-ken praise;
Well-spring of the joy of liv-ing, O-cean-depth of hap-py rest!
Fa-ther love is reign-ing o'er us, Broth-er love binds man to man.
Melt the clouds of sin and sad-ness; Drive the dark of doubt a-way;
Field and for-est, vale and moun-tain, Flow-ery mead-ow, flash-ing sea,
Thou our Fa-ther, Christ our broth-er, All who live in love are thine;
Ev-er sing-ing, march we on-ward, Vic-tors in the midst of strife;
Giv-er of im-mor-tal glad-ness, Fill us with the light of day!
Chant-ing bird and flow-ing foun-tain, Call us to re-joice in thee.
Teach us how to love each oth-er, Lift us to the joy di-vine.
Joy-ful mu-sic leads us sun-ward In the tri-umph song of life. A-men.

Let All on Earth Their Voices Raise

OLD 113TH 886.D.
Strassburger Kirchenamt, 1525
Probably by MATTHÄUS GREITER, c. 1500-1552
Harm. by V.E.C.

PSALM 96
ISAAC WATTS, 1674-1748

Unison
1. Let all on earth their voic - es raise, To
2. He framed the globe; he built the sky; He
3. Come, the great day, the glo - rious hour, When
sing the great Je - ho - vah's praise, And bless his ho - ly name:
made the shin - ing worlds on high, And reigns in glo - ry there:
earth shall feel his sav - ing power, All na - tions fear his name;
His glo - ry let the peo - ple know, His
His beams are maj - es - ty and light; His
Then shall the race of men con - fess The
won - ders to the na - tions show, His sav - ing grace pro - claim.
beau - ties, how di - vine - ly bright! His dwell - ing place, how fair!
beau - ty of his ho - li - ness, His sav - ing grace pro - claim. A - men.

Many and Great, O God

American Folk Hymn
Paraphrase by PHILIP FRAZIER

LACQUIPARLE Irregular
American Folk Hymn

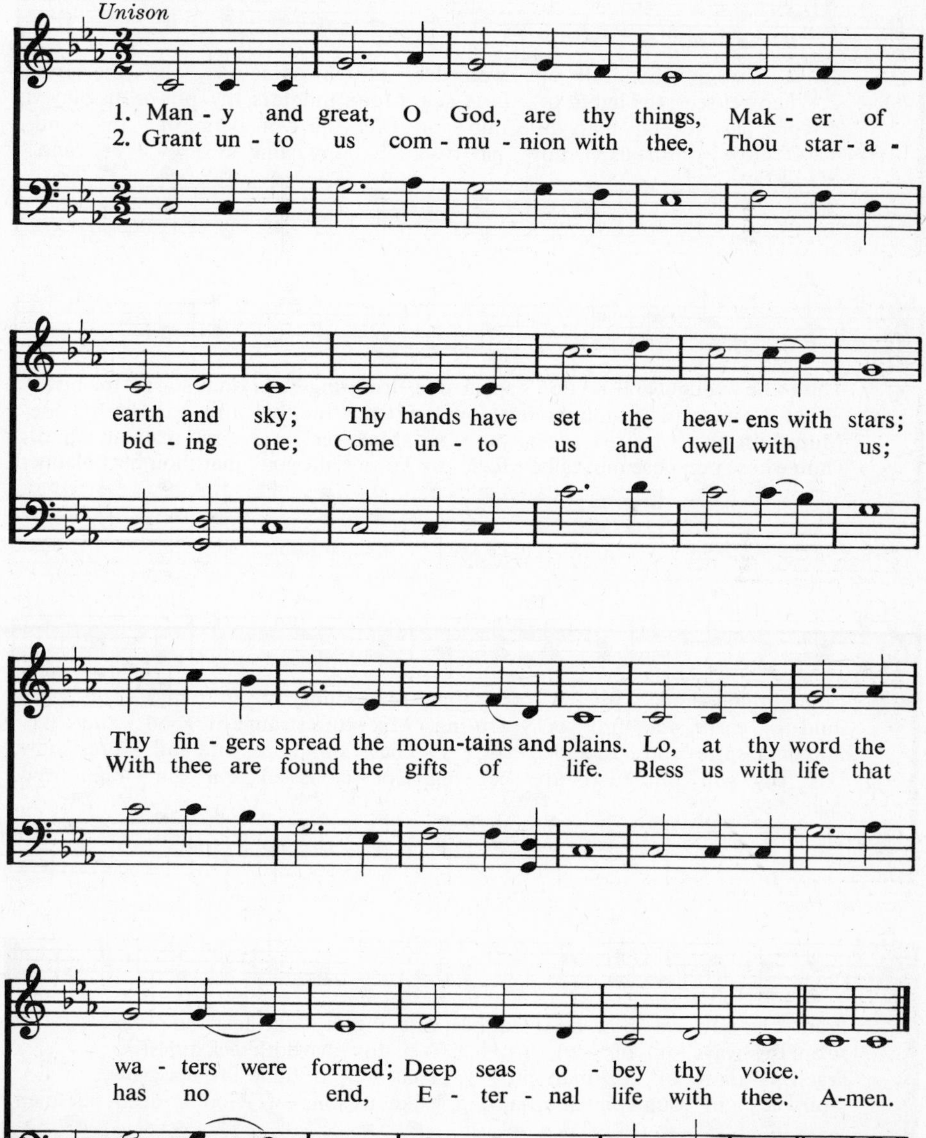
Unison
1. Man - y and great, O God, are thy things, Mak - er of
2. Grant un - to us com - mu - nion with thee, Thou star - a -
earth and sky; Thy hands have set the heav - ens with stars;
bid - ing one; Come un - to us and dwell with us;
Thy fin - gers spread the moun - tains and plains. Lo, at thy word the
With thee are found the gifts of life. Bless us with life that
wa - ters were formed; Deep seas o - bey thy voice.
has no end, E - ter - nal life with thee. A-men.

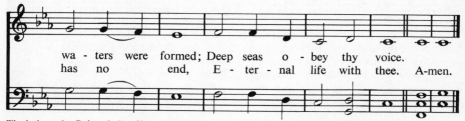

Words from the *Dakota Indian Hymnal,* copyright 1916 by Olive W. Riggs. Used by permission.

O How Glorious, Full of Wonder

HYMN TO JOY 87.87.D.
Arr. from LUDWIG VAN BEETHOVEN, 1770-1827
by EDWARD HODGES, 1796-1867

PSALM 8
CURTIS BEACH, 1914-

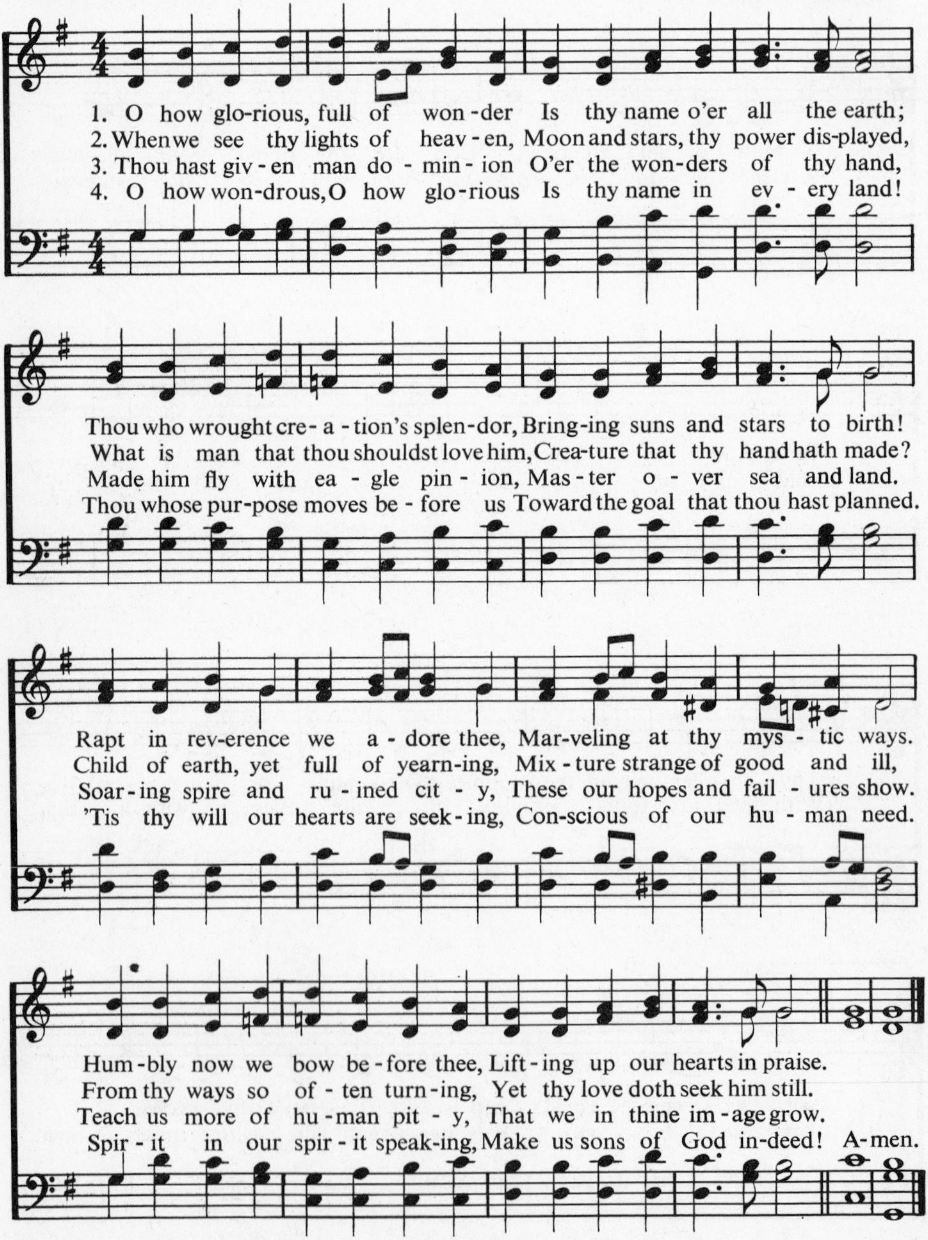
1. O how glo-rious, full of won-der Is thy name o'er all the earth;
2. When we see thy lights of heav-en, Moon and stars, thy power dis-played,
3. Thou hast giv-en man do-min-ion O'er the won-ders of thy hand,
4. O how won-drous, O how glo-rious Is thy name in ev-ery land!
Thou who wrought cre-a-tion's splen-dor, Bring-ing suns and stars to birth!
What is man that thou shouldst love him, Crea-ture that thy hand hath made?
Made him fly with ea-gle pin-ion, Mas-ter o-ver sea and land.
Thou whose pur-pose moves be-fore us Toward the goal that thou hast planned.
Rapt in rev-erence we a-dore thee, Mar-veling at thy mys-tic ways.
Child of earth, yet full of yearn-ing, Mix-ture strange of good and ill,
Soar-ing spire and ru-ined cit-y, These our hopes and fail-ures show.
'Tis thy will our hearts are seek-ing, Con-scious of our hu-man need.
Hum-bly now we bow be-fore thee, Lift-ing up our hearts in praise.
From thy ways so of-ten turn-ing, Yet thy love doth seek him still.
Teach us more of hu-man pit-y, That we in thine im-age grow.
Spir-it in our spir-it speak-ing, Make us sons of God in-deed! A-men.

42

Praise the Lord! Ye Heavens Adore Him

PSALM 148
The Foundling Hospital Collection, 1796

AUSTRIA 87.87.D.
FRANZ JOSEPH HAYDN, 1732-1809

1. Praise the Lord! ye heavens a-dore him; Praise him, an-gels, in the height;
2. Praise the Lord! for he is glo - rious; Nev - er shall his prom-ise fail;
Sun and moon, re - joice be - fore him; Praise him, all ye stars of light.
God hath made his saints vic - to - rious; Sin and death shall not pre - vail.
Praise the Lord! for he hath spo - ken; Worlds his might - y voice o-beyed;
Praise the God of our sal - va - tion! Hosts on high, his power pro-claim;
Laws which nev-er shall be bro - ken For their guid-ance hath he made.
Heaven, and earth, and all cre - a - tion, Laud and mag-ni - fy his name. A-men.

Alternate tune: HYFRYDOL

CREATION

The Spacious Firmament on High

CREATION LMD
The Choral, 1845
Adapt. from FRANZ JOSEPH HAYDN, 1732-1809

PSALM 19
JOSEPH ADDISON, 1672-1719

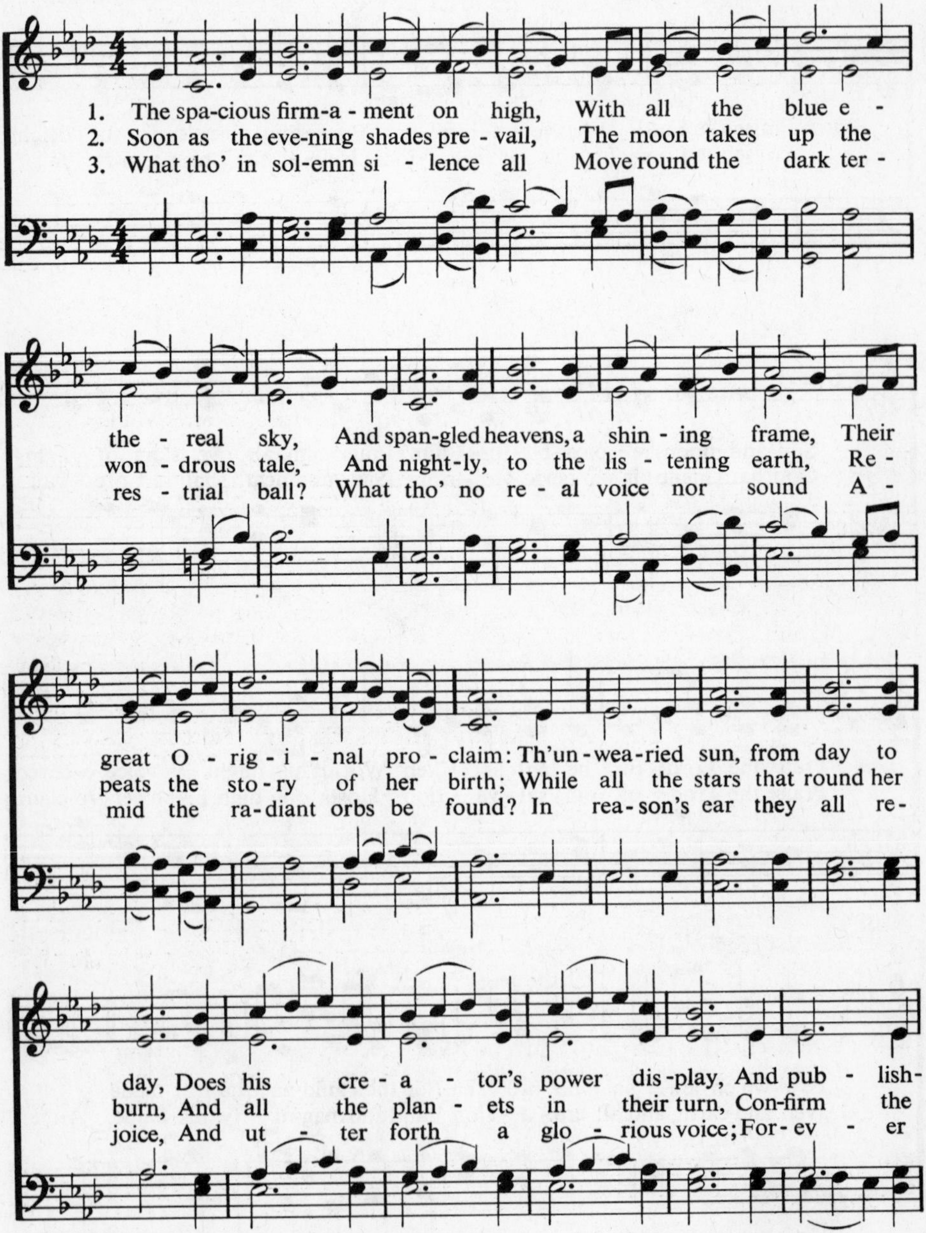
1. The spa-cious firm-a - ment on high, With all the blue e -
2. Soon as the eve-ning shades pre - vail, The moon takes up the
3. What tho' in sol-emn si - lence all Move round the dark ter -
the - real sky, And span-gled heavens, a shin - ing frame, Their
won - drous tale, And night-ly, to the lis - tening earth, Re -
res - trial ball? What tho' no re - al voice nor sound A -
great O - rig - i - nal pro - claim: Th'un-wea-ried sun, from day to
peats the sto - ry of her birth; While all the stars that round her
mid the ra-diant orbs be found? In rea-son's ear they all re-
day, Does his cre - a - tor's power dis-play, And pub - lish-
burn, And all the plan - ets in their turn, Con-firm the
joice, And ut - ter forth a glo - rious voice; For-ev - er

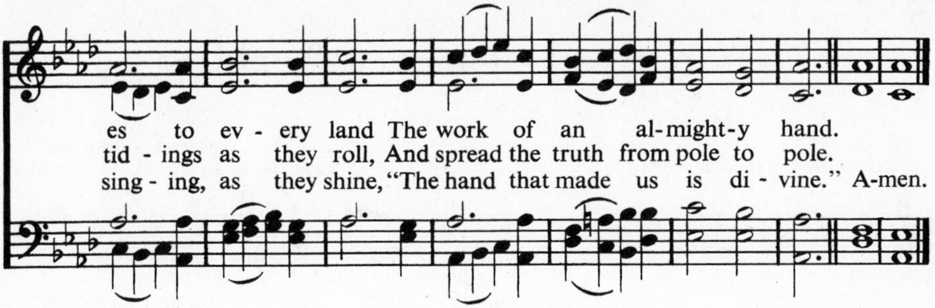
es to ev - ery land The work of an al-might-y hand.
tid - ings as they roll, And spread the truth from pole to pole.
sing - ing, as they shine, "The hand that made us is di - vine." A-men.

O Lord, Our Lord, in All the Earth

CHRISTUS, DER IST MEIN LEBEN CM
Ein schön geistlich Gesangbuch, Jena, 1609
MELCHIOR VULPIUS, c. 1560-1616

PSALM 8
The Psalter, 1912

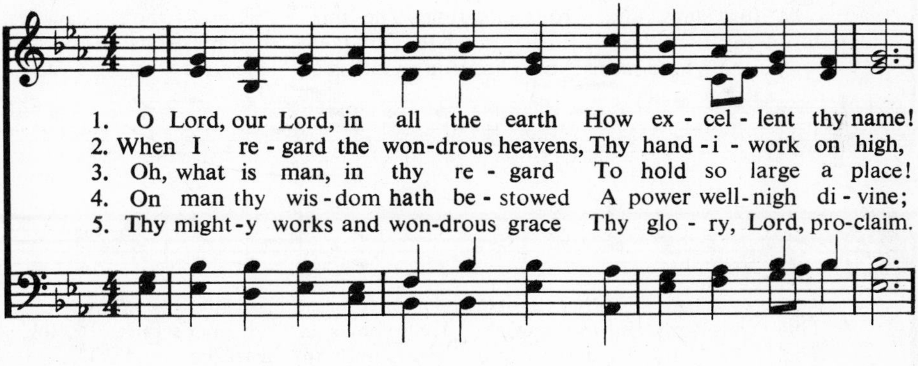
1. O Lord, our Lord, in all the earth How ex - cel - lent thy name!
2. When I re - gard the won-drous heavens, Thy hand - i - work on high,
3. Oh, what is man, in thy re - gard To hold so large a place!
4. On man thy wis - dom hath be - stowed A power well-nigh di - vine;
5. Thy might - y works and won-drous grace Thy glo - ry, Lord, pro-claim.

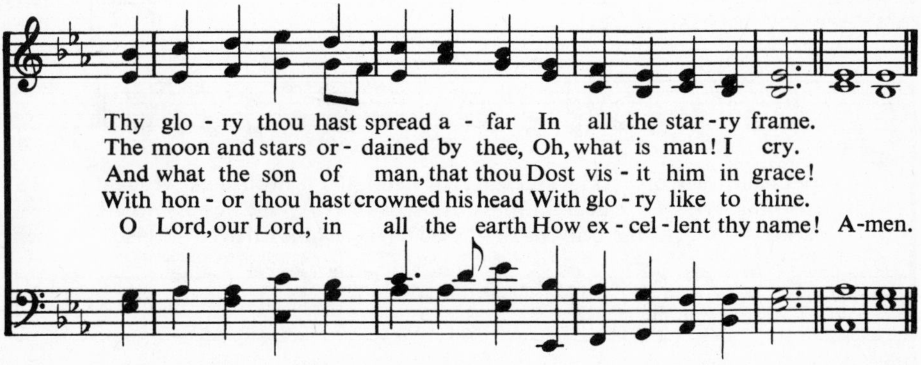
Thy glo - ry thou hast spread a - far In all the star - ry frame.
The moon and stars or - dained by thee, Oh, what is man! I cry.
And what the son of man, that thou Dost vis - it him in grace!
With hon - or thou hast crowned his head With glo - ry like to thine.
O Lord, our Lord, in all the earth How ex - cel - lent thy name! A-men.

45

This Is My Father's World

TERRA BEATA SMD

MALTBIE D. BABCOCK, 1858-1901 — FRANKLIN L. SHEPPARD, 1852-1930

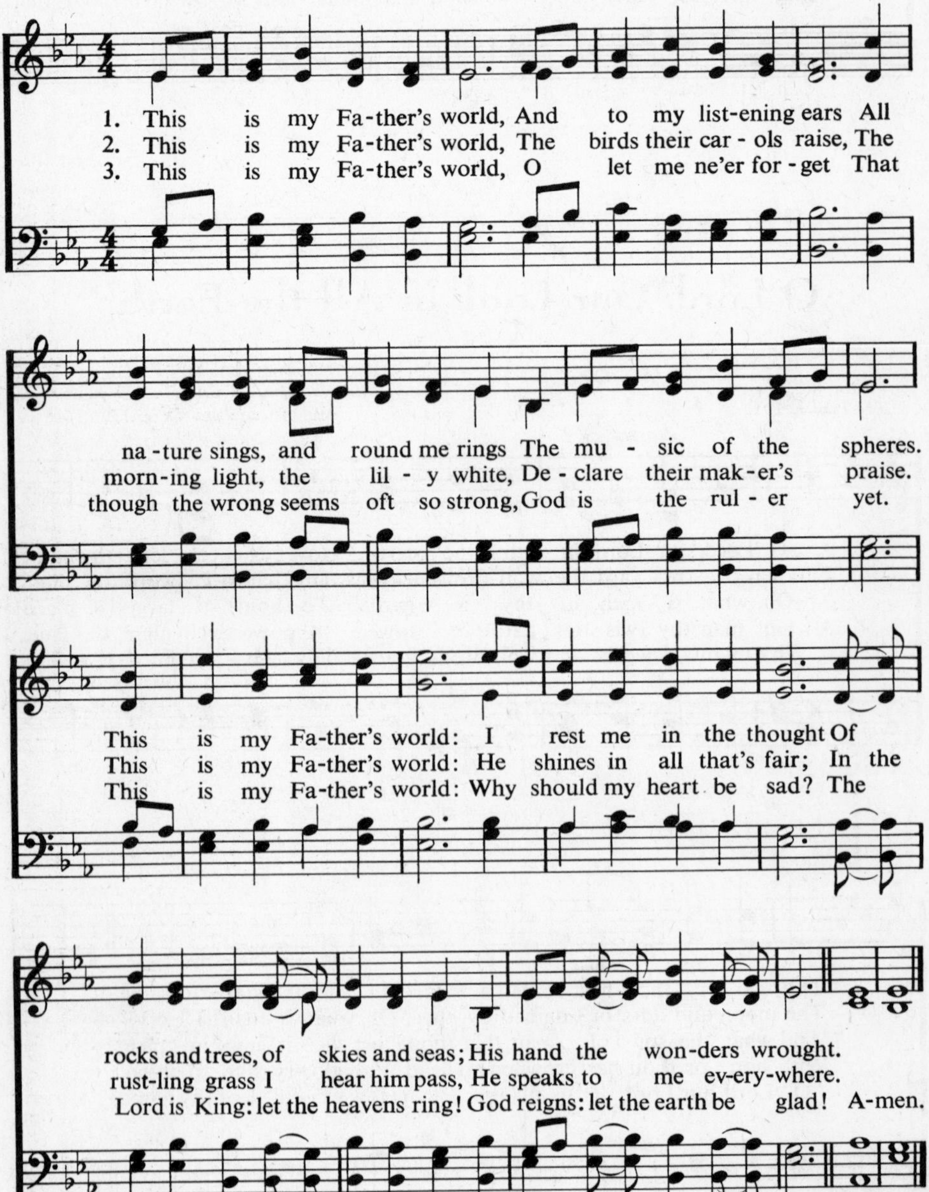
1. This is my Fa-ther's world, And to my list-ening ears All
2. This is my Fa-ther's world, The birds their car - ols raise, The
3. This is my Fa-ther's world, O let me ne'er for - get That
na - ture sings, and round me rings The mu - sic of the spheres.
morn-ing light, the lil - y white, De - clare their mak-er's praise.
though the wrong seems oft so strong, God is the rul - er yet.
This is my Fa-ther's world: I rest me in the thought Of
This is my Fa-ther's world: He shines in all that's fair; In the
This is my Fa-ther's world: Why should my heart be sad? The
rocks and trees, of skies and seas; His hand the won-ders wrought.
rust-ling grass I hear him pass, He speaks to me ev-ery-where.
Lord is King: let the heavens ring! God reigns: let the earth be glad! A-men.

Captain of Israel's Host

EISENACH 88.88.88.

EXODUS 13:21
CHARLES WESLEY, 1707-1788

JOHANN H. SCHEIN, 1586-1630
Harm. by J. S. BACH, 1685-1750

1. Cap-tain of Is-rael's host, and guide Of all who seek the
2. By thine un-err-ing spir-it led, We shall not in the
land a-bove, Be-neath thy sha-dow we a-bide, The
des-ert stray; We shall not full di-rec-tion need, Nor
cloud of thy pro-tect-ing love; Our strength, thy grace; our
miss our prov-i-den-tial way; As far from dan-ger
rule, thy word; Our end, the glo-ry of the Lord.
as from fear, While love, al-might-y love, is near. A-men.

PROVIDENCE

God of Our Life

SANDON 10 4.10 4.10 10.

HUGH T. KERR, 1872-1950

CHARLES H. PURDAY, 1799-1885

1. God of our life, through all the cir - cling years, We trust in thee;
2. God of the past, our times are in thy hand; With us a - bide.
3. God of the com - ing years, through paths un- known We fol - low thee;
In all the past, through all our hopes and fears, Thy hand we see.
Lead us by faith to hope's true prom-ised land; Be thou our guide.
When we are strong, Lord, leave us not a - lone; Our ref - uge be.
With each new day, when morn - ing lifts the veil, We
With thee to bless, the dark - ness shines as light, And
Be thou for us in life our dai - ly bread, Our
own thy mer - cies, Lord, which nev - er fail.
faith's fair vi - sion chang - es in - to sight.
heart's true home when all our years have sped. A - men.

How Firm a Foundation

II TIMOTHY 2:19; HEBREWS 13:5; ISAIAH 43:1-2
"K" IN RIPPON'S *A Selection of Hymns,* 1787

FOUNDATION 11 11. 11 11.
Early American Melody
Harm. by C.R.Y.

Unison
1. How firm a foun - da - tion, ye saints of the Lord, Is
2. "Fear not, I am with thee; O be not dis - mayed, For
3. "When through the deep wa - ters I call thee to go, The
4. "When through fi - ery tri - als thy path - ways shall lie, My
5. "The soul that on Je - sus still leans for re - pose, I
laid for your faith in his ex - cel - lent Word! What
I am thy God, and will still give thee aid; I'll
riv - ers of woe shall not thee o - ver - flow; For
grace, all - suf - fi - cient, shall be thy sup - ply; The
will not, I will not de - sert to his foes; That
more can he say than to you he hath said, To
strength - en thee, help thee, and cause thee to stand, Up -
I will be with thee thy trou - bles to bless, And
flame shall not hurt thee; I on - ly de - sign Thy
soul, though all hell should en - deav - or to shake, I'll
you who for ref - uge to Je - sus have fled?
held by my righ - teous, om - nip - o - tent hand.
sanc - ti - fy to thee thy deep - est dis - tress.
dross to con - sume, and thy gold to re - fine.
nev - er, no, nev - er, no, nev - er for - sake!" A - men.

Alternate tune: ADESTE FIDELES

PROVIDENCE

49

Now Thank We All Our God

ECCLESIASTICUS 50:22-24
MARTIN RINKART, 1586-1649
Trans. by CATHERINE WINKWORTH, 1827-1878

NUN DANKET 67.67.66.66.
JOHANN CRÜGER, 1598-1662
Harm. by FELIX MENDELSSOHN, 1809-1847

1. Now thank we all our God With heart and hands and voic - es,
2. O may this boun-teous God Through all our life be near us,
3. All praise and thanks to God The Fa - ther now be giv - en,
Who won-drous things hath done, In whom his world re - joic - es;
With ev - er joy - ful hearts And bless - ed peace to cheer us;
The Son, and him who reigns With them in high - est heav - en,
Who, from our moth - ers' arms, Hath blessed us on our way
And keep us in his grace, And guide us when per - plexed,
The one e - ter - nal God, Whom earth and heaven a - dore;
With count-less gifts of love, And still is ours to - day.
And free us from all ills In this world and the next.
For thus it was, is now, And shall be ev - er - more. A-men.

My God, I Thank Thee

ADELAIDE A. PROCTER, 1825-1864

WENTWORTH 84.84.84.
FREDERICK C. MAKER, 1844-1927

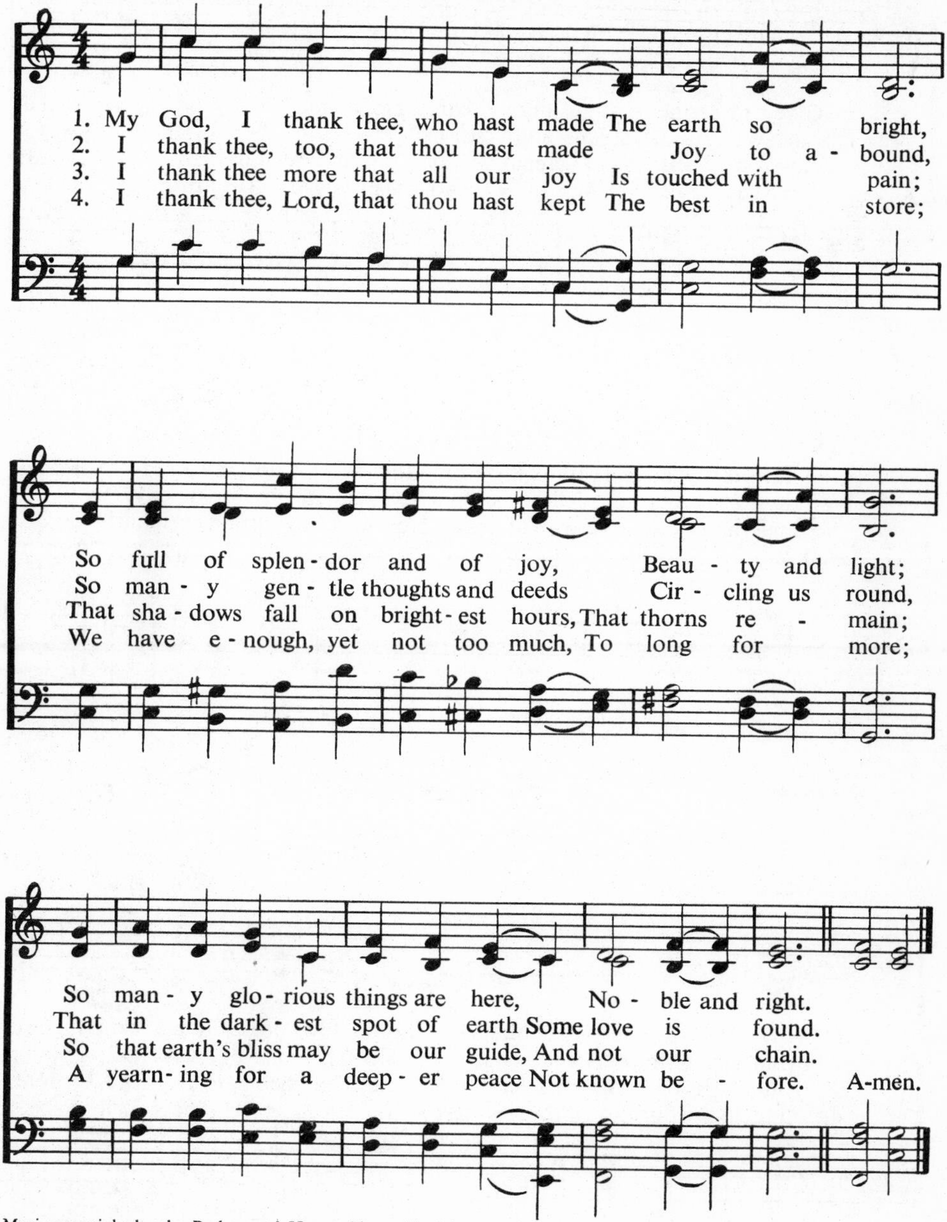
1. My God, I thank thee, who hast made The earth so bright,
2. I thank thee, too, that thou hast made Joy to a - bound,
3. I thank thee more that all our joy Is touched with pain;
4. I thank thee, Lord, that thou hast kept The best in store;
So full of splen - dor and of joy, Beau - ty and light;
So man - y gen - tle thoughts and deeds Cir - cling us round,
That sha - dows fall on bright - est hours, That thorns re - main;
We have e - nough, yet not too much, To long for more;
So man - y glo - rious things are here, No - ble and right.
That in the dark - est spot of earth Some love is found.
So that earth's bliss may be our guide, And not our chain.
A yearn - ing for a deep - er peace Not known be - fore. A-men.

51

Give to the Winds Thy Fears

PSALM 37:5
PAUL GERHARDT, 1607-1676
Trans. by JOHN WESLEY, 1703-1791

ST. BRIDE SM
SAMUEL HOWARD, 1710-1782

1. Give to the winds thy fears; Hope and be un - dis - mayed;
2. Through waves and clouds and storms, He gent - ly clears thy way;
3. Leave to his sov - ereign sway To choose and to com - mand;
4. Let us in life, in death, Thy stead - fast truth de - clare,

God hears thy sighs and counts thy tears, God shall lift up thy head.
Wait thou his time; so shall this night Soon end in joy - ous day.
So shall thou, wondering, own his way, How wise, how strong his hand!
And pub - lish with our lat - est breath Thy love and guard - ian care. A-men.

52

How Are Thy Servants Blest, O Lord

CAITHNESS CM
Scottish Psalter, 1635

JOSEPH ADDISON, 1672-1719

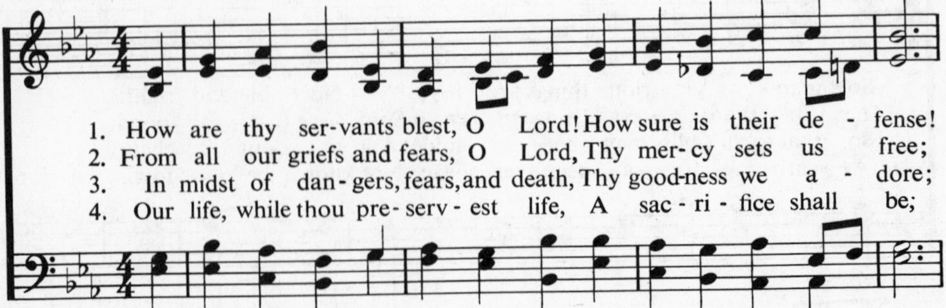
1. How are thy ser - vants blest, O Lord! How sure is their de - fense!
2. From all our griefs and fears, O Lord, Thy mer - cy sets us free;
3. In midst of dan - gers, fears, and death, Thy good-ness we a - dore;
4. Our life, while thou pre - serv - est life, A sac - ri - fice shall be;

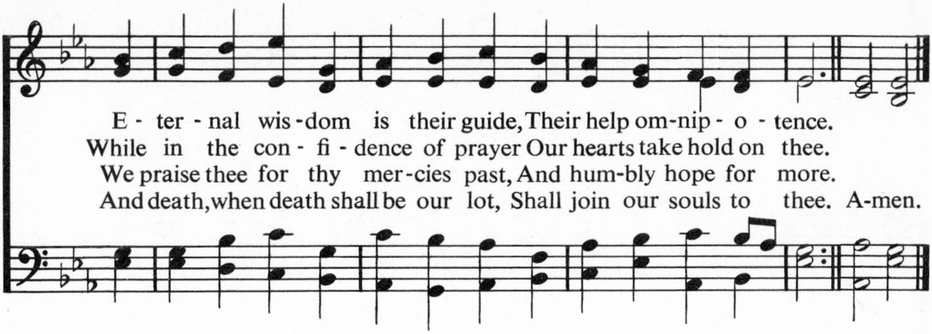
E - ter - nal wis - dom is their guide, Their help om-nip - o - tence.
While in the con - fi - dence of prayer Our hearts take hold on thee.
We praise thee for thy mer-cies past, And hum-bly hope for more.
And death, when death shall be our lot, Shall join our souls to thee. A-men.

53

How Gentle God's Commands

DENNIS SM

I PETER 5:7
PHILIP DODDRIDGE, 1702-1751

Arr. from JOHANN G. NÄGELI, 1768-1836
by LOWELL MASON, 1792-1872

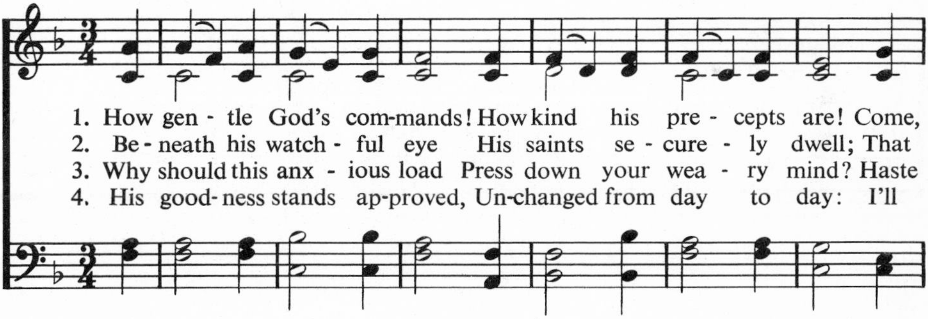
1. How gen - tle God's com-mands! How kind his pre - cepts are! Come,
2. Be - neath his watch - ful eye His saints se - cure - ly dwell; That
3. Why should this anx - ious load Press down your wea - ry mind? Haste
4. His good-ness stands ap-proved, Un-changed from day to day: I'll

cast your bur - dens on the Lord, And trust his con-stant care.
hand which bears all na - ture up Shall guard his chil - dren well.
to your heaven-ly Fa - ther's throne, And sweet re-fresh-ment find.
drop my bur - den at his feet, And bear a song a - way. A-men.

O Lord, Our Fathers Oft Have Told

WINCHESTER OLD CM
Est's *The Whole Booke of Psalmes,* 1592
Tune arrang. attr. to GEORGE KIRBYE, c. 1560-1634

PSALM 44 *New Version*
TATE AND BRADY, 1696

1. O Lord, our fa - thers oft have told, In
2. 'Twas not their cour - age nor their sword To
3. But thy right hand, thy power - ful arm, Whose
4. As thee their God our fa - thers owned, So
5. To thee the glo - ry we as - cribe, From

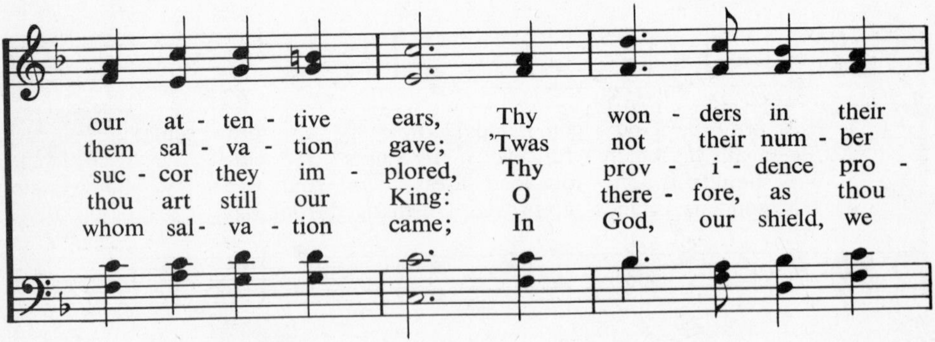
our at - ten - tive ears, Thy won - ders in their
them sal - va - tion gave; 'Twas not their num - ber
suc - cor they im - plored, Thy prov - i - dence pro -
thou art still our King: O there - fore, as thou
whom sal - va - tion came; In God, our shield, we

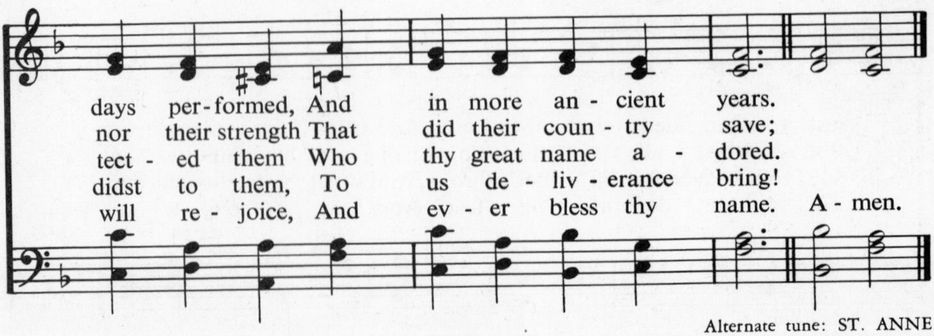
days per - formed, And in more an - cient years.
nor their strength That did their coun - try save;
tect - ed them Who thy great name a - dored.
didst to them, To us de - liv - erance bring!
will re - joice, And ev - er bless thy name. A - men.

Alternate tune: ST. ANNE

55

Praise to the Lord, the Almighty

PSALMS 103, 150
JOACHIM NEANDER, 1650-1680
Trans. by CATHERINE WINKWORTH, 1827-1878

LOBE DEN HERREN 14 14.478.
Stralsund Gesangbuch, 1665
Harm. from *The Chorale Book for England,* 1864

1. Praise to the Lord, the Al-might-y, the King of cre - a - tion!
2. Praise to the Lord, who o'er all things so won-drous - ly reign - eth,
3. Praise to the Lord, who doth pros-per thy work and de - fend thee;
4. Praise to the Lord! O let all that is in me a - dore him!
O my soul, praise him, for he is thy health and sal - va - tion!
Shield-eth thee un - der his wings, yea, so gent - ly sus - tain - eth!
Sure - ly his good-ness and mer - cy here dai - ly at - tend thee.
All that hath life and breath, come now with prais-es be - fore him!
All ye who hear, Now to his tem - ple draw near;
Hast thou not seen How thy de - sires e'er have been
Pon - der a - new What the Al - might - y can do,
Let the a - men Sound from his peo - ple a - gain;
Join me in glad ad - o - ra - - tion!
Grant - ed in what he or - dain - - eth?
If with his love he be - friend thee.
Glad - ly for - ev - er a - dore him. A - men.

PROVIDENCE

Through All the Changing Scenes of Life

IRISH CM

PSALM 34 *New Version*
TATE AND BRADY, 1696

A Collection of Hymns and Sacred Poems, 1749
Probably arr. by JOHN F. LAMPE, 1703-1751

1. Through all the chang - ing scenes of life, In trou - ble
2. O mag - ni - fy the Lord with me, With me ex-
3. O make but tri - al of his love; Ex - pe - rience
4. Fear him, ye saints, and you will then Have noth - ing
5. For God pre - serves the souls of those Who on his
and in joy, The prais - es of my God shall
alt his name; When in dis - tress to him I
will de - cide How blest are they, and on - ly
else to fear; Make you his serv - ice your de -
truth de - pend; To them and their pos - ter - i -
still My heart and tongue em - ploy.
called, He to my res - cue came.
they, Who in his truth con - fide.
light; Your wants shall be his care.
ty His bless - ing shall de - scend. A - men.

57

Unto the Hills I Lift Mine Eyes

PSALM 121
The Psalter, 1912

DUNFERMLINE CM
Scottish Psalter, 1615

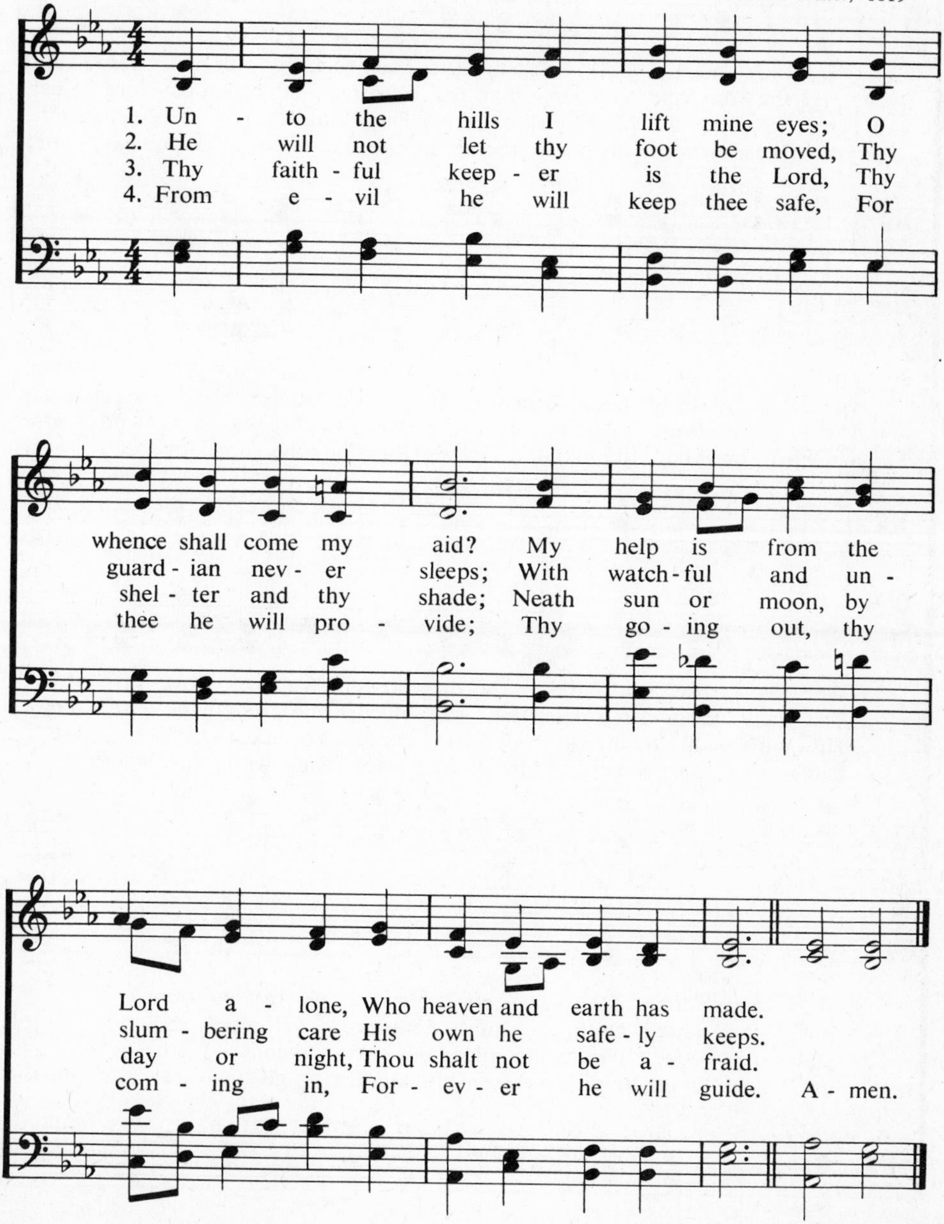

1. Un - to the hills I lift mine eyes; O
2. He will not let thy foot be moved, Thy
3. Thy faith - ful keep - er is the Lord, Thy
4. From e - vil he will keep thee safe, For
whence shall come my aid? My help is from the
guard - ian nev - er sleeps; With watch - ful and un -
shel - ter and thy shade; Neath sun or moon, by
thee he will pro - vide; Thy go - ing out, thy
Lord a - lone, Who heaven and earth has made.
slum - bering care His own he safe - ly keeps.
day or night, Thou shalt not be a - fraid.
com - ing in, For - ev - er he will guide. A - men.

PROVIDENCE

58

We Come unto Our Fathers' God

PSALM 90:1
THOMAS H. GILL, 1819-1906

NUN FREUT EUCH 87.87.887.
Klug's *Gesangbuch,* Wittenberg, 1535

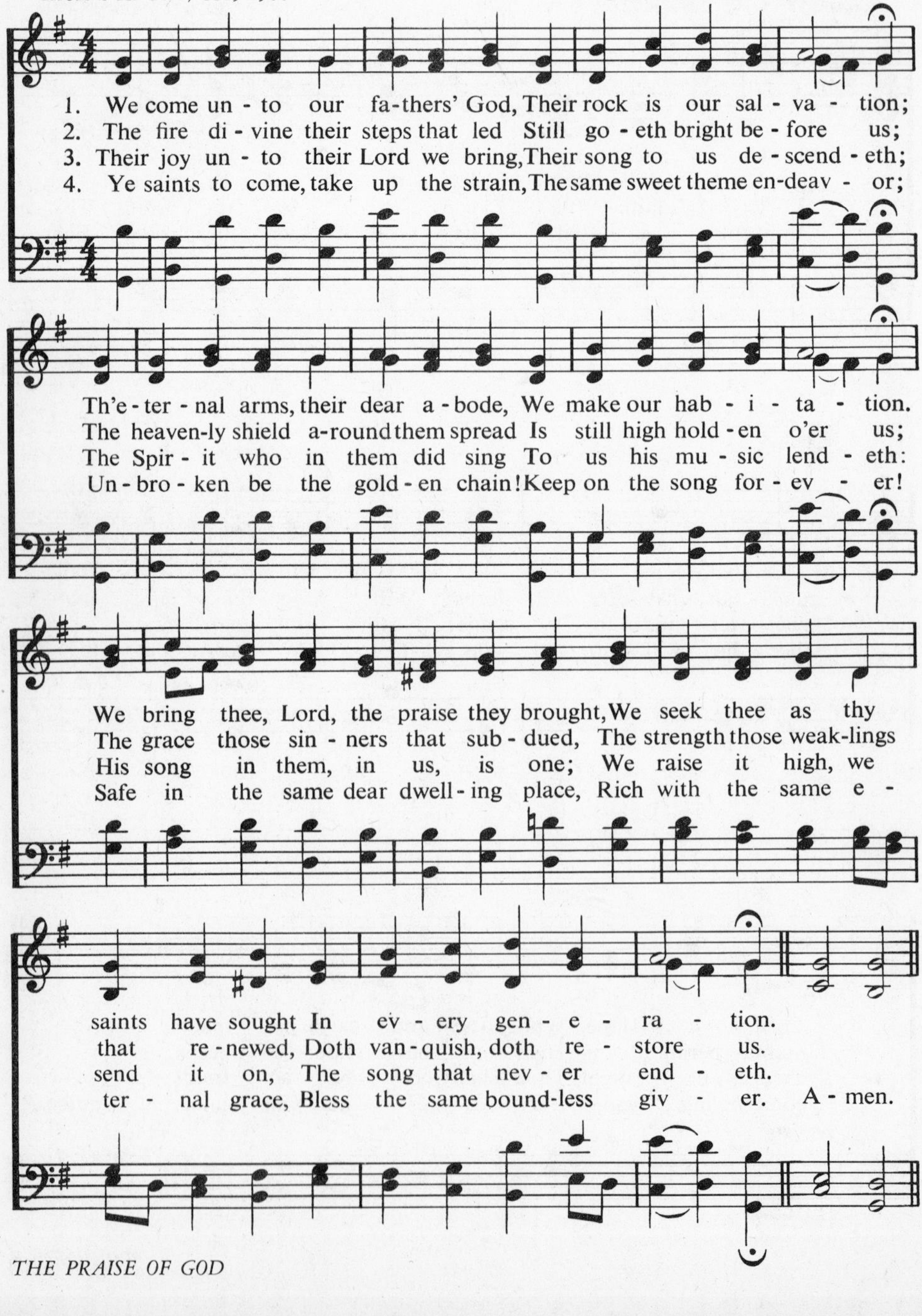
1. We come un - to our fa-thers' God, Their rock is our sal - va - tion;
2. The fire di - vine their steps that led Still go - eth bright be - fore us;
3. Their joy un - to their Lord we bring, Their song to us de - scend - eth;
4. Ye saints to come, take up the strain, The same sweet theme en-deav - or;
Th'e - ter - nal arms, their dear a - bode, We make our hab - i - ta - tion.
The heaven-ly shield a-round them spread Is still high hold - en o'er us;
The Spir - it who in them did sing To us his mu - sic lend - eth:
Un - bro - ken be the gold - en chain! Keep on the song for - ev - er!
We bring thee, Lord, the praise they brought, We seek thee as thy
The grace those sin - ners that sub - dued, The strength those weak-lings
His song in them, in us, is one; We raise it high, we
Safe in the same dear dwell - ing place, Rich with the same e -
saints have sought In ev - ery gen - e - ra - tion.
that re - newed, Doth van - quish, doth re - store us.
send it on, The song that nev - er end - eth.
ter - nal grace, Bless the same bound-less giv - er. A - men.

59

We Gather Together

Netherlands Folk Hymn
Trans. by THEODORE BAKER, 1851-1934

KREMSER Irregular
Nederlandtsch Gedenckclanck, 1626
Arr. by EDWARD KREMSER, 1838-1914

1. We gath - er to - geth - er to ask the Lord's bless - ing;
2. Be - side us to guide us, our God with us join - ing,
3. We all do ex - tol thee, thou lead - er tri - um - phant,
He chas - tens and has - tens his will to make known;
Or - dain - ing, main - tain - ing his king - dom di - vine;
And pray that thou still our de - fend - er wilt be.
The wick - ed op - press - ing now cease from dis - tress - ing,
So from the be - gin - ning the fight we were win - ning;
Let thy con - gre - ga - tion es - cape trib - u - la - tion;
Sing prais - es to his name: He for - gets not his own.
Thou, Lord, wast at our side, All glo - ry be thine!
Thy name be ev - er praised! O Lord, make us free! A-men.

Words by permission of G. Schirmer, Inc.

PROVIDENCE

All Creatures of Our God and King

LASST UNS ERFREUEN 88.44.88. with Alleluias
Melody from *Geistliche Kirchengesänge*, 1623
Harm. by R. VAUGHAN WILLIAMS, 1872-1958

FRANCIS OF ASSISI, 1182-1226
Trans. by WILLIAM H. DRAPER, 1855-1933

Unison
1. All crea - tures of our God and King, Lift
2. Thou rush - ing wind that art so strong, Ye
3. Thou flow - ing wa - ter, pure and clear, Make
4. Dear moth - er earth, who day by day Un -
5. And all ye men of ten - der heart, For -
6. And thou, most kind and gen - tle death, Wait -
7. Let all things their cre - a - tor bless, And
up your voice and with us sing Al - le - lu - ia! Al - le -
clouds that sail in heaven a - long, O praise him! Al - le -
mu - sic for thy Lord to hear, Al - le - lu - ia! Al - le -
fold - est bless - ings on our way, O praise him! Al - le -
giv - ing oth - ers, take your part, O sing ye! Al - le -
ing to hush our lat - est breath, O praise him! Al - le -
wor - ship him in hum - ble - ness, O praise him! Al - le -
lu - ia! Thou burn - ing sun with gold - en beam, Thou
lu - ia! Thou ris - ing morn, in praise re - joice, Ye
lu - ia! Thou fire so mas - ter - ful and bright, Thou
lu - ia! The flowers and fruits that in thee grow, Let
lu - ia! Ye who long pain and sor - row bear, Praise
lu - ia! Thou lead - est home the child of God, And
lu - ia! Praise, praise the Fa - ther, praise the Son, And

Words used by permission of J. Curwen & Sons, Ltd.
Music from *The English Hymnal* by permission of Oxford University Press.

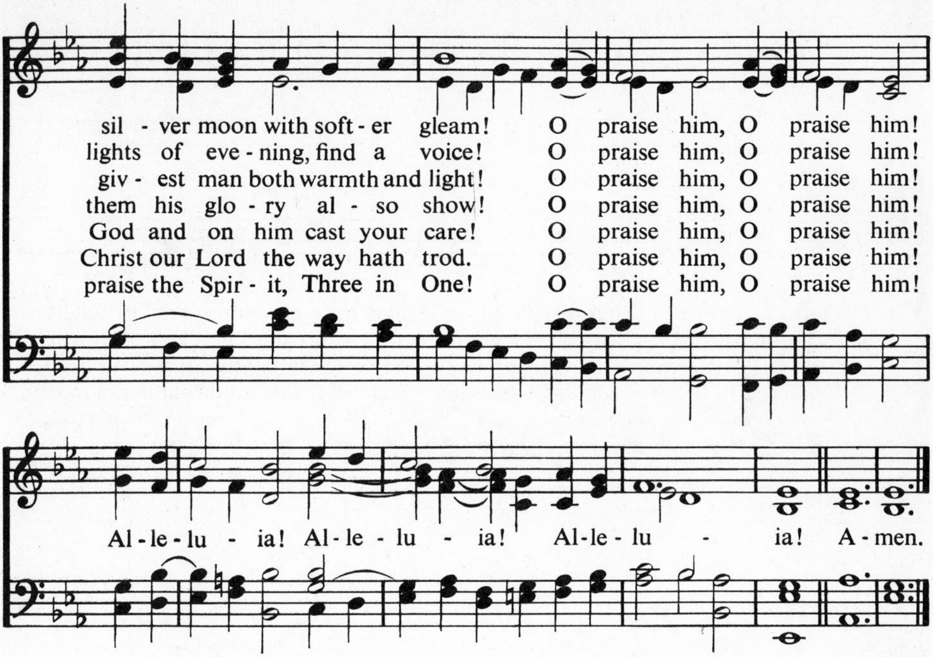
sil - ver moon with soft - er gleam! O praise him, O praise him!
lights of eve - ning, find a voice! O praise him, O praise him!
giv - est man both warmth and light! O praise him, O praise him!
them his glo - ry al - so show! O praise him, O praise him!
God and on him cast your care! O praise him, O praise him!
Christ our Lord the way hath trod. O praise him, O praise him!
praise the Spir - it, Three in One! O praise him, O praise him!
Al - le - lu - ia! Al - le - lu - ia! Al - le - lu - ia! A - men.

Let Us with a Gladsome Mind 61

INNOCENTS 77.77.
PSALM 136 — *The Parish Choir,* 1850
JOHN MILTON, 1608-1674 — W. H. MONK, 1823-1889

1. Let us with a glad - some mind Praise the Lord, for he is kind:
2. He, with all - com - mand - ing might, Filled the new - made world with light:
3. All things liv - ing he doth feed; His full hand sup - plies their need:
4. Let us then with glad - some mind Praise the Lord, for he is kind:
For his mer - cies shall en - dure, Ev - er faith - ful, ev - er sure. A - men.

God Is Love, by Him Upholden

WYLDE GREEN 87.87.47.
PETER CUTTS, 1937-

JOHN S. B. MONSELL, 1811-1875

Unison
1. God is love, by him up-hold-en Hang the glo-rious orbs of light,
2. Through that pre-cious love he sought us Wan-dering from his ho-ly ways;
3. Glad-some is the theme and glo-rious, Praise to Christ our gra-cious head;
4. Up to him let each af-fec-tion Dai-ly rise and round him move;

In their lan-guage, glad and gold-en, Speak-ing to us day and night
With that pre-cious life he bought us; Then let all our fu-ture days
Christ, the ris-en Christ, vic-tor-ious, Earth and hell hath cap-tive led.
Our whole lives one res-ur-rec-tion To the life of life a-bove;

Their great sto-ry, God is love, and God is light.
Tell this sto-ry, Love is life, our lives be praise.
Wel-come sto-ry! Love lives on, and death is dead.
Their glad sto-ry, God is life, and God is love. A-men.

Music used by permission of the Student Christian Movement of Great Britain and Ireland.

God Is Love; His Mercy Brightens

STUTTGART 87.87.
I JOHN 4:16 — *Psalmodia Sacra,* Gotha, 1715
JOHN BOWRING, 1792-1872 — Adapt. by HENRY J. GAUNTLETT, 1805-1876

1. God is love; his mercy brightens All the path in which we rove; Bliss he wakes and woe he lightens: God is wisdom, God is love.
2. Chance and change are busy ever; Man decays and ages move; But his mercy waneth never: God is wisdom, God is love.
3. E'en the hour that darkest seemeth Will his changeless goodness prove; Through the gloom his brightness streameth: God is wisdom, God is love.
4. He with earthly cares entwineth Hope and comfort from above; Everywhere his glory shineth: God is wisdom, God is love. A-men.

Lord of All Being

LOUVAN LM

OLIVER W. HOLMES, 1809-1894 VIRGIL C. TAYLOR, 1817-1891

1. Lord of all be - ing, throned a - far, Thy glo - ry
2. Sun of our life, thy quick - ening ray Sheds on our
3. Our mid - night is thy smile with-drawn; Our noon - tide
4. Lord of all life, be - low, a - bove, Whose light is
5. Grant us thy truth to make us free, And kin - dling
flames from sun and star; Cen - ter and soul of ev - ery
path the glow of day; Star of our hope, thy soft - ened
is thy gra - cious dawn; Our rain - bow arch thy mer - cy's
truth, whose warmth is love, Be - fore thy ev - er - blaz - ing
hearts that burn for thee; Till all thy liv - ing al - tars
sphere, Yet to each lov - ing heart how near!
light Cheers the long watch - es of the night.
sign; All, save the clouds of sin, are thine!
throne We ask no lus - ter of our own.
claim One ho - ly light, one heaven - ly flame. A - men.

O My Soul, Bless God the Father

STUTTGART 87.87.

PSALM 103

United Presbyterian Book of Psalms, 1871

Psalmodia Sacra, Gotha, 1715

Adapt. by HENRY J. GAUNTLETT, 1805-1876

1. O my soul, bless God the Fa - ther;
2. Who for - giv - eth thy trans - gres - sions,
3. Far as east from west is dis - tant,
4. As it was with - out be - gin - ning,
5. Un - to such as keep his cove - nant
6. Bless the Fa - ther, all his crea - tures,
All with - in me bless his name; Bless the Fa - ther,
Thy dis - eas - es all who heals; Who re - deems thee
He hath put a - way our sin; Like the pit - y
So it lasts with - out an end; To their chil - dren's
And are stead - fast in his way; Un - to those who
Ev - er un - der his con - trol; All through - out his
and for - get not All his mer - cies to pro - claim.
from de - struc - tion, Who with thee so kind - ly deals.
of a fa - ther Hath the Lord's com - pas - sion been.
chil - dren ev - er Shall his righ - teous - ness ex - tend:
still re - mem - ber His com - mand - ments, and o - bey.
vast do - min - ion Bless the Fa - ther, O my soul. A-men.

LOVE AND MERCY

Praise, My Soul, the King of Heaven

Psalm 103
Henry F. Lyte, 1793-1847

REGENT SQUARE 87.87.87.
Henry Smart, 1813-1879

1. Praise, my soul, the King of heav-en, To his feet thy
2. Praise him for his grace and fa-vor To our fa-thers
3. Fa-ther-like, he tends and spares us; Well our fee-ble
4. An-gels in the height, a-dore him; Ye be-hold him
trib-ute bring; Ran-somed, healed, re-stored, for-giv-en,
in dis-tress; Praise him, still the same as ev-er,
frame he knows; In his hands he gent-ly bears us,
face to face; Saints tri-um-phant, bow be-fore him,
Ev-er-more his prais-es sing. Al-le-lu-ia!
Slow to chide, and swift to bless. Al-le-lu-ia!
Res-cues us from all our foes. Al-le-lu-ia!
Gath-ered in from ev-ery race. Al-le-lu-ia!
Al-le-lu-ia! Praise the ev-er-last-ing King.
Al-le-lu-ia! Glo-rious in his faith-ful-ness.
Al-le-lu-ia! Wide-ly yet his mer-cy flows.
Al-le-lu-ia! Praise with us the God of grace. A-men.

Alternate tune: LAUDA ANIMA

The King of Love My Shepherd Is

Psalm 23
Henry W. Baker, 1821-1877

DOMINUS REGIT ME 87.87.
John B. Dykes, 1823-1876

1. The King of love my Shep - herd is, Whose
2. Where streams of liv - ing wa - ter flow, My
3. Per - verse and fool - ish oft I strayed, But
4. In death's dark vale I fear no ill With
5. Thou spreadst a ta - ble in my sight; Thy
6. And so through all the length of days Thy
good - ness fail - eth nev - er; I noth - ing lack if
ran - somed soul he lead - eth, And, where the ver - dant
yet in love he sought me, And on his shoul - der
thee, dear Lord, be - side me; Thy rod and staff my
unc - tion grace be - stow - eth; And oh, what trans - port
good - ness fail - eth nev - er: Good Shep - herd, may I
I am his And he is mine for - ev - er.
pas - tures grow, With food ce - les - tial feed - eth.
gent - ly laid, And home, re - joic - ing, brought me.
com - fort still, Thy cross be - fore to guide me.
of de - light From thy pure chal - ice flow - eth!
sing thy praise With - in thy house for - ev - er. A-men.

LOVE AND MERCY

The Lord's My Shepherd, I'll Not Want

EVAN CM
Arr. from WILLIAM HAVERGAL, 1793-1870
by LOWELL MASON, 1792-1872

PSALM 23
Scottish Psalter, 1650

1. The Lord's my Shep - herd, I'll not want; He
2. My soul he doth re - store a - gain; And
3. Yea, though I walk in death's dark vale, Yet
4. My ta - ble thou hast fur - nish - ed In
5. Good - ness and mer - cy all my life Shall
makes me down to lie In pas - tures green; he
me to walk doth make With - in the paths of
will I fear no ill; For thou art with me,
pres - ence of my foes; My head thou dost with
sure - ly fol - low me; And in God's house for -
lead - eth me The qui - et wa - ters by.
righ - teous - ness, E'en for his own name's sake.
and thy rod And staff me com - fort still.
oil a - noint, And my cup o - ver - flows.
ev - er - more My dwell - ing place shall be. A - men.

Alternate tune: MARTYRDOM

There's a Wideness in God's Mercy

IN BABILONE 87.87.D.
Trad. Dutch Melody

FREDERICK W. FABER, 1814-1863
Arr. by JULIUS RÖNTGEN, 1855-1932

1. There's a wide-ness in God's mer-cy, Like the wide-ness of the sea;
2. For the love of God is broad-er Than the meas-ure of man's mind;
There's a kind-ness in his jus-tice, Which is more than lib-er-ty.
And the heart of the E-ter-nal Is most won-der-ful-ly kind.
There is wel-come for the sin-ner, And more grac-es for the good;
If our love were but more sim-ple, We should take him at his word;
There is mer-cy with the Sav-ior; There is heal-ing in his blood.
And our lives would be all sun-shine In the sweet-ness of our Lord. A-men.

Music used by permission of Mrs. Engelbert Roentgen.

When All Thy Mercies, O My God

WINCHESTER OLD CM
Est's *The Whole Booke of Psalmes,* 1592
JOSEPH ADDISON, 1672-1719 — Tune arrang. attr. to GEORGE KIRBYE, c. 1560-1634

1. When all thy mer - cies, O my God, My
2. Un - num - bered com - forts to my soul Thy
3. When in the slip - pery paths of youth With
4. Through ev - ery per - iod of my life Thy
ris - ing soul sur - veys, Trans - port - ed with the
ten - der care be - stowed, Be - fore my in - fant
heed - less steps I ran, Thine arm, un - seen, con -
good - ness I'll pur - sue; And af - ter death, in
view, I'm lost In won - der, love, and praise.
heart could know From whom those com - forts flowed.
veyed me safe, And led me up to man.
dis - tant worlds, The glo - rious theme re - new. A - men.

Alternate tune: MANOAH

All Hail the Power of Jesus' Name

EDWARD PERRONET, 1726-1792
Alt. by JOHN RIPPON, 1751-1836

CORONATION CM
Union Harmony, 1793
OLIVER HOLDEN, 1765-1844

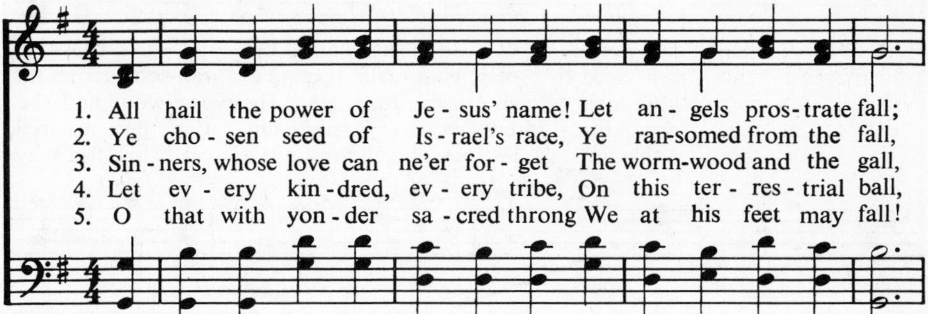
1. All hail the power of Je - sus' name! Let an - gels pros - trate fall;
2. Ye cho - sen seed of Is - rael's race, Ye ran-somed from the fall,
3. Sin - ners, whose love can ne'er for - get The worm-wood and the gall,
4. Let ev - ery kin - dred, ev - ery tribe, On this ter - res - trial ball,
5. O that with yon - der sa - cred throng We at his feet may fall!

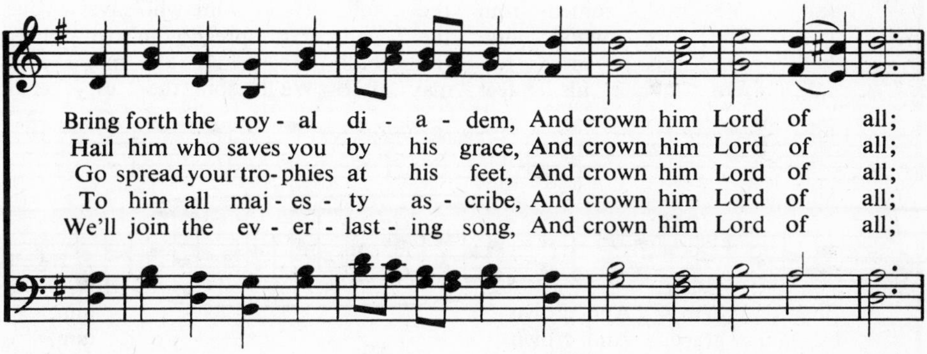
Bring forth the roy - al di - a - dem, And crown him Lord of all;
Hail him who saves you by his grace, And crown him Lord of all;
Go spread your tro - phies at his feet, And crown him Lord of all;
To him all maj - es - ty as - cribe, And crown him Lord of all;
We'll join the ev - er - last - ing song, And crown him Lord of all;

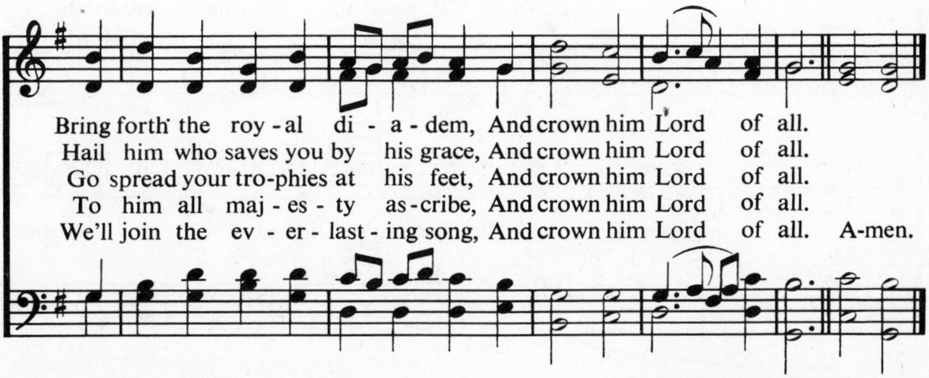
Bring forth the roy - al di - a - dem, And crown him Lord of all.
Hail him who saves you by his grace, And crown him Lord of all.
Go spread your tro - phies at his feet, And crown him Lord of all.
To him all maj - es - ty as - cribe, And crown him Lord of all.
We'll join the ev - er - last - ing song, And crown him Lord of all. A-men.

All Hail the Power of Jesus' Name

EDWARD PERRONET, 1726-1792
Alt. by JOHN RIPPON, 1751-1836

DIADEM CM
JAMES ELLOR, 1819-1899

1. All hail the power of Je - sus' name! Let an - gels pros-trate fall, Let an - gels pros - trate fall; Bring forth the roy - al di - a - dem, And crown him,
2. Ye cho - sen seed of Is - rael's race, Ye ran-somed from the fall, Ye ran - somed from the fall, Hail him who saves you by his grace, And crown him,
3. Sin-ners, whose love can ne'er for - get The worm-wood and the gall, The worm - wood and the gall, Go spread your tro - phies at his feet, And crown him,
4. Let ev - ery kin - dred, ev - ery tribe, On this ter - res-trial ball, On this ter - res - trial ball, To him all maj - es - ty as - cribe, And crown him,
5. O that with yon - der sa - cred throng We at his feet may fall, We at his feet may fall! We'll join the ev - er - last - ing song, And crown him,
crown him, crown him, crown him, crown him, crown
crown him, crown him, crown him, And crown him Lord of all. A-men.
him,

All Hail the Power of Jesus' Name

EDWARD PERRONET, 1726-1792
Alt. by JOHN RIPPON, 1751-1836

MILES' LANE CM
WILLIAM SHRUBSOLE, 1760-1806

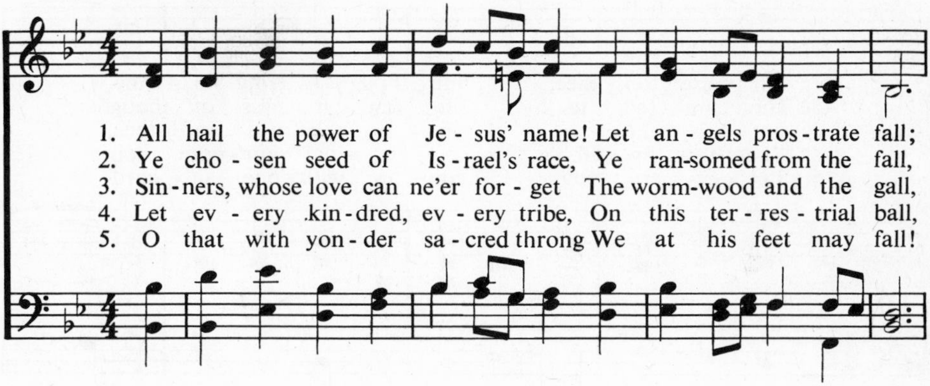
1. All hail the power of Je - sus' name! Let an - gels pros - trate fall;
2. Ye cho - sen seed of Is - rael's race, Ye ran-somed from the fall,
3. Sin - ners, whose love can ne'er for - get The worm-wood and the gall,
4. Let ev - ery kin - dred, ev - ery tribe, On this ter - res - trial ball,
5. O that with yon - der sa - cred throng We at his feet may fall!

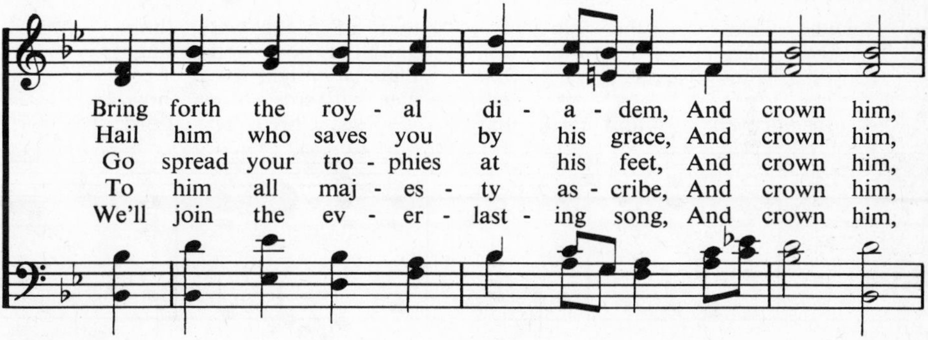
Bring forth the roy - al di - a - dem, And crown him,
Hail him who saves you by his grace, And crown him,
Go spread your tro - phies at his feet, And crown him,
To him all maj - es - ty as - cribe, And crown him,
We'll join the ev - er - last - ing song, And crown him,

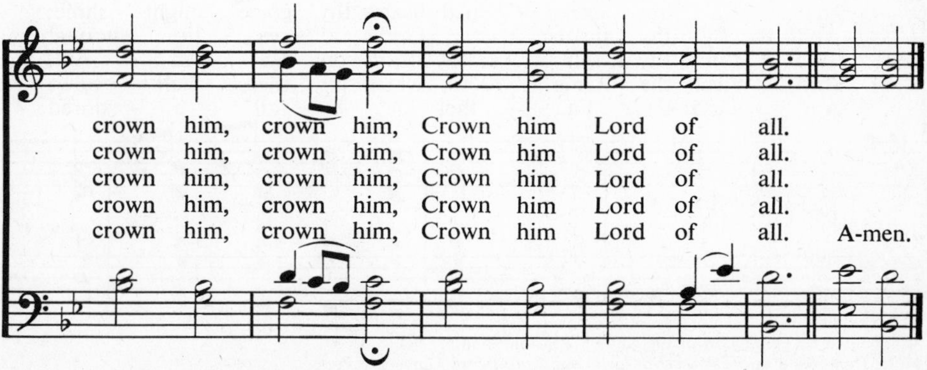
crown him, crown him, Crown him Lord of all.
crown him, crown him, Crown him Lord of all.
crown him, crown him, Crown him Lord of all.
crown him, crown him, Crown him Lord of all.
crown him, crown him, Crown him Lord of all. A-men.

All Praise to Thee, for Thou, O King Divine

PHILIPPIANS 2:5-11
F. BLAND TUCKER, 1895-

SINE NOMINE 10 10 10. with Alleluias
R. VAUGHAN WILLIAMS, 1872-1958

Unison
1. All praise to thee, for thou, O King di - vine,
2. Thou cam'st to us in low - li - ness of thought;
3. Let this mind be in us which was in thee,
4. Where-fore, by God's e - ter - nal pur - pose, thou
5. Let ev - ery tongue con - fess with one ac - cord
Didst yield the glo - ry that of right was thine,
By thee the out - cast and the poor were sought,
Who wast a ser - vant that we might be free,
Art ex - alt - ed o'er all crea - tures now,
In heaven and earth that Je - sus Christ is Lord;
That in our dark - ened hearts thy grace might shine:
And by thy death was God's sal - va - tion wrought:
Hum - bling thy - self to death on Cal - va - ry:
And given the name to which all knees shall bow:
And God the Fa - ther be by all a - dored:

Words used by permission of the Church Pension Fund.
Music from *The English Hymnal* by permission of Oxford University Press.

Al - le - lu - ia! Al - le - lu - ia! A-men.

Thou Art the Way: To Thee Alone 75

JOHN 14:6
GEORGE W. DOANE, 1799-1859

ST. BERNARD CM
Tochter Sion, Cologne, 1741
Arr. by JOHN RICHARDSON, 1816-1879

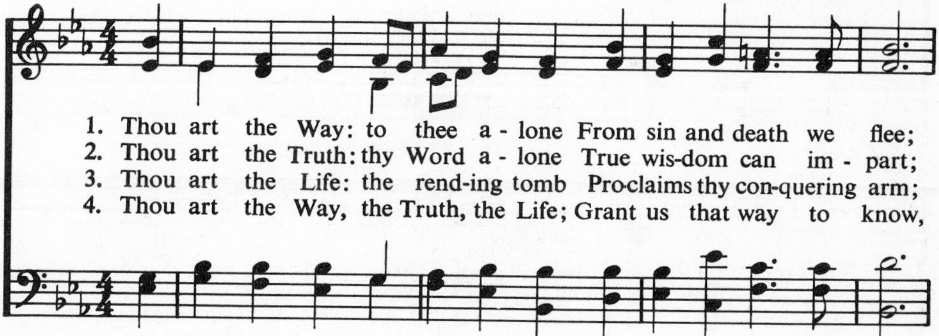
1. Thou art the Way: to thee a - lone From sin and death we flee;
2. Thou art the Truth: thy Word a - lone True wis-dom can im - part;
3. Thou art the Life: the rend-ing tomb Pro-claims thy con-quering arm;
4. Thou art the Way, the Truth, the Life; Grant us that way to know,

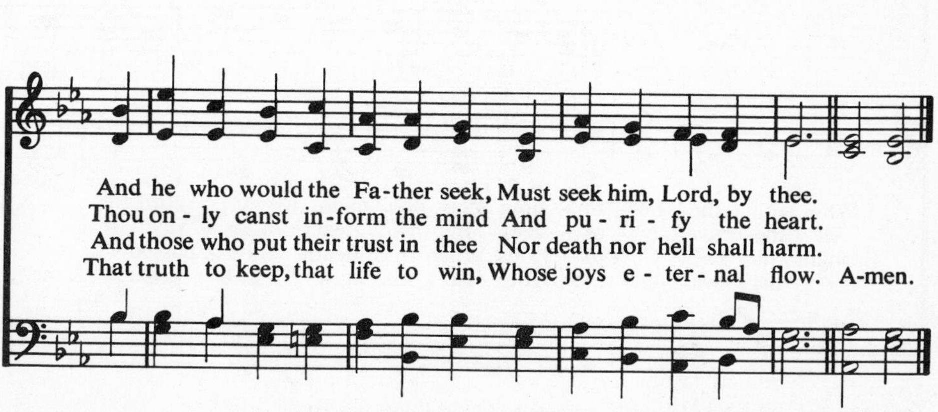
And he who would the Fa-ther seek, Must seek him, Lord, by thee.
Thou on - ly canst in-form the mind And pu - ri - fy the heart.
And those who put their trust in thee Nor death nor hell shall harm.
That truth to keep, that life to win, Whose joys e - ter - nal flow. A-men.

At the Name of Jesus

PHILIPPIANS 2:5-11
CAROLINE M. NOEL, 1817-1877

KING'S WESTON 65.65.D.
R. VAUGHAN WILLIAMS, 1872-1958

Unison
1. At the name of Je - sus Ev - ery knee shall bow,
2. At his voice cre - a - tion Sprang at once to sight,
3. Hum-bled for a sea - son, To re - ceive a name
4. In your hearts en - throne him; There let him sub - due
Ev - ery tongue con - fess him King of glo - ry now;
All the an - gel fac - es, All the hosts of light,
From the lips of sin - ners Un - to whom he came,
All that is not ho - ly, All that is not true:
'Tis the Fa - ther's plea - sure We should call him Lord,
Thrones and dom - i - na - tions, Stars up - on their way,
Faith - ful - ly he bore it Spot - less to the last,
Crown him as your cap - tain In temp - ta - tion's hour;
Who from the be - gin - ning Was the might - y Word.
All the heaven - ly or - ders, In their great ar - ray.
Brought it back vic - to - rious When from death he passed.
Let his will en - fold you In its light and power. A-men.

Music from *Enlarged Songs of Praise* by permission of Oxford University Press.

Come, Christians, Join to Sing

SPANISH HYMN 66.66.D.
Arr. by BENJAMIN CARR, 1768-1831
Harm. by A. C. L.

CHRISTIAN HENRY BATEMAN, 1813-1889

1. Come, Chris-tians, join to sing Al - le - lu - ia! A - men!
2. Come, lift your hearts on high; Al - le - lu - ia! A - men!
3. Praise yet the Lord a - gain; Al - le - lu - ia! A - men!
Loud praise to Christ our King; Al - le - lu - ia! A - men!
Let prais - es fill the sky; Al - le - lu - ia! A - men!
Life shall not end the strain; Al - le - lu - ia! A - men!
Let all, with heart and voice, Be - fore his throne re - joice;
He is our guide and friend; To us he'll con - des - cend,
On heav - en's bliss - ful shore His good - ness we'll a - dore,
Praise is his gra - cious choice: Al - le - lu - ia! A - men!
His love shall nev - er end: Al - le - lu - ia! A - men!
Sing - ing for - ev - er - more Al - le - lu - ia! A - men! A-men.

Creator of the Stars of Night

ANONYMOUS, Latin, 9th Century
Adapt. from JOHN M. NEALE, 1818-1866
in *The Hymnal,* 1940

CONDITOR ALME LM
Sarum Plainsong, Mode IV
Arr. by C. WINFRED DOUGLAS, 1867-1944

1. Cre - a - tor of the stars of night, Thy peo - ple's ev - er -
2. At the great name of Je - sus, now All knees must bend, all
3. Come in thy ho - ly might, we pray; Re - deem us for e -
4. To God the Fa - ther, God the Son, And God the Spir - it,
last - ing light, O Christ, thou Sav - ior of us all,
hearts must bow; And things ce - les - tial thee shall own,
ter - nal day From ev - ery power of dark - ness when
Three in One, Laud, hon - or, might, and glo - ry be
We pray thee, hear us when we call.
And things ter - res - trial, Lord a - lone.
Thou judg - est all the sons of men.
From age to age e - ter - nal - ly. A - men.

Used by permission of the Church Pension Fund.

Fairest Lord Jesus

ST. ELIZABETH 568.558.

ANONYMOUS in *Münster Gesangbuch,* 1677
Trans. ANONYMOUS

Schlesische Volkslieder, 1842
Arr. by RICHARD STORRS WILLIS, 1819-1900

1. Fair - est Lord Je - sus, Rul - er of all na - ture,
2. Fair are the mead - ows, Fair - er still the wood - lands,
3. Fair is the sun - shine, Fair - er still the moon - light,
O thou of God and man the son, Thee will I cher - ish,
Robed in the bloom - ing garb of spring: Je - sus is fair - er,
And all the twink - ling star - ry host: Je - sus shines bright - er,
Thee will I hon - or, Thou, my soul's glo - ry, joy, and crown.
Je - sus is pur - er, Who makes the woe - ful heart to sing.
Je - sus shines pur - er, Than all the an - gels heaven can boast. A-men.

How Beauteous Were the Marks

WINDHAM LM
A. Cleveland Coxe, 1818-1896 Daniel Read, 1757-1836

1. How beau - teous were the marks di - vine, That
2. O who like thee, so mild, so bright, Thou
3. O who like thee so hum - bly bore The
4. O won - drous Lord, my soul would be Still
in thy meek - ness used to shine, That lit thy lone - ly
Son of man, thou Light of light? O who like thee did
scorn, the scoffs of men, be - fore? So meek, so low - ly,
more and more con - formed to thee, And learn of thee, the
path - way, trod In won - drous love, O Son of God!
ev - er go, So pa - tient through a world of woe?
yet so high, So glo - rious in hu - mil - i - ty?
low - ly one, And like thee, all my jour - ney run. A-men.

Alternate tune: CANONBURY

How Sweet the Name of Jesus Sounds

SONG OF SOLOMON 1:3
JOHN NEWTON, 1725-1807

ST. PETER CM
ALEXANDER R. REINAGLE, 1799-1877

1. How sweet the name of Je - sus sounds In
2. It makes the wound - ed spir - it whole, And
3. Je - sus, my Sav - ior, shep - herd, friend, My
4. Weak is the ef - fort of my heart, And
5. Till then I would thy love pro - claim With
a be - liev - er's ear! It soothes his sor - rows,
calms the trou - bled breast; 'Tis man - na to the
pro - phet, priest, and king, My Lord, my life, my
cold my warm - est thought; But when I see thee
ev - ery fleet - ing breath; And may the mu - sic
heals his wounds, And drives a - way his fear.
hun - gry soul, And to the wea - ry, rest.
way, my end, Ac - cept the praise I bring.
as thou art, I'll praise thee as I ought.
of thy name Re - fresh my soul in death. A-men.

Jesus, the Very Thought of Thee

Latin, 12th Century
Trans. by EDWARD CASWALL, 1814-1878

ST. AGNES CM
JOHN B. DYKES, 1823-1876

1. Je - sus, the ver - y thought of thee
2. Nor voice can sing, nor heart can frame,
3. O Hope of ev - ery con - trite heart,
4. But what to those who find? Ah, this
5. Je - sus, our on - ly joy be thou,
With sweet - ness fills the breast; But sweet - er far thy
Nor can the mem - ory find A sweet - er sound than
O Joy of all the meek, To those who fall, how
Nor tongue nor pen can show: The love of Je - sus,
As thou our prize wilt be: Je - sus, be thou our
face to see, And in thy pres - ence rest.
thy blest name, O Sav - ior of man - kind!
kind thou art! How good to those who seek!
what it is None but his loved ones know.
glo - ry now, And through e - ter - ni - ty. A-men.

83

Majestic Sweetness Sits Enthroned

Song of Solomon 5:10-16
Samuel Stennett, 1727-1795

ORTONVILLE CM
Thomas Hastings, 1784-1872

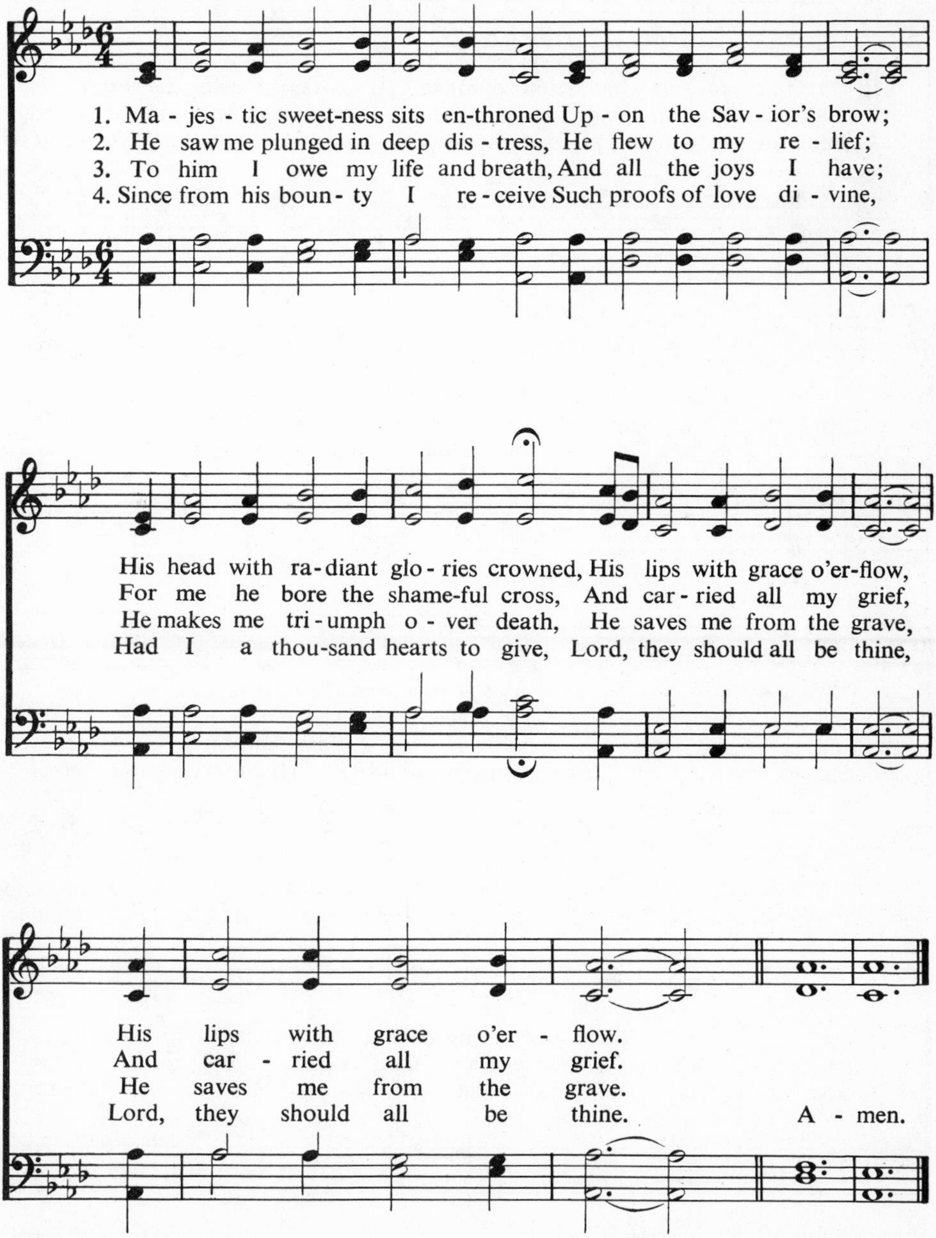
1. Ma - jes - tic sweet-ness sits en-throned Up - on the Sav - ior's brow;
2. He saw me plunged in deep dis - tress, He flew to my re - lief;
3. To him I owe my life and breath, And all the joys I have;
4. Since from his boun - ty I re - ceive Such proofs of love di - vine,
His head with ra - diant glo - ries crowned, His lips with grace o'er-flow,
For me he bore the shame-ful cross, And car - ried all my grief,
He makes me tri - umph o - ver death, He saves me from the grave,
Had I a thou-sand hearts to give, Lord, they should all be thine,
His lips with grace o'er - flow.
And car - ried all my grief.
He saves me from the grave.
Lord, they should all be thine.
A - men.

O Guide to Every Child

CLEMENT OF ALEXANDRIA, c. 160-215
Trans. by KENDRICK GROBEL, 1908-1965

NUN FREUT EUCH 87.87.887.
Klug's *Gesangbuch,* Wittenberg, 1535

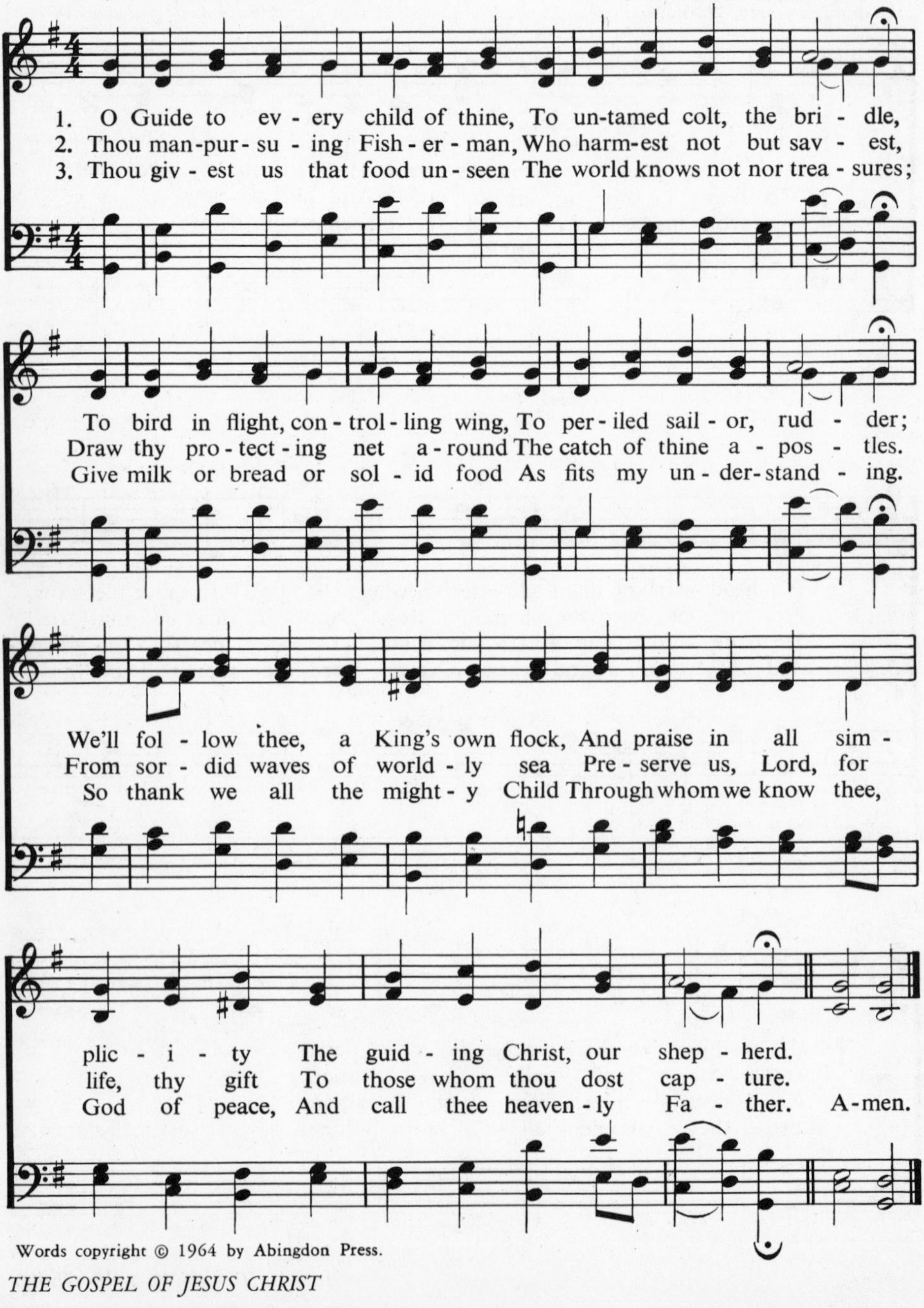
1. O Guide to ev - ery child of thine, To un-tamed colt, the bri - dle,
2. Thou man-pur - su - ing Fish - er - man, Who harm-est not but sav - est,
3. Thou giv - est us that food un - seen The world knows not nor trea - sures;
To bird in flight, con - trol - ling wing, To per - iled sail - or, rud - der;
Draw thy pro - tect - ing net a - round The catch of thine a - pos - tles.
Give milk or bread or sol - id food As fits my un - der-stand - ing.
We'll fol - low thee, a King's own flock, And praise in all sim -
From sor - did waves of world - ly sea Pre - serve us, Lord, for
So thank we all the might - y Child Through whom we know thee,
plic - i - ty The guid - ing Christ, our shep - herd.
life, thy gift To those whom thou dost cap - ture.
God of peace, And call thee heaven - ly Fa - ther. A-men.

O Son of God Incarnate

FAR-OFF LANDS 76.76.D.
Melody of the Bohemian Brethren

WILBUR FISK TILLETT, 1854-1936

Arr. by C. WINFRED DOUGLAS, 1867-1944

Unison
1. O Son of God in - car - nate, O Son of man di - vine!
2. O Mind of God in - car - nate, O Thought in flesh en - shrined!
3. O Heart of God in - car - nate, Love-bear - er to man - kind!
4. O Will of God in - car - nate, So hu - man, so di - vine!
In whom God's glo - ry dwell - eth, In whom man's vir - tues shine:
In hu - man form thou speak - est To men the Fa - ther's mind:
From thee we learn what love is, In thee love's ways we find:
Free wills to us thou giv - est, That we may make them thine:
God's light to earth thou bring - est To drive sin's night a - way,
God's thought to earth thou bring - est That men in thee may see
God's love to earth thou bring - est In liv - ing deeds that prove
God's will to earth thou bring - est That all who would o - bey,
And through thy life so ra - diant, Earth's dark-ness turns to day.
What God is like, and see - ing, Think God's thoughts af - ter thee.
How sweet to serve all oth - ers, When we all oth - ers love.
May learn from thee their du - ty, The truth, the life, the way. A-men.

Shepherd of Eager Youth

CLEMENT OF ALEXANDRIA, c. 160-215
Trans. by HENRY M. DEXTER, 1821-1890

HINMAN 664.6664.
AUSTIN C. LOVELACE, 1919-

Unison
1. Shep-herd of ea - ger youth, Guid - ing in
2. Thou art the great high priest; Thou hast pre -
3. Ev - er be thou our guide, Our shep - herd
4. So now, and till we die, Sound we thy
love and truth, Through de - vious ways;
pared the feast Of heaven - ly love;
and our pride, Our staff and song;
prais - es high, And joy - ful sing;
Christ our tri - um-phant King, We come thy name to sing,
While in our mor - tal pain None calls on thee in vain;
Je - sus, thou Christ of God, By thy pe - ren - nial Word,
Let all the ho - ly throng, Who to thy Church be - long,
Hith - er our chil-dren bring To shout thy praise.
Help thou dost not dis - dain, Help from a - bove.
Lead us where thou hast trod, Our faith make strong.
U - nite to swell the song To Christ our King! A-men.

Alternate tune: ITALIAN HYMN

Take the Name of Jesus with You

LYDIA BAXTER, 1809-1874

PRECIOUS NAME 87.87. with Refrain
WILLIAM H. DOANE, 1832-1915

1. Take the name of Je - sus with you, Child of sor - row and of woe;
2. Take the name of Je - sus ev - er, As a shield from ev - ery snare;
3. O the pre - cious name of Je - sus! How it thrills our souls with joy,
4. At the name of Je - sus bow - ing, Fall - ing pros - trate at his feet,
It will joy and com - fort give you; Take it, then, wher - e'er you go.
If temp - ta - tions round you gath - er, Breathe that ho - ly name in prayer.
When his lov - ing arms re - ceive us, And his songs our tongues employ!
King of kings in heaven we'll crown him, When our jour - ney is com - plete.
Refrain
Pre - cious name, O how sweet! Hope of
Pre - cious name, O how sweet!
earth and joy of heaven; Pre - cious name, O how
Pre - cious name, O how
sweet! Hope of earth and joy of heaven. A - men.
sweet, how sweet!

Tell Me the Stories of Jesus

STORIES OF JESUS 84.84.54.54.
FREDERIC A. CHALLINOR, 1866-1952

WILLIAM H. PARKER, 1845-1929

Unison
1. Tell me the sto - ries of Je - sus I love to hear;
2. First let me hear how the chil - dren Stood round his knee,
3. In - to the cit - y I'd fol - low The chil - dren's band,
Things I would ask him to tell me If he were here:
And I shall fan - cy his bless - ing Rest - ing on me;
Wav - ing a branch of the palm tree High in my hand;
Scenes by the way - side, Tales of the sea,
Words full of kind - ness, Deeds full of grace,
One of his her - alds, Yes, I would sing
Sto - ries of Je - sus, Tell them to me.
All in the love - light Of Je - sus' face.
Loud - est ho - san - nas, "Je - sus is King!"
A - men.

Used by permission of the National Sunday School Union.

Thou Hidden Source of Calm Repose

CHARLES WESLEY, 1707-1788

ST. PETERSBURG 88.88.88.
DIMITRI S. BORTNIANSKY, 1751-1825

1. Thou hid - den source of calm re - pose, Thou all - suf - fi - cient love di - vine, My help and ref - uge from my foes, Se - cure I am if thou art mine; And lo! from sin and grief and shame, I hide me, Je - sus, in thy name.
2. Thy might - y name sal - va - tion is, And keeps my hap - py soul a - bove; Com - fort it brings, and power and peace, And joy and ev - er - last - ing love: To me, with thy great name, are given Par - don and ho - li - ness and heaven.
3. Je - sus, my all - in - all thou art: My rest in toil, my ease in pain, The heal - ing of my bro - ken heart, In war my peace, in loss my gain, My smile be - neath the ty - rant's frown: In shame my glo - ry and my crown,
4. In want my plen - ti - ful sup - ply, In weak - ness my al - might - y power, In bonds my per - fect lib - er - ty, My light in Sa - tan's dark - est hour, In grief my joy un - speak - a - ble, My life in death, my heaven in hell. A - men.

90

We Would See Jesus

JOHN 12:21
J. EDGAR PARK, 1879-1956

CUSHMAN 11 10.11 10.
HERBERT B. TURNER, 1852-1927

1. We would see Je - sus; lo! his star is shin - ing
2. We would see Je - sus, Ma - ry's son most ho - ly,
3. We would see Je - sus, on the moun - tain teach - ing,
4. We would see Je - sus, in his work of heal - ing,
5. We would see Je - sus; in the ear - ly morn - ing
A - bove the sta - ble while the an - gels sing;
Light of the vil - lage life from day to day;
With all the lis - tening peo - ple gath - ered round;
At ev - en - tide be - fore the sun was set;
Still as of old he call - eth, "Fol - low me";
There in a man - ger on the hay re - clin - ing;
Shin - ing re - vealed through ev - ery task most low - ly,
While birds and flowers and sky a - bove are preach - ing
Di - vine and hu - man, in his deep re - veal - ing,
Let us a - rise, all mean - er serv - ice scorn - ing:
Haste, let us lay our gifts be - fore the King.
The Christ of God, the life, the truth, the way.
The bless - ed - ness which sim - ple trust has found.
Of God and man in lov - ing serv - ice met.
Lord, we are thine, we give our - selves to thee. A-men.

Words from *New Worship and Song.* Used by permission of the Pilgrim Press.

When Morning Gilds the Skies

ANONYMOUS, German, 19th Century
Trans. by EDWARD CASWALL, 1814-1878

LAUDES DOMINI 666.666.
JOSEPH BARNBY, 1838-1896

1. When morn - ing gilds the skies, My heart a - wak - ing cries,
2. The night be - comes as day, When from the heart we say,
3. Ye na - tions of man - kind, In this your con - cord find,
4. Be this, while life is mine, My can - ti - cle di - vine,
May Je - sus Christ be praised! A - like at work and prayer,
May Je - sus Christ be praised! The powers of dark - ness fear,
May Je - sus Christ be praised! Let all the earth a - round
May Je - sus Christ be praised! Be this th' e - ter - nal song
To Je - sus I re - pair; May Je - sus Christ be praised!
When this sweet chant they hear, May Je - sus Christ be praised!
Ring joy - ous with the sound, May Je - sus Christ be praised!
Through all the a - ges long, May Je - sus Christ be praised! A - men.

92 Amazing Grace! How Sweet the Sound

AMAZING GRACE CM
Early American Melody
Virginia Harmony, 1831
Harm. by A. C. L.

I CHRONICLES 17:16-17
JOHN NEWTON, 1725-1807

1. A - maz - ing grace! how sweet the sound That saved a
2. 'Twas grace that taught my heart to fear, And grace my
3. Through man - y dan - gers, toils, and snares, I have al -
4. The Lord has prom - ised good to me, His word my
5. Yea, when this flesh and heart shall fail, And mor - tal
wretch like me! I once was lost, but now am
fears re - lieved; How pre - cious did that grace ap -
read - y come; 'Tis grace hath brought me safe thus
hope se - cures; He will my shield and por - tion
life shall cease, I shall pos - sess, with - in the
found, Was blind, but now I see.
pear The hour I first be - lieved!
far, And grace will lead me home.
be As long as life en - dures.
veil, A life of joy and peace. A - men.

Come, Thou Fount of Every Blessing

NETTLETON 87.87.D.
American Folk Tune

ROBERT ROBINSON, 1735-1790

WYETH'S *Repository of Sacred Music, Part Second,* 1813

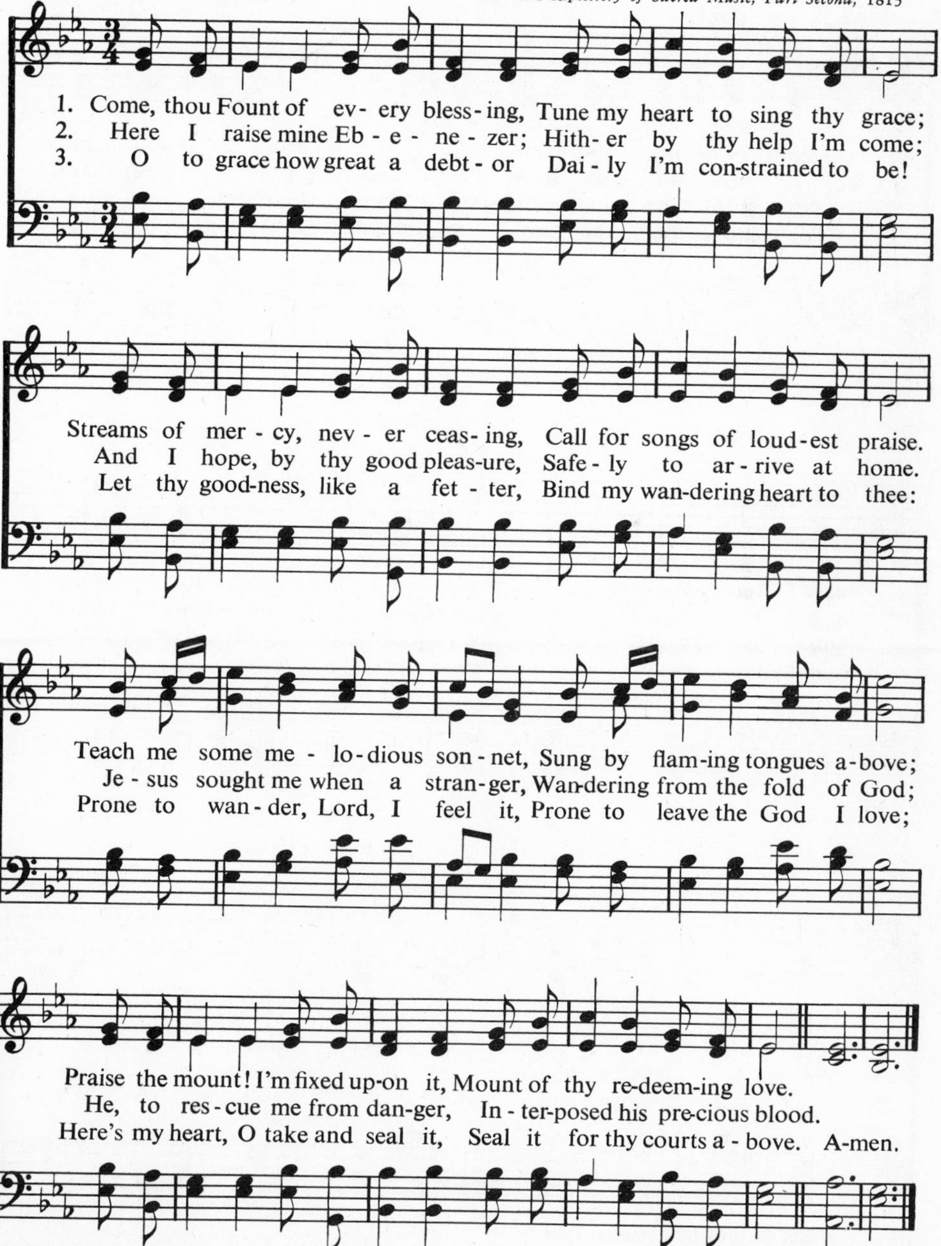
1. Come, thou Fount of ev- ery bless-ing, Tune my heart to sing thy grace;
2. Here I raise mine Eb - e - ne - zer; Hith- er by thy help I'm come;
3. O to grace how great a debt - or Dai - ly I'm con-strained to be!
Streams of mer - cy, nev - er ceas- ing, Call for songs of loud-est praise.
And I hope, by thy good pleas-ure, Safe - ly to ar - rive at home.
Let thy good-ness, like a fet - ter, Bind my wan-dering heart to thee:
Teach me some me - lo-dious son - net, Sung by flam-ing tongues a-bove;
Je - sus sought me when a stran- ger, Wan-dering from the fold of God;
Prone to wan - der, Lord, I feel it, Prone to leave the God I love;
Praise the mount! I'm fixed up-on it, Mount of thy re-deem-ing love.
He, to res - cue me from dan-ger, In - ter-posed his pre-cious blood.
Here's my heart, O take and seal it, Seal it for thy courts a - bove. A-men.

MERCY AND GRACE

Depth of Mercy

SEYMOUR 77.77.
Arr. from CARL M. VON WEBER, 1786-1826
by HENRY W. GREATOREX, 1813-1858
Harm. by V. E. C.

CHARLES WESLEY, 1707-1788

1. Depth of mer - cy! can there be Mer - cy still re -
2. I my Mas - ter have de - nied; I a - fresh have
3. Now in - cline me to re - pent; Let me now my
4. There for me the Sav - ior stands, Hold - ing forth his
served for me? Can my God his wrath for - bear,
cru - ci - fied, Oft pro - faned his hal - lowed name,
sins la - ment; Now my foul re - volt de - plore,
wound - ed hands; God is love! I know, I feel,
Me, the chief of sin - ners, spare?
Put him to an o - pen shame.
Weep, be - lieve, and sin no more.
Je - sus weeps and loves me still. A - men.

95

Heavenly Father, Bless Me Now

AUS DER TIEFE 77.77.

ALEXANDER CLARK, 1834-1879 — Attr. to MARTIN HERBST, 1654-1681

1. Heaven-ly Fa-ther, bless me now; At the cross of Christ I bow; Take my guilt and grief a-way; Hear and heal me now, I pray.
2. Now, O Lord, this ve-ry hour, Send thy grace and show thy power; While I rest up-on thy word, Come, and bless me now, O Lord!
3. Mer-cy now, O Lord, I plead In this hour of ut-ter need; Turn me not a-way un-blest; Calm my an-guish in-to rest.
4. O thou lov-ing, bless-ed One, Ris-ing o'er me like the sun, Light and life art thou with-in: Sav-ior, thou, from ev-ery sin! A-men.

Alternate tune: SEYMOUR

MERCY AND GRACE

I Sought the Lord

ANONYMOUS
The Pilgrim Hymnal, 1904

WACHUSETT 10 10.10 6.
KATHERINE K. DAVIS, 1892-

Unison
1. I sought the Lord, and af - ter - ward I knew
2. Thou didst reach forth thy hand and mine en - fold;
3. I find, I walk, I love, but oh, the whole
He moved my soul to seek him, seek - ing me;
I walked and sank not on the storm - vexed sea;
Of love is but my an - swer, Lord, to thee!
It was not I that found, O Sav - ior true;
'Twas not so much that I on thee took hold
For thou wert long be - fore - hand with my soul;
No, I was found of thee.
As thou, dear Lord, on me.
Al - ways thou lov - edst me. A - men.

97

Jesus Is All the World to Me

ELIZABETH Irregular

WILL L. THOMPSON, 1847-1909 WILL L. THOMPSON, 1847-1909

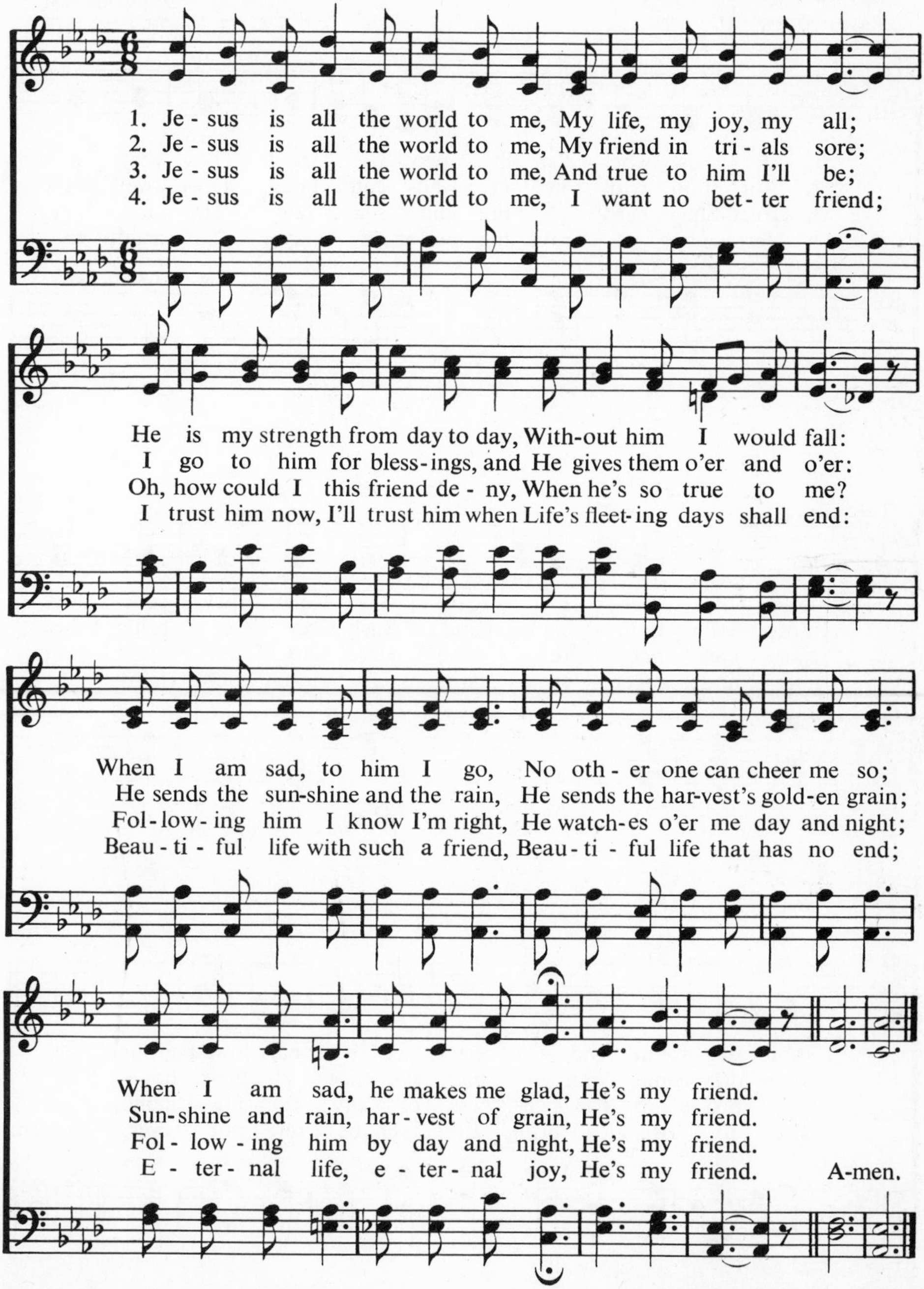
1. Je - sus is all the world to me, My life, my joy, my all;
2. Je - sus is all the world to me, My friend in tri - als sore;
3. Je - sus is all the world to me, And true to him I'll be;
4. Je - sus is all the world to me, I want no bet - ter friend;
He is my strength from day to day, With-out him I would fall:
I go to him for bless-ings, and He gives them o'er and o'er:
Oh, how could I this friend de - ny, When he's so true to me?
I trust him now, I'll trust him when Life's fleet-ing days shall end:
When I am sad, to him I go, No oth - er one can cheer me so;
He sends the sun-shine and the rain, He sends the har-vest's gold-en grain;
Fol-low-ing him I know I'm right, He watch-es o'er me day and night;
Beau - ti - ful life with such a friend, Beau - ti - ful life that has no end;
When I am sad, he makes me glad, He's my friend.
Sun-shine and rain, har-vest of grain, He's my friend.
Fol - low - ing him by day and night, He's my friend.
E - ter - nal life, e - ter - nal joy, He's my friend. A-men.

MERCY AND GRACE

98

Jesus, Where'er Thy People Meet

MALVERN LM

WILLIAM COWPER, 1731-1800 LOWELL MASON, 1792-1872

1. Je - sus, wher - e'er thy peo - ple meet, There they be -
2. For thou, with - in no walls con - fined, Dost dwell with
3. Great Shep - herd of thy cho - sen few, Thy for - mer
4. Here may we prove the power of prayer To strength - en
hold thy mer - cy seat; Wher - e'er they seek thee
those of hum - ble mind; Such ev - er bring thee
mer - cies here re - new; Here, to our wait - ing
faith and sweet - en care; To teach our faint de -
thou art found, And ev - ery place is hal - lowed ground.
where they come, And, go - ing, take thee to their home.
hearts, pro - claim The sweet - ness of thy sav - ing name.
sires to rise, And bring all heaven be - fore our eyes. A-men.

Art Thou Weary, Art Thou Languid

STEPHANOS 85.83.

Greek, 8th Century
John M. Neale, 1818-1866

Henry W. Baker, 1821-1877
Harm. by W. H. Monk, 1823-1889

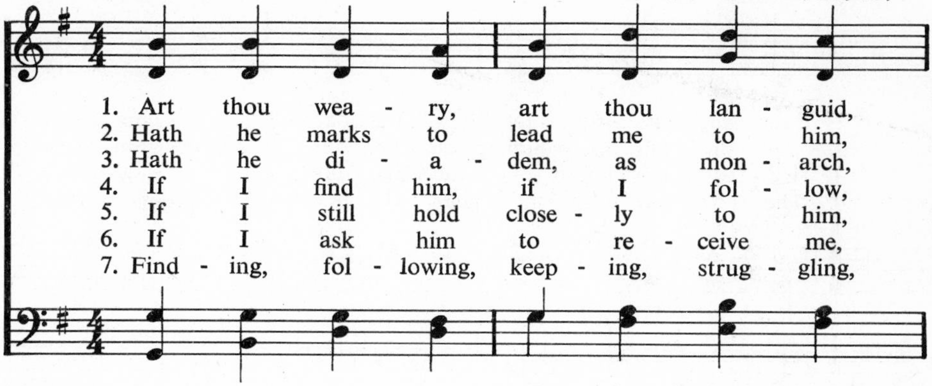
1. Art thou wea - ry, art thou lan - guid,
2. Hath he marks to lead me to him,
3. Hath he di - a - dem, as mon - arch,
4. If I find him, if I fol - low,
5. If I still hold close - ly to him,
6. If I ask him to re - ceive me,
7. Find - ing, fol - lowing, keep - ing, strug - gling,

Art thou sore dis - tressed? "Come to me," saith
If he be my guide? In his feet and
That his brow a - dorns? Yea, a crown, in
What his guer - don here? Many a sor - row,
What hath he at last? Sor - row van - quished,
Will he say me nay? Not till earth and
Is he sure to bless? Saints, a - pos - tles,

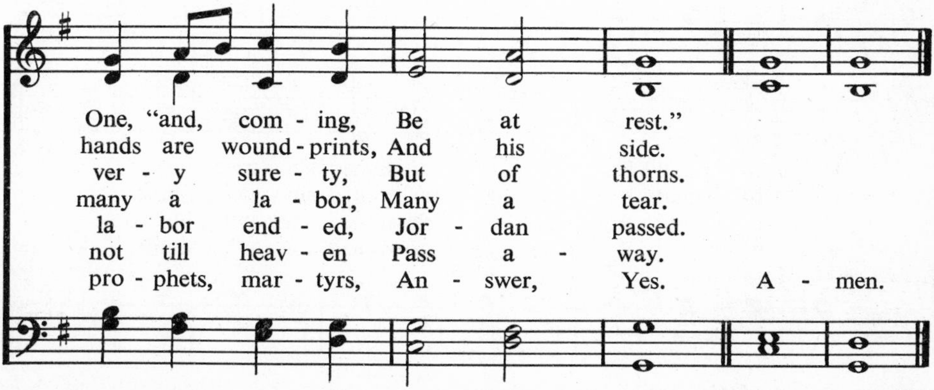
One, "and, com - ing, Be at rest."
hands are wound - prints, And his side.
ver - y sure - ty, But of thorns.
many a la - bor, Many a tear.
la - bor end - ed, Jor - dan passed.
not till heav - en Pass a - way.
pro - phets, mar - tyrs, An - swer, Yes. A - men.

CALL

Blow Ye the Trumpet, Blow

LENOX 66.66.88.
Chorister's Companion, c. 1782
LEWIS EDSON, 1748-1820

LEVITICUS 25:8-17
CHARLES WESLEY, 1707-1788

1. Blow ye the trum - pet, blow! The glad - ly sol - emn sound
2. Je - sus, our great high priest, Hath full a - tone - ment made;
3. Ex - tol the Lamb of God, The all - a - ton - ing Lamb;
4. The gos - pel trum - pet hear, The news of heaven - ly grace;
Let all the na - tions know, To earth's re - mot - est bound.
Ye wea - ry spir - its, rest; Ye mourn - ful souls, be glad.
Re - demp - tion in his blood Through-out the world pro - claim.
And, saved from earth, ap - pear Be - fore your Sav - ior's face.
The year of ju - bi - lee is come! The year of ju - bi -
The year of ju - bi - lee is come! The year of ju - bi -
The year of ju - bi - lee is come! The year of ju - bi -
The year of ju - bi - lee is come! The year of ju - bi -
lee is come! Re - turn, ye ran-somed sin - ners, home.
lee is come! Re - turn, ye ran-somed sin - ners, home.
lee is come! Re - turn, ye ran-somed sin - ners, home.
lee is come! Re - turn, ye ran-somed sin - ners, home. A-men.

Come, Every Soul by Sin Oppressed

STOCKTON 86.86. with Refrain

JOHN H. STOCKTON, 1813-1877 — JOHN H. STOCKTON, 1813-1877

1. Come, ev - ery soul by sin op-pressed, There's mer-cy with the Lord;
2. For Je - sus shed his pre-cious blood Rich bless-ings to be - stow;
3. Yes, Je - sus is the truth, the way, That leads you in - to rest;
4. Come then and join this ho - ly band, And on to glo - ry go,
And he will sure - ly give you rest, By trust - ing in his word.
Plunge now in - to the crim - son flood That wash - es white as snow.
Be - lieve in him with - out de - lay, And you are ful - ly blest.
To dwell in that ce - les - tial land, Where joys im - mor - tal flow.
Refrain
On - ly trust him, on - ly trust him, On - ly trust him now;
He will save you, he will save you, He will save you now. A-men.

CALL

Come, Sinners, to the Gospel Feast

WINCHESTER NEW LM
Musikalisches Handbuch, Hamburg, 1690
Arr. by WILLIAM HAVERGAL, 1793-1870

LUKE 14:16-24
CHARLES WESLEY, 1707-1788

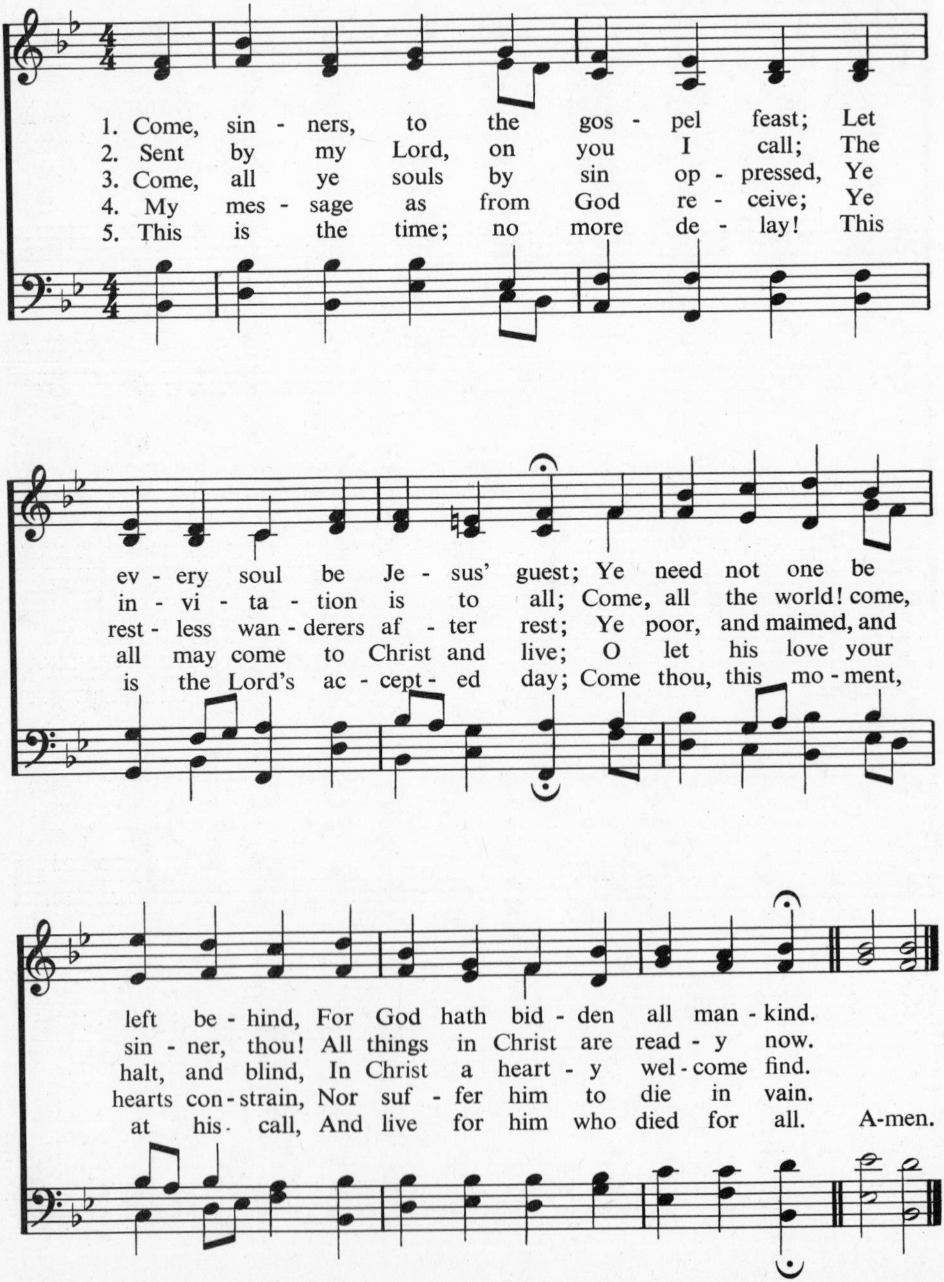
1. Come, sin - ners, to the gos - pel feast; Let
2. Sent by my Lord, on you I call; The
3. Come, all ye souls by sin op - pressed, Ye
4. My mes - sage as from God re - ceive; Ye
5. This is the time; no more de - lay! This
ev - ery soul be Je - sus' guest; Ye need not one be
in - vi - ta - tion is to all; Come, all the world! come,
rest - less wan - derers af - ter rest; Ye poor, and maimed, and
all may come to Christ and live; O let his love your
is the Lord's ac - cept - ed day; Come thou, this mo - ment,
left be - hind, For God hath bid - den all man - kind.
sin - ner, thou! All things in Christ are read - y now.
halt, and blind, In Christ a heart - y wel - come find.
hearts con - strain, Nor suf - fer him to die in vain.
at his call, And live for him who died for all. A-men.

Come, Ye Disconsolate

THOMAS MOORE, 1779-1852
Alt. by THOMAS HASTINGS, 1784-1872

CONSOLATOR 11 10.11 10.
A Collection of Motetts or Antiphons, London, 1792
SAMUEL WEBBE, SR., 1740-1816

1. Come, ye dis - con - so - late, wher - e'er ye lan - guish,
2. Joy of the des - o - late, light of the stray - ing,
3. Here see the bread of life; see wa - ters flow - ing
Come to the mer - cy seat, fer - vent - ly kneel.
Hope of the pen - i - tent, fade - less and pure!
Forth from the throne of God, pure from a - bove.
Here bring your wound - ed hearts, here tell your an - guish:
Here speaks the Com - fort - er, ten - der - ly say - ing,
Come to the feast of love; come, ev - er know - ing
Earth has no sor - row that heaven can - not heal.
"Earth has no sor - row that heaven can - not cure."
Earth has no sor - row but heaven can re - move. A-men.

CALL

Come, Ye Sinners, Poor and Needy

PLEADING SAVIOR 87.87.87.
The Christian Lyre, 1831

JOSEPH HART, 1712-1768

1. Come, ye sin - ners, poor and need - y, Weak and wound - ed,
2. Now, ye need - y, come and wel - come; God's free boun - ty
3. Let not con-science make you lin - ger, Nor of fit - ness
4. Come, ye wea - ry, hea - vy la - den, Bruised and man - gled
sick and sore; Je - sus read - y stands to save you,
glo - ri - fy; True be - lief and true re - pent - ance,
fond - ly dream; All the fit - ness he re - quir - eth
by the fall; If you tar - ry till you're bet - ter,
Full of pit - y, love, and power; He is a - ble,
Ev - ery grace that brings you nigh; With - out mon - ey,
Is to feel your need of him: This he gives you,
You will nev - er come at all; Not the righ - teous,
He is a - ble, He is will - ing; doubt no more.
With - out mon - ey, Come to Je - sus Christ and buy.
This he gives you; 'Tis the Spir - it's glim-mering beam.
Not the righ - teous; Sin - ners Je - sus came to call. A-men.

God Calling Yet! Shall I Not Hear

PSALM 95:7-8
GERHARD TERSTEEGEN, 1697-1769
Trans. by JANE BORTHWICK, 1813-1897

FEDERAL STREET LM
HENRY K. OLIVER, 1800-1885

1. God call - ing yet! Shall I not hear? Earth's plea-sures shall I
2. God call - ing yet! Shall I not rise? Can I his lov - ing
3. God call - ing yet! And shall he knock, And I my heart the
4. God call - ing yet! And shall I give No heed, but still in
5. God call - ing yet! I can - not stay; My heart I yield with-
still hold dear? Shall life's swift pass - ing years all fly,
voice de - spise, And base - ly his kind care re - pay?
clos - er lock? He still is wait - ing to re - ceive,
bond - age live? I wait, but he does not for - sake;
out de - lay; Vain world, fare-well, from thee I part;
And still my soul in slum - ber lie?
He calls me still; can I de - lay?
And shall I dare his spir - it grieve?
He calls me still; my heart, a - wake!
The voice of God hath reached my heart. A - men.

106

Holy Spirit, Faithful Guide

FAITHFUL GUIDE 77.77.D.

MARCUS M. WELLS, 1815-1895 — MARCUS M. WELLS, 1815-1895

1. Holy Spirit, faithful guide, Ever near the Christian's side,
2. Ever present, truest friend, Ever near thine aid to lend,
3. When our days of toil shall cease, Waiting still for sweet release,
Gently lead us by the hand, Pilgrims in a desert land;
Leave us not to doubt and fear, Groping on in darkness drear;
Nothing left but heaven and prayer, Wondering if our names were there;
Weary souls fore'er rejoice, While they hear that sweetest voice,
When the storms are raging sore, Hearts grow faint, and hopes give o'er,
Wading deep the dismal flood, Pleading naught but Jesus' blood,
Whispering softly, "Wanderer, come! Follow me, I'll guide thee home."
Whisper softly, "Wanderer, come! Follow me, I'll guide thee home."
Whisper softly, "Wanderer, come! Follow me, I'll guide thee home." Amen.

Jesus Calls Us O'er the Tumult

MATTHEW 4:18-22
CECIL FRANCES ALEXANDER, 1818-1895

GALILEE 87.87.
WILLIAM H. JUDE, 1851-1922

1. Je - sus calls us o'er the tu - mult Of our
2. As of old th' a - pos - tles heard it By the
3. Je - sus calls us from the wor - ship Of the
4. In our joys and in our sor - rows, Days of
5. Je - sus calls us! by thy mer - cies, Sav - ior,
life's wild, rest - less sea; Day by day his sweet voice
Gal - i - le - an lake, Turned from home and toil and
vain world's gold - en store, From each i - dol that would
toil and hours of ease, Still he calls, in cares and
may we hear thy call, Give our hearts to thine o -
sound - eth, Say - ing, "Chris - tian, fol - low me!"
kin - dred, Leav - ing all for Je - sus' sake.
keep us, Say - ing, "Chris - tian, love me more!"
plea - sures, "Chris-tian, love me more than these!"
be - dience, Serve and love thee best of all! A - men.

CALL

108

O Jesus, Thou Art Standing

ST. HILDA 76.76.D.

REVELATION 3:20
WILLIAM W. HOW, 1823-1897

JUSTIN H. KNECHT, 1752-1817
EDWARD HUSBAND, 1843-1908

1. O Je - sus, thou art stand - ing Out - side the fast - closed door,
2. O Je - sus, thou art knock - ing; And lo, that hand is scarred,
3. O Je - sus, thou art plead - ing In ac - cents meek and low,
In low - ly pa - tience wait - ing To pass the thresh - old o'er;
And thorns thy brow en - cir - cle, And tears thy face have marred.
"I died for you, my chil - dren, And will ye treat me so?"
Shame on us, Chris - tian breth - ren, His name and sign who bear;
O love that pass - eth knowl - edge, So pa - tient - ly to wait!
O Lord, with shame and sor - row We o - pen now the door;
O shame, thrice shame up - on us, To keep him stand - ing there!
O sin that hath no e - qual, So fast to bar the gate!
Dear Sav - ior, en - ter, en - ter, And leave us nev - er - more. A - men.

Sing Them Over Again to Me

WORDS OF LIFE 86.86.66. with Refrain

PHILIP P. BLISS, 1838-1876

PHILIP P. BLISS, 1838-1876

1. Sing them o - ver a - gain to me, Won-der - ful words of life;
2. Christ, the bless - ed one, gives to all Won-der - ful words of life;
3. Sweet - ly ech - o the gos - pel call, Won-der - ful words of life;
Let me more of their beau - ty see, Won-der - ful words of life;
Sin - ner, list to the lov - ing call, Won-der - ful words of life;
Of - fer par - don and peace to all, Won-der - ful words of life;
Words of life and beau - ty Teach me faith and du - ty.
All so free - ly giv - en, Woo - ing us to heav - en.
Je - sus, on - ly Sav - ior, Sanc - ti - fy for - ev - er.
Refrain
1.
2.
Beau-ti-ful words, won-der-ful words, Won-der-ful words of life; life.

CALL

Jesus Is Tenderly Calling

JESUS IS CALLING 10.8.10.7. with Refrain

FANNY J. CROSBY, 1820-1915

GEORGE C. STEBBINS, 1846-1945

1. Je - sus is ten - der - ly call - ing thee home,
2. Je - sus is call - ing the wea - ry to rest,
3. Je - sus is wait - ing, O come to him now,
4. Je - sus is plead - ing; O list to his voice:
Call - ing to - day, call - ing to - day; Why from the sun - shine of
Call - ing to - day, call - ing to - day; Bring him thy bur - den and
Wait - ing to - day, wait - ing to - day; Come with thy sins; at his
Hear him to - day, hear him to - day; They who be - lieve on his
love wilt thou roam Far - ther and far - ther a - way?
thou shalt be blest; He will not turn thee a - way.
feet low - ly bow; Come, and no long - er de - lay.
name shall re - joice; Quick - ly a - rise and a - way.
Refrain
Call - ing to - day, Call - ing to -
Call - ing, call - ing to - day, to - day, Call - ing, call - ing to -

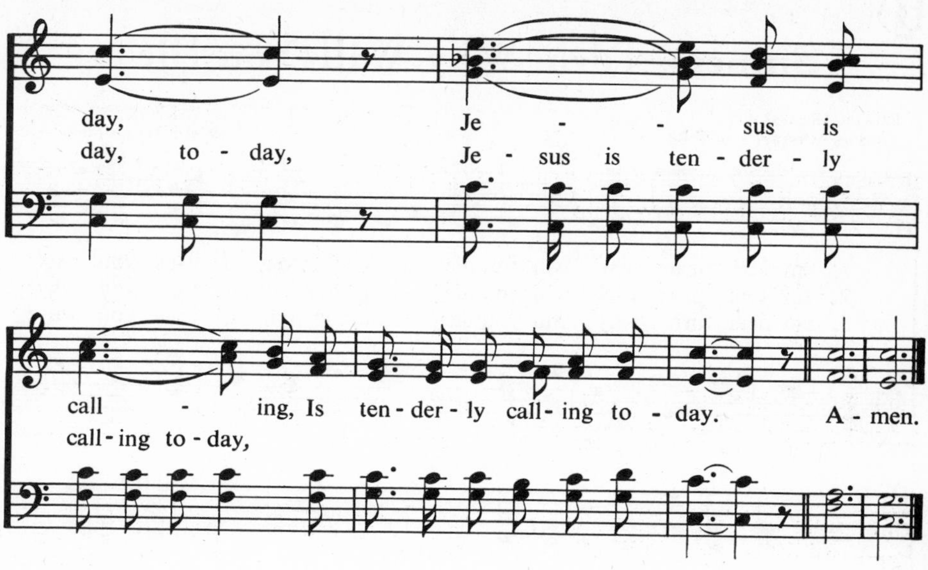
day, Je - - sus is
day, to - day, Je - sus is ten - der - ly
call - ing, Is ten - der - ly call - ing to - day. A - men.
call - ing to - day,

111

Come, Let Us, Who in Christ Believe

CAMPMEETING CM
Early American Melody
CHARLES WESLEY, 1707-1788
Harm. by ROBERT G. McCUTCHAN, 1877-1958

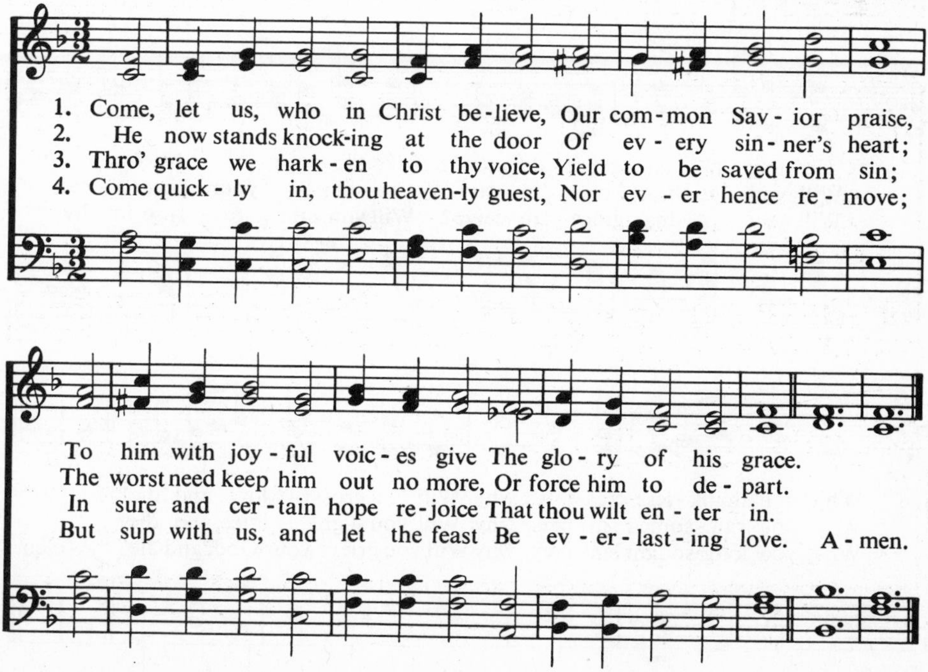
1. Come, let us, who in Christ be - lieve, Our com - mon Sav - ior praise,
2. He now stands knock - ing at the door Of ev - ery sin - ner's heart;
3. Thro' grace we hark - en to thy voice, Yield to be saved from sin;
4. Come quick - ly in, thou heaven - ly guest, Nor ev - er hence re - move;
To him with joy - ful voic - es give The glo - ry of his grace.
The worst need keep him out no more, Or force him to de - part.
In sure and cer - tain hope re - joice That thou wilt en - ter in.
But sup with us, and let the feast Be ev - er - last - ing love. A - men.

CALL

112

Sinners, Turn: Why Will You Die

EZEKIEL 18:31-32
CHARLES WESLEY, 1707-1788

ARFON 77.77.D.
Welsh Hymn Melody

1. Sin-ners, turn: why will you die? God, your Ma-ker, asks you why;
2. Sin-ners, turn: why will you die? God, your Sav-ior, asks you why;
3. Sin-ners, turn: why will you die? God, the Spir-it, asks you why;
God, who did your be-ing give, Made you with him-self to live;
God, who did your souls re-trieve, Died him-self, that you might live.
He, who all your lives hath strove, Wooed you to em-brace his love;
He the fa-tal cause de-mands, Asks the work of his own hands.
Will you let him die in vain? Cru-ci-fy your Lord a-gain?
Will you not his grace re-ceive? Will you still re-fuse to live?
Why, you thank-less crea-tures, why Will you cross his love, and die?
Why, you ran-somed sin-ners, why Will you slight his grace, and die?
Why, you long-sought sin-ners, why Will you grieve your God, and die? A-men.

By Thy Birth and by Thy Tears

ROBERT GRANT, 1779-1838
Alt. by THOMAS COTTERILL, 1779-1823, and others

REDHEAD 76 77.77.77.
RICHARD REDHEAD, 1820-1901

1. By thy birth and by thy tears, By thy hu - man griefs and fears, By thy con - flict in the hour Of the sub - tle temp-ter's power: Sav - ior, look with pity - ing eye; Sav - ior, help me, or I die.
2. By thy lone - ly hour of prayer, By thy fear - ful con - flict there, By thy cross and dy - ing cries, By thy one great sac - ri - fice: Sav - ior, look with pity - ing eye; Sav - ior, help me, or I die.
3. By thy tri - umph o'er the grave, By thy power the lost to save, By thy high, ma - jes - tic throne, By the em - pire all thine own: Sav - ior, look with pity - ing eye; Sav - ior, help me, or I die.
A-men.

How Can a Sinner Know

ST. MICHAEL SM
Genevan Psalter, 1551
Adapt. by WILLIAM CROTCH, 1775-1847

CHARLES WESLEY, 1707-1788

1. How can a sin - ner know His
2. What we have felt and seen With
3. We who in Christ be - lieve That
4. We by his spir - it prove And
sins on earth for - given? How can my gra - cious
con - fi - dence we tell; And pub - lish to the
he for us hath died, We all his un - known
know the things of God, The things which free - ly
Sav - ior show My name in - scribed in heaven?
sons of men The signs in - fal - li - ble.
peace re - ceive, And feel his blood ap - plied.
of his love He hath on us be - stowed. A - men.

115

How Happy Every Child of Grace

CLEANSING FOUNTAIN CMD

CHARLES WESLEY, 1707-1788

American Folk Melody

1. How hap - py ev - ery child of grace, Who knows his sins for - given!
2. O what a bless - ed hope is ours! While here on earth we stay.
"This earth," he cries, "is not my place; I seek my place in heaven:
We more than taste the heaven - ly powers, And an - te - date that day;
A coun - try far from mor - tal sight, Yet O by faith I see The
We feel the res - ur - rec - tion near, Our life in Christ con - cealed, And
land of rest, the saints' de - light, The heaven pre - pared for me."
with his glo - rious pres - ence here His life in us re - vealed. A - men.

I Am Coming to the Cross

COMING TO THE CROSS 77.77.

WILLIAM MCDONALD, 1820-1901 — WILLIAM G. FISCHER, 1835-1912

1. I am com - ing to the cross; I am
2. Long my heart has sighed for thee; Long has
3. Here I give my all to thee: Friends and
4. I am trust - ing, Lord, in thee, Bless - ed
5. Je - sus comes! He fills my soul! Per - fect -
poor and weak and blind; I am count - ing all but
e - vil reigned with - in; Je - sus sweet - ly speaks to
time and earth - ly store; Soul and bod - y thine to
Lamb of Cal - va - ry; Hum - bly at thy cross I
ed in him I am; I am ev - ery whit made
dross; I shall full sal - va - tion find.
me, "I will cleanse you from all sin."
be, Whol - ly thine for - ev - er - more.
bow, Save me, Je - sus, save me now.
whole; Glo - ry, glo - ry to the Lamb! A - men.

117

I Heard the Voice of Jesus Say

JOHN 1:16; MATTHEW 11:28;
JOHN 4:14; 8:12
HORATIUS BONAR, 1808-1889

VOX DILECTI CMD
JOHN B. DYKES, 1823-1876

1. I heard the voice of Je - sus say, "Come un - to me and rest;
2. I heard the voice of Je - sus say, "Be - hold, I free - ly give
3. I heard the voice of Je - sus say, "I am this dark world's light;
Lay down, thou wea - ry one, lay down Thy head up - on my breast."
The liv - ing wa - ter; thirst - y one, Stoop down and drink and live."
Look un - to me, thy morn shall rise, And all thy day be bright."
I came to Je - sus as I was, Wea - ry and worn and sad;
I came to Je - sus, and I drank Of that life - giv - ing stream;
I looked to Je - sus, and I found In him my star, my sun;
I found in him a rest-ing place, And he has made me glad.
My thirst was quenched, my soul re-vived, And now I live in him.
And in that light of life I'll walk Till travel-ing days are done. A-men.

Jesus, the Sinner's Friend, to Thee

GALATIANS 3:22
CHARLES WESLEY, 1707-1788

FEDERAL STREET LM
HENRY K. OLIVER, 1800-1885

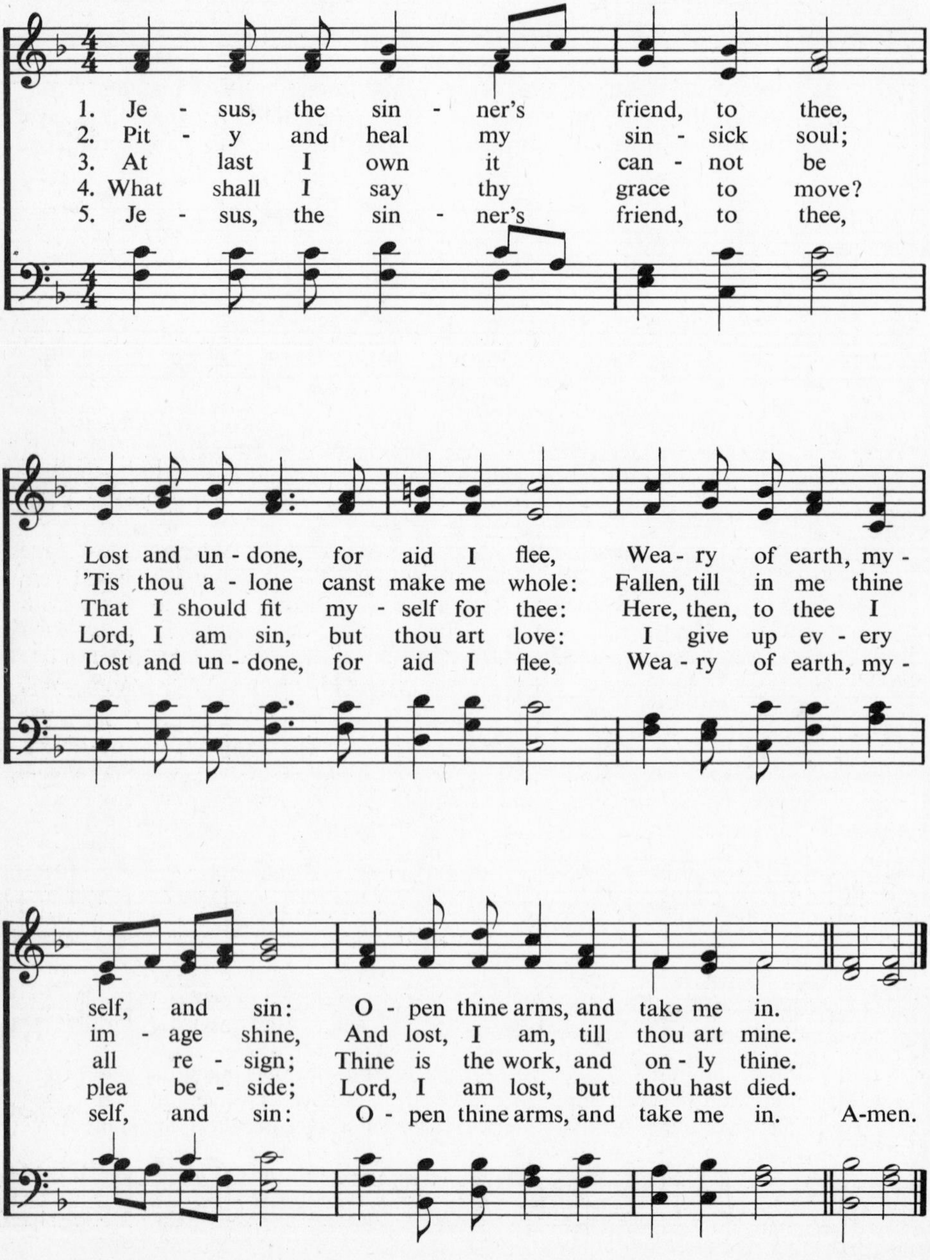
1. Je - sus, the sin - ner's friend, to thee,
2. Pit - y and heal my sin - sick soul;
3. At last I own it can - not be
4. What shall I say thy grace to move?
5. Je - sus, the sin - ner's friend, to thee,
Lost and un - done, for aid I flee, Wea - ry of earth, my -
'Tis thou a - lone canst make me whole: Fallen, till in me thine
That I should fit my - self for thee: Here, then, to thee I
Lord, I am sin, but thou art love: I give up ev - ery
Lost and un - done, for aid I flee, Wea - ry of earth, my -
self, and sin: O - pen thine arms, and take me in.
im - age shine, And lost, I am, till thou art mine.
all re - sign; Thine is the work, and on - ly thine.
plea be - side; Lord, I am lost, but thou hast died.
self, and sin: O - pen thine arms, and take me in. A-men.

Just as I Am, Without One Plea

JOHN 6:37
CHARLOTTE ELLIOTT, 1789-1871

WOODWORTH LM
WILLIAM B. BRADBURY, 1816-1868

1. Just as I am, with - out one plea,
2. Just as I am, and wait - ing not
3. Just as I am, though tossed a - bout
4. Just as I am, poor, wretch - ed, blind;
5. Just as I am, thou wilt re - ceive,
6. Just as I am, thy love un - known
But that thy blood was shed for me, And that thou bidst me
To rid my soul of one dark blot, To thee whose blood can
With many a con-flict, many a doubt, Fight - ings and fears with-
Sight, rich - es, heal - ing of the mind, Yea, all I need, in
Wilt wel - come, par - don, cleanse, re - lieve; Be - cause thy prom - ise
Hath bro - ken ev - ery bar - rier down; Now, to be thine, yea,
come to thee, O Lamb of God, I come, I come!
cleanse each spot, O Lamb of God, I come, I come!
in, with - out, O Lamb of God, I come, I come!
thee to find, O Lamb of God, I come, I come!
I be - lieve, O Lamb of God, I come, I come!
thine a - lone, O Lamb of God, I come, I come! A-men.

120

Rock of Ages, Cleft for Me

TOPLADY 77.77.77.

AUGUSTUS M. TOPLADY, 1740-1778 — THOMAS HASTINGS, 1784-1872

1. Rock of A - ges, cleft for me, Let me
2. Could my tears for - ev - er flow, Could my
3. While I draw this fleet - ing breath, When my
hide my - self in thee; Let the wa - ter and the blood,
zeal no lan - guor know, These for sin could not a - tone;
eyes shall close in death, When I rise to worlds un - known,
From thy wound - ed side which flowed, Be of sin the dou - ble
Thou must save, and thou a - lone. In my hand no price I
And be - hold thee on thy throne, Rock of A - ges, cleft for
cure, Save from wrath and make me pure.
bring; Sim - ply to thy cross I cling.
me, Let me hide my - self in thee. A - men.

Alternate tune: REDHEAD 76

Savior, Like a Shepherd Lead Us

BRADBURY 87.87.87.

Hymns for the Young, 1836
Attr. to DOROTHY A. THRUPP, 1779-1847

WILLIAM B. BRADBURY, 1816-1868
Arr. by V. E. C.

Unison
1. Sav-ior, like a shep-herd lead us, Much we need thy ten-der care;
2. We are thine, do thou be-friend us, Be the guard-ian of our way;
3. Thou hast prom-ised to re-ceive us, Poor and sin-ful though we be;
4. Ear-ly let us seek thy fa-vor, Ear-ly let us do thy will;

In thy pleas-ant pas-tures feed us, For our use thy folds pre-pare:
Keep thy flock, from sin de-fend us, Seek us when we go a-stray:
Thou hast mer-cy to re-lieve us, Grace to cleanse and power to free:
Bless-ed Lord and on-ly Sav-ior, With thy love our bos-oms fill:

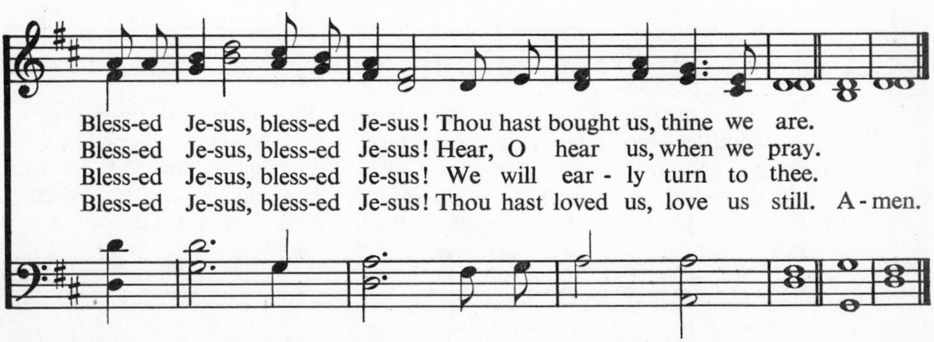
Bless-ed Je-sus, bless-ed Je-sus! Thou hast bought us, thine we are.
Bless-ed Je-sus, bless-ed Je-sus! Hear, O hear us, when we pray.
Bless-ed Je-sus, bless-ed Je-sus! We will ear-ly turn to thee.
Bless-ed Je-sus, bless-ed Je-sus! Thou hast loved us, love us still. A-men.

Arise, My Soul, Arise

LENOX 66.66.88.
Chorister's Companion, c. 1782
Lewis Edson, 1748-1820

Charles Wesley, 1707-1788

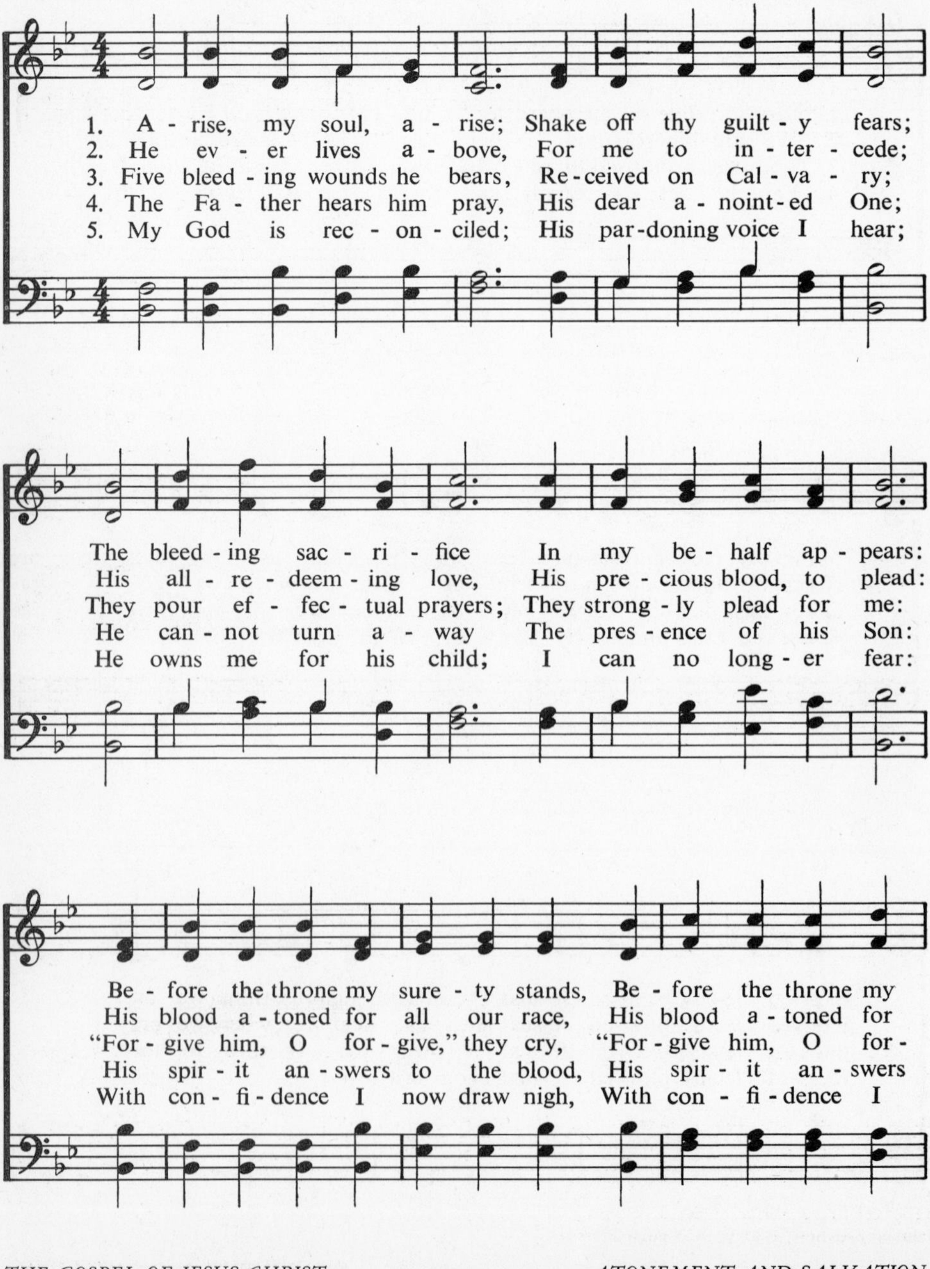
1. A - rise, my soul, a - rise; Shake off thy guilt - y fears;
2. He ev - er lives a - bove, For me to in - ter - cede;
3. Five bleed - ing wounds he bears, Re - ceived on Cal - va - ry;
4. The Fa - ther hears him pray, His dear a - noint - ed One;
5. My God is rec - on - ciled; His par-doning voice I hear;
The bleed - ing sac - ri - fice In my be - half ap - pears:
His all - re - deem - ing love, His pre - cious blood, to plead:
They pour ef - fec - tual prayers; They strong - ly plead for me:
He can - not turn a - way The pres - ence of his Son:
He owns me for his child; I can no long - er fear:
Be - fore the throne my sure - ty stands, Be - fore the throne my
His blood a - toned for all our race, His blood a - toned for
"For - give him, O for - give," they cry, "For - give him, O for -
His spir - it an - swers to the blood, His spir - it an - swers
With con - fi - dence I now draw nigh, With con - fi - dence I

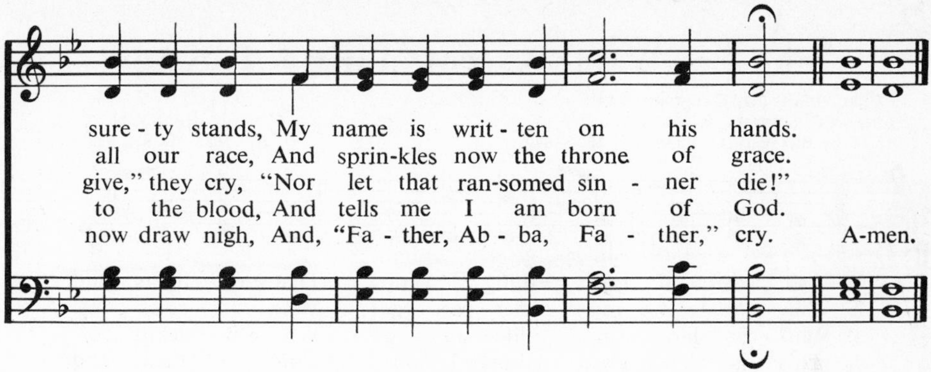
sure - ty stands, My name is writ - ten on his hands.
all our race, And sprin-kles now the throne of grace.
give," they cry, "Nor let that ran-somed sin - ner die!"
to the blood, And tells me I am born of God.
now draw nigh, And, "Fa - ther, Ab - ba, Fa - ther," cry. A-men.

123

I Know Not How That Bethlehem's Babe

SHIRLEYN CM
EARL E. HARPER, 1895-
Harm. by A. C. L.

HARRY WEBB FARRINGTON, 1880-1931

1. I know not how that Beth-lehem's babe Could in the God-head be;
2. I know not how that Cal - vary's cross A world from sin could free;
3. I know not how that Jo - seph's tomb Could solve death's mys-ter - y;

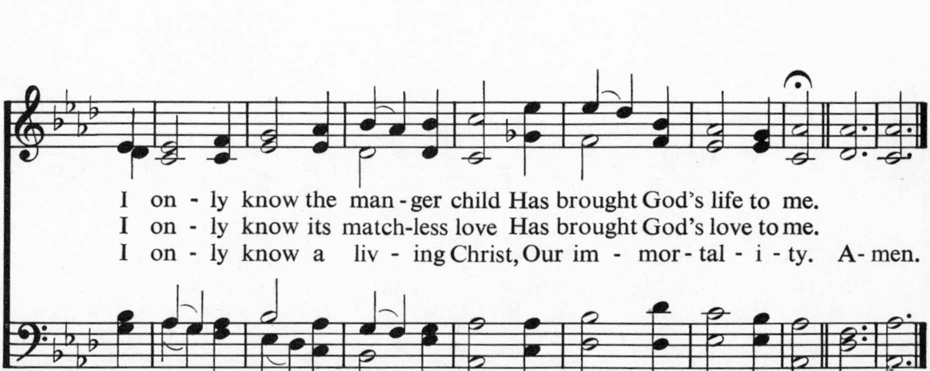
I on - ly know the man - ger child Has brought God's life to me.
I on - ly know its match-less love Has brought God's love to me.
I on - ly know a liv - ing Christ, Our im - mor - tal - i - ty. A- men.

124

Ask Ye What Great Thing I Know

I CORINTHIANS 2:2; GALATIANS 6:14
JOHANN C. SCHWEDLER, 1672-1730
Trans. by BENJAMIN H. KENNEDY, 1804-1889

HENDON 77.77.7.
H. A. CÉSAR MALAN, 1787-1864

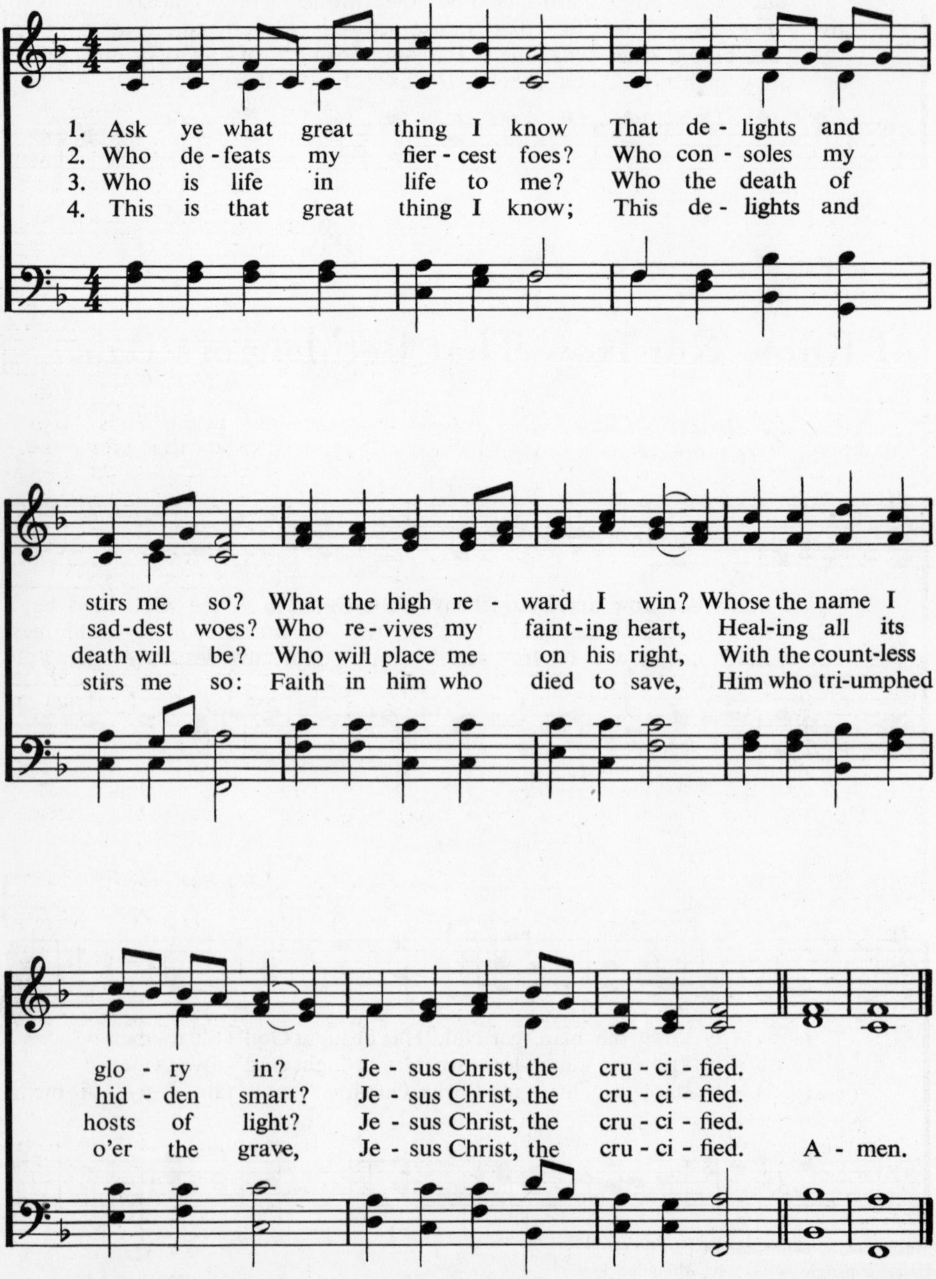
1. Ask ye what great thing I know That de - lights and stirs me so? What the high re - ward I win? Whose the name I glo - ry in? Je - sus Christ, the cru - ci - fied.
2. Who de - feats my fier - cest foes? Who con - soles my sad-dest woes? Who re - vives my faint-ing heart, Heal-ing all its hid - den smart? Je - sus Christ, the cru - ci - fied.
3. Who is life in life to me? Who the death of death will be? Who will place me on his right, With the count-less hosts of light? Je - sus Christ, the cru - ci - fied.
4. This is that great thing I know; This de - lights and stirs me so: Faith in him who died to save, Him who tri-umphed o'er the grave, Je - sus Christ, the cru - ci - fied. A - men.

Jesus, Lover of My Soul

ABERYSTWYTH 77.77.D.

CHARLES WESLEY, 1707-1788 — JOSEPH PARRY, 1841-1903

1. Je - sus, lov - er of my soul, Let me to thy bos-om fly,
2. Oth-er ref - uge have I none; Hangs my help-less soul on thee;
3. Thou, O Christ, art all I want; More than all in thee I find:
4. Plen-teous grace with thee is found, Grace to cov - er all my sin;
While the near-er wa-ters roll, While the tem-pest still is high:
Leave, ah! leave me not a - lone, Still sup - port and com-fort me.
Raise the fall - en, cheer the faint, Heal the sick, and lead the blind.
Let the heal - ing streams a - bound; Make and keep me pure with - in.
Hide me, O my Sav - ior, hide, Till the storm of life is past;
All my trust on thee is stayed; All my help from thee I bring;
Just and ho - ly is thy name; I am all un - righ - teous - ness;
Thou of life the foun-tain art; Free-ly let me take of thee:
Safe in - to the ha - ven guide; O re - ceive my soul at last!
Cov-er my de - fense-less head With the shad-ow of thy wing.
False and full of sin I am; Thou art full of truth and grace.
Spring thou up with - in my heart; Rise to all e - ter - ni - ty. A-men.

126

Jesus, Lover of My Soul

MARTYN 77.77.D.
SIMEON B. MARSH, 1798-1875

CHARLES WESLEY, 1707-1788

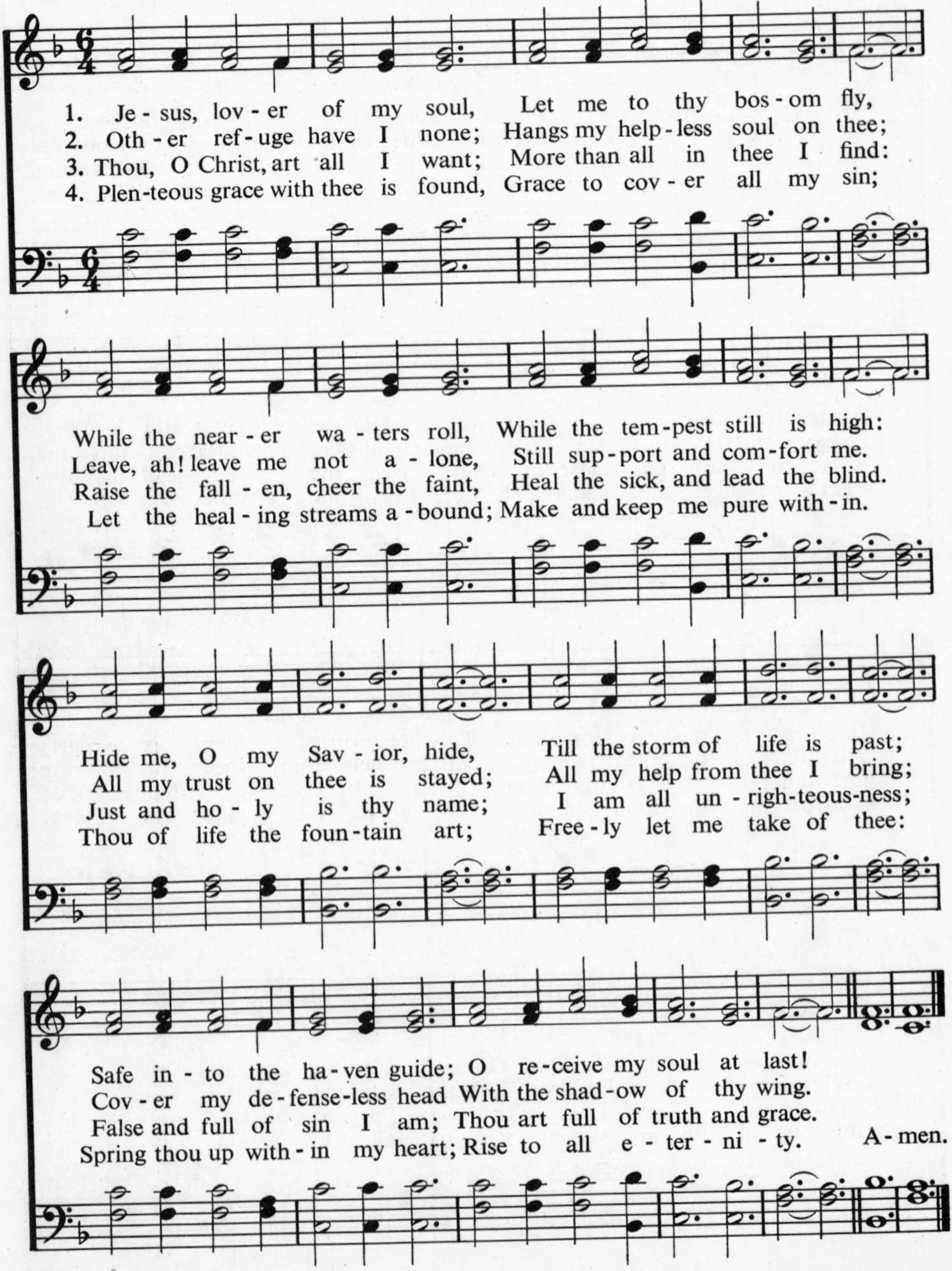

1. Je - sus, lov - er of my soul, Let me to thy bos - om fly,
2. Oth - er ref - uge have I none; Hangs my help - less soul on thee;
3. Thou, O Christ, art all I want; More than all in thee I find:
4. Plen-teous grace with thee is found, Grace to cov - er all my sin;
While the near - er wa - ters roll, While the tem - pest still is high:
Leave, ah! leave me not a - lone, Still sup - port and com - fort me.
Raise the fall - en, cheer the faint, Heal the sick, and lead the blind.
Let the heal - ing streams a - bound; Make and keep me pure with - in.
Hide me, O my Sav - ior, hide, Till the storm of life is past;
All my trust on thee is stayed; All my help from thee I bring;
Just and ho - ly is thy name; I am all un - righ - teous - ness;
Thou of life the foun - tain art; Free - ly let me take of thee:
Safe in - to the ha - ven guide; O re - ceive my soul at last!
Cov - er my de - fense - less head With the shad - ow of thy wing.
False and full of sin I am; Thou art full of truth and grace.
Spring thou up with - in my heart; Rise to all e - ter - ni - ty. A - men.

Jesus, Thy Blood and Righteousness

NICOLAUS VON ZINZENDORF, 1700-1760
Trans. by JOHN WESLEY, 1703-1791

HERR JESU CHRIST, MEIN'S LEBENS LICHT LM
As Hymnodus Sacer, Leipzig, 1625

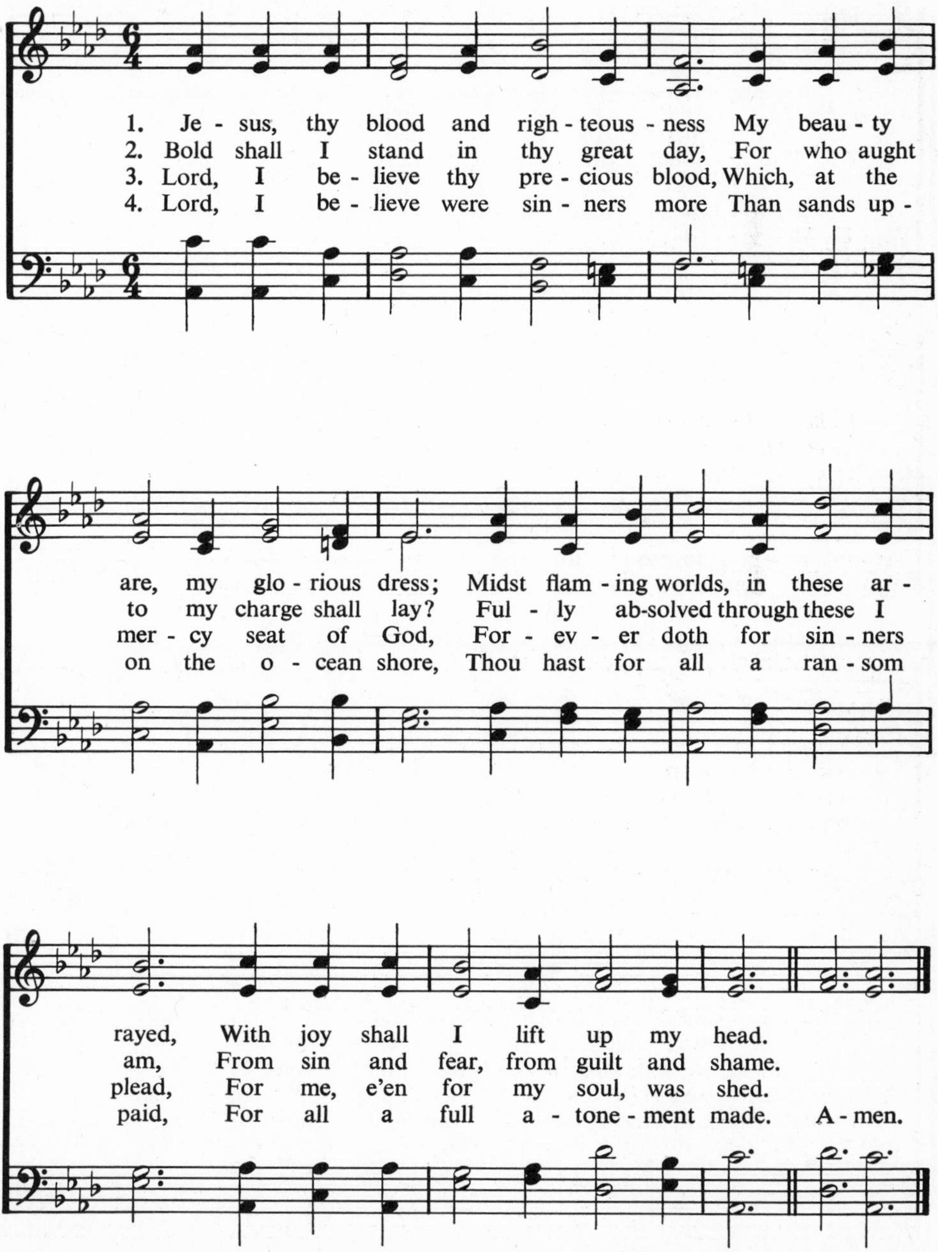
1. Je - sus, thy blood and righ - teous - ness My beau - ty
2. Bold shall I stand in thy great day, For who aught
3. Lord, I be - lieve thy pre - cious blood, Which, at the
4. Lord, I be - lieve were sin - ners more Than sands up -
are, my glo - rious dress; Midst flam - ing worlds, in these ar -
to my charge shall lay? Ful - ly ab-solved through these I
mer - cy seat of God, For - ev - er doth for sin - ners
on the o - cean shore, Thou hast for all a ran - som
rayed, With joy shall I lift up my head.
am, From sin and fear, from guilt and shame.
plead, For me, e'en for my soul, was shed.
paid, For all a full a - tone - ment made. A - men.

128

O Happy Day, That Fixed My Choice

HEBRON LM

PHILIP DODDRIDGE, 1702-1751 — LOWELL MASON, 1792-1872

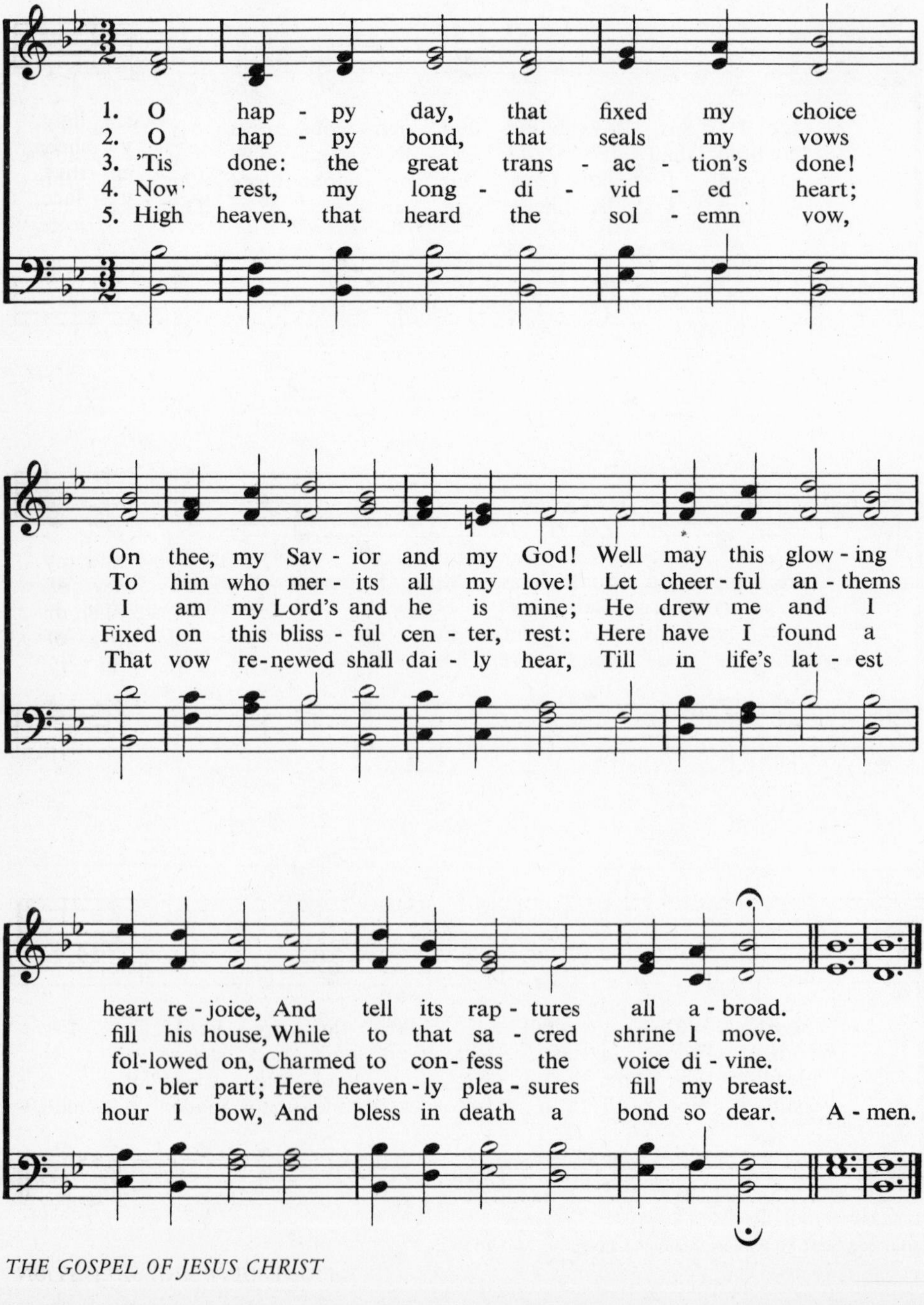
1. O hap - py day, that fixed my choice
2. O hap - py bond, that seals my vows
3. 'Tis done: the great trans - ac - tion's done!
4. Now rest, my long - di - vid - ed heart;
5. High heaven, that heard the sol - emn vow,
On thee, my Sav - ior and my God! Well may this glow - ing
To him who mer - its all my love! Let cheer - ful an - thems
I am my Lord's and he is mine; He drew me and I
Fixed on this bliss - ful cen - ter, rest: Here have I found a
That vow re - newed shall dai - ly hear, Till in life's lat - est
heart re - joice, And tell its rap - tures all a - broad.
fill his house, While to that sa - cred shrine I move.
fol - lowed on, Charmed to con - fess the voice di - vine.
no - bler part; Here heaven - ly plea - sures fill my breast.
hour I bow, And bless in death a bond so dear. A - men.

O Thou, in Whose Presence

DAVIS 11 8.11 8.
WYETH'S *Repository of Sacred Music, Part Second,* 1813
Harm. by A. C. L.

JOSEPH SWAIN, 1761-1796

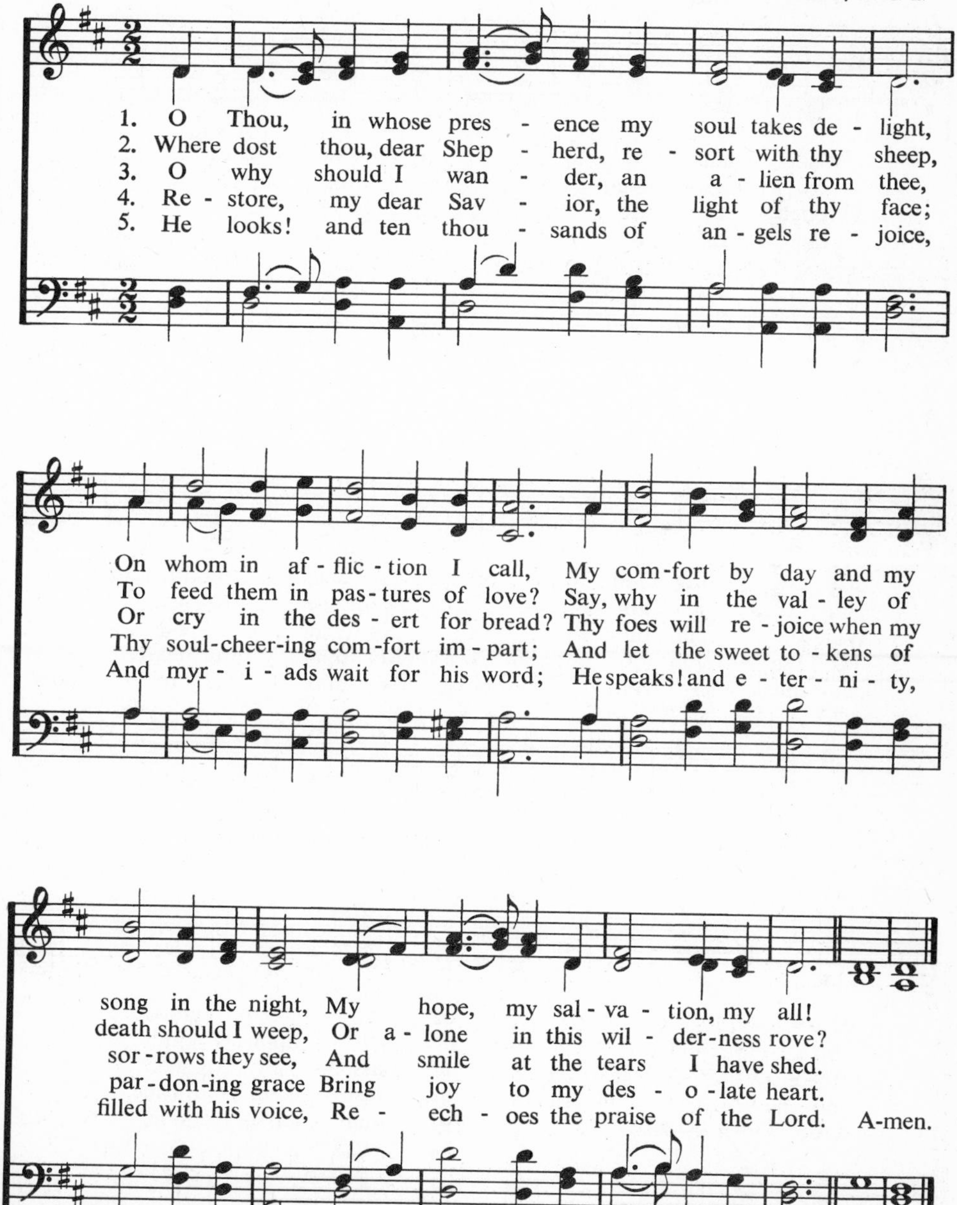
1. O Thou, in whose pres - ence my soul takes de - light,
2. Where dost thou, dear Shep - herd, re - sort with thy sheep,
3. O why should I wan - der, an a - lien from thee,
4. Re - store, my dear Sav - ior, the light of thy face;
5. He looks! and ten thou - sands of an - gels re - joice,
On whom in af - flic - tion I call, My com - fort by day and my
To feed them in pas - tures of love? Say, why in the val - ley of
Or cry in the des - ert for bread? Thy foes will re - joice when my
Thy soul-cheer-ing com - fort im - part; And let the sweet to - kens of
And myr - i - ads wait for his word; He speaks! and e - ter - ni - ty,
song in the night, My hope, my sal - va - tion, my all!
death should I weep, Or a - lone in this wil - der - ness rove?
sor - rows they see, And smile at the tears I have shed.
par - don - ing grace Bring joy to my des - o - late heart.
filled with his voice, Re - ech - oes the praise of the Lord. A-men.

What Shall I Do My God to Love

RICHMOND CM

CHARLES WESLEY, 1707-1788

THOMAS HAWEIS, 1734-1820

1. What shall I do my God to love,
2. Thy sov - ereign grace to all ex - tends,
3. Through - out the world its breadth is known,
4. Come quick - ly then, my Lord, and take
5. As - sert thy claim, re - ceive thy right,

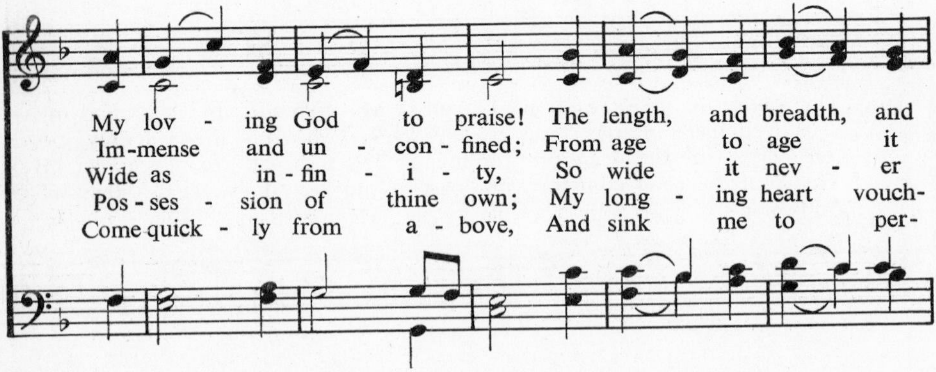
My lov - ing God to praise! The length, and breadth, and
Im-mense and un - con - fined; From age to age it
Wide as in - fin - i - ty, So wide it nev - er
Pos - ses - sion of thine own; My long - ing heart vouch-
Come quick - ly from a - bove, And sink me to per-

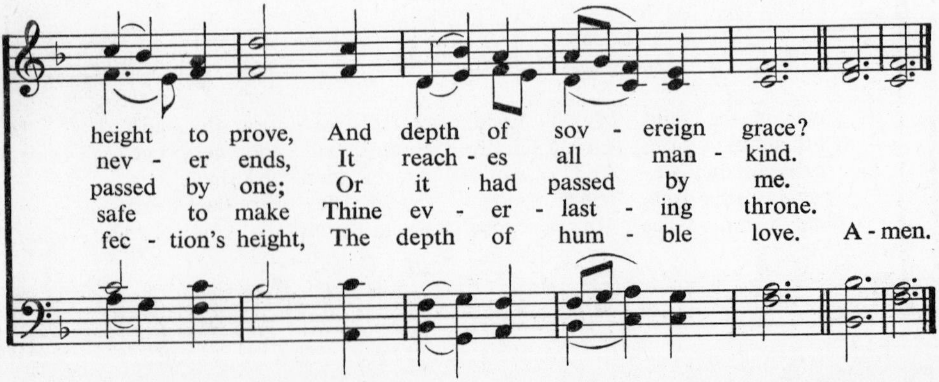
height to prove, And depth of sov - ereign grace?
nev - er ends, It reach - es all man - kind.
passed by one; Or it had passed by me.
safe to make Thine ev - er - last - ing throne.
fec - tion's height, The depth of hum - ble love. A - men.

Come, Holy Ghost, Our Hearts Inspire

Charles Wesley, 1707-1788

WINCHESTER OLD CM
Est's *The Whole Booke of Psalmes,* 1592

1. Come, Ho - ly Ghost, our hearts in - spire, Let
2. Come, Ho - ly Ghost, for moved by thee The
3. Ex - pand thy wings, ce - les - tial Dove, Brood
4. God, through him - self, we then shall know If
us thine in - fluence prove: Source of the old pro -
proph - ets wrote and spoke; Un - lock the truth, thy -
o'er our na - ture's night; On our dis - or - dered
thou with - in us shine, And sound with all thy
phet - ic fire, Foun - tain of life and love.
self the key, Un - seal the sa - cred book.
spir - its move, And let there now be light.
saints be - low, The depths of love di - vine. A - men.

THE HOLY SPIRIT

132

Holy Ghost, Dispel Our Sadness

Paul Gerhardt, 1607-1676
Trans. by John C. Jacobi, 1670-1750

HYFRYDOL 87.87.D.
Rowland H. Prichard, 1811-1887

1. Ho - ly Ghost, dis - pel our sad - ness; Pierce the clouds of
2. Au - thor of the new cre - a - tion, Come with unc - tion
na - ture's night; Come, thou source of joy and glad - ness,
and with power. Make our hearts thy hab - i - ta - tion;
Breathe thy life, and spread thy light. From the height which knows no
On our souls thy grac - es shower. Hear, O hear our sup - pli -
mea - sure, As a gra - cious shower de - scend, Bring-ing down the
ca - tion, Bless - ed Spir - it, God of peace! Rest up - on this

rich - est trea - sure Man can wish, or God can send.
con - gre - ga - tion, With the ful - ness of thy grace. A-men.

133

Breathe on Me, Breath of God

JOHN 20:22
EDWIN HATCH, 1835-1889

TRENTHAM SM
ROBERT JACKSON, 1842-1914

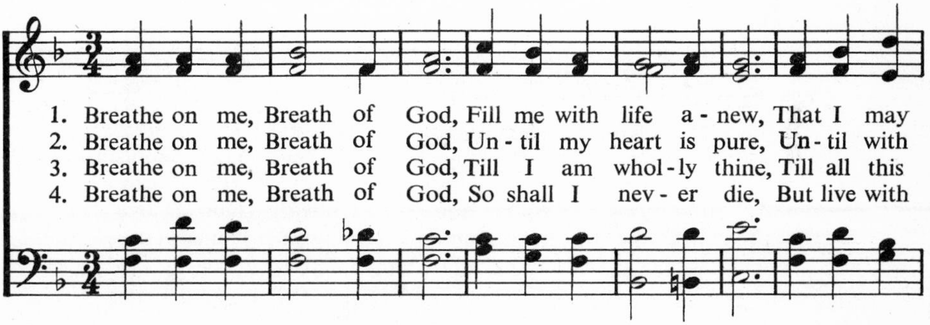
1. Breathe on me, Breath of God, Fill me with life a - new, That I may
2. Breathe on me, Breath of God, Un - til my heart is pure, Un - til with
3. Breathe on me, Breath of God, Till I am whol - ly thine, Till all this
4. Breathe on me, Breath of God, So shall I nev - er die, But live with

love what thou dost love, And do what thou wouldst do.
thee I will one will, To do and to en - dure.
earth - ly part of me Glows with thy fire di - vine.
thee the per - fect life Of thine e - ter - ni - ty. A-men.

Come, Holy Spirit, Heavenly Dove

GRÄFENBERG CM
Praxis Pietatis Melica, Berlin, 1653
JOHANN CRÜGER, 1598-1662

ISAAC WATTS, 1674-1748

1. Come, Ho - ly Spir - it, heaven - ly Dove,
2. Look how we grov - el here be - low,
3. In vain we tune our for - mal songs,
4. And shall we then for - ev - er live
5. Come, Ho - ly Spir - it, heaven - ly Dove,
With all thy quick - ening powers; Kin - dle a
Fond of these earth - ly toys; Our souls, how
In vain we strive to rise; Ho - san - nas
At this poor dy - ing rate? Our love so
With all thy quick - ening powers; Come, shed a -
flame of sa-cred love In these cold hearts of ours.
heav - i - ly they go, To reach e - ter - nal joys.
lan - guish on our tongues, And our de - vo - tion dies.
faint, so cold to thee, And thine to us so great!
broad a Sav-ior's love, And that shall kin - dle ours. A-men.

Holy Spirit, Truth Divine

Samuel Longfellow, 1819-1892

CANTERBURY 77.77.
Adapt. from Orlando Gibbons, 1583-1625

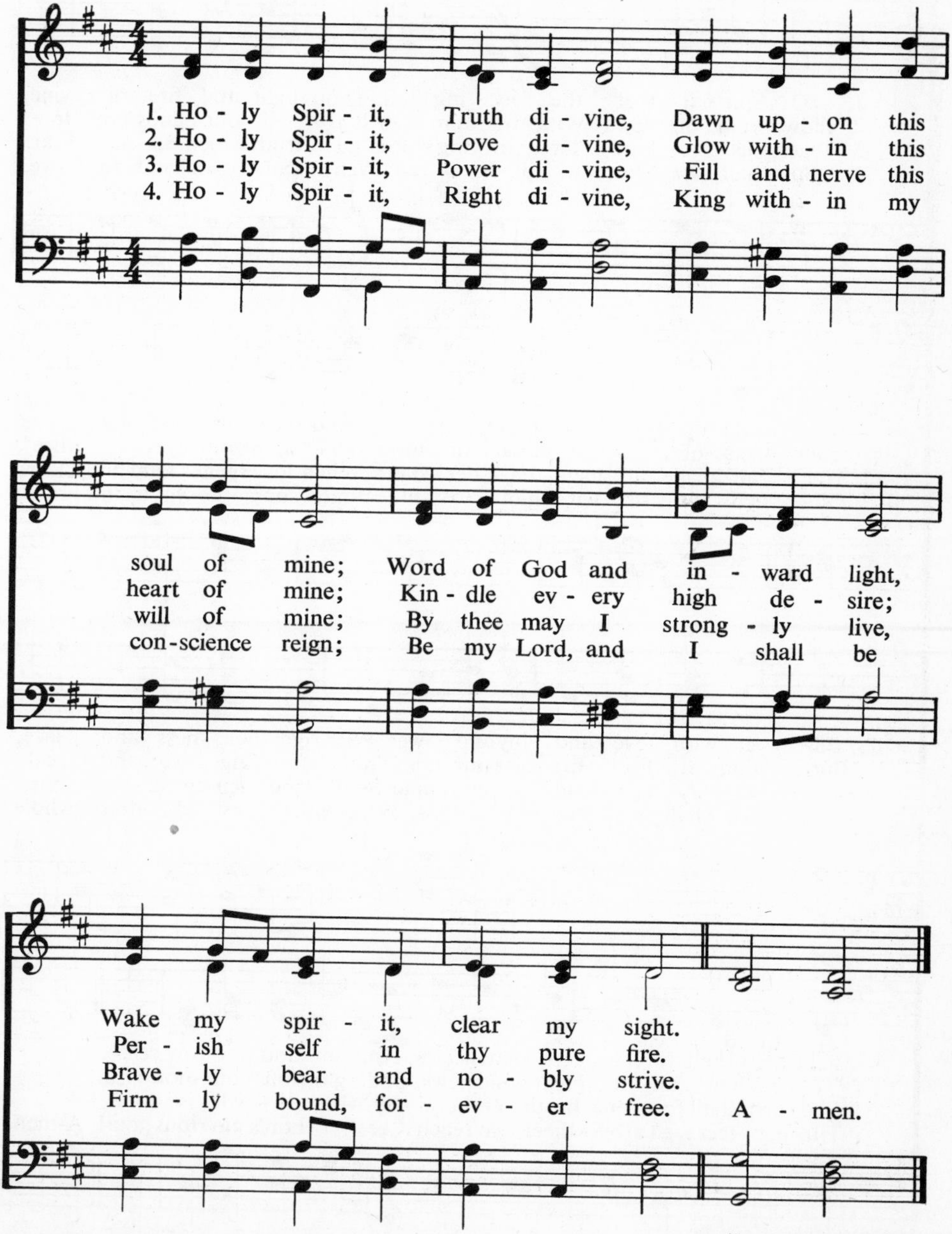
1. Ho - ly Spir - it, Truth di - vine, Dawn up - on this
2. Ho - ly Spir - it, Love di - vine, Glow with - in this
3. Ho - ly Spir - it, Power di - vine, Fill and nerve this
4. Ho - ly Spir - it, Right di - vine, King with - in my
soul of mine; Word of God and in - ward light,
heart of mine; Kin - dle ev - ery high de - sire;
will of mine; By thee may I strong - ly live,
con - science reign; Be my Lord, and I shall be
Wake my spir - it, clear my sight.
Per - ish self in thy pure fire.
Brave - ly bear and no - bly strive.
Firm - ly bound, for - ev - er free. A - men.

Alternate tune: MERCY

O Spirit of the Living God

HENRY H. TWEEDY, 1868-1953

LLANFYLLIN CMD
Trad. Welsh Melody

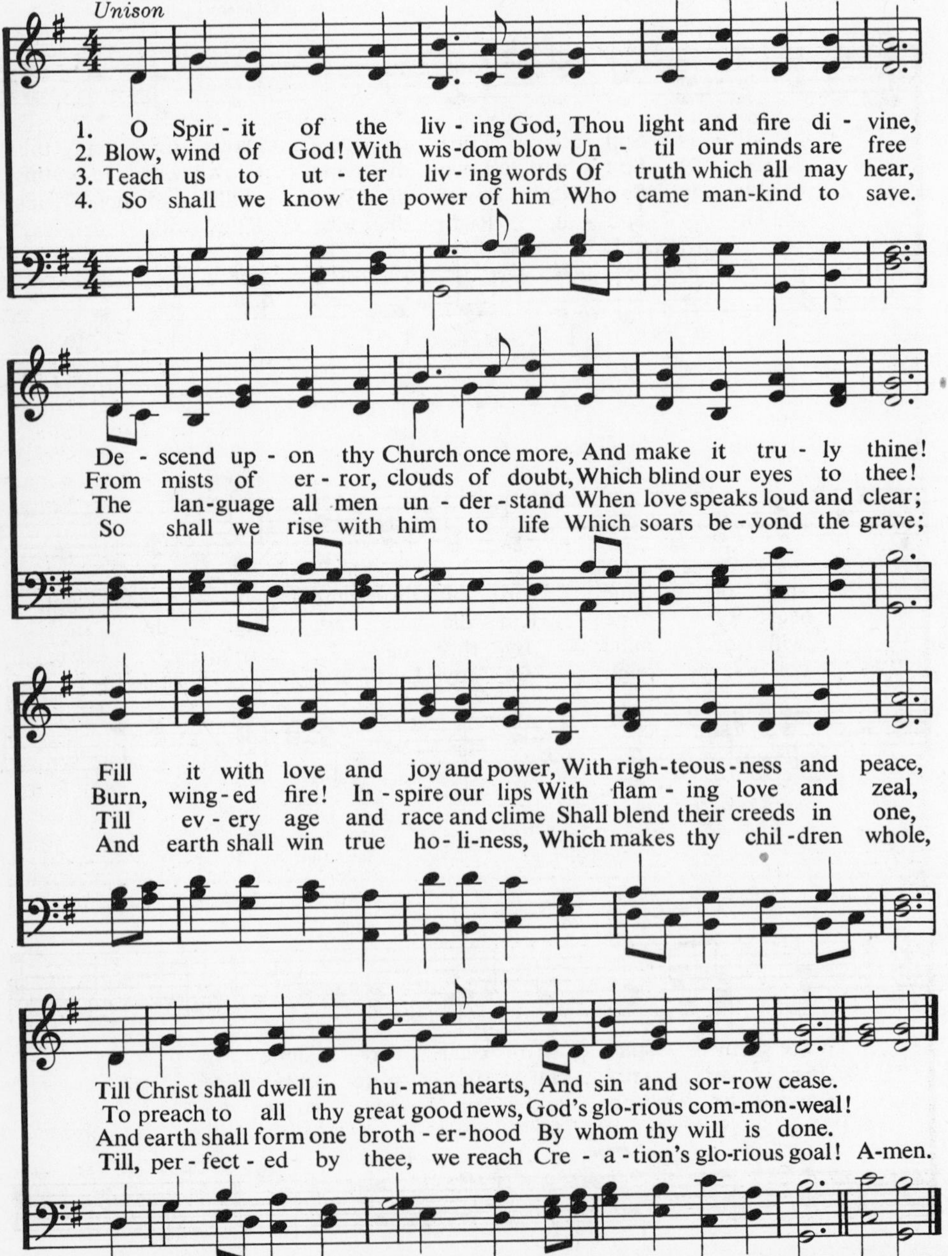
Unison
1. O Spir - it of the liv - ing God, Thou light and fire di - vine,
2. Blow, wind of God! With wis-dom blow Un - til our minds are free
3. Teach us to ut - ter liv - ing words Of truth which all may hear,
4. So shall we know the power of him Who came man-kind to save.
De - scend up - on thy Church once more, And make it tru - ly thine!
From mists of er - ror, clouds of doubt, Which blind our eyes to thee!
The lan-guage all men un - der - stand When love speaks loud and clear;
So shall we rise with him to life Which soars be - yond the grave;
Fill it with love and joy and power, With righ-teous-ness and peace,
Burn, wing-ed fire! In - spire our lips With flam - ing love and zeal,
Till ev - ery age and race and clime Shall blend their creeds in one,
And earth shall win true ho - li-ness, Which makes thy chil-dren whole,
Till Christ shall dwell in hu - man hearts, And sin and sor-row cease.
To preach to all thy great good news, God's glo-rious com-mon-weal!
And earth shall form one broth - er-hood By whom thy will is done.
Till, per - fect - ed by thee, we reach Cre - a - tion's glo-rious goal! A-men.

Spirit of Faith, Come Down

BEALOTH SMD
Mason's Sacred Harp, 1843
Harm. by A. C. L.

CHARLES WESLEY, 1707-1788

1. Spir - it of faith, come down, Re - veal the things of God;
2. No man can tru - ly say That Je - sus is the Lord,
3. O that the world might know The all - a - ton - ing Lamb!
4. In - spire the liv - ing faith, Which who - so - e'er re - ceives
And make to us the God-head known, And wit - ness with the blood.
Un - less thou take the veil a - way, And breathe the liv - ing Word.
Spir - it of faith, de - scend and show The vir - tue of his name.
The wit - ness in him - self he hath, And con - scious - ly be - lieves;
'Tis thine the blood to ap - ply And give us eyes to see,
Then, on - ly then, we feel Our in - terest in his blood,
The grace which all may find, The sav - ing power, im - part;
That faith that con - quers all, And doth the moun - tain move,
Who did for ev - ery sin - ner die Hath sure - ly died for me.
And cry, with joy un - speak - a - ble, "Thou art my Lord, my God!"
And tes - ti - fy to all man - kind, And speak in ev - ery heart.
And saves who - e'er on Je - sus call, And per - fects them in love. A - men.

138

Spirit of God, Descend upon My Heart

GALATIANS 5:25 MORECAMBE 10.10.10.10.
GEORGE CROLY, 1780-1860 FREDERICK C. ATKINSON, 1841-1897

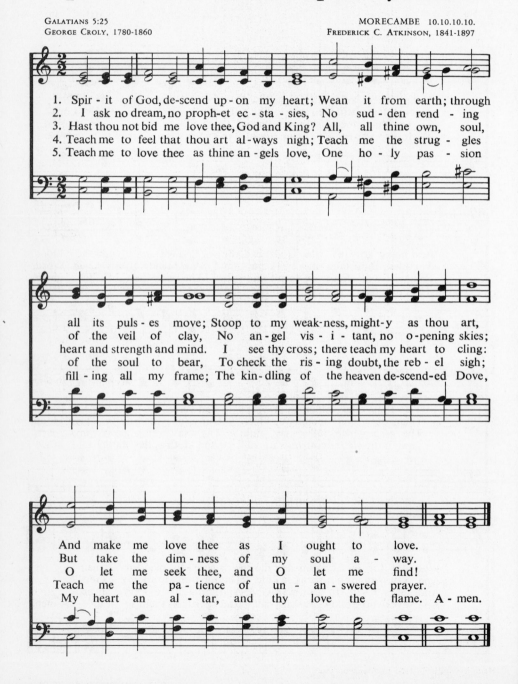

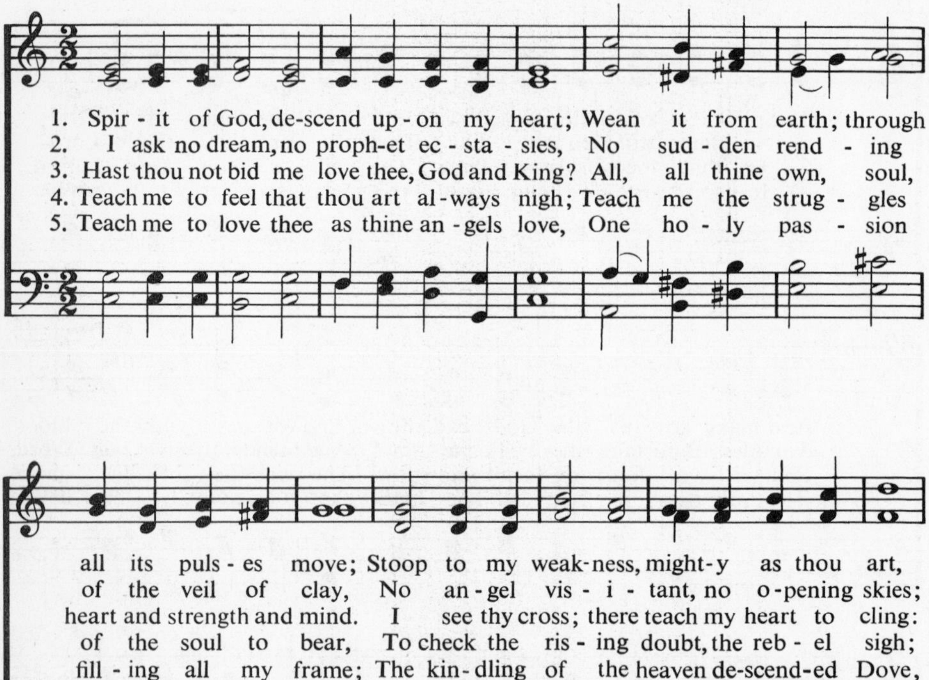
1. Spir - it of God, de-scend up - on my heart; Wean it from earth; through
2. I ask no dream, no proph-et ec - sta - sies, No sud - den rend - ing
3. Hast thou not bid me love thee, God and King? All, all thine own, soul,
4. Teach me to feel that thou art al - ways nigh; Teach me the strug - gles
5. Teach me to love thee as thine an - gels love, One ho - ly pas - sion
all its puls - es move; Stoop to my weak-ness, might-y as thou art,
of the veil of clay, No an-gel vis - i - tant, no o-pening skies;
heart and strength and mind. I see thy cross; there teach my heart to cling:
of the soul to bear, To check the ris - ing doubt, the reb - el sigh;
fill - ing all my frame; The kin-dling of the heaven de-scend-ed Dove,
And make me love thee as I ought to love.
But take the dim - ness of my soul a - way.
O let me seek thee, and O let me find!
Teach me the pa - tience of un - an - swered prayer.
My heart an al - tar, and thy love the flame. A - men.

Author of Faith, Eternal Word

HEBREWS 11
CHARLES WESLEY, 1707-1788

MAINZER LM
JOSEPH MAINZER, 1801-1851
Alt. and harm. by A. C. L.

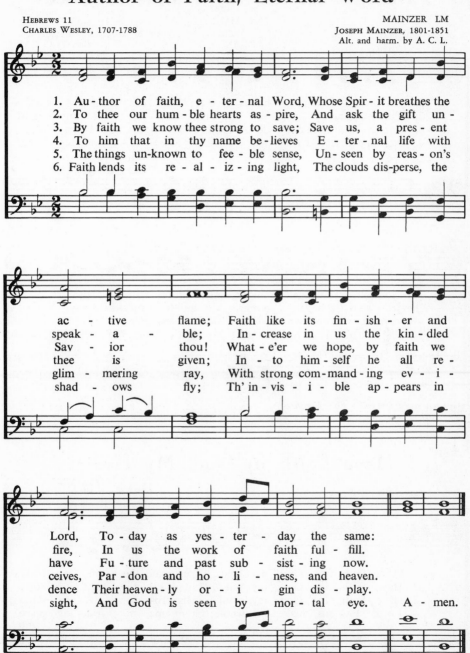

1. Au - thor of faith, e - ter - nal Word, Whose Spir - it breathes the
2. To thee our hum - ble hearts as - pire, And ask the gift un -
3. By faith we know thee strong to save; Save us, a pres - ent
4. To him that in thy name be - lieves E - ter - nal life with
5. The things un-known to fee - ble sense, Un - seen by reas - on's
6. Faith lends its re - al - iz - ing light, The clouds dis-perse, the
ac - tive flame; Faith like its fin - ish - er and
speak - a - ble; In - crease in us the kin - dled
Sav - ior thou! What - e'er we hope, by faith we
thee is given; In - to him - self he all re -
glim - mering ray, With strong com - mand - ing ev - i -
shad - ows fly; Th' in - vis - i - ble ap - pears in
Lord, To - day as yes - ter - day the same:
fire, In us the work of faith ful - fill.
have Fu - ture and past sub - sist - ing now.
ceives, Par - don and ho - li - ness, and heaven.
dence Their heaven - ly or - i - gin dis - play.
sight, And God is seen by mor - tal eye. A - men.

140

Father, I Stretch My Hands to Thee

NAOMI CM
JOHANN G. NÄGELI, 1768-1836
Arr. by LOWELL MASON, 1792-1872
Harm. by C. R. Y.

CHARLES WESLEY, 1707-1788

Unison
1. Fa-ther, I stretch my hands to thee; No oth-er help I know;
2. What did thine on-ly Son en-dure, Be-fore I drew my breath!
3. Sure-ly thou canst not let me die; O speak, and I shall live;
4. Au-thor of faith! to thee I lift My wea-ry, long-ing eyes;

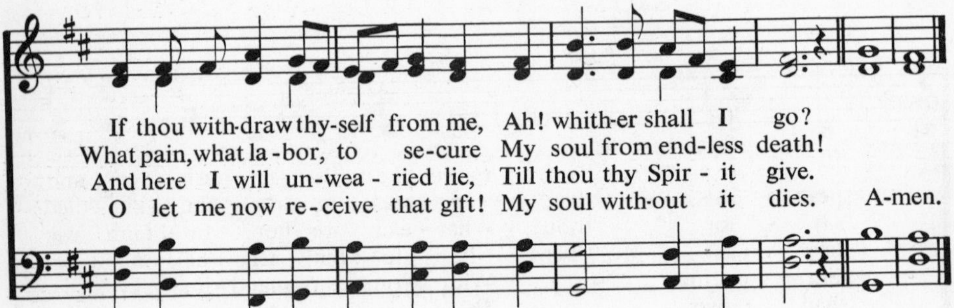
If thou with-draw thy-self from me, Ah! whith-er shall I go?
What pain, what la-bor, to se-cure My soul from end-less death!
And here I will un-wea-ried lie, Till thou thy Spir-it give.
O let me now re-ceive that gift! My soul with-out it dies. A-men.

141

Have Faith in God, My Heart

FRANCONIA SM
JOHANN B. KÖNIG, 1691-1758
Arr. by WILLIAM HAVERGAL, 1793-1870

BRYN AUSTIN REES, 1911-

1. Have faith in God, my heart, Trust and be un-a-fraid;
2. Have faith in God, my mind, Though oft thy light burns low;
3. Have faith in God, my soul, His cross for-ev-er stands;
4. Lord Je-sus, make me whole; Grant me no rest-ing place,

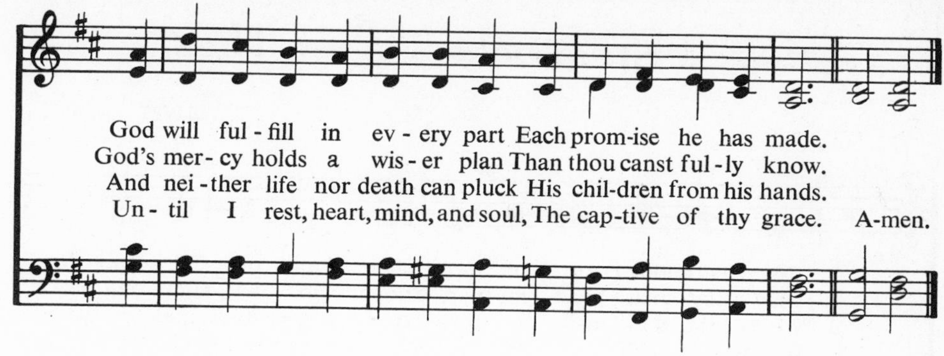
God will ful-fill in ev-ery part Each prom-ise he has made.
God's mer-cy holds a wis-er plan Than thou canst ful-ly know.
And nei-ther life nor death can pluck His chil-dren from his hands.
Un-til I rest, heart, mind, and soul, The cap-tive of thy grace. A-men.

142

O For a Faith that Will Not Shrink

PISGAH CM

LUKE 17:5
WILLIAM H. BATHURST, 1796-1877

Attr. to J. C. LOWRY in *Kentucky Harmony,* 1817
Harm. by A. C. L.

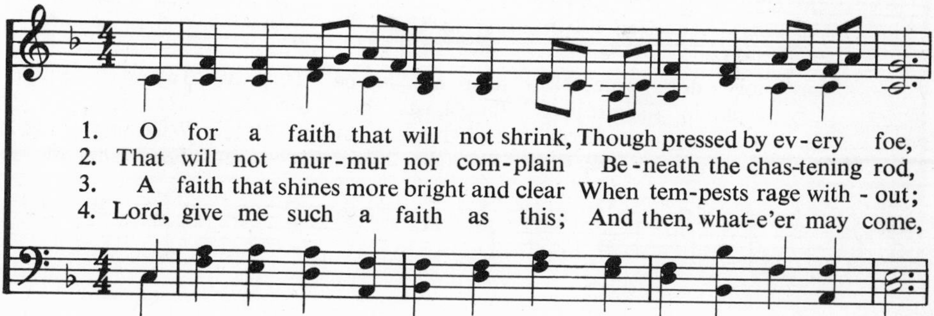
1. O for a faith that will not shrink, Though pressed by ev-ery foe,
2. That will not mur-mur nor com-plain Be-neath the chas-tening rod,
3. A faith that shines more bright and clear When tem-pests rage with-out;
4. Lord, give me such a faith as this; And then, what-e'er may come,

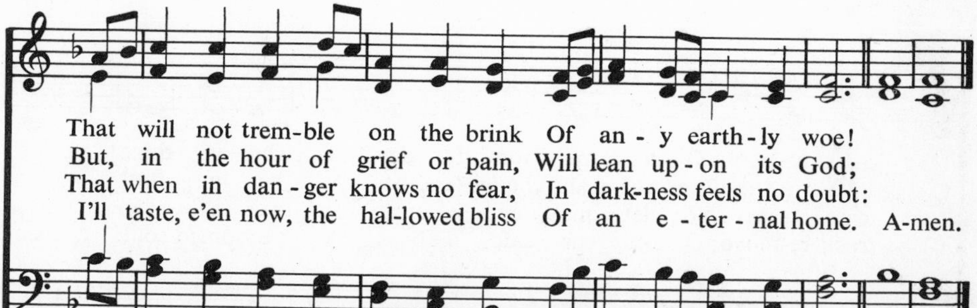
That will not trem-ble on the brink Of an-y earth-ly woe!
But, in the hour of grief or pain, Will lean up-on its God;
That when in dan-ger knows no fear, In dark-ness feels no doubt:
I'll taste, e'en now, the hal-lowed bliss Of an e-ter-nal home. A-men.

Alternate tune: ARLINGTON

My Faith Looks Up to Thee

OLIVET 664.6664.
LOWELL MASON, 1792-1872

RAY PALMER, 1808-1887

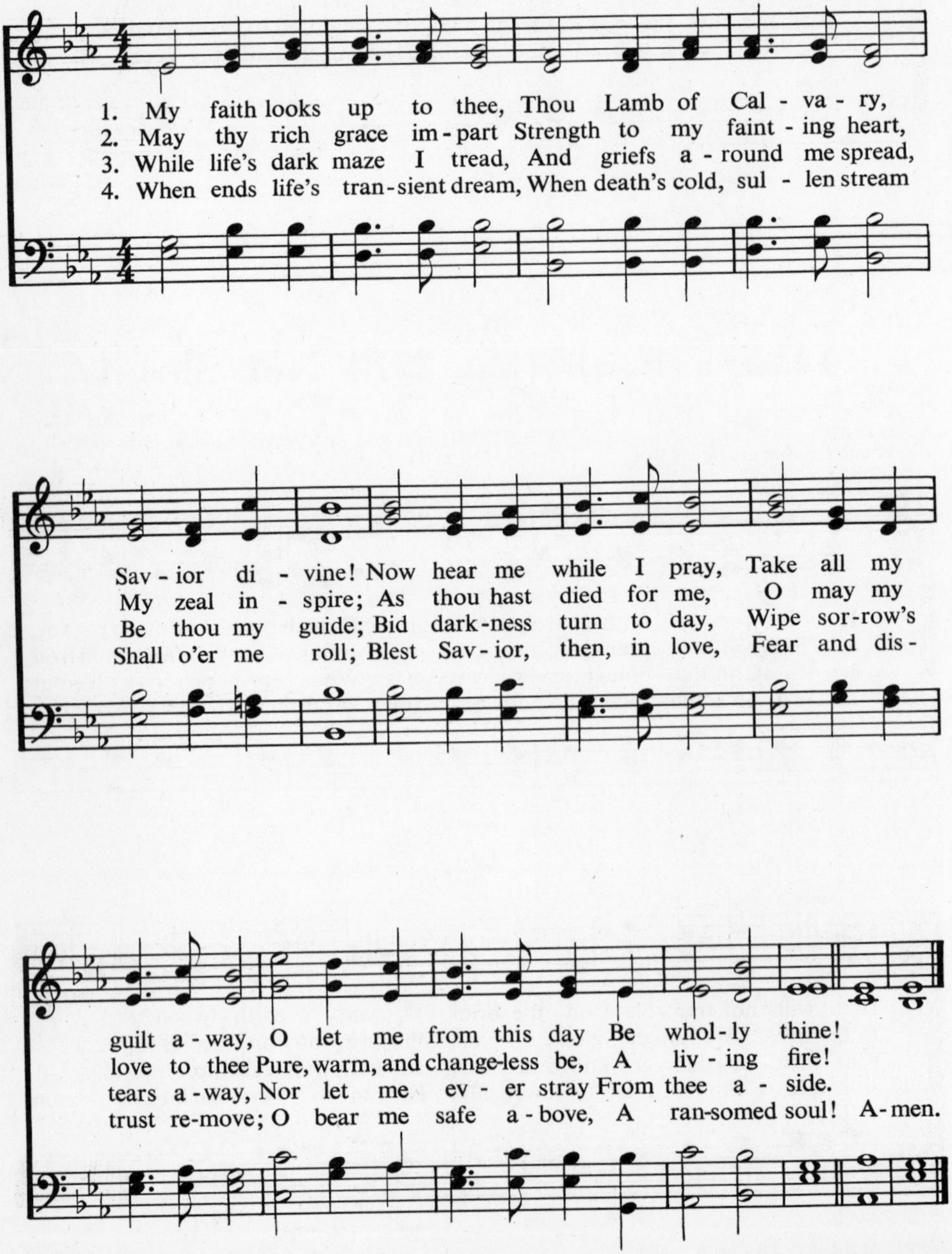
1. My faith looks up to thee, Thou Lamb of Cal - va - ry,
2. May thy rich grace im - part Strength to my faint - ing heart,
3. While life's dark maze I tread, And griefs a - round me spread,
4. When ends life's tran - sient dream, When death's cold, sul - len stream
Sav - ior di - vine! Now hear me while I pray, Take all my
My zeal in - spire; As thou hast died for me, O may my
Be thou my guide; Bid dark - ness turn to day, Wipe sor - row's
Shall o'er me roll; Blest Sav - ior, then, in love, Fear and dis -
guilt a - way, O let me from this day Be whol - ly thine!
love to thee Pure, warm, and change - less be, A liv - ing fire!
tears a - way, Nor let me ev - er stray From thee a - side.
trust re - move; O bear me safe a - bove, A ran - somed soul! A - men.

O Holy Savior, Friend Unseen

Charlotte Elliott, 1789-1871

FLEMMING 888.6.
Friedrich F. Flemming, 1778-1813

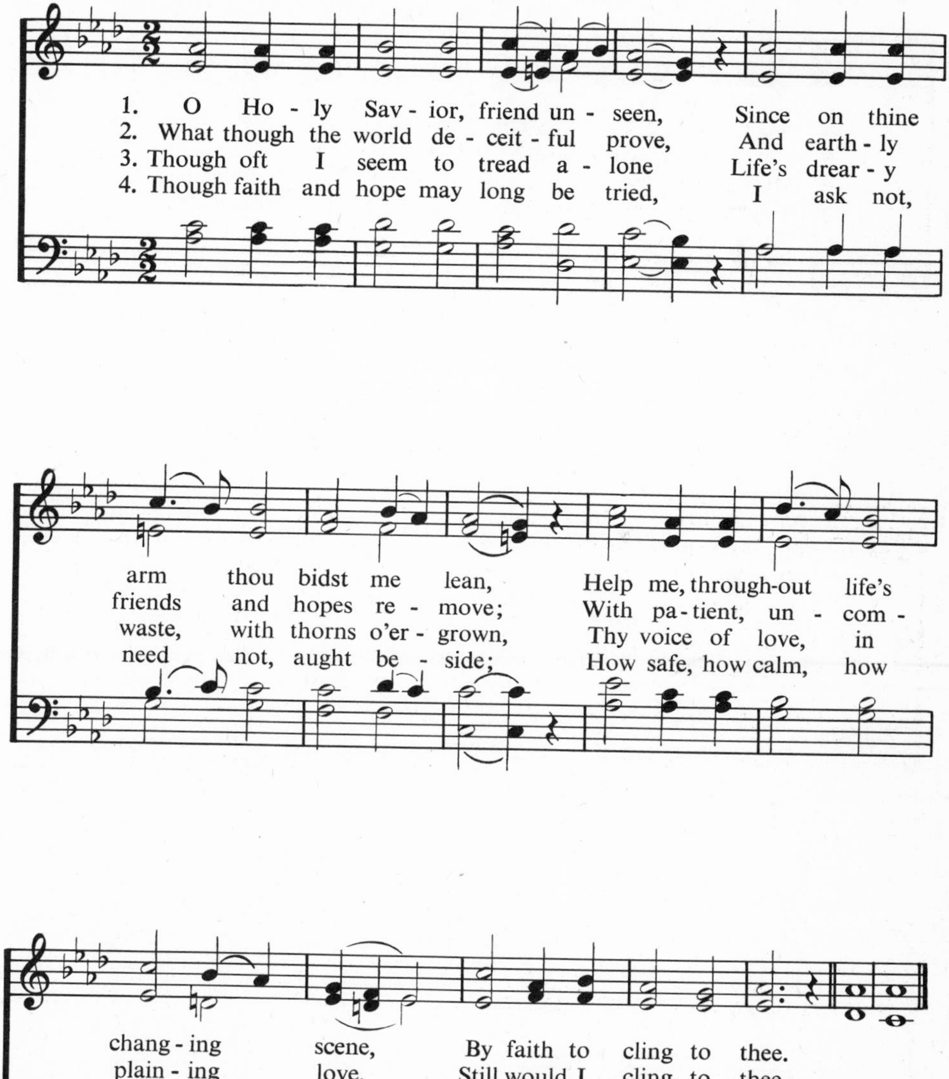
1. O Ho - ly Sav - ior, friend un - seen, Since on thine
2. What though the world de - ceit - ful prove, And earth - ly
3. Though oft I seem to tread a - lone Life's drear - y
4. Though faith and hope may long be tried, I ask not,
arm thou bidst me lean, Help me, through-out life's
friends and hopes re - move; With pa - tient, un - com -
waste, with thorns o'er - grown, Thy voice of love, in
need not, aught be - side; How safe, how calm, how
chang - ing scene, By faith to cling to thee.
plain - ing love, Still would I cling to thee.
gent - lest tone, Still whis-pers, "Cling to me!"
sat - is - fied, The soul that clings to thee! A-men.

145

Pass Me Not, O Gentle Savior

PASS ME NOT 85.85. with Refrain
WILLIAM H. DOANE, 1832-1915

FANNY J. CROSBY, 1820-1915

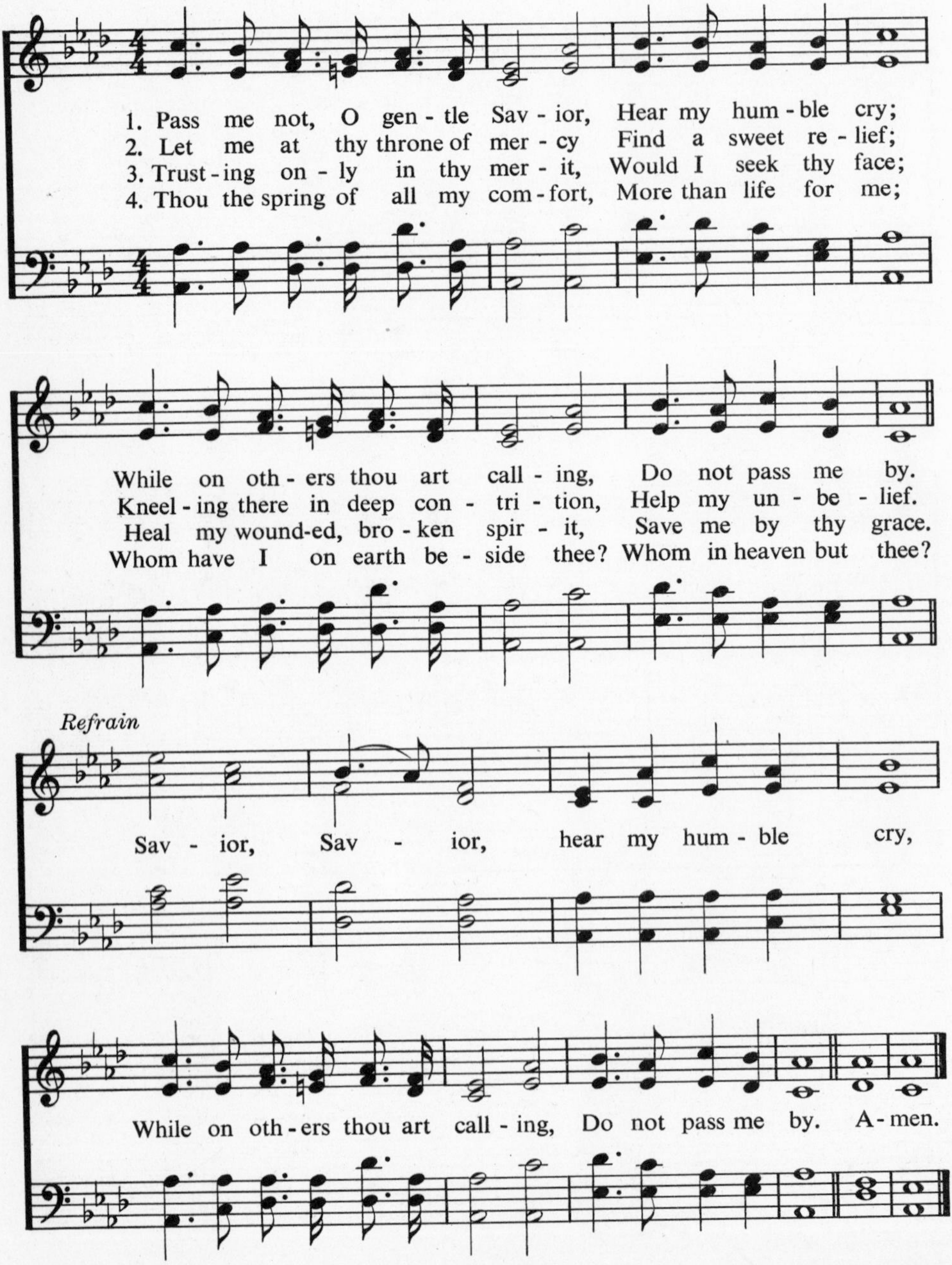
1. Pass me not, O gen-tle Sav-ior, Hear my hum-ble cry;
2. Let me at thy throne of mer-cy Find a sweet re-lief;
3. Trust-ing on-ly in thy mer-it, Would I seek thy face;
4. Thou the spring of all my com-fort, More than life for me;
While on oth-ers thou art call-ing, Do not pass me by.
Kneel-ing there in deep con-tri-tion, Help my un-be-lief.
Heal my wound-ed, bro-ken spir-it, Save me by thy grace.
Whom have I on earth be-side thee? Whom in heaven but thee?
Refrain
Sav-ior, Sav-ior, hear my hum-ble cry,
While on oth-ers thou art call-ing, Do not pass me by. A-men.

Strong Son of God, Immortal Love

KEBLE LM

ALFRED TENNYSON, 1809-1892

JOHN B. DYKES, 1823-1876
Harm. by A. C. L.

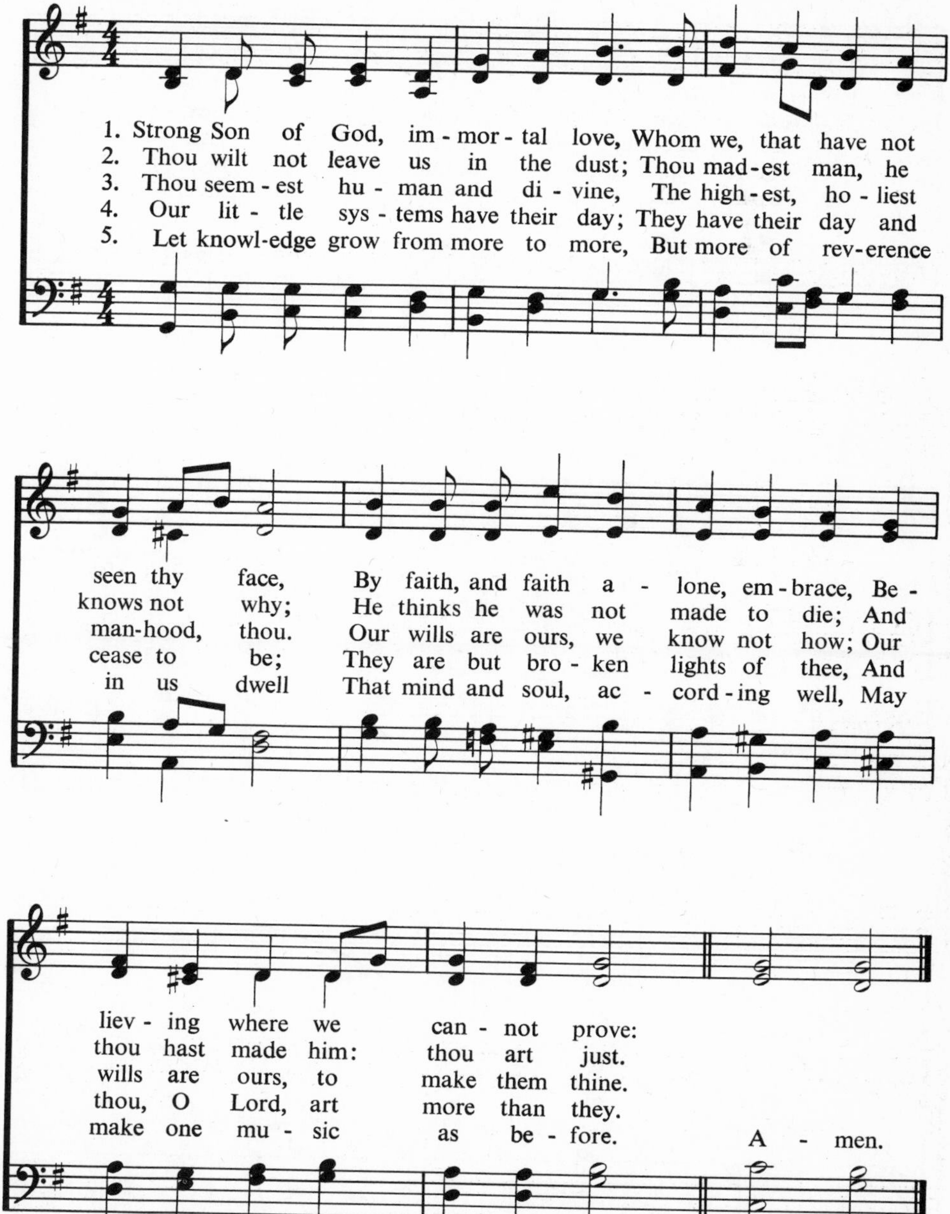
1. Strong Son of God, im - mor - tal love, Whom we, that have not
2. Thou wilt not leave us in the dust; Thou mad-est man, he
3. Thou seem - est hu - man and di - vine, The high - est, ho - liest
4. Our lit - tle sys - tems have their day; They have their day and
5. Let knowl-edge grow from more to more, But more of rev-erence
seen thy face, By faith, and faith a - lone, em - brace, Be -
knows not why; He thinks he was not made to die; And
man-hood, thou. Our wills are ours, we know not how; Our
cease to be; They are but bro - ken lights of thee, And
in us dwell That mind and soul, ac - cord - ing well, May
liev - ing where we can - not prove:
thou hast made him: thou art just.
wills are ours, to make them thine.
thou, O Lord, art more than they.
make one mu - sic as be - fore.
A - men.

147

If, on a Quiet Sea

VENICE SM

AUGUSTUS M. TOPLADY, 1740-1778

WILLIAM AMPS, 1824-1910

1. If, on a qui - et sea, Toward
2. But should the surg - es rise, And
3. Soon shall our doubts and fears All
4. Teach us, in ev - ery state, To

heaven we calm - ly sail, With grate-ful hearts, O
rest de - lay to come, Blest be the tem - pest,
yield to thy con - trol; Thy ten - der mer - cies
make thy will our own; And when the joys of

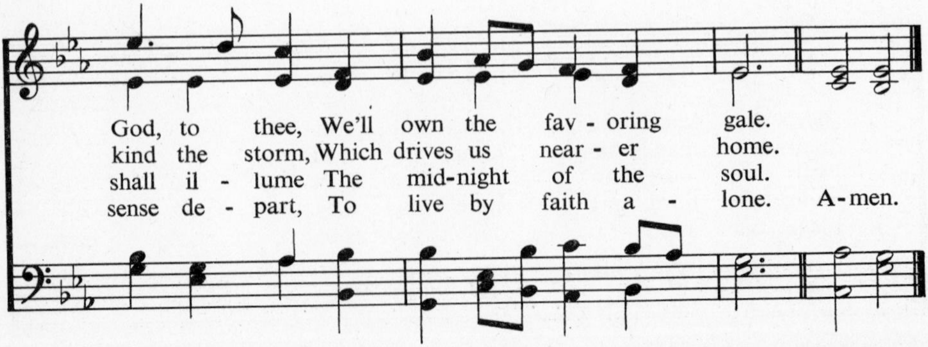
God, to thee, We'll own the fav - oring gale.
kind the storm, Which drives us near - er home.
shall il - lume The mid-night of the soul.
sense de - part, To live by faith a - lone. A-men.

148

Brightly Beams Our Father's Mercy

PHILIP P. BLISS, 1838-1876

LOWER LIGHTS 87.87. with Refrain
PHILIP P. BLISS, 1838-1876

1. Bright-ly beams our Fa-ther's mer-cy From his light-house ev - er-more;
2. Dark the night of sin has set-tled, Loud the an - gry bil-lows roar;
3. Trim your fee - ble lamp, my broth-er! Some poor sea-man, tem-pest-tossed,
But to us he gives the keep-ing Of the lights a - long the shore.
Ea - ger eyes are watch-ing, long-ing, For the lights a - long the shore.
Try - ing now to make the har - bor, In the dark-ness may be lost.
Refrain
Let the low - er lights be burn - ing! Send a
gleam a - cross the wave! Some poor faint - ing, strug-gling
sea - man You may res - cue, you may save. A - men.

I Love to Tell the Story

HANKEY 76.76.D. with Refrain

KATHERINE HANKEY, 1834-1911

WILLIAM G. FISCHER, 1835-1912

1. I love to tell the sto - ry Of un-seen things a -
2. I love to tell the sto - ry; More won-der-ful it
3. I love to tell the sto - ry; 'Tis pleas-ant to re -
4. I love to tell the sto - ry, For those who know it
bove, Of Je - sus and his glo - ry, Of Je - sus and his
seems Than all the gold - en fan - cies Of all our gold - en
peat What seems, each time I tell it, More won - der - ful - ly
best Seem hun - ger - ing and thirst - ing To hear it like the
love. I love to tell the sto - ry, Be - cause I know 'tis
dreams. I love to tell the sto - ry, It did so much for
sweet. I love to tell the sto - ry, For some have nev - er
rest. And when, in scenes of glo - ry, I sing the new, new
true; It sat - is - fies my long-ings As noth-ing else can do.
me; And that is just the rea - son I tell it now to thee.
heard The mes-sage of sal - va - tion From God's own ho - ly Word.
song, 'Twill be the old, old sto - ry That I have loved so long.

Refrain after last stanza

I love to tell the sto-ry, 'Twill be my theme in glo-ry,
To tell the old, old sto-ry Of Je-sus and his love. A-men.

A Charge to Keep I Have

150

LEVITICUS 8:35
CHARLES WESLEY, 1707-1788

BOYLSTON SM
LOWELL MASON, 1792-1872

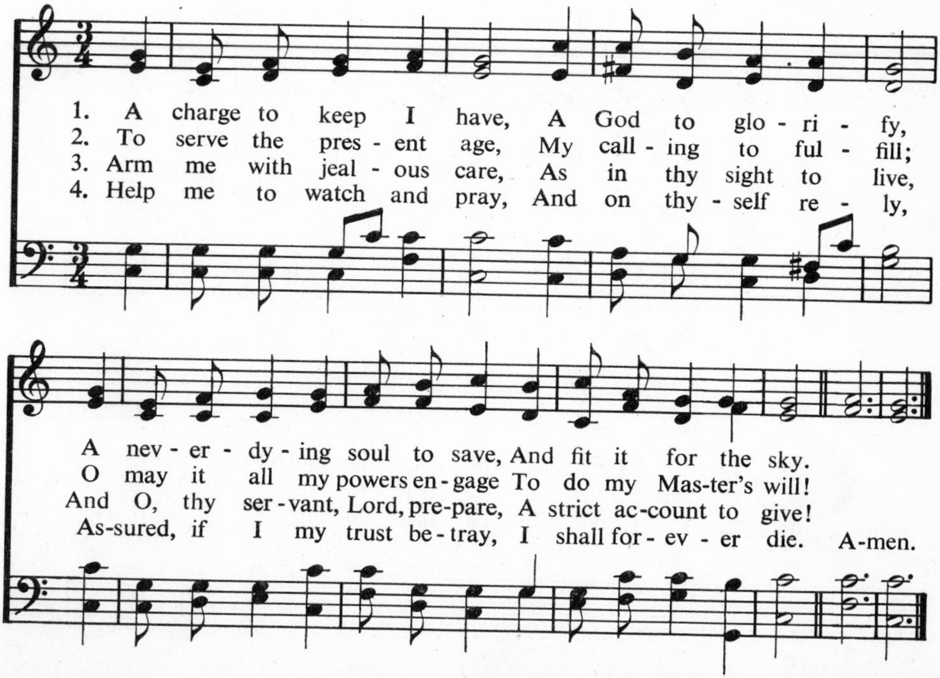
1. A charge to keep I have, A God to glo-ri-fy,
2. To serve the pres-ent age, My call-ing to ful-fill;
3. Arm me with jeal-ous care, As in thy sight to live,
4. Help me to watch and pray, And on thy-self re-ly,
A nev-er-dy-ing soul to save, And fit it for the sky.
O may it all my powers en-gage To do my Mas-ter's will!
And O, thy ser-vant, Lord, pre-pare, A strict ac-count to give!
As-sured, if I my trust be-tray, I shall for-ev-er die. A-men.

151

Faith of Our Fathers

ST. CATHERINE 88.88.88.
HENRI F. HEMY, 1818-1888
Adapt. by JAMES G. WALTON, 1821-1905

FREDERICK W. FABER, 1814-1863

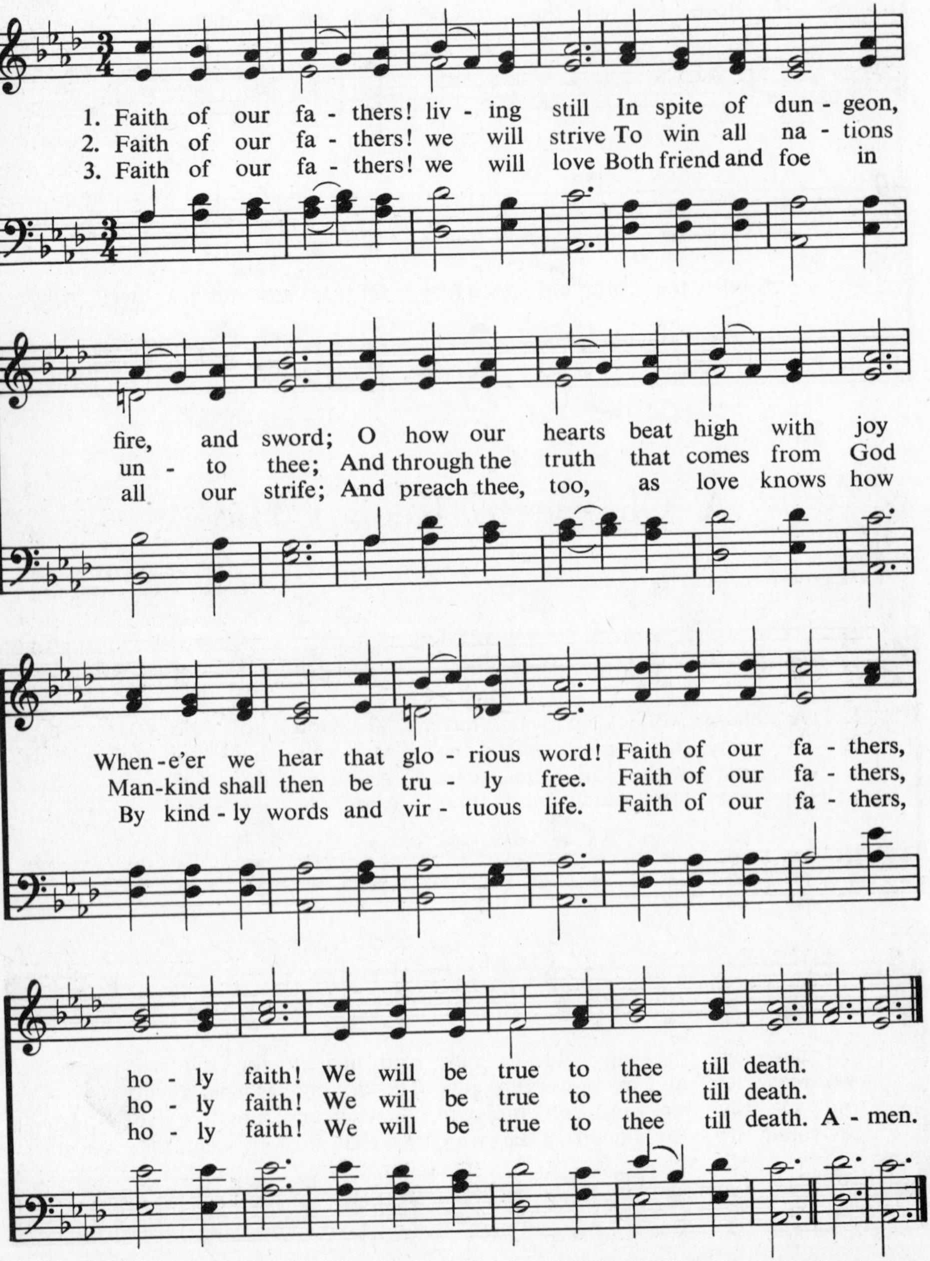
1. Faith of our fa - thers! liv - ing still In spite of dun - geon,
2. Faith of our fa - thers! we will strive To win all na - tions
3. Faith of our fa - thers! we will love Both friend and foe in
fire, and sword; O how our hearts beat high with joy
un - to thee; And through the truth that comes from God
all our strife; And preach thee, too, as love knows how
When-e'er we hear that glo - rious word! Faith of our fa - thers,
Man-kind shall then be tru - ly free. Faith of our fa - thers,
By kind - ly words and vir - tuous life. Faith of our fa - thers,
ho - ly faith! We will be true to thee till death.
ho - ly faith! We will be true to thee till death.
ho - ly faith! We will be true to thee till death. A - men.

Forth in Thy Name

KEBLE LM
JOHN B. DYKES, 1823-1876
Harm. by A. C. L.

CHARLES WESLEY, 1707-1788

1. Forth in thy name, O Lord, I go, My dai - ly la - bor
2. The task thy wis - dom hath as - signed, O let me cheer - ful -
3. Give me to bear thy ea - sy yoke, And ev - ery mo - ment
4. For thee de - light - ful - ly em - ploy What - e'er thy boun-teous
to pur - sue; Thee, on - ly thee, re - solved to know In
ly ful - fill; In all my works thy pres - ence find, And
watch and pray; And still to things e - ter - nal look, And
grace hath given; And run my course with e - ven joy, And
all I think or speak or do.
prove thy good and per - fect will.
has - ten to thy glo - rious day;
close - ly walk with thee to heaven. A - men.

153

God of Love and God of Power

UNSER HERRSCHER 77.77.77.

GERALD H. KENNEDY, 1907-

JOACHIM NEANDER, 1650-1680

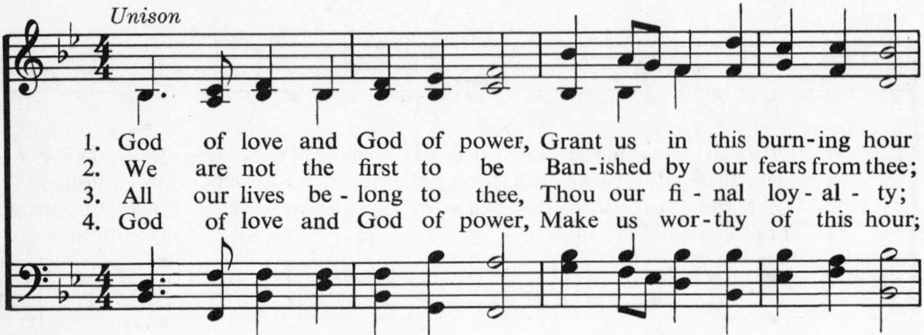
Unison
1. God of love and God of power, Grant us in this burn-ing hour
2. We are not the first to be Ban-ished by our fears from thee;
3. All our lives be-long to thee, Thou our fi-nal loy-al-ty;
4. God of love and God of power, Make us wor-thy of this hour;

Grace to ask these gifts of thee, Dar-ing hearts and spir-its free.
Give us cour-age, let us hear Heav-en's trum-pets ring-ing clear.
Slaves are we when-e'er we share That de-vo-tion an-y-where.
Offer-ing lives if it's thy will, Keep-ing free our spir-its still.

God of love and God of power, Thou hast called us for this hour.
God of love and God of power, Thou hast called us for this hour.
God of love and God of power, Thou hast called us for this hour.
God of love and God of power, Thou hast called us for this hour. A-men.

Have Thine Own Way, Lord

ADELAIDE 54.54.D.

ADELAIDE A. POLLARD, 1862-1934
GEORGE C. STEBBINS, 1846-1945

1. Have thine own way, Lord! Have thine own way! Thou art the
2. Have thine own way, Lord! Have thine own way! Search me and
3. Have thine own way, Lord! Have thine own way! Wound-ed and
4. Have thine own way, Lord! Have thine own way! Hold o'er my

pot - ter; I am the clay. Mold me and make me Af - ter thy
try me, Mas-ter, to - day! Whit - er than snow, Lord, Wash me just
wea - ry, Help me, I pray! Pow - er, all pow - er, Sure - ly is
be - ing Ab - so - lute sway! Fill with thy spir - it Till all shall

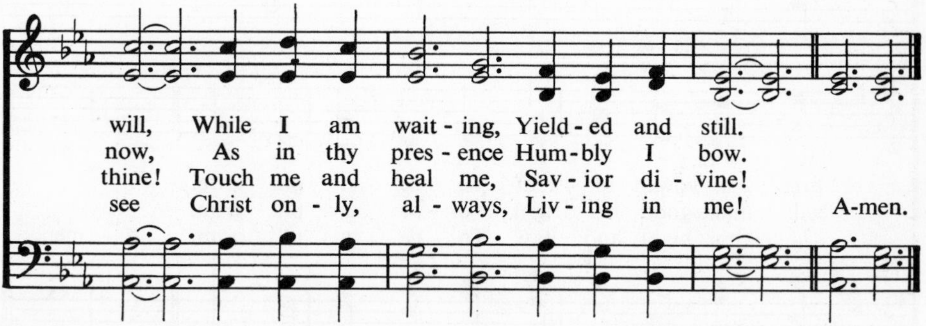
will, While I am wait - ing, Yield - ed and still.
now, As in thy pres - ence Hum - bly I bow.
thine! Touch me and heal me, Sav - ior di - vine!
see Christ on - ly, al - ways, Liv - ing in me!
A-men.

155

He Who Would Valiant Be

JOHN BUNYAN, 1628-1688
Adapt. by PERCY DEARMER, 1867-1936

ST. DUNSTAN'S 65.65.666.5.
C. WINFRED DOUGLAS, 1867-1944

1. He who would val - iant be 'Gainst all dis - as - ter,
2. Who so be - set him round With dis - mal sto - ries,
3. Since, Lord, thou dost de - fend Us with thy spir - it,
Let him in con - stan - cy Fol - low the Mas - ter. There's
Do but them - selves con-found, His strength the more is. No
We know we at the end Shall life in - her - it. Then
no dis - cour - age - ment Shall make him once re - lent His
foes shall stay his might, Though he with gi - ants fight; He
fan - cies flee a - way! I'll fear not what men say; I'll
first a - vowed in - tent To be a pil - grim.
will make good his right To be a pil - grim.
la - bor night and day To be a pil - grim. A - men.

I Would Be True

Howard A. Walter, 1883-1918

PEEK 11 10.11 10.
Joseph Y. Peek, 1843-1911

1. I would be true, for there are those who trust me;
2. I would be friend of all, the foe, the friend - less;
I would be pure, for there are those who care;
I would be giv - ing, and for - get the gift;
I would be strong, for there is much to suf - fer;
I would be hum - ble, for I know my weak - ness;
I would be brave, for there is much to dare,
I would look up, and laugh and love and lift,
I would be brave, for there is much to dare.
I would look up, and laugh and love and lift. A-men.

Immortal Love, Forever Full

AYRSHIRE CM

JOHN GREENLEAF WHITTIER, 1807-1892 KENNETH G. FINLAY, 1882-

1. Im - mor - tal Love, for - ev - er full, For - ev - er
2. We may not climb the heaven - ly steeps To bring the
3. But warm, sweet, ten - der, e - ven yet A pres - ent
4. The heal - ing of his seam - less dress Is by our
5. Through him the first fond prayers are said, Our lips of
6. O Lord and Mas - ter of us all: What-e'er our

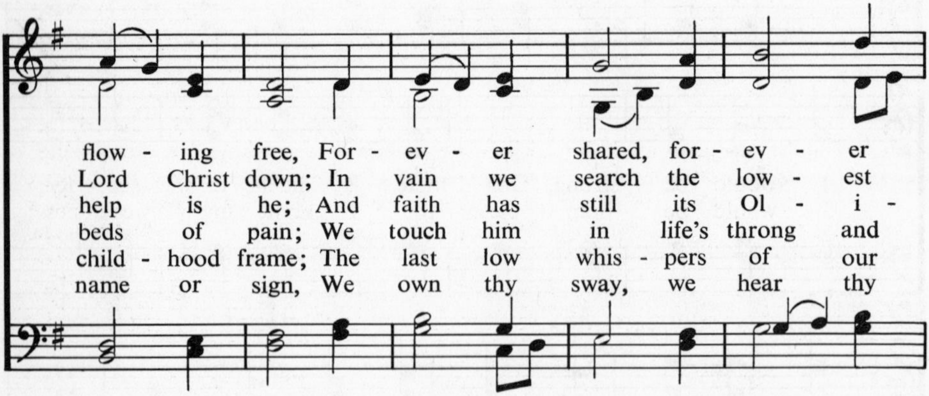
flow - ing free, For - ev - er shared, for - ev - er
Lord Christ down; In vain we search the low - est
help is he; And faith has still its Ol - i -
beds of pain; We touch him in life's throng and
child - hood frame; The last low whis - pers of our
name or sign, We own thy sway, we hear thy

whole, A nev - er - ebb - ing sea!
deeps, For him no depths can drown.
vet, And love its Gal - i - lee.
press, And we are whole a - gain.
dead Are bur - dened with his name.
call, We test our lives by thine. A - men.

Music used by permission of Kenneth G. Finlay.

158

Immortal Love, Forever Full

John Greenleaf Whittier, 1807-1892

SERENITY CM
Arr. from William V. Wallace, 1814-1865

1. Im - mor - tal Love, for - ev - er full, For -
2. We may not climb the heaven - ly steeps To
3. But warm, sweet, ten - der, e - ven yet A
4. The heal - ing of his seam - less dress Is
5. Through him the first fond prayers are said, Our
6. O Lord and Mas - ter of us all: What -
ev - er flow - ing free, For - ev - er shared, for -
bring the Lord Christ down; In vain we search the
pres - ent help is he; And faith has still its
by our beds of pain; We touch him in life's
lips of child - hood frame; The last low whis - pers
e'er our name or sign, We own thy sway, we
ev - er whole, A nev - er - ebb - ing sea!
low - est deeps, For him no depths can drown.
Ol - i - vet, And love its Gal - i - lee.
throng and press, And we are whole a - gain.
of our dead Are bur - dened with his name.
hear thy call, We test our lives by thine! A - men.

159

I Am Thine, O Lord

HEBREWS 10:22
FANNY J. CROSBY, 1820-1915

I AM THINE 10 7.10 7. with Refrain
WILLIAM H. DOANE, 1832-1915

1. I am thine, O Lord, I have heard thy voice, And it told thy love to me; But I long to rise in the arms of faith, And be clos - er drawn to thee.
2. Con - se - crate me now to thy ser - vice, Lord, By the power of grace di - vine; Let my soul look up with a stead - fast hope, And my will be lost in thine.
3. O the pure de - light of a sin - gle hour That be - fore thy throne I spend, When I kneel in prayer, and with thee, my God, I com - mune as friend with friend!
4. There are depths of love that I can - not know Till I cross the nar - row sea; There are heights of joy that I may not reach Till I rest in peace with thee.
Refrain
Draw me near - er, near - er, bless - ed Lord, To the cross where thou hast died; Draw me near - er, near - er,

near - er, bless - ed Lord, To thy pre-cious, bleed-ing side. A-men.

160

Take Up Thy Cross

MATTHEW 16:24-25
CHARLES W. EVEREST, 1814-1877

GERMANY LM
WILLIAM GARDINER'S *Sacred Melodies,* 1815

1. "Take up thy cross," the Sav - ior said, "If thou wouldst
2. Take up thy cross; let not its weight Fill thy weak
3. Take up thy cross, nor heed the shame; Nor let thy
4. Take up thy cross and fol - low Christ; Nor think till
my dis - ci - ple be; De - ny thy - self, the world for -
spir - it with a - larm; His strength shall bear thy spir - it
fool - ish pride re - bel; Thy Lord for thee the cross en -
death to lay it down; For on - ly he who bears the
sake, And hum - bly fol - low af - ter me."
up, And brace thy heart and nerve thine arm.
dured, To save thy soul from death and hell.
cross May hope to wear the glo - rious crown. A-men.

161

Hope of the World

VICAR 11 10.11 10.

GEORGIA HARKNESS, 1891- V. EARLE COPES, 1921-

Unison
1. Hope of the world, thou Christ of great com - pas - sion,
2. Hope of the world, God's gift from high - est heav - en,
3. Hope of the world, a - foot on dust - y high - ways,
4. Hope of the world, who by thy cross didst save us
5. Hope of the world, O Christ, o'er death vic - tor - ious,
Speak to our fear - ful hearts by con - flict rent.
Bring - ing to hun - gry souls the bread of life,
Show - ing to wan - dering souls the path of light;
From death and dark de - spair, from sin and guilt;
Who by this sign didst con - quer grief and pain,
Save us, thy peo - ple, from con - sum - ing pas - sion,
Still let thy spir - it un - to us be giv - en
Walk thou be - side us lest the tempt - ing by - ways
We ren - der back the love thy mer - cy gave us;
We would be faith - ful to thy gos - pel glo - rious:

Who by our own false hopes and aims are spent.
To heal earth's wounds and end her bit - ter strife.
Lure us a - way from thee to end - less night.
Take thou our lives, and use them as thou wilt.
Thou art our Lord! Thou dost for - ev - er reign! A-men.

Alternate tune: ANCIENT OF DAYS

162

Savior, Teach Me, Day by Day

I John 4:19
JANE E. LEESON, 1807-1882

ORIENTIS PARTIBUS 77.77.
Medieval French Melody
Harm. by RICHARD REDHEAD, 1820-1901

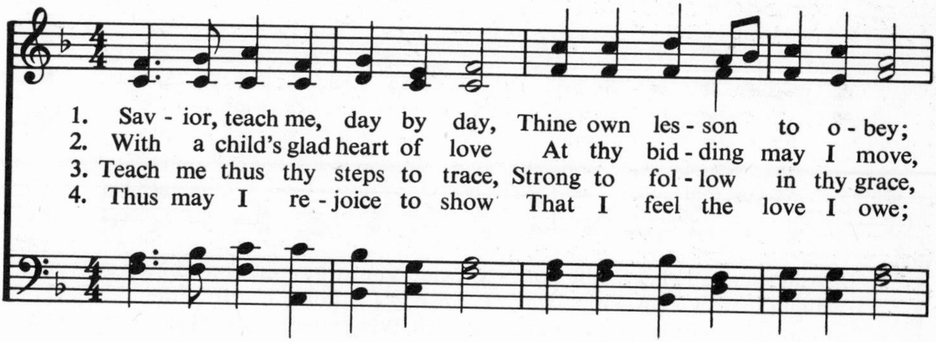
1. Sav - ior, teach me, day by day, Thine own les - son to o - bey;
2. With a child's glad heart of love At thy bid - ding may I move,
3. Teach me thus thy steps to trace, Strong to fol - low in thy grace,
4. Thus may I re - joice to show That I feel the love I owe;

Bet - ter les-son can-not be, Lov - ing him who first loved me.
Prompt to serve and fol-low thee, Lov - ing him who first loved me.
Learn-ing how to love from thee, Lov - ing him who first loved me.
Sing-ing, till thy face I see, Of his love who first loved me. A - men.

163

I've Found a Friend

FRIEND 87.87.D.

JAMES G. SMALL, 1817-1888

GEORGE C. STEBBINS, 1846-1945

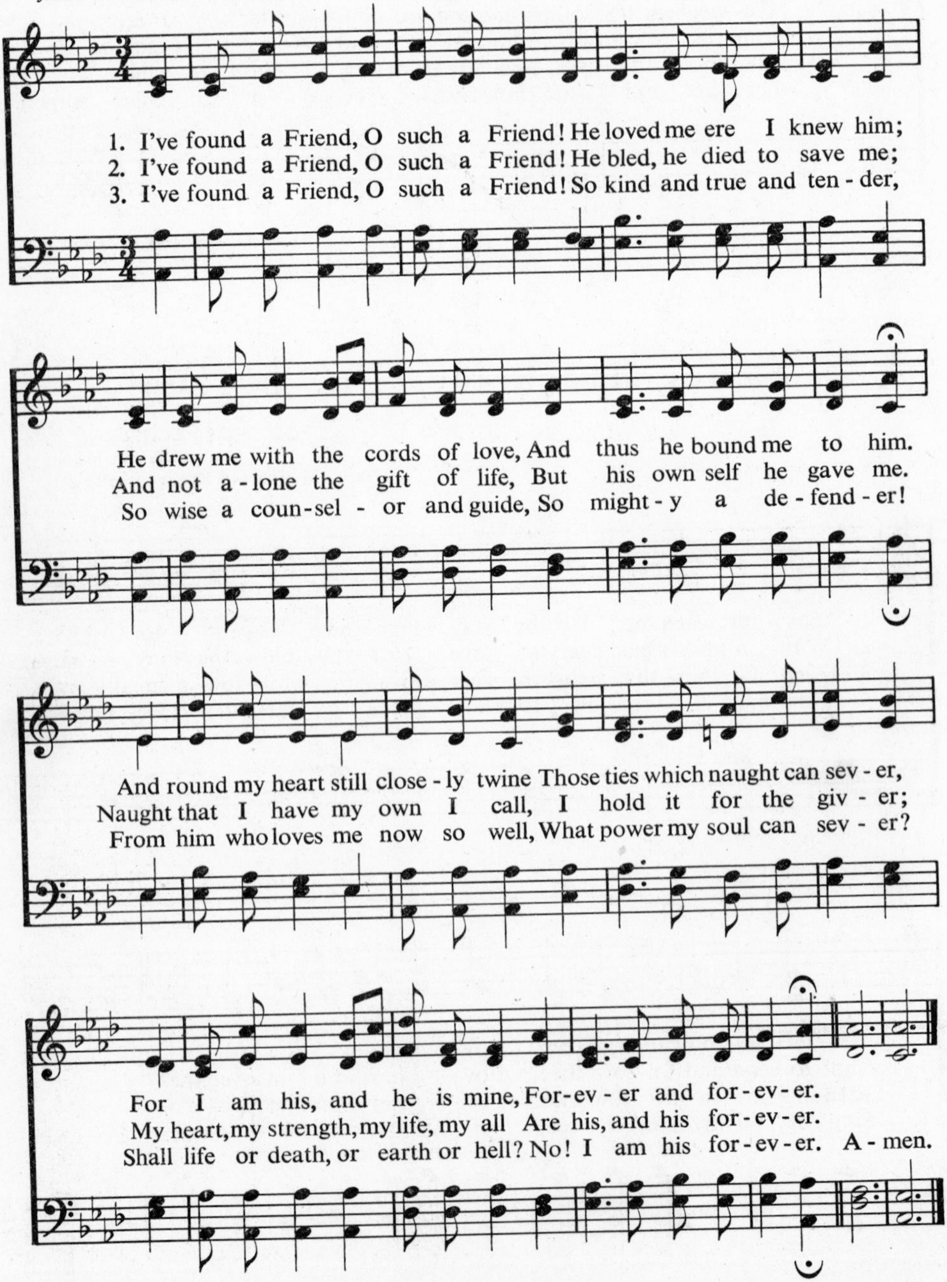
1. I've found a Friend, O such a Friend! He loved me ere I knew him;
2. I've found a Friend, O such a Friend! He bled, he died to save me;
3. I've found a Friend, O such a Friend! So kind and true and ten - der,
He drew me with the cords of love, And thus he bound me to him.
And not a - lone the gift of life, But his own self he gave me.
So wise a coun-sel - or and guide, So might - y a de - fend - er!
And round my heart still close - ly twine Those ties which naught can sev - er,
Naught that I have my own I call, I hold it for the giv - er;
From him who loves me now so well, What power my soul can sev - er?
For I am his, and he is mine, For-ev - er and for-ev - er.
My heart, my strength, my life, my all Are his, and his for-ev - er.
Shall life or death, or earth or hell? No! I am his for-ev - er. A - men.

O Jesus, I Have Promised

JOHN E. BODE, 1816-1874

ANGEL'S STORY 76.76.D.
ARTHUR H. MANN, 1850-1929

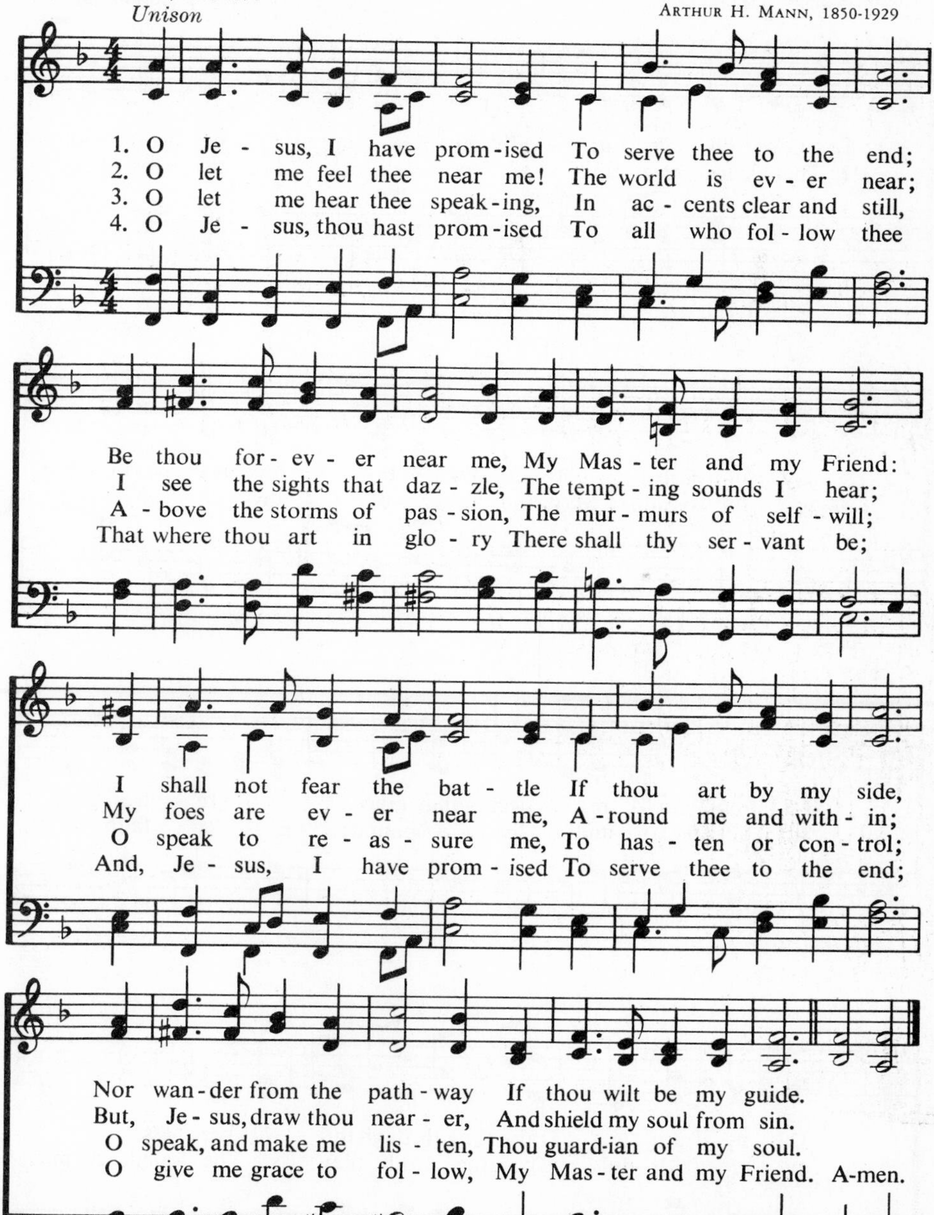
Unison
1. O Je - sus, I have prom-ised To serve thee to the end;
2. O let me feel thee near me! The world is ev - er near;
3. O let me hear thee speak-ing, In ac - cents clear and still,
4. O Je - sus, thou hast prom-ised To all who fol - low thee
Be thou for - ev - er near me, My Mas - ter and my Friend:
I see the sights that daz - zle, The tempt - ing sounds I hear;
A - bove the storms of pas - sion, The mur - murs of self - will;
That where thou art in glo - ry There shall thy ser - vant be;
I shall not fear the bat - tle If thou art by my side,
My foes are ev - er near me, A - round me and with - in;
O speak to re - as - sure me, To has - ten or con - trol;
And, Je - sus, I have prom - ised To serve thee to the end;
Nor wan-der from the path - way If thou wilt be my guide.
But, Je - sus, draw thou near - er, And shield my soul from sin.
O speak, and make me lis - ten, Thou guard-ian of my soul.
O give me grace to fol - low, My Mas - ter and my Friend. A-men.

Music used by permission of E. R. Goodliffe.

Lord, Dismiss Us with Thy Blessing

SICILIAN MARINERS 87.87.87.

JOHN FAWCETT, 1740-1817 — TATTERSALL'S *Psalmody,* 1794

1. Lord, dis - miss us with thy bless - ing; Fill our hearts with
2. Thanks we give and ad - o - ra - tion For thy Gos - pel's
joy and peace; Let us each, thy love pos - sess - ing,
joy - ful sound. May the fruits of thy sal - va - tion
Tri - umph in re - deem - ing grace. O re - fresh us,
In our hearts and lives a - bound; Ev - er faith - ful,
O re - fresh us, Trav - eling through this wil - der - ness.
ev - er faith - ful To the truth may we be found. A - men.

Lord Jesus, I Love Thee

WILLIAM R. FEATHERSTONE, 1842-1878

GORDON 11 11.11 11.
ADONIRAM J. GORDON, 1836-1895

1. Lord Je - sus, I love thee, I know thou art mine; For
2. I love thee, be - cause thou hast first lov - ed me, And
3. In man - sions of glo - ry and end - less de - light, I'll
thee all the fol - lies of sin I re - sign; My
pur - chased my par - don on Cal - va - ry's tree; I
ev - er a - dore thee in heav - en so bright; I'll
gra - cious Re - deem - er, my Sav - ior art thou; If
love thee for wear - ing the thorns on thy brow; If
sing with the glit - ter - ing crown on my brow; If
ev - er I loved thee, Lord Je - sus, 'tis now.
ev - er I loved thee, Lord Je - sus, 'tis now.
ev - er I loved thee, Lord Je - sus, 'tis now. A - men.

My Jesus, As Thou Wilt

MARK 14:36
BENJAMIN SCHMOLCK, 1672-1737
Trans. by JANE BORTHWICK, 1813-1897

MUNICH 66.66.D.
Gesangbuch, Meiningen, 1693
Harm. by FELIX MENDELSSOHN, 1809-1847

1. My Je - sus, as thou wilt! O may thy will be mine!
2. My Je - sus, as thou wilt! Though seen through many a tear,
3. My Je - sus, as thou wilt! All shall be well for me;
In - to thy hand of love I would my all re - sign.
Let not my star of hope Grow dim or dis - ap - pear.
Each chang-ing fu - ture scene I glad - ly trust with thee.
Through sor - row or through joy, Con - duct me as thine own;
Since thou on earth hast wept And sor-rowed oft a - lone,
Straight to my home a - bove I trav - el calm - ly on,
And help me still to say, "My Lord, thy will be done."
If I must weep with thee, "My Lord, thy will be done."
And sing, in life or death, "My Lord, thy will be done." A-men.

O Could I Speak the Matchless Worth

Samuel Medley, 1738-1799

ARIEL 886.D.
Arr. by Lowell Mason, 1792-1872

1. O could I speak the match - less worth,
2. I'd sing the char - ac - ters he bears,
3. Well, the de - light - ful day will come
O could I sound the glo - ries forth Which in my Sav - ior shine,
And all the forms of love he wears, Ex - alt - ed on his throne.
When my dear Lord will bring me home, And I shall see his face;
I'd sing his glo-rious righ-teous-ness, And mag - ni - fy the won-drous grace
In loft - iest songs of sweet-est praise, I would to ev - er - last-ing days
Then with my Sav - ior, broth-er, friend, A blest e - ter - ni - ty I'll spend,
Which made sal - va - tion mine, Which made sal - va - tion mine.
Make all his glo - ries known, Make all his glo - ries known.
Tri - um-phant in his grace, Tri - um-phant in his grace. A-men.

Just as I Am, Thine Own to Be

JUST AS I AM 888.6.

MARIANNE HEARN, 1834-1909 | JOSEPH BARNBY, 1838-1896

Unison
1. Just as I am, thine own to be, Friend of the
2. In the glad morn-ing of my day, My life to
3. I would live ev-er in the light, I would work
4. Just as I am, young, strong and free, To be the
young, who lov-est me, To con-se-crate my-
give, my vows to pay, With no re-serve and
ev-er for the right, I would serve thee with
best that I can be For truth and righ-teous-
self to thee, O Je-sus Christ, I come.
no de-lay, With all my heart, I come.
all my might, There-fore, to thee I come.
ness and thee, Lord of my life, I come. A-men.

O Master, Let Me Walk with Thee

MARYTON LM

WASHINGTON GLADDEN, 1836-1918 — H. PERCY SMITH, 1825-1898

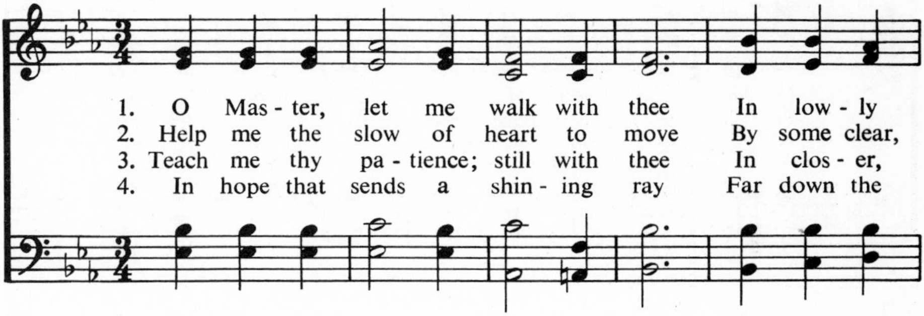
1. O Mas - ter, let me walk with thee In low - ly
2. Help me the slow of heart to move By some clear,
3. Teach me thy pa - tience; still with thee In clos - er,
4. In hope that sends a shin - ing ray Far down the

paths of ser - vice free; Tell me thy se - cret; help me
win - ning word of love; Teach me the way-ward feet to
dear - er com - pa - ny, In work that keeps faith sweet and
fu - ture's broad - ening way; In peace that on - ly thou canst

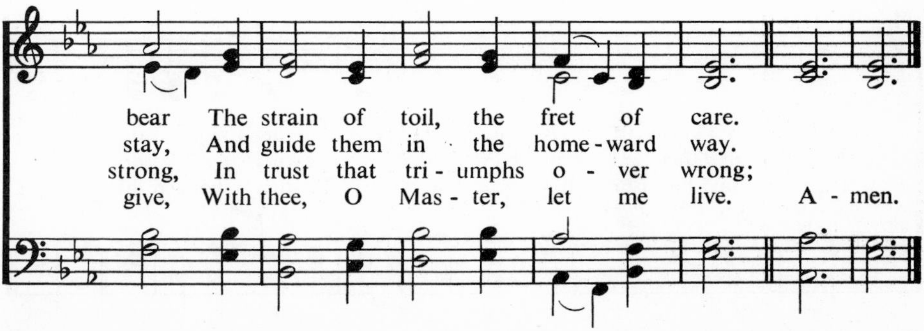
bear The strain of toil, the fret of care.
stay, And guide them in the home - ward way.
strong, In trust that tri - umphs o - ver wrong;
give, With thee, O Mas - ter, let me live. A - men.

171

O Master Workman of the Race

Jay T. Stocking, 1870-1936

ST. MICHEL'S CMD
W. Gawler's *Hymns and Psalms,* c. 1788

1. O Mas - ter Work-man of the race, Thou man of Gal - i - lee,
2. O Car - pen - ter of Naz - a - reth, Build - er of life di - vine,
3. O Thou who dost the vi - sion send And giv - est each his task,
Who with the eyes of ear - ly youth E - ter - nal things did see:
Who shap - est man to God's own law, Thy-self the fair de - sign:
And with the task suf - fi - cient strength: Show us thy will, we ask.
We thank thee for thy boy-hood faith That shone thy whole life through;
Build us a tower of Christ-like height, That we the land may view,
Give us a con-science bold and good; Give us a pur-pose true,
"Did ye not know it is my work My Fa-ther's work to do?"
And see, like thee, our no - blest work Our Fa-ther's work to do.
That it may be our high - est joy, Our Fa-ther's work to do. A-men.

O Thou Who Camest from Above

EISENACH LM

LEVITICUS 6:13
CHARLES WESLEY, 1707-1788

JOHANN H. SCHEIN, 1586-1630
Harm. by J. S. BACH, 1685-1750

1. O Thou who cam - est from a - bove, The
2. There let it for thy glo - ry burn With
3. Je - sus, con - firm my heart's de - sire To
4. Read - y for all thy per - fect will, My
pure ce - les - tial fire t'im-part, Kin - dle a flame of
in - ex - tin - guish - a - ble blaze, And trem - bling to its
work and speak and think for thee; Still let me guard the
acts of faith and love re - peat, Till death thy end - less
sa - cred love On the mean al - tar of my heart.
source re - turn, In hum - ble prayer and fer - vent praise.
ho - ly fire, And still stir up thy gift in me:
mer - cies seal, And make my sac - ri - fice com - plete. A-men.

173

O Young and Fearless Prophet

S. Ralph Harlow, 1885-

BLAIRGOWRIE 13 13.13 13.
John B. Dykes, 1823-1876

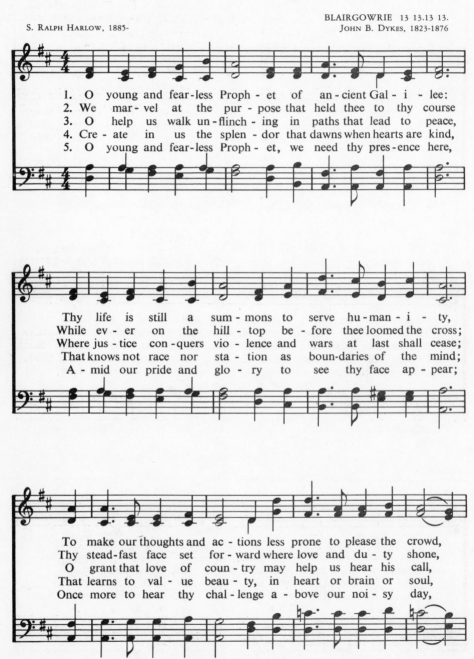

1. O young and fear-less Proph - et of an-cient Gal - i - lee:
2. We mar-vel at the pur - pose that held thee to thy course
3. O help us walk un-flinch - ing in paths that lead to peace,
4. Cre - ate in us the splen - dor that dawns when hearts are kind,
5. O young and fear-less Proph - et, we need thy pres-ence here,

Thy life is still a sum - mons to serve hu - man - i - ty,
While ev - er on the hill - top be - fore thee loomed the cross;
Where jus - tice con - quers vio - lence and wars at last shall cease;
That knows not race nor sta - tion as boun-daries of the mind;
A - mid our pride and glo - ry to see thy face ap - pear;

To make our thoughts and ac - tions less prone to please the crowd,
Thy stead-fast face set for - ward where love and du - ty shone,
O grant that love of coun - try may help us hear his call,
That learns to val - ue beau - ty, in heart or brain or soul,
Once more to hear thy chal - lenge a - bove our noi - sy day,

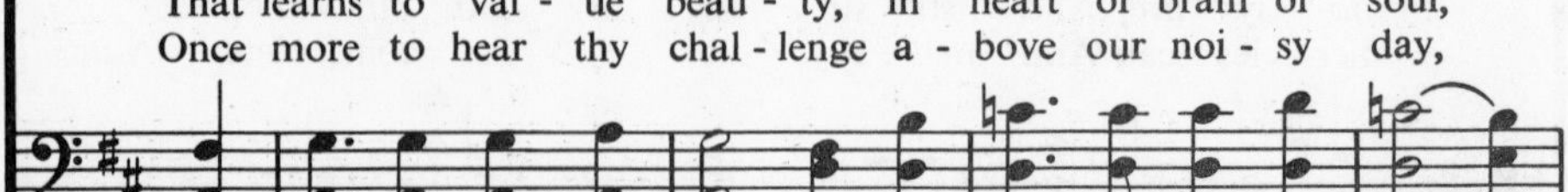

Words used by permission of S. Ralph Harlow.

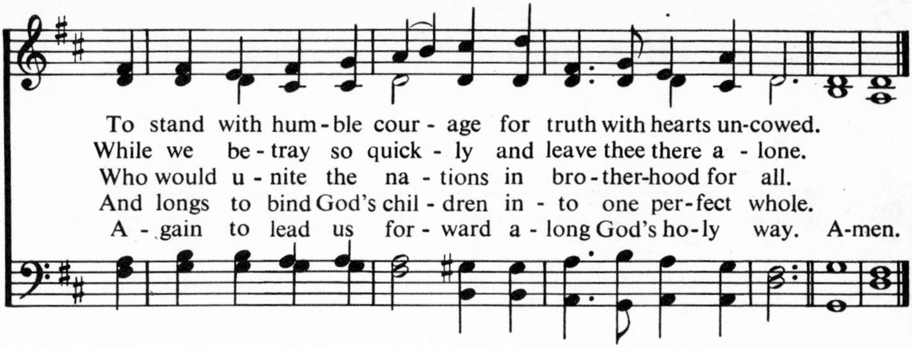
To stand with hum-ble cour-age for truth with hearts un-cowed.
While we be-tray so quick-ly and leave thee there a-lone.
Who would u-nite the na-tions in bro-ther-hood for all.
And longs to bind God's chil-dren in-to one per-fect whole.
A-gain to lead us for-ward a-long God's ho-ly way. A-men.

Rise Up, O Men of God

174

FESTAL SONG SM

WILLIAM P. MERRILL, 1867-1954

WILLIAM H. WALTER, 1825-1893

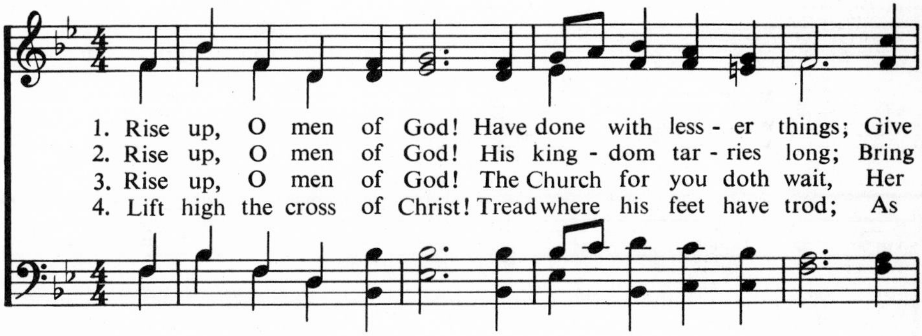
1. Rise up, O men of God! Have done with less-er things; Give
2. Rise up, O men of God! His king-dom tar-ries long; Bring
3. Rise up, O men of God! The Church for you doth wait, Her
4. Lift high the cross of Christ! Tread where his feet have trod; As

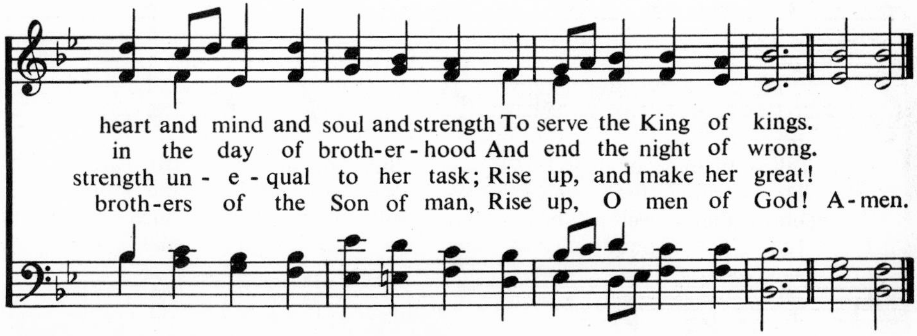
heart and mind and soul and strength To serve the King of kings.
in the day of broth-er-hood And end the night of wrong.
strength un-e-qual to her task; Rise up, and make her great!
broth-ers of the Son of man, Rise up, O men of God! A-men.

Words used by permission of *The Presbyterian Outlook.*

175

Rescue the Perishing

RESCUE 6 5 10.D.

FANNY J. CROSBY, 1820-1915 WILLIAM H. DOANE, 1832-1915

1. Res - cue the per - ish - ing, Care for the dy - ing,
2. Though they are slight - ing him, Still he is wait - ing,
3. Down in the hu - man heart, Crushed by the temp - ter,
4. Res - cue the per - ish - ing, Du - ty de - mands it;
Snatch them in pit - y from sin and the grave;
Wait - ing the pen - i - tent child to re - ceive;
Feel - ings lie bur - ied that grace can re - store;
Strength for thy la - bor the Lord will pro - vide;
Weep o'er the err - ing one, Lift up the fall - en,
Plead with them ear - nest - ly, Plead with them gent - ly;
Touched by a lov - ing heart, Wak - ened by kind - ness,
Back to the nar - row way Pa - tient - ly win them;
Tell them of Je - sus the might - y to save.
He will for - give if they on - ly be - lieve.
Chords that were bro - ken will vi - brate once more.
Tell the poor wan - derer a Sav - ior has died.

Refrain
Res - cue the per - ish - ing, Care for the dy - ing;
Je - sus is mer - ci - ful, Je - sus will save. A - men.

Thou My Everlasting Portion

176

FANNY J. CROSBY, 1820-1915

CLOSE TO THEE 87.87.
SILAS J. VAIL, 1818-1884

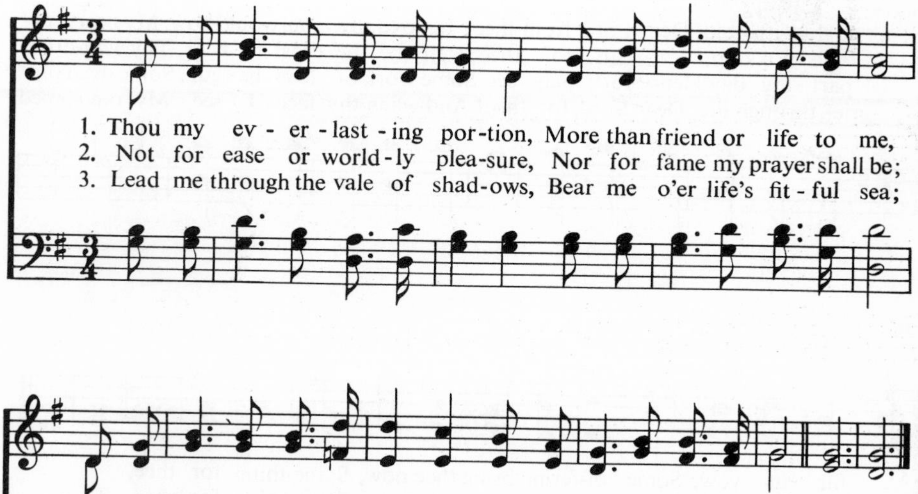
1. Thou my ev - er - last - ing por-tion, More than friend or life to me,
2. Not for ease or world - ly plea-sure, Nor for fame my prayer shall be;
3. Lead me through the vale of shad-ows, Bear me o'er life's fit - ful sea;
All a - long my pil-grim jour-ney, Sav - ior, let me walk with thee.
Glad - ly will I toil and suf - fer, On - ly let me walk with thee.
Then the gate of life e - ter - nal May I en-ter, Lord, with thee. A - men.

177

Savior, Thy Dying Love

ACTS 9:6
SYLVANUS D. PHELPS, 1816-1895

SOMETHING FOR JESUS 64.64.6664.
ROBERT LOWRY, 1826-1899

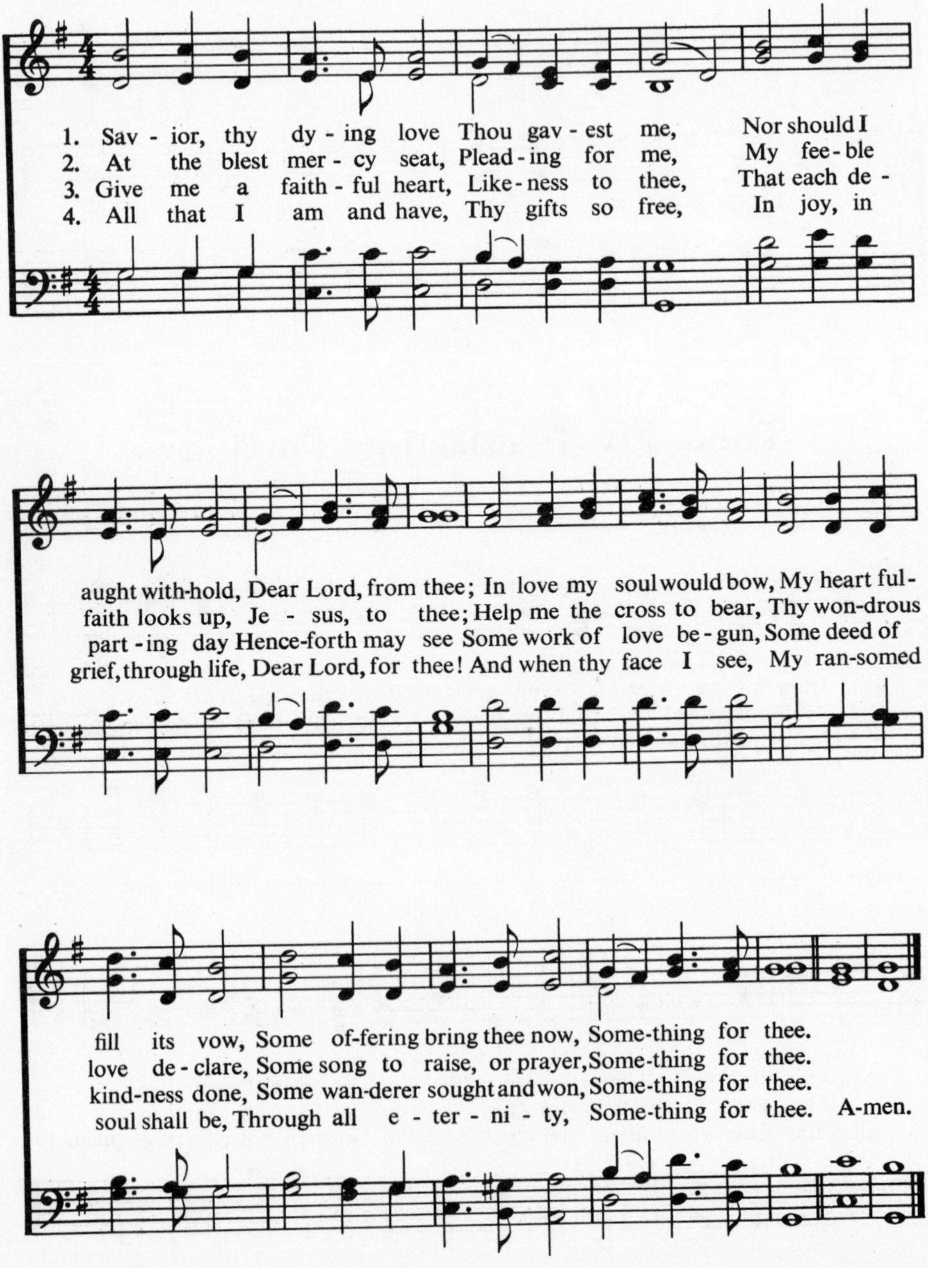
1. Sav - ior, thy dy - ing love Thou gav - est me, Nor should I
2. At the blest mer - cy seat, Plead - ing for me, My fee - ble
3. Give me a faith - ful heart, Like - ness to thee, That each de -
4. All that I am and have, Thy gifts so free, In joy, in
aught with-hold, Dear Lord, from thee; In love my soul would bow, My heart ful-
faith looks up, Je - sus, to thee; Help me the cross to bear, Thy won-drous
part - ing day Hence-forth may see Some work of love be - gun, Some deed of
grief, through life, Dear Lord, for thee! And when thy face I see, My ran-somed
fill its vow, Some of-fering bring thee now, Some-thing for thee.
love de - clare, Some song to raise, or prayer, Some-thing for thee.
kind-ness done, Some wan-derer sought and won, Some-thing for thee.
soul shall be, Through all e - ter - ni - ty, Some-thing for thee. A-men.

What Grace, O Lord, and Beauty Shone

Psalm 45:2
John S. B. Monsell, 1811-1875

CHRISTUS, DER IST MEIN LEBEN CM
Melchior Vulpius, c. 1560-1616

1. What grace, O Lord, and beau - ty shone A - round thy steps be - low; What pa - tient love was seen in all Thy life and death of woe!
2. Thy foes might hate, de - spise, re - vile, Thy friends un - faith - ful prove; Un - wea - ried in for - give - ness still, Thy heart could on - ly love.
3. O give us hearts to love like thee! Like thee, O Lord, to grieve Far more for oth - ers' sins than all The wrongs that we re - ceive.
4. One with thy - self, may ev - ery eye In us, thy breth - ren, see The gen - tle - ness and grace that spring From un - ion, Lord, with thee.
A - men.

179

Truehearted, Wholehearted

TRUEHEARTED 11 10.11 10. with Refrain

FRANCES R. HAVERGAL, 1836-1879

GEORGE C. STEBBINS, 1846-1945

1. True - heart - ed, whole - heart - ed, faith - ful and loy - al,
2. True - heart - ed, whole - heart - ed, full - est al - le - giance
3. True - heart - ed, whole - heart - ed, Sav - ior all - glo - rious!
King of our lives, by thy grace we will be;
Yield - ing hence - forth to our glo - ri - ous King;
Take thy great pow - er and reign there a - lone,
Un - der the stan - dard ex - alt - ed and roy - al,
Val - iant en - deav - or and lov - ing o - be - dience,
O - ver our wills and af - fec - tions vic - to - rious,
Strong in thy strength we will bat - tle for thee.
Free - ly and joy - ous - ly now would we bring.
Free - ly sur - ren - dered and whol - ly thine own.

Refrain
Peal out the watch-word! Si - lence it nev - er!
Song of our spir - its, re - joic - ing and free;
re - joic - ing
Peal out the watch-word! Loy - al for - ev - er!
King of our lives, By thy grace we will be.
A - men.

Awake, My Soul, and with the Sun

THOMAS KEN, 1637-1711

TALLIS' CANON LM
THOMAS TALLIS, c. 1505-1585

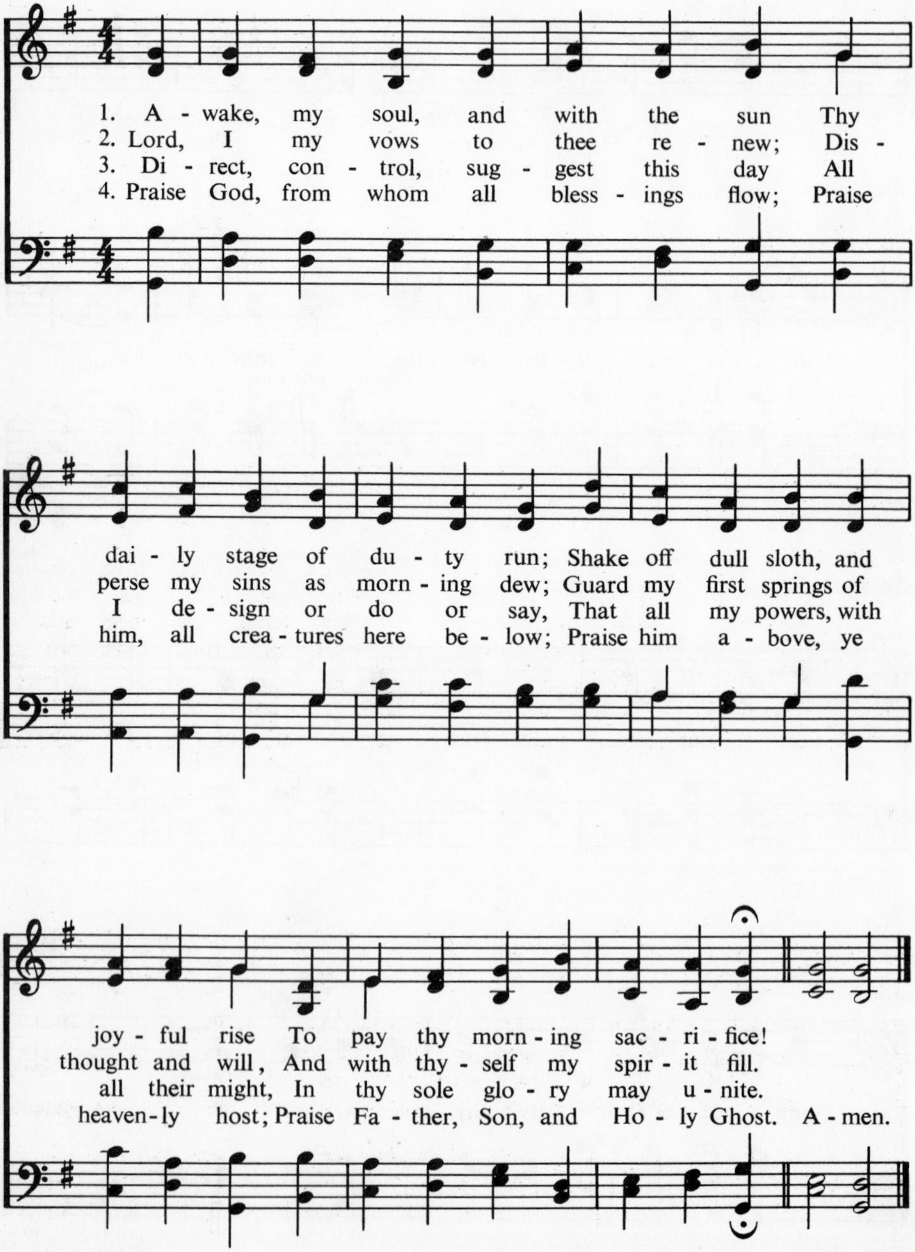
1. A - wake, my soul, and with the sun Thy
2. Lord, I my vows to thee re - new; Dis -
3. Di - rect, con - trol, sug - gest this day All
4. Praise God, from whom all bless - ings flow; Praise
dai - ly stage of du - ty run; Shake off dull sloth, and
perse my sins as morn - ing dew; Guard my first springs of
I de - sign or do or say, That all my powers, with
him, all crea - tures here be - low; Praise him a - bove, ye
joy - ful rise To pay thy morn - ing sac - ri - fice!
thought and will, And with thy - self my spir - it fill.
all their might, In thy sole glo - ry may u - nite.
heaven - ly host; Praise Fa - ther, Son, and Ho - ly Ghost. A - men.

We Give Thee But Thine Own

WILLIAM W. HOW, 1823-1897

SCHUMANN SM
Cantica Laudis, 1850

1. We give thee but thine own, What -
2. May we thy boun - ties thus As
3. To com - fort and to bless, To
4. And we be - lieve thy word, Though
e'er the gift may be: All that we have is
stew - ards true re - ceive, And glad - ly, as thou
find a balm for woe, To tend the lone and
dim our faith may be: What - e'er for thine we
thine a - lone, A trust, O Lord, from thee.
bless - est us, To thee our first fruits give.
fa - ther - less, Is an - gels' work be - low.
do, O Lord, We do it un - to thee. A - men.

182

Lord, in the Strength of Grace

FRANCONIA SM

I CHRONICLES 29:5
CHARLES WESLEY, 1707-1788

JOHANN B. KÖNIG, 1691-1758
Arr. by WILLIAM HAVERGAL, 1793-1870

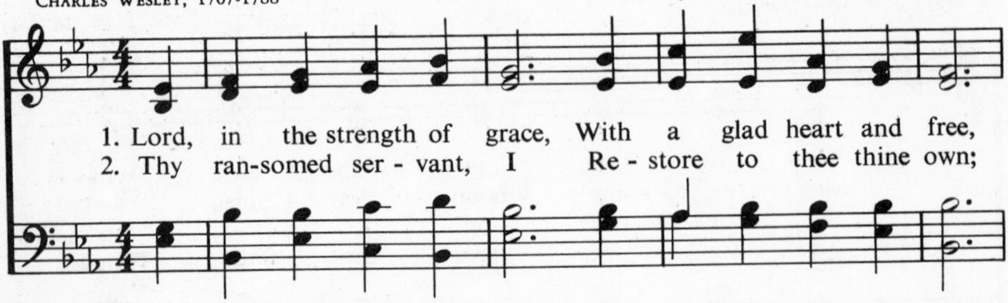
1. Lord, in the strength of grace, With a glad heart and free,
2. Thy ran-somed ser - vant, I Re - store to thee thine own;

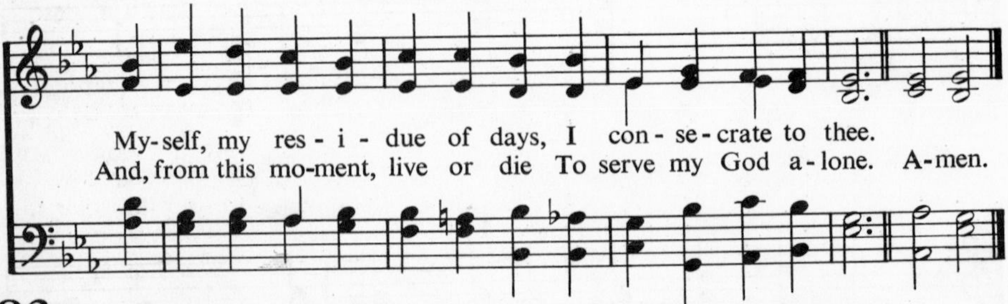
My-self, my res - i - due of days, I con - se - crate to thee.
And, from this mo-ment, live or die To serve my God a - lone. A-men.

183

Must Jesus Bear the Cross Alone

MAITLAND CM

THOMAS SHEPHERD, 1665-1739, and others

GEORGE N. ALLEN, 1812-1877

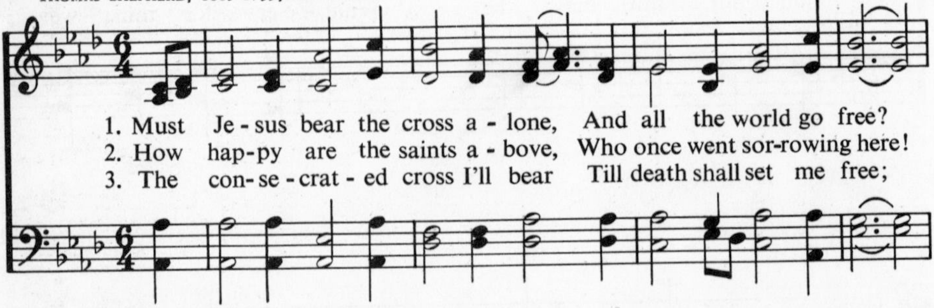
1. Must Je - sus bear the cross a - lone, And all the world go free?
2. How hap-py are the saints a - bove, Who once went sor-rowing here!
3. The con-se - crat - ed cross I'll bear Till death shall set me free;

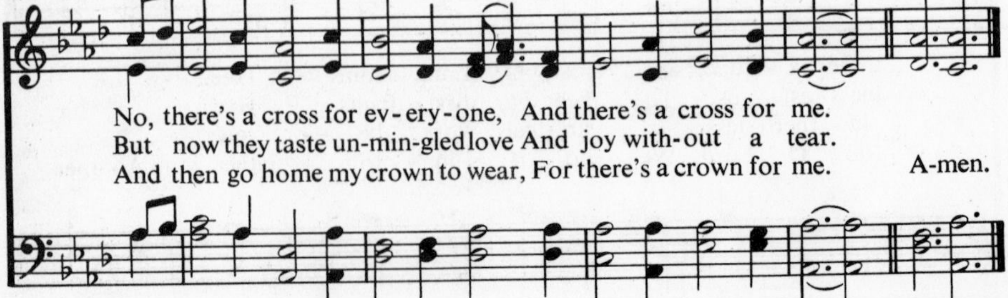
No, there's a cross for ev - ery - one, And there's a cross for me.
But now they taste un-min-gled love And joy with-out a tear.
And then go home my crown to wear, For there's a crown for me. A-men.

Make Me a Captive, Lord

EPHESIANS 3:1
GEORGE MATHESON, 1842-1906

DIADEMATA SMD
GEORGE J. ELVEY, 1816-1893

1. Make me a cap - tive, Lord, And then I shall be free;
2. My heart is weak and poor Un - til it mas - ter find;
3. My power is faint and low Till I have learned to serve;
4. My will is not my own Till thou hast made it thine;
Force me to ren - der up my sword, And I shall con-queror be.
It has no spring of ac - tion sure, It va - ries with the wind.
It wants the need - ed fire to glow, It wants the breeze to nerve;
If it would reach a mon-arch's throne, It must its crown re - sign;
I sink in life's a - larms When by my - self I stand; Im -
It can - not free - ly move Till thou hast wrought its chain; En -
It can - not drive the world, Un - til it - self be driven; Its
It on - ly stands un - bent, A - mid the clash - ing strife, When
pris - on me with - in thine arms, And strong shall be my hand.
slave it with thy match-less love, And death-less it shall reign.
flag can on - ly be un-furled When thou shalt breathe from heaven.
on thy bos - om it has leant And found in thee its life. A-men.

185

More Love to Thee, O Christ

MORE LOVE TO THEE 64.64.664.

ELIZABETH P. PRENTISS, 1818-1878

WILLIAM H. DOANE, 1832-1915

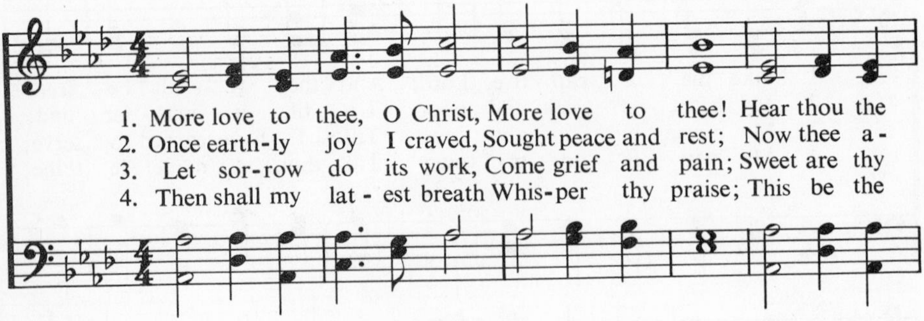
1. More love to thee, O Christ, More love to thee! Hear thou the
2. Once earth-ly joy I craved, Sought peace and rest; Now thee a -
3. Let sor-row do its work, Come grief and pain; Sweet are thy
4. Then shall my lat - est breath Whis-per thy praise; This be the

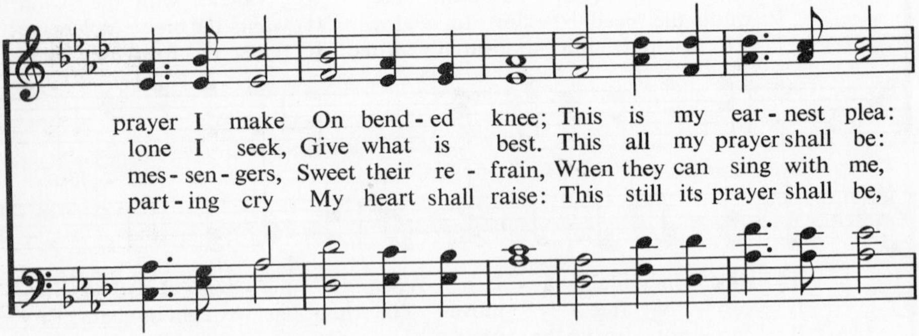
prayer I make On bend - ed knee; This is my ear - nest plea:
lone I seek, Give what is best. This all my prayer shall be:
mes - sen - gers, Sweet their re - frain, When they can sing with me,
part - ing cry My heart shall raise: This still its prayer shall be,

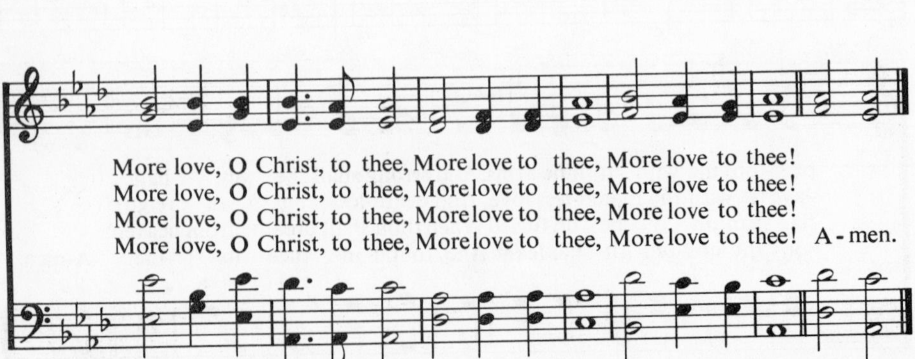
More love, O Christ, to thee, More love to thee, More love to thee!
More love, O Christ, to thee, More love to thee, More love to thee!
More love, O Christ, to thee, More love to thee, More love to thee!
More love, O Christ, to thee, More love to thee, More love to thee! A - men.

Servant of All, to Toil for Man

SHADDICK CM

CHARLES WESLEY, 1707-1788

BATES G. BURT, 1878-1948

1. Ser - vant of all, to toil for man Thou
2. Son of the car - pen - ter, re - ceive This
3. End of my ev - ery ac - tion thou, In
4. Thy bright ex - am - ple I pur - sue, To
5. Care - less through out - ward cares I go, From
didst not, Lord, re - fuse; Thy ma - jes - ty did
hum - ble work of mine; Worth to my mean - est
all things thee I see; Ac - cept my hal - lowed
thee in all things rise; And all I think or
all dis - trac - tion free; My hands are but en -
not dis - dain To be em - ployed for us.
la - bor give, By join - ing it to thine.
la - bor now, I do it un - to thee.
speak or do Is one great sac - ri - fice.
gaged be - low, My heart is still with thee. A - men.

Music used by permission of the Church Pension Fund.

187 Take My Life, and Let It Be Consecrated

MESSIAH 77.77.D.

ROMANS 12:1 LOUIS J. F. HEROLD, 1791-1833

FRANCES R. HAVERGAL, 1836-1879 Arr. by GEORGE KINGSLEY, 1811-1884

1. Take my life, and let it be Con-se-cra-ted, Lord, to thee.
2. Take my voice, and let me sing Al-ways, on-ly, for my King.
3. Take my will, and make it thine; It shall be no long-er mine.
Take my mo-ments and my days; Let them flow in cease-less praise.
Take my lips, and let them be Filled with mes-sag-es from thee.
Take my heart, it is thine own; It shall be thy roy-al throne.
Take my hands, and let them move At the im-pulse of thy love.
Take my sil-ver and my gold; Not a mite would I with-hold.
Take my love; my Lord, I pour At thy feet its trea-sure-store.
Take my feet, and let them be Swift and beau-ti-ful for thee.
Take my in-tel-lect, and use Ev-ery power as thou shalt choose.
Take my-self, and I will be Ev-er, on-ly, all for thee. A-men.

Draw Thou My Soul, O Christ

LUCY LARCOM, 1826-1893

ST. EDMUND 64.64.66.64.
ARTHUR S. SULLIVAN, 1842-1900

1. Draw thou my soul, O Christ, Clos - er to thine;
2. Lead forth my soul, O Christ, One with thine own,
3. Not for my - self a - lone May my prayer be;
Breathe in - to ev - ery wish Thy will di - vine!
Joy - ful to fol - low thee Through paths un - known!
Lift thou thy world, O Christ, Clos - er to thee!
Raise my low self a - bove, Won by thy death - less love;
In thee my strength re - new; Give me my work to do!
Cleanse it from guilt and wrong; Teach it sal - va - tion's song,
Ev - er, O Christ, through mine Let thy life shine.
Through me thy truth be shown, Thy love made known.
Till earth, as heaven, ful - fill God's ho - ly will. A - men.

189 At Length There Dawns the Glorious Day

CLONMEL CMD
Trad. Irish Melody
Harm. by A. C. L.

OZORA S. DAVIS, 1866-1931

Unison
1. At length there dawns the glo - rious day By proph - ets long fore - told;
2. For what are sun-dering strains of blood, Or an-cient caste and creed?
3. One com - mon faith u - nites us all, We seek one com-mon goal;
At length the cho - rus clear - er grows That shep-herds heard of old.
One claim u - nites all men in God To serve each hu - man need.
One ten - der com - fort broods up - on The strug-gling hu - man soul.
The day of dawn - ing broth - er - hood Breaks on our ea - ger eyes,
Then here to - geth - er, broth - er men, We pledge the Lord a - new
To this clear call of broth - er - hood Our hearts re - spon-sive ring;
And hu-man ha - treds flee be - fore The ra-diant east-ern skies.
Our loy - al love, our stal-wart faith, Our ser-vice strong and true.
We join the glo - rious new cru - sade Of our great Lord and King. A-men.

Alternate tune: ST. MICHEL'S

Awake, Awake to Love and Work

MORNING SONG 86.86.86.
WYETH'S *Repository of Sacred Music, Part Second,* 1813
Harm. by A. C. L.

G. A. STUDDERT-KENNEDY, 1883-1929

Unison
1. A-wake, a-wake to love and work, The lark is in the
2. Come, let thy voice be one with theirs, Shout with their shout of
3. To give and give, and give a-gain, What God hath giv-en
sky; The fields are wet with dia-mond dew, The
praise; See how the gi-ant sun soars up, Great
thee; To spend thy-self nor count the cost, To
worlds a-wake to cry Their bless-ings on the
lord of years and days! So let the love of
serve right glo-rious-ly The God who gave all
Lord of life, As he goes meek-ly by.
Je-sus come And set thy soul a-blaze:
worlds that are, And all that are to be. A-men.

Words from *The Unutterable Beauty* by G. A. Studdert-Kennedy. Used by permission of Hodder & Stoughton, Ltd.

God Send Us Men

KEDRON LM

FREDERICK J. GILLMAN, 1866-1949

PILSBURY'S *United States Harmony*, 1799

Unison
1. God send us men whose aim 'twill be Not
2. God send us men a - lert and quick His
3. God send us men of stead-fast will, Pa -
4. God send us men with hearts a - blaze, All

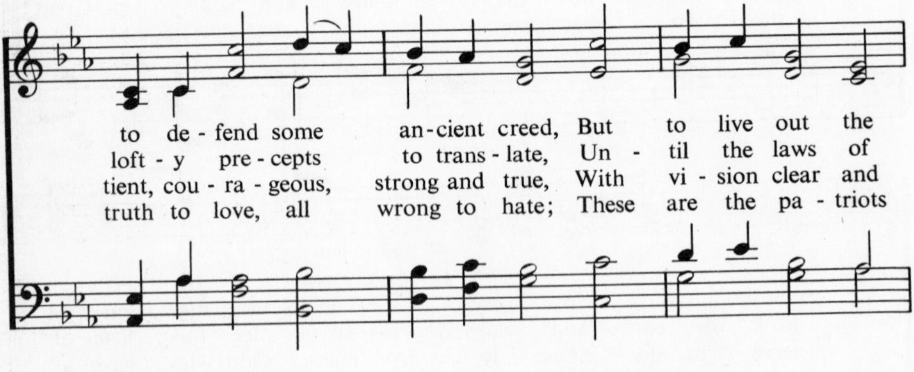
to de - fend some an-cient creed, But to live out the
loft - y pre - cepts to trans - late, Un - til the laws of
tient, cou - ra - geous, strong and true, With vi - sion clear and
truth to love, all wrong to hate; These are the pa - triots

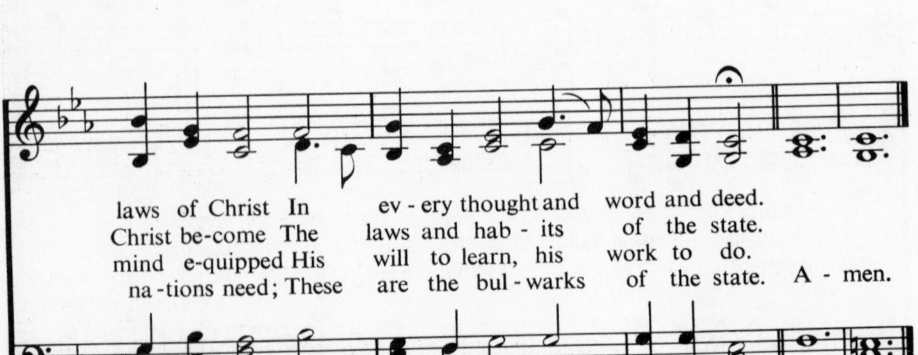
laws of Christ In ev - ery thought and word and deed.
Christ be-come The laws and hab - its of the state.
mind e-quipped His will to learn, his work to do.
na - tions need; These are the bul - warks of the state. A - men.

In Christ There Is No East or West

192

JOHN OXENHAM, 1852-1941

ST. PETER CM
ALEXANDER R. REINAGLE, 1799-1877

1. In Christ there is no east or west, In
2. In him shall true hearts ev - ery - where Their
3. Join hands, then, broth - ers of the faith, What -
4. In Christ now meet both east and west, In
him no south or north; But one great fel - low -
high com - mu - nion find; His ser - vice is the
e'er your race may be. Who serves my Fa - ther
him meet south and north; All Christ - ly souls are
ship of love Through-out the whole wide earth.
gold - en cord Close bind - ing all man - kind.
as a son Is sure - ly kin to me.
one in him Through-out the whole wide earth. A-men.

Words used by permission of Miss T. Oxenham.

Jesus, United by Thy Grace

ST. AGNES CM

CHARLES WESLEY, 1707-1788

JOHN B. DYKES, 1823-1876

1. Je - sus, u - nit - ed by thy grace,
2. Help us to help each oth - er, Lord,
3. Up un - to thee, our liv - ing Head,
4. Touched by the lode - stone of thy love,
5. To thee, in - sep - a - ra - bly joined,
6. This is the bond of per - fect - ness,
And each to each en - deared, With con - fi - dence we
Each oth - er's cross to bear; Let each his friend - ly
Let us in all things grow, Till thou hast made us
Let all our hearts a - gree; And ev - er toward each
Let all our spir - its cleave; O may we all the
Thy spot - less char - i - ty; O let us, still we
seek thy face, And know our prayer is heard.
aid af - ford, And feel his broth - er's care.
free in - deed And spot - less here be - low.
oth - er move, And ev - er move toward thee.
lov - ing mind That was in thee re - ceive.
pray, pos - sess The mind that was in thee. A - men.

Lift Up Our Hearts, O King of Kings

DEUS TUORUM MILITUM LM

JOHN H. B. MASTERMAN, 1867-1933

Grenoble Antiphoner, 1868

Unison
1. Lift up our hearts, O King of kings, To bright - er hopes and kind - lier things, To vi - sions of a larg - er good, And ho - lier dreams of broth - er - hood.
2. Thy world is wea - ry of its pain, Of self - ish greed and fruit - less gain, Of tar - nished hon - or, false - ly strong, And all its an - cient deeds of wrong.
3. Al - might - y Fa - ther, who dost give The gift of life to all who live, Look down on all earth's sin and strife, And lift us to a no - bler life. A - men.

195

Lord, Speak to Me

ROMANS 14:17
FRANCES R. HAVERGAL, 1836-1879

CANONBURY LM
Arr. from "Nachtstücke," ROBERT SCHUMANN, 1810-1856

1. Lord, speak to me, that I may speak In
2. O strength - en me, that while I stand Firm
3. O teach me, Lord, that I may teach The
4. O fill me with thy ful - ness, Lord, Un -
5. O use me, Lord, use ev - en me, Just

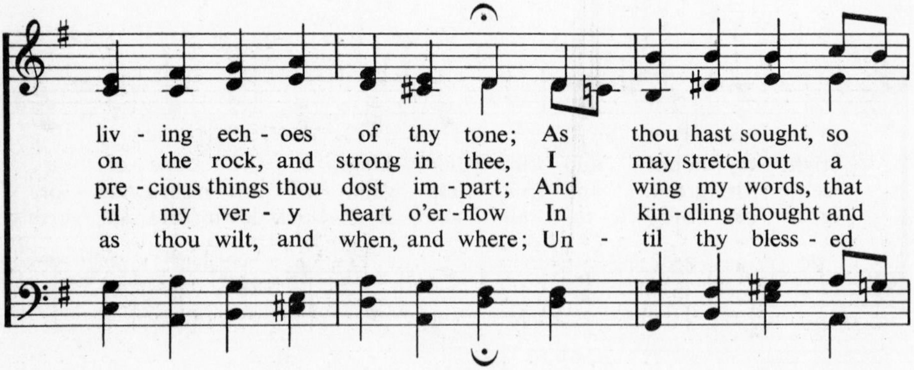
liv - ing ech - oes of thy tone; As thou hast sought, so
on the rock, and strong in thee, I may stretch out a
pre - cious things thou dost im - part; And wing my words, that
til my ver - y heart o'er - flow In kin - dling thought and
as thou wilt, and when, and where; Un - til thy bless - ed

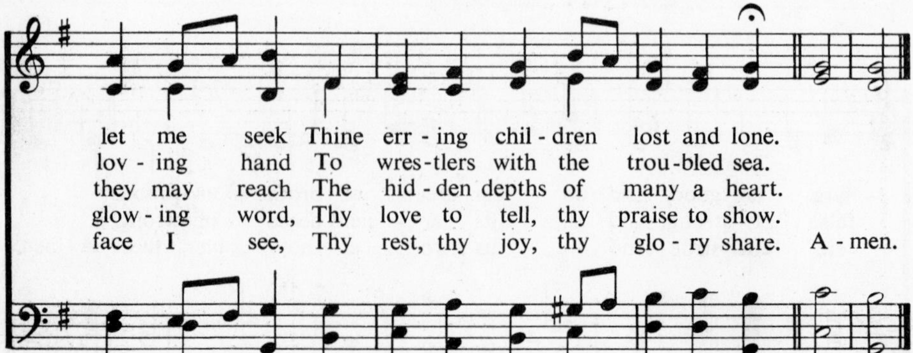
let me seek Thine err - ing chil - dren lost and lone.
lov - ing hand To wres - tlers with the trou - bled sea.
they may reach The hid - den depths of many a heart.
glow - ing word, Thy love to tell, thy praise to show.
face I see, Thy rest, thy joy, thy glo - ry share. A - men.

What Shall I Render to My God

Psalm 116: 12-18
Charles Wesley, 1707-1788

ARMENIA CM
Sylvanus B. Pond, 1792-1871
Harm. by A. C. L.

1. What shall I ren - der to my God For all his
2. The sa - cred cup of sav - ing grace I will with
3. My vows I will to his great name Be - fore his
4. The God of all - re - deem - ing grace My God I
5. Praise him, ye saints, the God of love Who hath my
mer - cy's store? I'll take the gifts he hath be -
thanks re - ceive, And all his prom - is - es em -
peo - ple pay, And all I have, and all I
will pro - claim, Of - fer the sac - ri - fice of
sins for - given, Till, gath - ered to the Church a -
stowed, And hum - bly ask for more.
brace, And to his glo - ry live.
am, Up - on his al - tar lay.
praise, And call up - on his name.
bove, We sing the songs of heaven. A - men.

O Son of Man, Thou Madest Known

CANONBURY LM

MILTON S. LITTLEFIELD, 1864-1934

Arr. from "Nachtstücke," ROBERT SCHUMANN, 1810-1856

1. O Son of Man, thou mad - est known, Through
2. O Work - man true, may we ful - fill In
3. Thou Mas - ter Work - man, grant us grace The
4. And thus, we pray in deed and word, Thy
qui - et work in shop and home, The sa - cred - ness of
dai - ly life thy Fa - ther's will; In du - ty's call, thy
chal - lenge of our tasks to face; By loy - al scorn of
king - dom come on earth, O Lord; In work that gives ef -
com - mon things, The chance of life that each day brings.
call we hear To full - er life, through work sin - cere.
sec - ond best, By ef - fort true, to meet each test.
fect to prayer, Thy pur - pose for thy world we share. A - men.

These Things Shall Be

TRURO LM

J. ADDINGTON SYMONDS, 1840-1893 | T. WILLIAMS' *Psalmodia Evangelica*, 1789

1. These things shall be: a loft - ier race Than e'er the
2. They shall be gen - tle, brave, and strong, To spill no
3. Na - tion with na - tion, land with land, In - armed shall
4. New arts shall bloom of loft - ier mold, And might - ier
world hath known shall rise With flame of free - dom in their
drop of blood, but dare All that may plant man's lord - ship
live as com-rades free; In ev - ery heart and brain shall
mu - sic thrill the skies, And ev - ery life shall be a
souls And light of knowl - edge in their eyes.
firm On earth and fire and sea and air.
throb The pulse of one fra - ter - ni - ty.
song, When all the earth is par - a - dise. A - men.

199

O Brother Man, Fold to Thy Heart

JAMES 1:27
JOHN GREENLEAF WHITTIER, 1807-1892

WELWYN 11 10.11 10.
ALFRED SCOTT-GATTY, 1847-1918

Unison

1. O brother-er man, fold to thy heart thy broth-er!
2. For he whom Je - sus loved hath tru-ly spo-ken:
3. Fol-low with rev - erent steps the great ex-am-ple
4. Then shall all shack - les fall; the storm-y clang-or
Where pit-y dwells, the peace of God is there; To
The ho-lier wor-ship which he deigns to bless Re-
Of him whose ho-ly work was do-ing good;
Of wild war mu-sic o'er the earth shall cease;
wor-ship right-ly is to love each oth-er,
stores the lost, and binds the spir-it bro-ken,
So shall the wide earth seem our Fa-ther's tem-ple,
Love shall tread out the bale-ful fire of an-ger,
Each smile a hymn, each kind-ly deed a prayer.
And feeds the wid - ow and the fa-ther-less.
Each lov-ing life a psalm of grat-i-tude.
And in its ash - es plant the tree of peace. A-men.

Music used by permission of the Abbot of Downside.

The Voice of God Is Calling

Isaiah 6:8
John Haynes Holmes, 1879-1964

MEIRIONYDD 76.76.D.
William Lloyd, 1786-1852

1. The voice of God is call - ing Its sum-mons un - to men;
2. I hear my peo - ple cry - ing In cot and mine and slum;
3. We heed, O Lord, thy sum-mons, And an-swer: Here are we!
4. From ease and plen - ty save us; From pride of place ab - solve;
As once he spake in Zi - on, So now he speaks a - gain.
No field or mart is si - lent, No cit - y street is dumb.
Send us up - on thine er - rand, Let us thy ser - vants be.
Purge us of low de - sire; Lift us to high re - solve;
Whom shall I send to suc - cor My peo - ple in their need?
I see my peo - ple fall - ing In dark-ness and de - spair.
Our strength is dust and ash - es, Our years a pass - ing hour;
Take us, and make us ho - ly; Teach us thy will and way.
Whom shall I send to loos - en The bonds of shame and greed?
Whom shall I send to shat - ter The fet - ters which they bear?
But thou canst use our weak - ness To mag - ni - fy thy power.
Speak, and, be-hold! we an - swer; Com-mand, and we o - bey! A-men.

201

O Thou Who Art the Shepherd

MUNICH 76.76.D.
Gesangbuch, Meiningen, 1693
Harm. by FELIX MENDELSSOHN, 1809-1847

JOHN W. SHACKFORD, 1878-

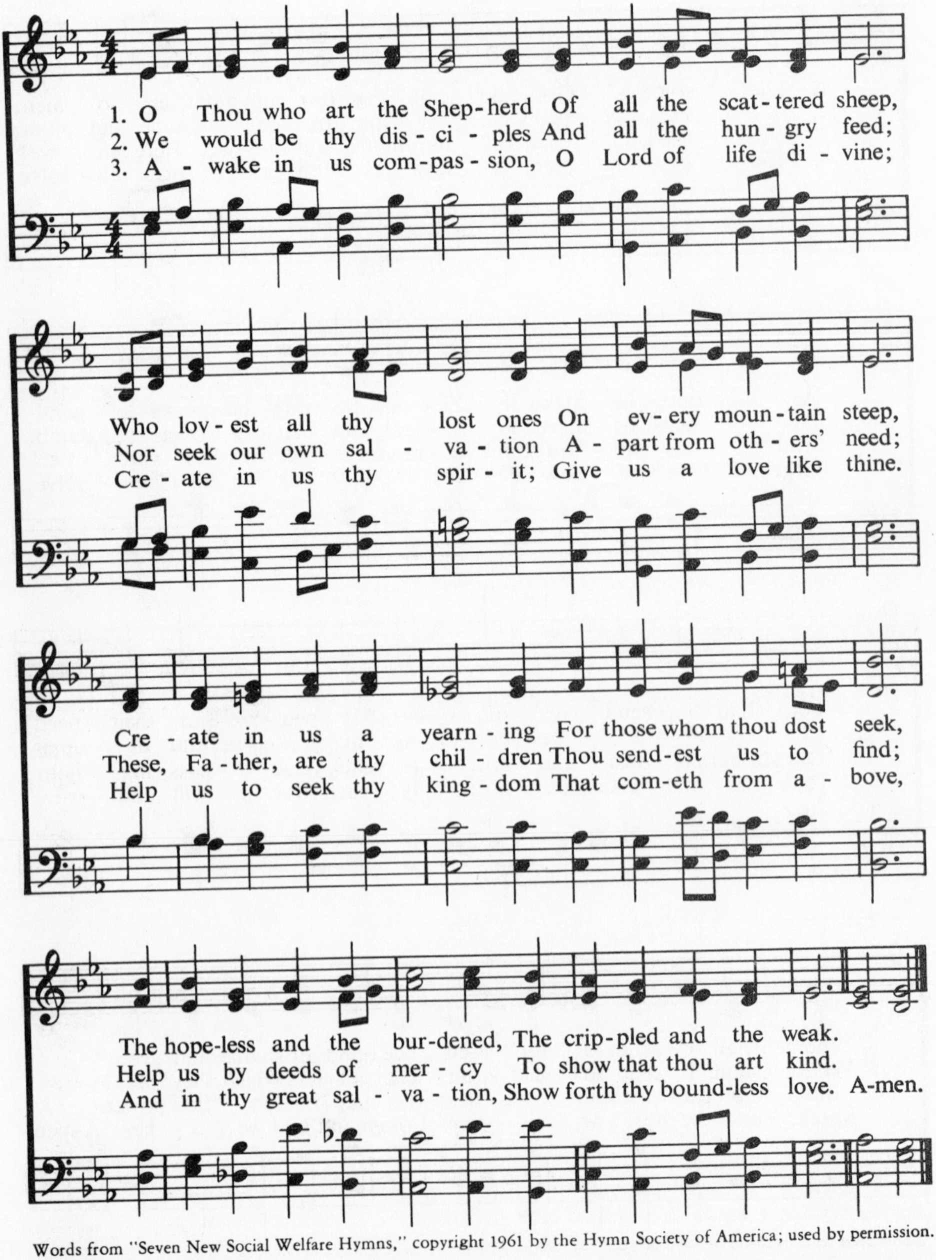
1. O Thou who art the Shep-herd Of all the scat-tered sheep,
2. We would be thy dis - ci - ples And all the hun-gry feed;
3. A - wake in us com-pas-sion, O Lord of life di - vine;
Who lov-est all thy lost ones On ev-ery moun-tain steep,
Nor seek our own sal - va - tion A - part from oth - ers' need;
Cre - ate in us thy spir - it; Give us a love like thine.
Cre - ate in us a yearn - ing For those whom thou dost seek,
These, Fa-ther, are thy chil - dren Thou send-est us to find;
Help us to seek thy king - dom That com-eth from a - bove,
The hope-less and the bur-dened, The crip-pled and the weak.
Help us by deeds of mer - cy To show that thou art kind.
And in thy great sal - va - tion, Show forth thy bound-less love. A-men.

We Bear the Strain of Earthly Care

OZORA S. DAVIS, 1866-1931

SHEPHERDS' PIPES CMD
ANNABETH MCCLELLAND GAY, 1925-

1. We bear the strain of earth-ly care, But bear it not a-lone;
2. The com-mon hopes that make us men Were his in Gal-i-lee;
Be-side us walks our broth-er Christ And makes our task his own.
The tasks he gives are those he gave Be-side the rest-less sea.
Through din of mar-ket, whirl of wheels, And thrust of driv-ing trade,
Our broth-er-hood still rests in him, The broth-er of us all,
We fol-low where the Mas-ter leads, Se-rene and un-a-fraid.
And o'er the cen-turies still we hear The Mas-ter's win-some call. A-men.

Alternate tune: AZMON

203

We Thank Thee, Lord

FIELD 10 10.10 10.

CALVIN W. LAUFER, 1874-1938 | CALVIN W. LAUFER, 1874-1938

1. We thank thee, Lord, thy paths of ser - vice lead
2. We've sought and found thee in the se - cret place
3. We've felt thy touch in sor - row's dark - ened way
4. We've seen thy glo - ry like a man - tle spread
To bla - zoned heights and down the slopes of need;
And mar - veled at the ra - diance of thy face;
A - bound with love and sol - ace for the day;
O'er hill and dale in saf - fron flame and red;
They reach thy throne, en - com - pass land and sea,
But of - ten in some far - off Gal - i - lee
And, neath the bur - dens there, thy sov - ereign - ty
But in the eyes of men, re - deemed and free,
And he who jour - neys in them walks with thee.
Be - held thee fair - er yet while serv - ing thee.
Has held our hearts en - thralled while serv - ing thee.
A splen - dor great - er yet while serv - ing thee. A - men.

Where Cross the Crowded Ways of Life

Matthew 22:9 — GERMANY LM
Frank Mason North, 1850-1935 — William Gardiner's *Sacred Melodies*, 1815

1. Where cross the crowd - ed ways of life, Where sound the
2. In haunts of wretch - ed - ness and need, On shad - owed
3. From ten - der child - hood's help - less - ness, From wo - man's
4. The cup of wa - ter given for thee Still holds the
5. O Mas - ter, from the moun - tain - side, Make haste to
6. Till sons of men shall learn thy love And fol - low
cries of race and clan, A - bove the noise of
thresh - olds dark with fears, From paths where hide the
grief, man's bur - dened toil, From fam - ished souls, from
fresh - ness of thy grace; Yet long these mul - ti -
heal these hearts of pain; A - mong these rest - less
where thy feet have trod; Till, glo - rious from thy
self - ish strife, We hear thy voice, O Son of man!
lures of greed, We catch the vi - sion of thy tears.
sor - row's stress Thy heart has nev - er known re - coil.
tudes to see The sweet com - pas - sion of thy face.
throngs a - bide, O tread the cit - y's streets a - gain,
heaven a - bove, Shall come the cit - y of our God! A - men.

All the Way My Savior Leads Me

ALL THE WAY 87.87.D.

FANNY J. CROSBY, 1820-1915

ROBERT LOWRY, 1826-1899

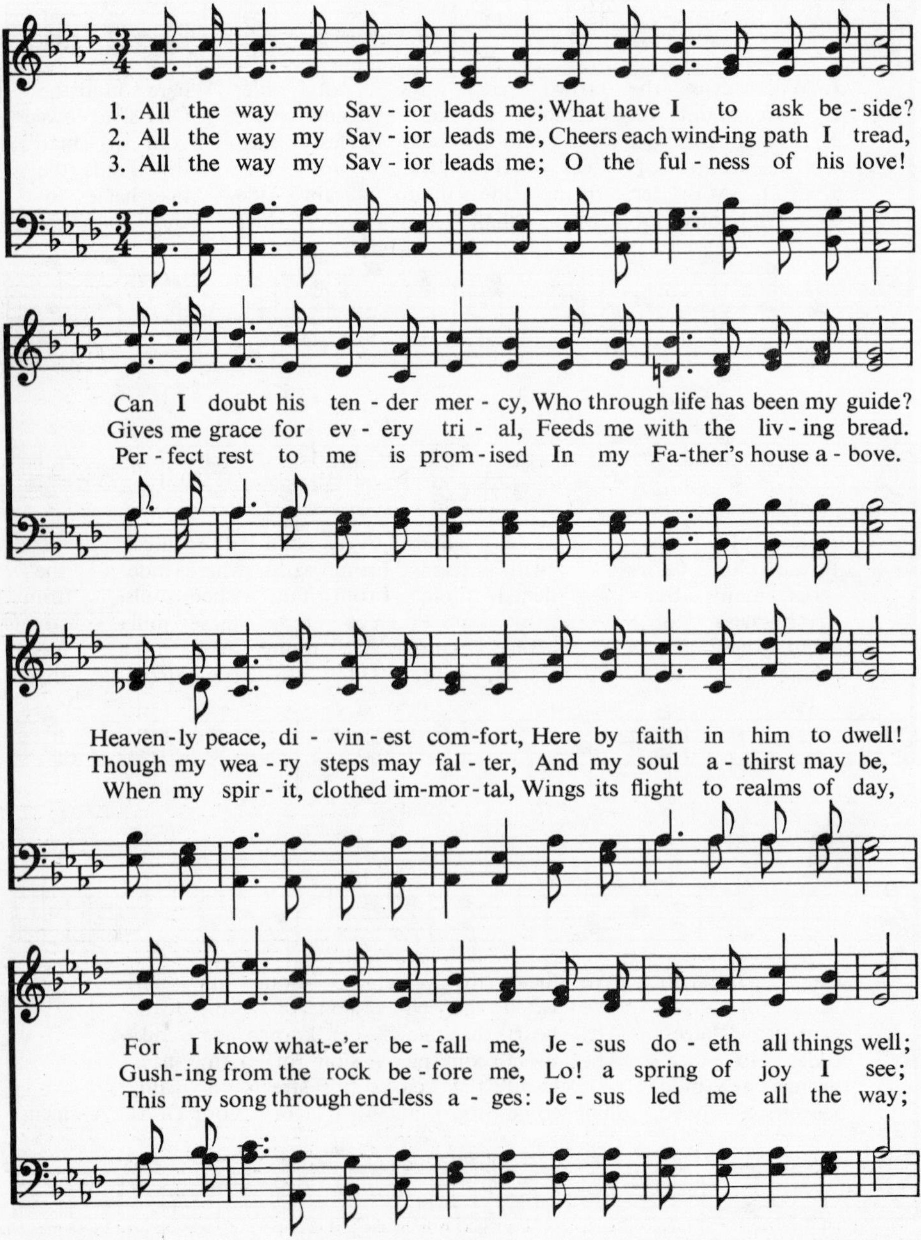
1. All the way my Sav - ior leads me; What have I to ask be - side?
2. All the way my Sav - ior leads me, Cheers each wind-ing path I tread,
3. All the way my Sav - ior leads me; O the ful - ness of his love!
Can I doubt his ten - der mer - cy, Who through life has been my guide?
Gives me grace for ev - ery tri - al, Feeds me with the liv - ing bread.
Per - fect rest to me is prom - ised In my Fa-ther's house a - bove.
Heaven - ly peace, di - vin - est com-fort, Here by faith in him to dwell!
Though my wea - ry steps may fal - ter, And my soul a - thirst may be,
When my spir - it, clothed im-mor - tal, Wings its flight to realms of day,
For I know what-e'er be - fall me, Je - sus do - eth all things well;
Gush-ing from the rock be - fore me, Lo! a spring of joy I see;
This my song through end-less a - ges: Je - sus led me all the way;

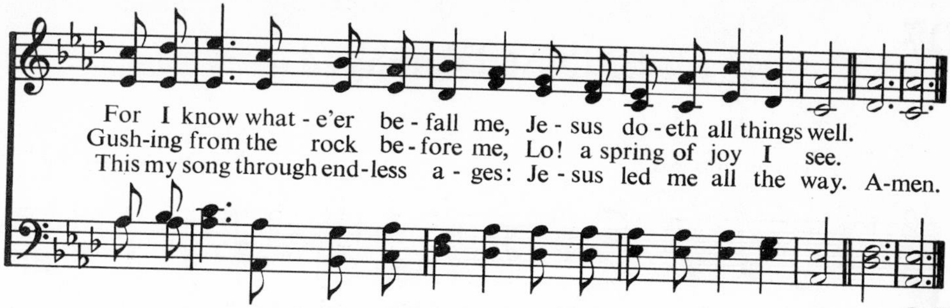
For I know what-e'er be-fall me, Je-sus do-eth all things well.
Gush-ing from the rock be-fore me, Lo! a spring of joy I see.
This my song through end-less a-ges: Je-sus led me all the way. A-men.

206

God of the Ages, by Whose Hand

ROCKINGHAM (MASON) LM
LOWELL MASON, 1792-1872
Harm. by A. C. L.

ELISABETH BURROWES, 1885-

1. God of the a-ges, by whose hand Through
2. Thou art the thought be-yond all thought, The
3. For-give our wa-vering trust in thee, Our
4. Though there be dark, un-chart-ed space, With
years long past our lives were led, Give us new cour-age
gift be-yond our ut-most prayer; No far-thest reach where
wild a-larms, our trem-bling fears; In thy strong hand e-
worlds on worlds be-yond our sight, Still may we trust thy
now to stand, New faith to find the paths a-head.
thou art not, No height but we may find thee there.
ter-nal-ly Rests the un-fold-ing of the years.
love and grace, And wait thy word, Let there be light. A-men.

207

Be Not Dismayed

MARTIN 86.86. with Refrain

CIVILLA D. MARTIN, 1869-1948 | W. STILLMAN MARTIN, 1862-1935

1. Be not dis-mayed what-e'er be-tide, God will take care of you;
2. Through days of toil when heart doth fail, God will take care of you;
3. All you may need he will pro-vide, God will take care of you;
4. No mat-ter what may be the test, God will take care of you;
Be-neath his wings of love a-bide, God will take care of you.
When dan-gers fierce your path as-sail, God will take care of you.
Noth-ing you ask will be de-nied, God will take care of you.
Lean, wea-ry one, up-on his breast, God will take care of you.
Refrain
God will take care of you, Through ev-ery day, o'er all the way;
He will take care of you, God will take care of you. A-men.

'Tis So Sweet to Trust in Jesus

Louisa M. R. Stead, c. 1850-1917

TRUST IN JESUS 87.87. with Refrain
William J. Kirkpatrick, 1838-1921

1. 'Tis so sweet to trust in Je - sus, And to take him at his word;
2. O how sweet to trust in Je - sus, Just to trust his cleans-ing blood;
3. Yes, 'tis sweet to trust in Je - sus, Just from sin and self to cease;
4. I'm so glad I learned to trust thee, Pre-cious Je - sus, Sav-ior, friend;
Just to rest up - on his prom-ise, And to know, "Thus saith the Lord."
And in sim - ple faith to plunge me Neath the heal - ing, cleans-ing flood!
Just from Je - sus sim-ply tak - ing Life and rest, and joy and peace.
And I know that thou art with me, Wilt be with me to the end.
Refrain
Je - sus, Je - sus, how I trust him! How I've proved him o'er and o'er!
Je - sus, Je - sus, pre-cious Je - sus! O for grace to trust him more! A-men.

209

Be Still, My Soul

Psalm 46:10
I Thessalonians 4:17
Katharina von Schlegel, b. 1697
Trans. by Jane Borthwick, 1813-1897

FINLANDIA 10 10.10 10.10 10.
Jean Sibelius, 1865-1957
Arr. for *The Hymnal*, 1933

1. Be still, my soul: the Lord is on thy side; Bear pa-tient-ly the
2. Be still, my soul: thy God doth un-der-take To guide the fu-ture
3. Be still, my soul: the hour is has-tening on When we shall be for-
cross of grief or pain; Leave to thy God to or-der and pro-vide;
as he has the past. Thy hope, thy con-fi-dence let noth-ing shake;
ev-er with the Lord, When dis-ap-point-ment, grief, and fear are gone,
In ev-ery change he faith-ful will re-main. Be still, my soul: thy
All now mys-te-rious shall be bright at last. Be still, my soul: the
Sor-row for-got, love's pur-est joys re-stored. Be still, my soul: when
best, thy heaven-ly friend Through thorn-y ways leads to a joy-ful end.
waves and winds still know His voice who ruled them while he dwelt be-low.
change and tears are past, All safe and bless-ed we shall meet at last. A-men.

210

If Thou But Suffer God to Guide Thee

Psalm 55:22
Georg Neumark, 1621-1681
Trans. by Catherine Winkworth, 1827-1878

WER NUR DEN LIEBEN GOTT 98.98.88.
Georg Neumark, 1621-1681

1. If thou but suf - fer God to guide thee, And hope in him through
2. On - ly be still, and wait his lei - sure In cheer - ful hope, with
3. Sing, pray, and keep his ways un - swerv - ing; So do thine own part
all thy ways, He'll give thee strength, what - e'er be - tide thee,
heart con - tent To take what - e'er thy Fa - ther's plea - sure
faith - ful - ly, And trust his word, though un - de - serv - ing;
And bear thee through the e - vil days; Who trusts in God's un -
And all - de - serv - ing love hath sent; Nor doubt our in - most
Thou yet shalt find it true for thee; God nev - er yet for -
chang - ing love Builds on the rock that naught can move.
wants are known To him who chose us for his own.
sook at need The soul that trust - ed him in - deed. A - men.

211

God Is My Strong Salvation

WEDLOCK 76.76.D.
The Sacred Harp, 1844
Harm. by A. C. L.

PSALM 27:1-3
JAMES MONTGOMERY, 1771-1854

Unison
1. God is my strong sal - va - tion: What foe have I to fear?
2. Place on the Lord re - li - ance; My soul, with cour - age wait;
In dark - ness and temp - ta - tion, My light, my help, is near.
His truth be thine af - fi - ance, When faint and des - o - late.
Though hosts en - camp a - round me, Firm in the fight I stand;
His might thy heart shall strength-en, His love thy joy in - crease;
What ter - ror can con - found me, With God at my right hand?
Mer - cy thy days shall length-en; The Lord will give thee peace. A - men.

Alternate tune: AURELIA

There Is a Balm in Gilead

JEREMIAH 8:22
American Folk Hymn

BALM IN GILEAD Irregular
American Folk Hymn
Arr. by DANIEL L. RIDOUT, 1898-

Unison
Refrain
There is a balm in Gil - e - ad, to make the wound-ed
Fine
whole; There is a balm in Gil - e - ad, to heal the sin - sick soul.
1. Some-times I feel dis - cour-aged, And think my work's in vain, But
2. If you can't preach like Pet - er, If you can't pray like Paul, Just
then the Ho - ly Spir - it Re-vives my soul a - gain. There is a
tell the love of Je - sus, And say he died for all.

Music arr. from *12 Negro Spirituals;* used by permission.

O Thou, to Whose All-Searching Sight

ROCKINGHAM (MASON) LM

Nicolaus von Zinzendorf, 1700-1760
Trans. by John Wesley, 1703-1791

Lowell Mason, 1792-1872
Harm. by A. C. L.

1. O Thou, to whose all - search - ing sight The
2. If in this dark - some wild I stray, Be
3. When ris - ing floods my soul o'er - flow, When
4. Sav - ior, wher - e'er thy steps I see, Daunt -
dark - ness shin - eth as the light: Search, prove my heart, it
thou my light, be thou my way; No foes, no vi - o -
sinks my heart in waves of woe, Je - sus, thy time - ly
less, un - tired, I fol - low thee; O let thy hand sup -
yearns for thee; O burst these bonds and set it free!
lence I fear, No fraud, while thou, my God, art near.
aid im - part, And raise my head, and cheer my heart.
port me still, And lead me to thy ho - ly hill! A - men.

The Righteous Ones

PSALM 1
Unknown Thai Christian
Trans. by VIDA RUMBAUGH, 1927-

SRI LAMPANG 10 8.10 8.
Thailand Folk Hymn

1. The righ-teous ones shall be for - ev - er blest. Their joy - ful,
2. They gai - ly bloom and pros - per cheer - ful - ly Like trees be -
3. Not like that go the men of un - be - lief, But are like
4. Their e - vil acts shall sure - ly come to naught. Past deeds shall
faith - ful hearts o - bey The laws of God in their de -
side a flow - ing stream; In drought their branch - es grow a -
chaff the wind doth blow. There-fore the e - vil shall re -
come and them en - snare. But righ - teous - ness in - spires those
ter-mined quest To fol - low in the saints' path - way.
bun - dant - ly, And in their time bear fruit su - preme.
ceive but grief; When God shall judge, their lot be woe.
who have sought To gain ful - fill-ment of their prayer. A - men.

God Moves in a Mysterious Way

WILLIAM COWPER, 1731-1800

DUNDEE (FRENCH) CM
Scottish Psalter, 1615

1. God moves in a mys - te - rious way His
2. Deep in un - fath - om - a - ble mines Of
3. Ye fear - ful saints, fresh cour - age take; The
4. Judge not the Lord by fee - ble sense, But
5. Blind un - be - lief is sure to err, And
won - ders to per - form; He plants his foot - steps
nev - er - fail - ing skill He trea - sures up his
clouds ye so much dread Are big with mer - cy,
trust him for his grace; Be - hind a frown - ing
scan his work in vain; God is his own in -
in the sea, And rides up - on the storm.
bright de - signs, And works his sov - ereign will.
and shall break In bless - ings on your head.
prov - i - dence He hides a smil - ing face.
ter - pre - ter, And he will make it plain. A - men.

The Man Who Once Has Found Abode

PSALM 91
United Presbyterian Book of Psalms, 1871

TALLIS' CANON LM
THOMAS TALLIS, c. 1505-1585

1. The man who once has found a - bode, With -
2. I of the Lord my God will say, "He
3. He shall with all - pro - tect - ing care Pre -
4. His out - spread pin - ions shall thee hide; Be -
5. No night - ly ter - rors shall a - larm; No
6. Be - cause thy trust is God a - lone, Thy
in the se - cret place of God, Shall with Al - might - y
is my ref - uge and my stay; To him for safe - ty
serve thee from the fowl - er's snare; When fear - ful plagues a -
neath his wings shalt thou con - fide; His faith - ful - ness shall
dead - ly shaft by day shall harm, Nor pes - ti - lence that
dwell - ing place the High - est One, No e - vil shall up -
God a - bide, And in his shad - ow safe - ly hide.
I will flee; My God, in him my trust shall be."
round pre - vail, No fa - tal stroke shall thee as - sail.
ev - er be A shield and buck - ler un - to thee.
walks by night, Nor plagues that waste in noon - day light.
on thee come, Nor plague ap - proach thy guard - ed home. A - men.

217

He Leadeth Me: O Blessed Thought

PSALM 23
JOSEPH H. GILMORE, 1834-1918

HE LEADETH ME LM with Refrain
WILLIAM B. BRADBURY, 1816-1868

1. He lead - eth me: O bless - ed thought! O
2. Some - times mid scenes of deep - est gloom, Some -
3. Lord, I would place my hand in thine, Nor
4. And when my task on earth is done, When
words with heaven - ly com - fort fraught! What - e'er I do, wher -
times where E - den's bow - ers bloom, By wa - ters still, o'er
ev - er mur - mur nor re - pine; Con - tent, what - ev - er
by thy grace the vic - tory's won, E'en death's cold wave I
e'er I be, Still 'tis God's hand that lead - eth me.
trou - bled sea, Still 'tis his hand that lead - eth me.
lot I see, Since 'tis my God that lead - eth me.
will not flee, Since God through Jor - dan lead - eth me.
Refrain
He lead - eth me, he lead - eth me, By

his own hand he lead - eth me; His faith - ful fol - lower
I would be, For by his hand he lead - eth me. A-men.

218

Lord, It Belongs Not to My Care

PHILIPPIANS 1:21
RICHARD BAXTER, 1615-1691

HORSLEY CM
WILLIAM HORSLEY, 1774-1858

1. Lord, it be-longs not to my care Wheth-er I die or live; To
2. If life be long, I will be glad That I may long o - bey; If
3. Christ leads me through no dark - er rooms Than he went through be-fore; He
4. Come, Lord, when grace hath made me meet Thy bless - ed face to see; For
5. My knowl-edge of that life is small; The eye of faith is dim; But
love and serve thee is my share, And this thy grace must give.
short, yet why should I be sad To soar to end - less day?
that in - to God's king-dom comes Must en - ter by this door.
if thy work on earth be sweet, What will thy glo - ry be?
'tis e-nough that Christ knows all, And I shall be with him. A-men.

I Look to Thee in Every Need

O JESU 86.86.88.
Hirschberger Gesangbuch, 1741
Altered

SAMUEL LONGFELLOW, 1819-1892

1. I look to thee in ev - ery need,
2. Dis - cour - aged in the work of life,
3. Thy calm - ness bends se - rene a - bove,
4. Em - bos - omed deep in thy dear love,
And nev - er look in vain; I feel thy strong and
Dis - heart - ened by its load, Shamed by its fail - ures
My rest - less - ness to still; A - round me flows thy
Held in thy law, I stand; Thy hand in all things
ten - der love, And all is well a - gain: The thought of thee is
or its fears, I sink be - side the road; But let me on - ly
quick-ening life, To nerve my fal-tering will: Thy pres-ence fills my
I be - hold, And all things in thy hand; Thou lead-est me by
might - ier far Than sin and pain and sor - row are.
think of thee, And then new heart springs up in me.
sol - i - tude; Thy prov - i - dence turns all to good.
un-sought ways, And turn'st my mourn-ing in - to praise. A - men.

220

Jesus, Priceless Treasure

JOHANN FRANCK, 1618-1677
Trans. by CATHERINE WINKWORTH, 1827-1878

JESU, MEINE FREUDE 665.665.786.
Trad. German Melody
Adapt. by JOHANN CRÜGER, 1598-1662

1. Je - sus, price - less trea - sure, Source of pur - est plea - sure,
2. In thine arm I rest me; Foes who would mo - lest me
3. Hence, all thoughts of sad - ness! For the Lord of glad - ness,
Tru-est friend to me, Long my heart hath pant-ed, Till it well-nigh
Can-not reach me here. Though the earth be shak-ing, Ev - ery heart be
Je - sus, en - ters in; Those who love the Fa - ther, Though the storms may
faint - ed, Thirst-ing af - ter thee. Thine I am, O spot-less Lamb,
quak - ing, God dis-pels our fear; Sin and hell in con-flict fell
gath - er, Still have peace with - in; Yea, what-e'er we here must bear,
I will suf-fer naught to hide thee, Ask for naught be-side thee.
With their heav-iest storms as-sail us; Je - sus will not fail us.
Still in thee lies pur-est plea - sure, Je - sus, price-less trea - sure! A-men.

221

Standing on the Promises

PROMISES 11 11.11 9. with Refrain

R. KELSO CARTER, 1849-1926 R. KELSO CARTER, 1849-1926

1. Stand - ing on the prom - is - es of Christ my King,
2. Stand - ing on the prom - is - es that can - not fail,
3. Stand - ing on the prom - is - es of Christ the Lord,
4. Stand - ing on the prom - is - es I can - not fall,
Through e - ter - nal a - ges let his prais - es ring;
When the howl - ing storms of doubt and fear as - sail,
Bound to him e - ter - nal - ly by love's strong cord,
Lis - tening ev - ery mo - ment to the Spir - it's call,
Glo - ry in the high - est, I will shout and sing,
By the liv - ing Word of God I shall pre - vail,
O - ver - com - ing dai - ly with the Spir - it's sword,
Rest - ing in my Sav - ior as my all - in - all,
Stand - ing on the prom - is - es of God.
Stand - ing on the prom - is - es of God.
Stand - ing on the prom - is - es of God.
Stand - ing on the prom - is - es of God.

Refrain
Stand - ing, stand - ing,
Stand - ing on the prom - is - es, stand - ing on the prom - is - es,
Stand - ing on the prom - is - es of God my Sav - ior;
Stand - ing, stand - ing, I'm
Stand - ing on the prom - is - es, stand - ing on the prom - is - es,
stand - ing on the prom - is - es of God. A - men.

My Hope Is Built

THE SOLID ROCK LM with Refrain

EDWARD MOTE, 1797-1874

WILLIAM B. BRADBURY, 1816-1868

1. My hope is built on noth - ing less Than Je - sus' blood and
2. When dark - ness veils his love - ly face, I rest on his un -
3. His oath, his cov - e - nant, his blood Sup - port me in the
4. When he shall come with trum - pet sound, O may I then in
righ - teous - ness; I dare not trust the sweet - est frame, But
chang - ing grace; In ev - ery high and storm - y gale, My
whelm - ing flood; When all a - round my soul gives way, He
him be found! Dressed in his righ - teous - ness a - lone, Fault -
whol - ly lean on Je - sus' name.
an - chor holds with - in the veil.
then is all my hope and stay.
less to stand be - fore the throne!
Refrain
On Christ, the sol - id rock, I stand; All
oth - er ground is sink - ing sand, All oth - er ground is sink - ing sand. A - men.

When We Walk with the Lord

JOHN H. SAMMIS, 1846-1919

TRUST AND OBEY 669.D. with Refrain
DANIEL B. TOWNER, 1850-1919

1. When we walk with the Lord In the light of his Word, What a
2. Not a bur-den we bear, Not a sor-row we share, But our
3. But we nev-er can prove The de-lights of his love Un-til
4. Then in fel-low-ship sweet We will sit at his feet, Or we'll
glo-ry he sheds on our way! While we do his good will, He a-
toil he doth rich-ly re-pay; Not a grief or a loss, Not a
all on the al-tar we lay; For the fa-vor he shows And the
walk by his side in the way; What he says we will do, Where he
bides with us still, And with all who will trust and o-bey.
frown or a cross, But is blest if we trust and o-bey.
joy he be-stows Are for them who will trust and o-bey.
sends we will go; Nev-er fear, on-ly trust and o-bey.
Refrain
Trust and o-bey, for there's no oth-er way To be
hap-py in Je-sus, but to trust and o-bey. A-men.

224

Blessed Assurance, Jesus Is Mine

ASSURANCE 9 10.9 9. with Refrain

FANNY J. CROSBY, 1820-1915

PHOEBE P. KNAPP, 1839-1908

1. Bless - ed as - sur - ance, Je - sus is mine! O what a
2. Per - fect sub - mis - sion, per - fect de - light, Vi - sions of
3. Per - fect sub - mis - sion, all is at rest; I in my
fore - taste of glo - ry di - vine! Heir of sal -
rap - ture now burst on my sight; An - gels de -
Sav - ior am hap - py and blest, Watch - ing and
va - tion, pur-chase of God, Born of his spir - it, washed in his blood.
scend - ing, bring from a - bove Ech - oes of mer - cy, whis-pers of love.
wait - ing, look - ing a - bove, Filled with his good-ness, lost in his love.
Refrain
This is my sto - ry, this is my song, Prais - ing my

Sav - ior all the day long; This is my sto - ry, this is my

song, Prais - ing my Sav - ior all the day long. A - men.

225

Mid All the Traffic of the Ways

HORSLEY CM

JOHN OXENHAM, 1852-1941

WILLIAM HORSLEY, 1774-1858

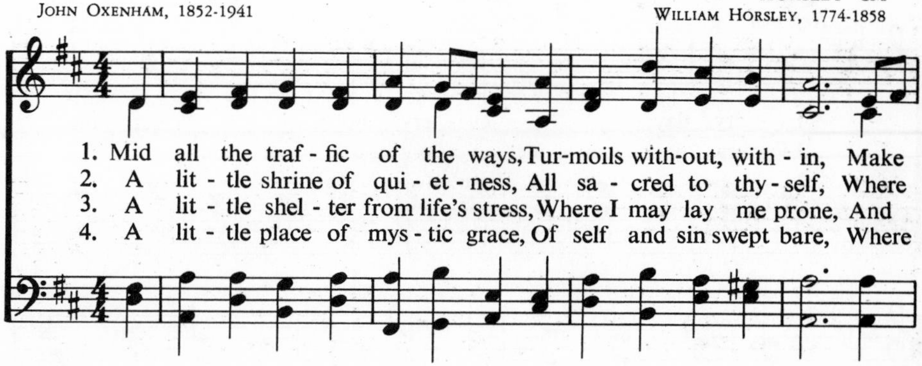
1. Mid all the traf - fic of the ways, Tur-moils with-out, with - in, Make
2. A lit - tle shrine of qui - et - ness, All sa - cred to thy - self, Where
3. A lit - tle shel - ter from life's stress, Where I may lay me prone, And
4. A lit - tle place of mys - tic grace, Of self and sin swept bare, Where

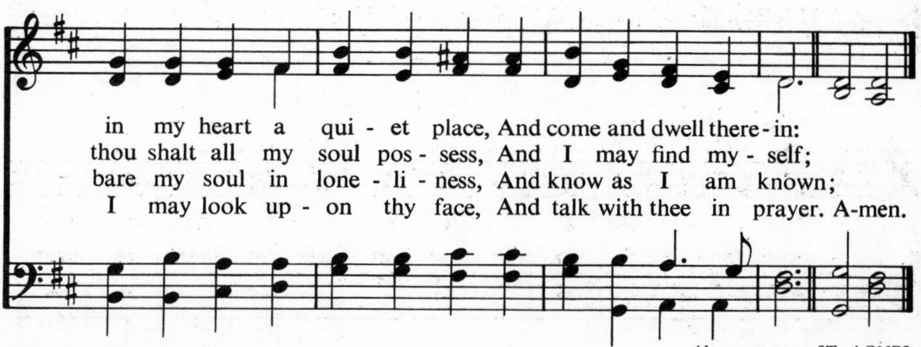
in my heart a qui - et place, And come and dwell there - in:
thou shalt all my soul pos - sess, And I may find my - self;
bare my soul in lone - li - ness, And know as I am known;
I may look up - on thy face, And talk with thee in prayer. A-men.

Words used by permission of Miss T. Oxenham.

Alternate tune: ST. AGNES

TRUST AND ASSURANCE

Savior, More Than Life to Me

Psalm 51:2
Fanny J. Crosby, 1820-1915

Every Day and Hour 79.79. with Refrain
William H. Doane, 1832-1915

1. Sav-ior, more than life to me, I am cling-ing, cling-ing close to thee;
2. Through this chang-ing world be-low, Lead me gent-ly, gent-ly as I go;
3. Let me love thee more and more, Till this fleet-ing, fleet-ing life is o'er;
Let thy pre-cious blood ap-plied Keep me ev-er, ev-er near thy side.
Trust-ing thee, I can-not stray; I can nev-er, nev-er lose my way.
Till my soul is lost in love, In a bright-er, bright-er world a-bove.
Refrain
Ev-ery day, ev-ery hour, Let me
Ev-ery day and hour, ev-ery day and hour,
feel thy cleans-ing power; May thy ten-der love to
me Bind me clos-er, clos-er, Lord, to thee. A-men.

O How Happy Are They

TRUE HAPPINESS 669.D.
Southern Harmony, 1835
Harm. by A. C. L.

CHARLES WESLEY, 1707-1788

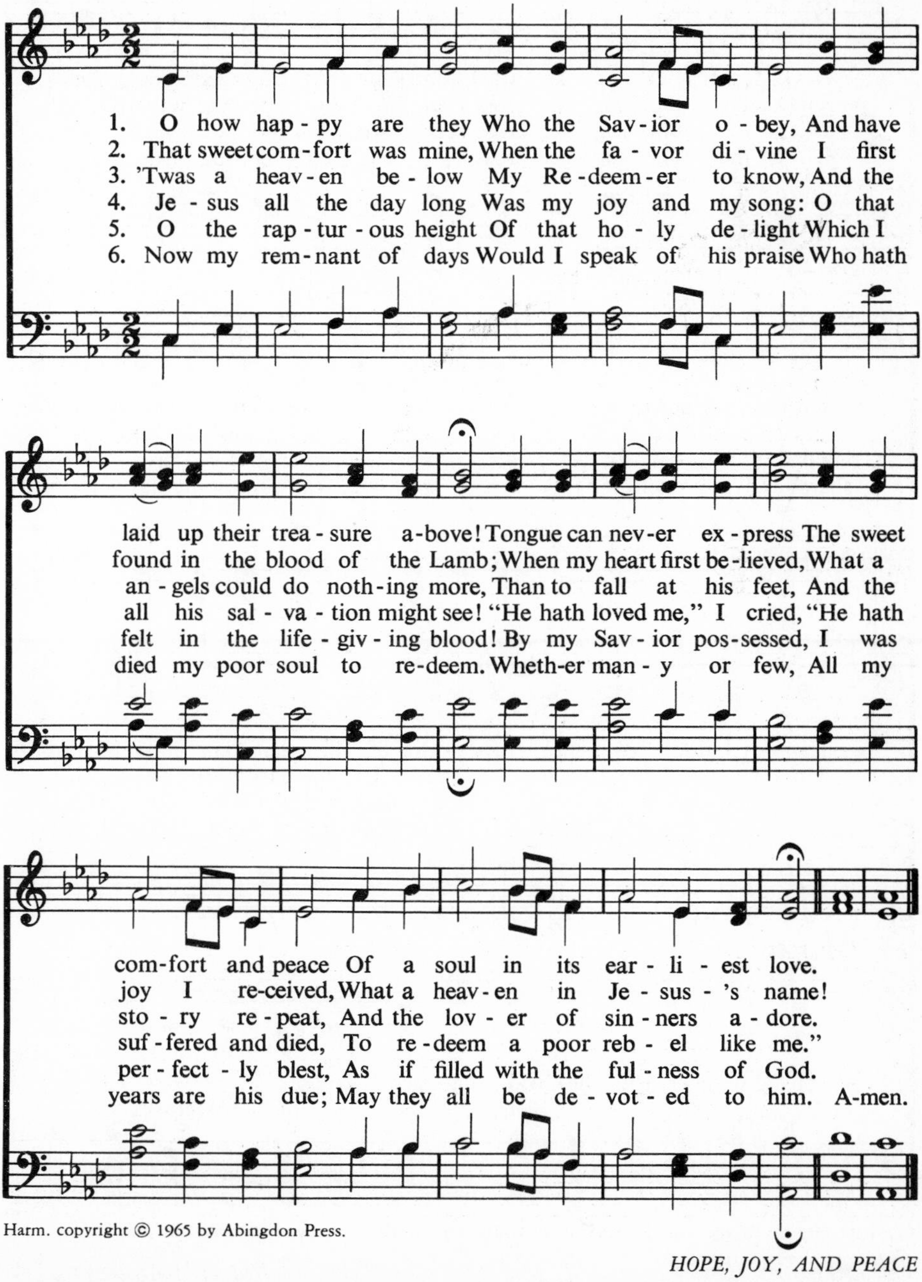
1. O how hap - py are they Who the Sav - ior o - bey, And have
2. That sweet com - fort was mine, When the fa - vor di - vine I first
3. 'Twas a heav - en be - low My Re - deem - er to know, And the
4. Je - sus all the day long Was my joy and my song: O that
5. O the rap - tur - ous height Of that ho - ly de - light Which I
6. Now my rem - nant of days Would I speak of his praise Who hath
laid up their trea - sure a - bove! Tongue can nev - er ex - press The sweet
found in the blood of the Lamb; When my heart first be - lieved, What a
an - gels could do noth - ing more, Than to fall at his feet, And the
all his sal - va - tion might see! "He hath loved me," I cried, "He hath
felt in the life - giv - ing blood! By my Sav - ior pos - sessed, I was
died my poor soul to re - deem. Wheth - er man - y or few, All my
com - fort and peace Of a soul in its ear - li - est love.
joy I re - ceived, What a heav - en in Je - sus - 's name!
sto - ry re - peat, And the lov - er of sin - ners a - dore.
suf - fered and died, To re - deem a poor reb - el like me."
per - fect - ly blest, As if filled with the ful - ness of God.
years are his due; May they all be de - vot - ed to him. A - men.

228

On a Hill Far Away

THE OLD RUGGED CROSS Irregular with Refrain

George Bennard, 1873-1958 George Bennard, 1873-1958

1. On a hill far a - way stood an old rug - ged cross, The
2. O that old rug - ged cross, so de - spised by the world, Has a
3. In the old rug - ged cross, stained with blood so di - vine, A
4. To the old rug - ged cross I will ev - er be true, Its
em-blem of suf-fering and shame; And I love that old cross where the
won-drous at-trac - tion for me; For the dear Lamb of God left his
won - drous beau - ty I see, For 'twas on that old cross Je - sus
shame and re-proach glad - ly bear; Then he'll call me some day to my
dear - est and best For a world of lost sin - ners was slain.
glo - ry a - bove, To bear it to dark Cal - va - ry.
suf - fered and died, To par - don and sanc - ti - fy me.
home far a - way, Where his glo - ry for - ev - er I'll share.
Refrain
So I'll cher - ish the old rug - ged cross, Till my
cross, the old rug - ged cross,

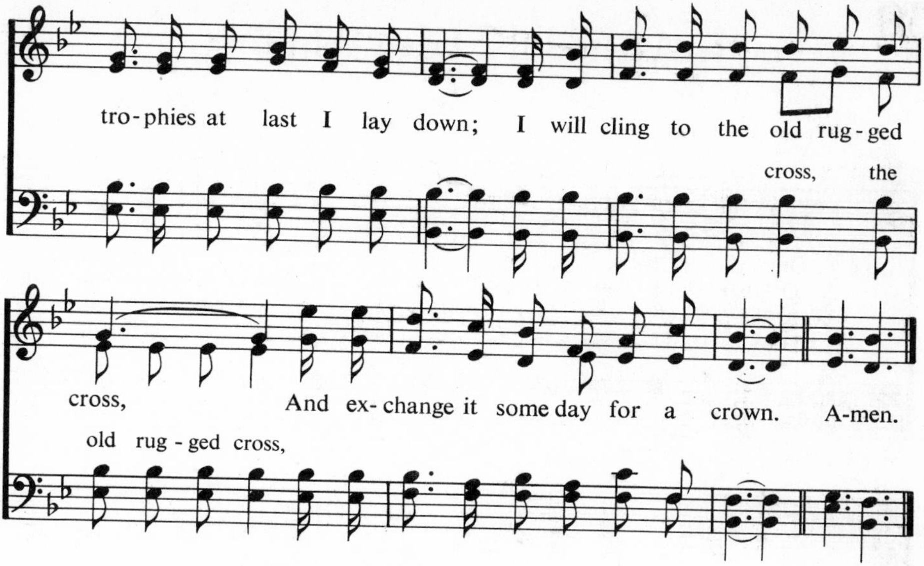
tro-phies at last I lay down; I will cling to the old rug-ged
cross, the
cross, And ex-change it some day for a crown. A-men.
old rug-ged cross,

229

Peace, Perfect Peace

ISAIAH 26:3
EDWARD H. BICKERSTETH, 1825-1906

SONG 46 10.10.
ORLANDO GIBBONS, 1583-1625

1. Peace, per-fect peace, in this dark world of sin? The blood of Je-sus whis-pers peace with-in.
2. Peace, per-fect peace, by throng-ing du-ties pressed? To do the will of Je-sus: this is rest.
3. Peace, per-fect peace, with sor-rows surg-ing round? On Je-sus' bos-om naught but calm is found.
4. Peace, per-fect peace, with loved ones far a-way? In Je-sus' keep-ing we are safe, and they.
5. Peace, per-fect peace, our fu-ture all un-known? Je-sus we know, and he is on the throne.
A-men.

In Heavenly Love Abiding

NYLAND 76.76.D.
Trad. Finnish Melody
Harm. by DAVID EVANS, 1874-1948

PSALM 23
ANNA L. WARING, 1823-1910

1. In heaven-ly love a - bid - ing, No change my heart shall fear;
2. Wher - ev - er he may guide me, No want shall turn me back;
3. Green pas-tures are be - fore me, Which yet I have not seen;
And safe is such con - fid - ing, For noth-ing chan - ges here.
My Shep-herd is be - side me, And noth-ing can I lack.
Bright skies will soon be o'er me, Where dark-est clouds have been.
The storm may roar with - out me, My heart may low be laid;
His wis-dom ev - er wak - eth, His sight is nev - er dim;
My hope I can - not mea - sure, My path to life is free;
But God is round a - bout me, And can I be dis - mayed?
He knows the way he tak - eth, And I will walk with him.
My Sav-ior has my trea - sure, And he will walk with me. A-men.

Music from *The Revised Church Hymnary* by permission of Oxford University Press.

Sometimes a Light Surprises

MATTHEW 6:25-34; HABAKKUK 3:17-18
WILLIAM COWPER, 1731-1800

LLANFYLLIN 76.76.D.
Trad. Welsh Melody

1. Some-times a light sur-pris - es The Chris-tian while he sings; It
2. In ho - ly con-tem-pla - tion We sweet-ly then pur-sue The
3. It can bring with it noth - ing But he will bear us through; Who
4. Though vine nor fig tree nei - ther Their wont-ed fruit should bear, Though
is the Lord, who ris - es With heal-ing in his wings. When
theme of God's sal-va - tion, And find it ev - er new; Set
gives the lil - ies cloth - ing Will clothe his peo-ple, too; Be -
all the field should with - er, Nor flocks nor herds be there; Yet
com-forts are de - clin - ing, He grants the soul a - gain A
free from pres - ent sor - row, We cheer-ful - ly can say, Let
neath the spread-ing heav - ens, No crea-ture but is fed; And
God the same a - bid - ing, His praise shall tune my voice, For
sea-son of clear shin - ing, To cheer it af - ter rain.
the un-known to - mor - row Bring with it what it may.
he who feeds the ra - vens Will give his chil-dren bread.
while in him con - fid - ing, I can-not but re - joice. A-men.

Alternate tune: AURELIA

HOPE, JOY, AND PEACE

232 From Every Stormy Wind That Blows

RETREAT LM

HUGH STOWELL, 1799-1865

THOMAS HASTINGS, 1784-1872

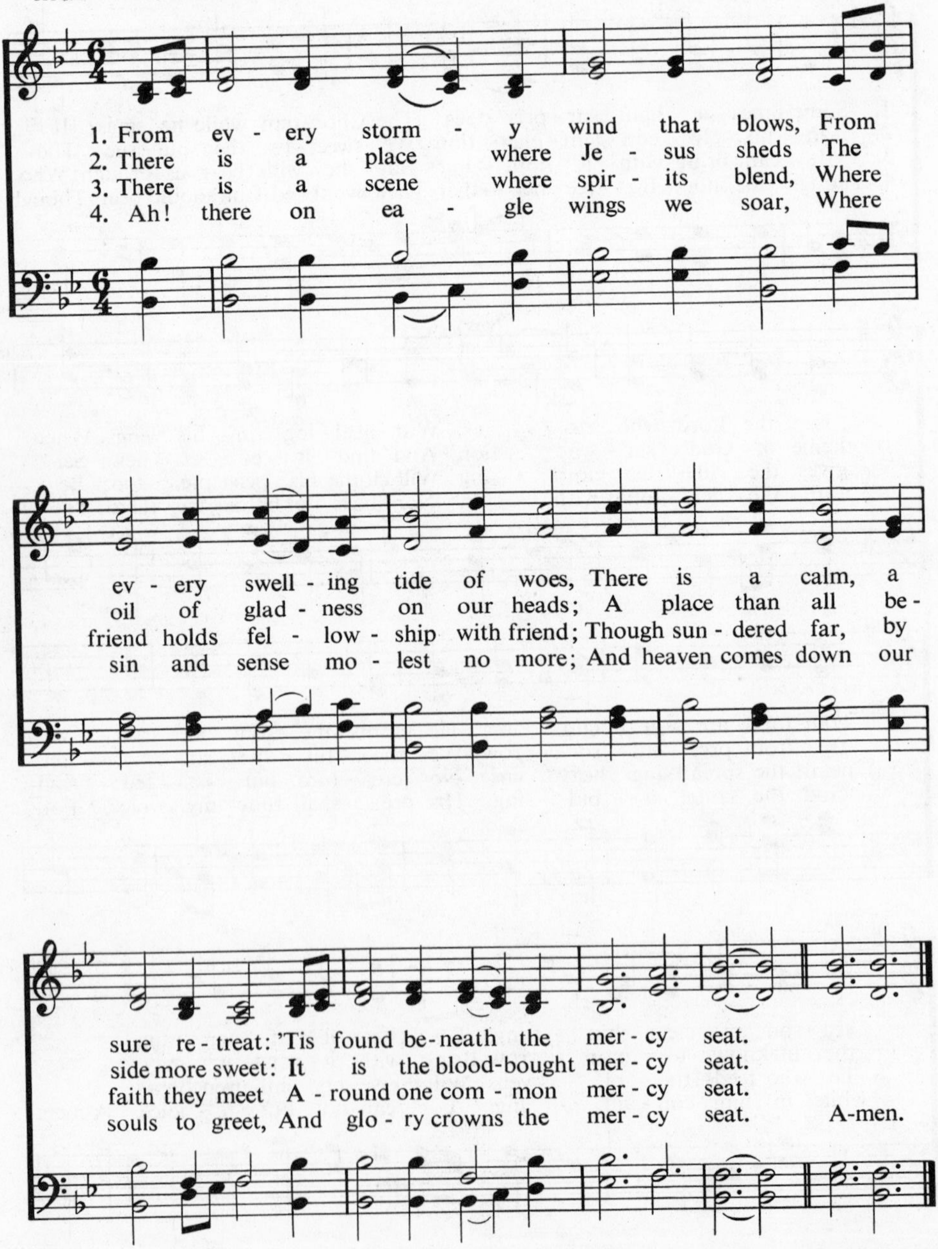
1. From ev - ery storm - y wind that blows, From
2. There is a place where Je - sus sheds The
3. There is a scene where spir - its blend, Where
4. Ah! there on ea - gle wings we soar, Where
ev - ery swell - ing tide of woes, There is a calm, a
oil of glad - ness on our heads; A place than all be -
friend holds fel - low - ship with friend; Though sun - dered far, by
sin and sense mo - lest no more; And heaven comes down our
sure re - treat: 'Tis found be - neath the mer - cy seat.
side more sweet: It is the blood-bought mer - cy seat.
faith they meet A - round one com - mon mer - cy seat.
souls to greet, And glo - ry crowns the mer - cy seat. A-men.

Rejoice, Ye Pure in Heart

PSALMS 20:4; 147:1; PHILIPPIANS 4:4
EDWARD H. PLUMPTRE, 1821-1891

MARION SM with Refrain
ARTHUR H. MESSITER, 1834-1916

1. Re - joice, ye pure in heart; Re - joice, give thanks and sing;
2. Bright youth and snow-crowned age, Strong men and maid - ens fair,
3. With voice as full and strong As o - cean's surg - ing praise,
4. Yes, on through life's long path, Still chant - ing as ye go;
5. Still lift your stan - dard high, Still march in firm ar - ray,
Your glo - rious ban - ner wave on high, The cross of Christ your King.
Raise high your free, ex - ult - ing song, God's won-drous praise de - clare.
Send forth the hymns our fa - thers loved, The psalms of an - cient days.
From youth to age, by night and day, In glad - ness and in woe.
As war - riors through the dark - ness toil Till dawns the gold - en day.
Refrain
Re - joice, re - joice, Re - joice, give thanks and sing. A - men.
Re - joice, re - joice,

234

O Love That Wilt Not Let Me Go

ST. MARGARET 88.886.
ALBERT L. PEACE, 1844-1912

GEORGE MATHESON, 1842-1906

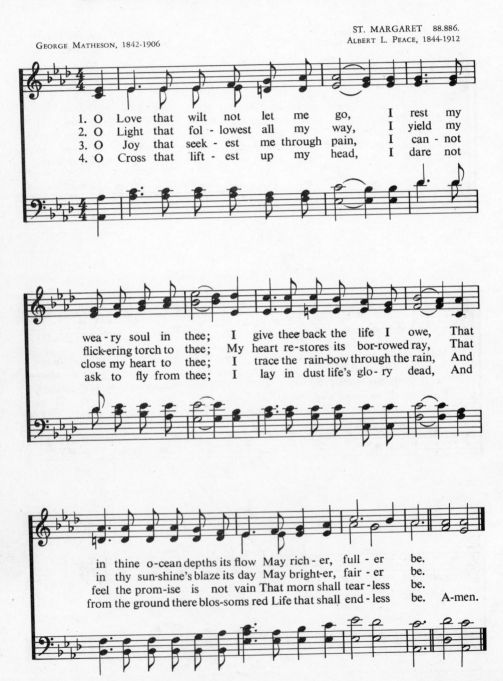

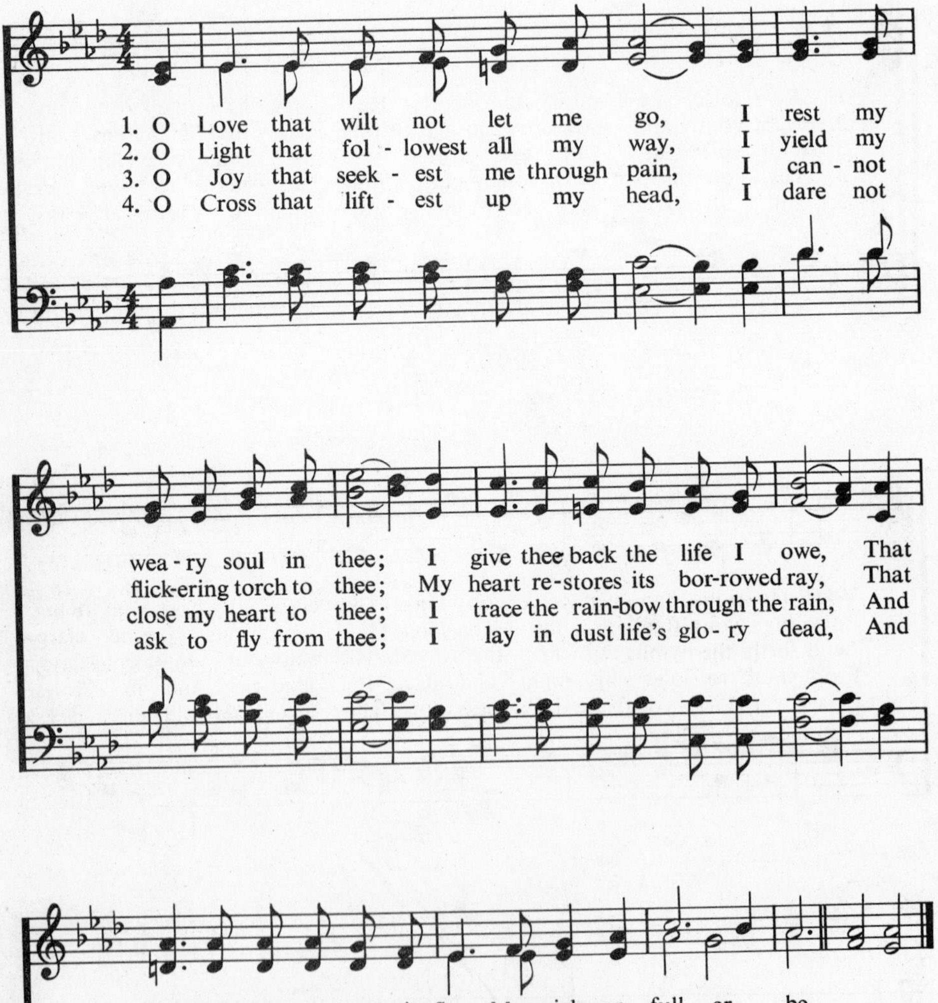
1. O Love that wilt not let me go, I rest my
2. O Light that fol - lowest all my way, I yield my
3. O Joy that seek - est me through pain, I can - not
4. O Cross that lift - est up my head, I dare not
wea - ry soul in thee; I give thee back the life I owe, That
flick-ering torch to thee; My heart re-stores its bor-rowed ray, That
close my heart to thee; I trace the rain-bow through the rain, And
ask to fly from thee; I lay in dust life's glo - ry dead, And
in thine o-cean depths its flow May rich - er, full - er be.
in thy sun-shine's blaze its day May bright-er, fair - er be.
feel the prom-ise is not vain That morn shall tear - less be.
from the ground there blos-soms red Life that shall end - less be. A-men.

Dear Lord and Father of Mankind

JOHN GREENLEAF WHITTIER, 1807-1892

REST 86.886.
FREDERICK C. MAKER, 1844-1927

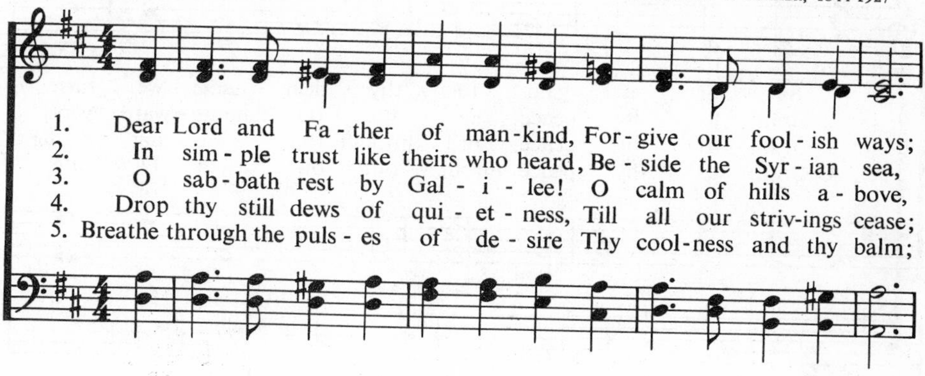
1. Dear Lord and Fa - ther of man-kind, For-give our fool - ish ways;
2. In sim - ple trust like theirs who heard, Be - side the Syr - ian sea,
3. O sab - bath rest by Gal - i - lee! O calm of hills a - bove,
4. Drop thy still dews of qui - et - ness, Till all our striv-ings cease;
5. Breathe through the puls - es of de - sire Thy cool-ness and thy balm;

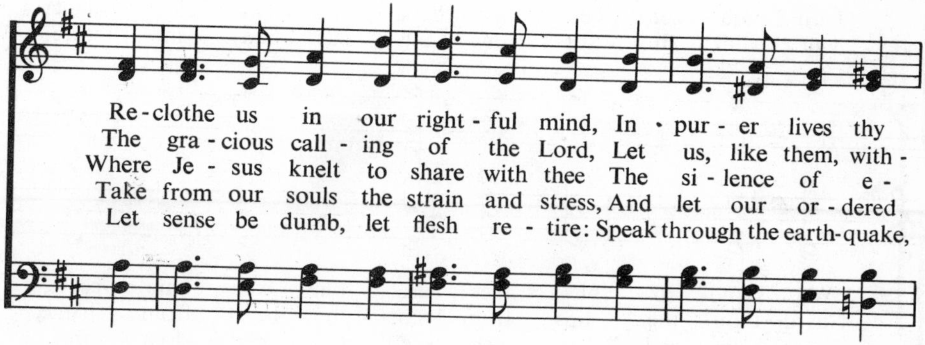
Re - clothe us in our right - ful mind, In pur - er lives thy
The gra - cious call - ing of the Lord, Let us, like them, with -
Where Je - sus knelt to share with thee The si - lence of e -
Take from our souls the strain and stress, And let our or - dered
Let sense be dumb, let flesh re - tire: Speak through the earth-quake,

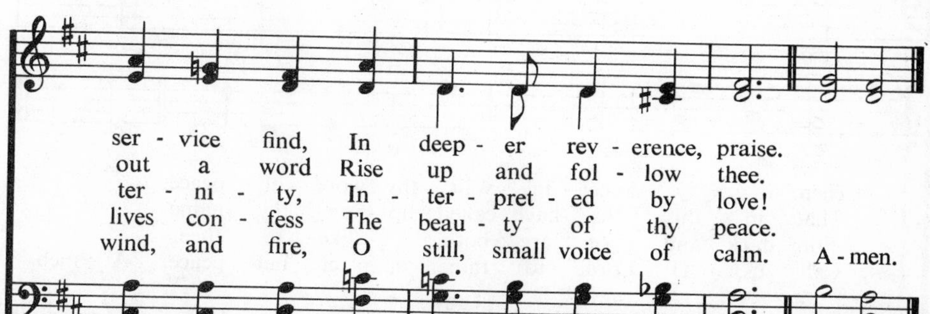
ser - vice find, In deep - er rev - erence, praise.
out a word Rise up and fol - low thee.
ter - ni - ty, In - ter - pret - ed by love!
lives con - fess The beau - ty of thy peace.
wind, and fire, O still, small voice of calm. A - men.

Savior, Again to Thy Dear Name

ELLERS 10 10.10 10.
EDWARD J. HOPKINS, 1818-1901

JOHN ELLERTON, 1826-1893

Unison
1. Sav - ior, a - gain to thy dear name we raise
2. Grant us thy peace up - on our home - ward way;
3. Grant us thy peace, Lord, through the com - ing night;
4. Grant us thy peace through - out our earth - ly life,
With one ac - cord our part - ing hymn of praise;
With thee be - gan, with thee shall end the day.
Turn thou for us its dark - ness in - to light;
Our balm in sor - row, and our stay in strife;
We stand to bless thee ere our wor - ship cease,
Guard thou the lips from sin, the hearts from shame,
From harm and dan - ger keep thy chil - dren free,
Then, when thy voice shall bid our con - flict cease,
Then, low - ly kneel - ing, wait thy word of peace.
That in this house have called up - on thy name.
For dark and light are both a - like to thee.
Call us, O Lord, to thine e - ter - nal peace. A - men.

In the Hour of Trial

Luke 22:32
James Montgomery, 1771-1854
Alt. by Frances A. Hutton, 1811-1877

PENITENCE 65.65.D.
Spencer Lane, 1843-1903

1. In the hour of tri - al, Je - sus, plead for me;
2. With for - bid - den plea - sures Would this vain world charm,
3. Should thy mer - cy send me Sor - row, toil, and woe,
4. When my last hour com - eth, Fraught with strife and pain,
Lest by base de - ni - al, I de - part from thee.
Or its sor - did trea - sures Spread to work me harm;
Or should pain at - tend me On my path be - low,
When my dust re - turn - eth To the dust a - gain,
When thou seest me wa - ver, With a look re - call,
Bring to my re - mem - brance Sad Geth - sem - a - ne,
Grant that I may nev - er Fail thy hand to see:
On thy truth re - ly - ing, Through that mor - tal strife:
Nor for fear or fa - vor Suf - fer me to fall.
Or, in dark - er sem - blance, Cross-crowned Cal - va - ry.
Grant that I may ev - er Cast my care on thee.
Je - sus, take me, dy - ing, To e - ter - nal life. A - men.

COURAGE IN CONFLICT

Christian, Dost Thou See Them

ANDREW OF CRETE, 660-732
Trans. by JOHN M. NEALE, 1818-1866

WALDA 65.65.D.
LLOYD A. PFAUTSCH, 1921-

Unison
1. Chris-tian, dost thou see them On the ho - ly ground,
2. Chris-tian, dost thou feel them, How they work with-in,
3. Chris-tian, dost thou hear them, How they speak thee fair?
4. Well I know thy trou-ble, O my ser - vant true;
How the powers of dark - ness Rage thy steps a - round?
Striv - ing, tempt-ing, lur - ing, Goad-ing in - to sin?
"Al - ways fast and vi - gil? Al - ways watch and prayer?"
Thou art ver - y wea - ry; I was wea - ry too;
Chris-tian, up and smite them, Count - ing gain but loss,
Chris-tian, nev - er trem - ble; Nev - er be down-cast;
Chris-tian, an - swer bold - ly, "While I breathe I pray!"
But that toil shall make thee Some day all mine own,

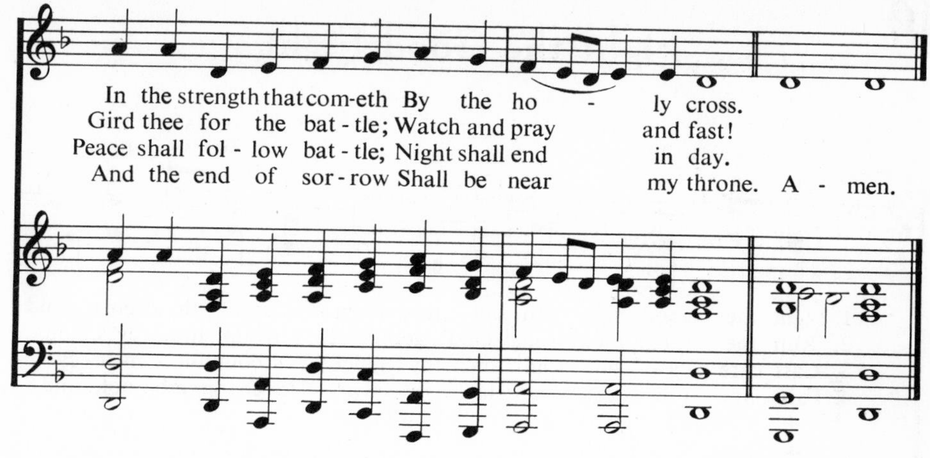
In the strength that com-eth By the ho - ly cross.
Gird thee for the bat - tle; Watch and pray and fast!
Peace shall fol - low bat - tle; Night shall end in day.
And the end of sor - row Shall be near my throne. A - men.

239

Am I a Soldier of the Cross

I Corinthians 16:13
Isaac Watts, 1674-1748

ARLINGTON CM
Thomas A. Arne, 1710-1778

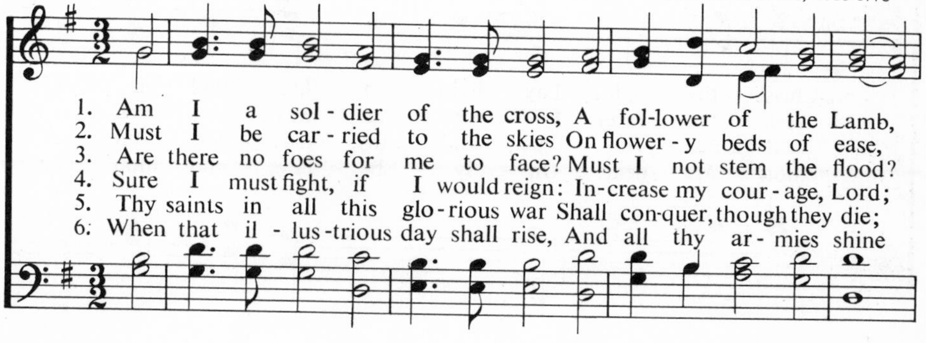
1. Am I a sol - dier of the cross, A fol-lower of the Lamb,
2. Must I be car - ried to the skies On flower - y beds of ease,
3. Are there no foes for me to face? Must I not stem the flood?
4. Sure I must fight, if I would reign: In-crease my cour - age, Lord;
5. Thy saints in all this glo - rious war Shall con-quer, though they die;
6. When that il - lus-trious day shall rise, And all thy ar - mies shine

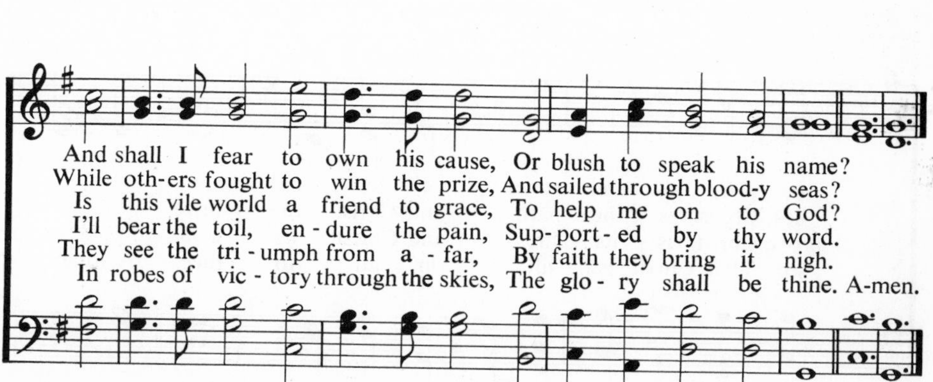
And shall I fear to own his cause, Or blush to speak his name?
While oth-ers fought to win the prize, And sailed through blood-y seas?
Is this vile world a friend to grace, To help me on to God?
I'll bear the toil, en - dure the pain, Sup - port - ed by thy word.
They see the tri - umph from a - far, By faith they bring it nigh.
In robes of vic - tory through the skies, The glo - ry shall be thine. A-men.

Fight the Good Fight

I Timothy 6:12
John S. B. Monsell, 1811-1875

GRACE CHURCH, GANANOQUE LM
Graham George, 1912-

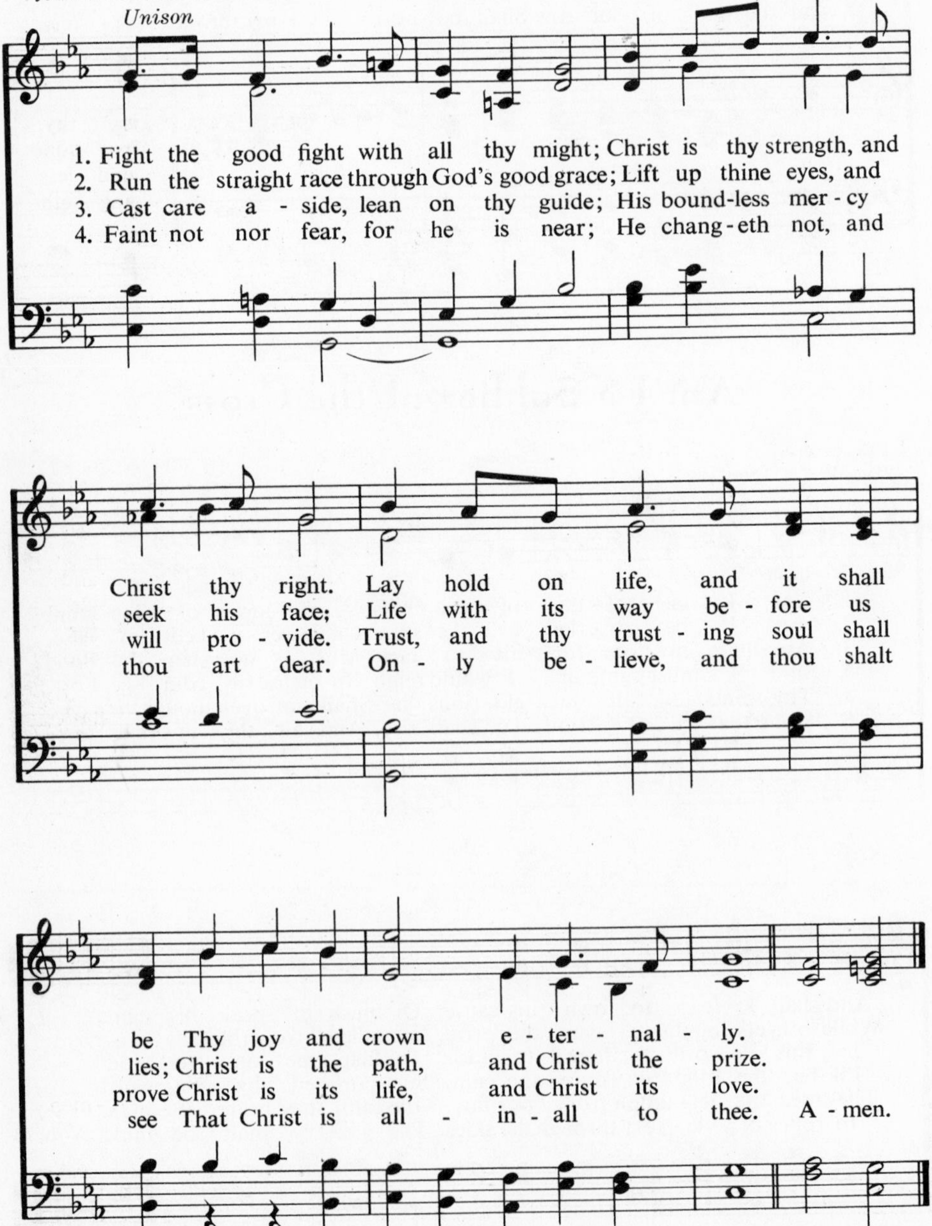
Unison
1. Fight the good fight with all thy might; Christ is thy strength, and
2. Run the straight race through God's good grace; Lift up thine eyes, and
3. Cast care a - side, lean on thy guide; His bound-less mer - cy
4. Faint not nor fear, for he is near; He chang - eth not, and
Christ thy right. Lay hold on life, and it shall
seek his face; Life with its way be - fore us
will pro - vide. Trust, and thy trust - ing soul shall
thou art dear. On - ly be - lieve, and thou shalt
be Thy joy and crown e - ter - nal - ly.
lies; Christ is the path, and Christ the prize.
prove Christ is its life, and Christ its love.
see That Christ is all - in - all to thee. A - men.

241

Fight the Good Fight

I Timothy 6:12
John S. B. Monsell, 1811-1875

PENTECOST LM
William Boyd, 1847-1928

1. Fight the good fight with all thy might; Christ is thy
2. Run the straight race through God's good grace; Lift up thine
3. Cast care a - side, lean on thy guide; His bound - less
4. Faint not nor fear, for he is near; He chang - eth
strength, and Christ thy right. Lay hold on life, and
eyes, and seek his face; Life with its way be -
mer - cy will pro - vide. Trust, and thy trust - ing
not, and thou art dear. On - ly be - lieve, and
it shall be Thy joy and crown e - ter - nal - ly.
fore us lies; Christ is the path, and Christ the prize.
soul shall prove Christ is its life, and Christ its love.
thou shalt see That Christ is all - in - all to thee. A - men.

Once to Every Man and Nation

EBENEZER 87.87.D.

James Russell Lowell, 1819-1891

Thomas J. Williams, 1869-1944

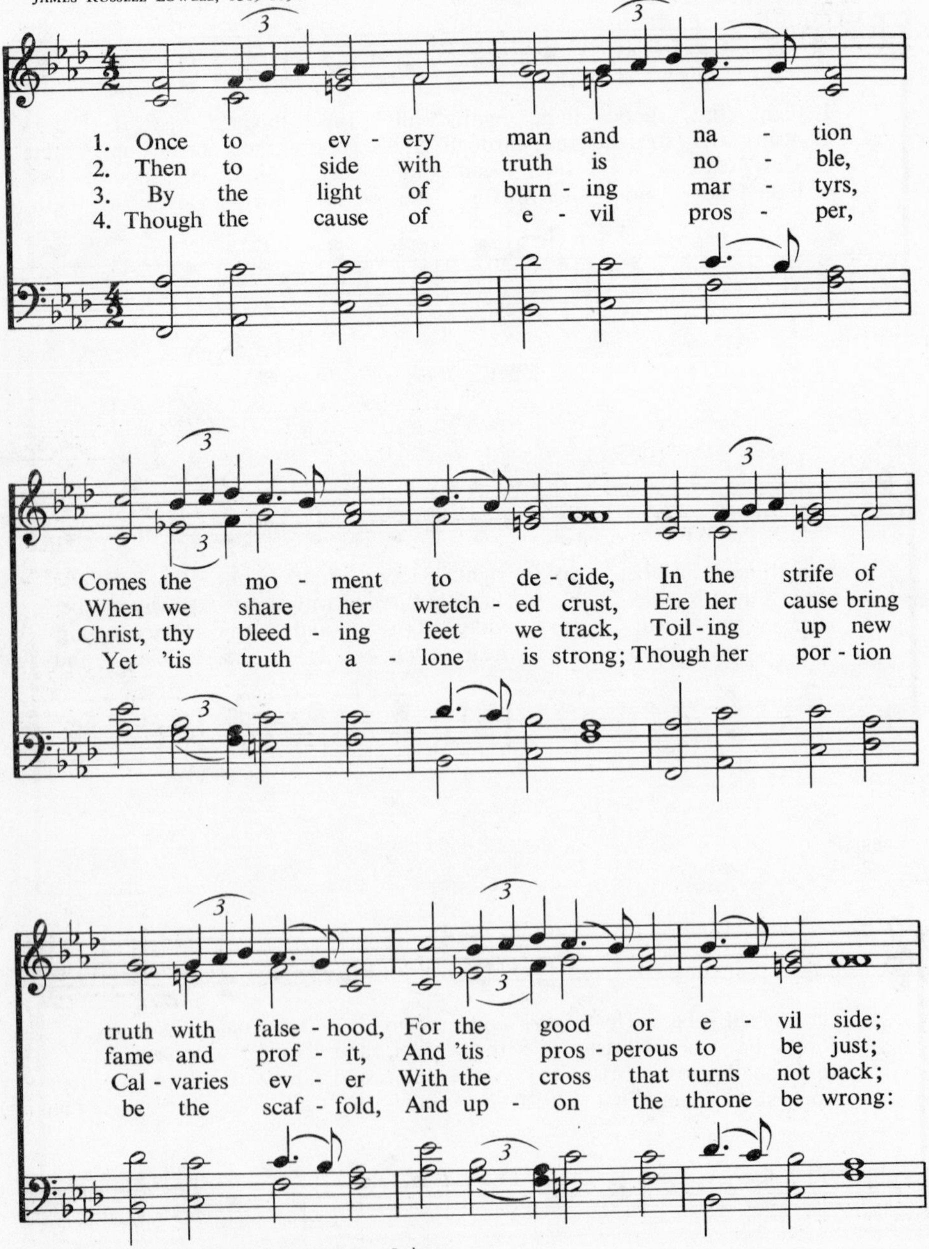
1. Once to ev - ery man and na - tion
2. Then to side with truth is no - ble,
3. By the light of burn - ing mar - tyrs,
4. Though the cause of e - vil pros - per,
Comes the mo - ment to de - cide, In the strife of
When we share her wretch - ed crust, Ere her cause bring
Christ, thy bleed - ing feet we track, Toil - ing up new
Yet 'tis truth a - lone is strong; Though her por - tion
truth with false - hood, For the good or e - vil side;
fame and prof - it, And 'tis pros - perous to be just;
Cal - varies ev - er With the cross that turns not back;
be the scaf - fold, And up - on the throne be wrong:

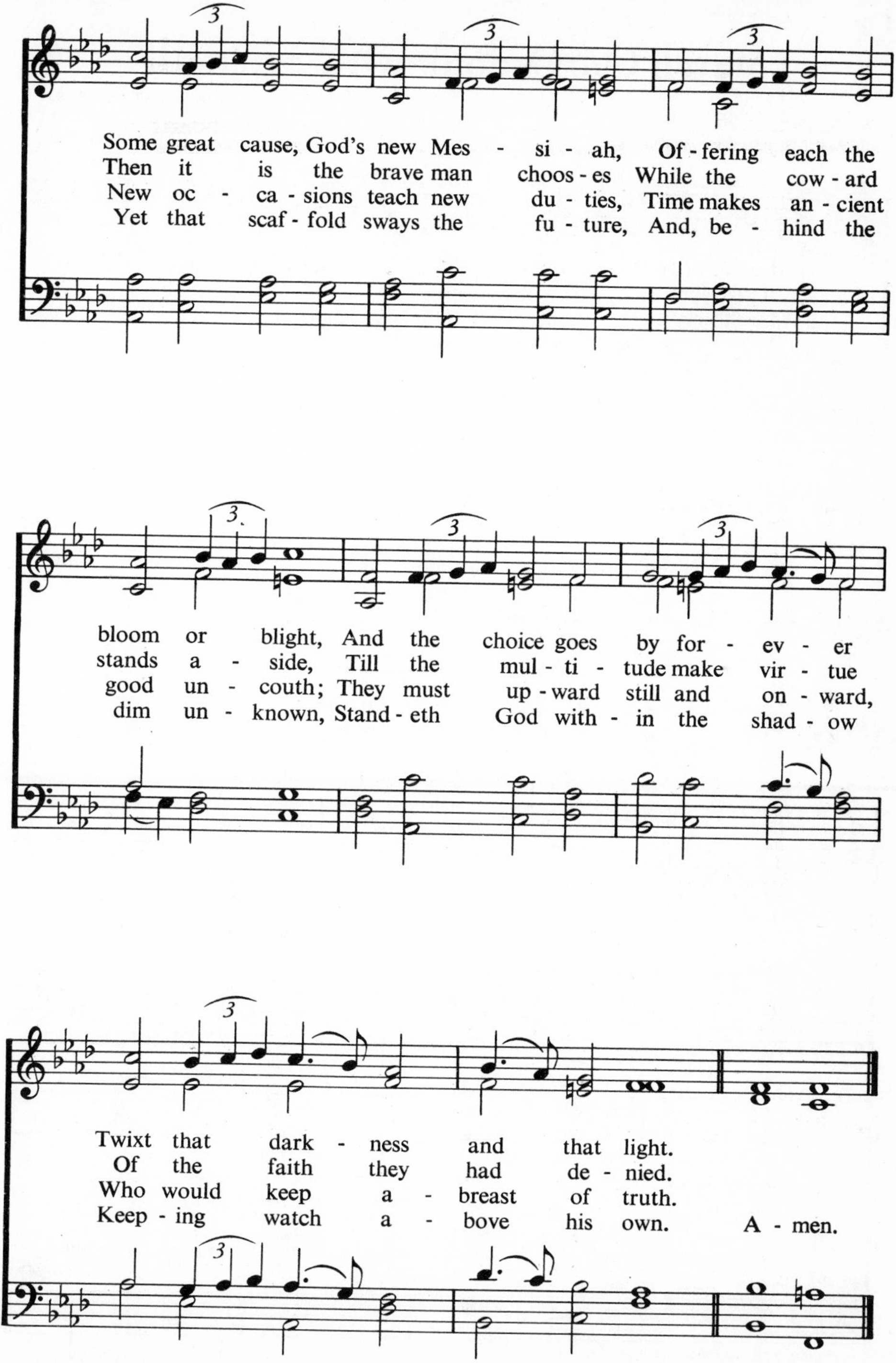
Some great cause, God's new Mes - si - ah, Of - fering each the
Then it is the brave man choos - es While the cow - ard
New oc - ca - sions teach new du - ties, Time makes an - cient
Yet that scaf - fold sways the fu - ture, And, be - hind the
bloom or blight, And the choice goes by for - ev - er
stands a - side, Till the mul - ti - tude make vir - tue
good un - couth; They must up - ward still and on - ward,
dim un - known, Stand - eth God with - in the shad - ow
Twixt that dark - ness and that light.
Of the faith they had de - nied.
Who would keep a - breast of truth.
Keep - ing watch a - bove his own. A - men.

March On, O Soul, with Strength

ARTHUR'S SEAT 66.66.88.
Arr. from JOHN GOSS, 1800-1880
by UZZIAH C. BURNAP, 1834-1900

JUDGES 5:21
GEORGE T. COSTER, 1835-1912

1. March on, O soul, with strength! Like those strong men of old
2. The sons of fa - thers we By whom our faith is taught
3. March on, O soul, with strength, As strong the bat - tle rolls!
4. Not long the con - flict, soon The ho - ly war shall cease,
Who gainst en - thron - ed wrong Stood con - fi - dent and
To fear no ill, to fight The ho - ly fight they
Gainst lies and lusts and wrongs, Let cour - age rule our
Faith's war - fare end - ed, won The home of end - less
bold; Who, thrust in prison or cast to flame, Still
fought: He - ro - ic war - riors, ne'er from Christ By
souls: In keen - est strife, Lord, may we stand, Up -
peace! Look up! the vic - tor's crown at length! March
made their glo - ry in thy name.
an - y lure or guile en - ticed.
held and strength - ened by thy hand.
on, O soul, march on, with strength! A - men.

When the Storms of Life Are Raging

STAND BY ME 83.83.77.83.

CHARLES A. TINDLEY, 1856-1933

CHARLES A. TINDLEY, 1856-1933
Arr. by DANIEL L. RIDOUT, 1898-

1. When the storms of life are ra - ging, Stand by me; When the
2. In the midst of trib - u - la - tion, Stand by me; In the
3. In the midst of faults and fail - ures, Stand by me; In the
4. When I'm grow - ing old and fee - ble, Stand by me; When I'm
storms of life are ra - ging, Stand by me. When the
midst of trib - u - la - tion, Stand by me. When the
midst of faults and fail - ures, Stand by me. When I've
grow - ing old and fee - ble, Stand by me. When my
world is toss - ing me Like a ship up - on the sea, Thou who
hosts of sin as - sail, And my strength be - gins to fail, Thou who
done the best I can, And my friends mis - un - der - stand, Thou who
life be - comes a bur - den, And I'm near - ing chill - y Jor - dan, O thou
rul - est wind and wa - ter, Stand by me.
nev - er lost a bat - tle, Stand by me.
know - est all a - bout me, Stand by me.
Lil - y of the Val - ley, Stand by me. A - men.

245

O Sometimes the Shadows Are Deep

PSALM 61:2
ERASTUS JOHNSON, 1826-1909

THE ROCK OF REFUGE 88.88. with Refrain
WILLIAM G. FISCHER, 1835-1912

1. O some-times the shad-ows are deep, And rough seems the path to the goal, And sor-rows, some-times how they sweep Like tem-pests down o-ver the soul!
2. O some-times how long seems the day, And some-times how wea-ry my feet; But toil-ing in life's dust-y way, The Rock's bless-ed shad-ow, how sweet!
3. O near to the Rock let me keep If bless-ings or sor-rows pre-vail, Or climb-ing the moun-tain way steep, Or walk-ing the shad-ow-y vale.
Refrain
O then to the Rock let me fly, let me fly, To the

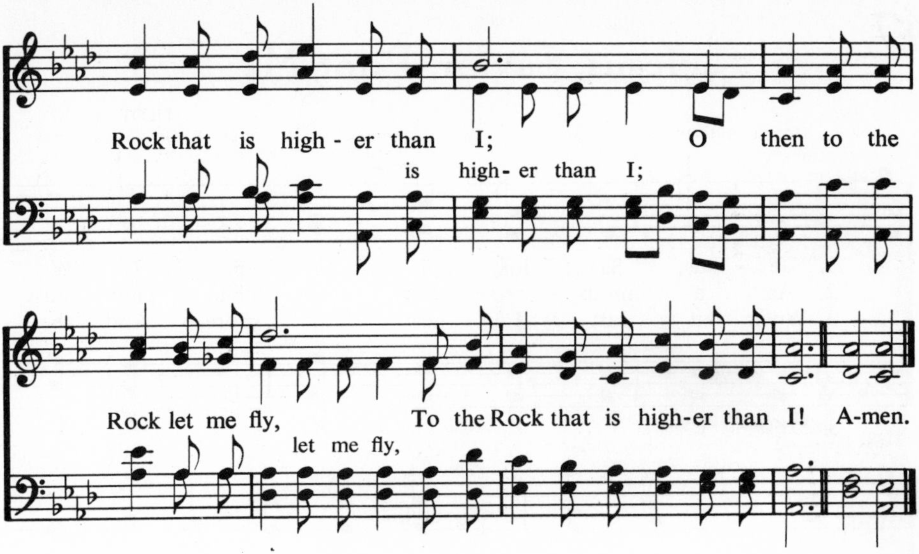
Rock that is high - er than I; O then to the
is high- er than I;
Rock let me fly, To the Rock that is high-er than I! A-men.
let me fly,

246

My Soul, Be on Thy Guard

LABAN SM

GEORGE HEATH, 1750-1822

LOWELL MASON, 1792-1872

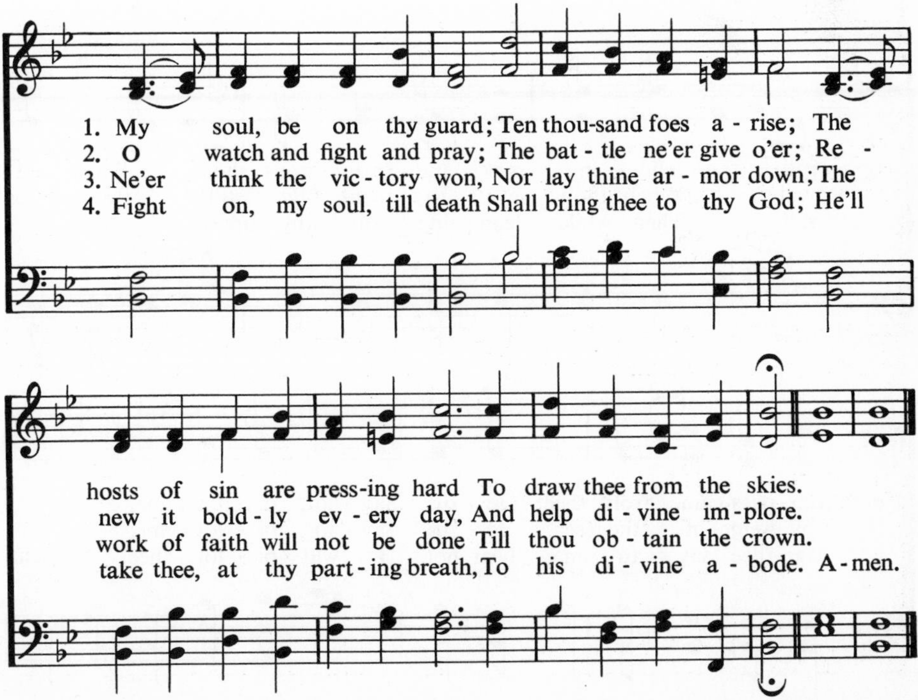
1. My soul, be on thy guard; Ten thou-sand foes a - rise; The
2. O watch and fight and pray; The bat - tle ne'er give o'er; Re -
3. Ne'er think the vic - tory won, Nor lay thine ar - mor down; The
4. Fight on, my soul, till death Shall bring thee to thy God; He'll
hosts of sin are press-ing hard To draw thee from the skies.
new it bold - ly ev - ery day, And help di - vine im - plore.
work of faith will not be done Till thou ob - tain the crown.
take thee, at thy part - ing breath, To his di - vine a - bode. A - men.

Jesus, Savior, Pilot Me

PILOT 77.77.77.

EDWARD HOPPER, 1816-1888 — JOHN E. GOULD, 1822-1875

3
1. Je - sus, Sav - ior, pi - lot me O - ver
2. As a moth - er stills her child, Thou canst
3. When at last I near the shore, And the
3
life's tem - pes - tuous sea; Un - known waves be - fore me
hush the o - cean wild; Bois - terous waves o - bey thy
fear - ful break - ers roar 'Twixt me and the peace - ful
roll, Hid - ing rock and treach-erous shoal; Chart and
will When thou sayest to them, "Be still!" Won-drous
rest, Then, while lean - ing on thy breast, May I
3
com - pass came from thee: Je - sus, Sav - ior, pi - lot me.
sov-ereign of the sea, Je - sus, Sav - ior, pi - lot me.
hear thee say to me, "Fear not, I will pi - lot thee." A - men.
3

Stand Up, Stand Up for Jesus

Ephesians 6:10-17
George Duffield, Jr., 1818-1888

WEBB 76.76.D.
George J. Webb, 1803-1887

1. Stand up, stand up for Je - sus, Ye sol - diers of the cross;
2. Stand up, stand up for Je - sus, The trum - pet call o - bey;
3. Stand up, stand up for Je - sus, Stand in his strength a - lone;
4. Stand up, stand up for Je - sus, The strife will not be long;
Lift high his roy - al ban - ner, It must not suf - fer loss;
Forth to the might - y con - flict, In this his glo - rious day;
The arm of flesh will fail you, Ye dare not trust your own;
This day the noise of bat - tle, The next, the vic - tor's song;
From vic - tory un - to vic - tory His ar - my shall he lead,
Ye that are men now serve him A - gainst un-num-bered foes;
Put on the gos - pel ar - mor, Each piece put on with prayer;
To him that o - ver - com - eth, A crown of life shall be;
Till ev - ery foe is van-quished, And Christ is Lord in - deed.
Let cour-age rise with dan - ger, And strength to strength op-pose.
Where du - ty calls or dan - ger, Be nev - er want - ing there.
He with the King of glo - ry Shall reign e - ter - nal - ly. A - men.

249 Awake, My Soul, Stretch Every Nerve

CHRISTMAS CM
WEYMAN'S *Melodia Sacra*, 1815
Arr. from GEORGE FREDERICK HANDEL, 1685-1759

PHILIPPIANS 3:12-14
PHILIP DODDRIDGE, 1702-1751

1. A - wake, my soul, stretch ev - ery nerve, And
2. A cloud of wit - ness - es a - round Holds
3. 'Tis God's all - an - i - mat - ing voice That
4. Blest Sav - ior, in - tro - duced by thee, Have

press with vig - or on; A heaven - ly race de - mands thy zeal,
thee in full sur - vey; For - get the steps al - read - y trod,
calls thee from on high; 'Tis his own hand pre - sents the prize
I my race be - gun; And, crowned with vic - tory, at thy feet

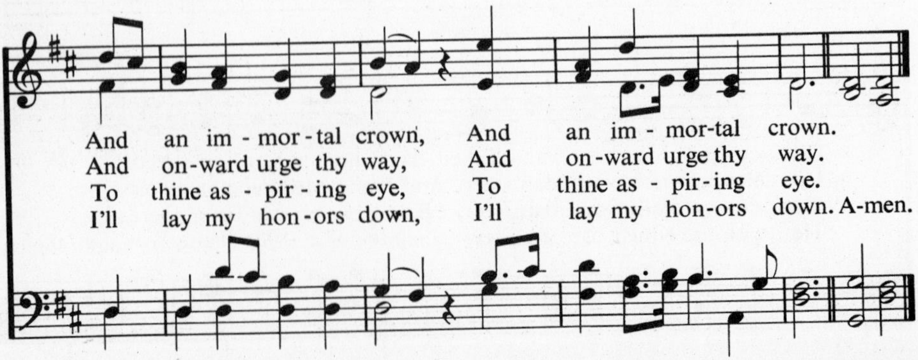
And an im - mor - tal crown, And an im - mor - tal crown.
And on - ward urge thy way, And on - ward urge thy way.
To thine as - pir - ing eye, To thine as - pir - ing eye.
I'll lay my hon - ors down, I'll lay my hon - ors down. A - men.

Soldiers of Christ, Arise

EPHESIANS 6:10-20
CHARLES WESLEY, 1707-1788

DIADEMATA SMD
GEORGE J. ELVEY, 1816-1893

1. Sol-diers of Christ, a-rise, And put your ar-mor on, Strong
2. Stand, then, in his great might, With all his strength en-dued; But
3. From strength to strength go on, Wres-tle and fight and pray; Tread
in the strength which God sup-plies Through his e-ter-nal Son;
take, to arm you for the fight, The pan-o-ply of God:
all the powers of dark-ness down, And win the well-fought day.
Strong in the Lord of hosts, And in his might-y power, Who
That, hav-ing all things done, And all your con-flicts passed, Ye
Still let the Spir-it cry, In all his sol-diers, "Come!" Till
in the strength of Je-sus trusts Is more than con-quer-or.
may o'er-come through Christ a-lone, And stand en-tire at last.
Christ the Lord de-scends from high, And takes the con-querors home. A-men.

251

Jesus, I My Cross Have Taken

ELLESDIE 87.87.D.

MARK 10:28 — *The Christian Lyre*, 1831

HENRY F. LYTE, 1793-1847 — Harm. by A. C. L.

1. Je - sus, I my cross have tak - en, All to leave and
2. Let the world de - spise and leave me; They have left my
3. Man may trou - ble and dis - tress me, 'Twill but drive me
4. Haste thee on from grace to glo - ry, Armed by faith and
fol - low thee; Des - ti - tute, de - spised, for - sak - en,
Sav - ior, too. Hu - man hearts and looks de - ceive me;
to thy breast; Life with tri - als hard may press me;
winged by prayer; Heaven's e - ter - nal day's be - fore thee,
Thou, from hence, my all shalt be. Per - ish ev - ery
Thou art not, like man, un - true. And, while thou shalt
Heaven will bring me sweet - er rest. O 'tis not in
God's own hand shall guide thee there. Soon shall close thy
fond am - bi - tion, All I've sought or hoped or known; Yet how rich is
smile up - on me, God of wis - dom, love, and might, Foes may hate, and
grief to harm me While thy love is left to me; O 'twere not in
earth - ly mis - sion; Swift shall pass thy pil - grim days; Hope shall change to

my con - di - tion: God and heaven are still my own!
friends may shun me; Show thy face, and all is bright.
joy to charm me, Were that joy un - mixed with thee.
glad fru - i - tion, Faith to sight, and prayer to praise. A - men.

252

Prayer Is the Soul's Sincere Desire

James Montgomery, 1771-1854

SHADDICK CM
Bates G. Burt, 1878-1948

1. Prayer is the soul's sin-cere de - sire, Un - ut - tered or ex-pressed, The
2. Prayer is the bur - den of a sigh, The fall - ing of a tear, The
3. Prayer is the sim - plest form of speech That in - fant lips can try; Prayer
4. Prayer is the con - trite sin-ner's voice, Re-turn - ing from his ways, While
5. Prayer is the Chris-tian's vi - tal breath, The Chris-tian's na-tive air, His
6. O Thou, by whom we come to God, The Life, the Truth, the Way; The

mo - tion of a hid - den fire That trem-bles in the breast.
up - ward glanc - ing of an eye, When none but God is near.
the sub - lim - est strains that reach The Ma - jes - ty on high.
an - gels in their songs re - joice And cry, "Be - hold, he prays!"
watch-word at the gates of death; He en - ters heaven with prayer.
path of prayer thy - self hast trod: Lord, teach us how to pray! A-men.

Jesus, My Strength, My Hope

ICH HALTE TREULICH STILL SMD

CHARLES WESLEY, 1707-1788

J. S. BACH, 1685-1750

1. Je - sus, my strength, my hope, On thee I cast my
2. I want a so - ber mind, A self - re - nounc - ing
3. I want a god - ly fear, A quick dis - cern - ing
4. I want a true re - gard, A sin - gle stead - y
care, With hum - ble con - fi - dence look up, And
will That tram - ples down and casts be - hind The
eye That looks to thee when sin is near, And
aim, Un - moved by threaten - ing or re - ward, To
know thou hearest my prayer. Give me on thee to wait,
baits of pleas - ing ill; A soul in - ured to pain,
sees the temp - ter fly; A spir - it still pre - pared,
thee and thy great name; A jeal - ous, just con - cern
Till I can all things do, On thee, al - might - y
To hard - ship, grief, and loss, Bold to take up, firm
And armed with jeal - ous care, For - ev - er stand - ing
For thine, im - mor - tal praise; A pure de - sire that

to cre - ate, Al - might - y to re - new.
to sus - tain The con - se - cra - ted cross.
on its guard, And watch - ing un - to prayer.
all may learn And glo - ri - fy thy grace. A-men.

Alternate tune: DIADEMATA

254

Dear Master, in Whose Life I See

HURSLEY LM

JOHN HUNTER, 1848-1917 — Adapt. from *Katholisches Gesangbuch*, Vienna, c. 1774

1. Dear Mas - ter, in whose life I see All that I
2. Though what I dream and what I do In my weak
would, but fail to be, Let thy clear light for -
days are al - ways two, Help me, op - pressed by
ev - er shine, To shame and guide this life of mine.
things un - done, O thou, whose deeds and dreams were one! A-men.

255 As Pants the Hart for Cooling Streams

Psalm 42 *New Version*
Tate and Brady, 1696
Alt. by Henry F. Lyte, 1793-1847

AYRSHIRE CM
Kenneth G. Finlay, 1882-

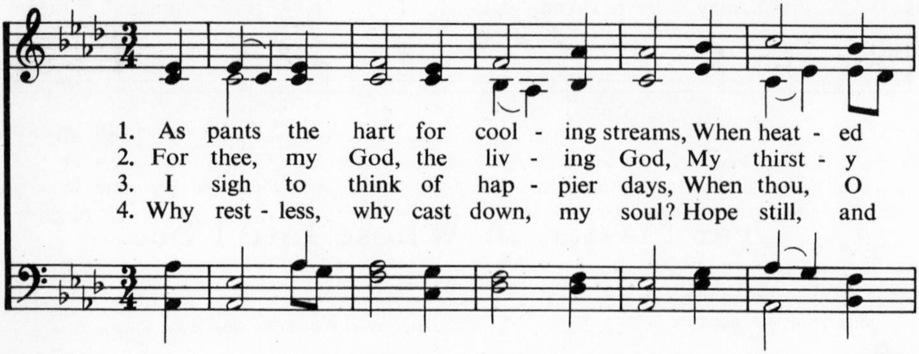
1. As pants the hart for cool - ing streams, When heat - ed
2. For thee, my God, the liv - ing God, My thirst - y
3. I sigh to think of hap - pier days, When thou, O
4. Why rest - less, why cast down, my soul? Hope still, and

in the chase, So longs my soul, O God, for
soul doth pine; O when shall I be - hold thy
Lord, wast nigh; When ev - ery heart was tuned to
thou shalt sing The praise of him who is thy

thee And thy re - fresh - ing grace.
face, Thou Maj - es - ty di - vine!
praise, And none more blest than I.
God, Thy Sav - ior, and thy King. A - men.

Music used by permission of Kenneth G. Finlay.

Be Thou My Vision

Ancient Irish
Trans. by MARY E. BYRNE, 1880-1931
Versed by ELEANOR H. HULL, 1860-1935

SLANE 10 10.9 10.
Trad. Irish Melody
Harm. by C. R. Y.

Unison
1. Be thou my Vi-sion, O Lord of my heart; Naught be all
2. Be thou my Wis-dom, and thou my true Word; I ev-er
3. Rich-es I heed not, nor man's emp-ty praise; Thou mine in-
4. High King of heav-en, my vic-to-ry won, May I reach

else to me, save that thou art; Thou my best thought, by day or by
with thee and thou with me, Lord; Thou my great Fa-ther, and I thy true
her-i-tance, now and al-ways; Thou and thou on-ly, first in my
heav-en's joys, O bright heaven's Sun! Heart of my own heart, what-ev-er be-

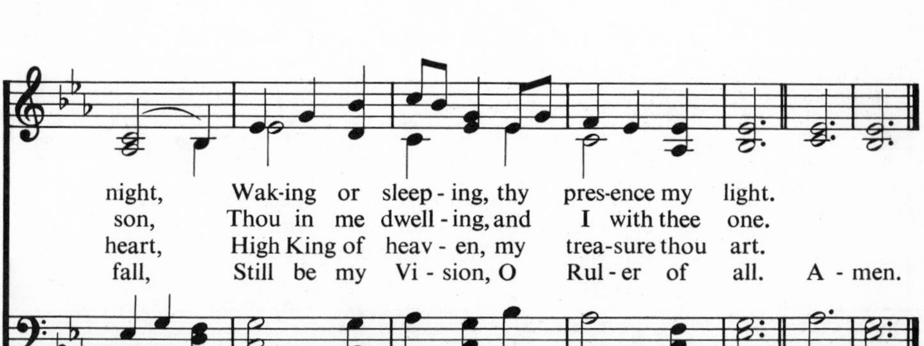
night, Wak-ing or sleep-ing, thy pres-ence my light.
son, Thou in me dwell-ing, and I with thee one.
heart, High King of heav-en, my trea-sure thou art.
fall, Still be my Vi-sion, O Rul-er of all. A-men.

257

Blessed Jesus, at Thy Word

TOBIAS CLAUSNITZER, 1619-1684
Trans. by CATHERINE WINKWORTH, 1827-1878

LIEBSTER JESU 78.78.88.
JOHANN R. AHLE, 1625-1673

1. Bless - ed Je - sus, at thy word We are gath - ered
2. All our knowl - edge, sense, and sight Lie in deep - est
3. Glo - rious Lord, thy - self im - part! Light of light, from
all to hear thee; Let our hearts and souls be stirred
dark - ness shroud - ed, Till thy spir - it breaks our night
God pro - ceed - ing, O - pen thou our ears and heart;
Now to seek and love and fear thee, By thy teach - ings
With the beams of truth un - cloud - ed. Thou a - lone to
Help us by thy spir - it's plead - ing; Hear the cry thy
sweet and ho - ly, Drawn from earth to love thee sole - ly.
God canst win us; Thou must work all good with - in us.
peo - ple rais - es; Hear, and bless our prayers and prais - es. A-men.

Come, My Soul, Thou Must Be Waking

FRIEDRICH R. L. VON CANITZ, 1654-1699
Trans. by HENRY J. BUCKOLL, 1803-1871

HAYDN 847.847.
Arr. from FRANZ JOSEPH HAYDN, 1732-1809
Harm. by A. C. L.

1. Come, my soul, thou must be wak - ing; Now is
2. Glad - ly hail the sun re - turn - ing; Read - y
3. Pray that he may pros - per ev - er Each en -
4. Our God's boun - teous gifts a - buse not, Light re -
break - ing O'er the earth an - oth - er day.
burn - ing Be the in - cense of thy powers;
deav - or, When thine aim is good and true;
fuse not, But his Spir - it's voice o - bey;
Come to him who made this splen - dor; See thou
For the night is safe - ly end - ed; God hath
But that he may ev - er thwart thee, And con -
Thou with him shalt dwell, be - hold - ing Light en -
ren - der All thy fee - ble strength can pay.
tend - ed With his care thy help - less hours.
vert thee, When thou e - vil wouldst pur - sue.
fold - ing All things in un - cloud - ed day. A - men.

259

Jesus, Thy Boundless Love to Me

PAUL GERHARDT, 1607-1676
Trans. by JOHN WESLEY, 1703-1791

ST. CATHERINE 88.88.88.
HENRI F. HEMY, 1818-1888
Adapt. by JAMES G. WALTON, 1821-1905

1. Je - sus, thy bound - less love to me No thought can reach, no
2. O Love, how cheer - ing is thy ray! All fear be - fore thy
3. In suf - fering be thy love my peace; In weak - ness be thy
tongue de - clare; O knit my thank - ful heart to thee,
pres - ence flies; Care, an - guish, sor - row, melt a - way,
love my power; And when the storms of life shall cease,
And reign with - out a ri - val there! Thine whol - ly, thine a -
Wher - e'er thy heal - ing beams a - rise: O Je - sus, noth - ing
O Je - sus, in that sol - emn hour, In death as life be
lone, I'd live, My - self to thee en - tire - ly give.
may I see, Noth - ing de - sire, or seek, but thee!
thou my guide, And save me, who for me hast died. A - men.

O Gracious Father of Mankind

260

HENRY H. TWEEDY, 1868-1953

LLANGLOFFAN CMD
Trad. Welsh Melody
Hymnau a Thonau, 1865

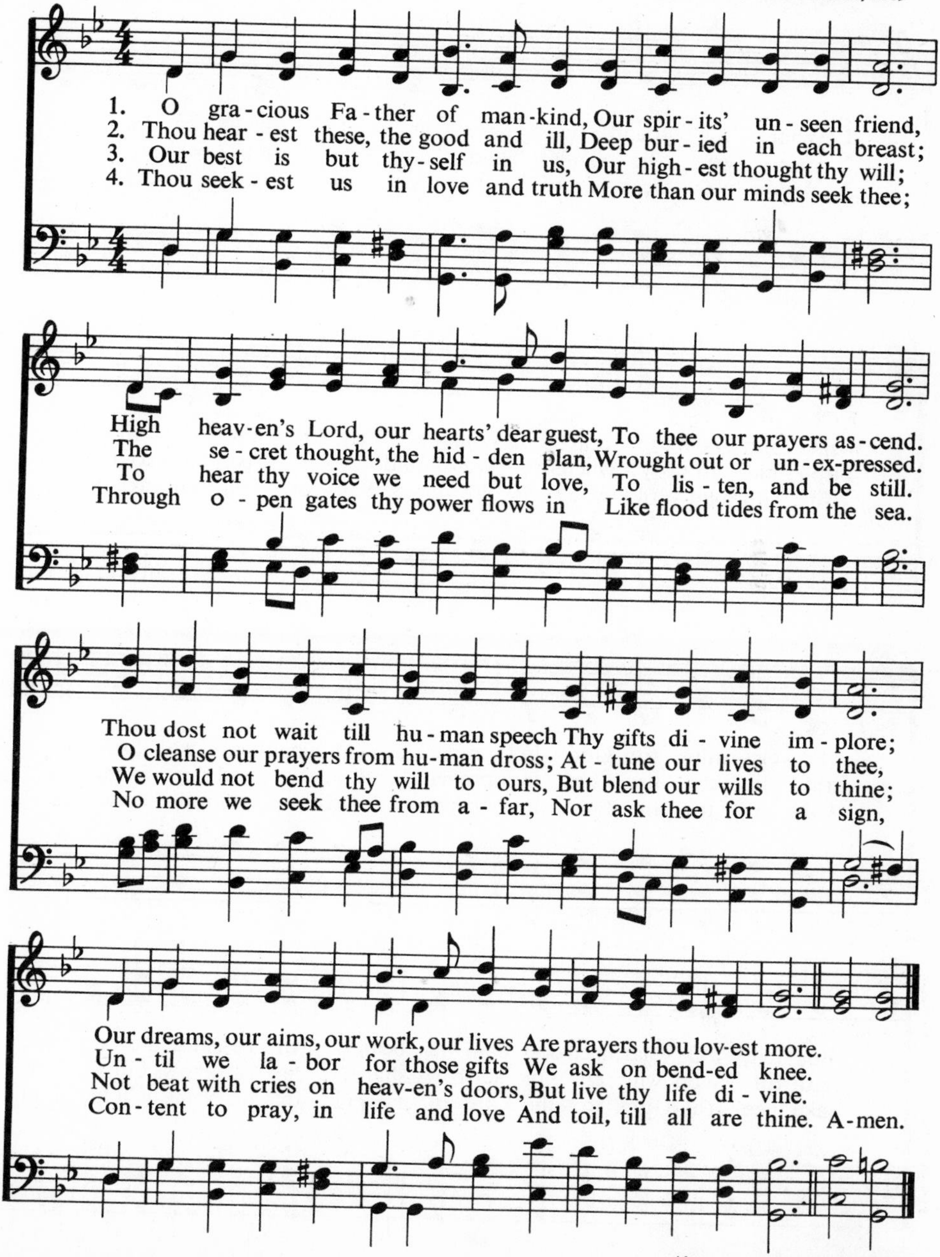

1. O gra-cious Fa-ther of man-kind, Our spir-its' un-seen friend,
2. Thou hear-est these, the good and ill, Deep bur-ied in each breast;
3. Our best is but thy-self in us, Our high-est thought thy will;
4. Thou seek-est us in love and truth More than our minds seek thee;
High heav-en's Lord, our hearts' dear guest, To thee our prayers as-cend.
The se-cret thought, the hid-den plan, Wrought out or un-ex-pressed.
To hear thy voice we need but love, To lis-ten, and be still.
Through o-pen gates thy power flows in Like flood tides from the sea.
Thou dost not wait till hu-man speech Thy gifts di-vine im-plore;
O cleanse our prayers from hu-man dross; At-tune our lives to thee,
We would not bend thy will to ours, But blend our wills to thine;
No more we seek thee from a-far, Nor ask thee for a sign,
Our dreams, our aims, our work, our lives Are prayers thou lov-est more.
Un-til we la-bor for those gifts We ask on bend-ed knee.
Not beat with cries on heav-en's doors, But live thy life di-vine.
Con-tent to pray, in life and love And toil, till all are thine. A-men.

Alternate tune: ST. MICHEL'S

What a Friend We Have in Jesus

CONVERSE 87.87.D.

JOSEPH M. SCRIVEN, 1820-1886

CHARLES C. CONVERSE, 1832-1918

1. What a friend we have in Je - sus, All our
2. Have we tri - als and temp - ta - tions? Is there
3. Are we weak and heav - y la - den, Cum - bered
sins and griefs to bear! What a priv - i - lege to car - ry
trou - ble an - y - where? We should nev - er be dis - cour - aged;
with a load of care? Pre - cious Sav - ior, still our ref - uge:
Ev - ery - thing to God in prayer! O what peace we of - ten
Take it to the Lord in prayer. Can we find a friend so
Take it to the Lord in prayer. Do thy friends de - spise, for -
for - feit, O what need - less pain we bear, All be - cause we do not
faith - ful Who will all our sor - rows share? Je - sus knows our ev - ery
sake thee? Take it to the Lord in prayer! In his arms he'll take and

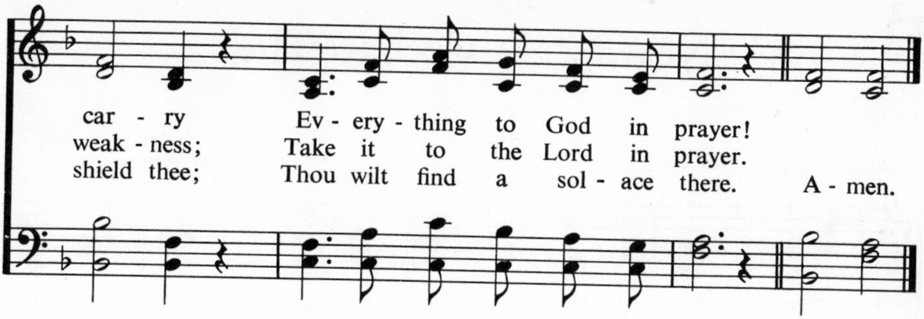
car - ry Ev - ery - thing to God in prayer!
weak - ness; Take it to the Lord in prayer.
shield thee; Thou wilt find a sol - ace there. A - men.

262

Talk with Us, Lord

GRÄFENBERG CM
JOHANN CRÜGER, 1598-1662
Praxis Pietatis Melica, Berlin, 1653

CHARLES WESLEY, 1707-1788

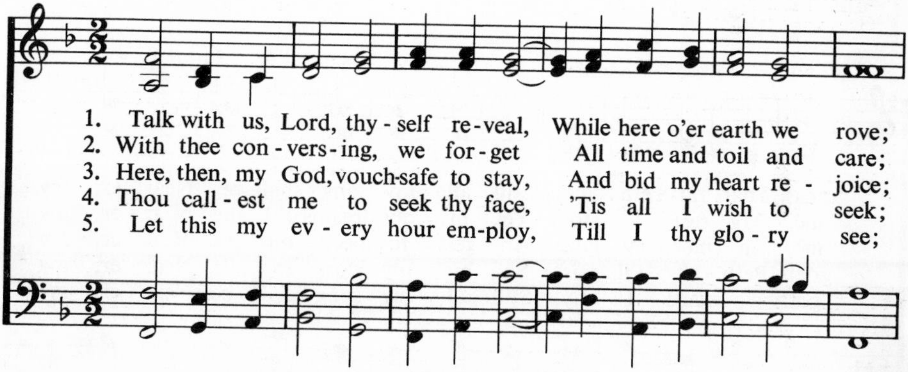
1. Talk with us, Lord, thy - self re - veal, While here o'er earth we rove;
2. With thee con - vers - ing, we for - get All time and toil and care;
3. Here, then, my God, vouch-safe to stay, And bid my heart re - joice;
4. Thou call - est me to seek thy face, 'Tis all I wish to seek;
5. Let this my ev - ery hour em - ploy, Till I thy glo - ry see;

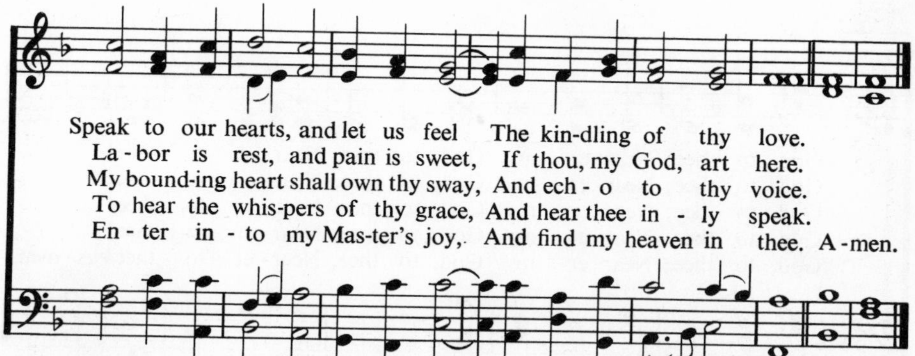
Speak to our hearts, and let us feel The kin - dling of thy love.
La - bor is rest, and pain is sweet, If thou, my God, art here.
My bound - ing heart shall own thy sway, And ech - o to thy voice.
To hear the whis - pers of thy grace, And hear thee in - ly speak.
En - ter in - to my Mas - ter's joy, And find my heaven in thee. A - men.

Nearer, My God, to Thee

GENESIS 28:10-22
SARAH F. ADAMS, 1805-1848

BETHANY 64.64.6664.
LOWELL MASON, 1792-1872

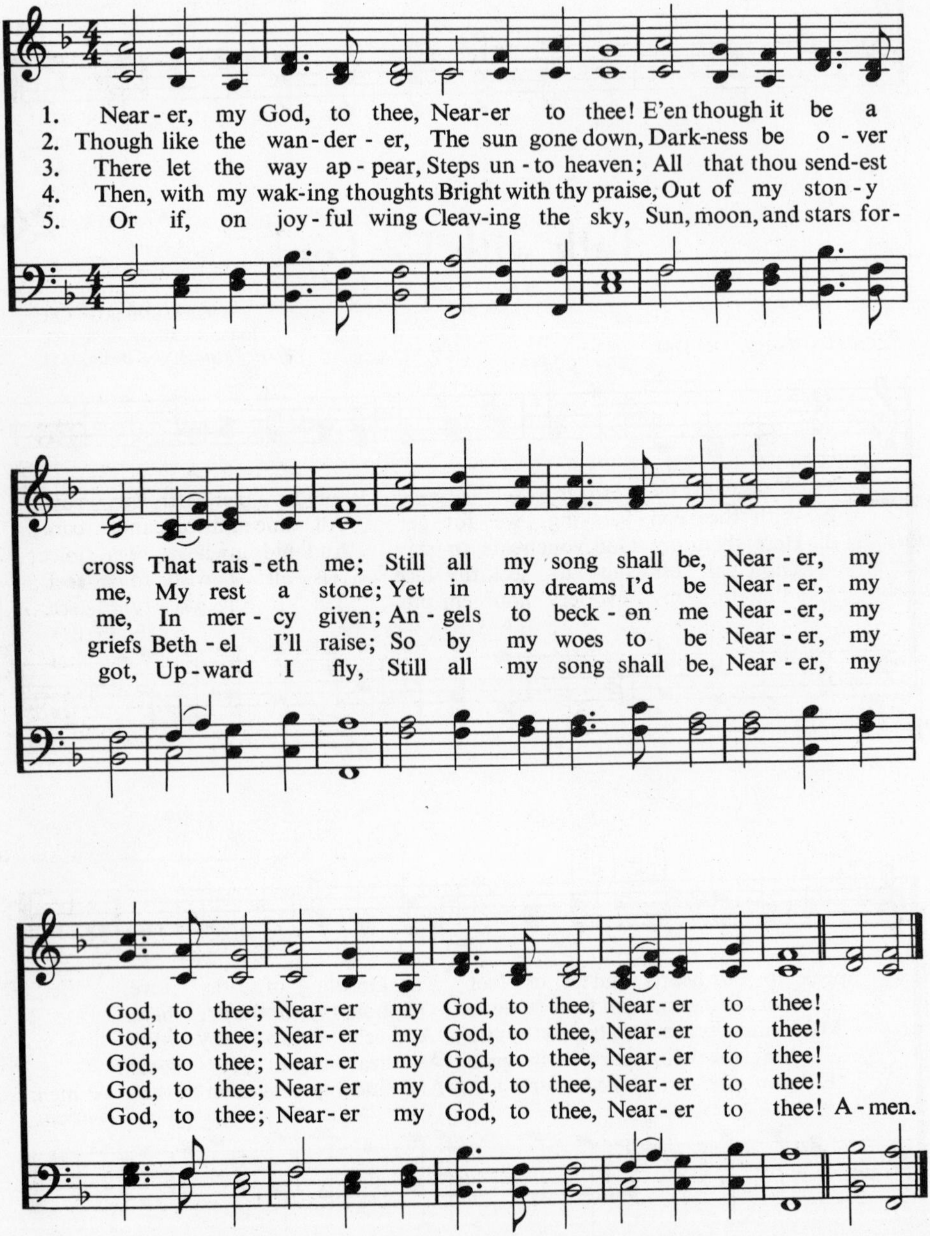
1. Near-er, my God, to thee, Near-er to thee! E'en though it be a
2. Though like the wan-der-er, The sun gone down, Dark-ness be o-ver
3. There let the way ap-pear, Steps un-to heaven; All that thou send-est
4. Then, with my wak-ing thoughts Bright with thy praise, Out of my ston-y
5. Or if, on joy-ful wing Cleav-ing the sky, Sun, moon, and stars for-
cross That rais-eth me; Still all my song shall be, Near-er, my
me, My rest a stone; Yet in my dreams I'd be Near-er, my
me, In mer-cy given; An-gels to beck-on me Near-er, my
griefs Beth-el I'll raise; So by my woes to be Near-er, my
got, Up-ward I fly, Still all my song shall be, Near-er, my
God, to thee; Near-er my God, to thee, Near-er to thee!
God, to thee; Near-er my God, to thee, Near-er to thee!
God, to thee; Near-er my God, to thee, Near-er to thee!
God, to thee; Near-er my God, to thee, Near-er to thee!
God, to thee; Near-er my God, to thee, Near-er to thee! A-men.

Still, Still with Thee

Psalm 139:18
Harriet B. Stowe, 1812-1896

CONSOLATION 11 10.11 10.
Arr. from Felix Mendelssohn, 1809-1847

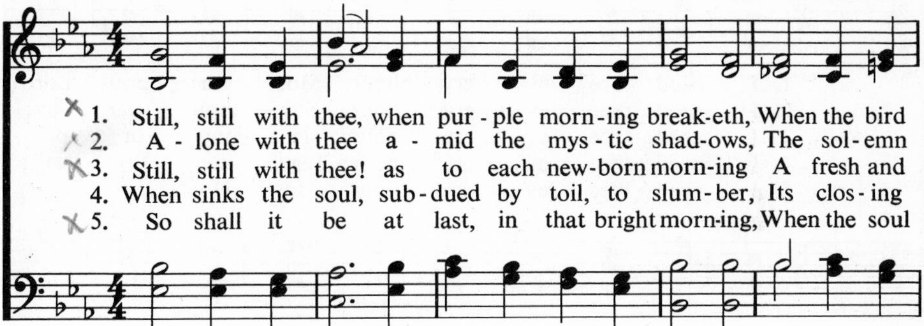
1. Still, still with thee, when pur - ple morn - ing break - eth, When the bird
2. A - lone with thee a - mid the mys - tic shad - ows, The sol - emn
3. Still, still with thee! as to each new - born morn - ing A fresh and
4. When sinks the soul, sub - dued by toil, to slum - ber, Its clos - ing
5. So shall it be at last, in that bright morn - ing, When the soul

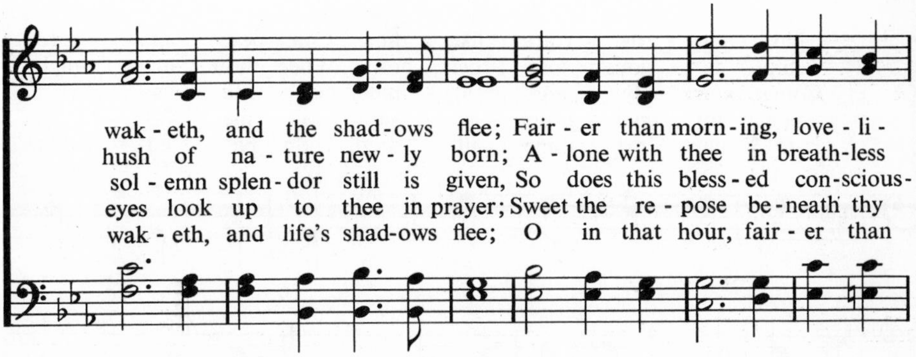
wak - eth, and the shad - ows flee; Fair - er than morn - ing, love - li -
hush of na - ture new - ly born; A - lone with thee in breath - less
sol - emn splen - dor still is given, So does this bless - ed con - scious -
eyes look up to thee in prayer; Sweet the re - pose be - neath thy
wak - eth, and life's shad - ows flee; O in that hour, fair - er than

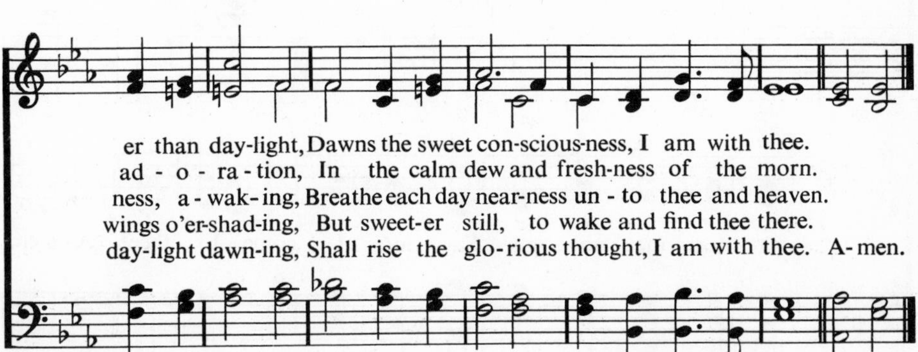
er than day - light, Dawns the sweet con - scious - ness, I am with thee.
ad - o - ra - tion, In the calm dew and fresh - ness of the morn.
ness, a - wak - ing, Breathe each day near - ness un - to thee and heaven.
wings o'er - shad - ing, But sweet - er still, to wake and find thee there.
day - light dawn - ing, Shall rise the glo - rious thought, I am with thee. A - men.

I Need Thee Every Hour

John 15:5
Annie S. Hawks, 1835-1918

NEED 64.64. with Refrain
Robert Lowry, 1826-1899

1. I need thee ev - ery hour, Most gra - cious Lord;
2. I need thee ev - ery hour; Stay thou near by;
3. I need thee ev - ery hour, In joy or pain;
4. I need thee ev - ery hour; Teach me thy will;
5. I need thee ev - ery hour, Most Ho - ly One;
No ten - der voice like thine Can peace af - ford.
Temp - ta - tions lose their power When thou art nigh.
Come quick - ly and a - bide, Or life is vain.
And thy rich prom - is - es In me ful - fill.
O make me thine in - deed, Thou bless - ed Son.
Refrain
I need thee, O I need thee, Ev - ery hour I need thee;
O bless me now, my Sav - ior, I come to thee! A - men.

Take Time to Be Holy

I PETER 1:16
WILLIAM D. LONGSTAFF, 1822-1894

HOLINESS 65.65.D.
GEORGE C. STEBBINS, 1846-1945

1. Take time to be ho - ly, Speak oft with thy Lord;
2. Take time to be ho - ly, The world rush - es on;
3. Take time to be ho - ly, Let him be thy guide,
4. Take time to be ho - ly, Be calm in thy soul,
A - bide in him al - ways, And feed on his Word;
Spend much time in se - cret With Je - sus a - lone;
And run not be - fore him, What - ev - er be - tide;
Each thought and each mo - tive Be - neath his con - trol;
Make friends of God's chil - dren, Help those who are weak,
By look - ing to Je - sus, Like him thou shalt be;
In joy or in sor - row, Still fol - low the Lord,
Thus led by his spir - it To foun - tains of love,
For - get - ting in noth - ing His bless - ing to seek.
Thy friends in thy con - duct His like - ness shall see.
And, look - ing to Je - sus, Still trust in his Word.
Thou soon shalt be fit - ted For ser - vice a - bove.
A - men.

Open My Eyes, That I May See

OPEN MY EYES 88.98. with Refrain

CLARA H. SCOTT, 1841-1897 | CLARA H. SCOTT, 1841-1897

1. O - pen my eyes, that I may see Glimps-es of truth thou
2. O - pen my ears, that I may hear Voic - es of truth thou
3. O - pen my mouth, and let me bear Glad - ly the warm truth
hast for me; Place in my hands the
send - est clear; And while the wave - notes
ev - ery - where; O - pen my heart and
won - der - ful key That shall un - clasp and set me free.
fall on my ear, Ev - ery - thing false will dis - ap - pear.
let me pre - pare Love with thy chil - dren thus to share.
Refrain
Si - lent - ly now I wait for thee, Read - y, my God thy will to see;
Si - lent - ly now I wait for thee, Read - y, my God thy will to see;
Si - lent - ly now I wait for thee, Read - y, my God thy will to see;

O - pen my eyes, il - lu - mine me, Spir - it di - vine!
O - pen my ears, il - lu - mine me, Spir - it di - vine!
O - pen my heart, il - lu - mine me, Spir - it di - vine! A-men.

268

O For a Closer Walk with God

NAOMI CM

Genesis 5:24
William Cowper, 1731-1800

Johann G. Nägeli, 1768-1836
Harm. by C. R. Y.

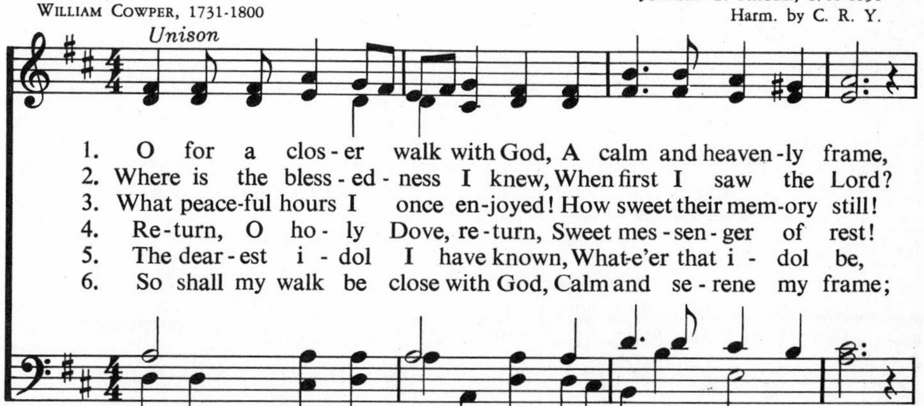
Unison
1. O for a clos - er walk with God, A calm and heaven - ly frame,
2. Where is the bless - ed - ness I knew, When first I saw the Lord?
3. What peace-ful hours I once en-joyed! How sweet their mem-ory still!
4. Re - turn, O ho - ly Dove, re - turn, Sweet mes - sen - ger of rest!
5. The dear - est i - dol I have known, What-e'er that i - dol be,
6. So shall my walk be close with God, Calm and se - rene my frame;

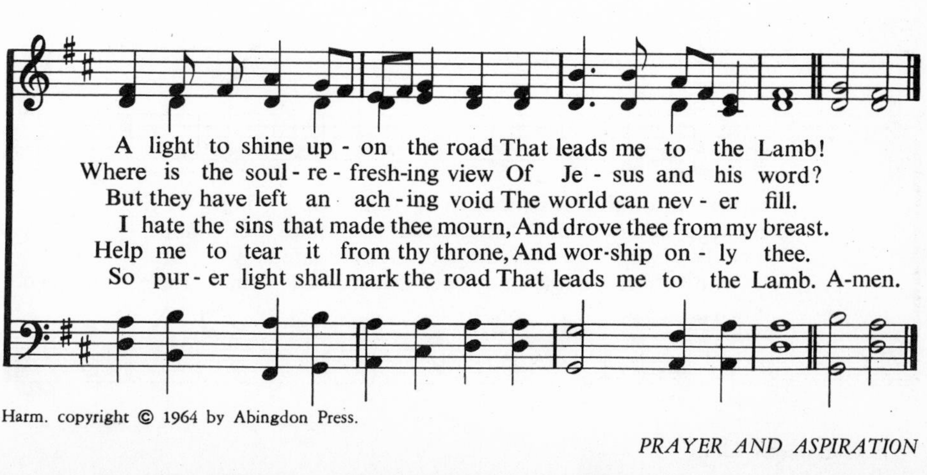
A light to shine up - on the road That leads me to the Lamb!
Where is the soul - re - fresh-ing view Of Je - sus and his word?
But they have left an ach - ing void The world can nev - er fill.
I hate the sins that made thee mourn, And drove thee from my breast.
Help me to tear it from thy throne, And wor-ship on - ly thee.
So pur - er light shall mark the road That leads me to the Lamb. A-men.

269

Lead Us, O Father

WILLIAM H. BURLEIGH, 1812-1871

LANGRAN 10 10.10 10.
JAMES LANGRAN, 1835-1909

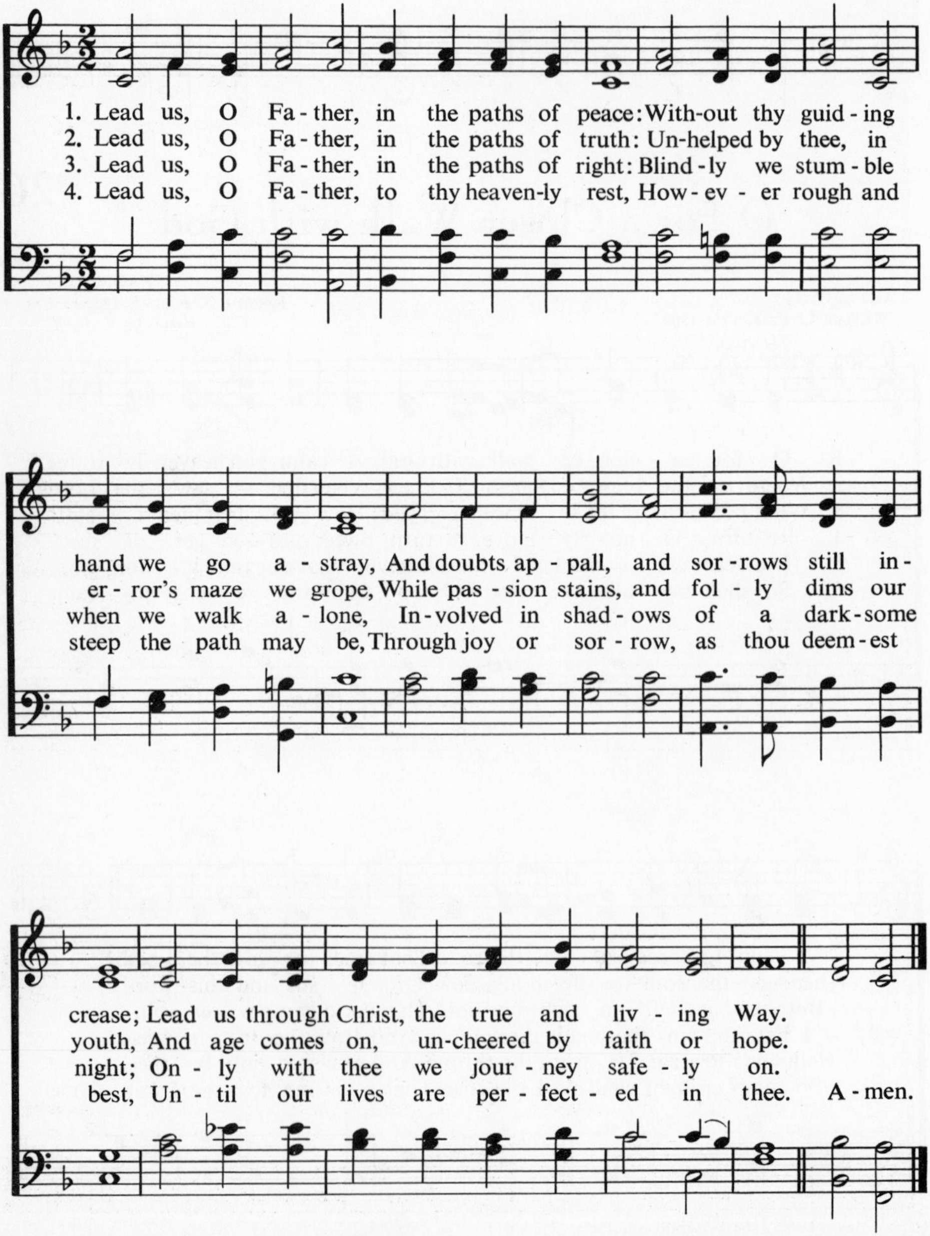
1. Lead us, O Fa-ther, in the paths of peace: With-out thy guid-ing
2. Lead us, O Fa-ther, in the paths of truth: Un-helped by thee, in
3. Lead us, O Fa-ther, in the paths of right: Blind-ly we stum-ble
4. Lead us, O Fa-ther, to thy heaven-ly rest, How-ev-er rough and
hand we go a-stray, And doubts ap-pall, and sor-rows still in-
er-ror's maze we grope, While pas-sion stains, and fol-ly dims our
when we walk a-lone, In-volved in shad-ows of a dark-some
steep the path may be, Through joy or sor-row, as thou deem-est
crease; Lead us through Christ, the true and liv-ing Way.
youth, And age comes on, un-cheered by faith or hope.
night; On-ly with thee we jour-ney safe-ly on.
best, Un-til our lives are per-fect-ed in thee. A-men.

O Love Divine, That Stooped to Share 270

Oliver W. Holmes, 1809-1894

HESPERUS LM
Henry Baker, 1835-1910

1. O Love di - vine, that stooped to share Our sharp - est
2. Though long the wea - ry way we tread, And sor - row
3. When droop - ing plea - sure turns to grief, And trem - bling
4. On thee we fling our bur-dening woe, O Love di -
pang, our bit - terest tear, On thee we cast each earth-born
crown each lin - gering year, No path we shun, no dark - ness
faith is changed to fear, The mur-muring wind, the quiv - ering
vine, for - ev - er dear, Con - tent to suf - fer while we
care; We smile at pain while thou art near.
dread, Our hearts still whis - pering, "Thou art near!"
leaf Shall soft - ly tell us thou art near!
know, Liv - ing and dy - ing, thou art near! A - men.

271 Guide Me, O Thou Great Jehovah

William Williams, 1717-1791
Stanza 1, trans. from the Welsh by Peter Williams, 1722-1796
Stanzas 2, 3, probably trans. by the author

CWM RHONDDA 87.87.87.
John Hughes, 1873-1932

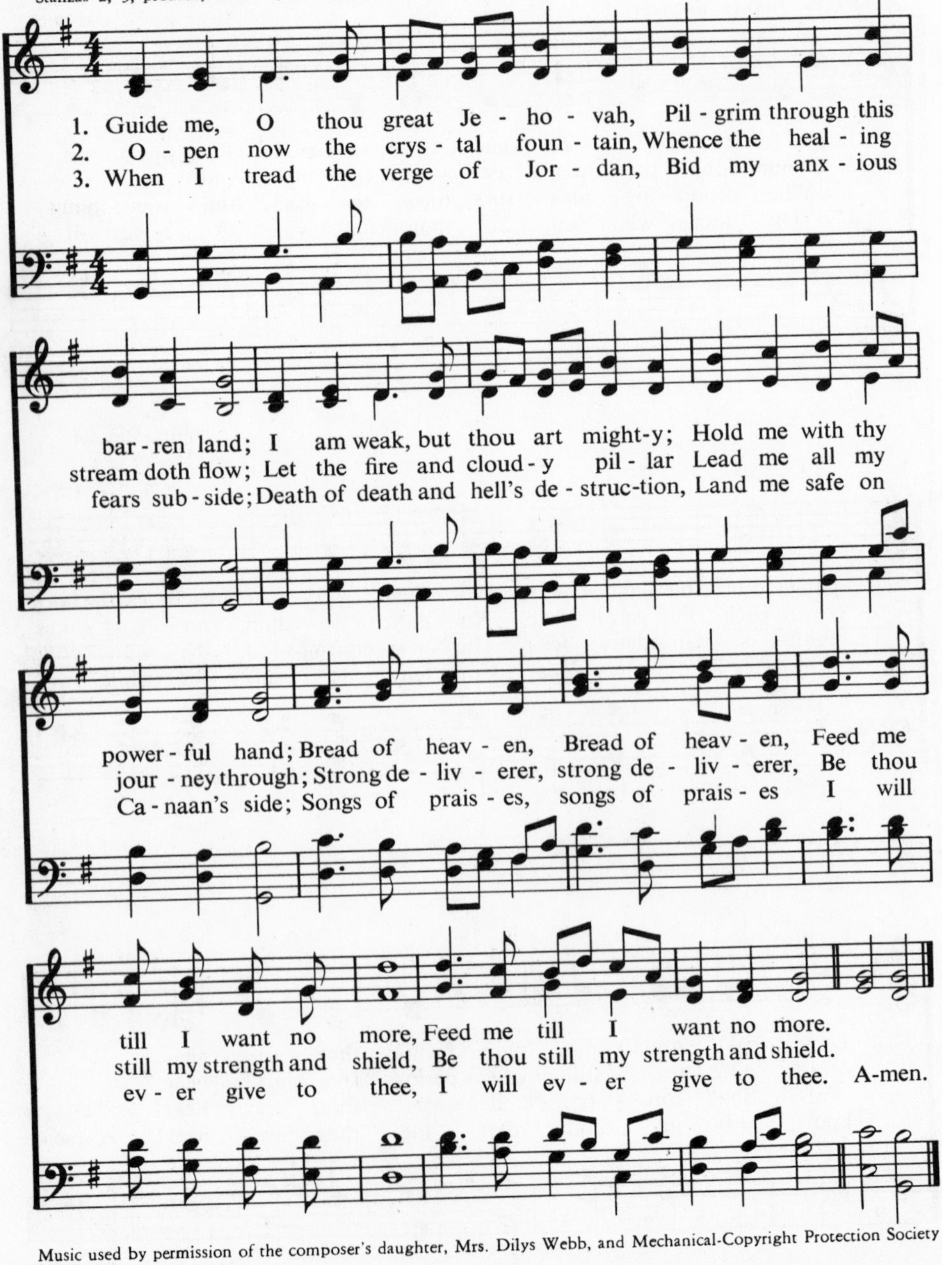
1. Guide me, O thou great Je - ho - vah, Pil - grim through this
2. O - pen now the crys - tal foun - tain, Whence the heal - ing
3. When I tread the verge of Jor - dan, Bid my anx - ious
bar - ren land; I am weak, but thou art might - y; Hold me with thy
stream doth flow; Let the fire and cloud - y pil - lar Lead me all my
fears sub - side; Death of death and hell's de - struc - tion, Land me safe on
power - ful hand; Bread of heav - en, Bread of heav - en, Feed me
jour - ney through; Strong de - liv - erer, strong de - liv - erer, Be thou
Ca - naan's side; Songs of prais - es, songs of prais - es I will
till I want no more, Feed me till I want no more.
still my strength and shield, Be thou still my strength and shield.
ev - er give to thee, I will ev - er give to thee. A-men.

272

Lead, Kindly Light

LUX BENIGNA 10 4.10 4.10 10.

JOHN HENRY NEWMAN, 1801-1890

JOHN B. DYKES, 1823-1876

1. Lead, kind - ly Light, a - mid th' en-cir - cling gloom, Lead thou me on!
2. I was not ev - er thus, nor prayed that thou Shouldst lead me on;
3. So long thy power hath blest me, sure it still Will lead me on
The night is dark, and I am far from home; Lead thou me on!
I loved to choose and see my path; but now Lead thou me on!
O'er moor and fen, o'er crag and tor - rent, till The night is gone;
Keep thou my feet; I do not ask to see
I loved the gar - ish day, and spite of fears,
And with the morn those an - gel fac - es smile,
The dis - tant scene; one step e - nough for me.
Pride ruled my will; re - mem - ber not past years.
Which I have loved long since and lost a - while! A-men.

Alternate tune: SANDON

PRAYER AND ASPIRATION

God, Who Touchest Earth with Beauty

BULLINGER 85.85.

MARY S. EDGAR, 1889-

ETHELBERT W. BULLINGER, 1837-1913

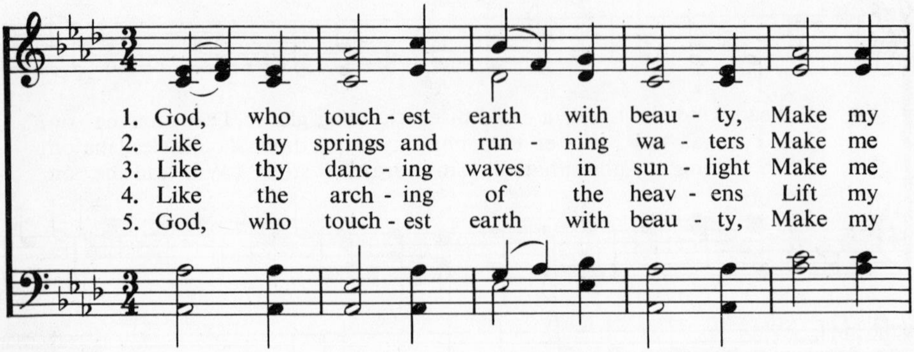
1. God, who touch - est earth with beau - ty, Make my
2. Like thy springs and run - ning wa - ters Make me
3. Like thy danc - ing waves in sun - light Make me
4. Like the arch - ing of the heav - ens Lift my
5. God, who touch - est earth with beau - ty, Make my

heart a - new; With thy spir - it re - cre -
crys - tal pure; Like thy rocks of tower - ing
glad and free; Like the straight - ness of the
thoughts a - bove; Turn my dreams to no - ble
heart a - new; Keep me ev - er, by thy

ate me, Pure and strong and true.
gran - deur Make me strong and sure.
pine trees Let me up - right be.
ac - tion, Min - is - tries of love.
spir - it, Pure and strong and true. A - men.

Words used by permission of Mary S. Edgar.

Master, Speak! Thy Servant Heareth

I Samuel 3:1-10
Frances R. Havergal, 1836-1879

AMEN, JESUS HAN SKAL RAADE 87.87.77.
Anton P. Berggreen, 1801-1880

1. Mas - ter, speak! thy ser - vant hear - eth, Wait - ing
2. Speak to me by name, O Mas - ter, Let me
3. Mas - ter, speak! though least and low - est, Let me
4. Mas - ter, speak! and make me read - y, When thy
for thy gra - cious word, Long - ing for thy voice that cheer - eth;
know it is to me; Speak, that I may fol - low fast - er,
not un - heard de - part; Mas - ter, speak! for O, thou know - est
voice is tru - ly heard, With o - be - dience glad and stead - y
Mas - ter, let it now be heard. I am lis - tening, Lord, for
With a step more firm and free, Where the Shep - herd leads the
All the yearn - ing of my heart, Know - est all its tru - est
Still to fol - low ev - ery word. I am lis - tening, Lord, for
thee: What hast thou to say to me?
flock, In the shad - ow of the rock.
need: Speak! and make me blest in - deed.
thee: Mas - ter, speak! O, speak to me! A - men.

275

Sweet Hour of Prayer

SWEET HOUR LMD

WILLIAM WALFORD, 1772-1850 — WILLIAM B. BRADBURY, 1816-1868

1. Sweet hour of prayer! sweet hour of prayer! That calls me from a
2. Sweet hour of prayer! sweet hour of prayer! The joys I feel, the
3. Sweet hour of prayer! sweet hour of prayer! Thy wings shall my pe -
world of care, And bids me at my Fa - ther's throne Make
bliss I share Of those whose anx - ious spir - its burn With
ti - tion bear To him whose truth and faith - ful - ness En -
all my wants and wish - es known; In sea - sons of dis - tress and
strong de - sires for thy re - turn! With such I has - ten to the
gage the wait - ing soul to bless; And since he bids me seek his
grief, My soul has of - ten found re - lief, And oft es-caped the
place Where God my Sav - ior shows his face, And glad - ly take my
face, Be - lieve his Word and trust his grace, I'll cast on him my

temp - ter's snare, By thy re - turn, sweet hour of prayer!
sta - tion there, And wait for thee, sweet hour of prayer!
ev - ery care, And wait for thee, sweet hour of prayer! A-men.

Blest Are the Pure in Heart

276

MATTHEW 5:8
JOHN KEBLE, 1792-1866

FRANCONIA SM
JOHANN B. KÖNIG, 1691-1758
Arr. by WILLIAM HAVERGAL, 1793-1870

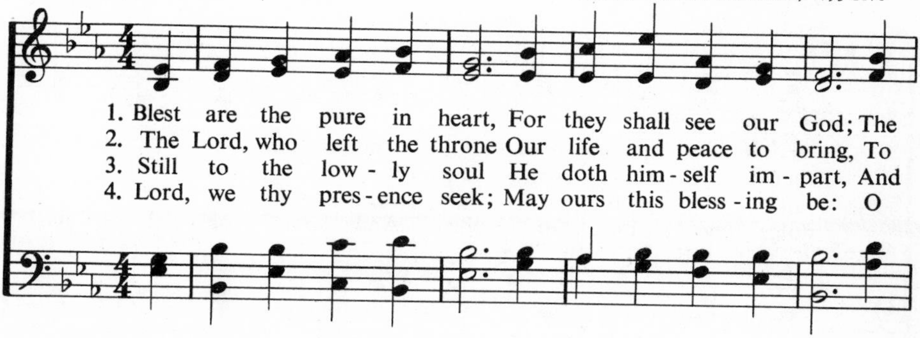
1. Blest are the pure in heart, For they shall see our God; The
2. The Lord, who left the throne Our life and peace to bring, To
3. Still to the low - ly soul He doth him - self im - part, And
4. Lord, we thy pres - ence seek; May ours this bless - ing be: O

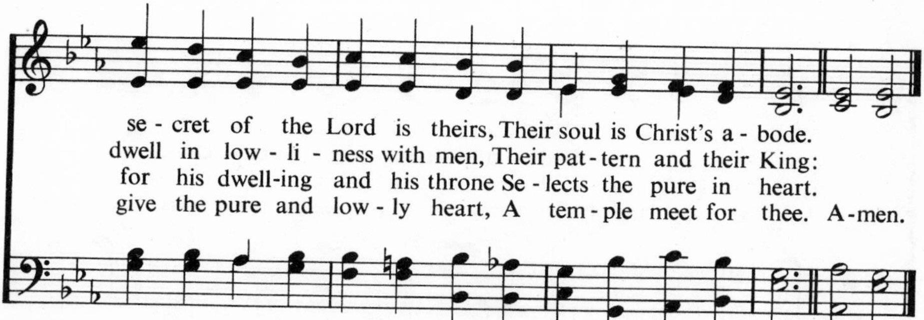
se - cret of the Lord is theirs, Their soul is Christ's a - bode.
dwell in low - li - ness with men, Their pat - tern and their King:
for his dwell-ing and his throne Se - lects the pure in heart.
give the pure and low - ly heart, A tem - ple meet for thee. A-men.

O Come, and Dwell in Me

ST. MICHAEL SM
Genevan Psalter, 1551

CHARLES WESLEY, 1707-1788
Adapt. by WILLIAM CROTCH, 1775-1847

1. O come, and dwell in me, Spir -
2. Has - ten the joy - ful day Which
3. I want the wit - ness, Lord, That
4. I ask no high - er state; In -
it of power with - in, And bring the glo - rious
shall my sins con - sume, When old things shall be
all I do is right, Ac - cord - ing to thy
dulge me but in this, And soon or la - ter
lib - er - ty From sor - row, fear, and sin.
done a - way, And all things new be - come.
mind and Word, Well - pleas - ing in thy sight.
then trans - late To my e - ter - nal bliss. A - men.

Jesus, Thine All-Victorious Love

AZMON CM

CHARLES WESLEY, 1707-1788

CARL G. GLÄSER, 1784-1829
Arr. by LOWELL MASON, 1792-1872

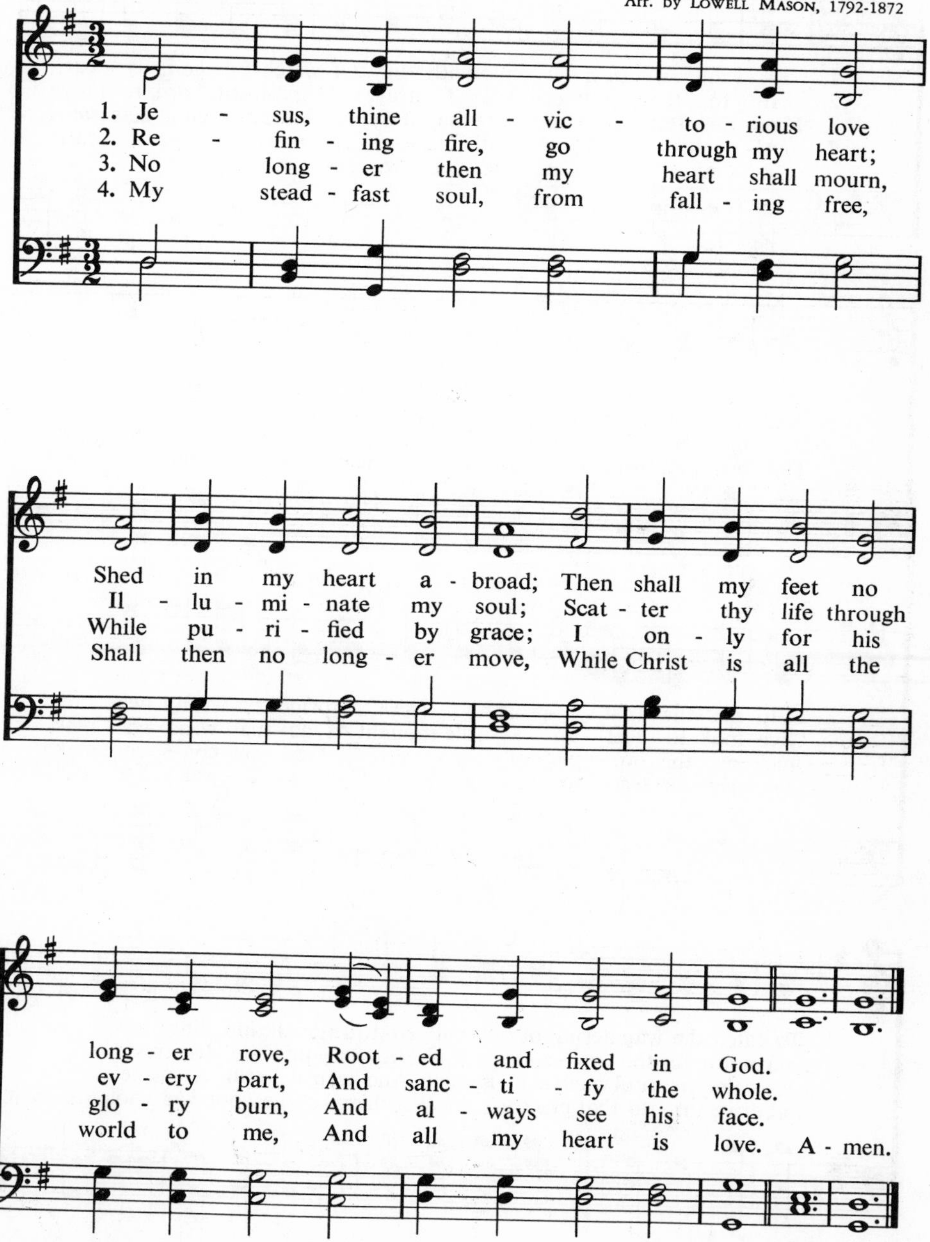
1. Je - sus, thine all - vic - to - rious love
2. Re - fin - ing fire, go through my heart;
3. No long - er then my heart shall mourn,
4. My stead - fast soul, from fall - ing free,
Shed in my heart a - broad; Then shall my feet no
Il - lu - mi - nate my soul; Scat - ter thy life through
While pu - ri - fied by grace; I on - ly for his
Shall then no long - er move, While Christ is all the
long - er rove, Root - ed and fixed in God.
ev - ery part, And sanc - ti - fy the whole.
glo - ry burn, And al - ways see his face.
world to me, And all my heart is love. A - men.

CHRISTIAN PERFECTION

I Want a Principle Within

GERALD CMD

CHARLES WESLEY, 1707-1788

Adapt. from LOUIS SPOHR, 1784-1859

1. I want a prin-ci-ple with-in Of watch-ful, god-ly fear,
2. If to the right or left I stray, That mo-ment, Lord, re-prove,
3. From thee that I no more may stray, No more thy good-ness grieve,
4. Al-might-y God of truth and love, To me thy power im-part;
A sen-si-bil-i-ty of sin, A pain to feel it near.
And let me weep my life a-way For hav-ing grieved thy love.
Grant me the fil-ial awe, I pray, The ten-der con-science give;
The bur-den from my soul re-move, The hard-ness from my heart.
Help me the first ap-proach to feel Of pride or wrong de-sire,
Give me to feel an i-dle thought As ac-tual wick-ed-ness,
Quick as the ap-ple of an eye, O God, my con-science make!
O may the least o-mis-sion pain My re-a-wak-ened soul,
To catch the wan-dering of my will, And quench the kin-dling fire.
And mourn for the mi-nut-est fault In ex-qui-site dis-tress.
A-wake my soul when sin is nigh, And keep it still a-wake.
And drive me to that grace a-gain, Which makes the wound-ed whole. A-men.

I Want a Principle Within

EUCLID CMD

CHARLES WESLEY, 1707-1788 LLOYD A. PFAUTSCH, 1921-

1. I want a prin - ci - ple with - in Of watch-ful, god - ly fear,
2. If to the right or left I stray, That mo-ment, Lord, re - prove,
3. From thee that I no more may stray, No more thy good-ness grieve,
4. Al - might - y God of truth and love, To me thy power im - part;
A sen - si - bil - i - ty of sin, A pain to feel it near.
And let me weep my life a - way For hav - ing grieved thy love.
Grant me the fil - ial awe, I pray, The ten - der con-science give;
The bur - den from my soul re - move, The hard-ness from my heart.
Help me the first ap - proach to feel Of pride or wrong de - sire,
Give me to feel an i - dle thought As ac - tual wick - ed - ness,
Quick as the ap - ple of an eye, O God, my con-science make!
O may the least o - mis - sion pain My re - a - wak-ened soul,
To catch the wan-dering of my will, And quench the kin-dling fire.
And mourn for the mi - nut - est fault In ex - qui - site dis - tress.
A-wake my soul when sin is nigh, And keep it still a - wake.
And drive me to that grace a-gain, Which makes the wound-ed whole. A - men.

God of All Power and Truth and Grace

VOM HIMMEL HOCH LM
Geistliche Lieder, Leipzig, 1539

CHARLES WESLEY, 1707-1788
ATTR. TO MARTIN LUTHER, 1483-1546

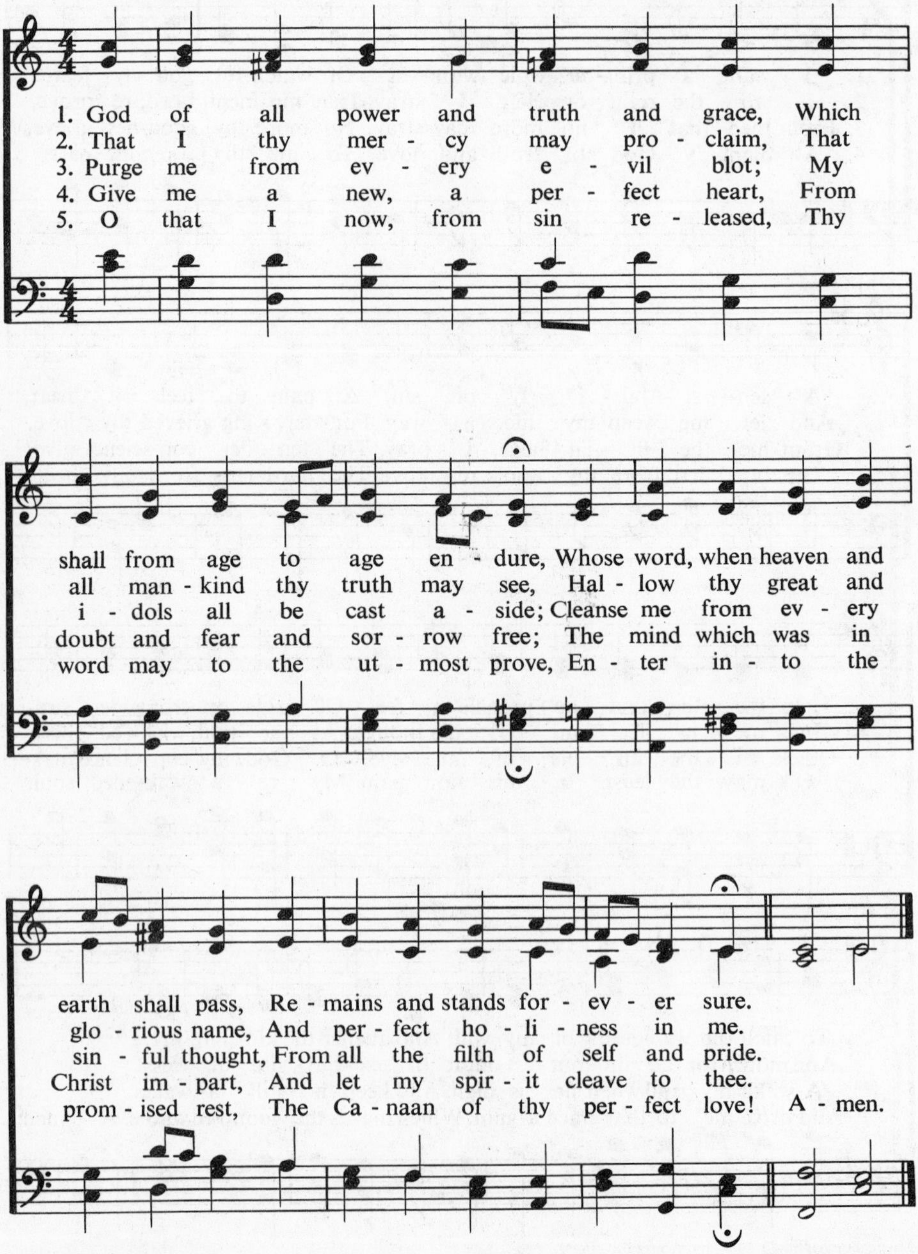
1. God of all power and truth and grace, Which
2. That I thy mer - cy may pro - claim, That
3. Purge me from ev - ery e - vil blot; My
4. Give me a new, a per - fect heart, From
5. O that I now, from sin re - leased, Thy
shall from age to age en - dure, Whose word, when heaven and
all man - kind thy truth may see, Hal - low thy great and
i - dols all be cast a - side; Cleanse me from ev - ery
doubt and fear and sor - row free; The mind which was in
word may to the ut - most prove, En - ter in - to the
earth shall pass, Re - mains and stands for - ev - er sure.
glo - rious name, And per - fect ho - li - ness in me.
sin - ful thought, From all the filth of self and pride.
Christ im - part, And let my spir - it cleave to thee.
prom - ised rest, The Ca - naan of thy per - fect love! A - men.

282

O For a Heart to Praise My God

PSALM 51:10
CHARLES WESLEY, 1707-1788

IRISH CM
A Collection of Hymns and Sacred Poems, 1749
Probably arr. by JOHN F. LAMPE, 1703-1751

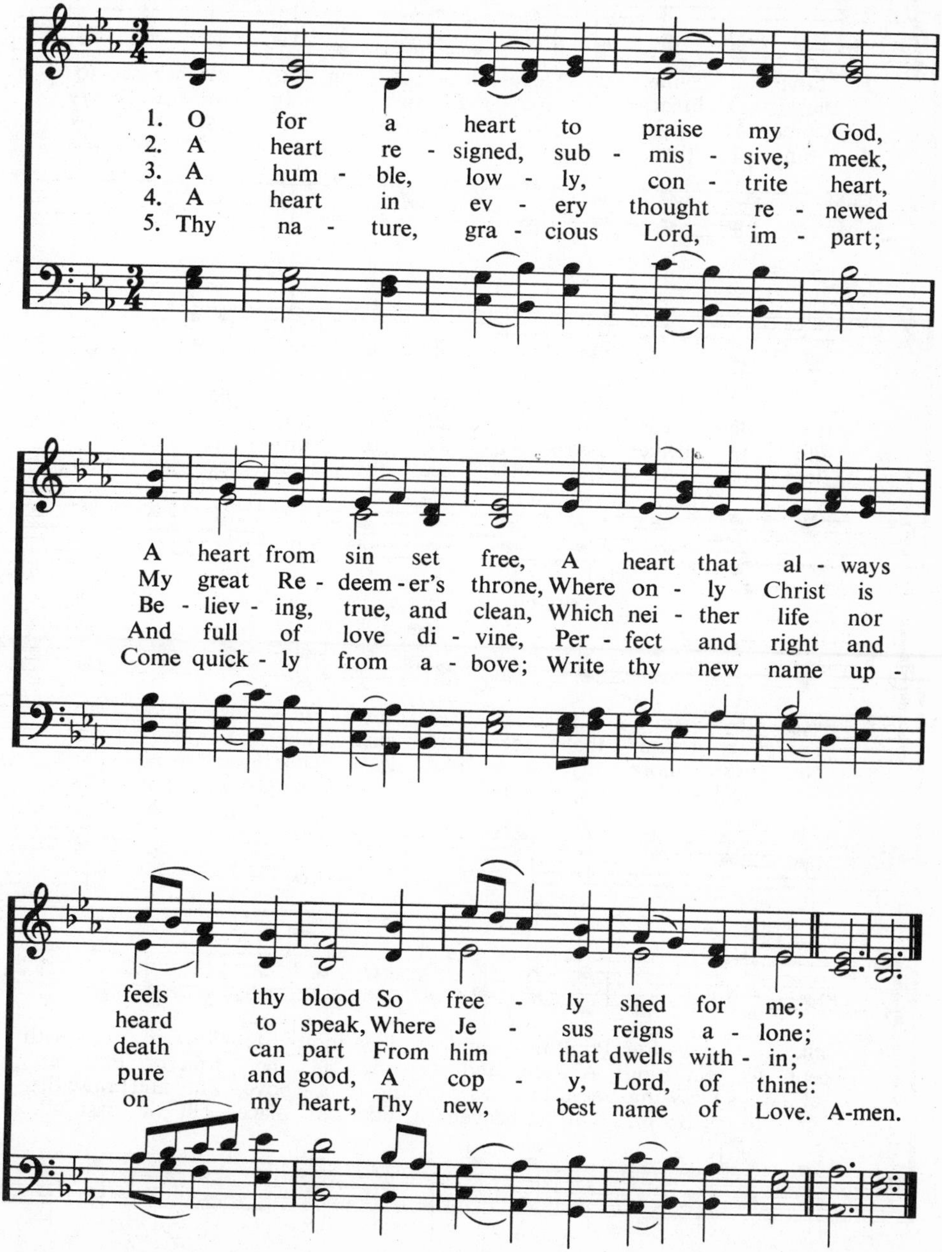

1. O for a heart to praise my God,
2. A heart resigned, sub - mis - sive, meek,
3. A hum - ble, low - ly, con - trite heart,
4. A heart in ev - ery thought re - newed
5. Thy na - ture, gra - cious Lord, im - part;
A heart from sin set free, A heart that al - ways
My great Re - deem - er's throne, Where on - ly Christ is
Be - liev - ing, true, and clean, Which nei - ther life nor
And full of love di - vine, Per - fect and right and
Come quick - ly from a - bove; Write thy new name up -
feels thy blood So free - ly shed for me;
heard to speak, Where Je - sus reigns a - lone;
death can part From him that dwells with - in;
pure and good, A cop - y, Lord, of thine:
on my heart, Thy new, best name of Love. A-men.

283

Love Divine, All Loves Excelling

BEECHER 87.87.D.

CHARLES WESLEY, 1707-1788

JOHN ZUNDEL, 1815-1882

1. Love di - vine, all loves ex - cell - ing, Joy of heaven, to
2. Breathe, O breathe thy lov - ing spir - it In - to ev - ery
3. Come, Al - might - y to de - liv - er, Let us all thy
4. Fin - ish, then, thy new cre - a - tion; Pure and spot - less
earth come down; Fix in us thy hum - ble dwell - ing;
trou - bled breast! Let us all in thee in - her - it;
life re - ceive; Sud - den - ly re - turn and nev - er,
let us be. Let us see thy great sal - va - tion
All thy faith - ful mer - cies crown! Je - sus, thou art
Let us find that sec - ond rest. Take a - way our
Nev - er - more thy tem - ples leave. Thee we would be
Per - fect - ly re - stored in thee: Changed from glo - ry
all com - pas - sion, Pure, un - bound - ed love thou art; Vis - it us with
bent to sin - ning; Al - pha and O - me - ga be; End of faith, as
al - ways bless - ing, Serve thee as thy hosts a - bove, Pray and praise thee
in - to glo - ry, Till in heaven we take our place, Till we cast our

thy sal - va - tion; En - ter ev - ery trem - bling heart.
its be - gin - ning, Set our hearts at lib - er - ty.
with - out ceas - ing, Glo - ry in thy per - fect love.
crowns be - fore thee, Lost in won - der, love, and praise. A - men.

Alternate tune: HYFRYDOL

284

Lord Jesus, Think on Me

SYNESIUS OF CYRENE, c. 375-430
Trans. by ALLEN W. CHATFIELD, 1808-1896

SOUTHWELL SM
Adapt. from DAMON'S *Psalmes*, 1579

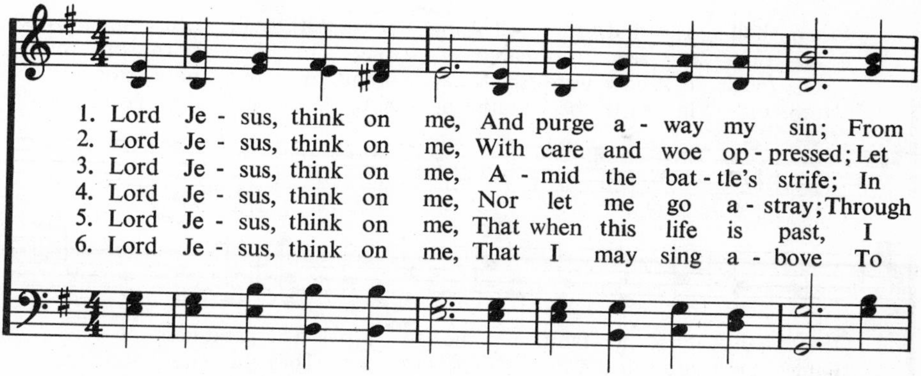
1. Lord Je - sus, think on me, And purge a - way my sin; From
2. Lord Je - sus, think on me, With care and woe op - pressed; Let
3. Lord Je - sus, think on me, A - mid the bat - tle's strife; In
4. Lord Je - sus, think on me, Nor let me go a - stray; Through
5. Lord Je - sus, think on me, That when this life is past, I
6. Lord Je - sus, think on me, That I may sing a - bove To

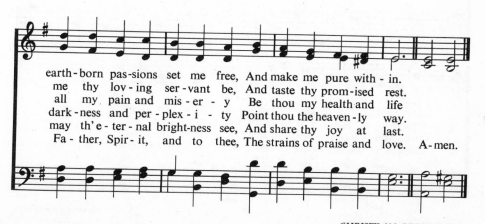

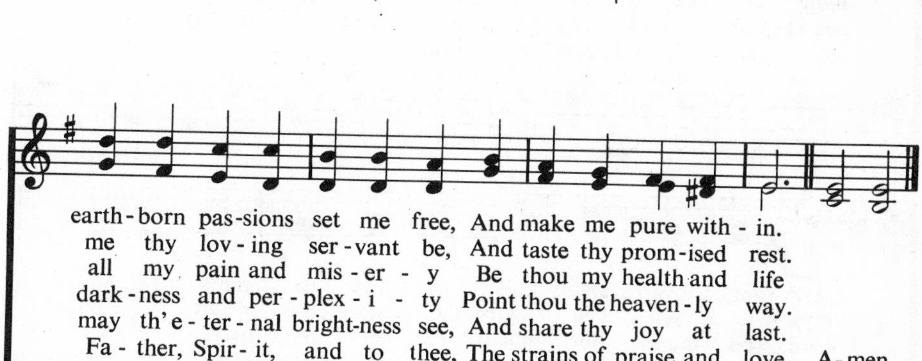
earth - born pas - sions set me free, And make me pure with - in.
me thy lov - ing ser - vant be, And taste thy prom - ised rest.
all my pain and mis - er - y Be thou my health and life.
dark - ness and per - plex - i - ty Point thou the heaven - ly way.
may th'e - ter - nal bright - ness see, And share thy joy at last.
Fa - ther, Spir - it, and to thee, The strains of praise and love. A - men.

285

O Love Divine, How Sweet Thou Art

ALLGÜTIGER, MEIN PREISGESANG 886.D.

CHARLES WESLEY, 1707-1788 — GEORG PETER WEIMAR, 1734-1800

1. O Love di - vine, how sweet thou art!
2. Strong - er his love than death or hell;
3. God on - ly knows the love of God;
4. Thy on - ly love do I re - quire,
When shall I find my will - ing heart All tak - en up by
Its rich - es are un - search - a - ble; The first - born sons of
O that it now were shed a - broad In this poor ston - y
Noth - ing in earth be - neath de - sire, Noth - ing in heaven a -
thee? I thirst, I faint, I die to prove The great-ness of re -
light De - sire in vain its depths to see; They can - not reach the
heart! For thee I long, for love di - vine; This on - ly por - tion,
bove; Let earth and heaven and all things go; Give me thy on - ly
deem - ing love, The love of Christ to me.
mys - ter - y, The length, the breadth, the height.
Lord, be mine; Be mine this bet - ter part!
love to know; Give me thy on - ly love. A - men.

Alternate tune: ARIEL

Lord, I Want to Be a Christian

American Folk Hymn

I WANT TO BE A CHRISTIAN Irregular
American Folk Hymn

1. Lord, I want to be a Chris-tian in my heart, in my heart; Lord, I want to be a Chris-tian in my heart, in my heart. In my heart, in my heart, Lord, I want to be a Chris-tian in my heart.
2. Lord, I want to be more lov-ing in my heart, in my heart; Lord, I want to be more lov-ing in my heart, in my heart. In my heart, in my heart, Lord, I want to be more lov-ing in my heart.
3. Lord, I want to be more ho-ly in my heart, in my heart; Lord, I want to be more ho-ly in my heart, in my heart. In my heart, in my heart, Lord, I want to be more ho-ly in my heart.
4. Lord, I want to be like Je-sus in my heart, in my heart; Lord, I want to be like Je-sus in my heart, in my heart. In my heart, in my heart, Lord, I want to be like Je-sus in my heart. A-men.
In my heart, In my heart,

We Are Climbing Jacob's Ladder

GENESIS 28:10-17
American Folk Hymn

JACOB'S LADDER 888.5.
American Folk Hymn

1. We are climb - ing Ja - cob's lad - der. We are
2. Ev - ery round goes high - er, high - er. Ev - ery
3. Sin - ner, do you love my Je - sus? Sin - ner,
4. If you love him, why not serve him? If you
5. We are climb - ing high - er, high - er. We are
climb - ing Ja - cob's lad - der. We are climb - ing
round goes high - er, high - er. Ev - ery round goes
do you love my Je - sus? Sin - ner, do you
love him, why not serve him? If you love him,
climb - ing high - er, high - er. We are climb - ing
Ja - cob's lad - der, Sol - diers of the cross.
high - er, high - er, Sol - diers of the cross.
love my Je - sus? Sol - diers of the cross.
why not serve him? Sol - diers of the cross.
high - er, high - er, Sol - diers of the cross. A - men.

Servant of God, Well Done

Charles Wesley, 1707-1788

DIADEMATA SMD
George J. Elvey, 1816-1893

1. Ser - vant of God, well done! Thy glo - rious war - fare's past;
2. O hap - py, hap - py soul! In ec - sta - sies of praise,
The bat - tle's fought, the race is won, And thou art crowned at last.
Long as e - ter - nal a - ges roll, Thou seest thy Sav - ior's face.
With saints en - throned on high, Thou dost thy Lord pro - claim,
Re - deemed from earth and pain, Ah! when shall we as - cend,
And still to God sal - va - tion cry, Sal - va - tion to the Lamb!
And all in Je - sus' pres - ence reign Through a - ges with - out end? A - men.

Abide with Me

LUKE 24:29
HENRY F. LYTE, 1793-1847

EVENTIDE 10 10.10 10.
W. H. MONK, 1823-1889

1. A - bide with me; fast falls the e - ven - tide;
2. Swift to its close ebbs out life's lit - tle day;
3. I need thy pres - ence ev - ery pass - ing hour;
4. I fear no foe, with thee at hand to bless;
5. Hold thou thy cross be - fore my clos - ing eyes;
The dark - ness deep - ens; Lord, with me a - bide!
Earth's joys grow dim; its glo - ries pass a - way;
What but thy grace can foil the temp - ter's power?
Ills have no weight, and tears no bit - ter - ness.
Shine through the gloom and point me to the skies;
When oth - er help - ers fail and com - forts flee,
Change and de - cay in all a - round I see;
Who, like thy - self, my guide and stay can be?
Where is death's sting? Where, grave, thy vic - to - ry?
Heaven's morn - ing breaks, and earth's vain shad - ows flee;

Help of the help - less, O a - bide with me.
O thou who chang - est not, a - bide with me.
Through cloud and sun - shine, Lord, a - bide with me.
I tri - umph still, if thou a - bide with me.
In life, in death, O Lord, a - bide with me. A - men.

I Know Not What the Future Hath 290

JOHN GREENLEAF WHITTIER, 1807-1892

COOLING CM
ALONZO J. ABBEY, 1825-1887

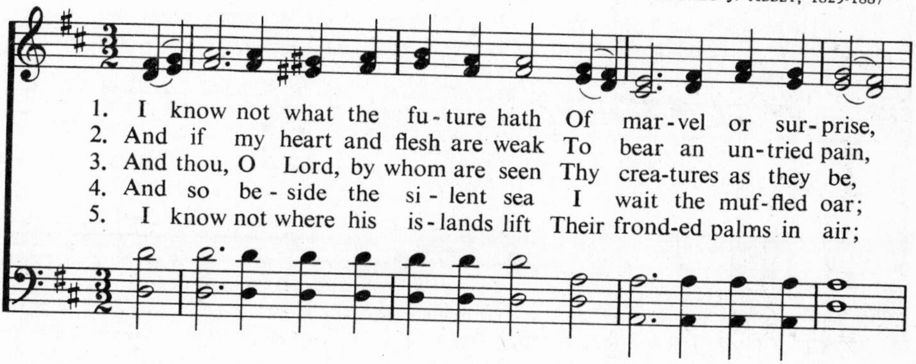
1. I know not what the fu - ture hath Of mar - vel or sur - prise,
2. And if my heart and flesh are weak To bear an un - tried pain,
3. And thou, O Lord, by whom are seen Thy crea - tures as they be,
4. And so be - side the si - lent sea I wait the muf - fled oar;
5. I know not where his is - lands lift Their frond - ed palms in air;

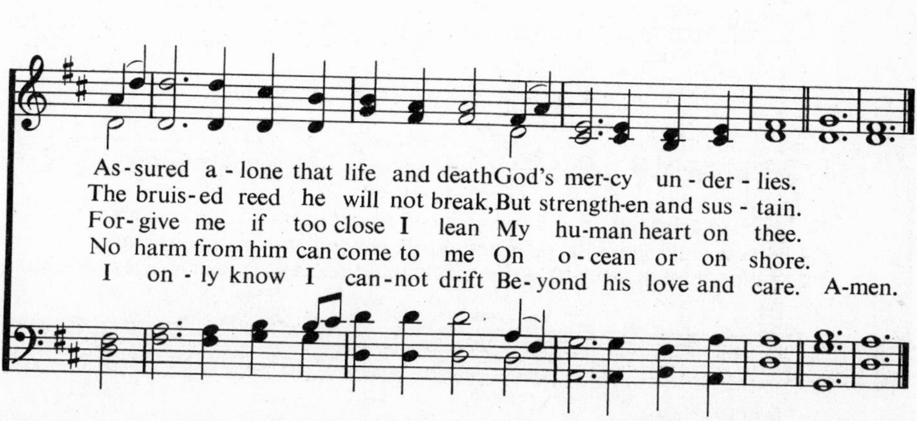
As - sured a - lone that life and death God's mer - cy un - der - lies.
The bruis - ed reed he will not break, But strength - en and sus - tain.
For - give me if too close I lean My hu - man heart on thee.
No harm from him can come to me On o - cean or on shore.
I on - ly know I can - not drift Be - yond his love and care. A - men.

On Jordan's Stormy Banks I Stand

PROMISED LAND CMD
American Folk Melody

SAMUEL STENNETT, 1727-1795

1. On Jor-dan's storm-y banks I stand, And cast a wish-ful eye
2. O'er all those wide-ex-tend-ed plains Shines one e-ter-nal day;
3. When I shall reach that hap-py place, I'll be for-ev-er blest,
To Ca-naan's fair and hap-py land, Where my pos-ses-sions lie.
There God the Son for-ev-er reigns, And scat-ters night a-way.
For I shall see my Fa-ther's face, And in his bos-om rest.
O the trans-port-ing rap-turous scene That ris-es to my sight:
No chill-ing winds of poi-sonous breath Can reach that health-ful shore;
Filled with de-light my rap-tured soul Lives out its earth-ly day;
Sweet fields ar-rayed in liv-ing green And riv-ers of de-light!
Sick-ness and sor-row, pain and death, Are felt and feared no more.
And then, though Jor-dan's waves may roll, I'll fear-less launch a-way. A-men.

Music may be played in E^b minor.

Christ for the World We Sing

ITALIAN HYMN 664.6664.
FELICE DE GIARDINI, 1716-1796
Harm. by V. E. C.

SAMUEL WOLCOTT, 1813-1886

1. Christ for the world we sing! The world to
2. Christ for the world we sing! The world to
3. Christ for the world we sing! The world to
4. Christ for the world we sing! The world to
Christ we bring, With lov - ing zeal; The poor, and
Christ we bring, With fer - vent prayer; The way - ward
Christ we bring, With one ac - cord; With us the
Christ we bring, With joy - ful song; The new - born
them that mourn, The faint and o - ver - borne,
and the lost, By rest - less pas - sions tossed,
work to share, With us re - proach to dare,
souls, whose days, Re - claimed from er - ror's ways,
Sin - sick and sor - row - worn, Whom Christ doth heal.
Re - deemed at count - less cost, From dark de - spair.
With us the cross to bear, For Christ our Lord.
In - spired with hope and praise, To Christ be - long. A - men.

NATURE AND MISSION

293

Glorious Things of Thee Are Spoken

ISAIAH 33:20-21; PSALM 87:3;
EXODUS 13:22
JOHN NEWTON, 1725-1807

AUSTRIA 87.87.D.
FRANZ JOSEPH HAYDN, 1732-1809

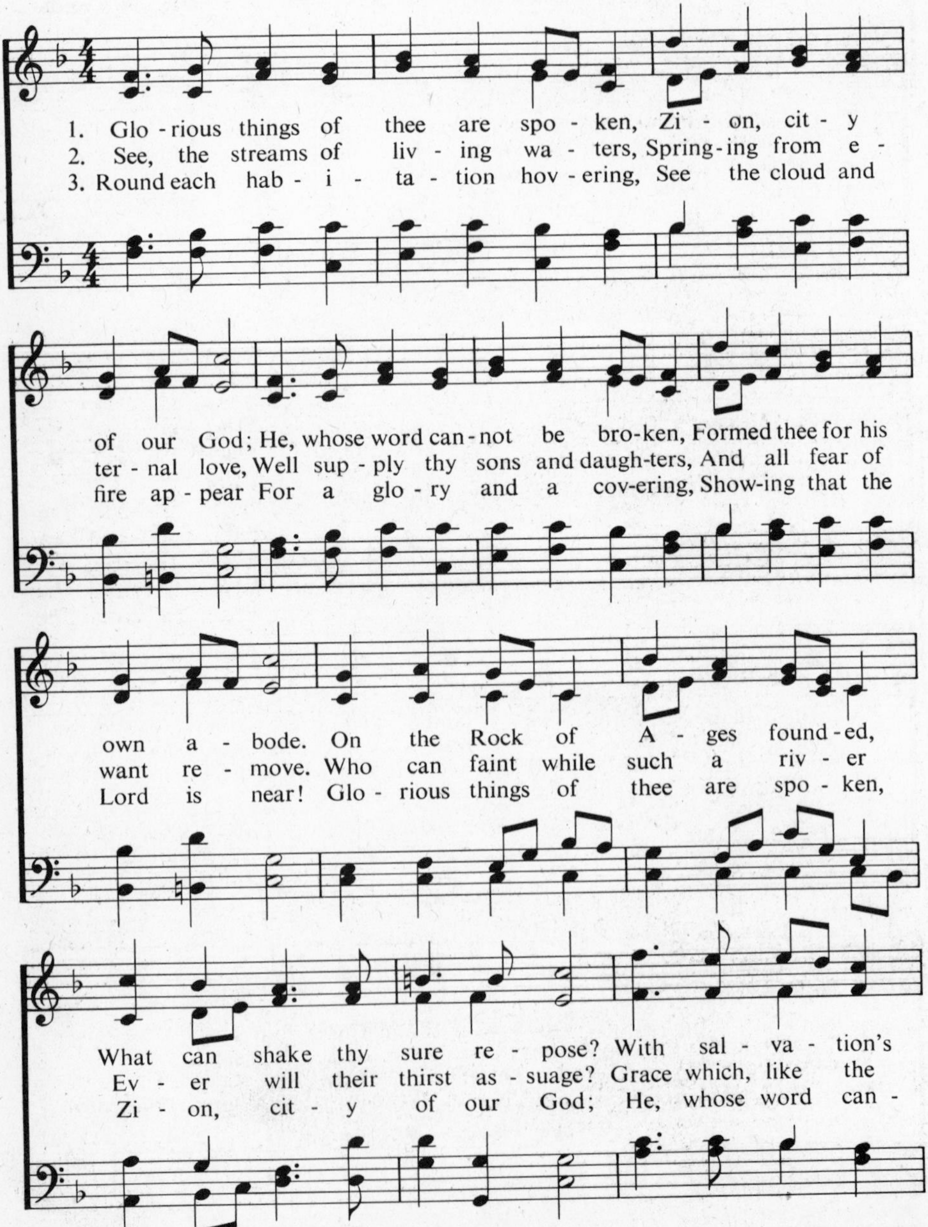
1. Glo - rious things of thee are spo - ken, Zi - on, cit - y
2. See, the streams of liv - ing wa - ters, Spring - ing from e -
3. Round each hab - i - ta - tion hov - ering, See the cloud and
of our God; He, whose word can - not be bro - ken, Formed thee for his
ter - nal love, Well sup - ply thy sons and daugh - ters, And all fear of
fire ap - pear For a glo - ry and a cov - ering, Show - ing that the
own a - bode. On the Rock of A - ges found - ed,
want re - move. Who can faint while such a riv - er
Lord is near! Glo - rious things of thee are spo - ken,
What can shake thy sure re - pose? With sal - va - tion's
Ev - er will their thirst as - suage? Grace which, like the
Zi - on, cit - y of our God; He, whose word can -

walls sur - round - ed, Thou mayst smile at all thy foes.
Lord, the giv - er, Nev - er fails from age to age.
not be bro - ken, Formed thee for his own a - bode. A - men.

294

I Love Thy Kingdom, Lord

TIMOTHY DWIGHT, 1752-1817

ST. THOMAS SM
AARON WILLIAMS, *The New Universal Psalmodist*, 1770

1. I love thy king - dom, Lord, The house of thine a - bode, The
2. I love thy Church, O God! Her walls be - fore thee stand Dear
3. For her my tears shall fall, For her my prayers as - cend, To
4. Be - yond my high - est joy I prize her heaven - ly ways, Her
5. Sure as thy truth shall last, To Zi - on shall be given The

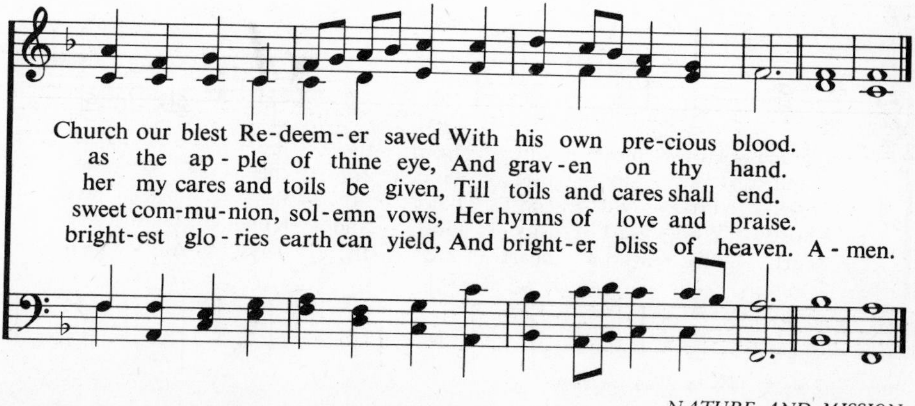
Church our blest Re - deem - er saved With his own pre - cious blood.
as the ap - ple of thine eye, And grav - en on thy hand.
her my cares and toils be given, Till toils and cares shall end.
sweet com - mu - nion, sol - emn vows, Her hymns of love and praise.
bright - est glo - ries earth can yield, And bright - er bliss of heaven. A - men.

How Lovely Is Thy Dwelling Place

SALZBURG CM

PSALM 84
Scottish Psalter, 1650

Adapt. from JOHANN MICHAEL HAYDN, 1737-1806
Harm. by V. E. C.

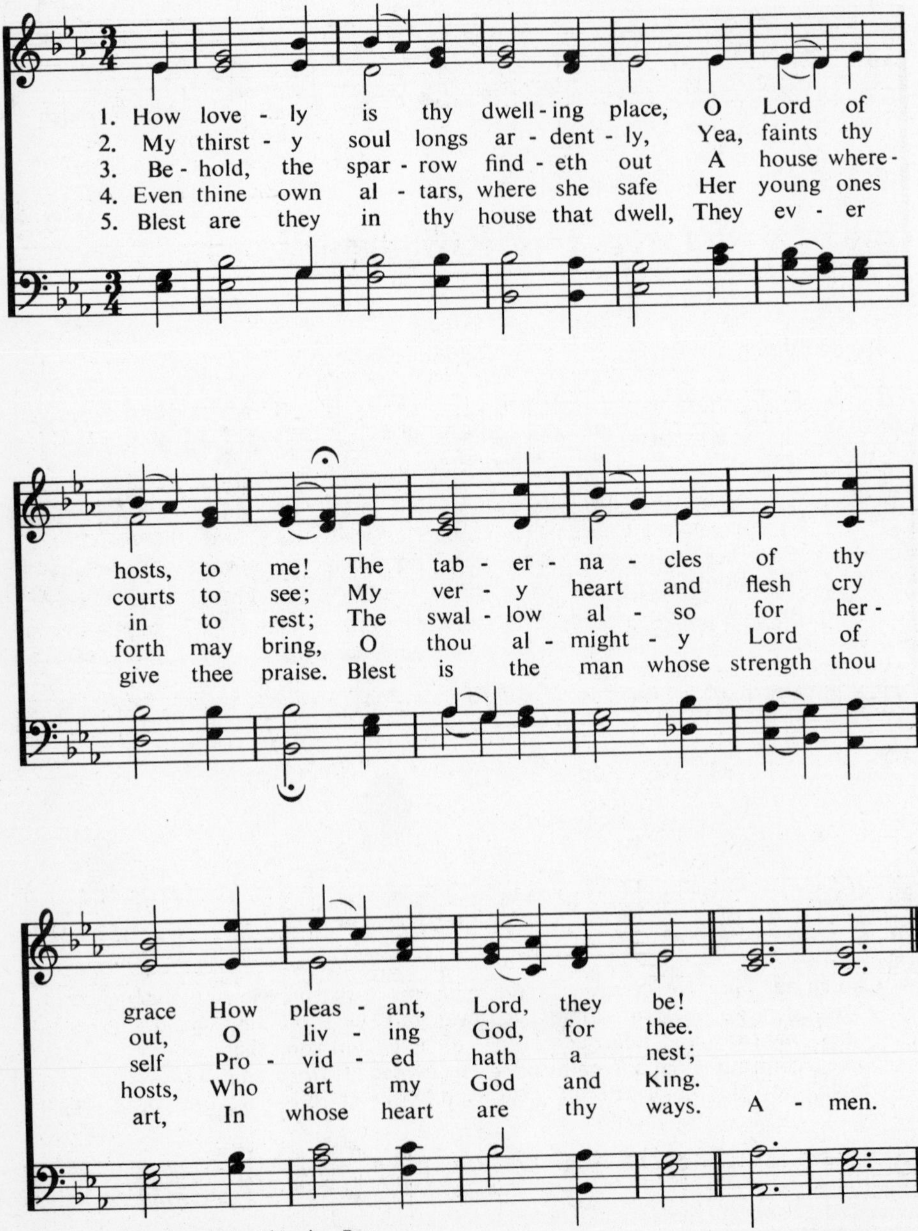
1. How love - ly is thy dwell - ing place, O Lord of
2. My thirst - y soul longs ar - dent - ly, Yea, faints thy
3. Be - hold, the spar - row find - eth out A house where -
4. Even thine own al - tars, where she safe Her young ones
5. Blest are they in thy house that dwell, They ev - er
hosts, to me! The tab - er - na - cles of thy
courts to see; My ver - y heart and flesh cry
in to rest; The swal - low al - so for her -
forth may bring, O thou al - might - y Lord of
give thee praise. Blest is the man whose strength thou
grace How pleas - ant, Lord, they be!
out, O liv - ing God, for thee.
self Pro - vid - ed hath a nest;
hosts, Who art my God and King.
art, In whose heart are thy ways. A - men.

One Holy Church of God Appears

SAMUEL LONGFELLOW, 1819-1892

ST. STEPHEN CM
WILLIAM JONES, 1726-1800

1. One ho - ly Church of God ap - pears Through
2. From old - est time, on far - thest shores, Be -
3. The truth is her pro - phet - ic gift, The
4. O liv - ing Church, thine er - rand speed; Ful -
ev - ery age and race, Un - wast - ed by the
neath the pine or palm, One un - seen Pres - ence
soul, her sa - cred page; And feet on mer - cy's
fill thy task sub - lime; With bread of life earth's
lapse of years, Un-changed by chang - ing place.
she a - dores, With si - lence, or with psalm.
er - rands swift Do make her pil - grim - age.
hun - ger feed; Re - deem the e - vil time! A - men.

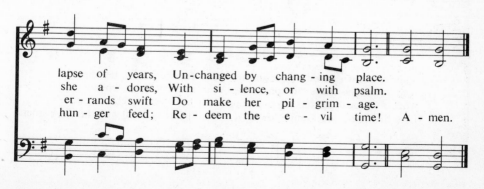

The Church's One Foundation

AURELIA 76.76.D.

SAMUEL J. STONE, 1839-1900

SAMUEL S. WESLEY, 1810-1876

1. The Church's one foun - da - tion Is Je - sus Christ her Lord;
2. E - lect from ev - ery na - tion, Yet one o'er all the earth,
3. Mid toil and trib - u - la - tion, And tu - mult of her war,
4. Yet she on earth hath un - ion With God the Three in One,
She is his new cre - a - tion By wa - ter and the word.
Her char - ter of sal - va - tion, One Lord, one faith, one birth;
She waits the con - sum - ma - tion Of peace for - ev - er - more;
And mys - tic sweet com - mu - nion With those whose rest is won.
From heaven he came and sought her To be his ho - ly bride;
One ho - ly name she bless - es, Par - takes one ho - ly food,
Till, with the vi - sion glo - rious, Her long - ing eyes are blest,
O hap - py ones and ho - ly! Lord, give us grace that we,
With his own blood he bought her, And for her life he died.
And to one hope she press - es, With ev - ery grace en - dued.
And the great Church vic - to - rious Shall be the Church at rest.
Like them, the meek and low - ly, On high may dwell with thee. A - men.

Christ Is Made the Sure Foundation

Ephesians 2:20-22
Latin, c. 7th Century
Trans. by John M. Neale, 1818-1866

REGENT SQUARE 87.87.87.
Henry Smart, 1813-1879

1. Christ is made the sure foun - da - tion, Christ the head and cor - ner - stone, Chos - en of the Lord and pre - cious, Bind - ing all the Church in one; Ho - ly Zi - on's help for - ev - er, And her con - fi - dence a - lone.
2. To this tem - ple, where we call thee, Come, O Lord of hosts, to - day! With thy wont - ed lov - ing - kind - ness Hear thy peo - ple as they pray; And thy full - est ben - e - dic - tion Shed with - in its walls al - way.
3. Here vouch - safe to all thy ser - vants What they ask of thee to gain: What they gain from thee for - ev - er With the bless - ed to re - tain, And here - af - ter in thy glo - ry Ev - er - more with thee to reign.
4. Laud and hon - or to the Fa - ther, Laud and hon - or to the Son, Laud and hon - or to the Spir - it, Ev - er Three and ev - er One; One in might, and One in glo - ry, While un - end - ing a - ges run. A - men.

O Zion, Haste

TIDINGS 11 10.11 10. with Refrain
JAMES WALCH, 1837-1901

MARY A. THOMPSON, 1834-1923

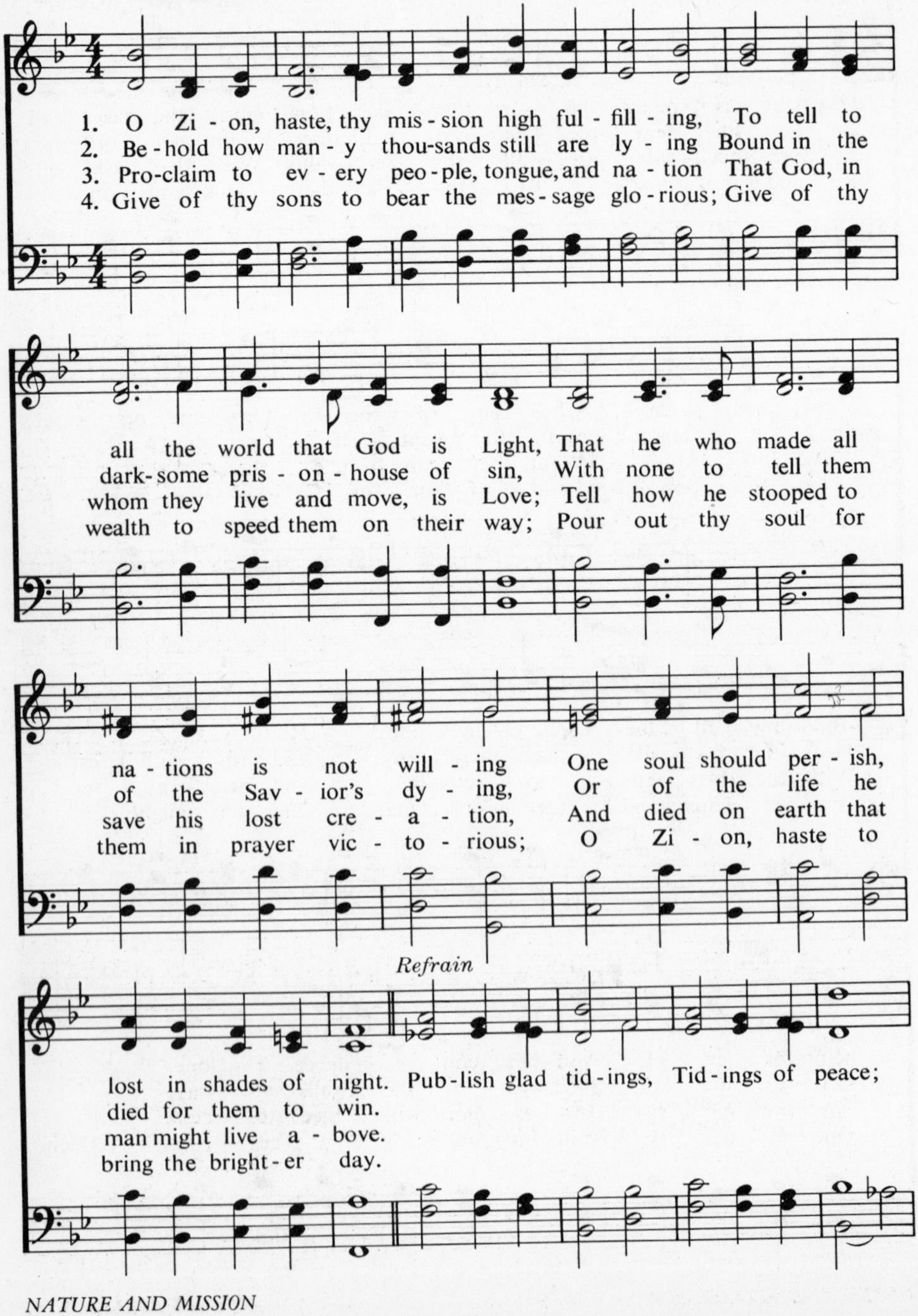
1. O Zi - on, haste, thy mis - sion high ful - fill - ing, To tell to
2. Be - hold how man - y thou-sands still are ly - ing Bound in the
3. Pro-claim to ev - ery peo - ple, tongue, and na - tion That God, in
4. Give of thy sons to bear the mes - sage glo - rious; Give of thy
all the world that God is Light, That he who made all
dark-some pris - on - house of sin, With none to tell them
whom they live and move, is Love; Tell how he stooped to
wealth to speed them on their way; Pour out thy soul for
na - tions is not will - ing One soul should per - ish,
of the Sav - ior's dy - ing, Or of the life he
save his lost cre - a - tion, And died on earth that
them in prayer vic - to - rious; O Zi - on, haste to
Refrain
lost in shades of night. Pub-lish glad tid - ings, Tid - ings of peace;
died for them to win.
man might live a - bove.
bring the bright - er day.

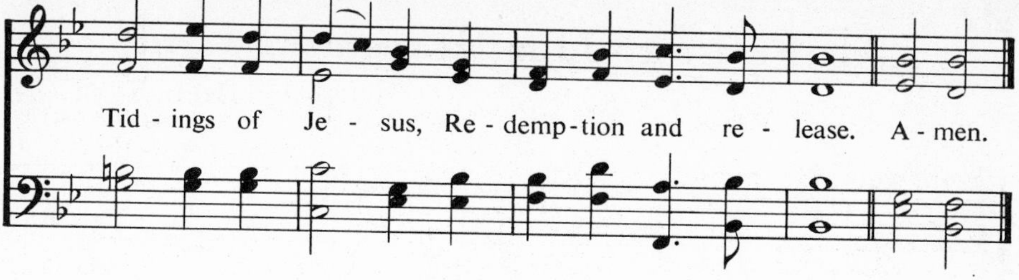
Tid - ings of Je - sus, Re - demp - tion and re - lease. A - men.

Children of the Heavenly King

300

John Cennick, 1718-1755

PLEYEL'S HYMN 77.77.
Ignace J. Pleyel, 1757-1831

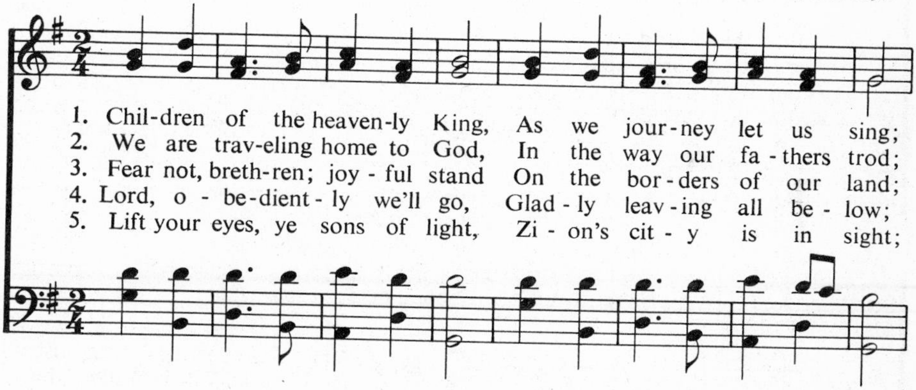
1. Chil-dren of the heaven-ly King, As we jour-ney let us sing;
2. We are trav-eling home to God, In the way our fa - thers trod;
3. Fear not, breth-ren; joy - ful stand On the bor-ders of our land;
4. Lord, o - be-dient - ly we'll go, Glad - ly leav - ing all be - low;
5. Lift your eyes, ye sons of light, Zi - on's cit - y is in sight;

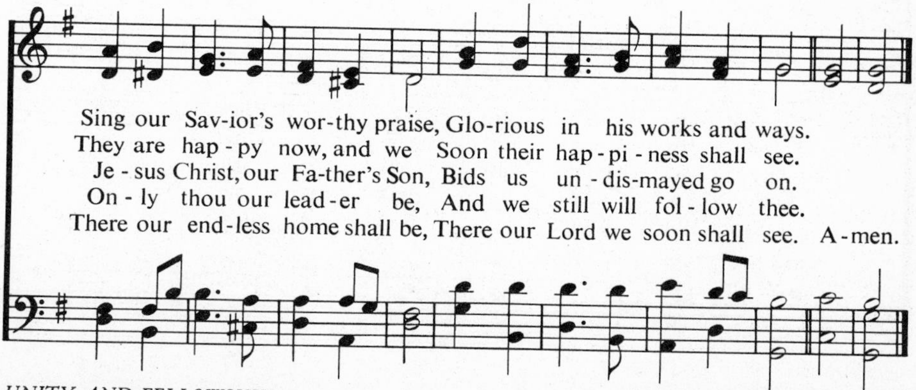
Sing our Sav-ior's wor-thy praise, Glo-rious in his works and ways.
They are hap - py now, and we Soon their hap - pi - ness shall see.
Je - sus Christ, our Fa-ther's Son, Bids us un - dis-mayed go on.
On - ly thou our lead - er be, And we still will fol - low thee.
There our end-less home shall be, There our Lord we soon shall see. A-men.

All Praise to Our Redeeming Lord

ARMENIA CM
SYLVANUS B. POND, 1792-1871
Harm. by A. C. L.

CHARLES WESLEY, 1707-1788

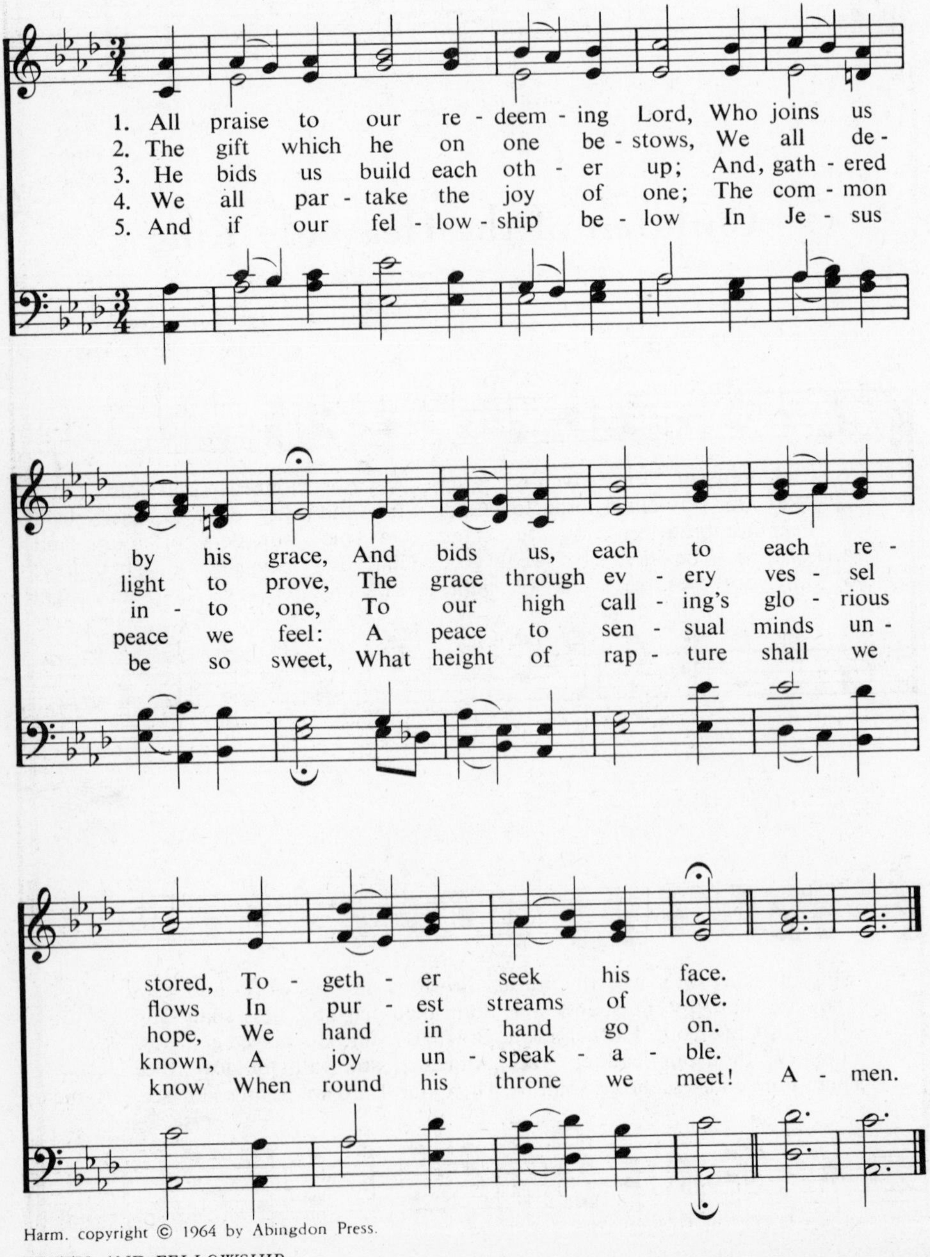
1. All praise to our re - deem - ing Lord, Who joins us
2. The gift which he on one be - stows, We all de -
3. He bids us build each oth - er up; And, gath - ered
4. We all par - take the joy of one; The com - mon
5. And if our fel - low - ship be - low In Je - sus
by his grace, And bids us, each to each re -
light to prove, The grace through ev - ery ves - sel
in - to one, To our high call - ing's glo - rious
peace we feel: A peace to sen - sual minds un -
be so sweet, What height of rap - ture shall we
stored, To - geth - er seek his face.
flows In pur - est streams of love.
hope, We hand in hand go on.
known, A joy un - speak - a - ble.
know When round his throne we meet! A - men.

Come, Let Us Join Our Friends Above

PISGAH CM
J. C. Lowry in *Kentucky Harmony*, 1817
Harm. by A. C. L.

Charles Wesley, 1707-1788

1. Come, let us join our friends a - bove Who
2. Let saints on earth u - nite to sing With
3. One fam - i - ly we dwell in him, One
4. One ar - my of the liv - ing God, To
5. E'en now by faith we join our hands With
have ob - tained the prize, And on the ea - gle
those to glo - ry gone; For all the ser - vants
Church a - bove, be - neath, Though now di - vid - ed
his com - mand we bow; Part of his host have
those that went be - fore, And greet the blood - re -
wings of love To joys ce - les - tial rise.
of our King, In earth and heaven, are one:
by the stream, The nar - row stream of death;
crossed the flood, And part are cross - ing now.
deem - ed bands On the e - ter - nal shore. A - men.

Alternate tune: DUNDEE (FRENCH)

Jerusalem the Golden

BERNARD OF CLUNY, 12th Century
Trans. by JOHN M. NEALE, 1818-1866

EWING 76.76.D.
ALEXANDER EWING, 1830-1895

1. Je - ru - sa - lem the gold - en, With milk and hon - ey blest!
2. They stand, those halls of Zi - on, All ju - bi - lant with song,
3. Strive, man, to win that glo - ry; Toil, man, to gain that light;
4. O sweet and bless - ed coun - try, The home of God's e - lect!
Be - neath thy con - tem - pla - tion Sink heart and voice op-pressed.
And bright with many an an - gel, And all the mar - tyr throng;
Send hope be - fore to grasp it, Till hope be lost in sight.
O sweet and bless - ed coun - try That ea - ger hearts ex - pect!
I know not, O I know not What joys a - wait us there;
The Prince is ev - er in them; The day - light is se - rene;
Ex - ult, O dust and ash - es; The Lord shall be thy part:
Je - sus, in mer - cy bring us To that dear land of rest;
What ra - dian - cy of glo - ry, What light be - yond com - pare.
The pas - tures of the bless - ed Are decked in glo - rious sheen.
His on - ly, his for - ev - er Thou shalt be, and thou art.
Who art, with God the Fa - ther And Spir - it, ev - er blest. A-men.

O Shepherd of the Nameless Fold

NORSE AIR CMD
Norse Folk Melody

MARY A. LATHBURY, 1841-1913

Arr. by WILLIAM J. KIRKPATRICK, 1838-1921

1. O Shep-herd of the name-less fold, The bless-ed Church to be, Our hearts with love and long-ing turn To find their rest in thee; "Thy king-dom come," its heaven-ly walls Un-seen a-round us rise, And deep in lov-ing hu-man hearts Its broad foun-da-tions rise.
2. O ho-ly king-dom, hap-py fold, The bless-ed Church to be, Our hearts in love and wor-ship turn To find them-selves in thee! Thy bounds are known to God a-lone, For they are set a-bove; The length, the breadth, the height are one, And mea-sured by his love. A-men.

305

Onward, Christian Soldiers

ST. GERTRUDE 65.65.D. with Refrain
ARTHUR S. SULLIVAN, 1842-1900

SABINE BARING-GOULD, 1834-1924

1. On-ward, Chris-tian sol - diers! March-ing as to war,
2. Like a might-y ar - my Moves the Church of God;
3. Crowns and thrones may per - ish, King-doms rise and wane,
4. On-ward, then, ye peo - ple, Join our hap-py throng,
With the cross of Je - sus Go-ing on be - fore.
Broth-ers, we are tread - ing Where the saints have trod;
But the Church of Je - sus Con-stant will re - main;
Blend with ours your voic - es In the tri-umph song;
Christ, the roy-al Mas - ter, Leads a - gainst the foe;
We are not di - vid - ed, All one bod - y we,
Gates of hell can nev - er Gainst that Church pre - vail;
Glo - ry, laud, and hon - or Un - to Christ the King;
For-ward in - to bat - tle, See his ban-ners go!
One in hope and doc - trine, One in char - i - ty.
We have Christ's own prom - ise, And that can - not fail.
This through count - less a - ges Men and an - gels sing.

Refrain
On-ward, Chris-tian sol-diers, March-ing as to war,
With the cross of Je-sus Go-ing on be-fore. A-men.

306

Blest Be the Tie That Binds

DENNIS SM
JOHANN G. NÄGELI, 1768-1836
Arr. by LOWELL MASON, 1792-1872

JOHN FAWCETT, 1740-1817

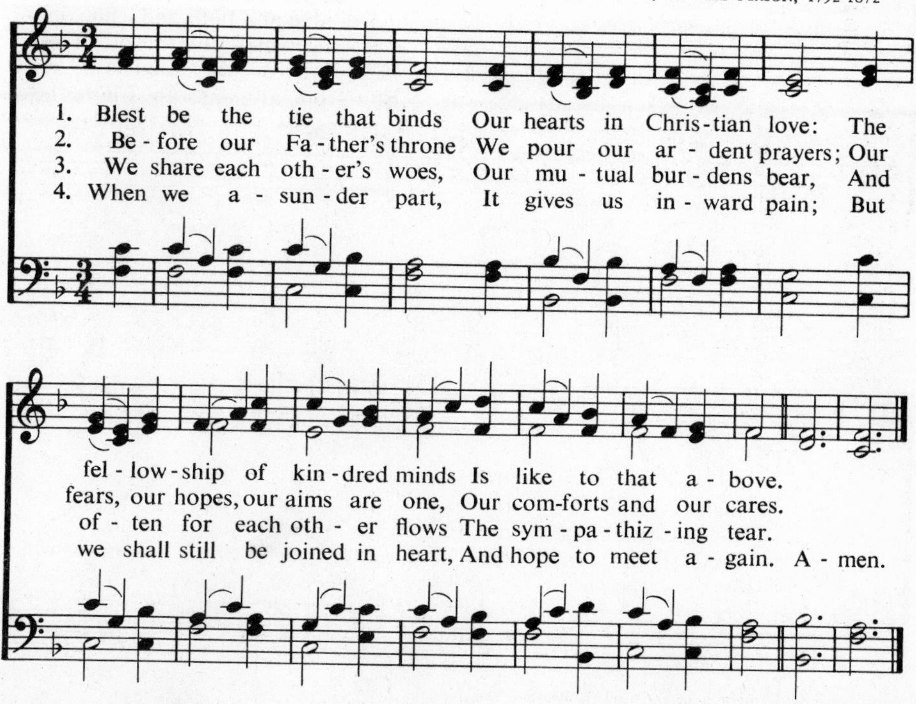
1. Blest be the tie that binds Our hearts in Chris-tian love: The fel-low-ship of kin-dred minds Is like to that a-bove.
2. Be-fore our Fa-ther's throne We pour our ar-dent prayers; Our fears, our hopes, our aims are one, Our com-forts and our cares.
3. We share each oth-er's woes, Our mu-tual bur-dens bear, And of-ten for each oth-er flows The sym-pa-thiz-ing tear.
4. When we a-sun-der part, It gives us in-ward pain; But we shall still be joined in heart, And hope to meet a-gain. A-men.

307 Father, We Thank Thee Who Hast Planted

COMMANDMENTS 98.98.

Didache, c. 110
Trans. by F. BLAND TUCKER, 1895-

Genevan Psalter, 1547
Attr. to LOUIS BOURGEOIS, c. 1510-c. 1561

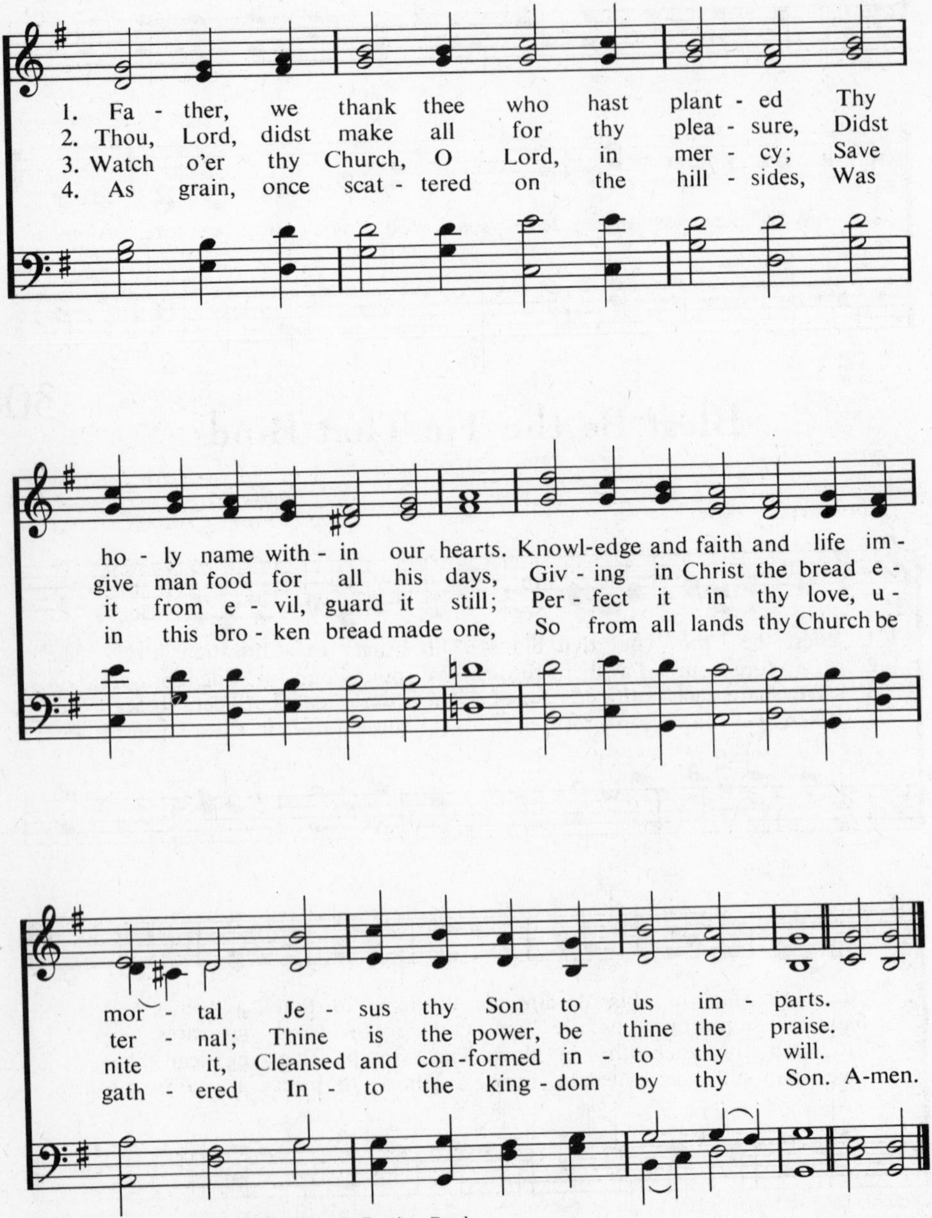
1. Fa - ther, we thank thee who hast plant - ed Thy ho - ly name with - in our hearts. Knowl-edge and faith and life im - mor - tal Je - sus thy Son to us im - parts.
2. Thou, Lord, didst make all for thy plea - sure, Didst give man food for all his days, Giv - ing in Christ the bread e - ter - nal; Thine is the power, be thine the praise.
3. Watch o'er thy Church, O Lord, in mer - cy; Save it from e - vil, guard it still; Per - fect it in thy love, u - nite it, Cleansed and con - formed in - to thy will.
4. As grain, once scat - tered on the hill - sides, Was in this bro - ken bread made one, So from all lands thy Church be gath - ered In - to the king - dom by thy Son. A-men.

Words used by permission of the Church Pension Fund.

O Where Are Kings and Empires Now

A. Cleveland Coxe, 1818-1896

ST. ANNE CM
Probably by William Croft, 1678-1727

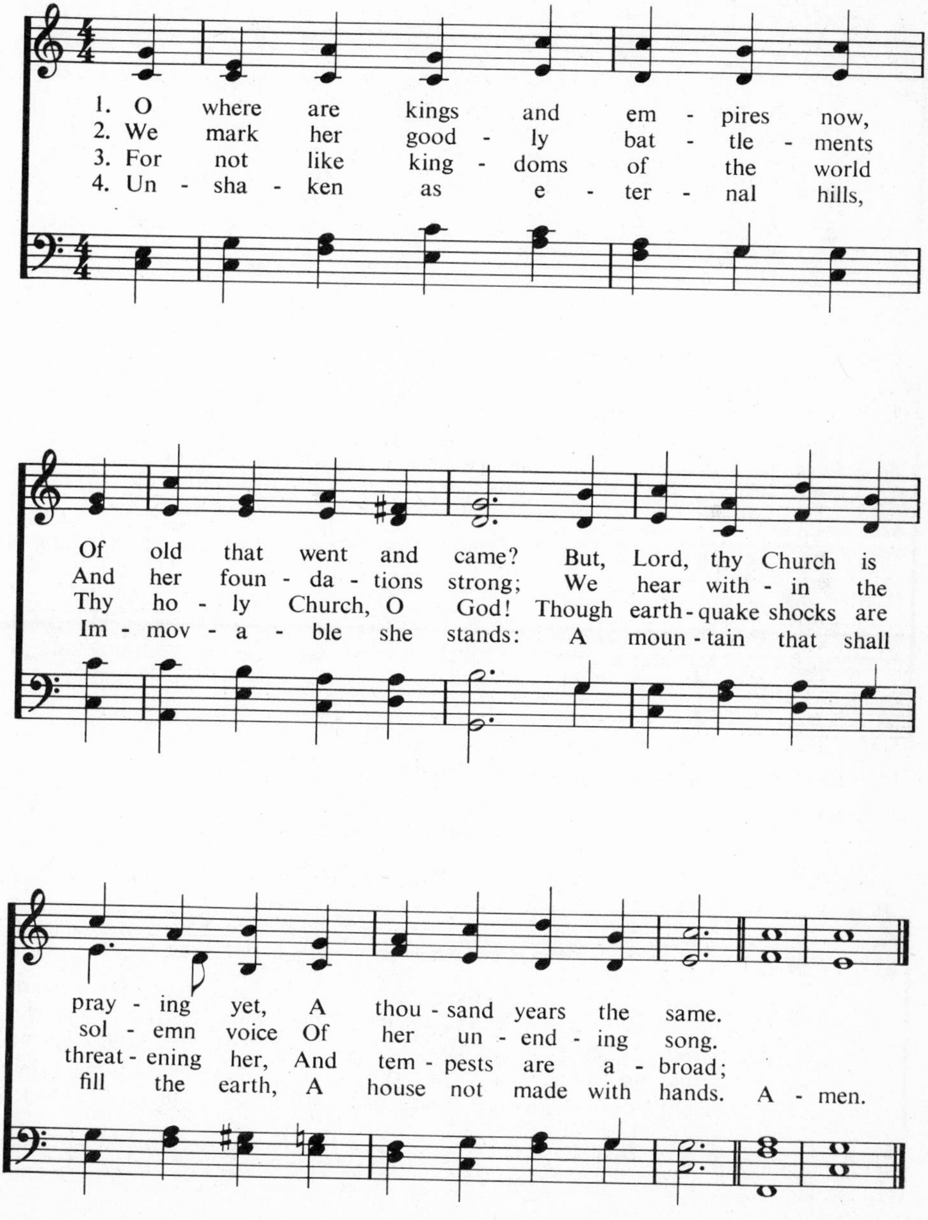
1. O where are kings and em - pires now,
2. We mark her good - ly bat - tle - ments
3. For not like king - doms of the world
4. Un - sha - ken as e - ter - nal hills,
Of old that went and came? But, Lord, thy Church is
And her foun - da - tions strong; We hear with - in the
Thy ho - ly Church, O God! Though earth - quake shocks are
Im - mov - a - ble she stands: A moun - tain that shall
pray - ing yet, A thou - sand years the same.
sol - emn voice Of her un - end - ing song.
threat - ening her, And tem - pests are a - broad;
fill the earth, A house not made with hands. A - men.

309

Jesus, Lord, We Look to Thee

SAVANNAH 77.77.
Foundery Collection, 1742

CHARLES WESLEY, 1707-1788

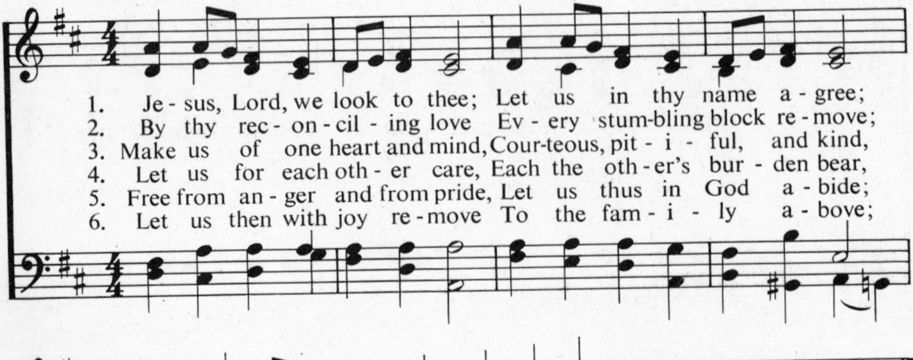
1. Je - sus, Lord, we look to thee; Let us in thy name a - gree;
2. By thy rec - on - cil - ing love Ev - ery stum-bling block re - move;
3. Make us of one heart and mind, Cour-teous, pit - i - ful, and kind,
4. Let us for each oth - er care, Each the oth - er's bur - den bear,
5. Free from an - ger and from pride, Let us thus in God a - bide;
6. Let us then with joy re - move To the fam - i - ly a - bove;

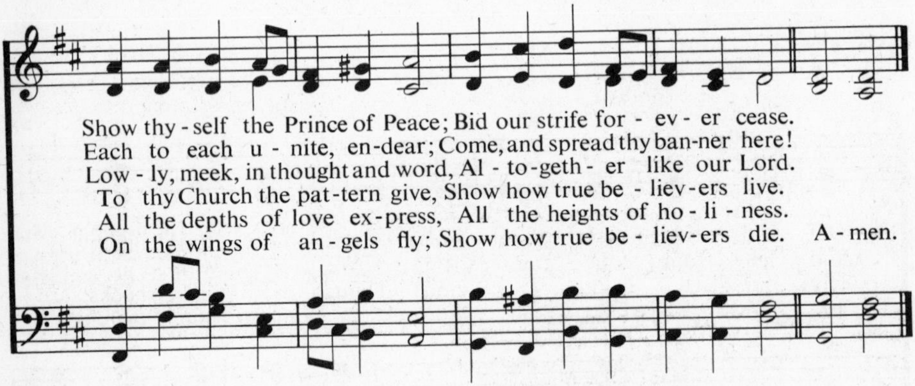
Show thy - self the Prince of Peace; Bid our strife for - ev - er cease.
Each to each u - nite, en - dear; Come, and spread thy ban - ner here!
Low - ly, meek, in thought and word, Al - to - geth - er like our Lord.
To thy Church the pat - tern give, Show how true be - liev - ers live.
All the depths of love ex - press, All the heights of ho - li - ness.
On the wings of an - gels fly; Show how true be - liev - ers die. A - men.

310

Jesus, We Look to Thee

MORNINGTON SM
Arr. from a chant by GARRET WELLESLEY, 1735-1781

CHARLES WESLEY, 1707-1788

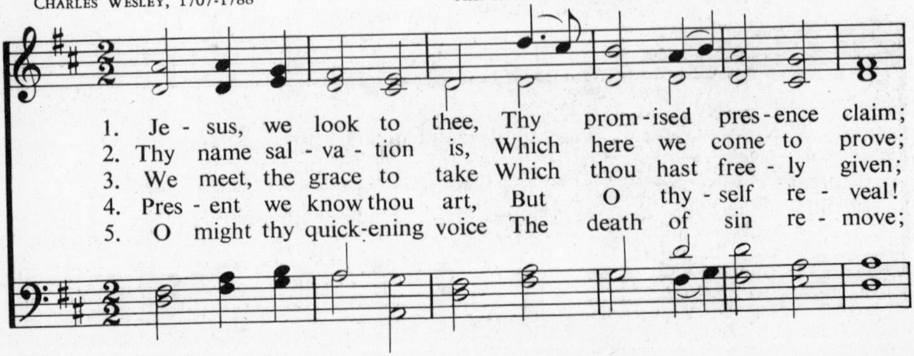
1. Je - sus, we look to thee, Thy prom - ised pres - ence claim;
2. Thy name sal - va - tion is, Which here we come to prove;
3. We meet, the grace to take Which thou hast free - ly given;
4. Pres - ent we know thou art, But O thy - self re - veal!
5. O might thy quick-ening voice The death of sin re - move;

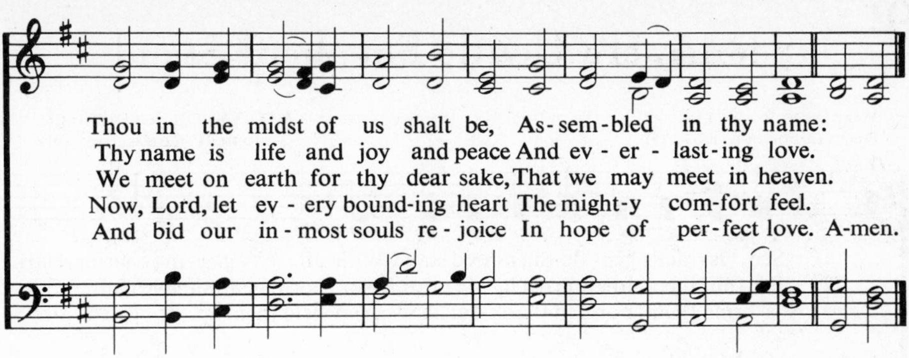
Thou in the midst of us shalt be, As-sem-bled in thy name:
Thy name is life and joy and peace And ev - er - last-ing love.
We meet on earth for thy dear sake, That we may meet in heaven.
Now, Lord, let ev - ery bound-ing heart The might-y com-fort feel.
And bid our in - most souls re - joice In hope of per-fect love. A-men.

Alternate tune: ST. THOMAS

311

Jesus, with Thy Church Abide

CANTERBURY 777.6.

THOMAS B. POLLOCK, 1836-1896

Adapt. from ORLANDO GIBBONS, 1583-1625

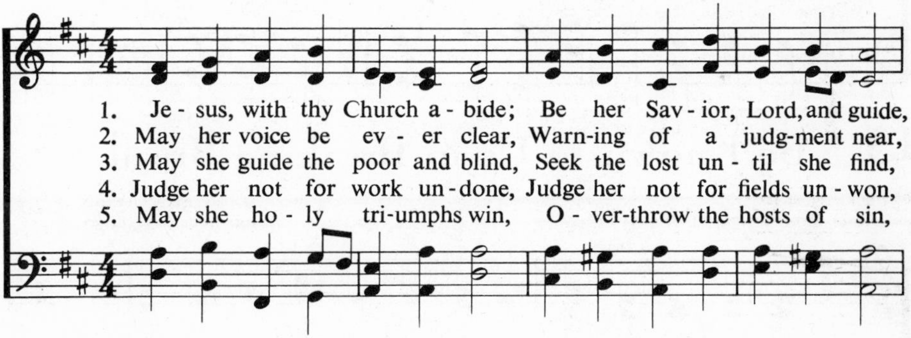
1. Je - sus, with thy Church a - bide; Be her Sav - ior, Lord, and guide,
2. May her voice be ev - er clear, Warn-ing of a judg-ment near,
3. May she guide the poor and blind, Seek the lost un - til she find,
4. Judge her not for work un - done, Judge her not for fields un - won,
5. May she ho - ly tri-umphs win, O - ver-throw the hosts of sin,

While on earth her faith is tried: We be-seech thee, hear us.
Tell-ing of a Sav - ior dear: We be-seech thee, hear us.
And the bro - ken-heart - ed bind: We be-seech thee, hear us.
Bless her works in thee be - gun: We be-seech thee, hear us.
Gath - er all the na - tions in: We be-seech thee, hear us. A-men.

312
See Israel's Gentle Shepherd Stand

MARK 10:13-16
PHILIP DODDRIDGE, 1702-1751

MEDITATION (GOWER) CM
JOHN H. GOWER, 1855-1922

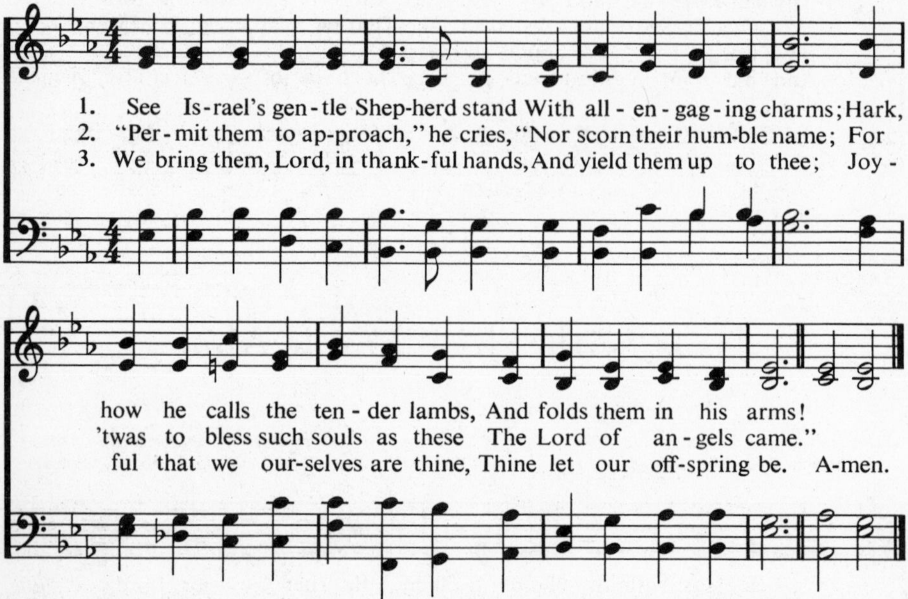
1. See Is-rael's gen-tle Shep-herd stand With all - en - gag - ing charms; Hark,
2. "Per-mit them to ap-proach," he cries, "Nor scorn their hum-ble name; For
3. We bring them, Lord, in thank-ful hands, And yield them up to thee; Joy -
how he calls the ten - der lambs, And folds them in his arms!
'twas to bless such souls as these The Lord of an - gels came."
ful that we our-selves are thine, Thine let our off-spring be. A-men.

313
Be Known to Us in Breaking Bread

LUKE 24:30-31
JAMES MONTGOMERY, 1771-1854

ST. FLAVIAN CM
Adapt. from *Day's Psalter*, 1562

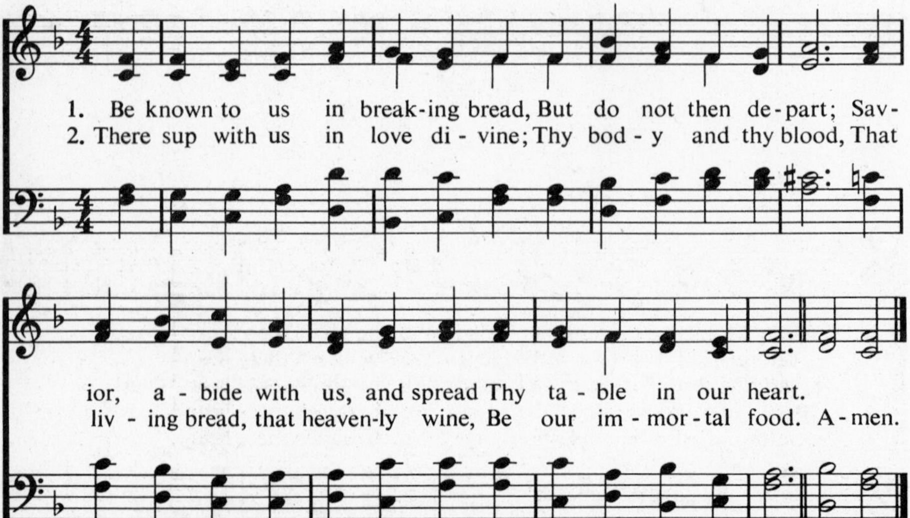
1. Be known to us in break-ing bread, But do not then de-part; Sav-
2. There sup with us in love di - vine; Thy bod - y and thy blood, That
ior, a - bide with us, and spread Thy ta - ble in our heart.
liv - ing bread, that heaven-ly wine, Be our im - mor - tal food. A - men.

Alternate tune: DUNDEE (FRENCH)

314

For the Bread, Which Thou Hast Broken

KINGDOM 87.87.

Louis F. Benson, 1855-1930

V. Earle Copes, 1921-

1. For the bread, which thou hast bro - ken, For the
2. By this pledge that thou dost love us, By thy
3. With our saint - ed ones in glo - ry Seat - ed
4. In thy ser - vice, Lord, de - fend us; In our
wine, which thou hast poured, For the words, which thou hast
gift of peace re - stored, By thy call to heaven a -
at our Fa - ther's board, May the Church that wait - eth
hearts keep watch and ward; In the world where thou dost
spo - ken, Now we give thee thanks, O Lord.
bove us, Hal - low all our lives, O Lord.
for thee Keep love's tie un - bro - ken, Lord.
send us Let thy king - dom come, O Lord. A - men.

315

Author of Life Divine

AUTHOR OF LIFE 66.66.88.

CHARLES WESLEY, 1707-1788 | ROBERT J. POWELL, 1932-

1. Au-thor of life di-vine, Who hast a ta-ble spread, Fur-nished with
2. Our need-y souls sus-tain With fresh sup-plies of love, Till all thy
mys-tic wine And ev-er-last-ing bread: Pre-serve the life thy-
life we gain, And all thy ful-ness prove, And, strength-ened by thy
self hast given, And feed and train us up for heaven.
per-fect grace, Be-hold with-out a veil thy face. A-men.

316

According to Thy Gracious Word

LUKE 22:19 | TALLIS' ORDINAL CM

JAMES MONTGOMERY, 1771-1854 | THOMAS TALLIS, c. 1505-1585

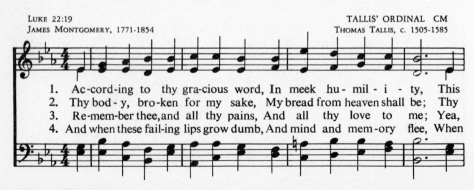

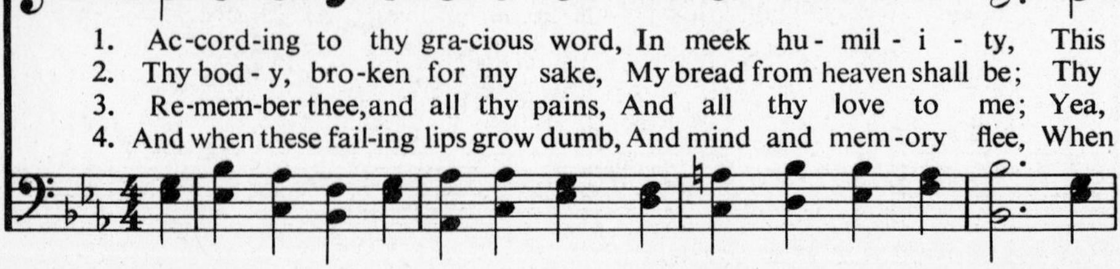
1. Ac-cord-ing to thy gra-cious word, In meek hu-mil-i-ty, This
2. Thy bod-y, bro-ken for my sake, My bread from heaven shall be; Thy
3. Re-mem-ber thee, and all thy pains, And all thy love to me; Yea,
4. And when these fail-ing lips grow dumb, And mind and mem-ory flee, When

will I do, my dy-ing Lord, I will re-mem-ber thee.
tes-ta-men-tal cup I take, And thus re-mem-ber thee.
while a breath, a pulse re-mains, Will I re-mem-ber thee!
thou shalt in thy king-dom come, Then, Lord, re-mem-ber me! A-men.

317

The Bread of Life, for All Men Broken

SHENG EN 98.98.

TIMOTHY TINGFANG LEW, 1892-1947
Trans. by WALTER REGINALD OXENHAM TAYLOR, 1890-

SU YIN-LAN, 1915-1937
Arr. by BLISS WIANT, 1895-

1. The bread of life, for all men bro-ken! He drank the
2. With god-ly fear we seek thy pres-ence; Our hearts dis-
3. O Lord, we pray, come thou a-mong us, Light-en our
cup on Gol-goth-a. His grace we trust, and spread with rev-erence
tressed by peo-ple's grief. Thy ho-ly face is stained with bitter tears;
eyes, bright-ly ap-pear! Im-man-u-el, heaven's joy un-end-ing,
This ho-ly feast, and thus re-mem-ber.
Our hu-man pain still bearest thou with us.
Our life with thine for-ev-er blend-ing. A-men.

Words used by permission of W. R. O. Taylor.

Deck Thyself, My Soul, with Gladness

JOHANN FRANCK, 1618-1677
Trans. by CATHERINE WINKWORTH, 1827-1878

SCHMÜCKE DICH 88.88.88.88.
JOHANN CRÜGER, 1598-1662

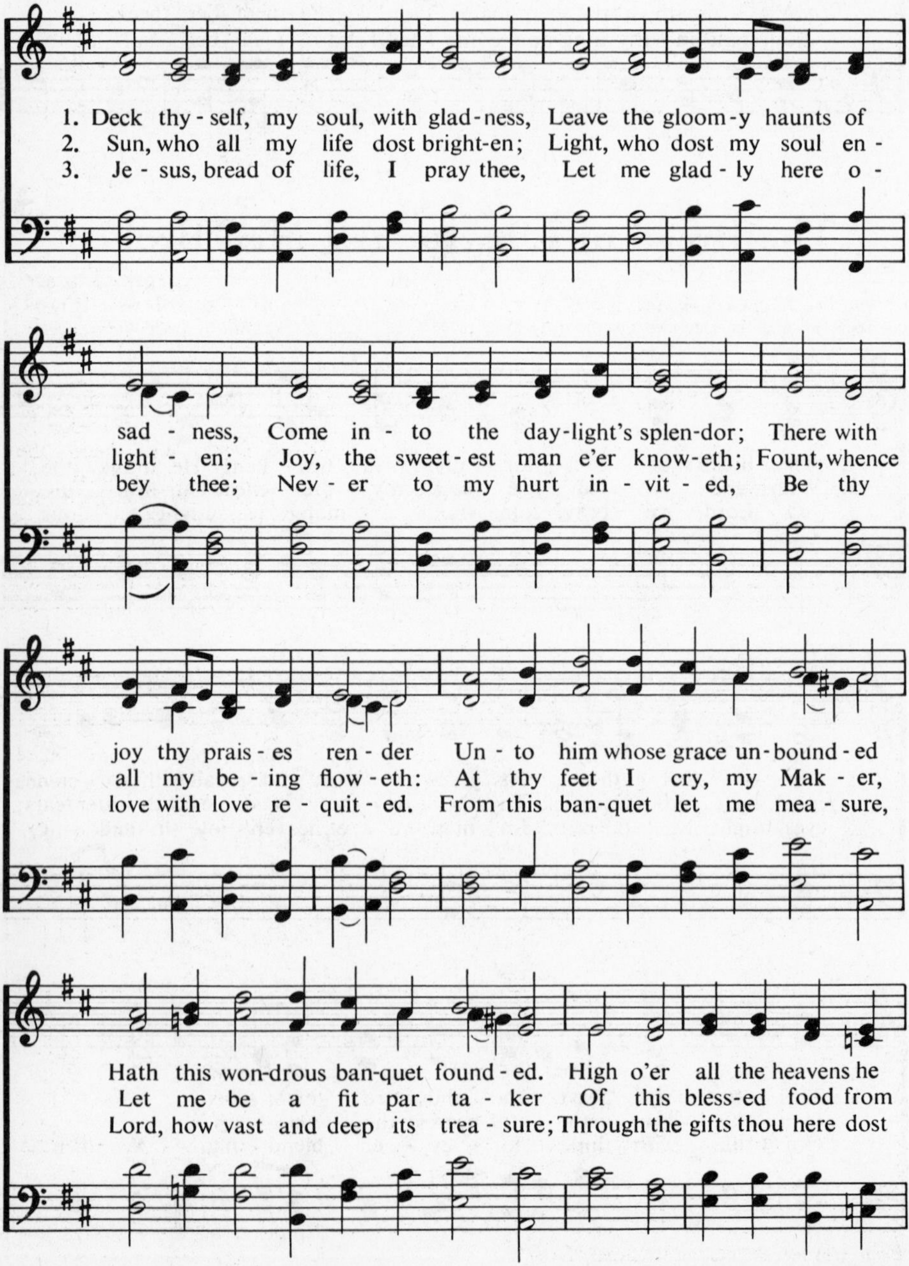
1. Deck thy - self, my soul, with glad - ness, Leave the gloom - y haunts of
2. Sun, who all my life dost bright - en; Light, who dost my soul en -
3. Je - sus, bread of life, I pray thee, Let me glad - ly here o -
sad - ness, Come in - to the day - light's splen - dor; There with
light - en; Joy, the sweet - est man e'er know - eth; Fount, whence
bey thee; Nev - er to my hurt in - vit - ed, Be thy
joy thy prais - es ren - der Un - to him whose grace un - bound - ed
all my be - ing flow - eth: At thy feet I cry, my Mak - er,
love with love re - quit - ed. From this ban - quet let me mea - sure,
Hath this won - drous ban - quet found - ed. High o'er all the heavens he
Let me be a fit par - ta - ker Of this bless - ed food from
Lord, how vast and deep its trea - sure; Through the gifts thou here dost

reign - eth, Yet to dwell with thee he deign - eth.
heav - en, For our good, thy glo - ry, giv - en.
give me, As thy guest in heaven re - ceive me. A-men.

319

In Memory of the Savior's Love

SALZBURG CM
Adapt. from JOHANN MICHAEL HAYDN, 1737-1806
Harm. by V. E. C.

THOMAS COTTERILL, 1779-1823

1. In mem - ory of the Sav - ior's love, We keep the
2. One fold, one faith, one hope, one Lord, One God a -
3. By faith we take the bread of life With which our
4. In faith and mem - ory thus we sing The won - ders
sa - cred feast, Where ev - ery hum - ble, con - trite
lone we know; As bre - thren, all, let ev - ery
souls are fed, The cup in to - ken of his
of his love, And thus an - tic - i - pate by
heart Is made a wel - come guest.
heart With kind af - fec - tion glow.
blood That was for sin - ners shed.
faith The heaven - ly feast a - bove. A - men.

320

Bread of the World

Reginald Heber, 1783-1826

EUCHARISTIC HYMN 98.98.
John S. B. Hodges, 1830-1915

1. Bread of the world in mer - cy bro - ken, Wine of the
2. Look on the heart by sor - row bro - ken, Look on the
soul in mer - cy shed, By whom the words of life were
tears by sin - ners shed; And be thy feast to us the
spo - ken, And in whose death our sins are dead:
to - ken That by thy grace our souls are fed! A - men.

321

Beneath the Forms of Outward Rite

James A. Blaisdell, 1867-1957

PERRY CM
Leo Sowerby, 1895-

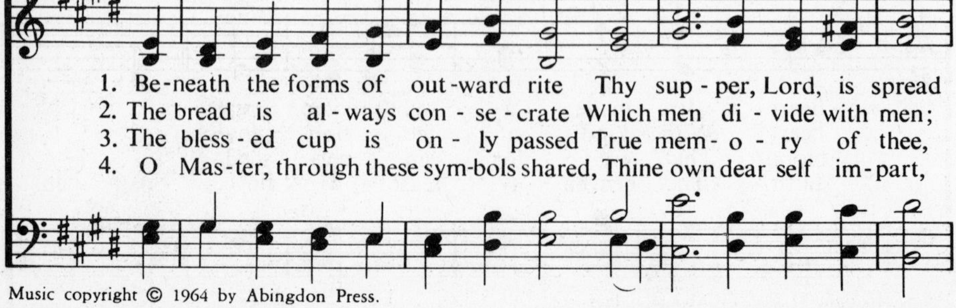
1. Be-neath the forms of out-ward rite Thy sup - per, Lord, is spread
2. The bread is al - ways con - se - crate Which men di - vide with men;
3. The bless - ed cup is on - ly passed True mem - o - ry of thee,
4. O Mas-ter, through these sym-bols shared, Thine own dear self im-part,

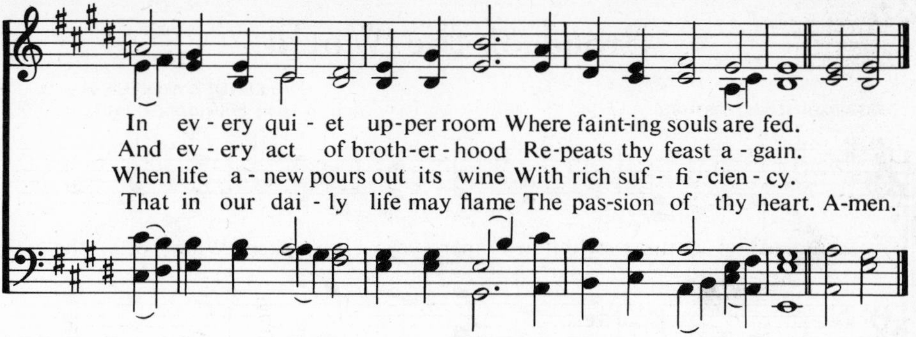

In ev - ery qui - et up-per room Where faint-ing souls are fed.
And ev - ery act of broth-er - hood Re-peats thy feast a - gain.
When life a - new pours out its wine With rich suf - fi - cien - cy.
That in our dai - ly life may flame The pas-sion of thy heart. A-men.

322

Bread of the World

Reginald Heber, 1783-1826

SRI LAMPANG 98.98.
Thailand Folk Melody

1. Bread of the world in mer - cy bro - ken, Wine of the soul in mer - cy shed, By whom the words of life were spo - ken, And in whose death our sins are dead:
2. Look on the heart by sor - row bro - ken, Look on the tears by sin - ners shed; And be thy feast to us the to - ken That by thy grace our souls are fed. A-men.

323

Bread of the World

RENDEZ À DIEU 98.98.D.

REGINALD HEBER, 1783-1826

Attr. to LOUIS BOURGEOIS, c. 1510-c. 1561

Unison
Bread of the world in mer - cy bro - ken, Wine of the
soul in mer - cy shed, By whom the words of life were spo - ken,
And in whose death our sins are dead: Look on the heart by sor - row
bro - ken, Look on the tears by sin - ners shed; And be thy
feast to us the to - ken That by thy grace our souls are fed. A-men.

Let All Mortal Flesh Keep Silence

Liturgy of St. James
Trans. by GERARD MOULTRIE, 1829-1885

PICARDY 87.87.87.
Trad. French Tune

Unison
1. Let all mor - tal flesh keep si - lence, And with fear and
2. King of kings, yet born of Ma - ry, As of old on
3. Rank on rank the host of heav - en Spreads its van - guard
4. At his feet the six - winged ser - aph, Cher - u - bim, with
trem - bling stand; Pon - der noth - ing earth - ly - mind - ed,
earth he stood, Lord of lords, in hu - man ves - ture,
on the way, As the Light of light de - scend - eth
sleep - less eye, Veil their fac - es to the pres - ence,
For with bless - ing in his hand, Christ our God to
In the bod - y and the blood, He will give to
From the realms of end - less day, That the powers of
As with cease - less voice they cry, Al - le - lu - ia,
earth de - scend - eth, Our full hom - age to de - mand.
all the faith - ful His own self for heaven - ly food.
hell may van - ish As the dark - ness clears a - way.
Al - le - lu - ia, Al - le - lu - ia, Lord most high! A - men.

325 The King of Heaven His Table Spreads

DUNDEE (FRENCH) CM

PHILIP DODDRIDGE, 1702-1751 — *Scottish Psalter*, 1615

1. The King of heaven his ta - ble spreads, And
2. Par - don and peace to dy - ing men And
3. Mil - lions of souls, in glo - ry now, Were
4. All things are rea - dy, come a - way, Nor
bless - ings crown the board; Not par - a - dise, with
end - less life are given, Through the rich blood that
fed and feast - ed here; And mil - lions more, still
weak ex - cus - es frame. Come to your plac - es
all its joys, Could such de - light af - ford.
Je - sus shed, To raise our souls to heaven.
on the way, A - round the board ap - pear.
at the feast, And bless the found - er's name. A - men.

Here, O My Lord, I See Thee

ADORO TE 10 10.10 10.

HORATIUS BONAR, 1808-1889

Benedictine Plainsong, Mode V, 13th Century

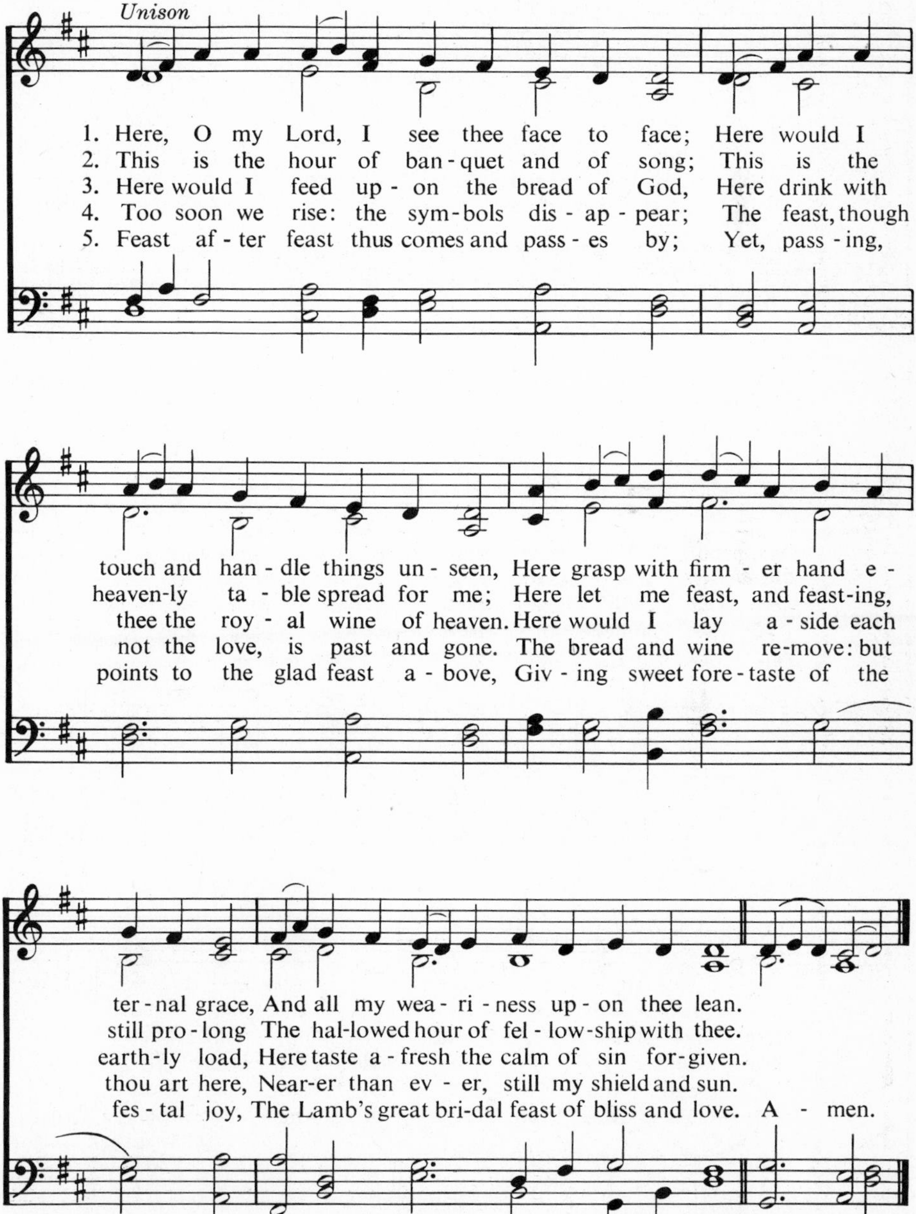
Unison
1. Here, O my Lord, I see thee face to face; Here would I
2. This is the hour of ban - quet and of song; This is the
3. Here would I feed up - on the bread of God, Here drink with
4. Too soon we rise: the sym - bols dis - ap - pear; The feast, though
5. Feast af - ter feast thus comes and pass - es by; Yet, pass - ing,
touch and han - dle things un - seen, Here grasp with firm - er hand e -
heaven-ly ta - ble spread for me; Here let me feast, and feast-ing,
thee the roy - al wine of heaven. Here would I lay a - side each
not the love, is past and gone. The bread and wine re-move: but
points to the glad feast a - bove, Giv - ing sweet fore - taste of the
ter - nal grace, And all my wea - ri - ness up - on thee lean.
still pro - long The hal-lowed hour of fel - low-ship with thee.
earth - ly load, Here taste a - fresh the calm of sin for - given.
thou art here, Near-er than ev - er, still my shield and sun.
fes - tal joy, The Lamb's great bri - dal feast of bliss and love. A - men.

327

Here, O My Lord, I See Thee

PENITENTIA 10 10.10 10.

HORATIUS BONAR, 1808-1889

EDWARD DEARLE, 1806-1891

1. Here, O my Lord, I see thee face to face;
2. This is the hour of ban - quet and of song;
3. Here would I feed up - on the bread of God,
4. Too soon we rise: the sym - bols dis - ap - pear;
5. Feast af - ter feast thus comes and pass - es by;
Here would I touch and han - dle things un - seen,
This is the heaven - ly ta - ble spread for me;
Here drink with thee the roy - al wine of heaven.
The feast, though not the love, is past and gone.
Yet, pass - ing, points to the glad feast a - bove,
Here grasp with firm - er hand e - ter - nal grace,
Here let me feast, and feast - ing, still pro - long
Here would I lay a - side each earth - ly load,
The bread and wine re - move: but thou art here,
Giv - ing sweet fore - taste of the fes - tal joy,

And all my wea - ri - ness up - on thee lean.
The hal - lowed hour of fel - low - ship with thee.
Here taste a - fresh the calm of sin for - given.
Near - er than ev - er, still my shield and sun.
The Lamb's great bri - dal feast of bliss and love. A - men.

How Happy Are Thy Servants, Lord

328

CHARLES WESLEY, 1707-1788

MARTYRDOM CM
HUGH WILSON, 1766-1824

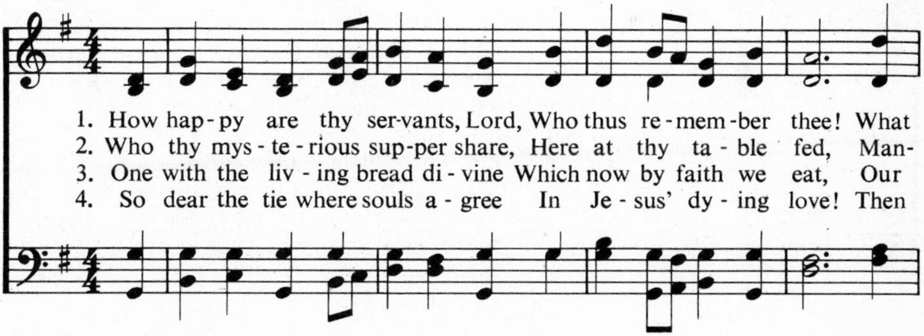
1. How hap - py are thy ser-vants, Lord, Who thus re - mem - ber thee! What
2. Who thy mys - te - rious sup-per share, Here at thy ta - ble fed, Man-
3. One with the liv - ing bread di - vine Which now by faith we eat, Our
4. So dear the tie where souls a - gree In Je - sus' dy - ing love! Then

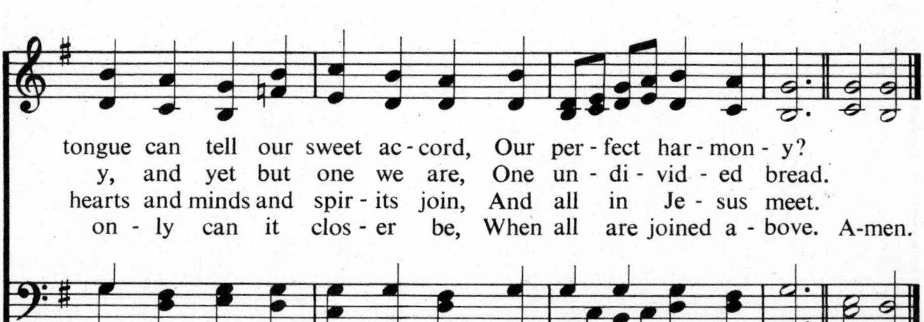
tongue can tell our sweet ac - cord, Our per - fect har - mon - y?
y, and yet but one we are, One un - di - vid - ed bread.
hearts and minds and spir - its join, And all in Je - sus meet.
on - ly can it clos - er be, When all are joined a - bove. A-men.

329

Jesus, Thou Joy of Loving Hearts

ROCKINGHAM (MASON) LM

Attr. to BERNARD OF CLAIRVAUX, 1091-1153
Trans. by RAY PALMER, 1808-1887

LOWELL MASON, 1792-1872
Harm. by A. C. L.

1. Je - sus, thou joy of lov - ing hearts! Thou fount of life! Thou
2. Thy truth un-changed hath ev - er stood; Thou sav - est those that
3. We taste thee, O thou liv - ing bread, And long to feast up -
4. Our rest - less spir - its yearn for thee Wher - e'er our change-ful
5. O Je - sus, ev - er with us stay; Make all our mo - ments
light of men! From the best bliss that earth im - parts,
on thee call; To them that seek thee, thou art good;
on thee still; We drink of thee, the foun - tain - head,
lot is cast, Glad, when thy gra - cious smile we see,
calm and bright; Chase the dark night of sin a - way;
We turn un - filled to thee a - gain.
To them that find thee, all - in - all.
And thirst our souls from thee to fill!
Blest, when our faith can hold thee fast.
Shed o'er the world thy ho - ly light! A - men.

330

Let Us Break Bread Together

LET US BREAK BREAD 10 10. with Refrain
American Folk Hymn
Harm. by C. R. Y.

American Folk Hymn

Unison
1. Let us break bread to - geth - er on our knees;
2. Let us drink wine to - geth - er on our knees;
3. Let us praise God to - geth - er on our knees;
Let us break bread to - geth - er on our knees.
Let us drink wine to - geth - er on our knees.
Let us praise God to - geth - er on our knees.
Refrain
When I fall on my knees, With my face to the ris - ing
When I fall on my knees, With my face to the ris - ing
When I fall on my knees, With my face to the ris - ing
sun, O Lord, have mer - cy on me.
sun, O Lord, have mer - cy on me.
sun, O Lord, have mer - cy on me. A - men.

331

Jesus Spreads His Banner o'er Us

AUTUMN 87.87.D.

ROSWELL PARK, 1807-1869 — Arr. from FRANÇOIS H. BARTHÉLÉMON, 1741-1808

1. Je - sus spreads his ban - ner o'er us, Cheers our fam-ished souls with food;
2. In thy ho - ly in - car - na - tion, When the an - gels sang thy birth,
He the ban-quet spreads be-fore us, Of his mys - tic flesh and blood.
In thy fast - ing and temp - ta - tion, In thy la - bors on the earth,
Pre-cious ban-quet, bread of heav - en, Wine of glad - ness, flow-ing free,
In thy tri - al and re - jec - tion, In thy suf-ferings on the tree,
May we taste it, kind - ly giv - en, In re-mem-brance, Lord, of thee.
In thy glo-rious res - ur - rec - tion, May we, Lord, re-mem-ber thee. A-men.

Alternate tune: HYFRYDOL

O the Depth of Love Divine

BARNABAS 76.76.77.76.

CHARLES WESLEY, 1707-1788 — Adapt. from *French Psalter*, 1561

1. O the depth of love di - vine, Th' un-fath - o - ma - ble grace!
2. Let the wis - est mor - tal show How we the grace re - ceive;
3. How can heaven-ly spir - its rise, By earth - ly mat - ter fed,
4. Sure and re - al is the grace, The man - ner be un - known;
Who shall say how bread and wine God in - to man con - veys!
Fee - ble el - e - ments be - stow A power not theirs to give.
Drink here - with di - vine sup - plies, And eat im - mor - tal bread?
On - ly meet us in thy ways And per - fect us in one.
How the bread his flesh im - parts, How the wine trans-mits his blood,
Who ex-plains the won-drous way, How through these the vir - tue came?
Ask the Fa - ther's wis - dom how; Him that did the means or - dain!
Let us taste the heaven - ly powers; Lord, we ask for noth - ing more.
Fills his faith-ful peo - ple's hearts With all the life of God!
These the vir - tue did con - vey, Yet still re - main the same.
An - gels round our al - tars bow To search it out in vain.
Thine to bless, 'tis on - ly ours To won - der and a - dore. A-men.

333

O Perfect Love

PERFECT LOVE 11 10.11 10.

DOROTHY B. GURNEY, 1858-1932

Arr. from JOSEPH BARNBY, 1838-1896

1. O per - fect Love, all hu - man thought tran - scend - ing,
2. O per - fect Life, be thou their full as - sur - ance
3. Grant them the joy which bright - ens earth - ly sor - row;
Low - ly we kneel in prayer be - fore thy throne,
Of ten - der char - i - ty and stead - fast faith,
Grant them the peace which calms all earth - ly strife,
That theirs may be the love which knows no end - ing,
Of pa - tient hope and qui - et, brave en - dur - ance,
And to life's day the glo - rious un - known mor - row
Whom thou for - ev - er - more dost join in one.
With child - like trust that fears nor pain nor death.
That dawns up - on e - ter - nal love and life. A - men.

MARRIAGE

334

May the Grace of Christ Our Savior

II CORINTHIANS 13:14
JOHN NEWTON, 1725-1807

STUTTGART 87.87.
Psalmodia Sacra, Gotha, 1715
Adapt. by HENRY J. GAUNTLETT, 1805-1876

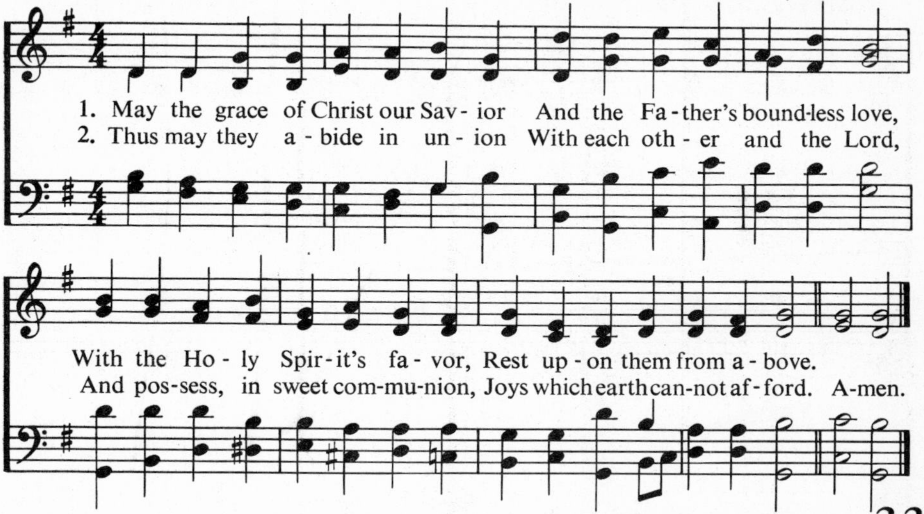
1. May the grace of Christ our Sav - ior And the Fa - ther's bound-less love,
2. Thus may they a - bide in un - ion With each oth - er and the Lord,
With the Ho - ly Spir - it's fa - vor, Rest up - on them from a - bove.
And pos - sess, in sweet com - mu - nion, Joys which earth can - not af - ford. A - men.

335

Let Zion's Watchmen All Awake

HEBREWS 13:17
PHILIP DODDRIDGE, 1702-1751

ARLINGTON CM
THOMAS A. ARNE, 1710-1778

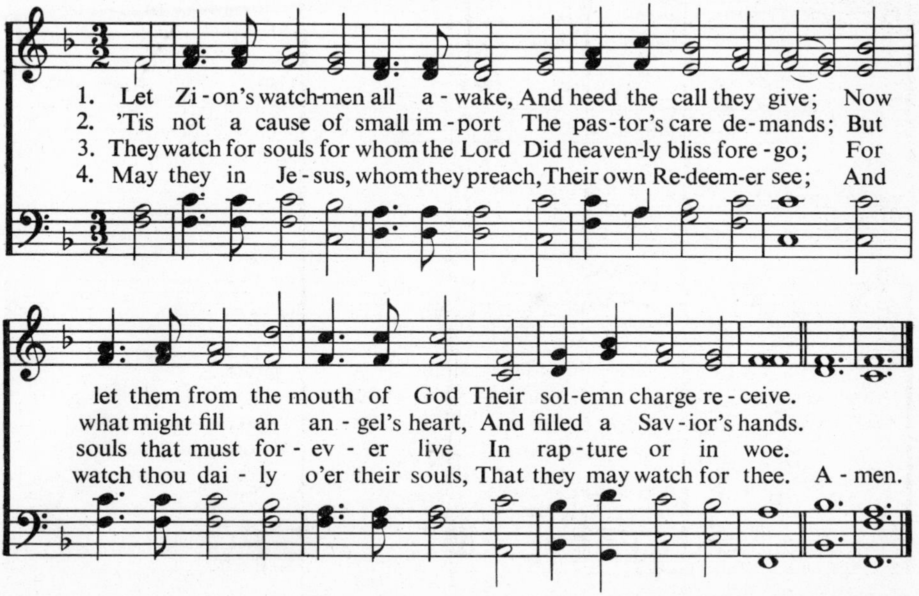
1. Let Zi - on's watch-men all a - wake, And heed the call they give; Now
2. 'Tis not a cause of small im - port The pas - tor's care de - mands; But
3. They watch for souls for whom the Lord Did heaven-ly bliss fore - go; For
4. May they in Je - sus, whom they preach, Their own Re - deem - er see; And
let them from the mouth of God Their sol - emn charge re - ceive.
what might fill an an - gel's heart, And filled a Sav - ior's hands.
souls that must for - ev - er live In rap - ture or in woe.
watch thou dai - ly o'er their souls, That they may watch for thee. A - men.

336

And Are We Yet Alive

DENNIS SM
Arr. from JOHANN G. NÄGELI, 1768-1836
by LOWELL MASON, 1792-1872

CHARLES WESLEY, 1707-1788

1. And are we yet a - live, And see each
2. What trou - bles have we seen, What might - y
3. Yet out of all the Lord Hath brought us
4. Then let us make our boast Of his re -
5. Let us take up the cross, Till we the
oth - er's face? Glo - ry and thanks to Je - sus
con - flicts past, Fight - ings with - out, and fears with -
by his love; And still he doth his help af -
deem - ing power, Which saves us to the ut - ter -
crown ob - tain, And glad - ly reck - on all things
give, For his al - might - y grace.
in, Since we as - sem - bled last!
ford, And hides our life a - bove.
most, Till we can sin no more.
loss, So we may Je - sus gain. A - men.

Pour Out Thy Spirit from on High

HERR JESU CHRIST, MEIN'S LEBENS LICHT LM

JAMES MONTGOMERY, 1771-1854

As Hymnodus Sacer, Leipzig, 1625

1. Pour out thy spir - it from on high; Lord, thine or -
2. With - in thy tem - ple when they stand To teach the
3. Wis - dom and zeal and faith im - part, Firm - ness with
4. To watch and pray, and nev - er faint; By day and
5. Then, when their work is fin - ished here, In hum - ble
dain - ed ser - vants bless; Grac - es and gifts to each sup -
truth, as taught by thee, Sav - ior, like stars in thy right
meek - ness from a - bove, To bear thy peo - ple on their
night strict guard to keep; To warn the sin - ner, cheer the
hope their charge re - sign. When the chief Shep - herd shall ap -
ply, And clothe them with thy righ - teous - ness.
hand Thy ser - vants in the church - es be.
heart, And love the souls whom thou dost love:
saint, Nour - ish thy lambs, and feed thy sheep.
pear, O God, may they and we be thine. A - men.

338 Blest Be the Dear Uniting Love

EVAN CM
Arr. from WILLIAM HAVERGAL, 1793-1870
by LOWELL MASON, 1792-1872

CHARLES WESLEY, 1707-1788

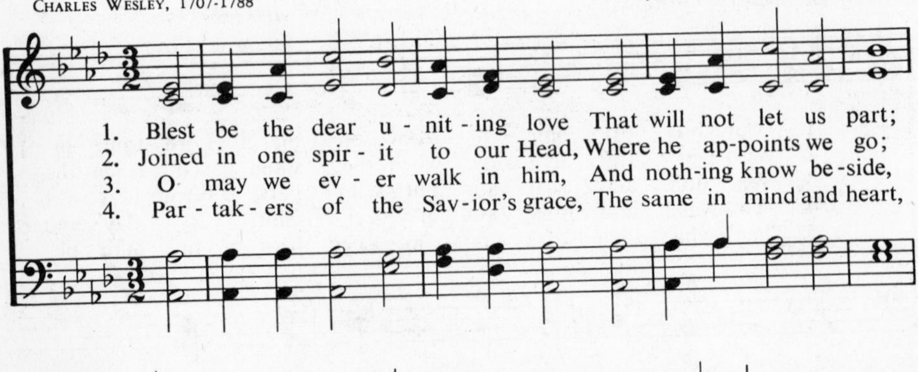
1. Blest be the dear u - nit - ing love That will not let us part;
2. Joined in one spir - it to our Head, Where he ap-points we go;
3. O may we ev - er walk in him, And noth-ing know be-side,
4. Par - tak-ers of the Sav-ior's grace, The same in mind and heart,

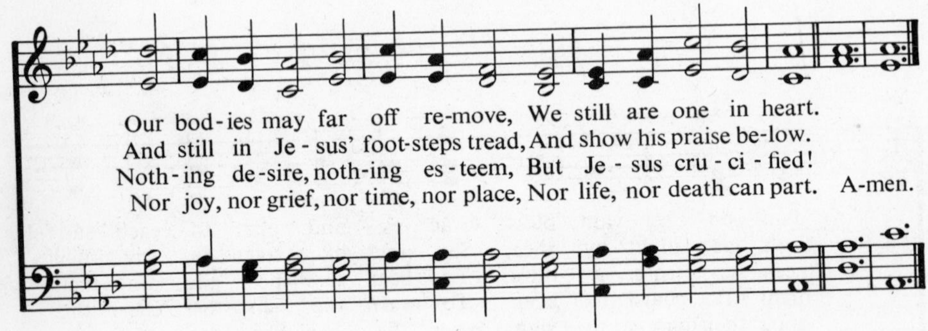
Our bod-ies may far off re-move, We still are one in heart.
And still in Je - sus' foot-steps tread, And show his praise be-low.
Noth-ing de-sire, noth-ing es-teem, But Je - sus cru - ci - fied!
Nor joy, nor grief, nor time, nor place, Nor life, nor death can part. A-men.

339 Lord of the Harvest, Hear

ST. BRIDE SM
SAMUEL HOWARD, 1710-1782

MATTHEW 9:37-38
CHARLES WESLEY, 1707-1788

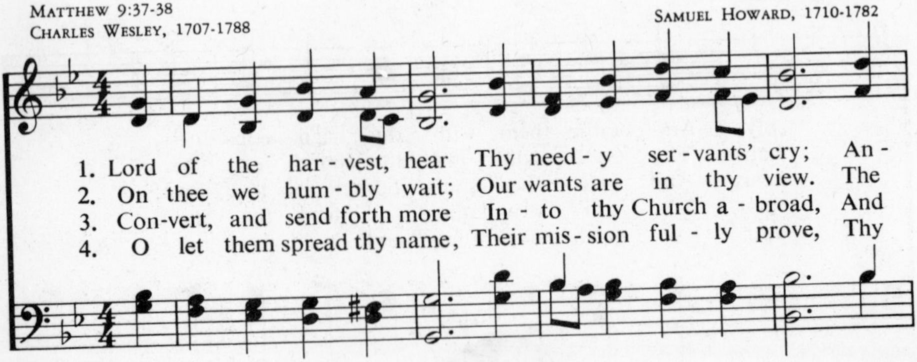
1. Lord of the har - vest, hear Thy need - y ser - vants' cry; An -
2. On thee we hum - bly wait; Our wants are in thy view. The
3. Con-vert, and send forth more In - to thy Church a - broad, And
4. O let them spread thy name, Their mis - sion ful - ly prove, Thy

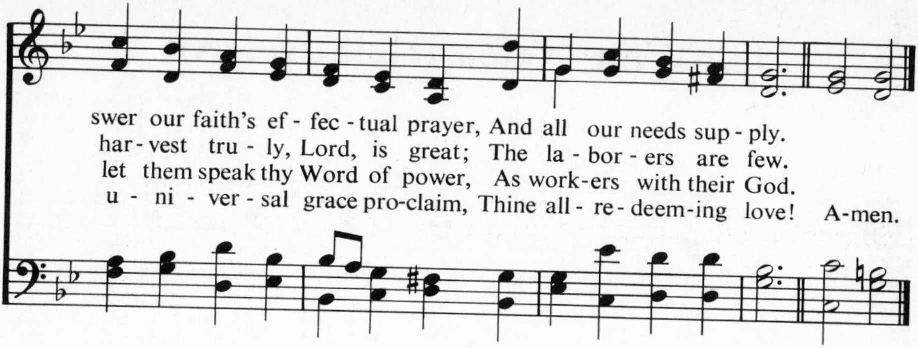
swer our faith's ef - fec - tual prayer, And all our needs sup - ply.
har - vest tru - ly, Lord, is great; The la - bor - ers are few.
let them speak thy Word of power, As work-ers with their God.
u - ni - ver - sal grace pro-claim, Thine all - re - deem-ing love! A-men.

With Thine Own Pity, Savior

340

GRÄFENBERG CM
Praxis Pietatis Melica, Berlin, 1653
JOHANN CRÜGER, 1598-1662

RAY PALMER, 1808-1887

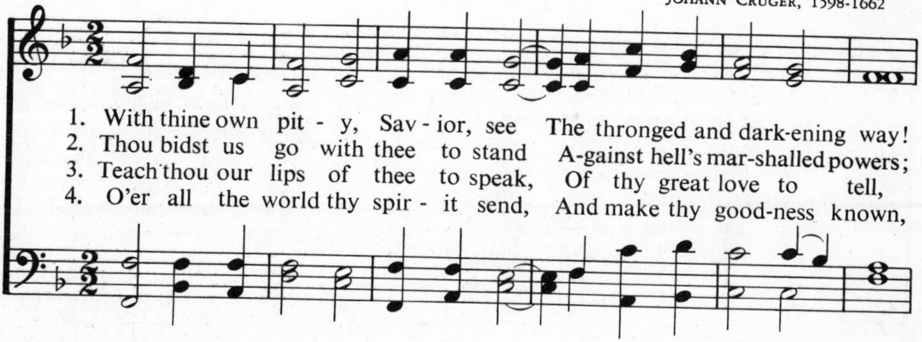
1. With thine own pit - y, Sav - ior, see The thronged and dark-ening way!
2. Thou bidst us go with thee to stand A-gainst hell's mar-shalled powers;
3. Teach thou our lips of thee to speak, Of thy great love to tell,
4. O'er all the world thy spir - it send, And make thy good-ness known,

We go to win the lost to thee; O, help us, Lord, we pray!
And heart to heart, and hand to hand, To make thine hon - or ours.
Till they who wan - der far shall seek And find and serve thee well.
Till earth and heaven to-geth - er blend Their prais-es at thy throne. A-men.

Jesus! the Name High over All

GRÄFENBERG CM
Praxis Pietatis Melica, Berlin, 1653
CHARLES WESLEY, 1707-1788 JOHANN CRÜGER, 1598-1662

1. Je - sus! the name high o - ver all,
2. Je - sus! the name to sin - ners dear,
3. O that the world might taste and see
4. Thee I shall con - stant - ly pro - claim,
5. His on - ly righ - teous - ness I show,
6. Hap - py, if with my lat - est breath
In hell or earth or sky; An - gels and men be -
The name to sin - ners given; It scat - ters all their
The rich - es of his grace! The arms of love that
Though earth and hell op - pose, Bold to con - fess thy
His sav - ing grace pro - claim; 'Tis all my busi - ness
I may but gasp his name; Preach him to all and
fore it fall, And dev - ils fear and fly.
guilt - y fear; It turns their hell to heaven.
com - pass me Would all man - kind em - brace.
glo - rious name Be - fore a world of foes.
here be - low To cry, "Be - hold the Lamb!"
cry in death, "Be - hold, be - hold the Lamb!" A-men.

Go, Make of All Disciples

MATTHEW 28:19-20
LEON M. ADKINS, 1896-

LANCASHIRE 76.76.D.
HENRY SMART, 1813-1879

1. "Go, make of all dis - ci - ples." We hear the call, O Lord,
2. "Go, make of all dis - ci - ples," Bap - tiz - ing in the name
3. "Go, make of all dis - ci - ples." We at thy feet would stay
4. "Go, make of all dis - ci - ples." We wel-come thy com-mand.
That comes from thee, our Fa - ther, In thy e - ter - nal Word.
Of Fa - ther, Son, and Spir - it From age to age the same.
Un - til each life's vo - ca - tion Ac - cents thy ho - ly way.
"Lo, I am with you al - way." We take thy guid - ing hand.
In - spire our ways of learn - ing Through ear-nest, fer - vent prayer,
We call each new dis - ci - ple To fol - low thee, O Lord,
We cul - ti - vate the na - ture God plants in ev - ery heart,
The task looms large be - fore us; We fol - low with-out fear.
And let our dai - ly liv - ing Re - veal thee ev - ery-where.
Re-deem-ing soul and bod - y By wa - ter and the Word.
Re - veal-ing in our wit - ness The mas - ter teach - er's art.
In heaven and earth thy pow - er Shall bring God's king-dom here. A-men.

343 All Nature's Works His Praise Declare

BETHLEHEM CMD

HENRY WARE, JR., 1794-1843 GOTTFRIED W. FINK, 1783-1846

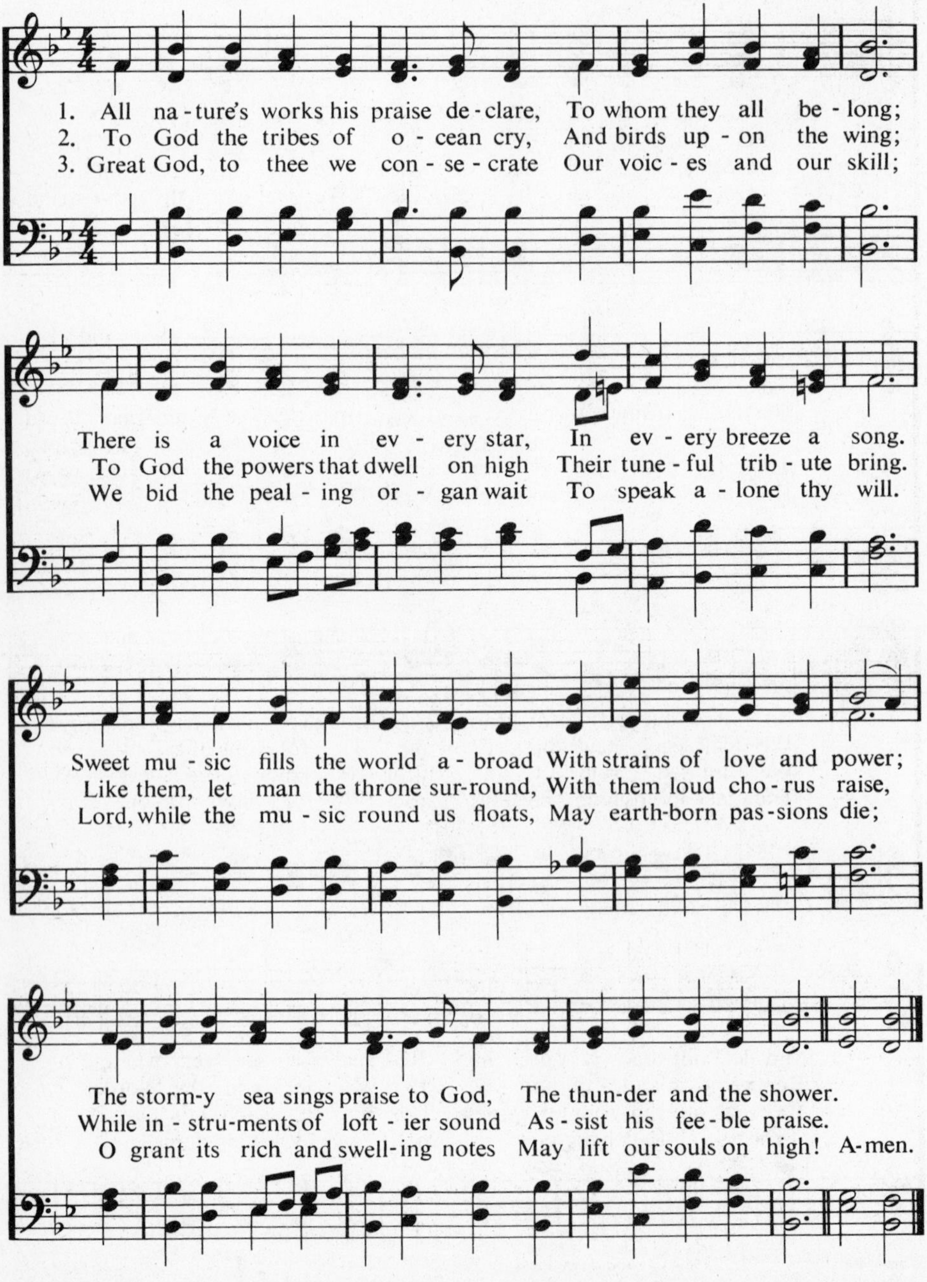

1. All na-ture's works his praise de-clare, To whom they all be-long;
2. To God the tribes of o-cean cry, And birds up-on the wing;
3. Great God, to thee we con-se-crate Our voic-es and our skill;
There is a voice in ev-ery star, In ev-ery breeze a song.
To God the powers that dwell on high Their tune-ful trib-ute bring.
We bid the peal-ing or-gan wait To speak a-lone thy will.
Sweet mu-sic fills the world a-broad With strains of love and power;
Like them, let man the throne sur-round, With them loud cho-rus raise,
Lord, while the mu-sic round us floats, May earth-born pas-sions die;
The storm-y sea sings praise to God, The thun-der and the shower.
While in-stru-ments of loft-ier sound As-sist his fee-ble praise.
O grant its rich and swell-ing notes May lift our souls on high! A-men.

Come, Father, Son, and Holy Ghost

ST. CATHERINE 88.88.88.

CHARLES WESLEY, 1707-1788

HENRI F. HEMY, 1818-1888
Adapt. by JAMES G. WALTON, 1821-1905

1. Come, Fa - ther, Son, and Ho - ly Ghost, To whom we for our chil - dren cry; The good de - sired and want - ed most Out of thy rich - est grace sup - ply; The sa - cred dis - ci - pline be given, To train and bring them up for heaven.
2. Er - ror and ig - no - rance re - move, Their blind-ness both of heart and mind; Give them the wis - dom from a - bove, Spot - less and peace - a - ble and kind; In knowl-edge pure their mind re - new, And store with thoughts di - vine - ly true.
3. U - nite the pair so long dis - joined, Knowl-edge and vi - tal pi - e - ty; Learn - ing and ho - li - ness com - bined, And truth and love let all men see In these, whom up to thee we give, Thine, whol - ly thine, to die and live.
4. Fa - ther, ac - cept them in thy Son, And ev - er by thy Spir - it guide! Thy wis - dom in their lives be shown, Thy name con - fessed and glo - ri - fied; Thy power and love dif - fused a - broad, Till all our earth is filled with God. A - men.

345 Thou, Whose Unmeasured Temple Stands

DUNDEE (FRENCH) CM
Scottish Psalter, 1615

William C. Bryant, 1794-1878

1. Thou, whose un - mea - sured tem - ple stands, Built
2. And let the com - fort - er and friend, Thy
3. May they who err be guid - ed here To
4. May faith grow firm, and love grow warm, And
o - ver earth and sea, Ac - cept the walls that
Ho - ly Spir - it, meet With those who here in
find the bet - ter way; And they who mourn, and
pure de - vo - tion rise, While round these hal - lowed
hu - man hands Have raised, O God, to thee.
wor - ship bend Be - fore thy mer - cy seat.
they who fear, Be strength - ened as they pray.
walls the storm Of earth - born pas - sion dies. A - men.

The Lord Our God Alone Is Strong

Caleb T. Winchester, 1847-1920

TRURO LM
T. Williams' *Psalmodia Evangelica,* 1789

1. The Lord our God a - lone is strong; His hands built not for one brief day; His won - drous works, through a - ges long, His wis - dom and his power dis - play.
2. His moun - tains lift their sol - emn forms To watch in si - lence o'er the land; The roll - ing o - cean, rocked with storms, Sleeps in the hol - low of his hand.
3. Thou sov - ereign God, re - ceive this gift Thy will - ing ser - vants of - fer thee; Ac - cept the prayers that thou - sands lift, And let these halls thy tem - ple be.
4. And let those learn, who here shall meet, True wis - dom is with rev - erence crowned, And sci - ence walks with hum - ble feet To seek the God that faith hath found. A - men.

All Things Are Thine

HERR JESU CHRIST, DICH ZU LM
Pensum Sacrum, Görlitz, 1648
Harm. from *Cantionale Sacrum*, Gotha, 1651

JOHN GREENLEAF WHITTIER, 1807-1892

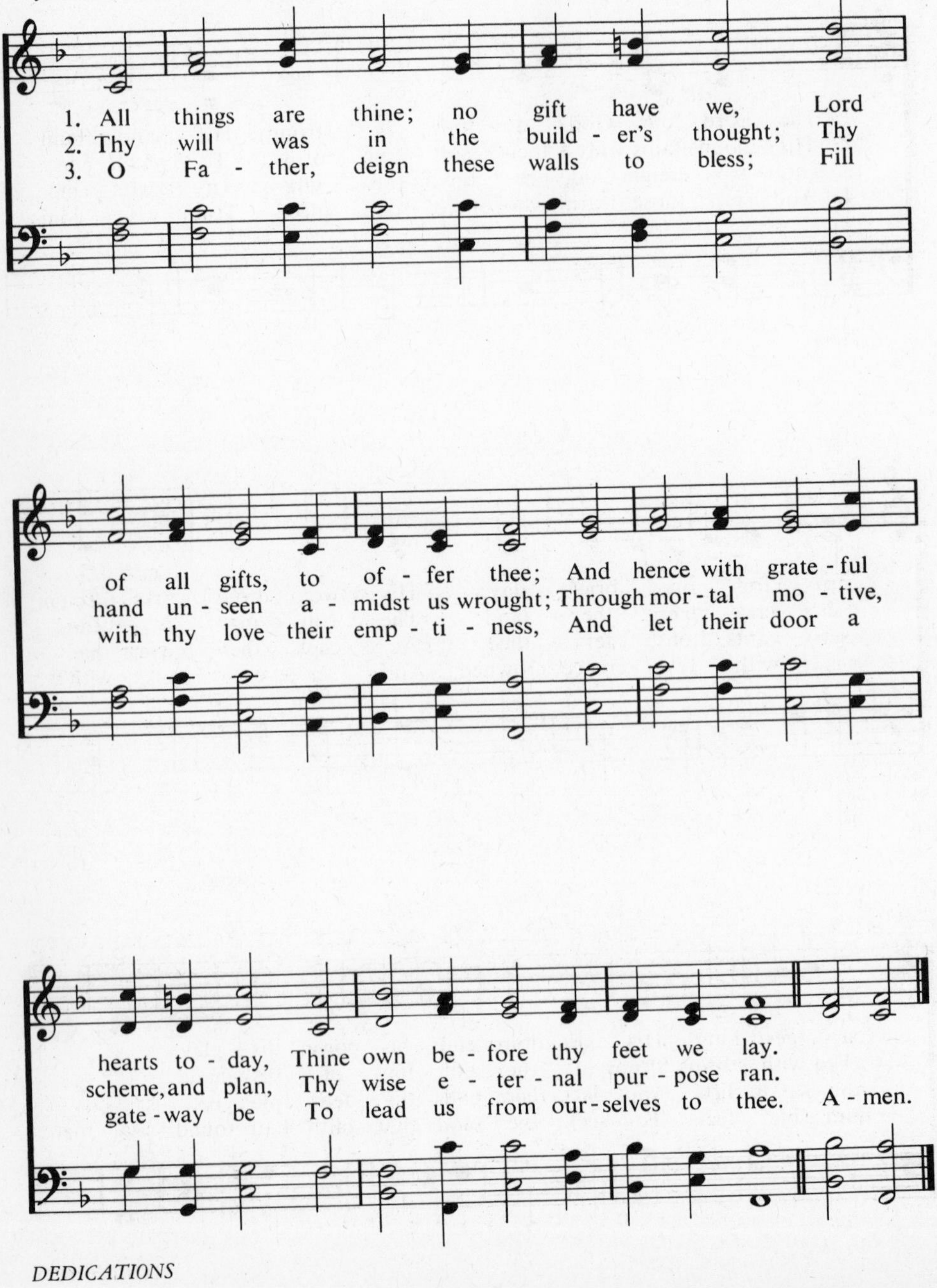
1. All things are thine; no gift have we, Lord
2. Thy will was in the build - er's thought; Thy
3. O Fa - ther, deign these walls to bless; Fill
of all gifts, to of - fer thee; And hence with grate - ful
hand un - seen a - midst us wrought; Through mor - tal mo - tive,
with thy love their emp - ti - ness, And let their door a
hearts to - day, Thine own be - fore thy feet we lay.
scheme, and plan, Thy wise e - ter - nal pur - pose ran.
gate - way be To lead us from our - selves to thee. A - men.

On This Stone Now Laid with Prayer

348

John Pierpont, 1785-1866

PLEYEL'S HYMN 77.77.
Ignace J. Pleyel, 1757-1831

1. On this stone now laid with prayer Let thy
2. May thy spir - it here give rest To the
3. O - pen wide, O God, thy door For the
4. By wise mas - ter build - ers squared, Here be
Church rise, strong and fair; Ev - er, Lord, thy name be
heart by sin op - pressed, And the seeds of truth be
out - cast and the poor; May they know this house their
liv - ing stones pre - pared For the tem - ple near thy
known, Where we lay this cor - ner - stone.
sown, Where we lay this cor - ner - stone.
own, Where we lay this cor - ner - stone.
throne, Je - sus Christ, its cor - ner - stone. A - men.

O Living Christ, Chief Cornerstone

ST. PETER CM

MAUD M. CUNINGGIM, 1874-1965 — ALEXANDER R. REINAGLE, 1799-1877

1. O liv - ing Christ, chief cor - ner - stone Of
2. These walls for thine own sake, O Lord, Be
3. May ben - e - dic - tions here at - tend The
4. To God the Fa - ther, God the Son, And
God's great tem - ple thou: As here with joy this
pleased to bless, we pray; In grate - ful ser - vice
teach - ing of thy word, And Christ, with love's per -
Spir - it we a - dore; All praise and hon - or,
stone we lay, Vouch - safe thy pres - ence now!
would we now Their strong foun - da - tion lay.
sua - sive power, Here make his mes - sage heard.
glo - ry, power Be now and ev - er - more! A - men.

Alternate tune: ARLINGTON

DEDICATIONS

How Blessed Is This Place

KENT LM

ERNEST E. RYDEN, 1886- JOHN F. LAMPE, 1703-1751

1. How bless - ed is this place, O Lord, Where
2. Here let thy sa - cred fire of old De -
3. Here gath - er us a - round thy board To
4. Here let the wea - ry one find rest, The
5. Here thine an - gel - ic spir - its send Their
thou art wor-shiped and a - dored; In faith we here an
scend to kin - dle spir - its cold; And may our prayers, when
keep the feast with thee, dear Lord, And when in faith our
trou - bled heart thy com - fort blest, The guil - ty soul a
sol - emn praise with ours to blend, And grant the vi - sion,
al - tar raise To thy great glo - ry, God of praise!
here we bend, Like in - cense sweet to thee as - cend.
souls draw near, May we dis - cern thy pres - ence here.
sure re - treat, The sin - ner par - don at thy feet.
in - ly given, Of this thy house, the gate of heaven. A - men.

351

Eternal God and Sovereign Lord

GERMANY LM

Costen J. Harrell, 1885-

William Gardiner's *Sacred Melodies*, 1815

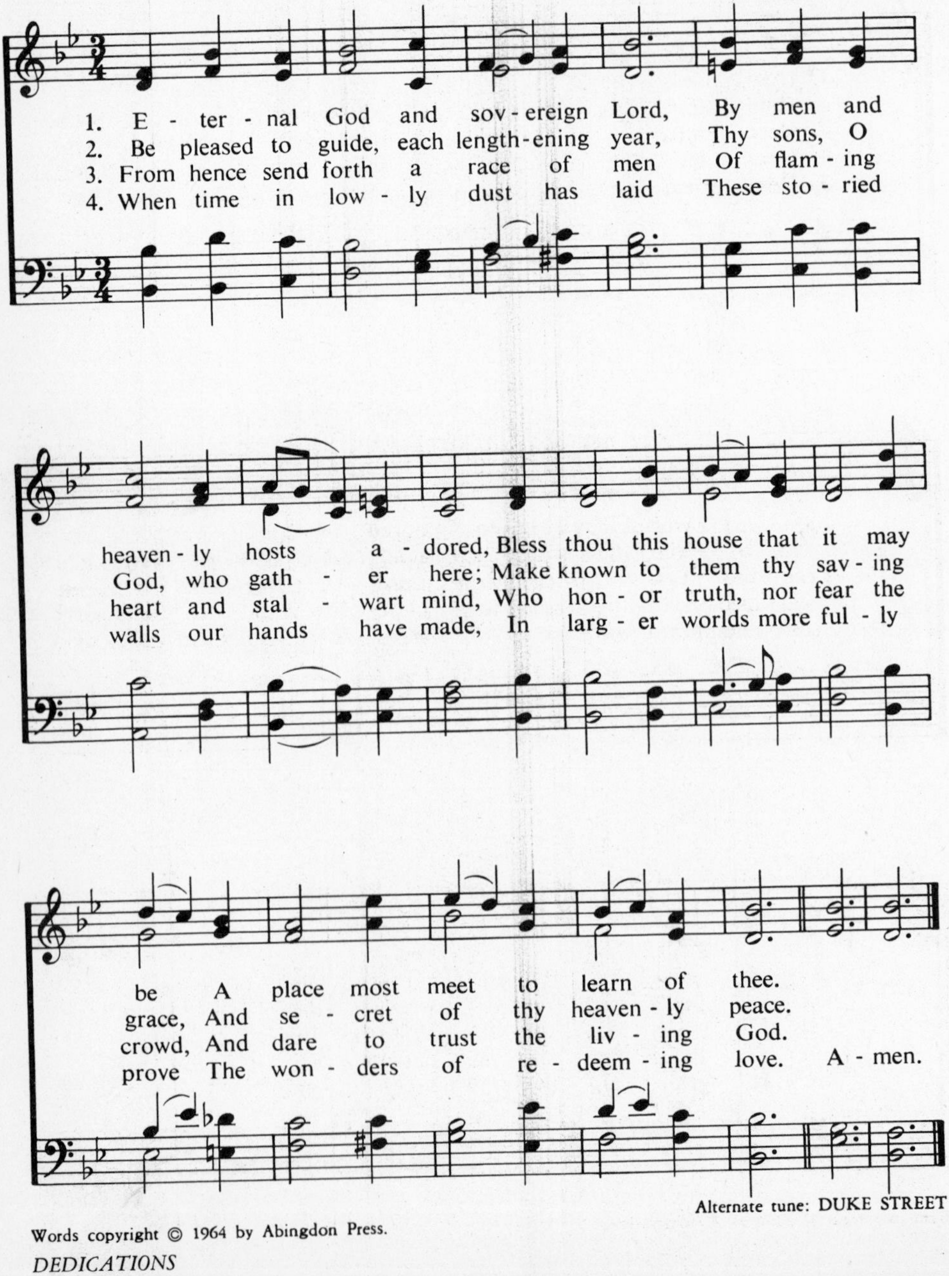
1. E - ter - nal God and sov - ereign Lord, By men and
2. Be pleased to guide, each length - ening year, Thy sons, O
3. From hence send forth a race of men Of flam - ing
4. When time in low - ly dust has laid These sto - ried
heaven - ly hosts a - dored, Bless thou this house that it may
God, who gath - er here; Make known to them thy sav - ing
heart and stal - wart mind, Who hon - or truth, nor fear the
walls our hands have made, In larg - er worlds more ful - ly
be A place most meet to learn of thee.
grace, And se - cret of thy heaven - ly peace.
crowd, And dare to trust the liv - ing God.
prove The won - ders of re - deem - ing love. A - men.

Alternate tune: DUKE STREET

DEDICATIONS

Come, O Thou God of Grace

ITALIAN HYMN 664.6664.
FELICE DE GIARDINI, 1716-1796
Harm. by V. E. C.

WILLIAM E. EVANS, 1851-1915

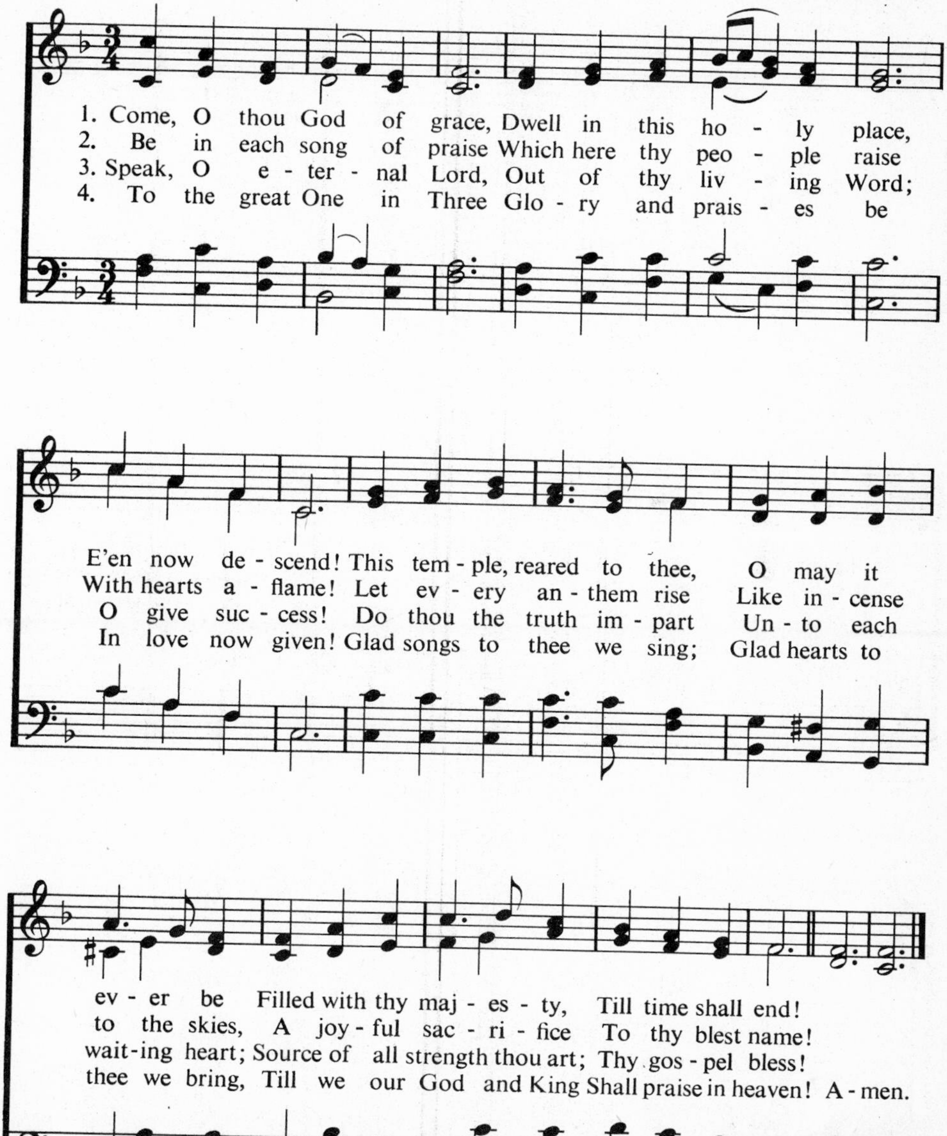
1. Come, O thou God of grace, Dwell in this ho - ly place,
2. Be in each song of praise Which here thy peo - ple raise
3. Speak, O e - ter - nal Lord, Out of thy liv - ing Word;
4. To the great One in Three Glo - ry and prais - es be
E'en now de - scend! This tem - ple, reared to thee, O may it
With hearts a - flame! Let ev - ery an - them rise Like in - cense
O give suc - cess! Do thou the truth im - part Un - to each
In love now given! Glad songs to thee we sing; Glad hearts to
ev - er be Filled with thy maj - es - ty, Till time shall end!
to the skies, A joy - ful sac - ri - fice To thy blest name!
wait - ing heart; Source of all strength thou art; Thy gos - pel bless!
thee we bring, Till we our God and King Shall praise in heaven! A - men.

353 The King Shall Come

ANONYMOUS Greek
Trans. by JOHN BROWNLIE, 1859-1925

ST. STEPHEN CM
WILLIAM JONES, 1726-1800

1. The King shall come when morn - ing dawns And
2. Not as of old a lit - tle child, To
3. O bright - er than the ris - ing morn When
4. O bright - er than that glo - rious morn Shall
5. The King shall come when morn - ing dawns And

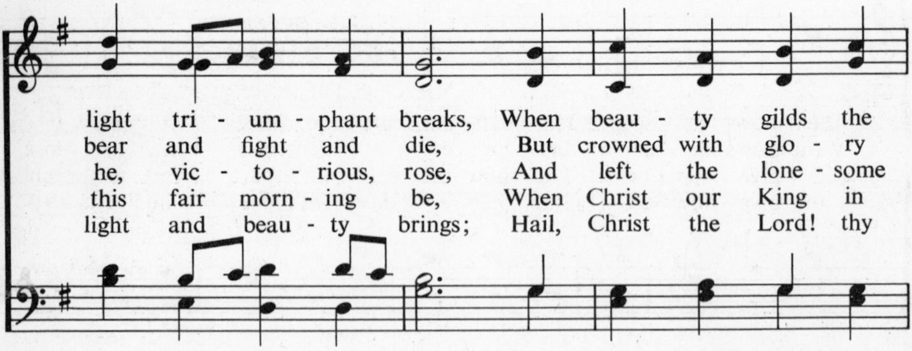
light tri - um - phant breaks, When beau - ty gilds the
bear and fight and die, But crowned with glo - ry
he, vic - to - rious, rose, And left the lone - some
this fair morn - ing be, When Christ our King in
light and beau - ty brings; Hail, Christ the Lord! thy

east - ern hills And life to joy a - wakes.
like the sun That lights the morn - ing sky.
place of death, De - spite the rage of foes.
beau - ty comes, And we his face shall see!
peo - ple pray, Come quick - ly, King of kings! A - men.

O Come, O Come, Emmanuel

Latin, 12th Century
Stanzas 1, 4, trans. by JOHN M. NEALE, 1818-1866
Stanzas 2, 3, trans. by HENRY S. COFFIN, 1877-1954

VENI EMMANUEL LM with Refrain
Adapt. from Plainsong, Mode I
by THOMAS HELMORE, 1811-1890

Unison
1. O come, O come, Em-man - u - el, And ran-som cap-tive
2. O come, thou Wis-dom from on high, And or-der all things,
3. O come, De-sire of na - tions, bind All peo-ples in one
4. O come, thou Day-spring, come and cheer Our spir-its by thine
Is - ra - el, That mourns in lone-ly ex - ile here
far and nigh; To us the path of knowl - edge show,
heart and mind; Bid en-vy, strife, and quar - rels cease;
ad - vent here; Dis-perse the gloom-y clouds of night,
Un-til the Son of God ap-pear.
And cause us in her ways to go.
Fill the whole world with heav - en's peace.
And death's dark shad-ows put to flight.
Refrain
Re-joice! Re-joice! Em-man - u - el Shall come to thee, O Is - ra - el!
A-men.

355

Lord Christ, When First Thou Cam'st

KIRKEN DEN ER ET GAMMELT HUS 87.87.887.
LUDWIG M. LINDEMAN, 1812-1887

WALTER RUSSELL BOWIE, 1882-

Unison
1. Lord Christ, when first thou cam'st to men, Up - on a cross they
2. O aw - ful love, which found no room In life where sin de -
3. New ad - vent of the love of Christ, Shall we a - gain re -
4. O wound - ed hands of Je - sus, build In us thy new cre -
bound thee, And mocked thy sav - ing king - ship then
nied thee, And, doomed to death, must bring to doom
fuse thee, Till in the night of hate and war
a - tion; Our pride is dust; our vaunt is stilled;
By thorns with which they crowned thee. And still our wrongs may
The power which cru - ci - fied thee, Till not a stone was
We per - ish as we lose thee? From old un - faith our
We wait thy rev - e - la - tion. O love that tri - umphs
weave thee now New thorns to pierce that stead - y brow,
left on stone, And all a na - tion's pride o'er - thrown
souls re - lease To seek the king - dom of thy peace,
o - ver loss, We bring our hearts be - fore thy cross,

ADVENT SEASON

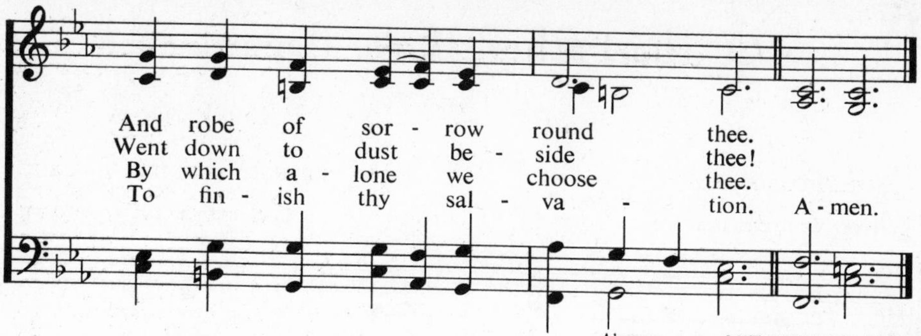
And robe of sor - row round thee.
Went down to dust be - side thee!
By which a - lone we choose thee.
To fin - ish thy sal - va - tion. A - men.

Alternate tune: MIT FREUDEN ZART

Break Forth, O Living Light of God 356

FRANK VON CHRISTIERSON, 1900-

ST. STEPHEN CM
WILLIAM JONES, 1726-1800

1. Break forth, O liv - ing light of God, Up - on the world's dark hour! Show us the way the Mas - ter trod; Re - veal his sav - ing power.
2. Re - move the veil of an - cient words, Their mes - sage long ob - scure; Re - store to us thy truth, O God, And make its mean - ing sure.
3. O let thy Word be light a - new To ev - ery na - tion's life; U - nite us in thy will, O Lord, And end all sin - ful strife.
4. O may one Lord, one faith, one Word, One Spir - it lead us still; And one great Church go forth in might To work God's per - fect will. A - men.

Words from "Ten New Bible Hymns," copyright 1952 by the Hymn Society of America; used by permission.

357

Of the Father's Love Begotten

AURELIUS CLEMENS PRUDENTIUS, 348-c. 413
Trans. by JOHN M. NEALE, 1818-1866 and
HENRY W. BAKER, 1821-1877

DIVINUM MYSTERIUM 87.87.887.
13th Century Plainsong, Mode V
Arr. by C. WINFRED DOUGLAS, 1867-1944

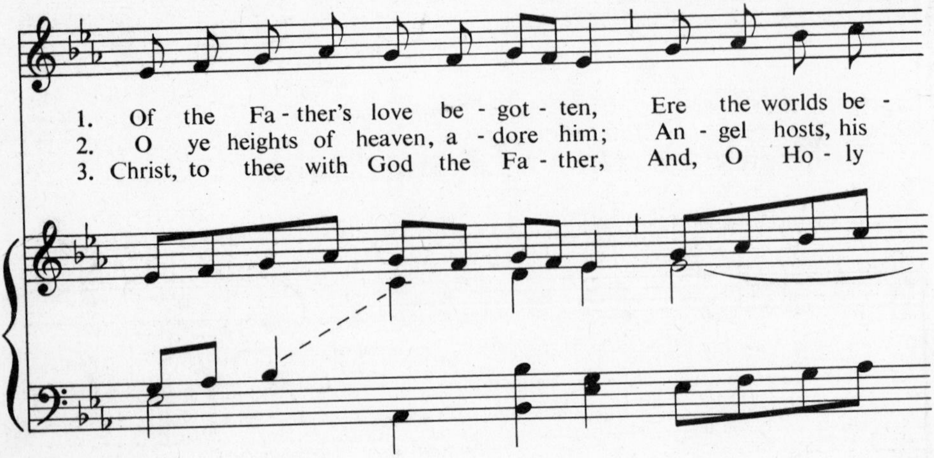
1. Of the Fa - ther's love be - got - ten, Ere the worlds be -
2. O ye heights of heaven, a - dore him; An - gel hosts, his
3. Christ, to thee with God the Fa - ther, And, O Ho - ly

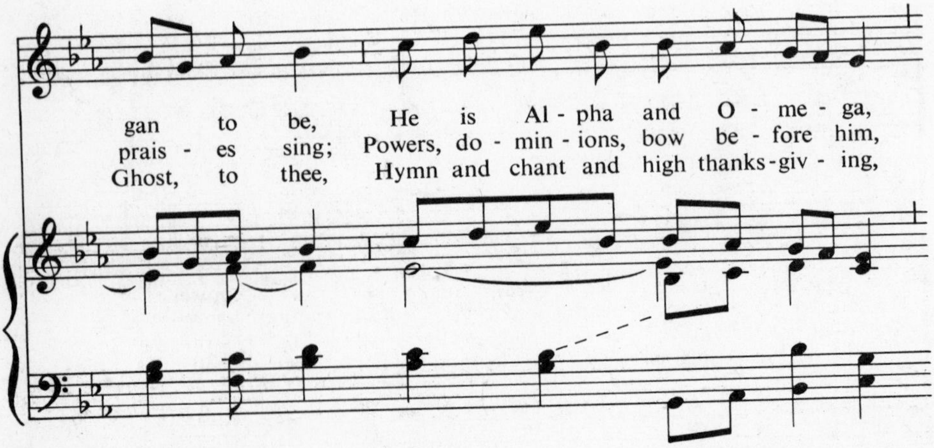
gan to be, He is Al - pha and O - me - ga,
prais - es sing; Powers, do - min - ions, bow be - fore him,
Ghost, to thee, Hymn and chant and high thanks - giv - ing,

He the source, the end - ing he; Of the things that are, that
And ex - tol our God and King; Let no tongue on earth be
And un - wea - ried prais - es be: Hon - or, glo - ry, and do -
have been, And that fu - ture years shall see,
si - lent, Ev - ery voice in con - cert ring,
min - ion, And e - ter - nal vic - to - ry,
Ev - er - more and ev - er - more.
Ev - er - more and ev - er - more.
Ev - er - more and ev - er - more. A - men.

Watchman, Tell Us of the Night

Isaiah 21:11-12
John Bowring, 1792-1872

ABERYSTWYTH 77.77.D.
Joseph Parry, 1841-1903

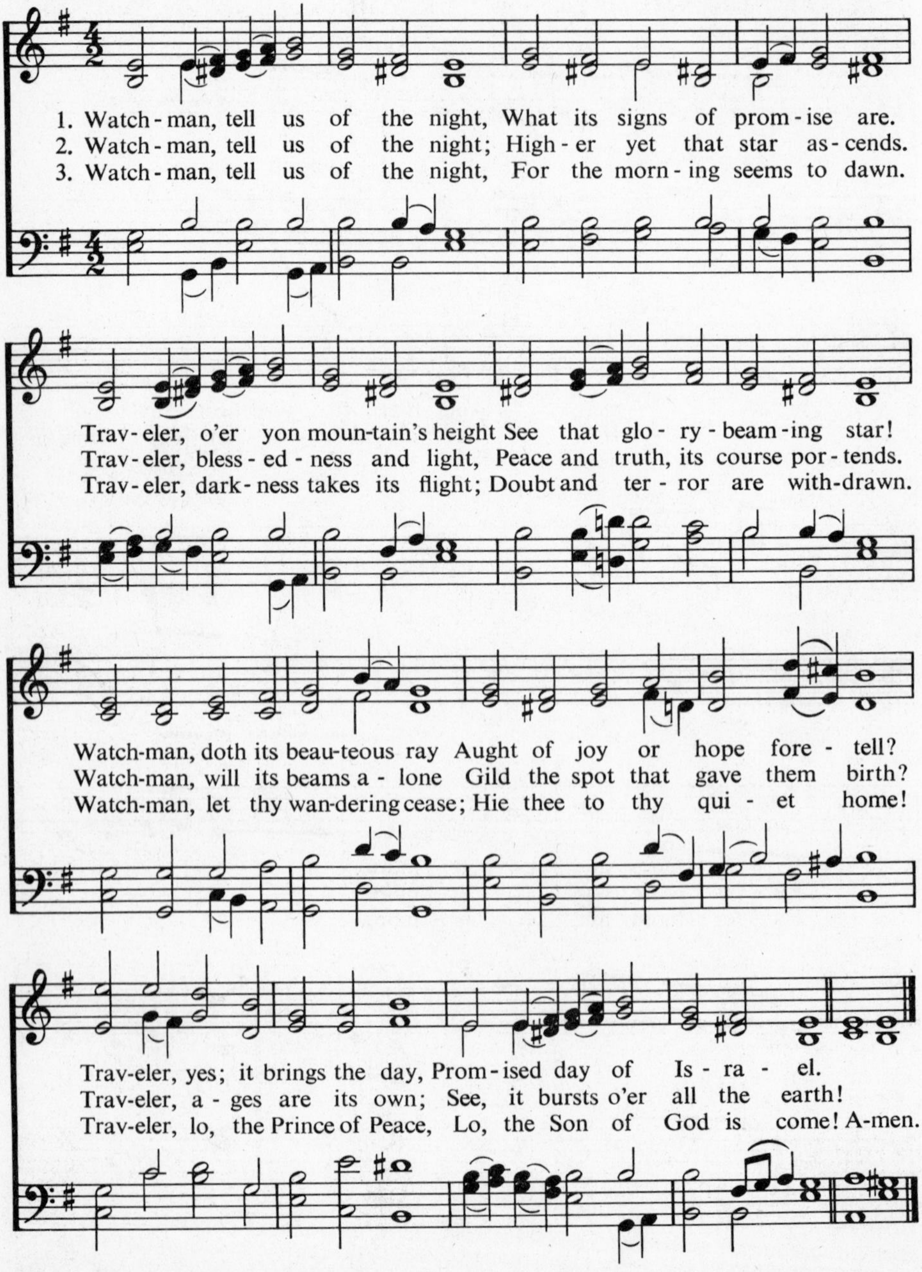
1. Watch-man, tell us of the night, What its signs of prom-ise are.
2. Watch-man, tell us of the night; High-er yet that star as-cends.
3. Watch-man, tell us of the night, For the morn-ing seems to dawn.
Trav-eler, o'er yon moun-tain's height See that glo-ry-beam-ing star!
Trav-eler, bless-ed-ness and light, Peace and truth, its course por-tends.
Trav-eler, dark-ness takes its flight; Doubt and ter-ror are with-drawn.
Watch-man, doth its beau-teous ray Aught of joy or hope fore-tell?
Watch-man, will its beams a-lone Gild the spot that gave them birth?
Watch-man, let thy wan-dering cease; Hie thee to thy qui-et home!
Trav-eler, yes; it brings the day, Prom-ised day of Is-ra-el.
Trav-eler, a-ges are its own; See, it bursts o'er all the earth!
Trav-eler, lo, the Prince of Peace, Lo, the Son of God is come! A-men.

Hail to the Lord's Anointed

PSALM 72
JAMES MONTGOMERY, 1771-1854

ELLACOMBE 76.76.D.
Gesangbuch der H. W. K. Hofkapelle, 1784

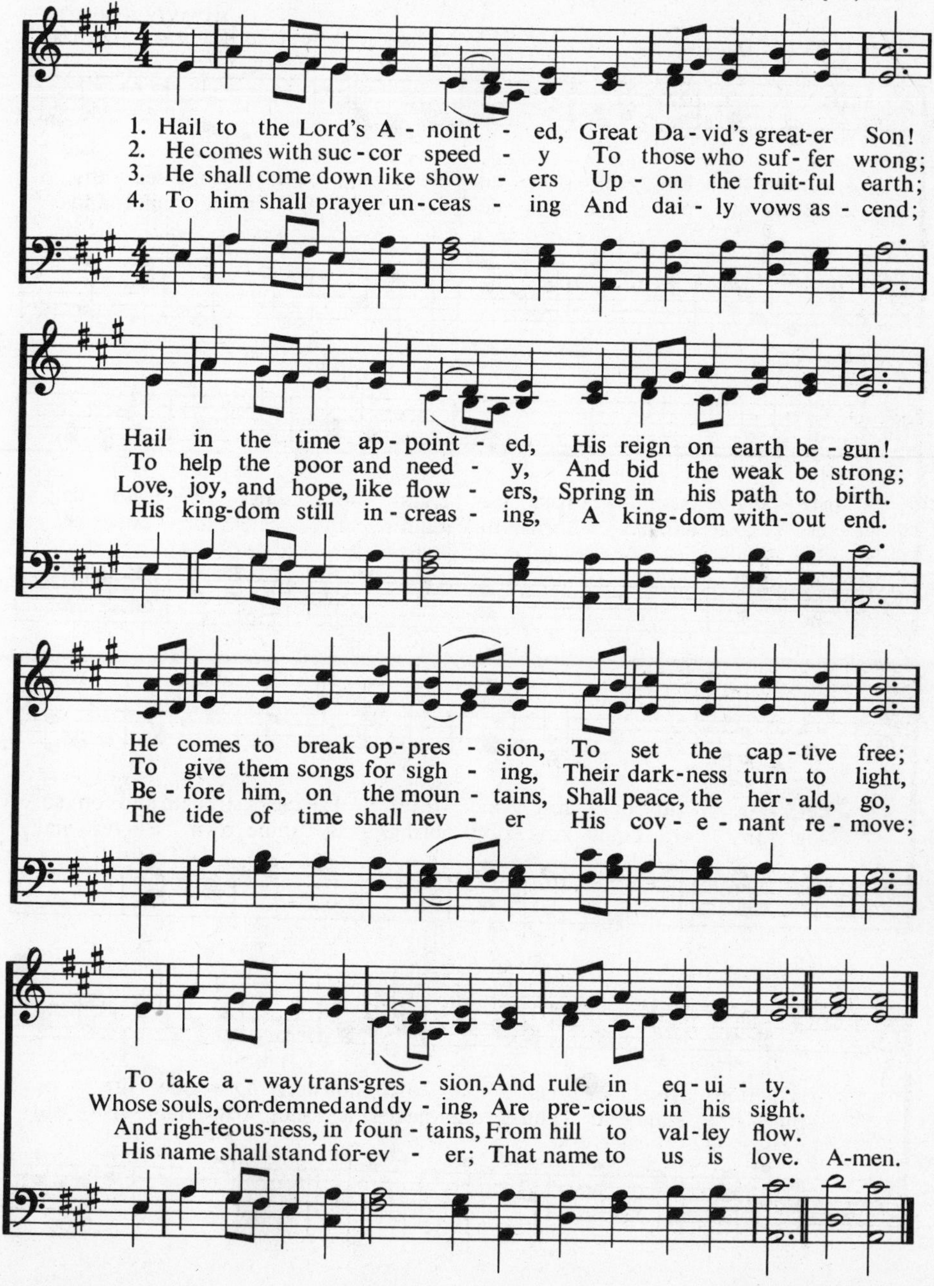
1. Hail to the Lord's A - noint - ed, Great Da - vid's great - er Son!
2. He comes with suc - cor speed - y To those who suf - fer wrong;
3. He shall come down like show - ers Up - on the fruit - ful earth;
4. To him shall prayer un - ceas - ing And dai - ly vows as - cend;
Hail in the time ap - point - ed, His reign on earth be - gun!
To help the poor and need - y, And bid the weak be strong;
Love, joy, and hope, like flow - ers, Spring in his path to birth.
His king - dom still in - creas - ing, A king - dom with - out end.
He comes to break op - pres - sion, To set the cap - tive free;
To give them songs for sigh - ing, Their dark - ness turn to light,
Be - fore him, on the moun - tains, Shall peace, the her - ald, go,
The tide of time shall nev - er His cov - e - nant re - move;
To take a - way trans - gres - sion, And rule in eq - ui - ty.
Whose souls, con - demned and dy - ing, Are pre - cious in his sight.
And righ - teous - ness, in foun - tains, From hill to val - ley flow.
His name shall stand for - ev - er; That name to us is love. A - men.

360

Come, Thou Long-Expected Jesus

HYFRYDOL 87.87.D.

CHARLES WESLEY, 1707-1788

Melody by ROWLAND H. PRICHARD, 1811-1887

1. Come, thou long - ex - pect - ed Je - sus, Born to set thy
2. Born thy peo - ple to de - liv - er, Born a child and
peo - ple free; From our fears and sins re - lease us;
yet a King, Born to reign in us for - ev - er,
Let us find our rest in thee. Is - rael's strength and con - so -
Now thy gra - cious king - dom bring. By thine own e - ter - nal
la - tion, Hope of all the earth thou art; Dear de - sire of
spir - it Rule in all our hearts a - lone; By thine all - suf-

ev - ery na - tion, Joy of ev - ery long - ing heart.
fi - cient mer - it, Raise us to thy glo - rious throne. A - men.

Alternate tune: STUTTGART

361

The People That in Darkness Sat

ISAIAH 9:2-8
JOHN MORISON, 1750-1798
Scottish Paraphrases, 1781

CAITHNESS CM
Scottish Psalter, 1635

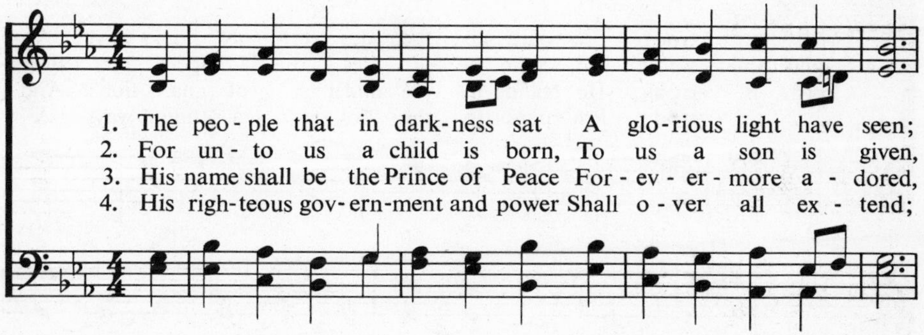
1. The peo - ple that in dark - ness sat A glo - rious light have seen;
2. For un - to us a child is born, To us a son is given,
3. His name shall be the Prince of Peace For - ev - er - more a - dored,
4. His righ - teous gov - ern - ment and power Shall o - ver all ex - tend;

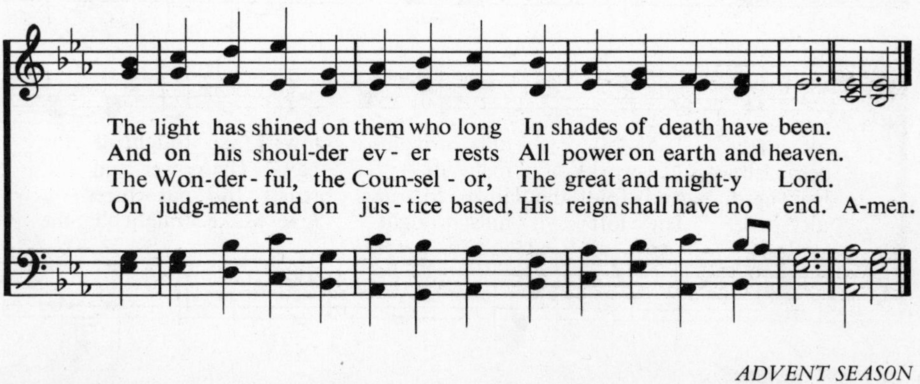
The light has shined on them who long In shades of death have been.
And on his shoul - der ev - er rests All power on earth and heaven.
The Won - der - ful, the Coun - sel - or, The great and might - y Lord.
On judg - ment and on jus - tice based, His reign shall have no end. A - men.

362 There's a Voice in the Wilderness Crying

HEREFORD Irregular

JAMES L. MILLIGAN, 1876-1961

FRANCIS D. HEINS, 1878-1949

1. There's a voice in the wil - der - ness cry - ing, A call from the
2. O Zi - on, that bring-est good ti - dings, Get thee up to the
3. But the word of our God en - dur - eth, The arm of the
4. There's a voice in the wil - der - ness cry - ing, A call from the
ways un - trod: Pre - pare in the des - ert a high - way, A
heights and sing! Pro - claim to a des - o - late peo - ple The
Lord is strong; He stands in the midst of na - tions, And
ways un - trod: Pre - pare in the des - ert a high - way, A
high - way for our God! The val - leys shall be ex -
com - ing of their King. Like the flowers of the field they
he will right the wrong. He shall feed his flock like a
high - way for our God! The val - leys shall be ex -
alt - ed, The loft - y hills brought low; Make straight all the
per - ish, The works of men de - cay, The power and
shep - herd, And fold the lambs to his breast; In pas - tures of
alt - ed, The loft - y hills brought low; Make straight all the

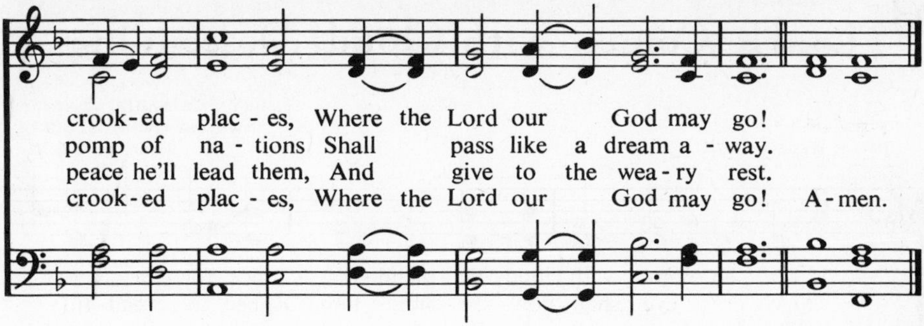
crook-ed plac-es, Where the Lord our God may go!
pomp of na-tions Shall pass like a dream a-way.
peace he'll lead them, And give to the wea-ry rest.
crook-ed plac-es, Where the Lord our God may go! A-men.

363

Lift Up Your Heads, Ye Mighty Gates

Psalm 24
Georg Weissel, 1590-1635
Trans. by Catherine Winkworth, 1827-1878

TRURO LM
T. Williams' *Psalmodia Evangelica*, 1789

1. Lift up your heads, ye might-y gates; Be-hold, the King of glo-ry waits; The King of kings is draw-ing near; The Sav-ior of the world is here!
2. Fling wide the por-tals of your heart; Make it a tem-ple, set a-part From earth-ly use for heaven's em-ploy, A-dorned with prayer and love and joy.
3. Re-deem-er, come, with us a-bide; Our hearts to thee we o-pen wide; Let us thy in-ner pres-ence feel; Thy grace and love in us re-veal. A-men.

364

Lo, He Comes with Clouds Descending

BRYN CALFARIA 87.87.47.

REVELATION 1:7
CHARLES WESLEY, 1707-1788

WILLIAM OWEN, 1814-1893
Harm. by C.R.Y.

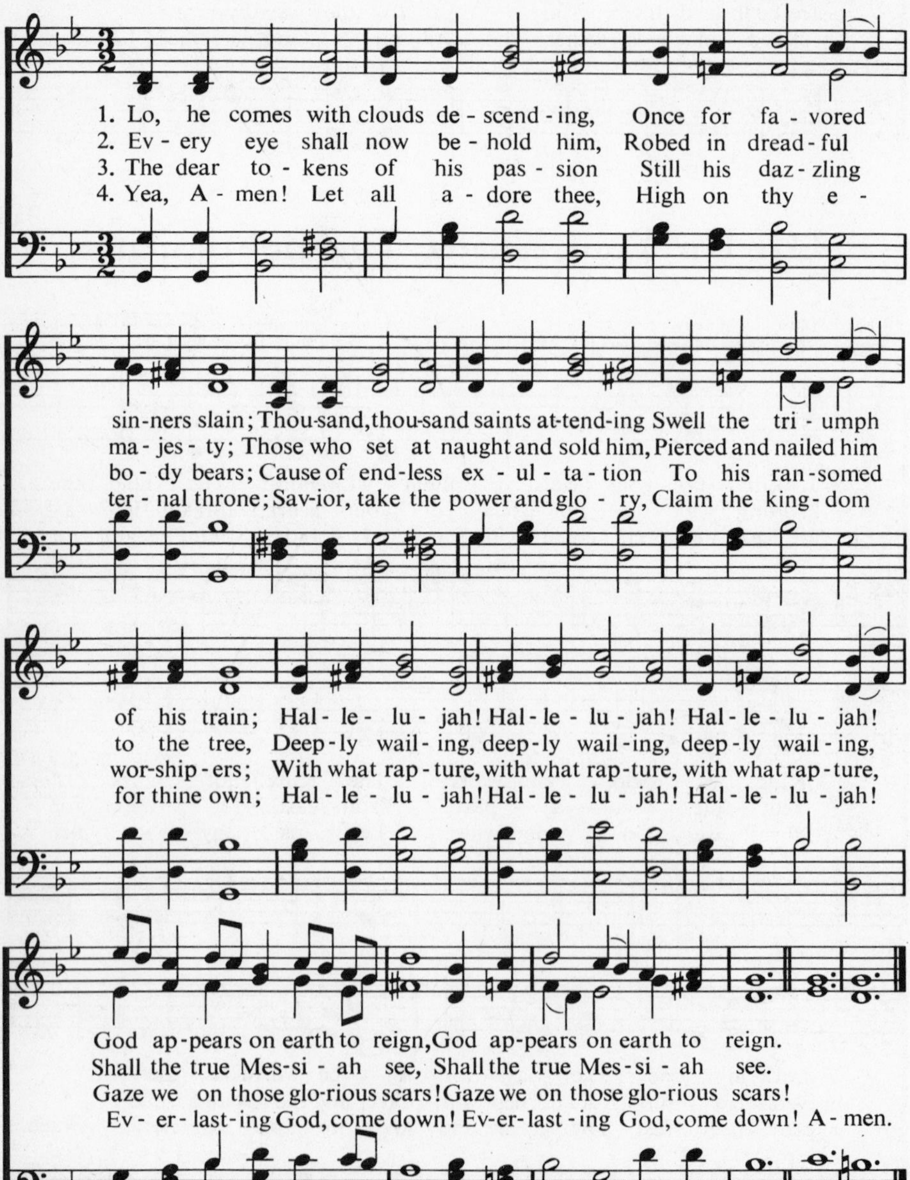
1. Lo, he comes with clouds de - scend - ing, Once for fa - vored
2. Ev - ery eye shall now be - hold him, Robed in dread - ful
3. The dear to - kens of his pas - sion Still his daz - zling
4. Yea, A - men! Let all a - dore thee, High on thy e -
sin-ners slain; Thou-sand, thou-sand saints at-tend-ing Swell the tri - umph
ma - jes - ty; Those who set at naught and sold him, Pierced and nailed him
bo - dy bears; Cause of end-less ex - ul - ta - tion To his ran-somed
ter - nal throne; Sav-ior, take the power and glo - ry, Claim the king-dom
of his train; Hal - le - lu - jah! Hal - le - lu - jah! Hal - le - lu - jah!
to the tree, Deep-ly wail-ing, deep-ly wail-ing, deep-ly wail-ing,
wor-ship-ers; With what rap-ture, with what rap-ture, with what rap-ture,
for thine own; Hal - le - lu - jah! Hal - le - lu - jah! Hal - le - lu - jah!
God ap-pears on earth to reign, God ap-pears on earth to reign.
Shall the true Mes-si - ah see, Shall the true Mes-si - ah see.
Gaze we on those glo-rious scars! Gaze we on those glo-rious scars!
Ev - er-last-ing God, come down! Ev-er-last - ing God, come down! A - men.

ADVENT SEASON

The Heavens Declare Thy Glory, Lord

PSALM 19:1-6
ISAAC WATTS, 1674-1748

HEBRON LM
LOWELL MASON, 1792-1872

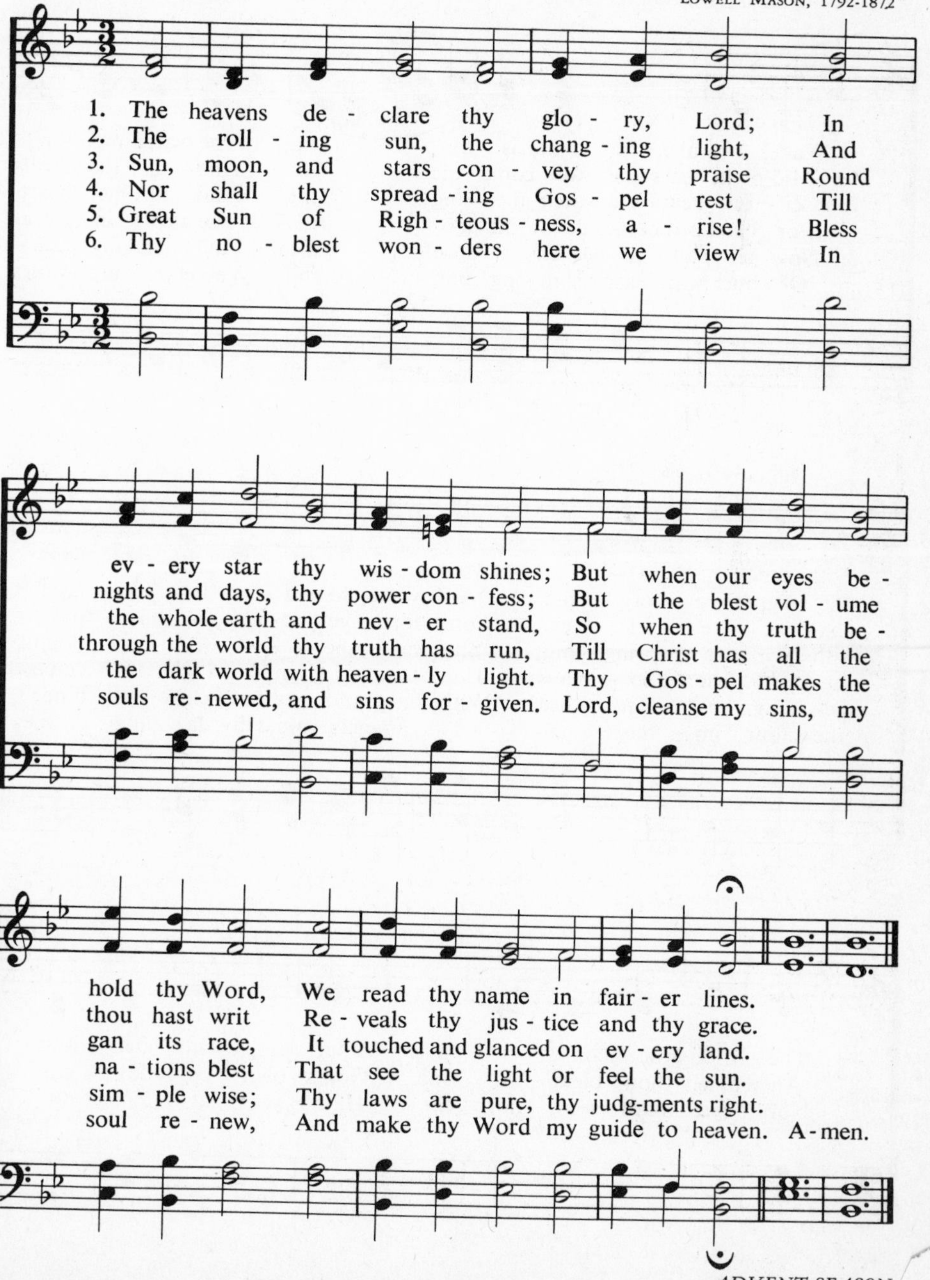
1. The heavens de - clare thy glo - ry, Lord; In
2. The roll - ing sun, the chang - ing light, And
3. Sun, moon, and stars con - vey thy praise Round
4. Nor shall thy spread - ing Gos - pel rest Till
5. Great Sun of Righ - teous - ness, a - rise! Bless
6. Thy no - blest won - ders here we view In
ev - ery star thy wis - dom shines; But when our eyes be -
nights and days, thy power con - fess; But the blest vol - ume
the whole earth and nev - er stand, So when thy truth be -
through the world thy truth has run, Till Christ has all the
the dark world with heaven - ly light. Thy Gos - pel makes the
souls re - newed, and sins for - given. Lord, cleanse my sins, my
hold thy Word, We read thy name in fair - er lines.
thou hast writ Re - veals thy jus - tice and thy grace.
gan its race, It touched and glanced on ev - ery land.
na - tions blest That see the light or feel the sun.
sim - ple wise; Thy laws are pure, thy judg-ments right.
soul re - new, And make thy Word my guide to heaven. A - men.

366

Wake, Awake, for Night Is Flying

PHILIPP NICOLAI, 1556-1608
Trans. by CATHERINE WINKWORTH, 1827-1878

WACHET AUF Irregular
PHILIPP NICOLAI, 1556-1608

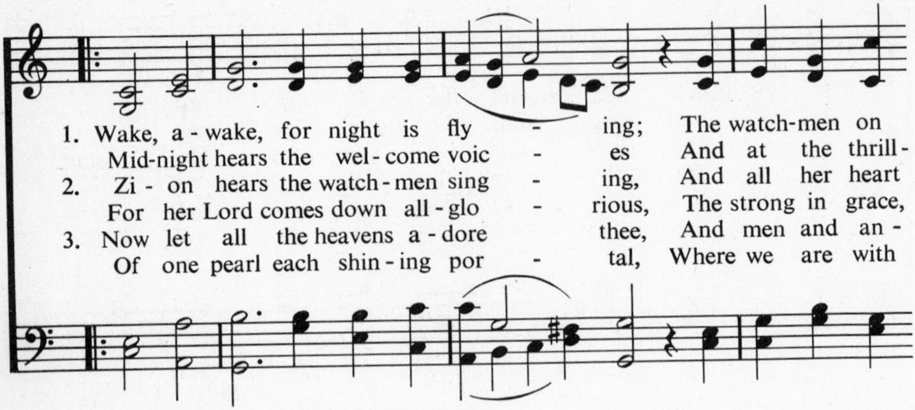

1. Wake, a-wake, for night is fly - ing; The watch-men on
Mid-night hears the wel-come voic - es And at the thrill-
2. Zi - on hears the watch-men sing - ing, And all her heart
For her Lord comes down all-glo - rious, The strong in grace,
3. Now let all the heavens a-dore thee, And men and an-
Of one pearl each shin-ing por - tal, Where we are with

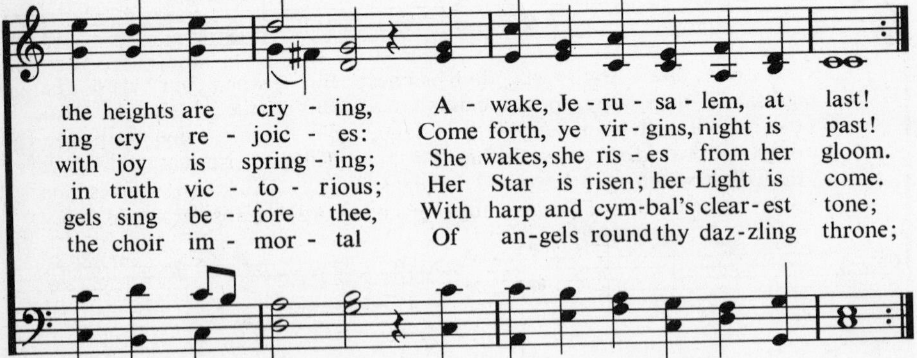

the heights are cry - ing, A - wake, Je - ru - sa - lem, at last!
ing cry re - joic - es: Come forth, ye vir-gins, night is past!
with joy is spring - ing; She wakes, she ris - es from her gloom.
in truth vic - to - rious; Her Star is risen; her Light is come.
gels sing be - fore thee, With harp and cym-bal's clear-est tone;
the choir im - mor - tal Of an-gels round thy daz-zling throne;

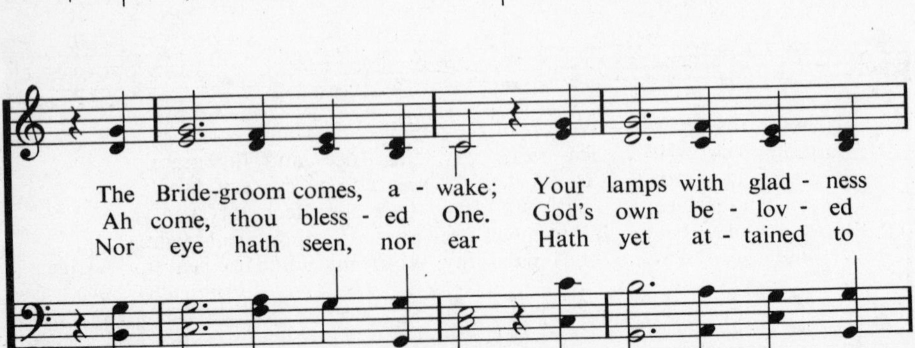

The Bride-groom comes, a - wake; Your lamps with glad - ness
Ah come, thou bless - ed One. God's own be - lov - ed
Nor eye hath seen, nor ear Hath yet at - tained to

ADVENT SEASON

take; Al - le - lu - ia! And for his mar - riage feast pre -
Son, Al - le - lu - ia! We fol - low till the halls we
hear What there is ours; But we re - joice, and sing to
pare, For ye must go to meet him there.
see Where thou hast bid us sup with thee.
thee Our hymn of joy e - ter - nal - ly. A - men.

367

Father of Mercies, in Thy Word

ANNE STEELE, 1716-1778

TALLIS' ORDINAL CM
THOMAS TALLIS, c. 1505-1585

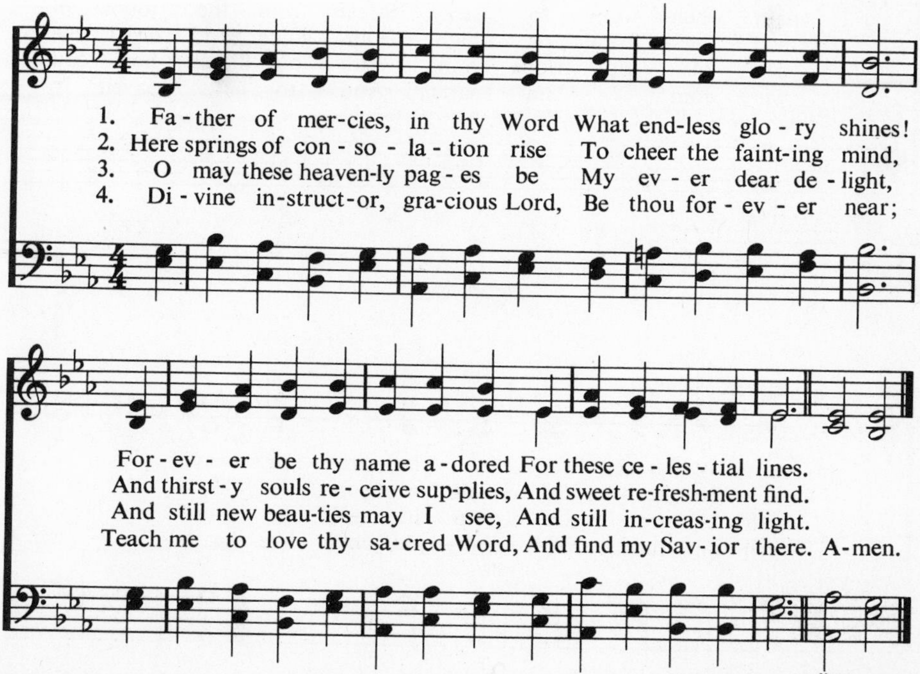
1. Fa - ther of mer - cies, in thy Word What end - less glo - ry shines!
2. Here springs of con - so - la - tion rise To cheer the faint - ing mind,
3. O may these heaven - ly pag - es be My ev - er dear de - light,
4. Di - vine in - struct - or, gra - cious Lord, Be thou for - ev - er near;
For - ev - er be thy name a - dored For these ce - les - tial lines.
And thirst - y souls re - ceive sup - plies, And sweet re - fresh - ment find.
And still new beau - ties may I see, And still in - creas - ing light.
Teach me to love thy sa - cred Word, And find my Sav - ior there. A - men.

Alternate tune: GRÄFENBERG

HOLY SCRIPTURE

Lamp of Our Feet

EVAN CM
Arr. from WILLIAM HAVERGAL, 1793-1870
by LOWELL MASON, 1792-1872

BERNARD BARTON, 1784-1849

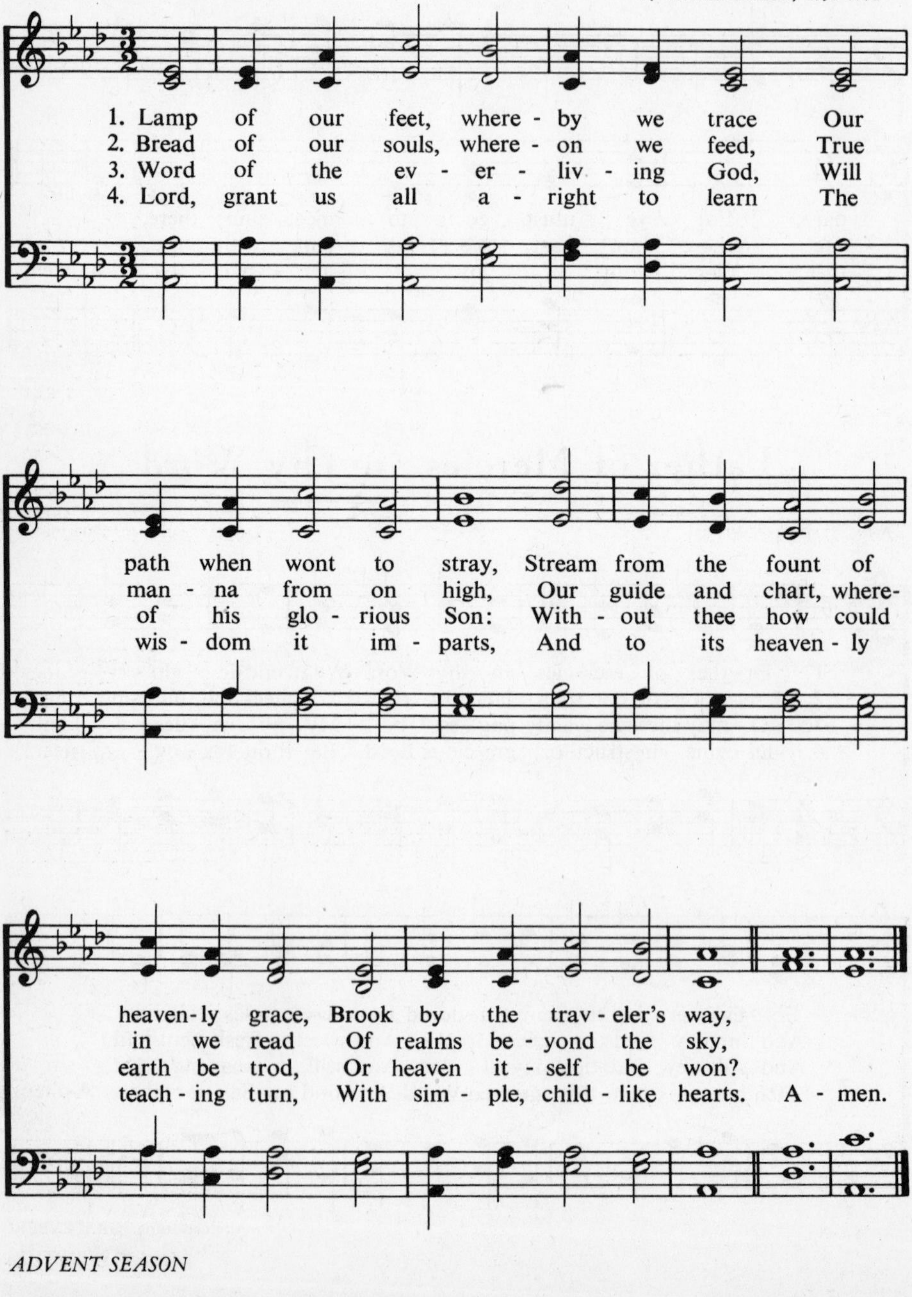
1. Lamp of our feet, where - by we trace Our
2. Bread of our souls, where - on we feed, True
3. Word of the ev - er - liv - ing God, Will
4. Lord, grant us all a - right to learn The
path when wont to stray, Stream from the fount of
man - na from on high, Our guide and chart, whereof his glo - rious Son: With - out thee how could
wis - dom it im - parts, And to its heaven - ly
heaven-ly grace, Brook by the trav - eler's way,
in we read Of realms be - yond the sky,
earth be trod, Or heaven it - self be won?
teach - ing turn, With sim - ple, child - like hearts. A - men.

ADVENT SEASON

369

Break Thou the Bread of Life

MARY A. LATHBURY, 1841-1913

BREAD OF LIFE 64.64.D.
WILLIAM F. SHERWIN, 1826-1888

1. Break thou the bread of life, Dear Lord, to me,
2. Bless thou the truth, dear Lord, To me, to me,
As thou didst break the loaves Be - side the sea;
As thou didst bless the bread By Gal - i - lee;
Be - yond the sa - cred page I seek thee, Lord;
Then shall all bond - age cease, All fet - ters fall;
My spir - it pants for thee, O liv - ing Word!
And I shall find my peace, My all - in - all. A-men.

370

Book of Books, Our People's Strength

LIEBSTER JESU 78.78.88.

PERCY DEARMER, 1867-1936 JOHANN R. AHLE, 1625-1673

1. Book of books, our peo - ple's strength, States-man's, teach - er's,
2. Thank we those who toiled in thought, Man - y di - verse
3. Praise we God, who hath in - spired Those whose wis - dom
he - ro's trea - sure, Bring - ing free - dom, spread - ing truth,
scrolls com - plet - ing: Po - ets, proph - ets, schol - ars, saints,
still di - rects us; Praise him for the Word made flesh,
Shed - ding light that none can mea - sure: Wis - dom comes to
Each his word from God re - peat - ing; Till they came, who
For the Spir - it which pro - tects us. Light of knowl - edge,
those who know thee; All the best we have we owe thee.
told the sto - ry Of the Word, and showed his glo - ry.
ev - er burn - ing, Shed on us thy death - less learn - ing. A - men.

Words from *Enlarged Songs of Praise* by permission of Oxford University Press.

O God of Light, Thy Word, a Lamp

WELYWN 11 10.11 10.

SARAH E. TAYLOR, 1883-1954

ALFRED SCOTT-GATTY, 1847-1918

1. O God of light, thy Word, a lamp un - fail - ing,
2. From days of old, through swift - ly roll - ing a - ges,
3. Un-dimmed by time, the Word is still re - veal - ing
4. To all the world the mes - sage thou art send - ing,
Shines through the dark - ness of our earth - ly way, O'er
Thou hast re - vealed thy will to mor - tal men,
To sin - ful men thy jus - tice and thy grace; And
To ev - ery land, to ev - ery race and clan, And
fear and doubt, o'er black de - spair pre - vail - ing,
Speak - ing to saints, to proph - ets, kings, and sag - es,
quest - ing hearts that long for peace and heal - ing
myr - iad tongues, in one great an - them blend - ing,
Guid - ing our steps to thine e - ter - nal day.
Who wrote the mes - sage with im - mor - tal pen.
See thy com - pas - sion in the Sav - ior's face.
Ac - claim with joy thy won - drous gift to man. A - men.

HOLY SCRIPTURE

372

O Word of God Incarnate

MUNICH 76.76.D.

PSALM 119:105; PROVERBS 6:23
WILLIAM W. HOW, 1823-1897

Gesangbuch, Meiningen, 1693
Harm. by FELIX MENDELSSOHN, 1809-1847

1. O Word of God in - car - nate, O Wis-dom from on high,
2. The Church from thee, her Mas - ter, Re-ceived the gift di - vine,
3. It float - eth like a ban - ner Be - fore God's host un - furled;
4. O make thy Church, dear Sav - ior, A lamp of pur - est gold,
O Truth un-changed, un-chang - ing, O Light of our dark sky:
And still that light she lift - eth O'er all the earth to shine.
It shin - eth like a bea - con A - bove the dark - ling world.
To bear be - fore the na - tions Thy true light as of old.
We praise thee for the ra - diance That from the hal - lowed page,
It is the sa - cred cas - ket, Where gems of truth are stored;
It is the chart and com - pass That o'er life's surg - ing sea,
O teach thy wan-dering pil - grims By this their path to trace,
A lan - tern to our foot-steps, Shines on from age to age.
It is the heaven-drawn pic-ture Of thee, the liv - ing Word.
Mid mists and rocks and quick-sands, Still guides, O Christ, to thee.
Till, clouds and dark-ness end - ed, They see thee face to face. A - men.

Break Forth, O Beauteous Heavenly Light

JOHANN RIST, 1607-1667
Trans. ANONYMOUS

ERMUNTRE DICH 87.87.88.77.
JOHANN SCHOP, c. 1590-1664
Harm. by J. S. BACH, 1685-1750

1. Break forth, O beau-teous heaven-ly light, And ush-er in the
morn - ing; Ye shep-herds, shrink not with af-fright, But
hear the an - gel's warn - ing. This child, now weak in
in - fan - cy, Our con - fi - dence and joy shall be, The
power of Sa-tan break - ing, Our peace e-ter-nal mak - ing.

CHRISTMASTIDE

374

Angels We Have Heard on High

Trad. French Carol

GLORIA 77.77. with Refrain
Trad. French Carol
Harm. by A. C. L.

1. Angels we have heard on high Sweetly singing o'er the plains,
2. Shepherds, why this jubilee? Why your joyous strains prolong?
3. Come to Bethlehem and see Him whose birth the angels sing;
4. See him in a manger laid, Whom the choirs of angels praise;
And the mountains in reply Echoing their joyous strains.
What the gladsome tidings be Which inspire your heavenly song?
Come, adore on bended knee Christ the Lord, the newborn King.
Mary, Joseph, lend your aid, While our hearts in love we raise.
Refrain
Glo - - - - - ri - a in excelsis Deo,
Glo - - - - -

CHRISTMASTIDE

- - - ri - a in ex-cel-sis De - o.

Love Came Down at Christmas

GARTON 67.67.
Trad. Irish Melody
Harm. by A. C. L.

CHRISTINA G. ROSSETTI, 1830-1894

1. Love came down at Christ - mas, Love all love - ly, Love di-vine;
2. Wor-ship we the God - head, Love in - car - nate, Love di-vine;
3. Love shall be our to - ken; Love be yours and love be mine,

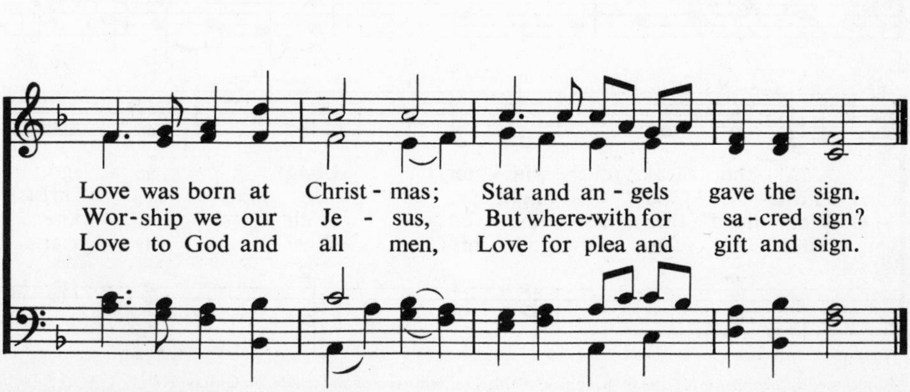
Love was born at Christ - mas; Star and an - gels gave the sign.
Wor-ship we our Je - sus, But where-with for sa - cred sign?
Love to God and all men, Love for plea and gift and sign.

In the Bleak Midwinter

CRANHAM Irregular
GUSTAV HOLST, 1874-1934

CHRISTINA G. ROSSETTI, 1830-1894

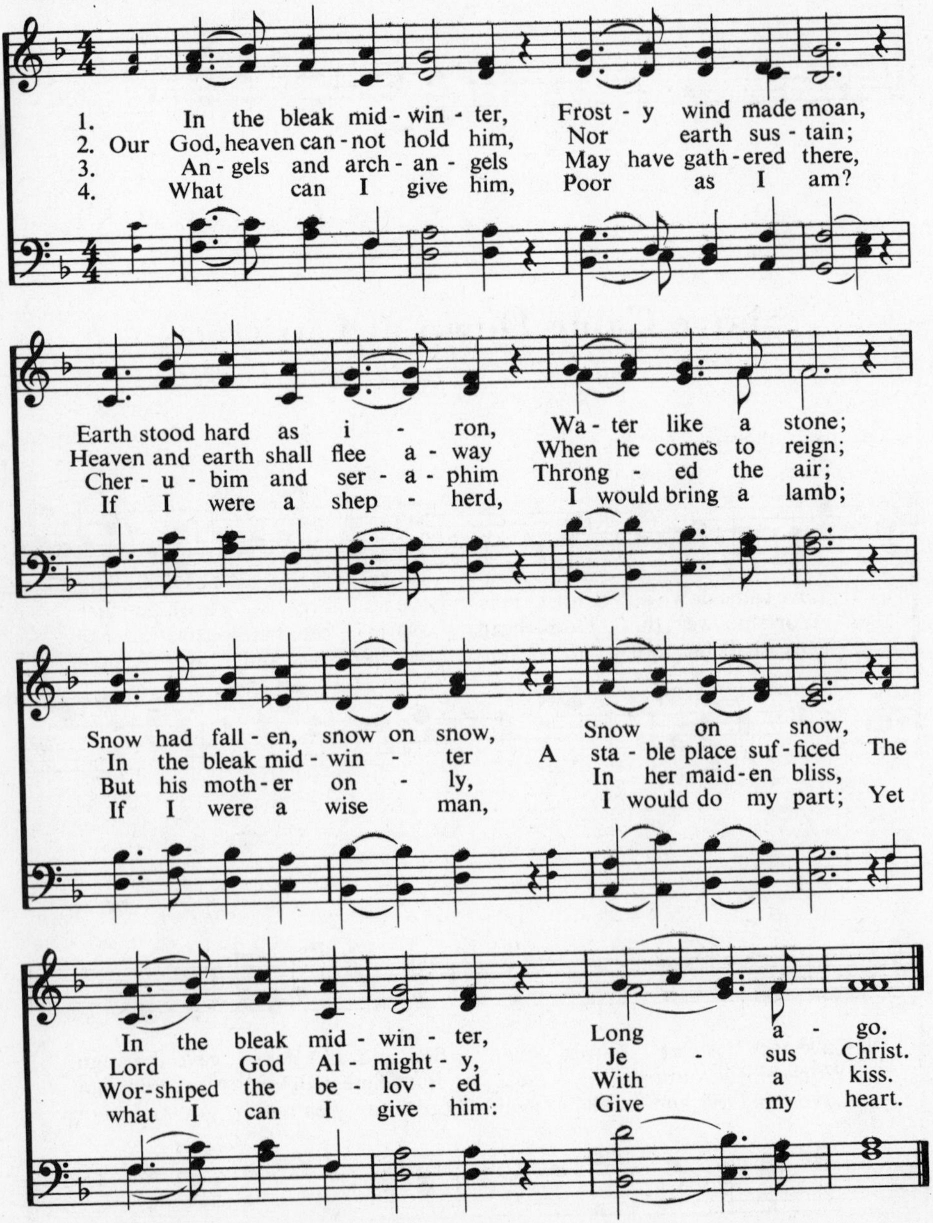
1. In the bleak mid - win - ter, Frost - y wind made moan,
2. Our God, heaven can - not hold him, Nor earth sus - tain;
3. An - gels and arch - an - gels May have gath - ered there,
4. What can I give him, Poor as I am?
Earth stood hard as i - ron, Wa - ter like a stone;
Heaven and earth shall flee a - way When he comes to reign;
Cher - u - bim and ser - a - phim Throng - ed the air;
If I were a shep - herd, I would bring a lamb;
Snow had fall - en, snow on snow, Snow on snow,
In the bleak mid - win - ter A sta - ble place suf - ficed The
But his moth - er on - ly, In her maid - en bliss,
If I were a wise man, I would do my part; Yet
In the bleak mid - win - ter, Long a - go.
Lord God Al - might - y, Je - sus Christ.
Wor - shiped the be - lov - ed With a kiss.
what I can I give him: Give my heart.

CHRISTMASTIDE

In Bethlehem Neath Starlit Skies

WAITS' CAROL 88.888. with Alleluias

GRACE M. STUTSMAN, 1886-

GRACE M. STUTSMAN, 1886-

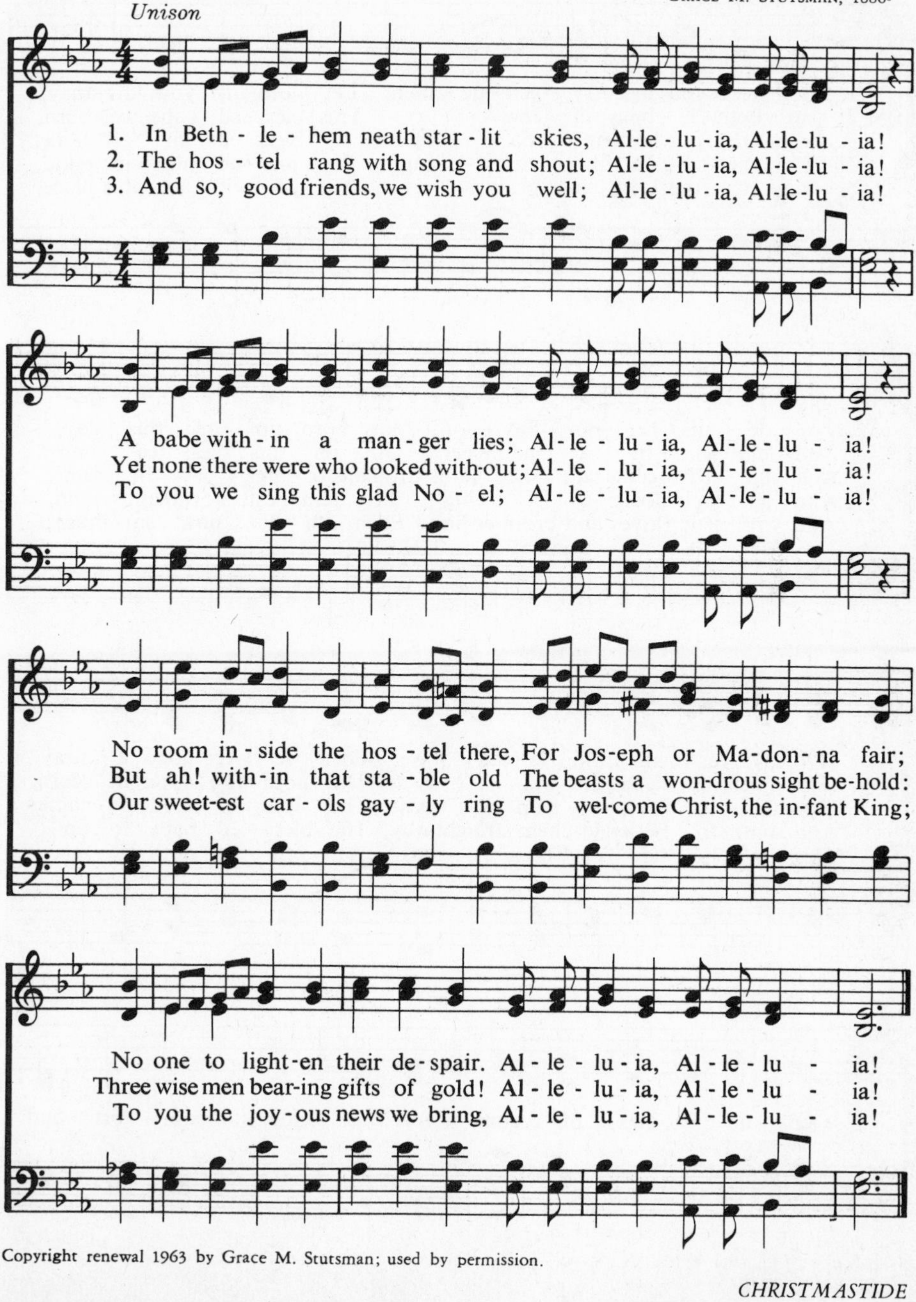
Unison
1. In Beth - le - hem neath star - lit skies, Al-le - lu - ia, Al-le-lu - ia!
2. The hos - tel rang with song and shout; Al-le - lu - ia, Al-le-lu - ia!
3. And so, good friends, we wish you well; Al-le - lu - ia, Al-le-lu - ia!
A babe with - in a man - ger lies; Al - le - lu - ia, Al - le - lu - ia!
Yet none there were who looked with-out; Al - le - lu - ia, Al - le - lu - ia!
To you we sing this glad No - el; Al - le - lu - ia, Al - le - lu - ia!
No room in - side the hos - tel there, For Jos-eph or Ma-don- na fair;
But ah! with-in that sta - ble old The beasts a won-drous sight be-hold:
Our sweet-est car - ols gay - ly ring To wel-come Christ, the in-fant King;
No one to light-en their de-spair. Al - le - lu - ia, Al - le - lu - ia!
Three wise men bear-ing gifts of gold! Al - le - lu - ia, Al - le - lu - ia!
To you the joy-ous news we bring, Al - le - lu - ia, Al - le - lu - ia!

378

God Rest You Merry, Gentlemen

GOD REST YOU MERRY Irregular with Refrain

18th Century Trad. English Carol

Trad. English Melody

Unison
1. God rest you mer - ry, gen - tle - men, Let noth - ing you dis - may,
2. In Beth - le - hem in Jew - ry This bless - ed babe was born,
3. From God our heaven - ly Fa - ther A bless - ed an - gel came,
4. The shep - herds at those tid - ings Re - joic - ed much in mind,
5. Now to the Lord sing prais - es, All you with - in this place,
For Je - sus Christ our Sav - ior Was born up - on this day,
And laid with - in a man - ger Up - on this bless - ed morn:
And un - to cer - tain shep - herds Brought tid - ings of the same,
And left their flocks a - feed - ing In tem - pest, storm, and wind,
And with true love and broth - er - hood Each oth - er now em - brace;
To save us all from Sa - tan's power When we were gone a - stray.
The which his moth - er Ma - ry Did noth - ing take in scorn.
How that in Beth - le - hem was born The Son of God by name.
And went to Beth - le - hem straight - way, The bless - ed babe to find.
This ho - ly tide of Christ - mas All oth - er doth de - face.
Refrain
O tid - ings of com - fort and joy, com - fort and

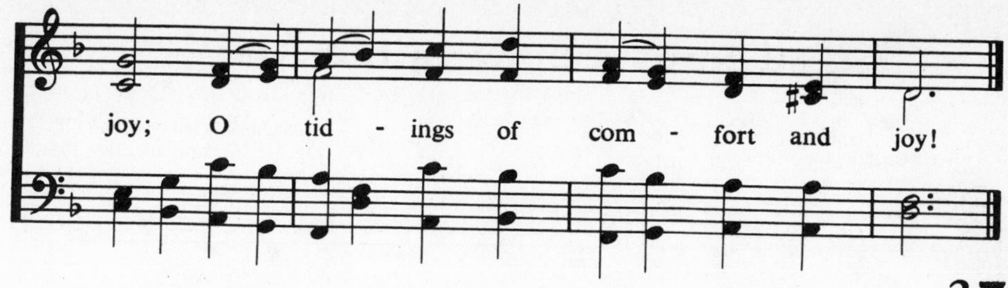
joy; O tid - ings of com - fort and joy!

379

All My Heart This Night Rejoices

PAUL GERHARDT, 1607-1676
Trans. by CATHERINE WINKWORTH, 1827-1878

WARUM SOLLT ICH MICH DENN GRÄMEN 8336.D.
JOHANN G. EBELING, 1637-1676

1. All my heart this night re - joic - es, As I hear, Far and near,
2. Hark! a voice from yon - der man - ger, Soft and sweet, Doth en - treat:
3. Come, then, let us has - ten yon - der; Here let all, Great and small,
Sweet - est an - gel voic - es: "Christ is born," their choirs are
"Flee from woe and dan - ger; Bre - thren, come; from all that
Kneel in awe and won - der; Love him, who with love is
sing - ing, Till the air, Ev - ery-where, Now with joy is ring - ing.
grieves you, You are freed; All you need I will sure - ly give you."
yearn - ing; Hail the star, That from far Bright with hope is burn - ing!

There's a Song in the Air

CHRISTMAS SONG 66.66.12 12.

JOSIAH G. HOLLAND, 1819-1881

KARL P. HARRINGTON, 1861-1953

1. There's a song in the air! There's a star in the sky!
2. There's a tu - mult of joy O'er the won - der - ful birth,
3. In the light of that star Lie the a - ges im - pearled;
4. We re - joice in the light, And we ech - o the song
There's a moth - er's deep prayer And a ba - by's low cry!
For the vir - gin's sweet boy Is the Lord of the earth.
And that song from a - far Has swept o - ver the world.
That comes down through the night From the heav - en - ly throng.
And the star rains its fire while the beau - ti - ful sing,
Ay! the star rains its fire while the beau - ti - ful sing,
Ev - ery hearth is a - flame, and the beau - ti - ful sing
Ay! we shout to the love - ly e - van - gel they bring,
For the man - ger of Beth - le - hem cra - dles a King!
For the man - ger of Beth - le - hem cra - dles a King!
In the homes of the na - tions that Je - sus is King!
And we greet in his cra - dle our Sav - ior and King!

CHRISTMASTIDE

381

O Little Town of Bethlehem

PHILLIPS BROOKS, 1835-1893

ST. LOUIS 86.86.76.86.
LEWIS H. REDNER, 1830-1908

1. O lit - tle town of Beth - le - hem, How still we see thee lie!
2. For Christ is born of Ma - ry, And gath - ered all a - bove,
3. How si - lent - ly, how si - lent - ly The won - drous gift is given!
4. O ho - ly Child of Beth - le - hem, De - scend to us, we pray;
A - bove thy deep and dream - less sleep The si - lent stars go by;
While mor - tals sleep, the an - gels keep Their watch of won - dering love.
So God im - parts to hu - man hearts The bless - ings of his heaven.
Cast out our sin, and en - ter in, Be born in us to - day.
Yet in thy dark streets shin - eth The ev - er - last - ing light; The
O morn - ing stars, to - geth - er Pro - claim the ho - ly birth, And
No ear may hear his com - ing, But in this world of sin, Where
We hear the Christ - mas an - gels The great glad tid - ings tell; O
hopes and fears of all the years Are met in thee to - night.
prais - es sing to God the King, And peace to men on earth!
meek souls will re - ceive him, still The dear Christ en - ters in.
come to us, a - bide with us, Our Lord Em - man - u - el! A - men.

Alternate tune: FOREST GREEN

CHRISTMASTIDE

Angels, from the Realms of Glory

REGENT SQUARE 87.87.87.

JAMES MONTGOMERY, 1771-1854

HENRY SMART, 1813-1879

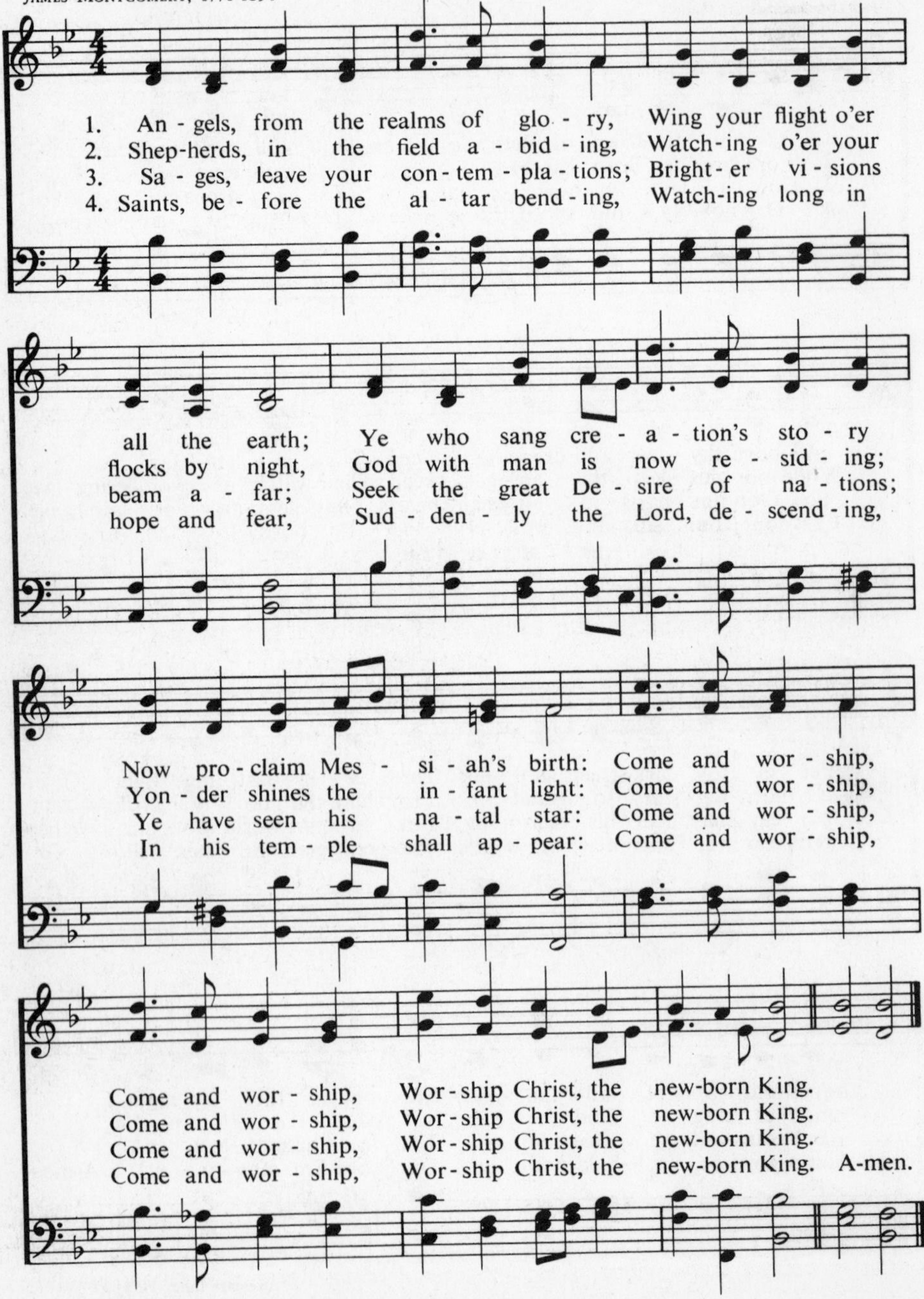
1. An - gels, from the realms of glo - ry, Wing your flight o'er
2. Shep-herds, in the field a - bid - ing, Watch-ing o'er your
3. Sa - ges, leave your con - tem - pla - tions; Bright - er vi - sions
4. Saints, be - fore the al - tar bend - ing, Watch-ing long in
all the earth; Ye who sang cre - a - tion's sto - ry
flocks by night, God with man is now re - sid - ing;
beam a - far; Seek the great De - sire of na - tions;
hope and fear, Sud - den - ly the Lord, de - scend - ing,
Now pro - claim Mes - si - ah's birth: Come and wor - ship,
Yon - der shines the in - fant light: Come and wor - ship,
Ye have seen his na - tal star: Come and wor - ship,
In his tem - ple shall ap - pear: Come and wor - ship,
Come and wor - ship, Wor - ship Christ, the new-born King.
Come and wor - ship, Wor - ship Christ, the new-born King.
Come and wor - ship, Wor - ship Christ, the new-born King.
Come and wor - ship, Wor - ship Christ, the new-born King. A-men.

CHRISTMASTIDE

The First Noel

Trad. English Carol

THE FIRST NOEL Irregular with Refrain
Trad. English Melody

1. The first No - el, the an - gel did say, Was to cer - tain poor
2. They look - ed up and saw a star Shin - ing in the
3. And by the light of that same star Three wise men
4. This star drew nigh to the north - west, O'er Beth - le -
5. Then en - tered in those wise men three, Full rev - erent -
shep - herds in fields as they lay; In fields where they lay
east, be - yond them far; And to the earth it
came from coun - try far; To seek for a king was
hem it took its rest, And there it did both
ly up - on the knee, And of - fered there, in
keep - ing their sheep, On a cold win - ter's night that was so deep.
gave great light, And so it con - tin - ued both day and night.
their in - tent, And to fol - low the star wher - ev - er it went.
stop and stay, Right o - ver the place where Je - sus lay.
his pres - ence, Their gold and myrrh and frank - in - cense.
Refrain
No - el, No - el, No - el, No - el, Born is the King of Is - ra - el.

Away in a Manger

AWAY IN A MANGER 11 11.11 11.
JAMES R. MURRAY, 1841-1905

ANONYMOUS

1. A - way in a man - ger, no crib for a bed,
2. The cat - tle are low - ing, the ba - by a - wakes,
3. Be near me, Lord Je - sus, I ask thee to stay
The lit - tle Lord Je - sus laid down his sweet head.
But lit - tle Lord Je - sus, no cry - ing he makes.
Close by me for - ev - er, and love me, I pray.
The stars in the sky looked down where he lay,
I love thee, Lord Je - sus, look down from the sky,
Bless all the dear chil - dren in thy ten - der care,
The lit - tle Lord Je - sus, a - sleep on the hay.
And stay by my cra - dle till morn - ing is nigh.
And fit us for heav - en to live with thee there. A - men.

CHRISTMASTIDE

What Child Is This

William C. Dix, 1837-1898

GREENSLEEVES 87.87. with Refrain
16th Century English Melody

1. What child is this, who, laid to rest, On Ma-ry's lap is sleep-ing?
2. Why lies he in such mean es-tate Where ox and ass are feed-ing?
3. So bring him in - cense, gold, and myrrh, Come, peas-ant, King, to own him;
Whom an-gels greet with an-thems sweet, While shep-herds watch are keep-ing?
Good Chris-tian, fear, for sin-ners here The si - lent Word is plead-ing.
The King of kings sal - va - tion brings, Let lov - ing hearts en-throne him.
Refrain
This, this is Christ the King, Whom shep-herds guard and an - gels sing;
Haste, haste to bring him laud, The babe, the son of Ma - ry.

386

O Come, All Ye Faithful

ANONYMOUS, Latin, 18th Century
Trans. by FREDERICK OAKELEY, 1802-1880, and others

ADESTE FIDELES Irregular with Refrain
JOHN F. WADE, c. 1710-1786

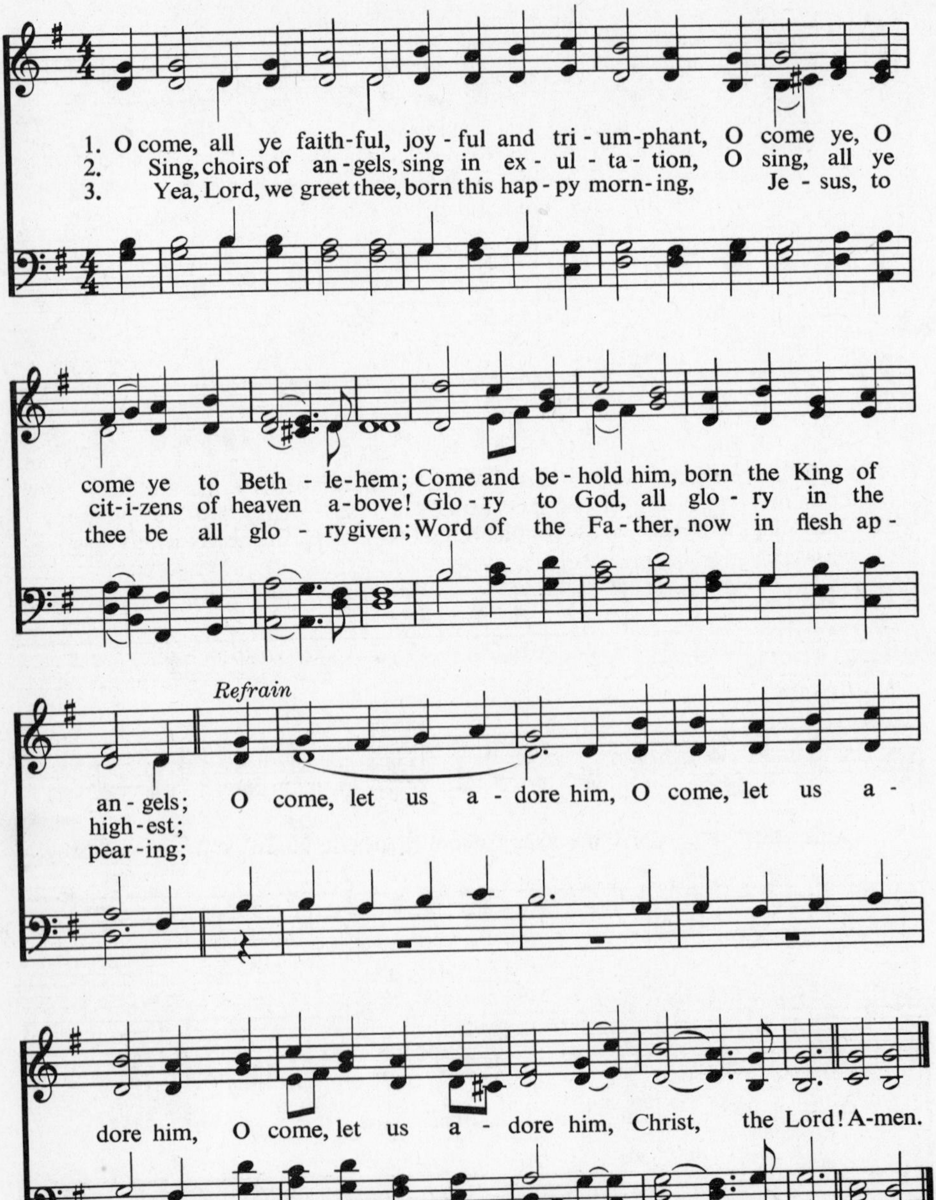
1. O come, all ye faith-ful, joy-ful and tri - um-phant, O come ye, O
2. Sing, choirs of an-gels, sing in ex - ul - ta - tion, O sing, all ye
3. Yea, Lord, we greet thee, born this hap - py morn-ing, Je - sus, to
come ye to Beth - le-hem; Come and be - hold him, born the King of
cit-i-zens of heaven a-bove! Glo - ry to God, all glo - ry in the
thee be all glo - rygiven; Word of the Fa-ther, now in flesh ap -
Refrain
an-gels; O come, let us a - dore him, O come, let us a -
high-est;
pear-ing;
dore him, O come, let us a - dore him, Christ, the Lord! A-men.

387

Hark! the Herald Angels Sing

CHARLES WESLEY, 1707-1788
Alt. by GEORGE WHITEFIELD, 1714-1770

EASTER HYMN 77.77.D.
Lyra Davidica, 1708

1. Hark! the her-ald an-gels sing, "Glo-ry to the new-born King;
2. Christ, by high-est heaven a-dored; Christ, the ev-er-last-ing Lord!
3. Hail the heaven-born Prince of Peace! Hail the Sun of Righ-teous-ness!
Peace on earth, and mer-cy mild, God and sin-ners rec-on-ciled!"
Late in time be-hold him come, Off-spring of the vir-gin's womb.
Light and life to all he brings, Risen with heal-ing in his wings,
Joy-ful, all ye na-tions, rise, Join the tri-umph of the skies;
Veiled in flesh the God-head see; Hail th' in-car-nate De-i-ty,
Mild he lays his glo-ry by, Born that man no more may die,
With th'an-gel-ic host pro-claim, "Christ is born in Beth-le-hem!"
Pleased as man with men to dwell, Je-sus, our Em-man-u-el.
Born to raise the sons of earth, Born to give them sec-ond birth. A-men.

388

Hark! the Herald Angels Sing

MENDELSSOHN 77.77.D. with Refrain

CHARLES WESLEY, 1707-1788
Alt. by GEORGE WHITEFIELD, 1714-1770

FELIX MENDELSSOHN, 1809-1847
Adapt. by WILLIAM H. CUMMINGS, 1831-1915

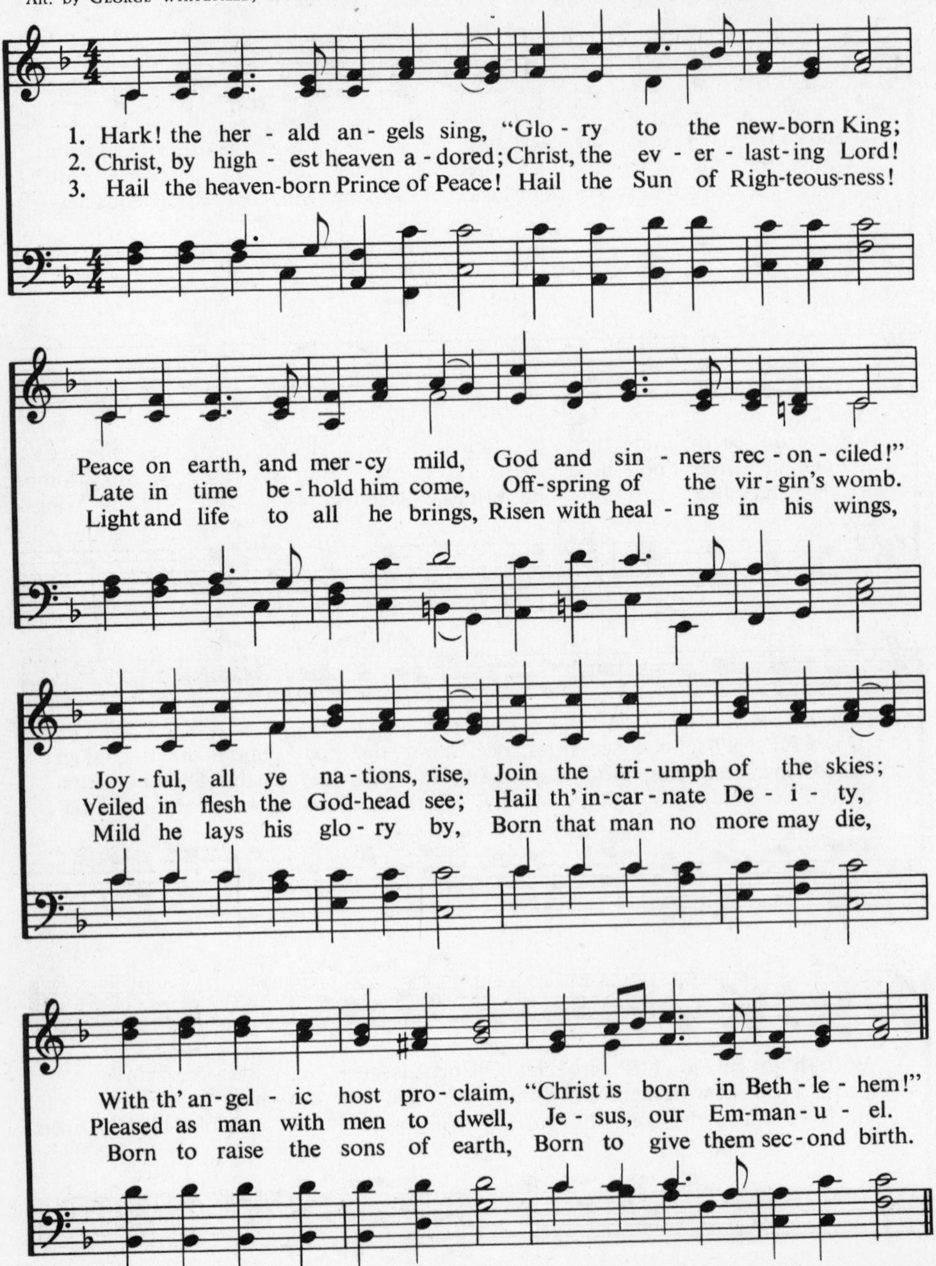
1. Hark! the her - ald an - gels sing, "Glo - ry to the new-born King;
2. Christ, by high - est heaven a - dored; Christ, the ev - er - last - ing Lord!
3. Hail the heaven-born Prince of Peace! Hail the Sun of Righ-teous-ness!
Peace on earth, and mer - cy mild, God and sin - ners rec - on - ciled!"
Late in time be - hold him come, Off - spring of the vir - gin's womb.
Light and life to all he brings, Risen with heal - ing in his wings,
Joy - ful, all ye na - tions, rise, Join the tri - umph of the skies;
Veiled in flesh the God-head see; Hail th' in - car - nate De - i - ty,
Mild he lays his glo - ry by, Born that man no more may die,
With th' an - gel - ic host pro - claim, "Christ is born in Beth - le - hem!"
Pleased as man with men to dwell, Je - sus, our Em - man - u - el.
Born to raise the sons of earth, Born to give them sec - ond birth.

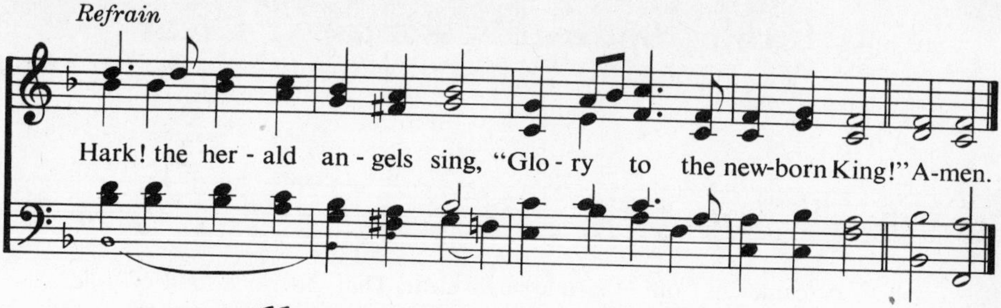
Refrain
Hark! the her - ald an - gels sing, “Glo - ry to the new-born King!” A-men.

Let All Together Praise Our God 389

NICOLAUS HERMANN, c. 1485-1561
Trans. by ARTHUR TOZER RUSSELL, 1806-1874

LOBT GOTT, IHR CHRISTEN CM
NICOLAUS HERMANN, c. 1485-1561
Harm. by A. C. L.

1. Let all to - geth - er praise our God Up - on his loft - y
2. He lays a - side his maj - es - ty And seems as noth - ing
3. Be - hold the won - der - ful ex - change Our Lord with us doth
4. The glo - rious gates of par - a - dise The an - gel guards no
throne; For he un - clos - es heaven to - day And
worth, And takes on him a ser - vant's form, Who
make! Lo, he as - sumes our flesh and blood, And
more; This day a - gain those gates un - fold. With
gives to us his Son, And gives to us his Son.
made the heaven and earth, Who made the heaven and earth.
we of heaven par - take, And we of heaven par - take.
praise our God a - dore, With praise our God a - dore! A-men.

390

It Came upon the Midnight Clear

LUKE 2:13-14
EDMUND H. SEARS, 1810-1876

CAROL CMD
RICHARD STORRS WILLIS, 1819-1900

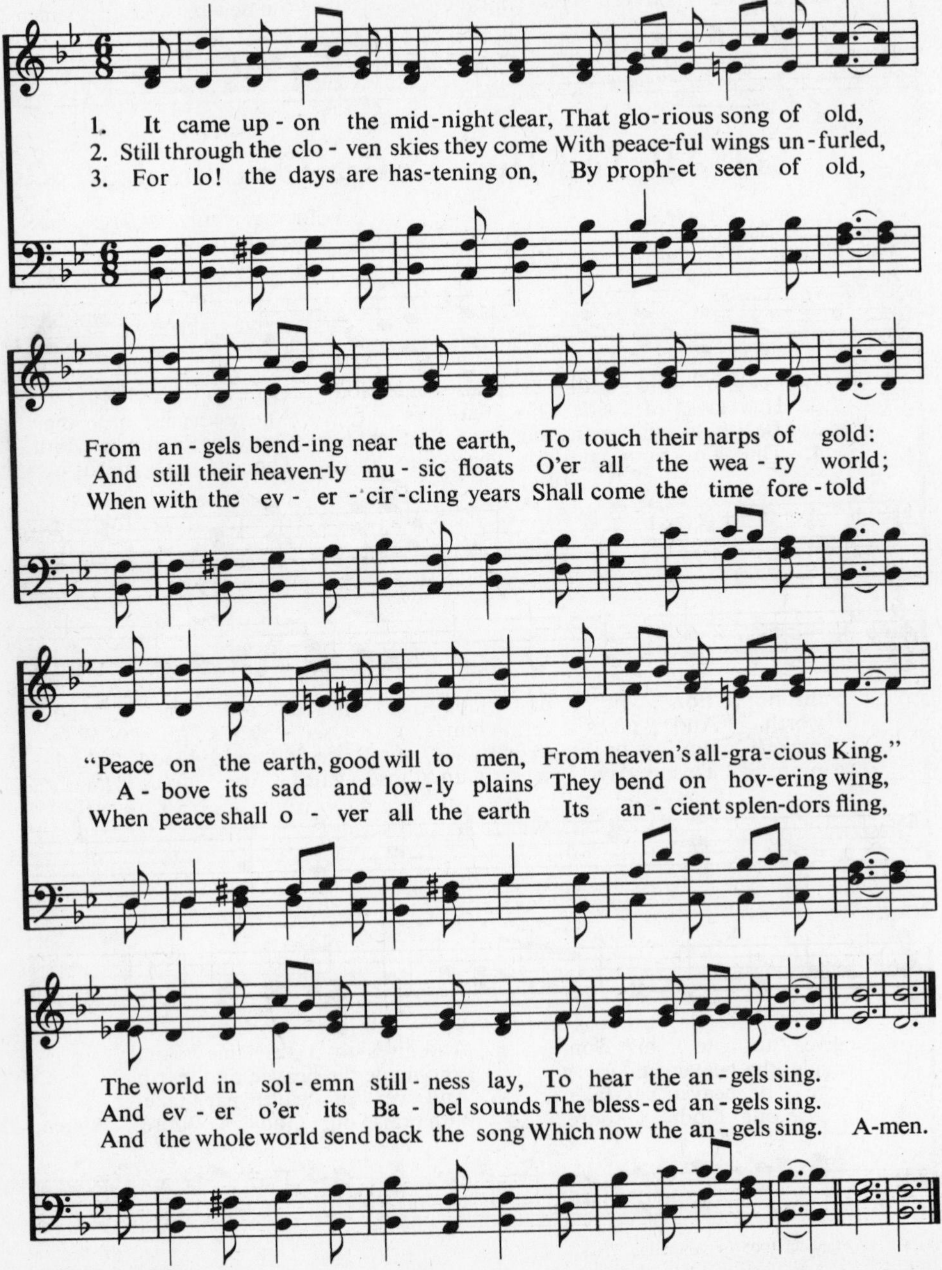
1. It came up - on the mid-night clear, That glo-rious song of old,
2. Still through the clo - ven skies they come With peace-ful wings un-furled,
3. For lo! the days are has-tening on, By proph-et seen of old,
From an-gels bend-ing near the earth, To touch their harps of gold:
And still their heaven-ly mu - sic floats O'er all the wea - ry world;
When with the ev - er - cir-cling years Shall come the time fore-told
"Peace on the earth, good will to men, From heaven's all-gra-cious King."
A - bove its sad and low-ly plains They bend on hov-ering wing,
When peace shall o - ver all the earth Its an - cient splen-dors fling,
The world in sol - emn still - ness lay, To hear the an - gels sing.
And ev - er o'er its Ba - bel sounds The bless-ed an - gels sing.
And the whole world send back the song Which now the an - gels sing. A-men.

Good Christian Men, Rejoice

Latin, 14th Century
Paraphrase by JOHN M. NEALE, 1818-1866

IN DULCI JUBILO 66.77.78.55.
14th Century German Melody
Harm. by V. E. C.

Unison
1. Good Chris-tian men, re - joice, With heart and soul and voice;
2. Good Chris-tian men, re - joice, With heart and soul and voice;
3. Good Chris-tian men, re - joice, With heart and soul and voice;
Give ye heed to what we say: Je - sus Christ is born to - day.
Now ye hear of end - less bliss; Je - sus Christ was born for this!
Now ye need not fear the grave; Je - sus Christ was born to save!
Ox and ass be - fore him bow, And he is in the
He hath oped the heaven - ly door, And man is bless - ed
Calls you one and calls you all, To gain his ev - er -
man - ger now. Christ is born to - day, Christ is born to - day!
ev - er - more. Christ was born for this, Christ was born for this!
last - ing hall. Christ was born to save, Christ was born to save!

CHRISTMASTIDE

392

Joy to the World

ANTIOCH CM

Psalm 98
Isaac Watts, 1674-1748

Arr. from George Frederick Handel, 1685-1759
by Lowell Mason, 1792-1872

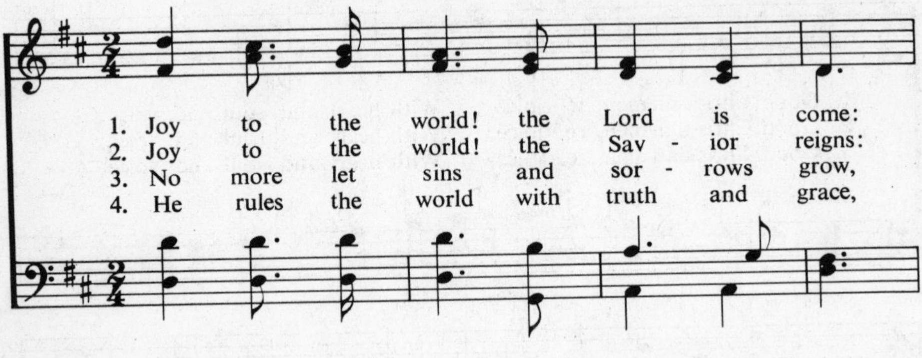
1. Joy to the world! the Lord is come:
2. Joy to the world! the Sav - ior reigns:
3. No more let sins and sor - rows grow,
4. He rules the world with truth and grace,

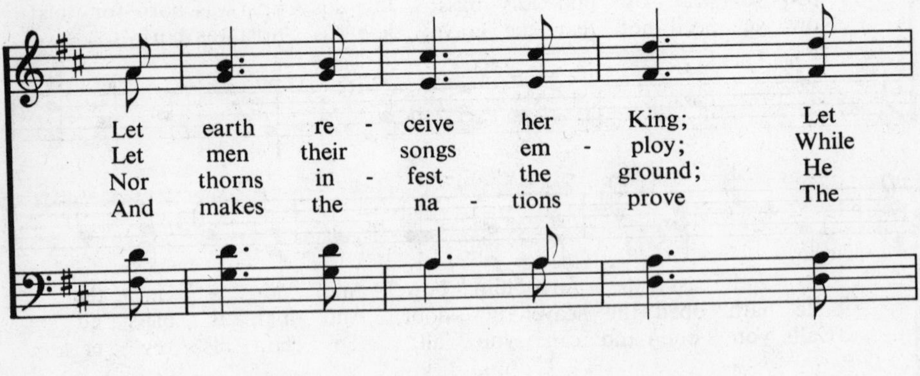
Let earth re - ceive her King; Let
Let men their songs em - ploy; While
Nor thorns in - fest the ground; He
And makes the na - tions prove The

ev - ery heart pre - pare him room,
fields and floods, rocks, hills, and plains
comes to make his bless - ings flow
glo - ries of his righ - teous - ness,

And heaven and na - ture sing, And
Re - peat the sound - ing joy, Re -
Far as the curse is found, Far
And won - ders of his love, And
And heaven and na - ture
Re - peat the sound - ing
Far as the curse is
And won - ders of his
heaven and na - ture sing, And
peat the sound - ing joy, Re -
as the curse is found, Far
won - ders of his love, And
sing,
joy,
found,
love,
And heaven and na - ture
Re - peat the sound - ing
Far as the curse is
And won - ders of his
heaven, and heaven and na - ture sing.
peat, re - peat the sound - ing joy.
as, far as the curse is found.
won - ders, won - ders of his love. A - men.
sing,
joy,
found,
love,

CHRISTMASTIDE

Silent Night, Holy Night

JOSEPH MOHR, 1792-1848
Trans. by JOHN F. YOUNG, 1820-1885

STILLE NACHT Irregular
FRANZ GRUBER, 1787-1863

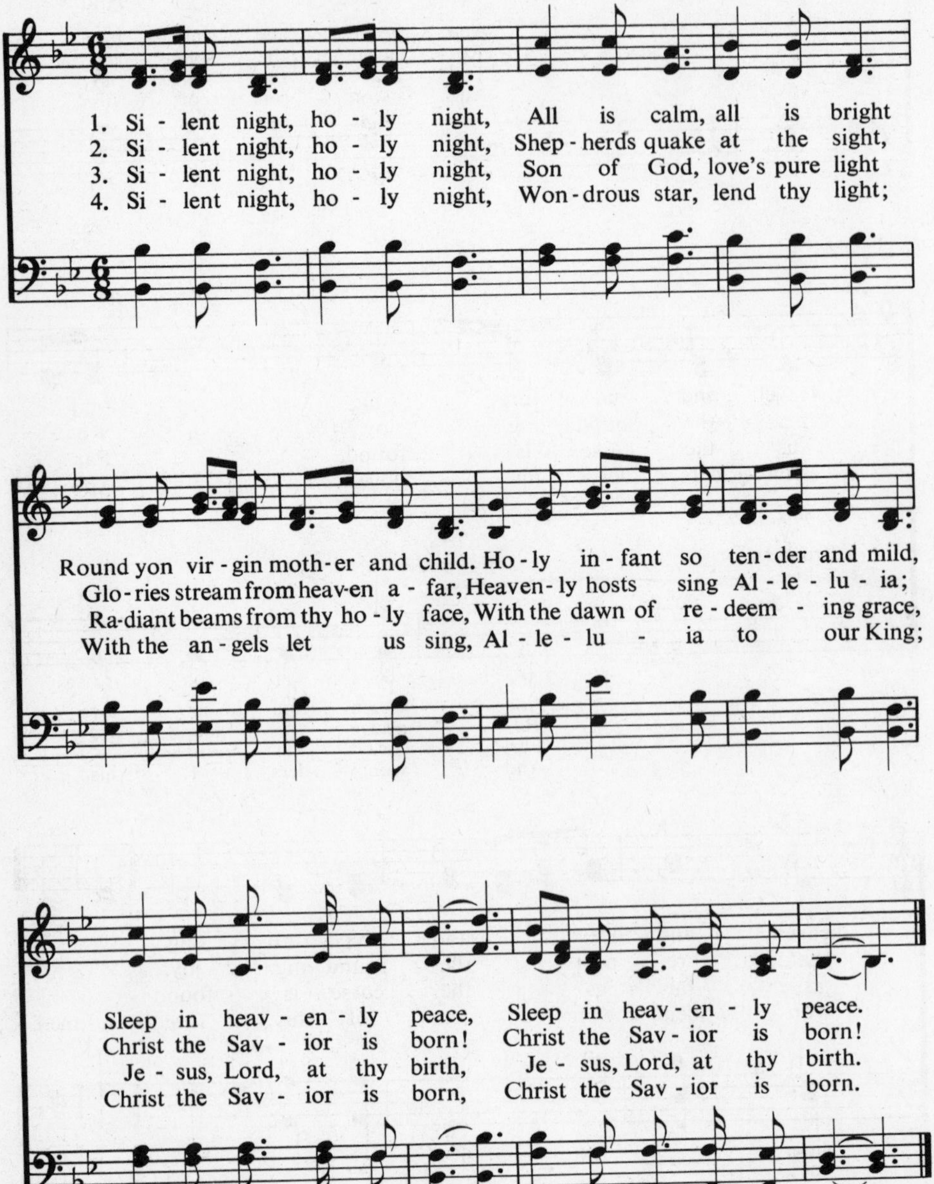
1. Si - lent night, ho - ly night, All is calm, all is bright
2. Si - lent night, ho - ly night, Shep - herds quake at the sight,
3. Si - lent night, ho - ly night, Son of God, love's pure light
4. Si - lent night, ho - ly night, Won - drous star, lend thy light;
Round yon vir - gin moth - er and child. Ho - ly in - fant so ten - der and mild,
Glo - ries stream from heav-en a - far, Heaven - ly hosts sing Al - le - lu - ia;
Ra-diant beams from thy ho - ly face, With the dawn of re - deem - ing grace,
With the an - gels let us sing, Al - le - lu - ia to our King;
Sleep in heav - en - ly peace, Sleep in heav - en - ly peace.
Christ the Sav - ior is born! Christ the Sav - ior is born!
Je - sus, Lord, at thy birth, Je - sus, Lord, at thy birth.
Christ the Sav - ior is born, Christ the Sav - ior is born.

While Shepherds Watched Their Flocks

LUKE 2:8-14
NAHUM TATE, 1652-1715

WINCHESTER OLD CM
Est's *The Whole Booke of Psalmes*, 1592
Tune arrang. attr. to GEORGE KIRBYE, c. 1560-1634

1. While shep - herds watched their flocks by night, All
2. "Fear not!" said he, for might - y dread Had
3. "To you, in Da - vid's town, this day Is
4. "The heaven - ly babe you there shall find To
5. Thus spake the ser - aph; and forth - with Ap -
6. "All glo - ry be to God on high, And
seat - ed on the ground, The an - gel of the
seized their trou - bled mind, "Glad tid - ings of great
born of Da - vid's line The Sav - ior, who is
hu - man view dis - played, All mean - ly wrapped in
peared a shin - ing throng Of an - gels prais - ing
to the earth be peace; Good will hence - forth from
Lord came down, And glo - ry shone a - round.
joy I bring To you and all man - kind.
Christ the Lord; And this shall be the sign:
swath - ing bands, And in a man - ger laid."
God on high, Who thus ad - dressed their song:
heaven to men Be - gin and nev - er cease!" A - men.

Alternate tune: CHRISTMAS

CHRISTMASTIDE

Gentle Mary Laid Her Child

TEMPUS ADEST FLORIDUM 76.76.D.
Piae Cantiones, 1582
JOSEPH S. COOK, 1859-1933
Harm. by ERNEST MACMILLAN, 1893-

1. Gen - tle Ma - ry laid her child Low - ly in a man - ger;
2. An - gels sang a - bout his birth; Wise men sought and found him;
3. Gen - tle Ma - ry laid her child Low - ly in a man - ger;
There he lay, the un - de - filed, To the world a stran - ger.
Heav-en's star shone bright-ly forth, Glo - ry all a - round him.
He is still the un - de - filed, But no more a stran - ger.
Such a babe in such a place, Can he be the Sav - ior?
Shep-herds saw the won-drous sight, Heard the an - gels sing - ing;
Son of God, of hum-ble birth, Beau - ti - ful the sto - ry;
Ask the saved of all the race Who have found his fa - vor.
All the plains were lit that night; All the hills were ring - ing.
Praise his name in all the earth; Hail the King of glo - ry! A-men.

CHRISTMASTIDE

Infant Holy, Infant Lowly

Polish Carol
Paraphrase by E. M. G. Reed, 1885-1933

W̦ ZLOBIE LEZY 447.447.44447.
Arr. by E. M. G. Reed, 1885-1933
Harm. by A. C. L.

Unison
1. In - fant ho - ly, In - fant low - ly, For his bed a cat - tle stall; Ox - en low - ing, Lit - tle know - ing Christ the babe is Lord of all. Swift are wing - ing An - gels sing - ing, No - els ring - ing, Tid - ings bring - ing: Christ the babe is Lord of all.
2. Flocks were sleep - ing; Shep - herds keep - ing Vig - il till the morn - ing new Saw the glo - ry, Heard the sto - ry, Tid - ings of a Gos - pel true. Thus re - joic - ing, Free from sor - row, Prais - es voic - ing Greet the mor - row: Christ the babe was born for you.

As with Gladness Men of Old

DIX 77.77.77.

Matthew 2:1-11
William C. Dix, 1837-1898

Arr. from Conrad Kocher, 1786-1872
by W. H. Monk, 1823-1889

1. As with glad - ness men of old Did the guid - ing
2. As with joy - ous steps they sped To that low - ly
3. As they of - fered gifts most rare At that man - ger
4. Ho - ly Je - sus, ev - ery day Keep us in the
star be - hold; As with joy they hailed its light,
man - ger bed, There to bend the knee be - fore
rude and bare, So may we with ho - ly joy,
nar - row way; And, when earth - ly things are past,
Lead - ing on - ward, beam - ing bright; So, most gra - cious
Him whom heaven and earth a - dore; So may we with
Pure and free from sin's al - loy, All our cost - liest
Bring our ran - somed souls at last Where they need no
Lord, may we Ev - er - more be led to thee.
will - ing feet Ev - er seek thy mer - cy seat.
trea - sures bring, Christ, to thee, our heaven-ly King.
star to guide, Where no clouds thy glo - ry hide. A - men.

Light of the World, We Hail Thee

COMPLAINER 76.76.D.
WILLIAM WALKER, 1809-1875
Harm. by C. R. Y.

JOHN S. B. MONSELL, 1811-1875

Unison
1. Light of the world, we hail thee, Flood-ing the east-ern skies;
2. Light of the world, thy beau-ty Steals in-to ev-ery heart,
3. Light of the world, il-lu-mine This dark-ened earth of thine,
Nev-er shall dark-ness veil thee A-gain from hu-man eyes;
And glo-ri-fies with du-ty Life's poor-est, hum-blest part;
Till ev-ery-thing that's hu-man Be filled with the di-vine;
Too long, a-las, with-hold-en, Now spread from shore to shore;
Thou rob-est in thy splen-dor The sim-plest ways of men,
Till ev-ery tongue and na-tion, From sin's do-min-ion free,
Thy light, so glad and gold-en, Shall set on earth no more.
And help-est them to ren-der Light back to thee a-gain.
Rise in the new cre-a-tion Which springs from love and thee. A-men.

399

O Morning Star, How Fair and Bright

Psalm 45
Philipp Nicolai, 1556-1608
Trans. by Catherine Winkworth, 1827-1878

WIE SCHÖN LEUCHTET DER MORGENSTERN 887.887.4.84.8.
Philipp Nicolai, 1556-1608
Harm. by J. S. Bach, 1685-1750

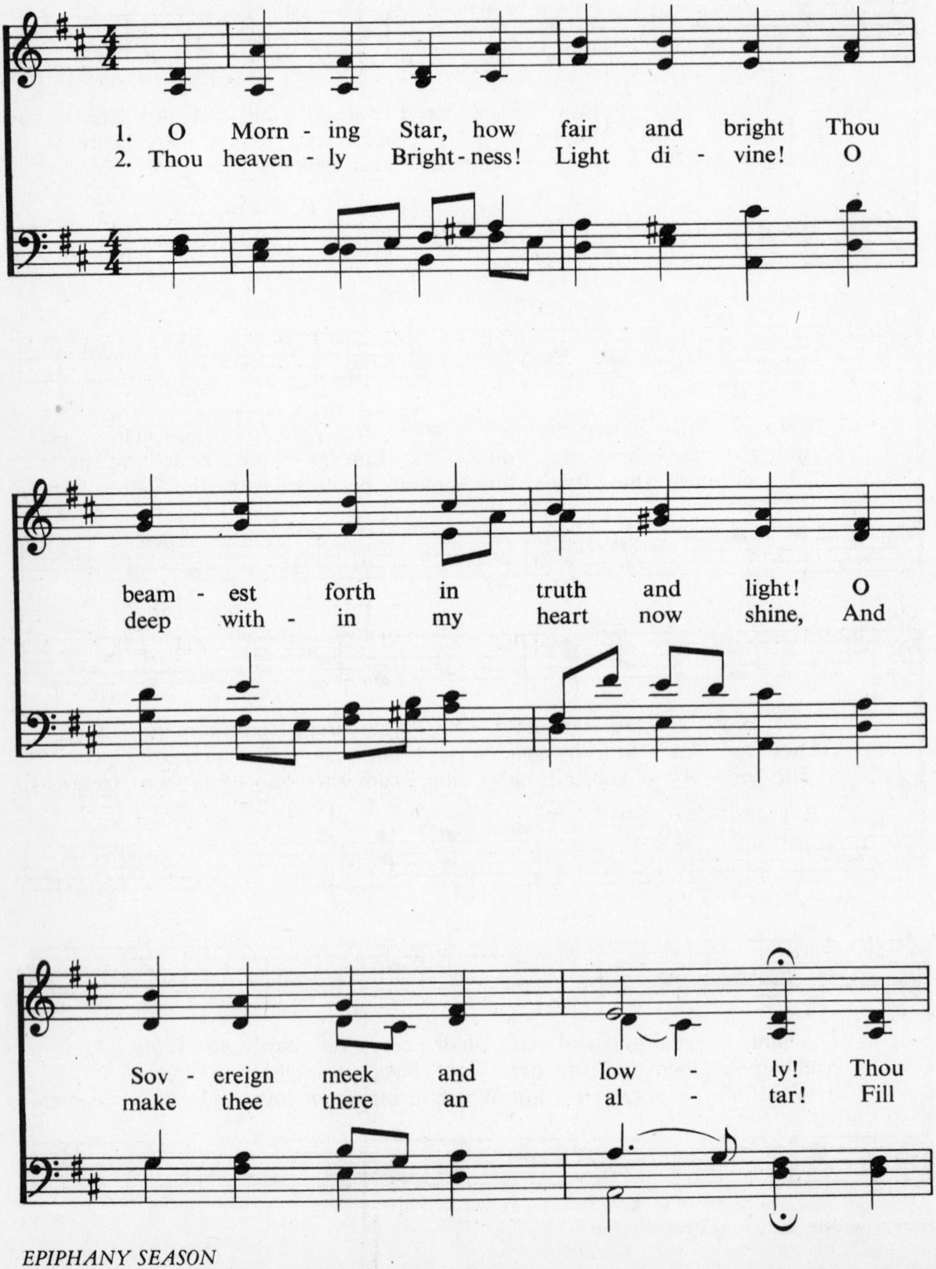
1. O Morn - ing Star, how fair and bright Thou
2. Thou heaven - ly Bright - ness! Light di - vine! O
beam - est forth in truth and light! O
deep with - in my heart now shine, And
Sov - ereign meek and low - ly! Thou
make thee there an al - tar! Fill

Root of Jes - se, Da - vid's Son, My Lord and Mas - ter,
me with joy and strength to be Thy mem - ber, ev - er
thou has won My heart to serve thee sole - ly! Thou art
joined to thee In love that can - not fal - ter; Toward thee
ho - ly, Fair and glo - rious, all - vic - to - rious, Rich in bless -
long - ing Doth pos - sess me; turn and bless me; Here in sad -
ing, Rule and might o'er all pos - sess - ing.
ness Eye and heart long for thy glad - ness! A - men.

Brightest and Best

MATTHEW 2:1-11
REGINALD HEBER, 1783-1826

MORNING STAR 11 10.11 10.
JAMES P. HARDING, c. 1850-1911

1. Bright - est and best of the sons of the morn - ing,
2. Cold on his cra - dle the dew - drops are shin - ing;
3. Say, shall we yield him, in cost - ly de - vo - tion,
4. Vain - ly we of - fer each am - ple ob - la - tion;
5. Bright - est and best of the sons of the morn - ing,
Dawn on our dark - ness and lend us thine aid;
Low lies his head with the beasts of the stall;
O - dors of E - dom and of - ferings di - vine,
Vain - ly with gifts would his fa - vor se - cure;
Dawn on our dark - ness and lend us thine aid;
Star of the East, the ho - ri - zon a - dorn - ing,
An - gels a - dore him in slum - ber re - clin - ing,
Gems of the moun - tain and pearls of the o - cean,
Rich - er by far is the heart's ad - o - ra - tion;
Star of the East, the ho - ri - zon a - dorn - ing,
Guide where our in - fant Re - deem - er is laid.
Mak - er and Mon - arch and Sav - ior of all.
Myrrh from the for - est and gold from the mine?
Dear - er to God are the prayers of the poor.
Guide where our in - fant Re - deem - er is laid. A - men.

Christ, Whose Glory Fills the Skies

RATISBON 77.77.77.
Arr. from J. G. WERNER'S *Choralbuch*, 1815
by W. H. MONK, 1823-1889

CHARLES WESLEY, 1707-1788

1. Christ, whose glo - ry fills the skies, Christ, the true, the
2. Dark and cheer - less is the morn Un - ac - com - pa -
3. Vis - it, then, this soul of mine; Pierce the gloom of
on - ly light, Sun of Righ - teous - ness, a - rise,
nied by thee; Joy - less is the day's re - turn
sin and grief; Fill me, Ra - dian - cy di - vine;
Tri - umph o'er the shades of night; Day - spring from on
Till thy mer - cy's beams I see; Till they in - ward
Scat - ter all my un - be - lief; More and more thy -
high, be near; Day - star, in my heart ap - pear.
light im - part, Cheer my eyes and warm my heart.
self dis - play, Shin - ing to the per - fect day. A - men.

EPIPHANY SEASON

We Three Kings

MATTHEW 2:1-11
JOHN H. HOPKINS, JR., 1820-1891

KINGS OF ORIENT 88.44.6. with Refrain
JOHN H. HOPKINS, JR., 1820-1891

1. We three kings of O - ri - ent are; Bear - ing
2. Born a King on Beth - le - hem's plain, Gold I
3. Frank - in - cense to of - fer have I; In - cense
4. Myrrh is mine: its bit - ter per - fume Breathes a
5. Glo - rious now be - hold him a - rise, King and
gifts we tra - verse a - far, Field and foun - tain,
bring to crown him a - gain, King for - ev - er,
owns a De - i - ty nigh; Prayer and prais - ing
life of gath - er - ing gloom: Sor - rowing, sigh - ing,
God and sac - ri - fice; Al - le - lu - ia,
moor and moun - tain, Fol - low - ing yon - der star.
ceas - ing nev - er O - ver us all to reign.
all men rais - ing, Wor - ship him, God on high.
bleed - ing, dy - ing, Sealed in the stone - cold tomb.
Al - le - lu - ia! Sounds through the earth and skies.

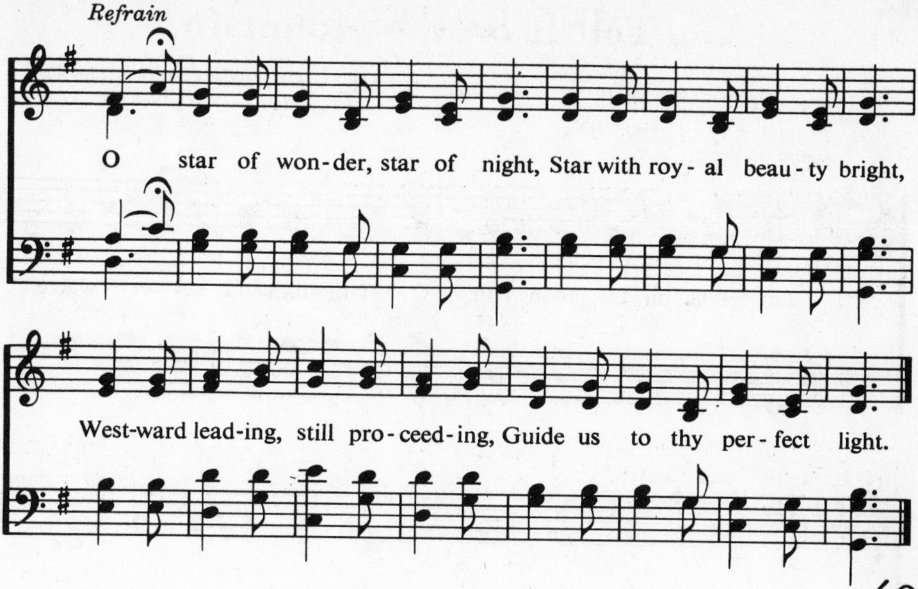
Refrain
O star of won-der, star of night, Star with roy-al beau-ty bright,
West-ward lead-ing, still pro-ceed-ing, Guide us to thy per-fect light.

403

Walk in the Light

I JOHN 1:7
BERNARD BARTON, 1784-1849

MANOAH CM
HENRY W. GREATOREX'S *Collection of Church Music*, 1851

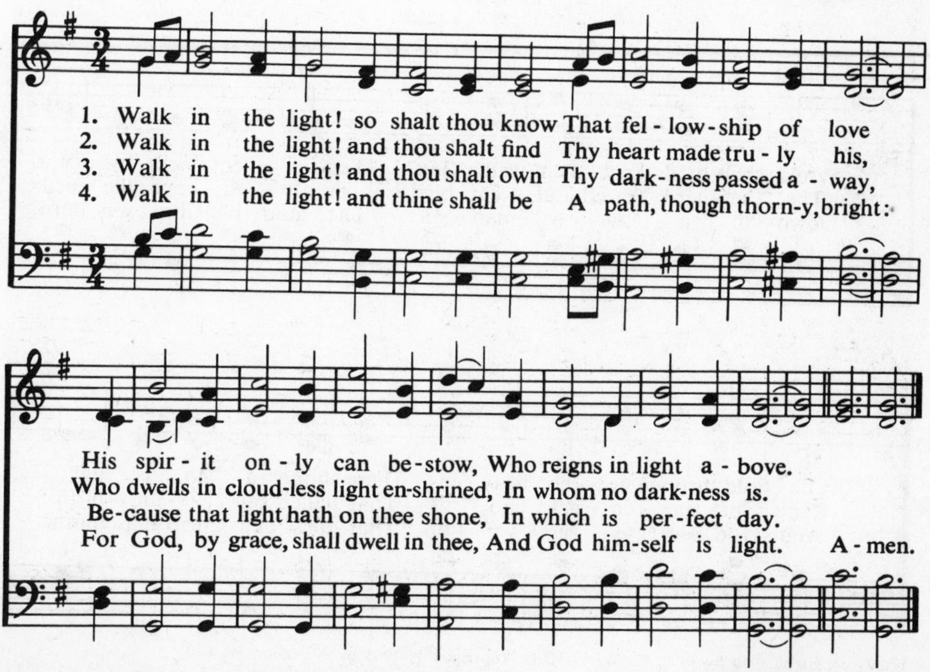
1. Walk in the light! so shalt thou know That fel-low-ship of love
2. Walk in the light! and thou shalt find Thy heart made tru-ly his,
3. Walk in the light! and thou shalt own Thy dark-ness passed a-way,
4. Walk in the light! and thine shall be A path, though thorn-y, bright:
His spir-it on-ly can be-stow, Who reigns in light a-bove.
Who dwells in cloud-less light en-shrined, In whom no dark-ness is.
Be-cause that light hath on thee shone, In which is per-fect day.
For God, by grace, shall dwell in thee, And God him-self is light. A-men.

404

Go, Tell It on the Mountain

GO TELL IT ON THE MOUNTAIN Irregular
American Folk Hymn
Arr. by JOHN W. WORK, 1901-

American Folk Hymn
Adapt. by JOHN W. WORK, 1901-

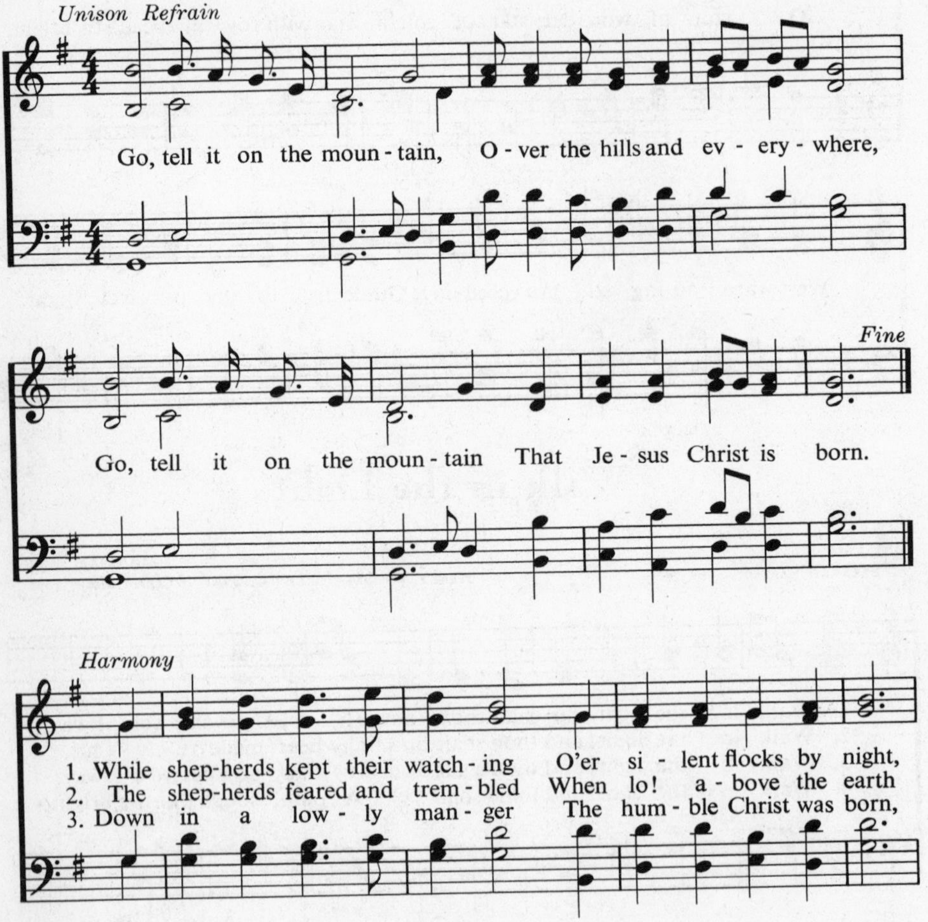

Unison Refrain
Go, tell it on the moun-tain, O-ver the hills and ev-ery-where,
Go, tell it on the moun-tain That Je-sus Christ is born.
Fine
Harmony
1. While shep-herds kept their watch-ing O'er si-lent flocks by night,
2. The shep-herds feared and trem-bled When lo! a-bove the earth
3. Down in a low-ly man-ger The hum-ble Christ was born,
Be-hold through-out the heav-ens There shone a ho-ly light.
Rang out the an-gel cho-rus That hailed our Sav-ior's birth.
And God sent us sal-va-tion That bless-ed Christ-mas morn.
D.C.

Earth Has Many a Noble City

MATTHEW 2:1-11
AURELIUS CLEMENS PRUDENTIUS, 348-c. 413
Trans. by EDWARD CASWALL, 1814-1878

STUTTGART 87.87.
Psalmodia Sacra, Gotha, 1715
Adapt. by HENRY J. GAUNTLETT, 1805-1876

1. Earth has many a no - ble cit - y;
2. Fair - er than the sun at morn - ing
3. East - ern sa - ges at his cra - dle
4. Sa - cred gifts of mys - tic mean - ing:
5. Je - sus, whom the Gen - tiles wor - shiped
Beth-lehem, thou dost all ex - cel; Out of thee the
Was the star that told his birth, To the world its
Make ob - la - tions rich and rare; See them give, in
In - cense doth their God dis - close; Gold the King of
At thy glad e - piph - a - ny, Un - to thee, with
Lord from heav - en Came to rule his Is - ra - el.
God an-nounc-ing Seen in flesh - ly form on earth.
deep de - vo - tion, Gold and frank - in - cense and myrrh.
kings pro-claim-eth; Myrrh his sep - ul - cher fore-shows.
God the Fa - ther And the Spir - it, glo - ry be. A-men.

Heralds of Christ

NATIONAL HYMN 10 10.10 10.
GEORGE W. WARREN, 1828-1902

LAURA S. COPENHAVER, 1868-1941

1. Her - alds of Christ, who bear the King's com - mands,
2. Through des - ert ways, dark fen, and deep mo - rass,
3. Lord, give us faith and strength the road to build,
Im - mor - tal ti - dings in your mor - tal hands,
Through jun - gles, slug - gish seas, and moun - tain pass,
To see the prom - ise of the day ful - filled,
Pass on and car - ry swift the news ye bring:
Build ye the road, and fal - ter not, nor stay;
When war shall be no more and strife shall cease
Make straight, make straight the high - way of the King.
Pre - pare a - cross the earth the King's high - way.
Up - on the high - way of the Prince of Peace. A-men.

O Master of the Waking World

MELITA 88.88.88.

FRANK MASON NORTH, 1850-1935

JOHN B. DYKES, 1823-1876

1. O Mas - ter of the wak - ing world, Who hast the na - tions
2. We hear the throb of surg - ing life, The clank of chains, the
3. Thy wit - ness in the souls of men, Thy Spir - it's cease - less,
in thy heart, The heart that bled and broke to send
curse of greed, The moan of pain, the fu - tile cries
brood - ing power, In lands, where shad - ows hide the light,
God's love to earth's re - mot - est part: Show us a - new in
Of su - per - sti - tion's cru - el creed; The peo - ples hun - ger
A - wait a new cre - a - tive hour: O might - y God, set
Cal - va - ry The won - drous power that makes men free.
for thee, Lord; The world is wait - ing for thy Word.
us a - flame To show the glo - ry of thy name. A-men.

408

Christ Is the World's True Light

GEORGE W. BRIGGS, 1875-1959

SURETTE 67.67.66.66.
KATHERINE K. DAVIS, 1892-

1. Christ is the world's true light, Its cap - tain of sal - va - tion,
2. In Christ all rac - es meet, Their an - cient feuds for - get - ting,
3. One Lord, in one great name U - nite us all who own thee;
The Day - star clear and bright Of ev - ery man and na - tion;
The whole round world com - plete, From sun - rise to its set - ting;
Cast out our pride and shame That hin - der to en - throne thee;
New life, new hope a - wakes Where - e'er men own his sway;
When Christ is throned as Lord, Men shall for - sake their fear; To
The world has wait - ed long, Has tra - vailed long in pain; To
Free - dom her bond - age breaks, And night is turned to day.
plow - share beat the sword, To prun - ing - hook the spear.
heal its an - cient wrong, Come, Prince of Peace, and reign. A - men.

Ye Servants of God

REVELATION 7:9-12
CHARLES WESLEY, 1707-1788

HANOVER 10 10.11 11.
Probably by WILLIAM CROFT, 1678-1727

1. Ye ser - vants of God, your Mas - ter pro - claim,
2. God rul - eth on high, al - might - y to save;
3. "Sal - va - tion to God, who sits on the throne!"
4. Then let us a - dore and give him his right,
And pub - lish a - broad his won - der - ful name;
And still he is nigh, his pres - ence we have;
Let all cry a - loud and hon - or the Son:
All glo - ry and power, all wis - dom and might,
The name all - vic - to - rious of Je - sus ex - tol;
The great con - gre - ga - tion his tri - umph shall sing,
The prais - es of Je - sus the an - gels pro - claim,
All hon - or and bless - ing, with an - gels a - bove,
His king - dom is glo - rious and rules o - ver all.
As - crib - ing sal - va - tion to Je - sus, our King.
Fall down on their fac - es and wor - ship the Lamb.
And thanks nev - er ceas - ing, and in - fi - nite love. A - men.

We've a Story to Tell to the Nations

H. Ernest Nichol, 1862-1928

MESSAGE 10 8.87. with Refrain
H. Ernest Nichol, 1862-1928

1. We've a sto - ry to tell to the na - tions,
2. We've a song to be sung to the na - tions,
3. We've a mes - sage to give to the na - tions,
4. We've a Sav - ior to show to the na - tions,
That shall turn their hearts to the right, A
That shall lift their hearts to the Lord, A
That the Lord who reign - eth a - bove Hath
Who the path of sor - row hath trod, That
sto - ry of truth and mer - cy, A
song that shall con - quer e - vil And
sent us his Son to save us, And
all of the world's great peo - ples Might

sto - ry of peace and light, A sto - ry of peace and light.
shat - ter the spear and sword, And shat - ter the spear and sword.
show us that God is love, And show us that God is love.
come to the truth of God, Might come to the truth of God!
Refrain
For the dark - ness shall turn to dawn - ing,
And the dawn-ing to noon - day bright, And Christ's great king-dom shall
come on earth, The king - dom of love and light. A - men.

O God, Whose Will Is Life

TALLIS' ORDINAL CM

HARDWICKE D. RAWNSLEY, 1851-1920

THOMAS TALLIS, c. 1505-1585

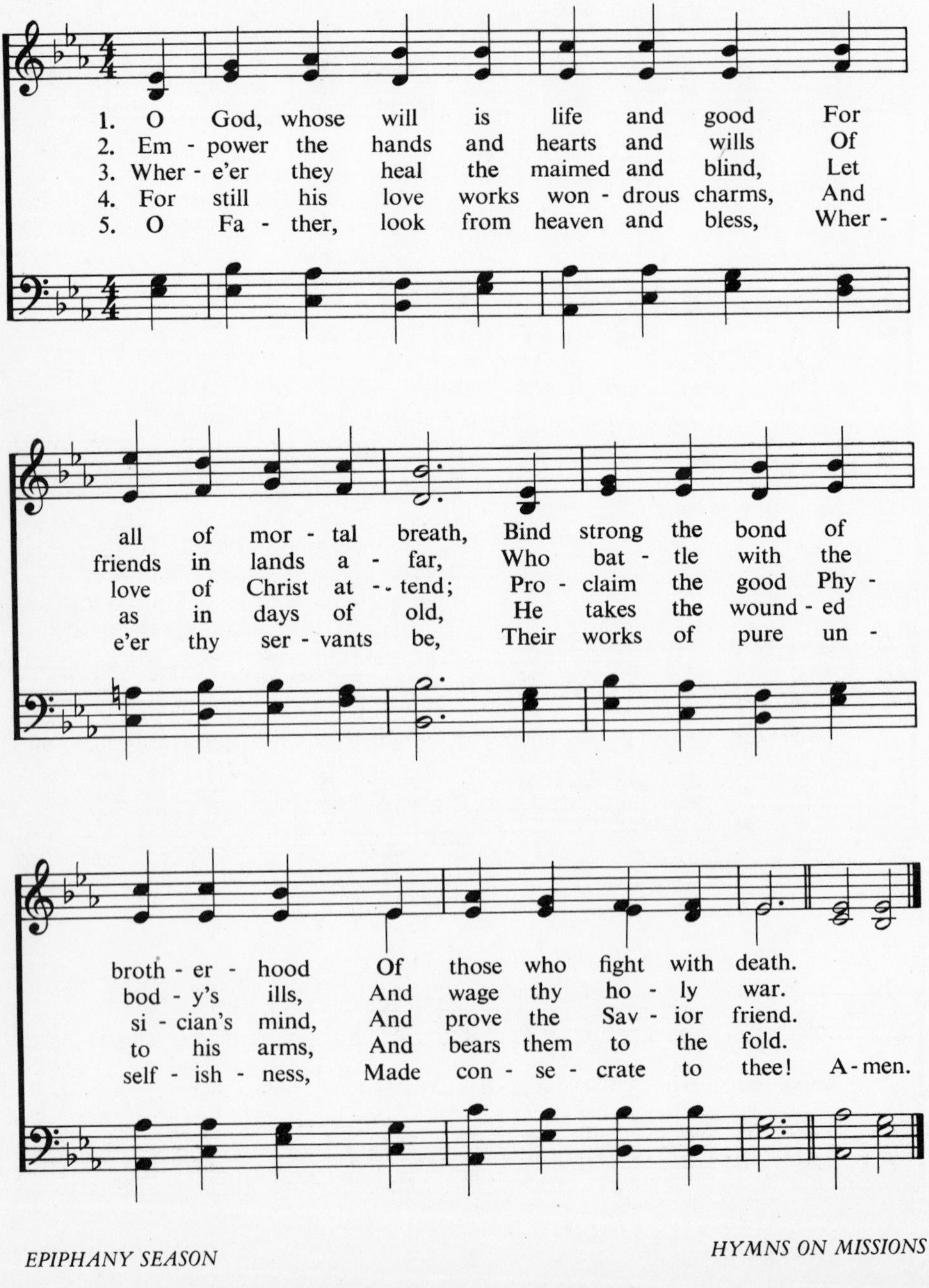
1. O God, whose will is life and good For
2. Em - power the hands and hearts and wills Of
3. Wher - e'er they heal the maimed and blind, Let
4. For still his love works won - drous charms, And
5. O Fa - ther, look from heaven and bless, Wher -
all of mor - tal breath, Bind strong the bond of
friends in lands a - far, Who bat - tle with the
love of Christ at - tend; Pro - claim the good Phy -
as in days of old, He takes the wound - ed
e'er thy ser - vants be, Their works of pure un -
broth - er - hood Of those who fight with death.
bod - y's ills, And wage thy ho - ly war.
si - cian's mind, And prove the Sav - ior friend.
to his arms, And bears them to the fold.
self - ish - ness, Made con - se - crate to thee! A - men.

Ah, Holy Jesus

JOHANN HEERMANN, 1585-1647
Trans. by ROBERT S. BRIDGES, 1844-1930

HERZLIEBSTER JESU 11 11 11.5.
JOHANN CRÜGER, 1598-1662

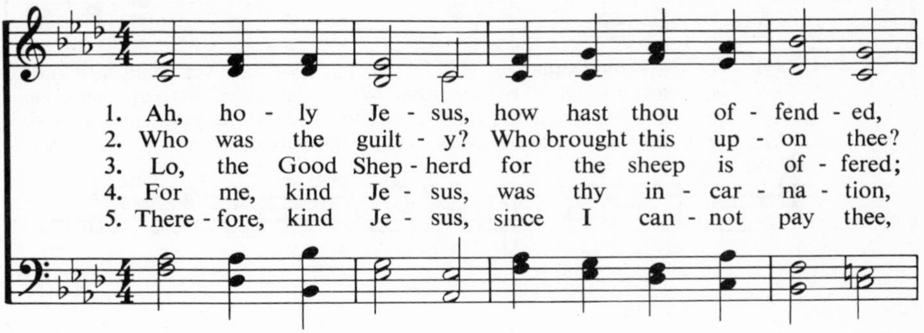
1. Ah, ho - ly Je - sus, how hast thou of - fend - ed,
2. Who was the guilt - y? Who brought this up - on thee?
3. Lo, the Good Shep - herd for the sheep is of - fered;
4. For me, kind Je - sus, was thy in - car - na - tion,
5. There - fore, kind Je - sus, since I can - not pay thee,

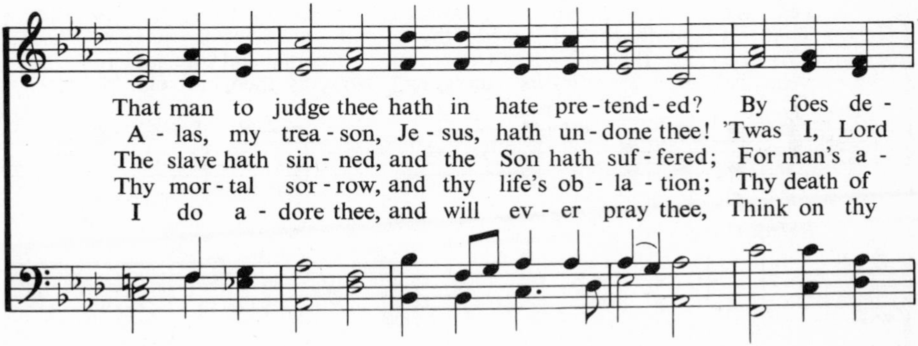
That man to judge thee hath in hate pre - tend - ed? By foes de -
A - las, my trea - son, Je - sus, hath un - done thee! 'Twas I, Lord
The slave hath sin - ned, and the Son hath suf - fered; For man's a -
Thy mor - tal sor - row, and thy life's ob - la - tion; Thy death of
I do a - dore thee, and will ev - er pray thee, Think on thy

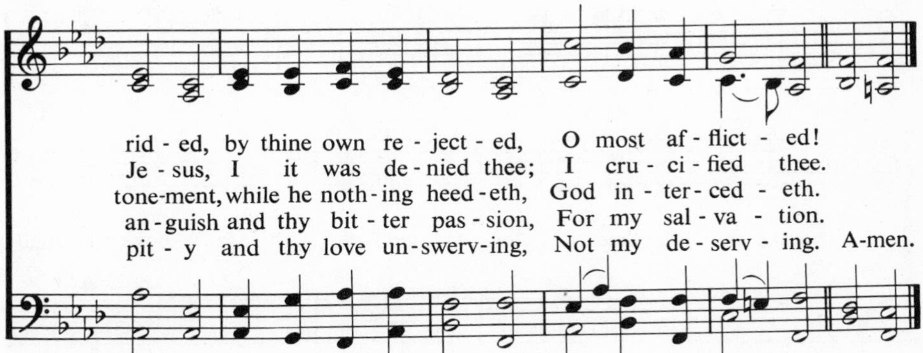
rid - ed, by thine own re - ject - ed, O most af - flict - ed!
Je - sus, I it was de - nied thee; I cru - ci - fied thee.
tone-ment, while he noth - ing heed - eth, God in - ter - ced - eth.
an - guish and thy bit - ter pas - sion, For my sal - va - tion.
pit - y and thy love un - swerv - ing, Not my de - serv - ing. A-men.

Are Ye Able

MARK 10:35-40
EARL MARLATT, 1892-

BEACON HILL Irregular
HARRY S. MASON, 1881-1964

1. "Are ye a - ble," said the Mas - ter, "To be cru - ci - fied with me?"
2. Are ye a - ble to re - mem - ber, When a thief lifts up his eyes,
3. Are ye a - ble when the shad - ows Close a - round you with the sod,
4. Are ye a - ble? Still the Mas - ter Whis - pers down e - ter - ni - ty,
"Yea," the sturd - y dream - ers an - swered, "To the death we fol - low thee."
That his par - doned soul is wor - thy Of a place in par - a - dise?
To be - lieve that spir - it tri - umphs, To com - mend your soul to God?
And he - ro - ic spir - its an - swer Now, as then, in Gal - i - lee.
Refrain
Lord, we are a - ble. Our spir - its are thine. Re - mold them,
make us, Like thee, di - vine. Thy guid - ing ra - diance A - bove us shall

Words used by permission of Earl Marlatt.

LENTEN SEASON

be A bea - con to God, To love, and loy - al - ty. A-men.

There Is a Green Hill Far Away

414

WINDSOR CM

Cecil Frances Alexander, 1818-1895

William Damon's *Booke of Musicke*, 1591

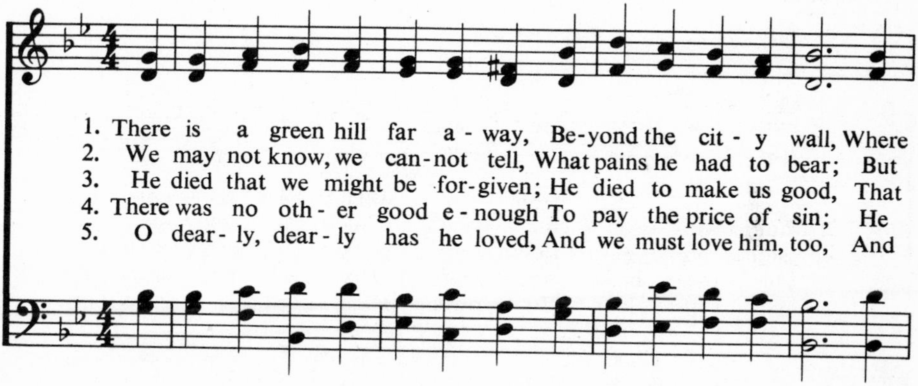
1. There is a green hill far a - way, Be-yond the cit - y wall, Where
2. We may not know, we can-not tell, What pains he had to bear; But
3. He died that we might be for-given; He died to make us good, That
4. There was no oth - er good e - nough To pay the price of sin; He
5. O dear- ly, dear - ly has he loved, And we must love him, too, And

the dear Lord was cru - ci - fied, Who died to save us all.
we be - lieve it was for us He hung and suf - fered there.
we might go at last to heaven, Saved by his pre - cious blood.
on - ly could un - lock the gate Of heaven and let us in.
trust in his re - deem - ing blood, And try his works to do. A-men.

415

Alas! and Did My Savior Bleed

MARTYRDOM CM

ISAAC WATTS, 1674-1748 — HUGH WILSON, 1766-1824

1. A - las! and did my Sav - ior bleed, And
2. Was it for crimes that I have done, He
3. Well might the sun in dark - ness hide, And
4. Thus might I hide my blush - ing face While
5. But drops of grief can ne'er re - pay The
did my Sov - ereign die? Would he de - vote that
groaned up - on the tree? A - maz - ing pit - y!
shut his glo - ries in, When God, the might - y
his dear cross ap - pears; Dis - solve my heart in
debt of love I owe; Here, Lord, I give my-
sa - cred head For sin - ners such as I?
Grace un - known! And love be - yond de - gree!
mak - er, died For man the crea - ture's sin.
thank - ful - ness, And melt mine eyes to tears.
self a - way; 'Tis all that I can do. A - men.

In the Cross of Christ I Glory

GALATIANS 6:14
JOHN BOWRING, 1792-1872

RATHBUN 87.87.
ITHAMAR CONKEY, 1815-1867

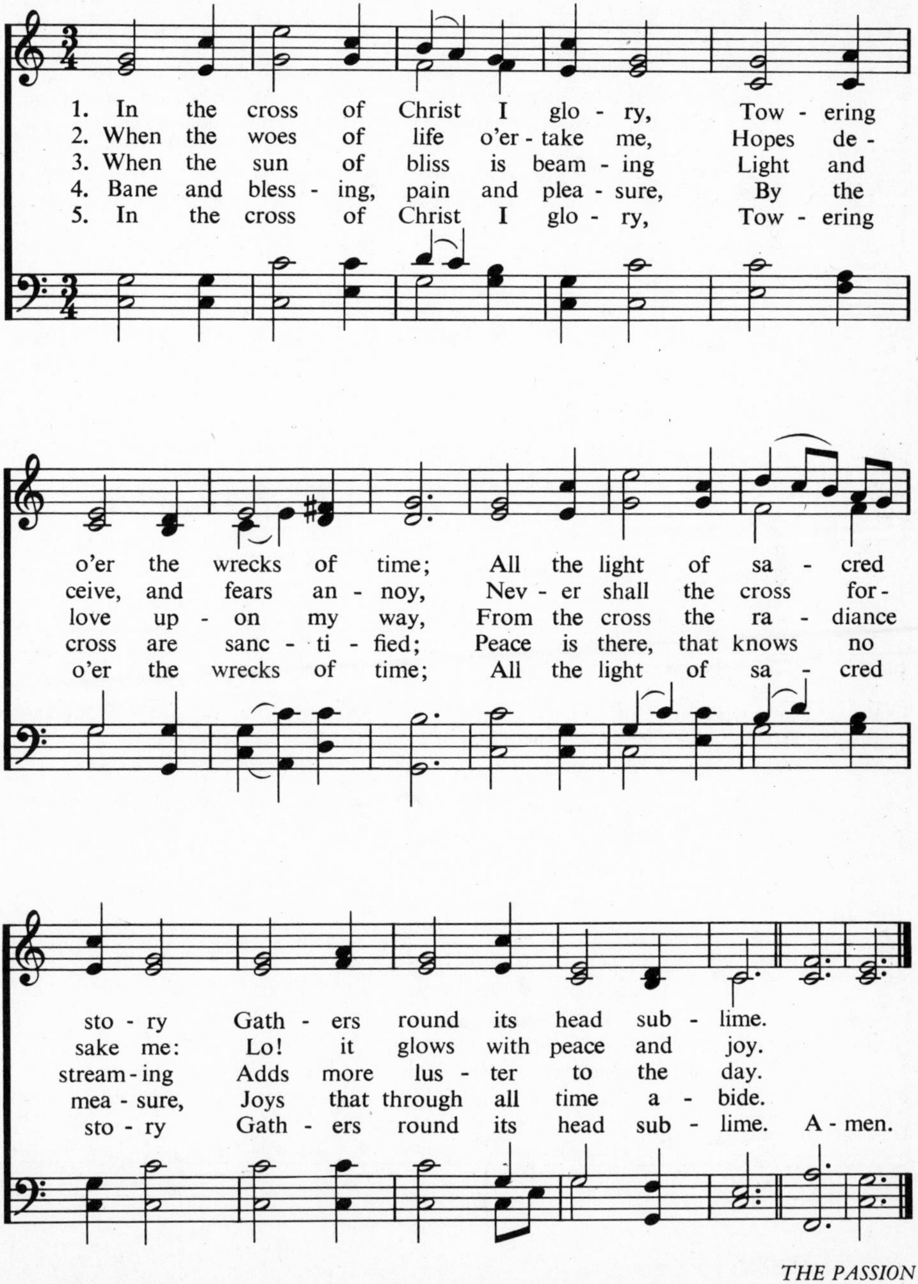
1. In the cross of Christ I glo - ry, Tow - ering
2. When the woes of life o'er - take me, Hopes de -
3. When the sun of bliss is beam - ing Light and
4. Bane and bless - ing, pain and plea - sure, By the
5. In the cross of Christ I glo - ry, Tow - ering
o'er the wrecks of time; All the light of sa - cred
ceive, and fears an - noy, Nev - er shall the cross for -
love up - on my way, From the cross the ra - diance
cross are sanc - ti - fied; Peace is there, that knows no
o'er the wrecks of time; All the light of sa - cred
sto - ry Gath - ers round its head sub - lime.
sake me: Lo! it glows with peace and joy.
stream - ing Adds more lus - ter to the day.
mea - sure, Joys that through all time a - bide.
sto - ry Gath - ers round its head sub - lime. A - men.

417

Beneath the Cross of Jesus

ST. CHRISTOPHER 76.86.86.86.

ELIZABETH C. CLEPHANE, 1830-1869

FREDERICK C. MAKER, 1844-1927

1. Be-neath the cross of Je - sus I fain would take my stand, The
2. Up - on that cross of Je - sus Mine eye at times can see The
3. I take, O cross, thy shad-ow For my a - bid - ing place; I
shad-ow of a might-y rock With - in a wea - ry land; A
ver - y dy - ing form of One Who suf - fered there for me; And
ask no oth - er sun-shine than The sun-shine of his face; Con-
home with - in the wil - der - ness, A rest up - on the way, From the
from my strick-en heart with tears Two won-ders I con - fess: The
tent to let the world go by, To know no gain nor loss, My
burn-ing of the noon-tide heat, And the bur - den of the day.
won-ders of re-deem-ing love And my un - wor - thi - ness.
sin - ful self my on - ly shame, My glo - ry all the cross. A-men.

LENTEN SEASON

418

O Sacred Head, Now Wounded

ANONYMOUS Latin
Trans. by PAUL GERHARDT, 1607-1676
Trans. by JAMES W. ALEXANDER, 1804-1859

PASSION CHORALE 76.76.D.
HANS L. HASSLER, 1564-1612
Harm. by J. S. BACH, 1685-1750

1. O sa - cred Head, now wound-ed, With grief and shame weighed down,
2. What thou, my Lord, hast suf - fered Was all for sin - ners' gain;
3. What lan-guage shall I bor - row To thank thee, dear - est friend,
Now scorn - ful - ly sur - round - ed With thorns, thine on - ly crown:
Mine, mine was the trans - gres - sion, But thine the dead - ly pain.
For this thy dy - ing sor - row, Thy pit - y with - out end?
How pale thou art with an - guish, With sore a - buse and scorn!
Lo, here I fall, my Sav - ior! 'Tis I de-serve thy place;
O make me thine for - ev - er; And should I faint-ing be,
How does that vis - age lan - guish Which once was bright as morn!
Look on me with thy fa - vor, Vouch - safe to me thy grace.
Lord, let me nev - er, nev - er Out - live my love to thee. A-men.

419 The Son of God Goes Forth to War

REGINALD HEBER, 1783-1826

ALL SAINTS NEW CMD
HENRY S. CUTLER, 1824-1902

1. The Son of God goes forth to war, A king-ly crown to gain;
2. The mar-tyr first, whose ea-gle eye Could pierce be-yond the grave,
3. A glo-rious band, the cho-sen few On whom the Spir-it came,
His blood-red ban-ner streams a-far; Who fol-lows in his train?
Who saw his Mas-ter in the sky, And called on him to save:
Twelve val-iant saints, their hope they knew, And mocked the cross and flame;
Who best can drink his cup of woe, Tri-um-phant o-ver pain,
Like him, with par-don on his tongue, In midst of mor-tal pain,
They climbed the steep as-cent of heaven Through per-il, toil, and pain:
Who pa-tient bears his cross be-low, He fol-lows in his train.
He prayed for them that did the wrong: Who fol-lows in his train?
O God, to us may grace be given To fol-low in their train! A-men.

Alternate tune: LLANGLOFFAN

420

O Love Divine, What Hast Thou Done

SELENA 88.88.88.

CHARLES WESLEY, 1707-1788

ISAAC B. WOODBURY, 1819-1858

1. O Love di - vine, what hast thou done! Th'in - car - nate
2. Is cru - ci - fied for me and you, To bring us
3. Be - hold him, all ye that pass by, The bleed - ing
God hath died for me! The Fa - ther's co - e - ter - nal
reb - els near to God; Be - lieve, be - lieve the rec - ord
Prince of life and peace! Come, sin - ners, see your Sav - ior
Son Bore all my sins up - on the tree! The Son of
true, Ye all are bought with Je - sus' blood; Par - don for
die, And say, was ev - er grief like his? Come, feel with
God for me hath died: My Lord, my Love, is cru - ci - fied:
all flows from his side: My Lord, my Love, is cru - ci - fied.
me his blood ap - plied: My Lord, my Love, is cru - ci - fied. A-men.

Alternate tune: WER NUR DEN LIEBEN GOTT

421

There Is a Fountain Filled with Blood

ZECHARIAH 13:1
WILLIAM COWPER, 1731-1800

CLEANSING FOUNTAIN CMD
American Folk Melody

1. There is a foun - tain filled with blood Drawn
2. The dy - ing thief re - joiced to see That
3. Dear dy - ing Lamb, thy pre - cious blood Shall
4. E'er since, by faith, I saw the stream Thy
5. Then in a no - bler, sweet - er song, I'll
from Em - man - uel's veins; And sin - ners, plunged be - neath that flood,
foun - tain in his day; And there may I, though vile as he,
nev - er lose its power, Till all the ran - somed Church of God
flow - ing wounds sup - ply, Re - deem - ing love has been my theme,
sing thy power to save, When this poor lisp - ing, stam-mering tongue
Lose all their guilt - y stains, Lose all their guilt - y stains,
Wash all my sins a - way, Wash all my sins a - way,
Be saved, to sin no more, Be saved, to sin no more,
And shall be till I die, And shall be till I die,
Lies si - lent in the grave, Lies si - lent in the grave,
Lose all their guilt - y stains; And sin - ners, plunged be -
Wash all my sins a - way; And there may I, though
Be saved, to sin no more; Till all the ran - somed
And shall be till I die; Re - deem - ing love has
Lies si - lent in the grave; When this poor lisp - ing,

neath that flood, Lose all their guilt - y stains.
vile as he, Wash all my sins a - way.
Church of God Be saved, to sin no more.
been my theme, And shall be till I die.
stam-mering tongue Lies si - lent in the grave. A - men.

422

So Lowly Doth the Savior Ride

EPWORTH CHURCH CM

ALMER T. PENNEWELL, 1876-

V. EARLE COPES, 1921-

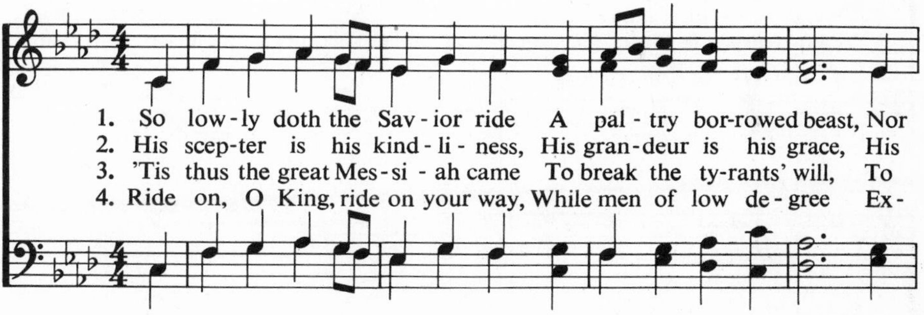
1. So low-ly doth the Sav-ior ride A pal-try bor-rowed beast, Nor
2. His scep-ter is his kind-li-ness, His gran-deur is his grace, His
3. 'Tis thus the great Mes-si-ah came To break the ty-rants' will, To
4. Ride on, O King, ride on your way, While men of low de-gree Ex-

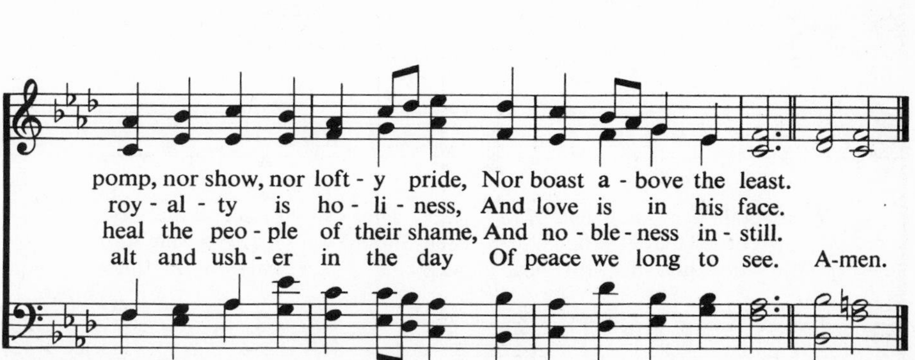
pomp, nor show, nor loft-y pride, Nor boast a-bove the least.
roy-al-ty is ho-li-ness, And love is in his face.
heal the peo-ple of their shame, And no-ble-ness in-still.
alt and ush-er in the day Of peace we long to see. A-men.

423

Hosanna, Loud Hosanna

MARK 11:1-10
JEANNETTE THRELFALL, 1821-1880

ELLACOMBE 76.76.D.
Gesangbuch der H. W. K. Hofkapelle, 1784

1. Ho - san - na, loud ho - san - na The lit - tle chil - dren sang;
2. From Ol - i - vet they fol - lowed Mid an ex - ult - ant crowd,
3. "Ho - san - na in the high - est!" That an - cient song we sing,
Through pil - lared court and tem - ple The love - ly an - them rang;
The vic - tor palm branch wav - ing, And chant - ing clear and loud;
For Christ is our Re - deem - er, The Lord of heaven our King.
To Je - sus, who had blessed them Close fold - ed to his breast,
The Lord of men and an - gels Rode on in low - ly state,
O may we ev - er praise him With heart and life and voice,
The chil - dren sang their prais - es, The sim - plest and the best.
Nor scorned that lit - tle chil - dren Should on his bid - ding wait.
And in his bliss - ful pres - ence E - ter - nal - ly re - joice! A - men.

All Glory, Laud, and Honor

Matthew 21:1-11
Theodulph of Orleans, d. 821
Trans. by John M. Neale, 1818-1866

ST. THEODULPH 76.76.D.
Melchior Teschner, 1584-1635

1. All glo - ry, laud, and hon - or To thee, Re-deem - er, King,
2. The com - pa - ny of an - gels Are prais - ing thee on high,
3. To thee, be - fore thy pas - sion They sang their hymns of praise;
To whom the lips of chil - dren Made sweet ho - san - nas ring.
And mor - tal men and all things Cre - a - ted make re - ply.
To thee, now high ex - alt - ed, Our mel - o - dy we raise.
Thou art the King of Is - ra - el, Thou Da - vid's roy - al Son,
The peo - ple of the He - brews With palms be - fore thee went;
Thou didst ac - cept their prais - es; Ac - cept the prayers we bring,
Who in the Lord's name com - est, The King and bless - ed One.
Our praise and prayer and an - thems Be - fore thee we pre - sent.
Who in all good de - light - est, Thou good and gra - cious King. A-men.

PALM SUNDAY

Ride On, Ride On in Majesty

JOHN 12:12-15
HENRY H. MILMAN, 1791-1868

THE KING'S MAJESTY LM
GRAHAM GEORGE, 1912-

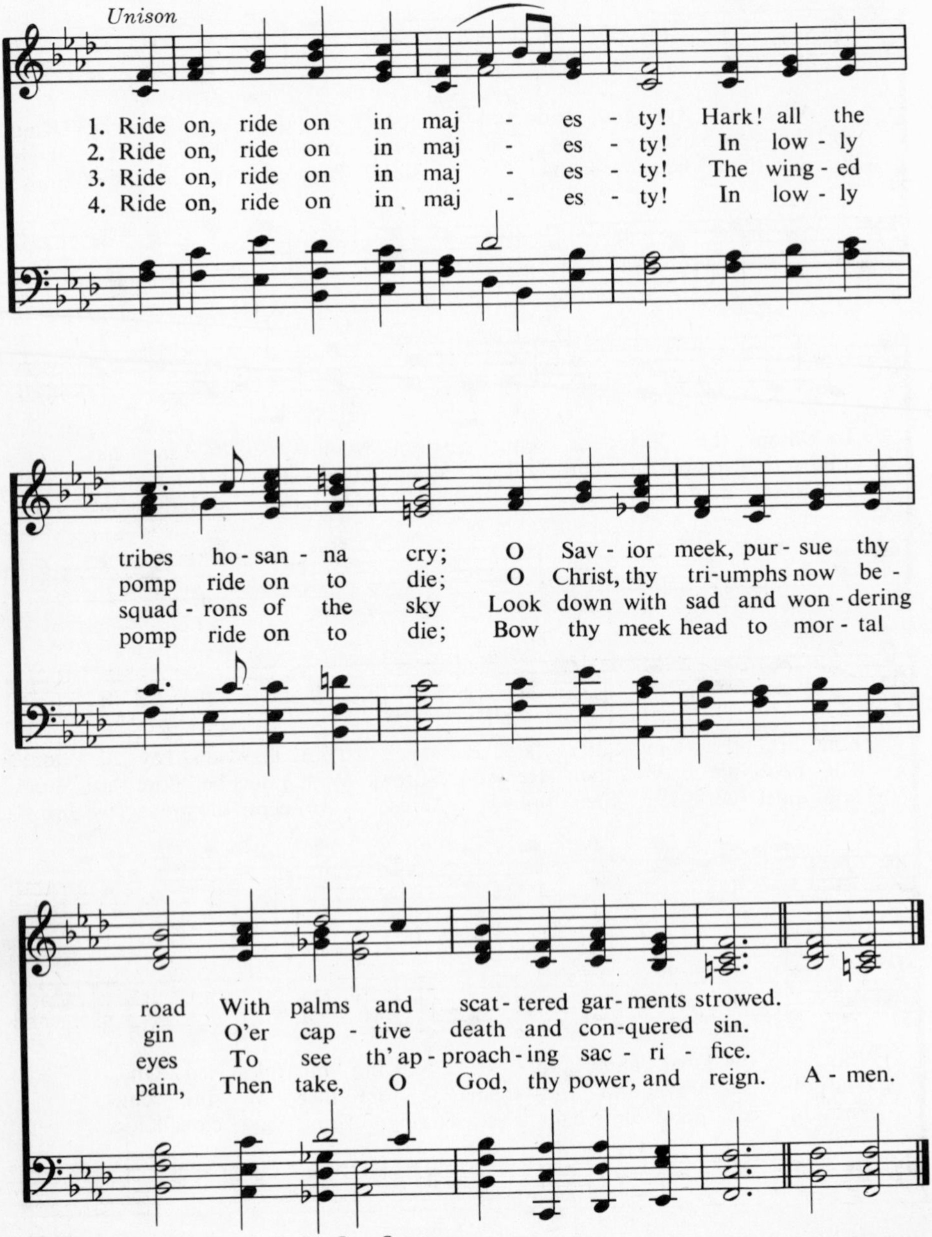
Unison
1. Ride on, ride on in maj - es - ty! Hark! all the tribes ho - san - na cry; O Sav - ior meek, pur - sue thy road With palms and scat - tered gar - ments strowed.
2. Ride on, ride on in maj - es - ty! In low - ly pomp ride on to die; O Christ, thy tri - umphs now be - gin O'er cap - tive death and con - quered sin.
3. Ride on, ride on in maj - es - ty! The wing - ed squad - rons of the sky Look down with sad and won - dering eyes To see th' ap - proach - ing sac - ri - fice.
4. Ride on, ride on in maj - es - ty! In low - ly pomp ride on to die; Bow thy meek head to mor - tal pain, Then take, O God, thy power, and reign. A - men.

Cross of Jesus, Cross of Sorrow

CHARLESTOWN 87.87.
STEPHEN JENKS'S *American Compiler of Sacred Harmony, No. 1,* 1803
Harm. by C. R. Y.

WILLIAM J. S. SIMPSON, 1860-1952

Unison
1. Cross of Je - sus, cross of sor - row, Where the
2. Here the King of all the a - ges, Throned in
3. O mys - te - rious con - de - scend - ing! O a -
4. Cross of Je - sus, cross of sor - row, Where the
blood of Christ was shed, Per - fect man on thee did
light ere worlds could be, Robed in mor - tal flesh is
ban - don - ment sub - lime! Ver - y God him - self is
blood of Christ was shed, Per - fect man on thee did
suf - fer, Per - fect God on thee has bled!
dy - ing, Cru - ci - fied by sin for me.
bear - ing All the suf - fer - ings of time!
suf - fer, Per - fect God on thee has bled! A - men.

427

Alone Thou Goest Forth

Peter Abelard, 1079-1142
Trans. by F. Bland Tucker, 1895-

BANGOR CM
William Tans'ur, 1706-1783

1. A - lone thou go - est forth, O Lord, In sac - ri - fice to die;
2. Our sins, not thine, thou bear - est, Lord; Make us thy sor-row feel,
3. This is earth's dark - est hour, but thou Dost light and life re - store;
4. Give us com - pas - sion for thee, Lord, That, as we share this hour,

Is this thy sor-row naught to us Who pass un-heed-ing by?
Till through our pit - y and our shame Love an-swers love's ap-peal.
Then let all praise be giv - en thee Who liv - est ev - er - more.
Thy cross may bring us to thy joy And res - ur - rec - tion power. A-men.

Alternate tune: WINDSOR

428

Behold the Savior of Mankind

WINDSOR CM

Samuel Wesley, 1662-1735

William Damon's *Booke of Musicke*, 1591

1. Be - hold the Sav - ior of man - kind Nailed to the shame - ful tree!
2. Hark, how he groans, while na - ture shakes, And earth's strong pil - lars bend!
3. 'Tis done! the pre - cious ran - som's paid! "Re - ceive my soul!" he cries;
4. But soon he'll break death's en - vious chain, And in full glo - ry shine;

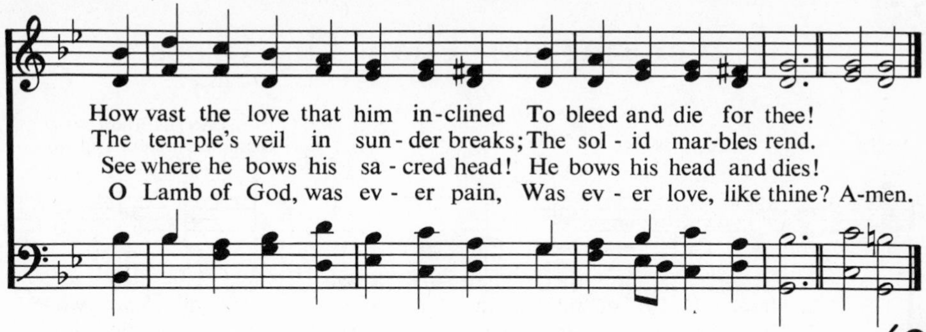
How vast the love that him in-clined To bleed and die for thee!
The tem-ple's veil in sun-der breaks; The sol-id mar-bles rend.
See where he bows his sa-cred head! He bows his head and dies!
O Lamb of God, was ev-er pain, Was ev-er love, like thine? A-men.

429

'Tis Finished! The Messiah Dies

JOHN 19:30
CHARLES WESLEY, 1707-1788

WINCHESTER NEW LM
Musikalisches Handbuch, Hamburg, 1690
Arr. by WILLIAM HAVERGAL, 1793-1870

1. 'Tis fin-ished! The Mes-si-ah dies, Cut
2. The veil is rent in Christ a-lone; The
3. The reign of sin and death is o'er, And
off for sins, but not his own. Ac-com-plished is the
liv-ing way to heaven is seen; The mid-dle wall is
all may live from sin set free; Sa-tan hath lost his
sac-ri-fice; The great re-deem-ing work is done.
bro-ken down, And all man-kind may en-ter in.
mor-tal power; 'Tis swal-lowed up in vic-to-ry. A-men.

430

Never Further Than Thy Cross

CANTERBURY 77.77.

ELIZABETH R. CHARLES, 1828-1896

Adapt. from ORLANDO GIBBONS, 1583-1625

1. Nev - er fur - ther than thy cross, Nev - er high - er
2. Here, O Christ, our sins we see, Learn thy love while
3. Here we learn to serve and give, And, re - joic - ing,
4. Press - ing on - ward as we can, Still to this our
5. Till a - mid the hosts of light, We in thee re -
than thy feet; Here earth's pre - cious things seem dross;
gaz - ing thus; Sin, which laid the cross on thee,
self de - ny; Here we gath - er love to live;
hearts must tend; Where our ear - liest hopes be - gan,
deemed, com - plete, Through thy cross made pure and white,
Here earth's bit - ter things grow sweet.
Love, which bore the cross for us.
Here we gath - er faith to die.
There our last as - pir - ings end;
Cast our crowns be - fore thy feet. A - men.

LENTEN SEASON

'Tis Midnight, and on Olive's Brow

MARK 14:32-42
WILLIAM B. TAPPAN, 1794-1849

OLIVE'S BROW LM
WILLIAM B. BRADBURY, 1816-1868

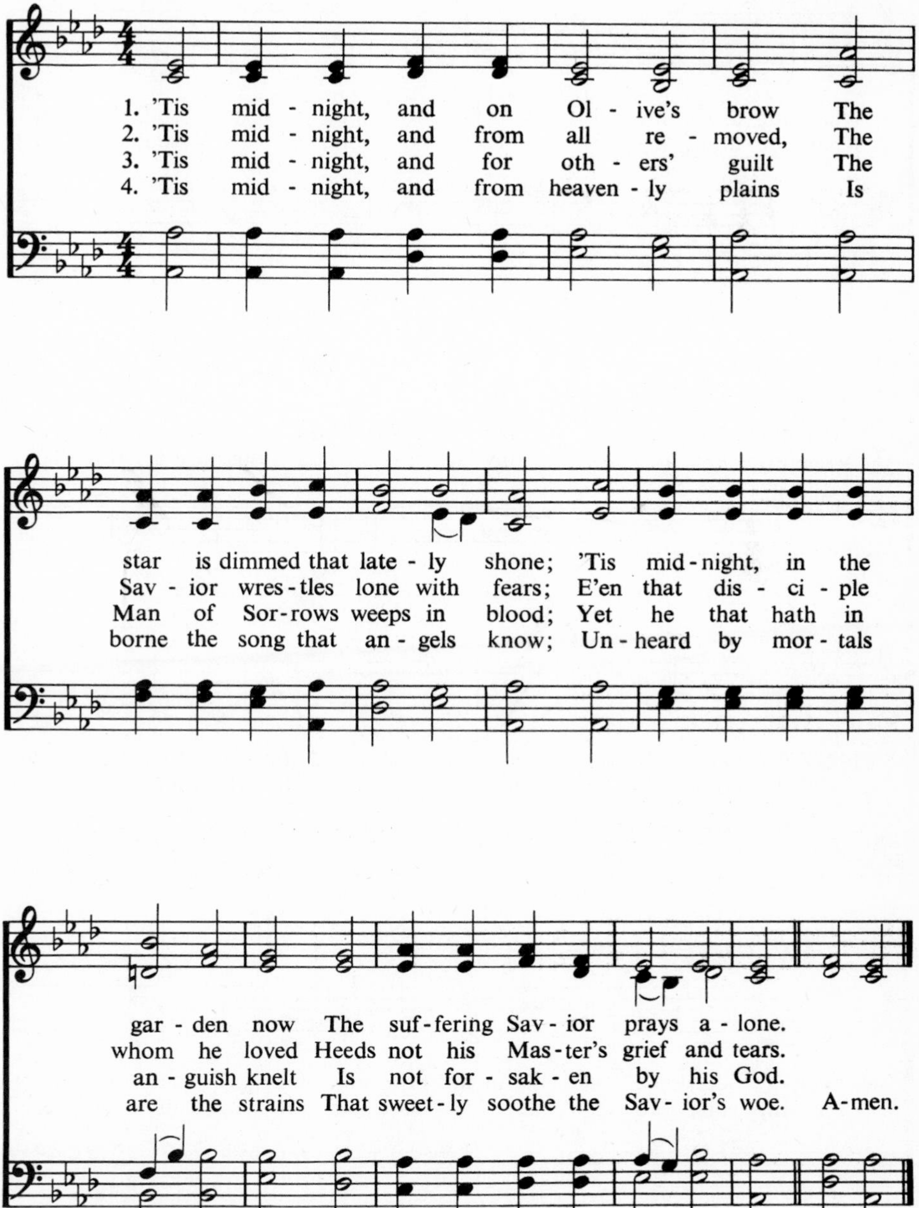
1. 'Tis mid - night, and on Ol - ive's brow The
2. 'Tis mid - night, and from all re - moved, The
3. 'Tis mid - night, and for oth - ers' guilt The
4. 'Tis mid - night, and from heaven - ly plains Is
star is dimmed that late - ly shone; 'Tis mid - night, in the
Sav - ior wres - tles lone with fears; E'en that dis - ci - ple
Man of Sor - rows weeps in blood; Yet he that hath in
borne the song that an - gels know; Un - heard by mor - tals
gar - den now The suf - fering Sav - ior prays a - lone.
whom he loved Heeds not his Mas - ter's grief and tears.
an - guish knelt Is not for - sak - en by his God.
are the strains That sweet - ly soothe the Sav - ior's woe. A - men.

432

What Wondrous Love Is This

WONDROUS LOVE 12 9.12 9.
Southern Harmony, 1835
Harm. by C. R. Y.

American Folk Hymn

Unison
1. What won-drous love is this, O my soul, O my soul, What won-drous love is this, O my soul! What won-drous love is this that caused the Lord of bliss To bear the dread-ful curse for my soul, for my soul, To bear the dread-ful curse for my soul.
2. What won-drous love is this, O my soul, O my soul, What won-drous love is this, O my soul! What won-drous love is this that caused the Lord of life To lay a-side his crown for my soul, for my soul, To lay a-side his crown for my soul. A-men.

LENTEN SEASON

Jesus, Keep Me Near the Cross

NEAR THE CROSS 76.76. with Refrain

FANNY J. CROSBY, 1820-1915

WILLIAM H. DOANE, 1832-1915

1. Je - sus, keep me near the cross; There a pre - cious foun - tain,
2. Near the cross, a trem - bling soul, Love and mer - cy found me;
3. Near the cross! O Lamb of God, Bring its scenes be - fore me;
4. Near the cross I'll watch and wait, Hop - ing, trust - ing ev - er,
Free to all, a heal - ing stream, Flows from Cal - vary's moun - tain.
There the bright and morn - ing star Shed its beams a - round me.
Help me walk from day to day With its shad - ow o'er me.
Till I reach the gold - en strand Just be - yond the riv - er.
Refrain
In the cross, in the cross, Be my glo - ry ev - er,
Till my rap - tured soul shall find Rest be - yond the riv - er. A - men.

Go to Dark Gethsemane

REDHEAD 76 77.77.77.

JAMES MONTGOMERY, 1771-1854 RICHARD REDHEAD, 1820-1901

1. Go to dark Geth-sem-a-ne, Ye that feel the
2. See him at the judg-ment hall, Beat-en, bound, re-
3. Cal-vary's mourn-ful moun-tain climb; There a-dor-ing
4. Ear-ly has-ten to the tomb Where they laid his
temp-ter's power; Your Re-deem-er's con-flict see;
viled, ar-raigned; See him meek-ly bear-ing all!
at his feet, Mark that mir-a-cle of time,
breath-less clay: All is sol-i-tude and gloom;
Watch with him one bit-ter hour; Turn not from his
Love to man his soul sus-tained. Shun not suf-fering,
God's own sac-ri-fice com-plete; "It is fin-ished!"
Who hath tak-en him a-way? Christ is risen! He
griefs a-way; Learn of Je-sus Christ to pray.
shame, or loss; Learn of Christ to bear the cross.
hear him cry; Learn of Je-sus Christ to die.
meets our eyes. Sav-ior, teach us so to rise. A-men.

When I Survey the Wondrous Cross

GALATIANS 6:14
ISAAC WATTS, 1674-1748

HAMBURG LM
Ancient Chant
Arr. by LOWELL MASON, 1792-1872

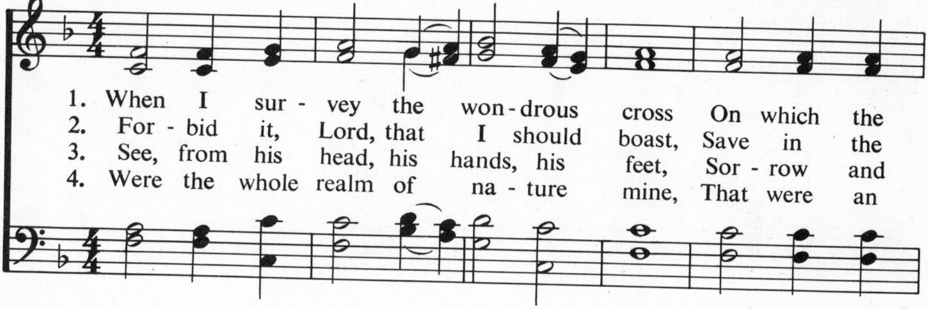
1. When I sur - vey the won - drous cross On which the
2. For - bid it, Lord, that I should boast, Save in the
3. See, from his head, his hands, his feet, Sor - row and
4. Were the whole realm of na - ture mine, That were an

Prince of Glo - ry died, My rich - est gain I
death of Christ, my God; All the vain things that
love flow min - gled down; Did e'er such love and
of - fering far too small; Love so a - maz - ing,

count but loss, And pour con-tempt on all my pride.
charm me most, I sac - ri - fice them to his blood.
sor - row meet, Or thorns com-pose so rich a crown?
so di - vine, De-mands my soul, my life, my all. A-men.

Were You There

American Folk Hymn

WERE YOU THERE Irregular
American Folk Hymn

1. Were you there when they cru - ci - fied my Lord? Were you
2. Were you there when they nailed him to the tree? Were you
3. Were you there when they laid him in the tomb? Were you
there when they cru - ci - fied my Lord? Oh!
there when they nailed him to the tree? Oh!
there when they laid him in the tomb? Oh!
Some-times it caus - es me to trem - ble, trem - ble, trem - ble.
Some-times it caus - es me to trem - ble, trem - ble, trem - ble.
Some-times it caus - es me to trem - ble, trem - ble, trem - ble.
Were you there when they cru - ci - fied my Lord?
Were you there when they nailed him to the tree?
Were you there when they laid him in the tomb?

The Day of Resurrection

JOHN OF DAMASCUS, 8th Century
Trans. by JOHN M. NEALE, 1818-1866

LANCASHIRE 76.76.D.
HENRY SMART, 1813-1879

1. The day of res - ur - rec - tion! Earth, tell it out a - broad;
2. Our hearts be pure from e - vil, That we may see a - right
3. Now let the heavens be joy - ful! Let earth her song be - gin!
The pass - o - ver of glad - ness, The pass - o - ver of God.
The Lord in rays e - ter - nal Of res - ur - rec - tion light;
Let the round world keep tri - umph, And all that is there - in!
From death to life e - ter - nal, From earth un - to the sky,
And lis-tening to his ac - cents, May hear, so calm and plain,
Let all things seen and un - seen Their notes in glad-ness blend,
Our Christ hath brought us o - ver With hymns of vic - to - ry.
His own "All hail!" and, hear - ing, May raise the vic - tor strain.
For Christ the Lord hath ris - en, Our joy that hath no end. A-men.

438 Christ Jesus Lay in Death's Strong Bands

MARTIN LUTHER, 1483-1546
Trans. by RICHARD MASSIE, 1800-1887

CHRIST LAG IN TODESBANDEN 87.87.78.74.
JOHANN WALTHER'S *Geistliches Gesangbüchlein*, Wittenberg, 1524

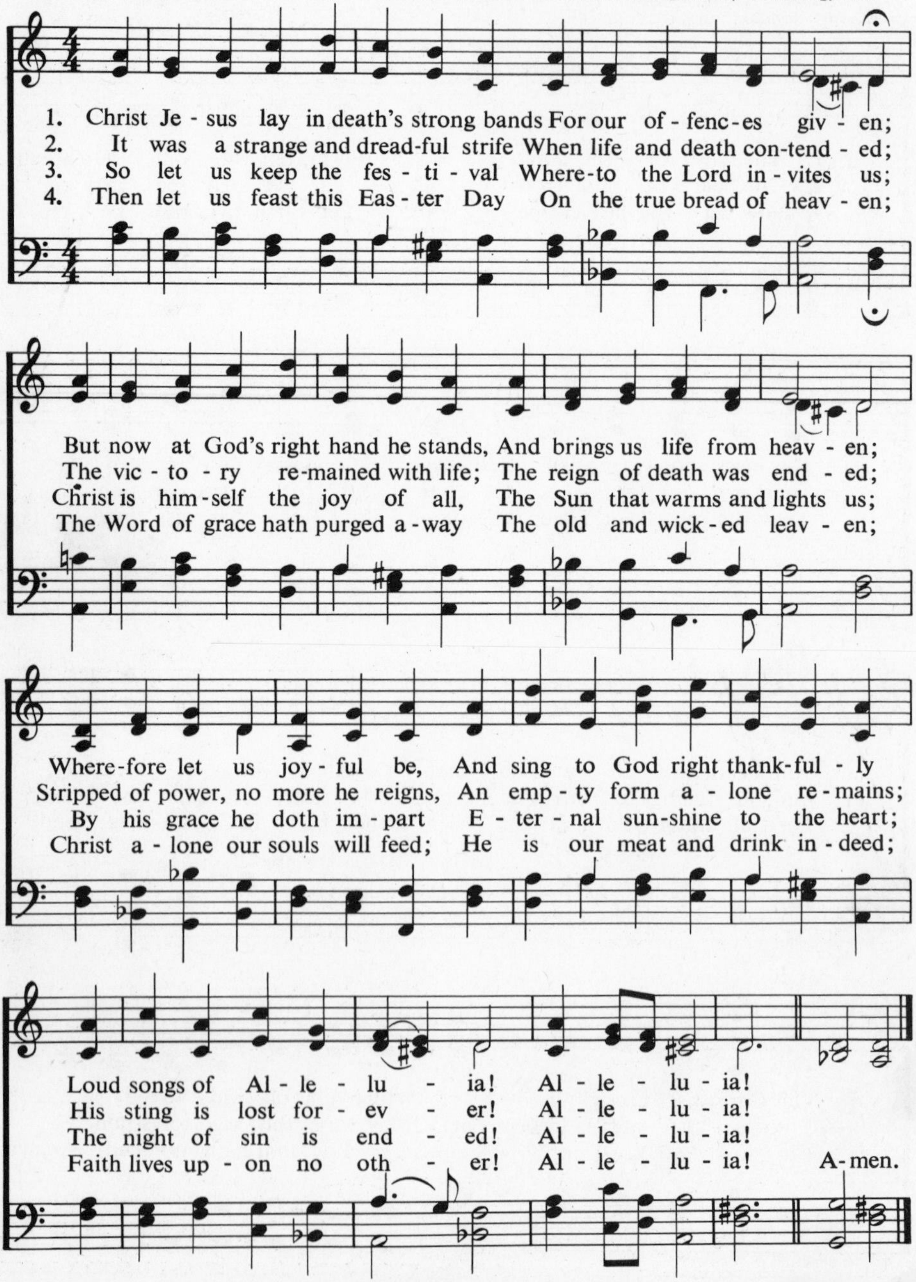
1. Christ Je - sus lay in death's strong bands For our of - fenc - es giv - en;
2. It was a strange and dread-ful strife When life and death con-tend - ed;
3. So let us keep the fes - ti - val Where-to the Lord in - vites us;
4. Then let us feast this Eas - ter Day On the true bread of heav - en;
But now at God's right hand he stands, And brings us life from heav - en;
The vic - to - ry re-mained with life; The reign of death was end - ed;
Christ is him-self the joy of all, The Sun that warms and lights us;
The Word of grace hath purged a - way The old and wick - ed leav - en;
Where-fore let us joy - ful be, And sing to God right thank-ful - ly
Stripped of power, no more he reigns, An emp - ty form a - lone re - mains;
By his grace he doth im - part E - ter - nal sun-shine to the heart;
Christ a - lone our souls will feed; He is our meat and drink in - deed;
Loud songs of Al - le - lu - ia! Al - le - lu - ia!
His sting is lost for - ev - er! Al - le - lu - ia!
The night of sin is end - ed! Al - le - lu - ia!
Faith lives up - on no oth - er! Al - le - lu - ia! A-men.

EASTERTIDE

Christ the Lord Is Risen Today

EASTER HYMN 77.77. with Alleluias

CHARLES WESLEY, 1707-1788, and others

Lyra Davidica, 1708

1. Christ the Lord is risen to - day, Al - le - lu - ia!
2. Lives a - gain our glo - rious King, Al - le - lu - ia!
3. Love's re - deem - ing work is done, Al - le - lu - ia!
4. Soar we now where Christ has led, Al - le - lu - ia!
Sons of men and an - gels say, Al - le - lu - ia!
Where, O death, is now thy sting? Al - le - lu - ia!
Fought the fight, the bat - tle won, Al - le - lu - ia!
Fol - lowing our ex - alt - ed Head, Al - le - lu - ia!
Raise your joys and tri - umphs high, Al - le - lu - ia!
Once he died, our souls to save, Al - le - lu - ia!
Death in vain for - bids him rise, Al - le - lu - ia!
Made like him, like him we rise, Al - le - lu - ia!
Sing, ye heavens, and earth re - ply, Al - le - lu - ia!
Where's thy vic - tory, boast - ing grave? Al - le - lu - ia!
Christ hath o - pened par - a - dise, Al - le - lu - ia!
Ours the cross, the grave, the skies, Al - le - lu - ia! A - men.

440

Sing with All the Sons of Glory

HYMN TO JOY 87.87.D.

I CORINTHIANS 15:20
WILLIAM J. IRONS, 1812-1883

Arr. from LUDWIG VAN BEETHOVEN, 1770-1827
by EDWARD HODGES, 1796-1867

1. Sing with all the sons of glo - ry, Sing the res - ur - rec - tion song!
2. O what glo - ry, far ex - ceed - ing All that eye has yet per - ceived!
3. Life e - ter - nal! heaven re - joic - es: Je - sus lives who once was dead;
4. Life e - ter - nal! O what won - ders Crowd on faith; what joy un - known,
Death and sor - row, earth's dark sto - ry, To the for - mer
Ho - liest hearts for a - ges plead - ing, Nev - er that full
Join, O man, the death - less voic - es; Child of God, lift
When, a - midst earth's clos - ing thun - ders, Saints shall stand be -
days be - long. All a - round the clouds are break - ing,
joy con - ceived. God has prom - ised, Christ pre - pares it,
up thy head! Pa - triarchs from the dis - tant a - ges,
fore the throne! O to en - ter that bright por - tal,
Soon the storms of time shall cease; In God's like - ness,
There on high our wel - come waits; Ev - ery hum - ble
Saints all long - ing for their heaven, Proph - ets, psalm - ists,
See that glow - ing fir - ma - ment, Know, with thee, O

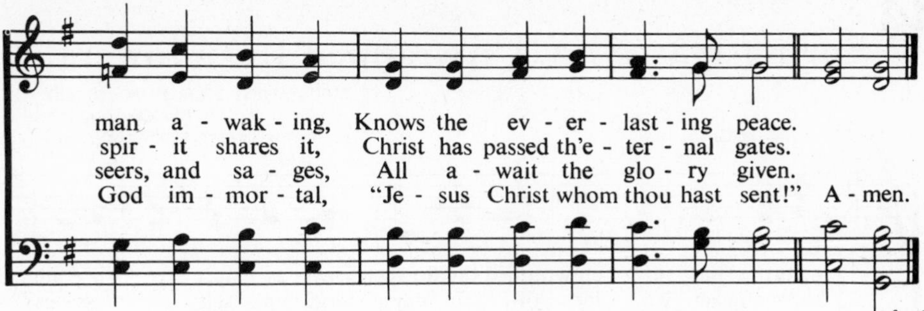
man a - wak - ing, Knows the ev - er - last - ing peace.
spir - it shares it, Christ has passed th'e - ter - nal gates.
seers, and sa - ges, All a - wait the glo - ry given.
God im - mor - tal, "Je - sus Christ whom thou hast sent!" A - men.

Now the Green Blade Riseth 441

FRENCH CAROL 11 10.10 11.

Trad. French Carol, "Noël Nouvelet"

J. M. C. CRUM, 1872-1958 Harm. by MARTIN SHAW, 1875-1958

1. Now the green blade ris - eth from the bur - ied grain, Wheat that in
2. In the grave they laid him, Love whom men had slain, Think-ing that
3. Forth he came at Eas - ter, like the ris - en grain, He that for
4. When our hearts are win - try, griev-ing, or in pain, Thy touch can

dark earth man - y days has lain; Love lives a - gain, that
nev - er he would wake a - gain, Laid in the earth like
three days in the grave had lain; Quick from the dead my
call us back to life a - gain, Fields of our hearts that

Refrain
with the dead has been:
grain that sleeps un - seen:
ris - en Lord is seen:
dead and bare have been:
Love is come a-gain like wheat that spring-eth green.

From *The Oxford Book of Carols* by permission of Oxford University Press.

442

Spring Has Now Unwrapped the Flowers

TEMPUS ADEST FLORIDUM 76.76.D.
Piae Cantiones, 1582
The Oxford Book of Carols, 1928 Arr. by ERNEST MACMILLAN, 1893-

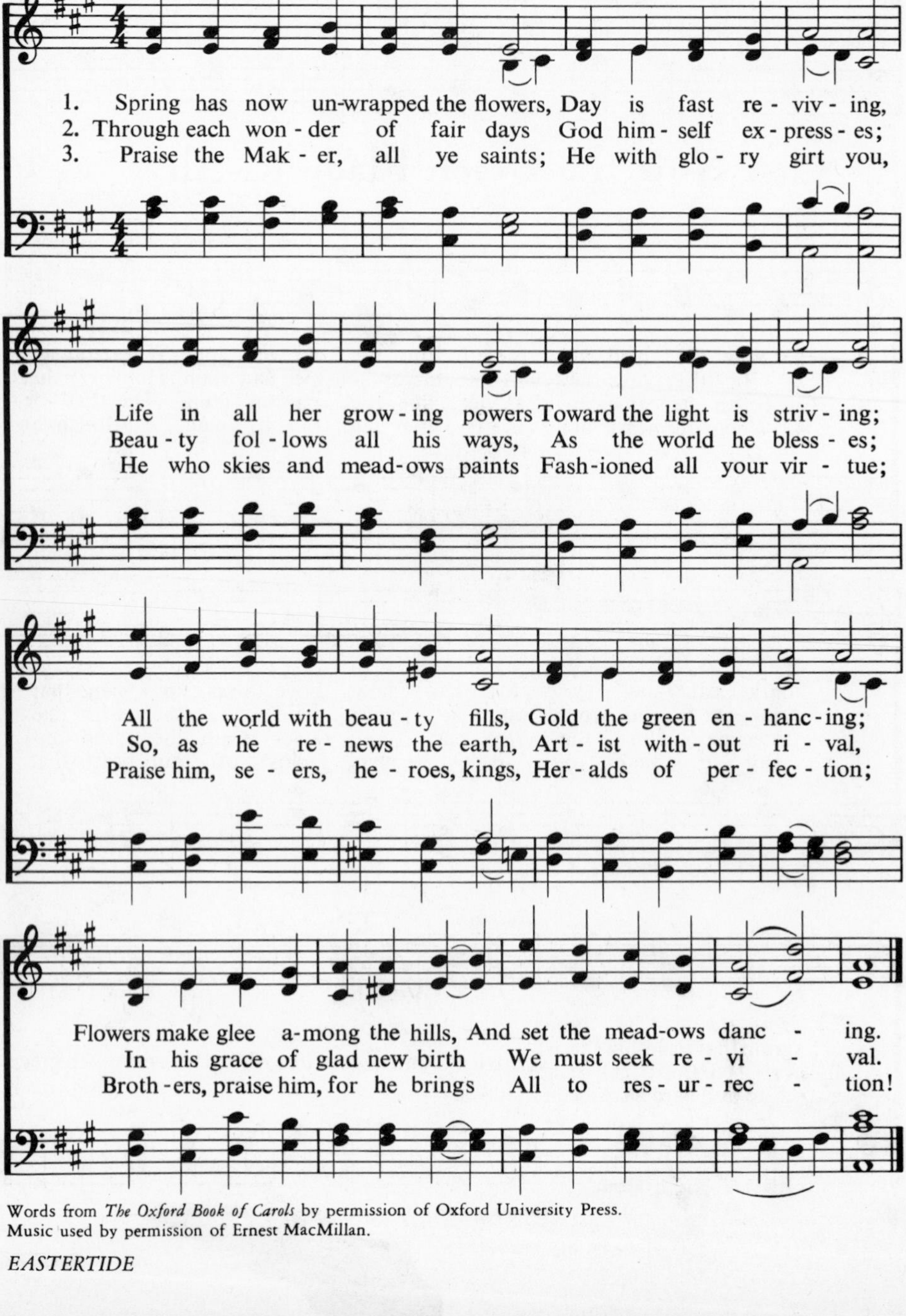
1. Spring has now un-wrapped the flowers, Day is fast re - viv - ing,
2. Through each won - der of fair days God him - self ex - press - es;
3. Praise the Mak - er, all ye saints; He with glo - ry girt you,
Life in all her grow - ing powers Toward the light is striv - ing;
Beau - ty fol - lows all his ways, As the world he bless - es;
He who skies and mead - ows paints Fash - ioned all your vir - tue;
All the world with beau - ty fills, Gold the green en - hanc - ing;
So, as he re - news the earth, Art - ist with - out ri - val,
Praise him, se - ers, he - roes, kings, Her - alds of per - fec - tion;
Flowers make glee a - mong the hills, And set the mead - ows danc - ing.
In his grace of glad new birth We must seek re - vi - val.
Broth - ers, praise him, for he brings All to res - ur - rec - tion!

Words from *The Oxford Book of Carols* by permission of Oxford University Press.
Music used by permission of Ernest MacMillan.

EASTERTIDE

Jesus Christ Is Risen Today

Latin, 14th Century
Trans. in *Lyra Davidica*, 1708
Stanza 2, JOHN ARNOLD'S *Compleat Psalmodist*, 1749
Stanza 3, CHARLES WESLEY, 1707-1788

LLANFAIR 77.77. with Alleluias
ROBERT WILLIAMS, c. 1781-1821
Harm. by DAVID EVANS, 1874-1948

1. Je - sus Christ is risen to - day, Al - le - lu - ia!
2. Hymns of praise then let us sing, Al - le - lu - ia!
3. Sing we to our God a - bove, Al - le - lu - ia!
Our tri - um - phant ho - ly day, Al - le - lu - ia!
Un - to Christ, our heaven - ly King, Al - le - lu - ia!
Praise e - ter - nal as his love; Al - le - lu - ia!
Who did once, up - on the cross, Al - le - lu - ia!
Who en - dured the cross and grave, Al - le - lu - ia!
Praise him, all ye heaven - ly host, Al - le - lu - ia!
Suf - fer to re - deem our loss. Al - le - lu - ia!
Sin - ners to re - deem and save. Al - le - lu - ia!
Fa - ther, Son, and Ho - ly Ghost. Al - le - lu - ia! A - men.

444

Low in the Grave He Lay

CHRIST AROSE 65.64.with Refrain

ROBERT LOWRY, 1826-1899 ROBERT LOWRY, 1826-1899

1. Low in the grave he lay, Je - sus my Sav - ior!
2. Vain - ly they watch his bed, Je - sus my Sav - ior!
3. Death can - not keep his prey, Je - sus my Sav - ior!
Wait - ing the com - ing day, Je - sus my Lord!
Vain - ly they seal the dead, Je - sus my Lord!
He tore the bars a - way, Je - sus my Lord!
Refrain
Up from the grave he a - rose, With a
he a - rose
might - y tri - umph o'er his foes; He a -
o'er his foes
rose a vic - tor from the dark do - main, And he

EASTERTIDE

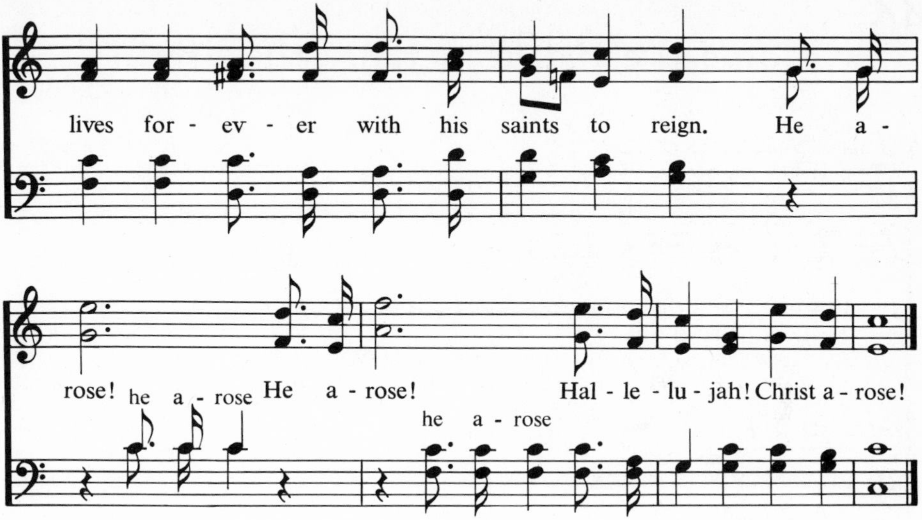
lives for - ev - er with his saints to reign. He a -
rose! he a - rose He a - rose! Hal - le - lu - jah! Christ a - rose!
he a - rose

445

I Know That My Redeemer Lives

JOB 19:25
SAMUEL MEDLEY, 1738-1799

TRURO LM
T. WILLIAMS' *Psalmodia Evangelica*, 1789

1. I know that my Re-deem-er lives: What joy the blest as - sur-ance gives!
2. He lives, to bless me with his love; He lives, to plead for me a - bove;
3. He lives, and grants me dai - ly breath; He lives, and I shall con-quer death;
4. He lives, all glo - ry to his name; He lives, my Sav-ior, still the same;
He lives, he lives, who once was dead; He lives, my ev - er - last-ing Head!
He lives, my hun-gry soul to feed; He lives, to help in time of need.
He lives, my man-sion to pre-pare; He lives, to bring me safe-ly there.
What joy the blest as - sur - ance gives: I know that my Re-deem-er lives! A-men.

Come, Ye Faithful, Raise the Strain

EXODUS 15
JOHN OF DAMASCUS, 8th Century
Trans. by JOHN M. NEALE, 1818-1866

ST. KEVIN 76.76.D.
ARTHUR S. SULLIVAN, 1842-1900

1. Come, ye faith - ful, raise the strain Of tri - um - phant glad - ness;
2. 'Tis the spring of souls to - day; Christ hath burst his pris - on,
3. Now the queen of sea - sons, bright With the day of splen - dor,
4. Neith - er might the gates of death, Nor the tomb's dark por - tal,
5. "Al - le - lu - ia!" now we cry To our King im - mor - tal,
God hath brought his Is - ra - el In - to joy from sad - ness;
And from three days' sleep in death As a sun hath ris - en;
With the roy - al feast of feasts, Comes its joy to ren - der;
Nor the watch - ers, nor the seal Hold thee as a mor - tal;
Who, tri - um - phant, burst the bars Of the tomb's dark por - tal;
Loosed from Phar - aoh's bit - ter yoke Ja - cob's sons and daugh - ters;
All the win - ter of our sins, Long and dark, is fly - ing
Comes to glad Je - ru - sa - lem Who with true af - fec - tion
But to - day a - midst the twelve Thou didst stand, be - stow - ing
"Al - le - lu - ia" with the Son, God the Fa - ther prais - ing;

EASTERTIDE

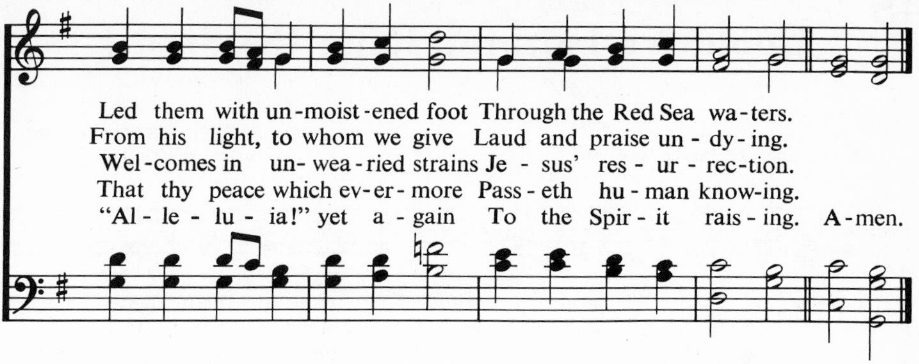
Led them with un-moist-ened foot Through the Red Sea wa-ters.
From his light, to whom we give Laud and praise un-dy-ing.
Wel-comes in un-wea-ried strains Je-sus' res-ur-rec-tion.
That thy peace which ev-er-more Pass-eth hu-man know-ing.
"Al-le-lu-ia!" yet a-gain To the Spir-it rais-ing. A-men.

447

The Strife Is O'er, the Battle Done

VICTORY 888. with Alleluia

ANONYMOUS Latin
Trans. by FRANCIS POTT, 1832-1909

Arr. from GIOVANNI P. DA PALESTRINA, c. 1525-1594
by W. H. MONK, 1823-1889

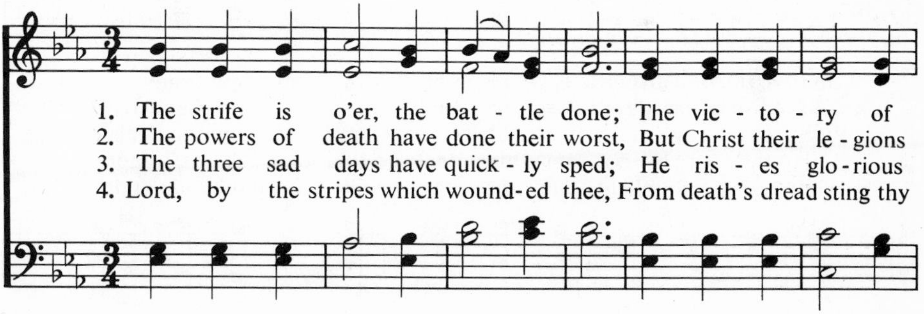
1. The strife is o'er, the bat-tle done; The vic-to-ry of
2. The powers of death have done their worst, But Christ their le-gions
3. The three sad days have quick-ly sped; He ris-es glo-rious
4. Lord, by the stripes which wound-ed thee, From death's dread sting thy

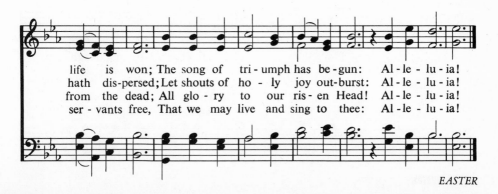

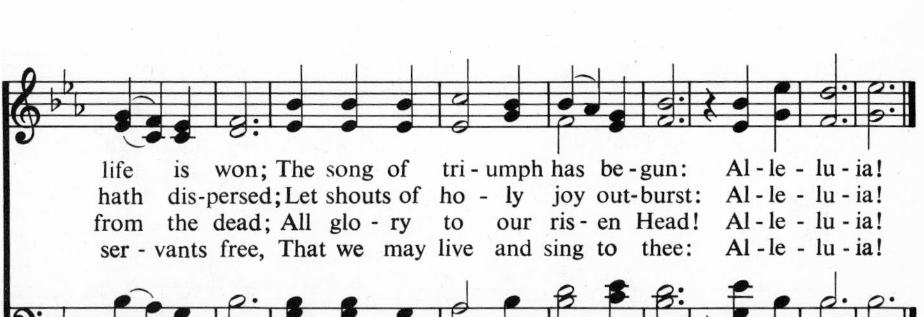
life is won; The song of tri-umph has be-gun: Al-le-lu-ia!
hath dis-persed; Let shouts of ho-ly joy out-burst: Al-le-lu-ia!
from the dead; All glo-ry to our ris-en Head! Al-le-lu-ia!
ser-vants free, That we may live and sing to thee: Al-le-lu-ia!

448

Come, Ye Faithful, Raise the Strain

Exodus 15
John of Damascus, 8th Century
Trans. by John M. Neale, 1818-1866

AVE VIRGO VIRGINUM 76.76.D.
Leisentritt's *Gesangbuch*, 1584

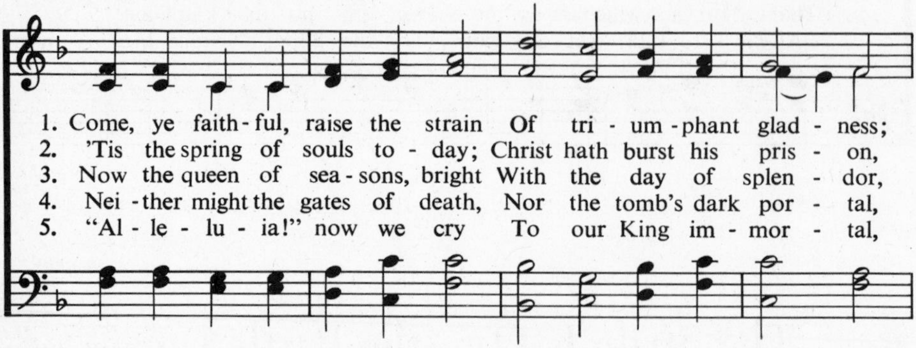
1. Come, ye faith - ful, raise the strain Of tri - um - phant glad - ness;
2. 'Tis the spring of souls to - day; Christ hath burst his pris - on,
3. Now the queen of sea - sons, bright With the day of splen - dor,
4. Nei - ther might the gates of death, Nor the tomb's dark por - tal,
5. "Al - le - lu - ia!" now we cry To our King im - mor - tal,

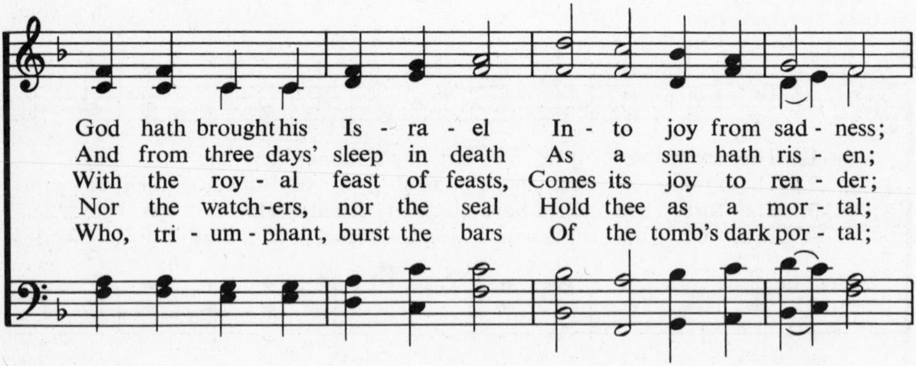
God hath brought his Is - ra - el In - to joy from sad - ness;
And from three days' sleep in death As a sun hath ris - en;
With the roy - al feast of feasts, Comes its joy to ren - der;
Nor the watch - ers, nor the seal Hold thee as a mor - tal;
Who, tri - um - phant, burst the bars Of the tomb's dark por - tal;

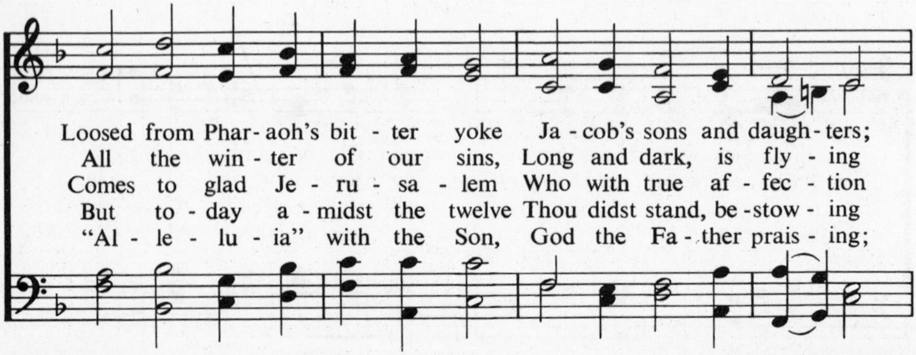
Loosed from Phar - aoh's bit - ter yoke Ja - cob's sons and daugh - ters;
All the win - ter of our sins, Long and dark, is fly - ing
Comes to glad Je - ru - sa - lem Who with true af - fec - tion
But to - day a - midst the twelve Thou didst stand, be - stow - ing
"Al - le - lu - ia" with the Son, God the Fa - ther prais - ing;

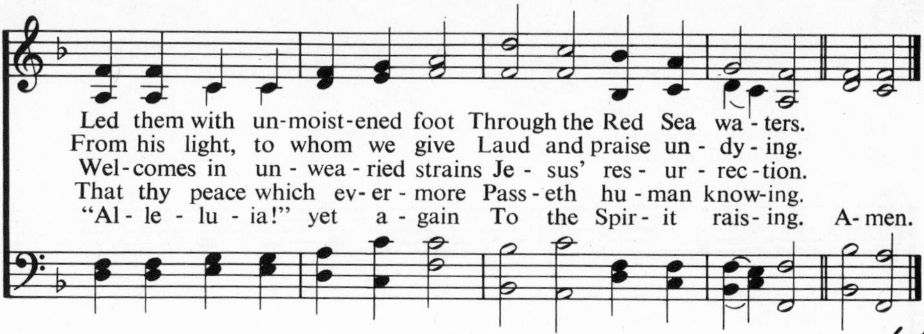
Led them with un-moist-ened foot Through the Red Sea wa - ters.
From his light, to whom we give Laud and praise un - dy - ing.
Wel-comes in un - wea - ried strains Je - sus' res - ur - rec - tion.
That thy peace which ev - er - more Pass - eth hu - man know-ing.
"Al - le - lu - ia!" yet a - gain To the Spir - it rais - ing. A - men.

449

Good Christian Men, Rejoice and Sing

GELOBT SEI GOTT 888. with Alleluias

CYRIL A. ALINGTON, 1872-1955

MELCHIOR VULPIUS, c. 1560-1616

1. Good Chris - tian men, re - joice and sing! Now is the tri - umph
2. The Lord of life is risen for aye; Bring flowers of song to
3. Praise we in songs of vic - to - ry That love, that life which
4. Thy name we bless, O ris - en Lord, And sing to - day with

of our King! To all the world glad news we bring:
strew his way; Let all man - kind re - joice and say:
can - not die, And sing with hearts up - lift - ed high:
one ac - cord The life laid down, the life re - stored:

Refrain
Al - le - lu - ia! Al - le - lu - ia! Al - le - lu - ia!

Thine Is the Glory

EDMOND L. BUDRY, 1854-1932
Trans. by R. BIRCH HOYLE, 1875-1939

JUDAS MACCABEUS 55.65.65.65. with Refrain
GEORGE FREDERICK HANDEL, 1685-1759

1. Thine is the glo-ry, Ris-en, con-quering Son; End-less is the vic-tory Thou o'er death hast won. An-gels in bright rai-ment Rolled the stone a-way, Kept the fold-ed grave-clothes Where thy bod-y lay.
2. Lo! Je-sus meets thee, Ris-en from the tomb; Lov-ing-ly he greets thee, Scat-ters fear and gloom; Let his church with glad-ness Hymns of tri-umph sing, For her Lord now liv-eth; Death hath lost its sting.
3. No more we doubt thee, Glo-rious Prince of life! Life is naught with-out thee; Aid us in our strife; Make us more than con-querors, Through thy death-less love; Bring us safe through Jor-dan To thy home a-bove.
Refrain
Thine is the glo-ry, Ris-en, con-quering Son;

EASTERTIDE

End-less is the vic-tory Thou o'er death hast won. A-men.

451

O Sons and Daughters, Let Us Sing

Jean Tisserand, d. 1494
Trans. by John M. Neale, 1818-1866

O FILII ET FILIAE 888. with Alleluias
French Carol, c. 15th Century

1. O sons and daugh-ters, let us sing! The King of heaven, the glo-rious King, O'er death to-day rose tri-umph-ing,
2. That Eas-ter morn at break of day, The faith-ful wom-en went their way To seek the tomb where Je-sus lay,
3. An an-gel clad in white they see, Who sat and spake un-to the three, "Your Lord doth go to Gal-i-lee,"
4. How blest are they who have not seen, And yet whose faith hath con-stant been; For they e-ter-nal life shall win,
5. On this most ho-ly day of days, Our hearts and voic-es, Lord, we raise To thee, in ju-bi-lee and praise,
Al-le-lu-ia! Al-le-lu-ia!

Welcome, Happy Morning

VENANTIUS FORTUNATUS, c. 530-609
Trans. by JOHN ELLERTON, 1826-1893

HERMAS 65.65.D.
FRANCES R. HAVERGAL, 1836-1879

1. "Wel-come, hap - py morn - ing!" Age to age shall say:
2. Earth with joy con - fess - es, Cloth - ing her for spring,
3. Thou, of life the au - thor, Death didst un - der - go,
4. "Wel-come, hap - py morn - ing!" Age to age shall say:
"Hell to - day is van - quished, Heaven is won to - day."
All good gifts re - turned with Her re - turn - ing King.
Tread the path of dark - ness, Sav - ing strength to show;
"Hell to - day is van - quished, Heaven is won to - day."
Lo! the dead is liv - ing, God for - ev - er - more!
Bloom in ev - ery mead - ow, Leaves on ev - ery bough,
Come then, true and faith - ful, Now ful - fill thy word;
Lo! the dead is liv - ing, God for - ev - er - more!
Him, their true cre - a - tor, All his works a - dore.
Speak his sor - rows end - ed; Hail his tri - umph now.
'Tis thine own third morn - ing, Rise, O bur - ied Lord!
Him, their true cre - a - tor, All his works a - dore. A-men.

Alternate tune: ST. GERTRUDE

Look, Ye Saints! The Sight Is Glorious

REVELATION 11:15
THOMAS KELLY, 1769-1854

BRYN CALFARIA 87.87.47.
WILLIAM OWEN, 1814-1893
Harm. by C. R. Y.

1. Look, ye saints! The sight is glo-rious; See the Man of Sor-rows now;
2. Crown the Sav-ior, an-gels, crown him; Rich the tro-phies Je-sus brings;
3. Sin-ners in de-ri-sion crowned him, Mock-ing thus the Sav-ior's claim;
4. Hark, those bursts of ac-cla-ma-tion! Hark, those loud tri-um-phant chords!
From the fight re-turned vic-to-rious, Ev-ery knee to him shall bow:
In the seat of power en-throne him, While the vault of heav-en rings:
Saints and an-gels crowd a-round him, Own his ti-tle, praise his name:
Je-sus takes the high-est sta-tion; O what joy the sight af-fords!
Crown him, crown him, Crown him, crown him, Crown him, crown him.
Crown him, crown him, Crown him, crown him, Crown him, crown him.
Crown him, crown him, Crown him, crown him, Crown him, crown him.
Crown him, crown him, Crown him, crown him, Crown him, crown him.
Crowns be-come the vic-tor's brow, Crowns be-come the vic-tor's brow.
Crown the Sav-ior King of kings, Crown the Sav-ior King of kings.
Spread a-broad the vic-tor's fame, Spread a-broad the vic-tor's fame.
King of kings, and Lord of lords! King of kings, and Lord of lords! A-men.

454

Hail, Thou Once Despised Jesus

IN BABILONE 87.87.D.

Probably by JOHN BAKEWELL, 1721-1819 — Trad. Dutch Melody

Probably alt. by MARTIN MADAN, 1726-1790 — Arr. by JULIUS RÖNTGEN, 1855-1932

1. Hail, thou once de - spis - ed Je - sus! Hail, thou Gal - i - le - an King!
2. Pas - chal Lamb, by God ap - point - ed, All our sins on thee were laid;
3. Je - sus, hail! en - throned in glo - ry, There for - ev - er to a - bide;
4. Wor - ship, hon - or, power, and bless - ing Christ is wor - thy to re - ceive;
Thou didst suf - fer to re - lease us; Thou didst free sal - va - tion bring.
By al - might - y love ap - point - ed, Thou hast full a - tone - ment made.
All the heaven - ly hosts a - dore thee, Seat - ed at thy Fa - ther's side.
Loud - est prais - es, with - out ceas - ing, Meet it is for us to give.
Hail, thou u - ni - ver - sal Sav - ior, Who hast borne our sin and shame!
Ev - ery sin may be for - giv - en, Through the vir - tue of thy blood;
There for sin - ners thou art plead - ing; There thou dost our place pre - pare;
Help, ye bright an - gel - ic spir - its, Bring your sweet - est, no - blest lays;
By thy mer - its we find fa - vor; Life is giv - en through thy name.
O - pened is the gate of heav - en; Peace is made twixt man and God.
Thou for saints art in - ter - ced - ing Till in glo - ry they ap - pear.
Help to sing of Je - sus' mer - its, Help to chant Em - man - uel's praise! A - men.

Alternate tune: AUTUMN

Music used by permission of Mrs. Engelbert Roentgen.

EASTERTIDE

Crown Him with Many Crowns

REVELATION 19:12
MATTHEW BRIDGES, 1800-1894 and
GODFREY THRING, 1823-1903

DIADEMATA SMD
GEORGE J. ELVEY, 1816-1893

1. Crown him with man - y crowns, The Lamb up - on his throne;
2. Crown him the Lord of life, Who tri-umphed o'er the grave,
3. Crown him the Lord of peace, Whose power a scep - ter sways
4. Crown him the Lord of love; Be - hold his hands and side,
Hark! how the heaven - ly an - them drowns All mu - sic but its own.
And rose vic - to - rious in the strife For those he came to save;
From pole to pole, that wars may cease, And all be prayer and praise;
Those wounds, yet vis - i - ble a - bove, In beau - ty glo - ri - fied.
A - wake, my soul, and sing Of him who died for thee,
His glo - ries now we sing Who died, and rose on high,
His reign shall know no end, And round his pierc - ed feet
All hail, Re - deem - er, hail! For thou hast died for me;
And hail him as thy match-less King Through all e - ter - ni - ty.
Who died, e - ter - nal life to bring, And lives, that death may die.
Fair flowers of par - a - dise ex - tend Their fra-grance ev - er sweet.
Thy praise and glo - ry shall not fail Through-out e - ter - ni - ty. A-men.

456

And Have the Bright Immensities

HALIFAX CMD
George Frederick Handel, 1685-1759
Harm. by A. C. L.

Howard Chandler Robbins, 1876-1952

1. And have the bright im - men - si - ties Re-ceived our ris - en Lord, Where
2. The heaven that hides him from our sight Knows nei-ther near nor far: An
light-years frame the Plei - a - des And point O - ri - on's sword? Do
al - tar can - dle sheds its light As sure - ly as a star; And
flam - ing suns his foot-steps trace Through cor - ri - dors sub - lime, The
where his lov - ing peo - ple meet To share the gift di - vine, There
Lord of in - ter - stel - lar space And con-quer - or of time?
stands he with un - hur-rying feet; There heaven-ly splen-dors shine. A - men.

Alternate tune: FOREST GREEN

Words used by permission of Howard Chandler Robbins and the Morehouse-Barlow Company.

EASTERTIDE

Come, Let Us Rise with Christ

CHARLES WESLEY, 1707-1788

ST. MATTHEW CMD
Probably by WILLIAM CROFT, 1678-1727

1. Come, let us rise with Christ our Head And seek the things a - bove,
2. En-throned at God's right hand he sits, Main-tain - er of our cause,
3. To him our will - ing hearts we give Who gives us power and peace,
By the al-might - y Spir - it led And filled with faith and love; Our
Till ev - ery van-quished foe sub - mits To his vic - to - rious cross; Wor-
And dead to sin, his mem-bers live The life of righ-teous-ness; The
hearts de-tached from all be - low Should af - ter him as - cend, And
thy to be ex - alt - ed thus, The Lamb for sin - ners slain, The
hid - den life of Christ is ours With Christ con-cealed a - bove, And
on - ly wish the joy to know Of our tri - um-phant friend.
Lord our King, who reigns for us, And shall for - ev - er reign.
tast - ing the ce - les - tial powers, We ban - quet on his love. A-men.

458

The Head That Once Was Crowned

HEBREWS 2:9-10
THOMAS KELLY, 1769-1854

ST. MAGNUS CM
JEREMIAH CLARK, c. 1670-1707

1. The head that once was crowned with thorns Is
2. The high - est place that heaven af - fords Be -
3. The joy of all who dwell a - bove, The
4. To them the cross with all its shame, With
5. They suf - fer with their Lord be - low; They
6. The cross he bore is life and health, Though
crowned with glo - ry now; A roy - al di - a -
longs to him by right; The King of kings, and
joy of all be - low, To whom he man - i -
all its grace, is given; Their name an ev - er -
reign with him a - bove; Their prof - it and their
shame and death to him, His peo - ple's hope, his
dem a - dorns The might - y vic - tor's brow.
Lord of lords, And heaven's e - ter - nal light.
fests his love, And grants his name to know.
last - ing name; Their joy the joy of heaven.
joy to know The mys - tery of his love.
peo - ple's wealth, Their ev - er - last - ing theme. A - men.

Ancient of Days

ANCIENT OF DAYS 11 10.11 10.
J. ALBERT JEFFERY, 1854-1929
Harm. by V. E. C.

DANIEL 7:9-10
WILLIAM C. DOANE, 1832-1913

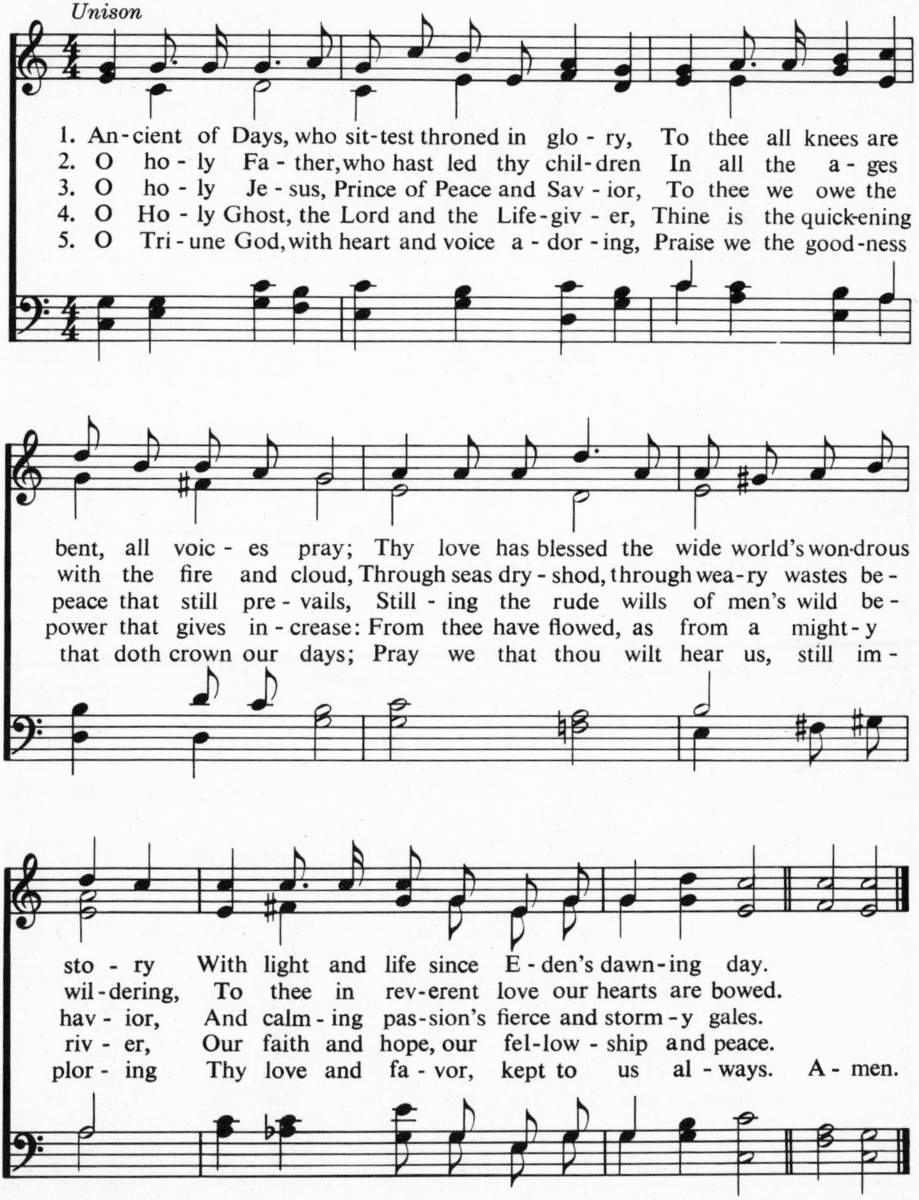
Unison
1. An-cient of Days, who sit-test throned in glo - ry, To thee all knees are
2. O ho - ly Fa - ther, who hast led thy chil-dren In all the a - ges
3. O ho - ly Je - sus, Prince of Peace and Sav - ior, To thee we owe the
4. O Ho - ly Ghost, the Lord and the Life-giv - er, Thine is the quick-ening
5. O Tri - une God, with heart and voice a - dor - ing, Praise we the good-ness
bent, all voic - es pray; Thy love has blessed the wide world's won-drous
with the fire and cloud, Through seas dry - shod, through wea-ry wastes be -
peace that still pre - vails, Still - ing the rude wills of men's wild be -
power that gives in - crease: From thee have flowed, as from a might - y
that doth crown our days; Pray we that thou wilt hear us, still im -
sto - ry With light and life since E - den's dawn-ing day.
wil-dering, To thee in rev-erent love our hearts are bowed.
hav - ior, And calm - ing pas-sion's fierce and storm - y gales.
riv - er, Our faith and hope, our fel-low - ship and peace.
plor - ing Thy love and fa - vor, kept to us al - ways. A - men.

460

God Hath Spoken by His Prophets

EBENEZER 87.87.D.

GEORGE W. BRIGGS, 1875-1959 THOMAS J. WILLIAMS, 1869-1944

1. God hath spo-ken by his proph - ets, Spo-ken his un -
2. God hath spo-ken by Christ Je - sus, Christ, the ev - er -
3. God yet speak-eth by his Spir - it, Speak-eth to the
chang - ing Word, Each from age to age pro - claim - ing
last - ing Son, Bright-ness of the Fa - ther's glo - ry,
hearts of men, In the age - long Word ex - pound - ing
God, the one, the righ - teous Lord. 'Mid the world's de-spair and tur-moil,
With the Fa - ther ev - er one; Spo-ken by the Word in - car-nate,
God's own mes - sage, now as then; Through the rise and fall of na - tions
One firm an - chor hold - eth fast; God is King, his
God of God, ere time be - gan, Light of Light, to
One sure faith yet stand - ing fast, God a - bides, his

Words from "Ten New Hymns on the Bible," copyright 1953 by the Hymn Society of America; used by permission. Music used by permission of Gwenlyn Evans, Ltd.

PENTECOST SEASON

throne e - ter - nal, God the first, and God the last.
earth de - scend - ing, Man, re - veal - ing God to man.
Word un - chang - ing, God the first, and God the last. A - men.
3
3
3

Alternate tune: AUSTRIA

461

Spirit Divine, Attend Our Prayers

BALLERMA CM

FRANÇOIS H. BARTHÉLÉMON, 1741-1808

Adapt. by ROBERT SIMPSON, 1790-1832

ANDREW REED, 1787-1862

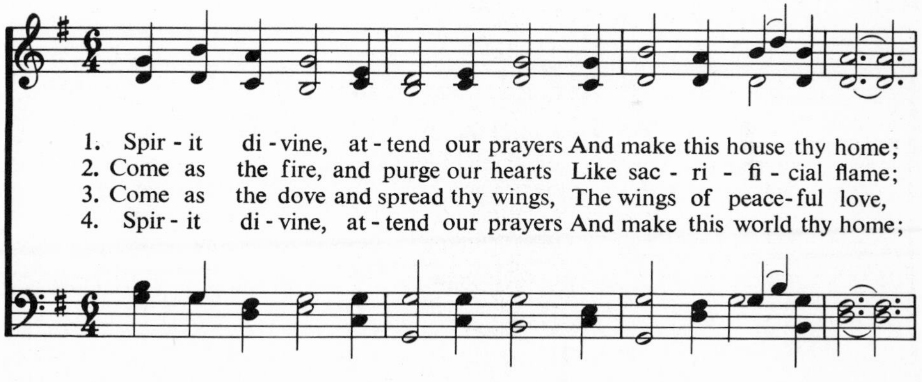
1. Spir - it di - vine, at - tend our prayers And make this house thy home;
2. Come as the fire, and purge our hearts Like sac - ri - fi - cial flame;
3. Come as the dove and spread thy wings, The wings of peace - ful love,
4. Spir - it di - vine, at - tend our prayers And make this world thy home;

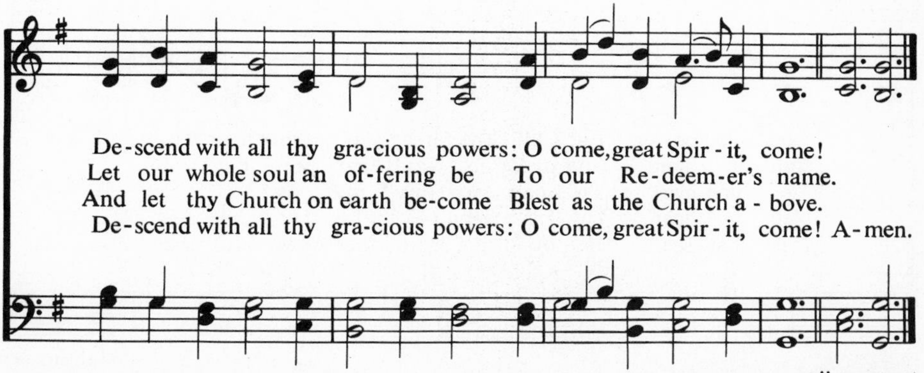
De - scend with all thy gra - cious powers: O come, great Spir - it, come!
Let our whole soul an of - fering be To our Re - deem - er's name.
And let thy Church on earth be - come Blest as the Church a - bove.
De - scend with all thy gra - cious powers: O come, great Spir - it, come! A - men.

Alternate tune: GRÄFENBERG

462

Spirit of Life, in This New Dawn

MARYTON LM

EARL MARLATT, 1892- H. PERCY SMITH, 1825-1898

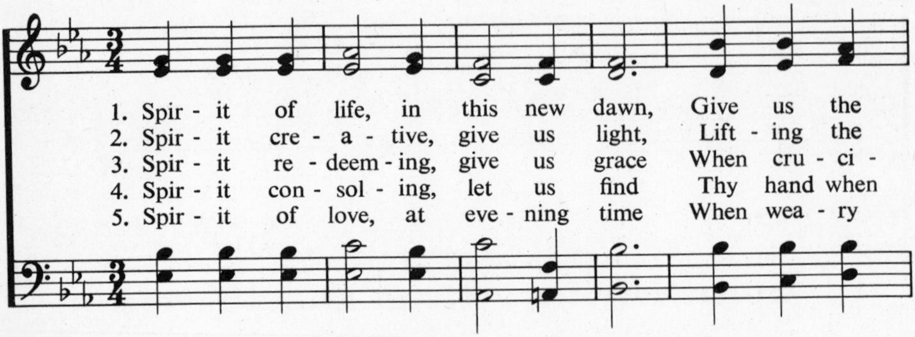
1. Spir - it of life, in this new dawn, Give us the
2. Spir - it cre - a - tive, give us light, Lift - ing the
3. Spir - it re - deem - ing, give us grace When cru - ci -
4. Spir - it con - sol - ing, let us find Thy hand when
5. Spir - it of love, at eve - ning time When wea - ry

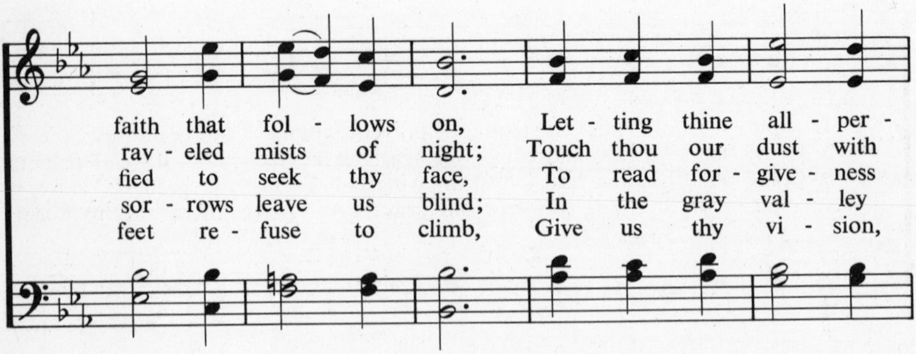
faith that fol - lows on, Let - ting thine all - per -
rav - eled mists of night; Touch thou our dust with
fied to seek thy face, To read for - give - ness
sor - rows leave us blind; In the gray val - ley
feet re - fuse to climb, Give us thy vi - sion,

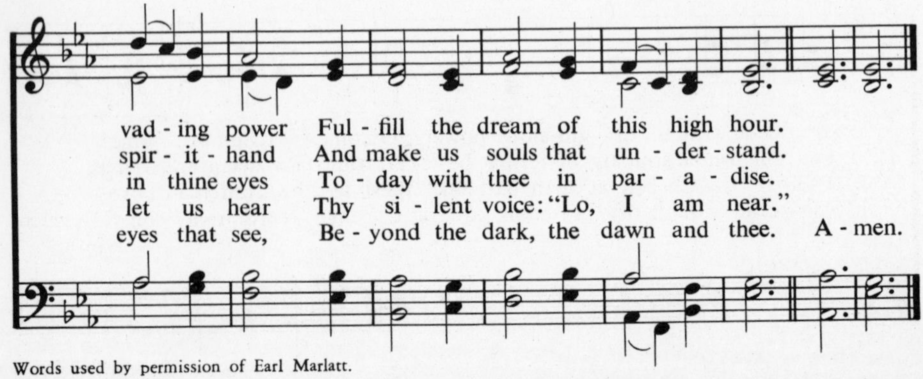
vad - ing power Ful - fill the dream of this high hour.
spir - it - hand And make us souls that un - der - stand.
in thine eyes To - day with thee in par - a - dise.
let us hear Thy si - lent voice: "Lo, I am near."
eyes that see, Be - yond the dark, the dawn and thee. A - men.

Words used by permission of Earl Marlatt.

PENTECOST SEASON

We Believe in One True God

TOBIAS CLAUSNITZER, 1619-1684
Trans. by CATHERINE WINKWORTH, 1827-1878

RATISBON 77.77.77.
Arr. from J. G. WERNER'S *Choralbuch*, 1815
by W. H. MONK, 1823-1889

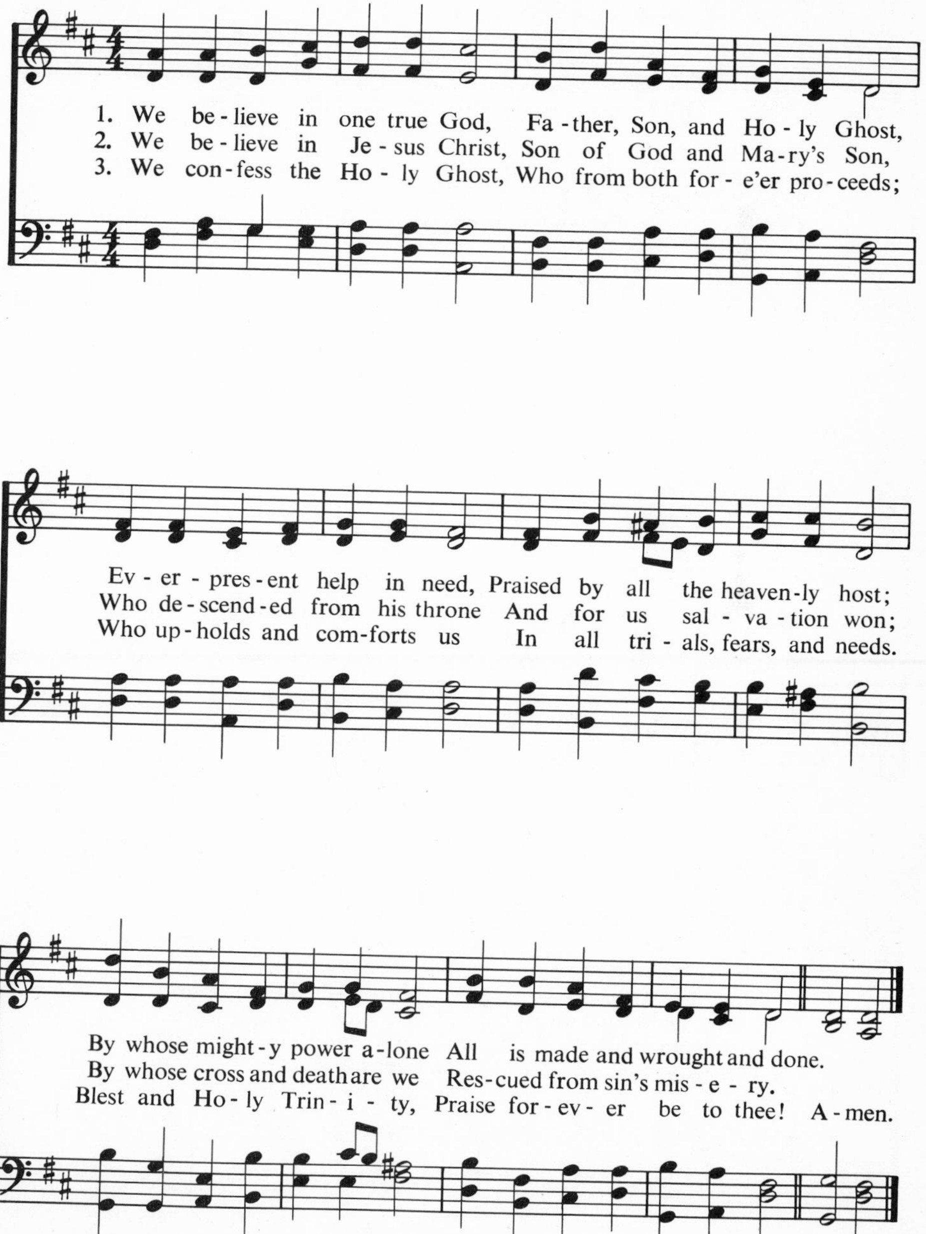
1. We be - lieve in one true God, Fa - ther, Son, and Ho - ly Ghost,
2. We be - lieve in Je - sus Christ, Son of God and Ma - ry's Son,
3. We con - fess the Ho - ly Ghost, Who from both for - e'er pro - ceeds;
Ev - er - pres - ent help in need, Praised by all the heaven - ly host;
Who de - scend - ed from his throne And for us sal - va - tion won;
Who up - holds and com - forts us In all tri - als, fears, and needs.
By whose might - y power a - lone All is made and wrought and done.
By whose cross and death are we Res - cued from sin's mis - e - ry.
Blest and Ho - ly Trin - i - ty, Praise for - ev - er be to thee! A - men.

Alternate tune: ARFON

464

See How Great a Flame Aspires

ARFON (MAJOR) 77.77.D.
Welsh Hymn Melody
Harm. by C. R. Y.

CHARLES WESLEY, 1707-1788

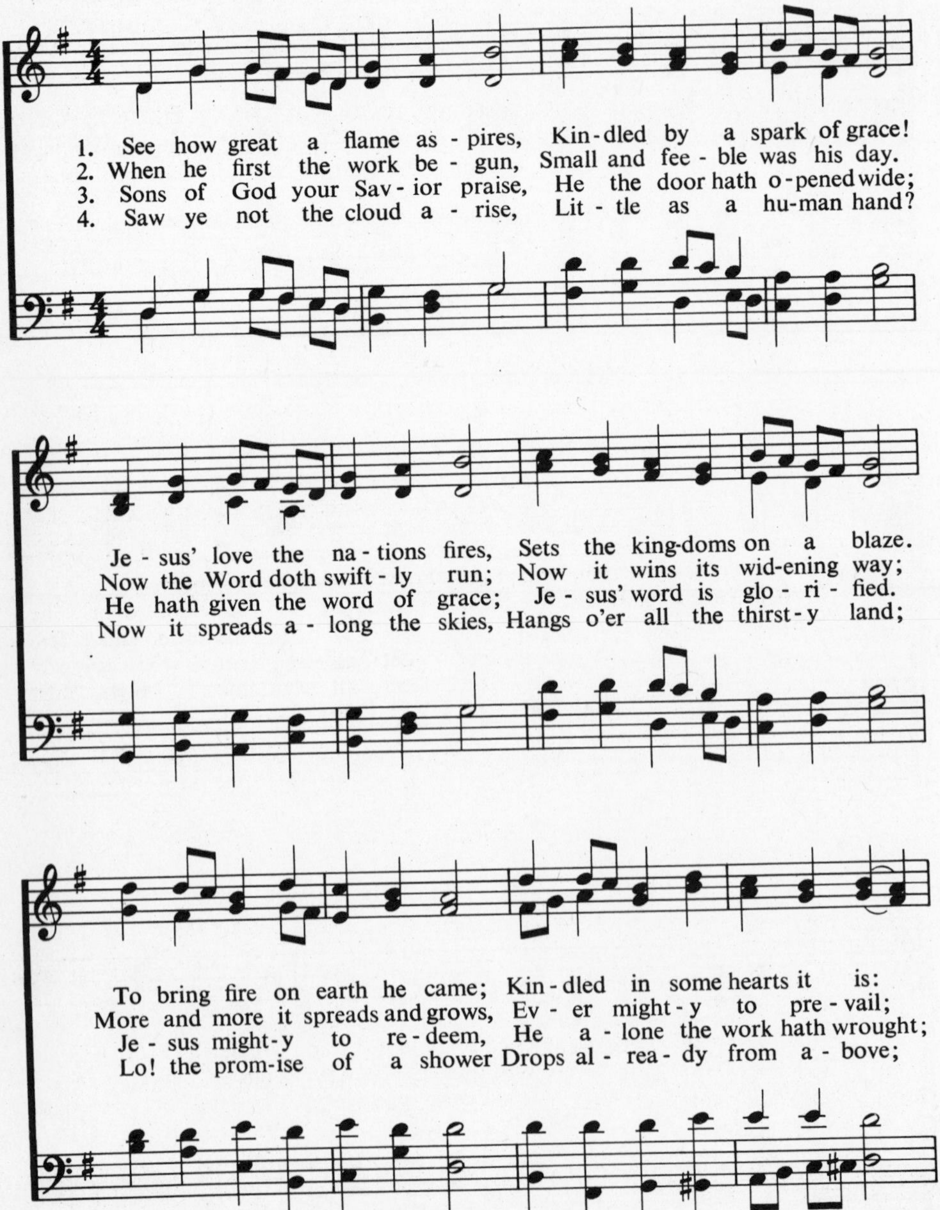

1. See how great a flame as - pires, Kin-dled by a spark of grace!
2. When he first the work be - gun, Small and fee - ble was his day.
3. Sons of God your Sav - ior praise, He the door hath o-pened wide;
4. Saw ye not the cloud a - rise, Lit - tle as a hu-man hand?
Je - sus' love the na - tions fires, Sets the king-doms on a blaze.
Now the Word doth swift - ly run; Now it wins its wid-ening way;
He hath given the word of grace; Je - sus' word is glo - ri - fied.
Now it spreads a - long the skies, Hangs o'er all the thirst - y land;
To bring fire on earth he came; Kin - dled in some hearts it is:
More and more it spreads and grows, Ev - er might - y to pre - vail;
Je - sus might - y to re - deem, He a - lone the work hath wrought;
Lo! the prom-ise of a shower Drops al - rea - dy from a - bove;

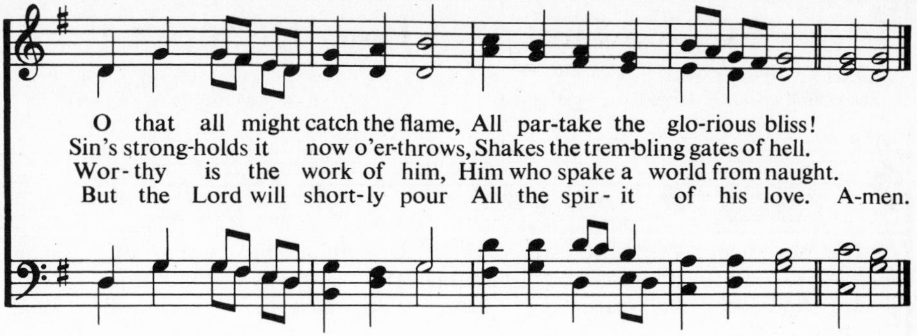
O that all might catch the flame, All par-take the glo-rious bliss!
Sin's strong-holds it now o'er-throws, Shakes the trem-bling gates of hell.
Wor-thy is the work of him, Him who spake a world from naught.
But the Lord will short-ly pour All the spir-it of his love. A-men.

465

Father, in Whom We Live

CHARLES WESLEY, 1707-1788

ST. BRIDE SM
SAMUEL HOWARD, 1710-1782

1. Fa-ther, in whom we live, In whom we are, and move, The
2. In-car-nate De-i-ty, Let all the ran-somed race Ren-
3. Spir-it of ho-li-ness, Let all thy saints a-dore Thy
4. E-ter-nal, Tri-une Lord, Let all the hosts a-bove, Let

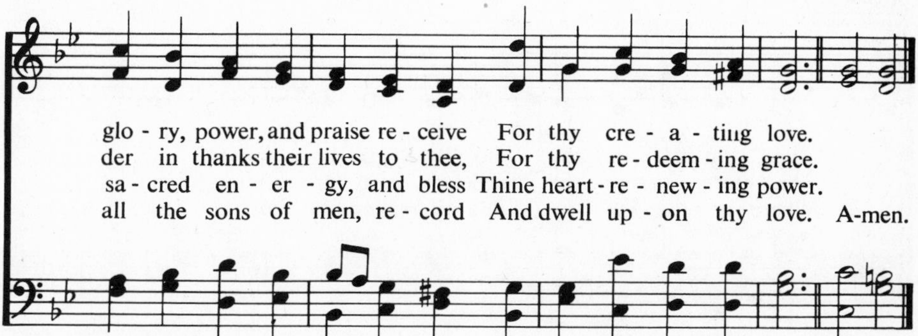
glo-ry, power, and praise re-ceive For thy cre-a-ting love.
der in thanks their lives to thee, For thy re-deem-ing grace.
sa-cred en-er-gy, and bless Thine heart-re-new-ing power.
all the sons of men, re-cord And dwell up-on thy love. A-men.

466

Come Down, O Love Divine

Bianco da Siena, d. 1434
Trans. by Richard F. Littledale, 1833-1890

DOWN AMPNEY 6 6 11.D.
R. Vaughan Williams, 1872-1958

1. Come down, O Love di - vine, Seek thou this soul of mine,
2. O let it free - ly burn, Till earth - ly pas - sions turn
3. And so the yearn - ing strong, With which the soul will long,
And vis - it it with thine own ar - dor glow - ing;
To dust and ash - es in its heat con - sum - ing;
Shall far out - pass the power of hu - man tell - ing;
O Com - fort - er, draw near, With - in my heart ap - pear,
And let thy glo - rious light Shine ev - er on my sight,
For none can guess its grace, Till he be - come the place
And kin - dle it, thy ho - ly flame be - stow - ing.
And clothe me round the while my path il - lum - ing.
Where - in the Ho - ly Spir - it makes his dwell - ing. A - men.

Music from *The English Hymnal* by permission of Oxford University Press.

PENTECOST SEASON

Come, Holy Ghost, Our Souls Inspire

Attr. to RHABANUS MAURUS, c. 776-856
Trans. by JOHN COSIN, 1594-1672

VENI CREATOR LM
Plainsong, *Vesperale Romanum*, Mechlin, 1848

Unison
1. Come, Ho - ly Ghost, our souls in - spire, And light - en with ce -
2. Thy bless - ed unc - tion from a - bove Is com - fort, life, and
3. A - noint and cheer our soil - ed face With the a - bun - dance
4. Teach us to know the Fa - ther, Son, And Thee, of both, to
les - tial fire; Thou the a - noint - ing Spir - it art,
fire of love; En - a - ble with per - pet - ual light
of thy grace; Keep far our foes; give peace at home;
be but One; That through the a - ges all a - long
After last stanza
Who dost thy seven-fold gifts im - part.
The dull - ness of our blind - ed sight.
Where thou art guide, no ill can come.
This, this may be our end - less song: Praise to thy e -
ter - nal mer - it, Fa - ther, Son, and Ho - ly Spir - it. A - men.

The Lord Will Come and Not Be Slow

OLD 107TH CMD

PSALMS 85, 82, 86 — *Genevan Psalter*, 1547

JOHN MILTON, 1608-1674 — Harm. adapt. from CLAUDE GOUDIMEL, c. 1514-1572

1. The Lord will come and not be slow, His foot-steps can-not err;
2. Sure-ly to such as do him fear Sal-va-tion is at hand!
3. The na-tions all whom thou hast made Shall come, and all shall frame
Be-fore him righ-teous-ness shall go, His roy-al har-bin-ger.
And glo-ry shall ere long ap-pear To dwell with-in our land.
To bow them low be-fore thee, Lord, And glo-ri-fy thy name.
Truth from the earth, like to a flower, Shall bud and blos-som then; And
Rise, God, judge thou the earth in might, This wick-ed earth re-dress; For
For great thou art, and won-ders great By thy strong hand are done: Thou
jus-tice, from her heaven-ly bower, Look down on mor-tal men.
thou art he who shall by right The na-tions all pos-sess.
in thy ev-er-last-ing seat Re-main-est God a-lone. A-men.

Father Eternal, Ruler of Creation

GENEVA 124 11 10.11 10.10.

LAURENCE HOUSMAN, 1865-1959

Genevan Psalter, 1551

Unison
1. Fa-ther e - ter - nal, Rul - er of cre - a - tion, Spir - it of
2. Rac - es and peo - ples, lo, we stand di - vid - ed, And shar - ing
3. En - vious of heart, blind-eyed, with tongues con-found-ed, Na - tion by
4. How shall we love thee, ho - ly, hid - den Be - ing, If we love
life, which moved ere form was made, Through the thick dark - ness
not our griefs, no joy can share; By wars and tu - mults
na - tion still goes un - for - given; In wrath and fear, by
not the world which thou hast made? O give us broth - er
cov - ering ev - ery na - tion, Light to man's blind-ness, O be thou our
love is mocked, de - rid - ed, His con-quering cross no king-dom wills to
jeal - ous - ies sur - round - ed, Build - ing proud towers which shall not reach to
love for bet - ter see - ing Thy Word made flesh, and in a man - ger
aid: Thy king - dom come, O Lord, thy will be done.
bear: Thy king - dom come, O Lord, thy will be done.
heaven: Thy king - dom come, O Lord, thy will be done.
laid: Thy king - dom come, O Lord, thy will be done. A - men.

470

God of Grace and God of Glory

CWM RHONDDA 87.87.87.

HARRY EMERSON FOSDICK, 1878- | JOHN HUGHES, 1873-1932

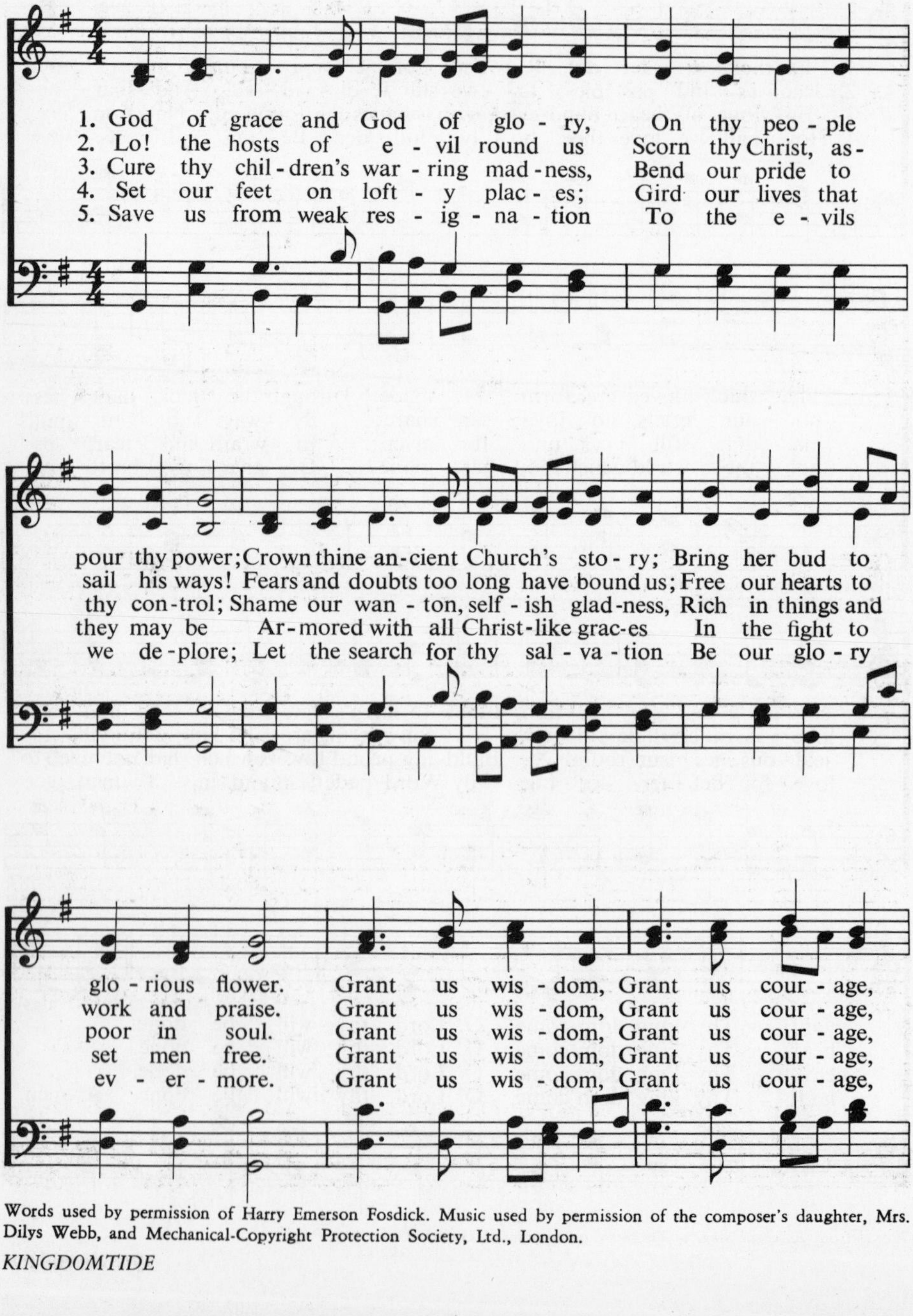
1. God of grace and God of glo - ry, On thy peo - ple
2. Lo! the hosts of e - vil round us Scorn thy Christ, as-
3. Cure thy chil - dren's war - ring mad - ness, Bend our pride to
4. Set our feet on loft - y plac - es; Gird our lives that
5. Save us from weak res - ig - na - tion To the e - vils
pour thy power; Crown thine an - cient Church's sto - ry; Bring her bud to
sail his ways! Fears and doubts too long have bound us; Free our hearts to
thy con - trol; Shame our wan - ton, self - ish glad - ness, Rich in things and
they may be Ar - mored with all Christ - like grac - es In the fight to
we de - plore; Let the search for thy sal - va - tion Be our glo - ry
glo - rious flower. Grant us wis - dom, Grant us cour - age,
work and praise. Grant us wis - dom, Grant us cour - age,
poor in soul. Grant us wis - dom, Grant us cour - age,
set men free. Grant us wis - dom, Grant us cour - age,
ev - er - more. Grant us wis - dom, Grant us cour - age,

KINGDOMTIDE

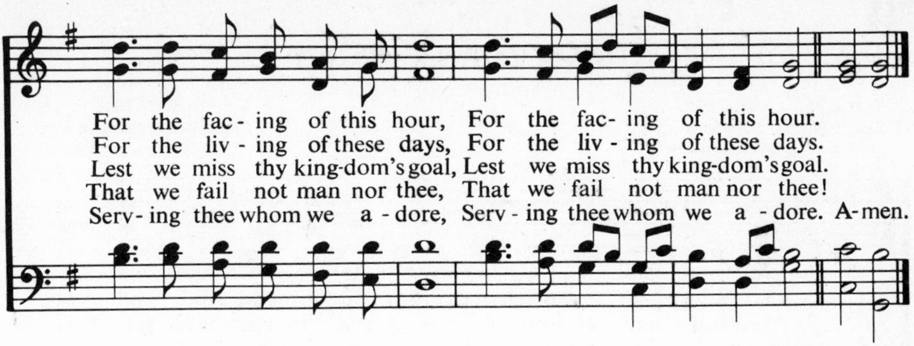
For the fac - ing of this hour, For the fac - ing of this hour.
For the liv - ing of these days, For the liv - ing of these days.
Lest we miss thy king-dom's goal, Lest we miss thy king-dom's goal.
That we fail not man nor thee, That we fail not man nor thee!
Serv - ing thee whom we a - dore, Serv - ing thee whom we a - dore. A - men.

471

Eternal Son, Eternal Love

HEBRON LM

Charles Wesley, 1707-1788

Lowell Mason, 1792-1872

1. E - ter - nal Son, e - ter - nal Love, Take
2. The tri - umphs of thy love dis - play; In
3. Spir - it of grace and health and power, Foun -
4. In - flame our hearts with per - fect love; In
to thy - self thy might - y power; Let all earth's sons thy
ev - ery heart reign thou a - lone, Till all thy foes con -
tain of light and love be - low, A - broad thy heal - ing
us the work of faith ful - fill, So not heaven's host shall
mer - cy prove; Let all thy sav - ing grace a - dore.
fess thy sway, And glo - ry ends what grace be - gun.
in-fluence shower, O'er all the na - tions let it flow.
swift - er move Than we on earth, to do thy will. A - men.

Jesus Shall Reign

PSALM 72
ISAAC WATTS, 1674-1748

DUKE STREET LM
JOHN HATTON, d. 1793

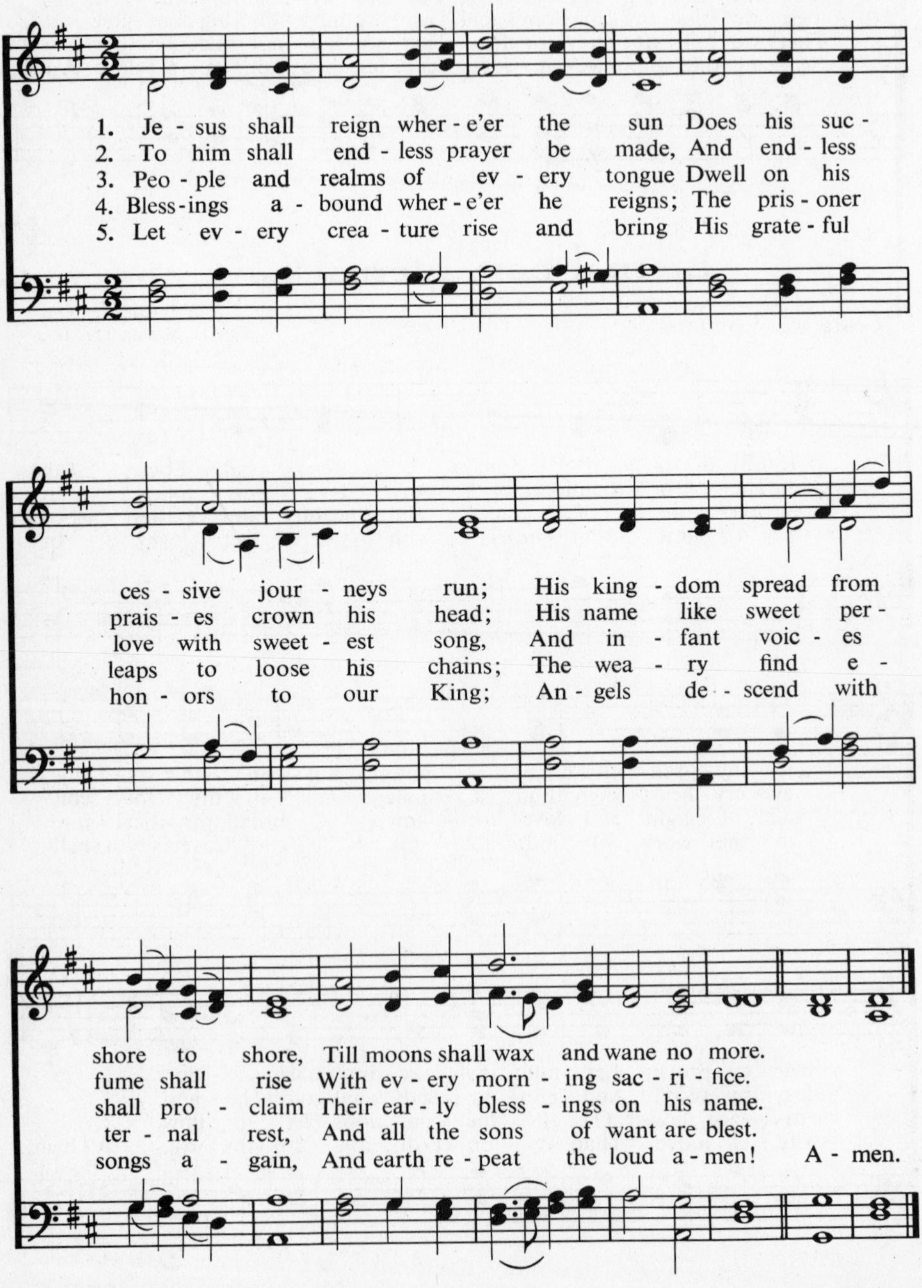
1. Je - sus shall reign wher - e'er the sun Does his suc -
2. To him shall end - less prayer be made, And end - less
3. Peo - ple and realms of ev - ery tongue Dwell on his
4. Bless - ings a - bound wher - e'er he reigns; The pris - oner
5. Let ev - ery crea - ture rise and bring His grate - ful
ces - sive jour - neys run; His king - dom spread from
prais - es crown his head; His name like sweet per -
love with sweet - est song, And in - fant voic - es
leaps to loose his chains; The wea - ry find e -
hon - ors to our King; An - gels de - scend with
shore to shore, Till moons shall wax and wane no more.
fume shall rise With ev - ery morn - ing sac - ri - fice.
shall pro - claim Their ear - ly bless - ings on his name.
ter - nal rest, And all the sons of want are blest.
songs a - gain, And earth re - peat the loud a - men! A - men.

O Worship the King

PSALM 104
ROBERT GRANT, 1779-1838

LYONS 10 10.11 11.
Adapt. from JOHANN MICHAEL HAYDN, 1737-1806

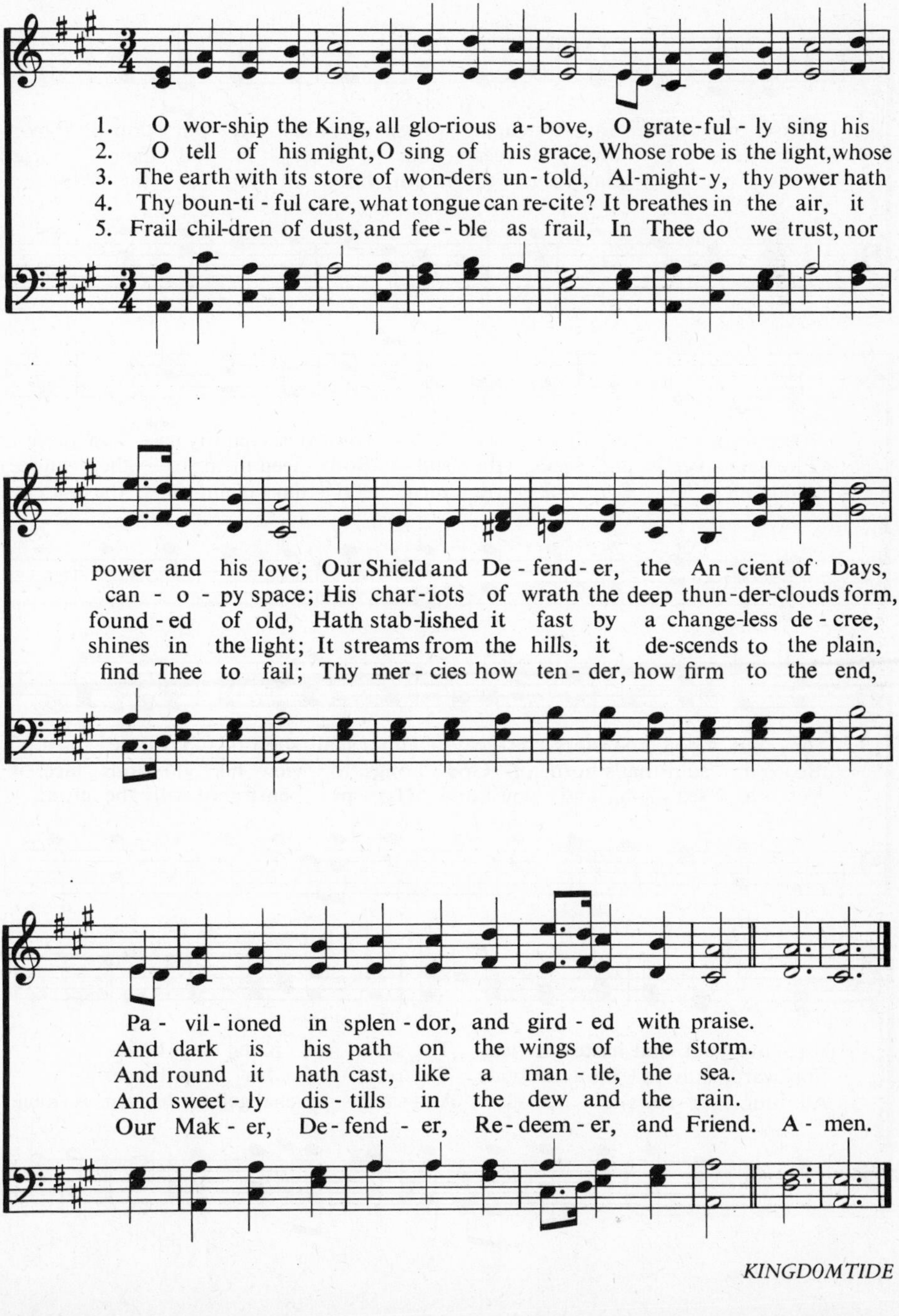
1. O wor-ship the King, all glo-rious a - bove, O grate-ful - ly sing his
2. O tell of his might, O sing of his grace, Whose robe is the light, whose
3. The earth with its store of won-ders un - told, Al-might - y, thy power hath
4. Thy boun-ti - ful care, what tongue can re-cite? It breathes in the air, it
5. Frail chil-dren of dust, and fee - ble as frail, In Thee do we trust, nor
power and his love; Our Shield and De - fend - er, the An - cient of Days,
can - o - py space; His char - iots of wrath the deep thun - der-clouds form,
found - ed of old, Hath stab-lished it fast by a change-less de - cree,
shines in the light; It streams from the hills, it de-scends to the plain,
find Thee to fail; Thy mer - cies how ten - der, how firm to the end,
Pa - vil - ioned in splen - dor, and gird - ed with praise.
And dark is his path on the wings of the storm.
And round it hath cast, like a man - tle, the sea.
And sweet - ly dis - tills in the dew and the rain.
Our Mak - er, De - fend - er, Re - deem - er, and Friend. A - men.

Rise, My Soul

AMSTERDAM 76.76.77.76.

ROBERT SEAGRAVE, 1693-1759 *Foundery Collection*, 1742

1. Rise, my soul, and stretch thy wings, Thy bet - ter por - tion trace;
2. Riv - ers to the o - cean run, Nor stay in all their course;
3. Cease, ye pil - grims, cease to mourn, Press on - ward to the prize;
Rise from tran - si - to - ry things Toward heaven, thy na - tive place.
Fire as - cend - ing seeks the sun; Both speed them to their source:
Soon our Sav - ior will re - turn, Tri - um - phant in the skies:
Sun and moon and stars de - cay; Time shall soon this earth re - move;
So a soul that's born of God Longs to view his glo - rious face,
Yet a sea - son, and you know Hap - py en - trance will be given,
Rise, my soul, and haste a - way To seats pre - pared a - bove.
For - ward tends to his a - bode, To rest in his em - brace.
All our sor - rows left be - low, And earth ex - changed for heaven. A - men.

KINGDOMTIDE

Turn Back, O Man

GENEVA 124 10 10.10 10.10.

Clifford Bax, 1886-1962

Genevan Psalter, 1551

Unison
1. Turn back, O man, for-swear thy fool-ish ways. Old now is
2. Earth might be fair and all men glad and wise. Age af-ter
3. Earth shall be fair, and all her peo-ple one; Nor till that
earth, and none may count her days; Yet thou, her child, whose
age their trag-ic em-pires rise, Built while they dream, and
hour shall God's whole will be done. Now, e-ven now, once
head is crowned with flame, Still wilt not hear thine in-ner God pro-
in that dream-ing weep; Would man but wake from out his haunt-ed
more from earth to sky, Peals forth in joy man's old un-daunt-ed
claim: "Turn back, O man, for-swear thy fool-ish ways!"
sleep, Earth might be fair and all men glad and wise.
cry: "Earth shall be fair, and all her folk be one!" A-men.

Words used by permission of A. D. Peters.

Eternal God, Whose Power Upholds

HALIFAX CMD
GEORGE FREDERICK HANDEL, 1685-1759
Harm. by A. C. L.

HENRY H. TWEEDY, 1868-1953

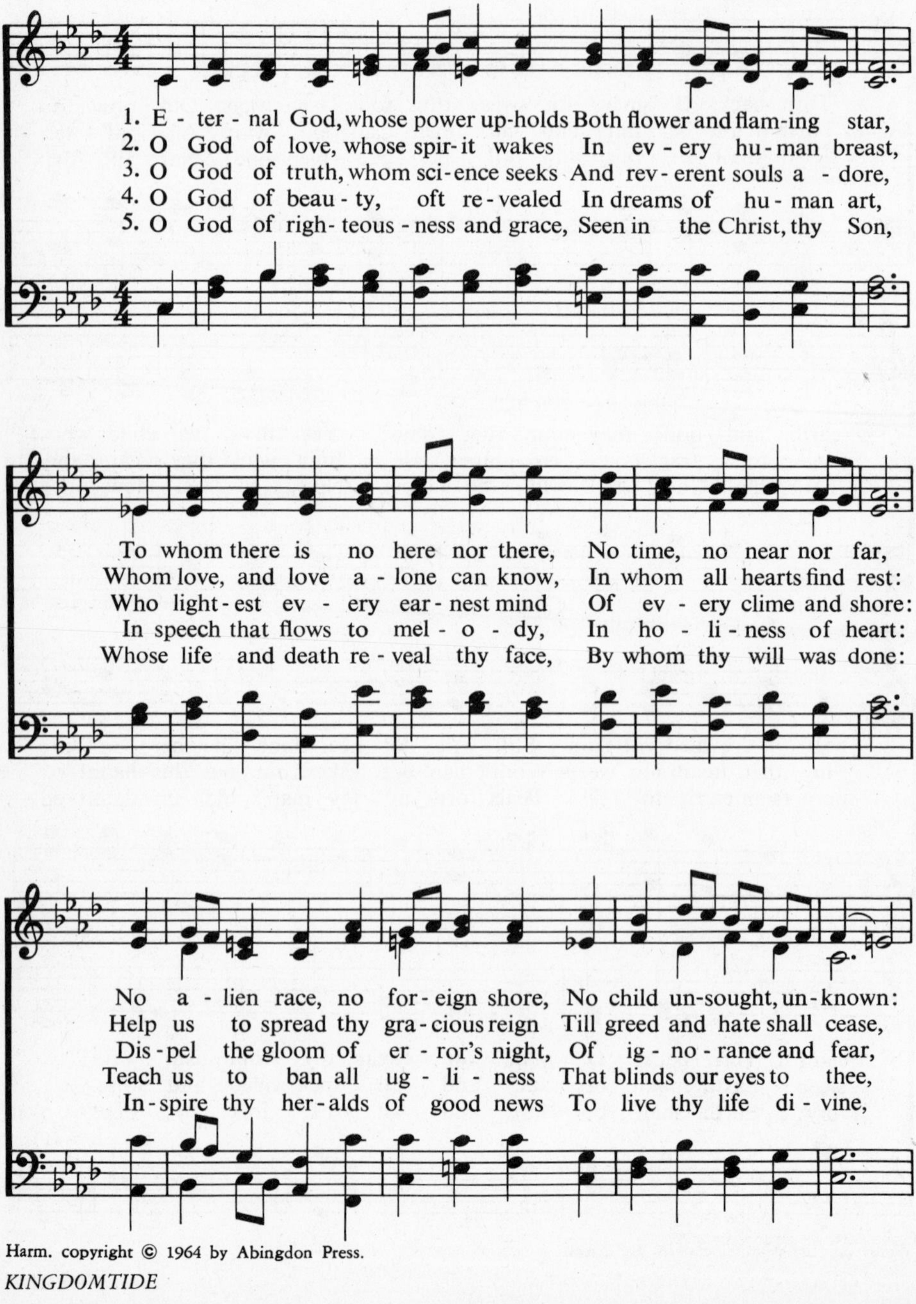
1. E - ter - nal God, whose power up-holds Both flower and flam-ing star,
2. O God of love, whose spir - it wakes In ev - ery hu - man breast,
3. O God of truth, whom sci - ence seeks And rev - erent souls a - dore,
4. O God of beau - ty, oft re - vealed In dreams of hu - man art,
5. O God of righ - teous - ness and grace, Seen in the Christ, thy Son,
To whom there is no here nor there, No time, no near nor far,
Whom love, and love a - lone can know, In whom all hearts find rest:
Who light - est ev - ery ear - nest mind Of ev - ery clime and shore:
In speech that flows to mel - o - dy, In ho - li - ness of heart:
Whose life and death re - veal thy face, By whom thy will was done:
No a - lien race, no for - eign shore, No child un-sought, un - known:
Help us to spread thy gra - cious reign Till greed and hate shall cease,
Dis - pel the gloom of er - ror's night, Of ig - no - rance and fear,
Teach us to ban all ug - li - ness That blinds our eyes to thee,
In - spire thy her - alds of good news To live thy life di - vine,

KINGDOMTIDE

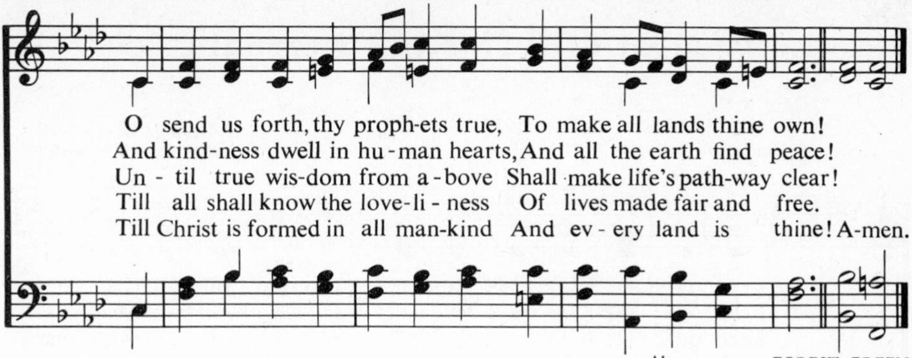
O send us forth, thy proph-ets true, To make all lands thine own!
And kind-ness dwell in hu-man hearts, And all the earth find peace!
Un-til true wis-dom from a-bove Shall make life's path-way clear!
Till all shall know the love-li-ness Of lives made fair and free.
Till Christ is formed in all man-kind And ev-ery land is thine! A-men.

Alternate tune: FOREST GREEN

477

O Day of God, Draw Nigh

ST. MICHAEL SM
Genevan Psalter, 1551

ROBERT B. Y. SCOTT, 1899- Adapt. by WILLIAM CROTCH, 1775-1847

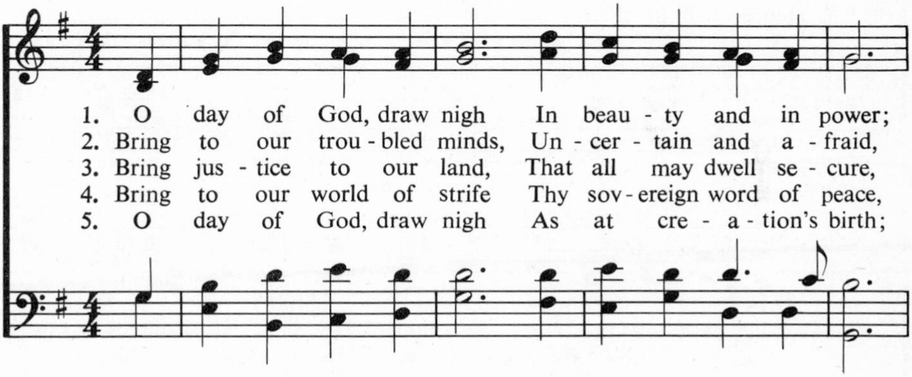
1. O day of God, draw nigh In beau-ty and in power;
2. Bring to our trou-bled minds, Un-cer-tain and a-fraid,
3. Bring jus-tice to our land, That all may dwell se-cure,
4. Bring to our world of strife Thy sov-ereign word of peace,
5. O day of God, draw nigh As at cre-a-tion's birth;

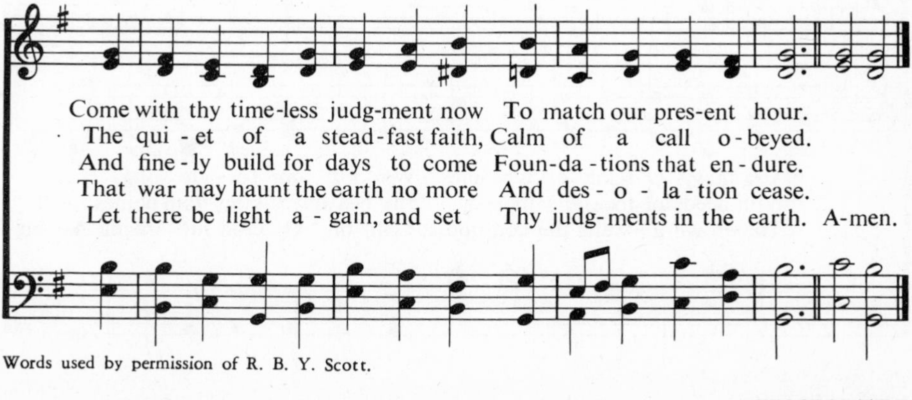
Come with thy time-less judg-ment now To match our pres-ent hour.
The qui-et of a stead-fast faith, Calm of a call o-beyed.
And fine-ly build for days to come Foun-da-tions that en-dure.
That war may haunt the earth no more And des-o-la-tion cease.
Let there be light a-gain, and set Thy judg-ments in the earth. A-men.

Words used by permission of R. B. Y. Scott.

478

Lead On, O King Eternal

LANCASHIRE 76.76.D.

ERNEST W. SHURTLEFF, 1862-1917

HENRY SMART, 1813-1879

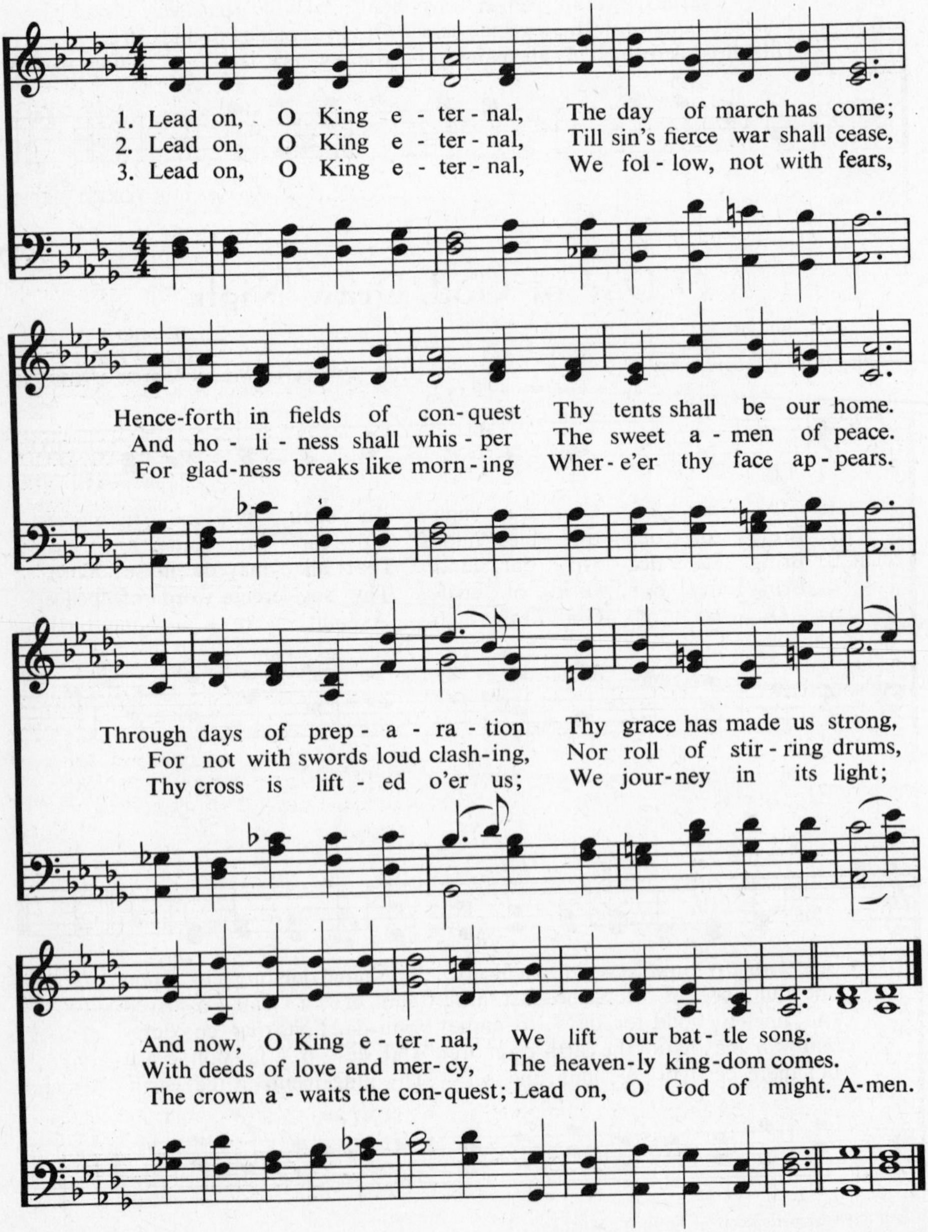
1. Lead on, O King e - ter - nal, The day of march has come;
2. Lead on, O King e - ter - nal, Till sin's fierce war shall cease,
3. Lead on, O King e - ter - nal, We fol - low, not with fears,
Hence-forth in fields of con - quest Thy tents shall be our home.
And ho - li - ness shall whis - per The sweet a - men of peace.
For glad-ness breaks like morn - ing Wher - e'er thy face ap - pears.
Through days of prep - a - ra - tion Thy grace has made us strong,
For not with swords loud clash-ing, Nor roll of stir - ring drums,
Thy cross is lift - ed o'er us; We jour-ney in its light;
And now, O King e - ter - nal, We lift our bat - tle song.
With deeds of love and mer - cy, The heaven-ly king-dom comes.
The crown a - waits the con-quest; Lead on, O God of might. A-men.

KINGDOMTIDE

Lord, Whose Love Through Humble Service

ALBERT F. BAYLY, 1901-

BEECHER 87.87.D.
JOHN ZUNDEL, 1815-1882

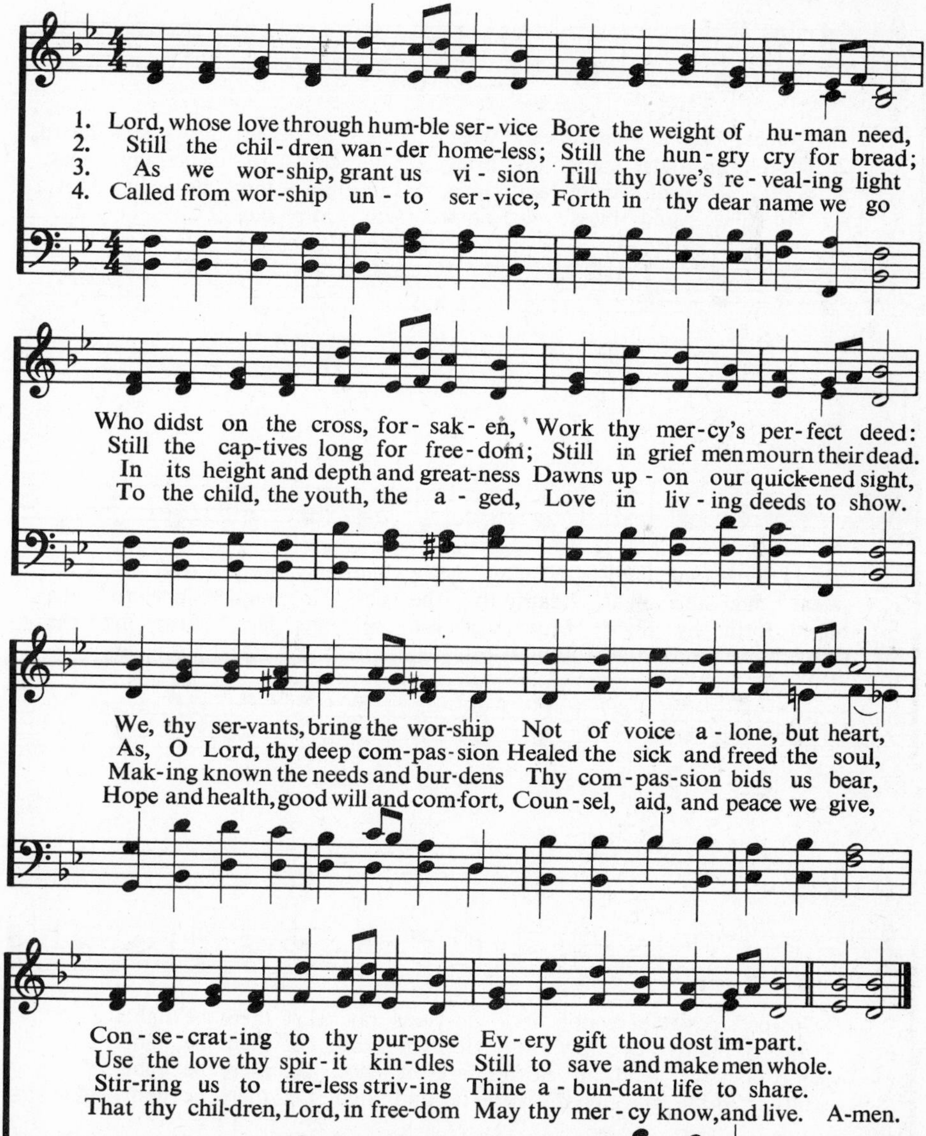
1. Lord, whose love through hum-ble ser-vice Bore the weight of hu-man need,
2. Still the chil-dren wan-der home-less; Still the hun-gry cry for bread;
3. As we wor-ship, grant us vi-sion Till thy love's re-veal-ing light
4. Called from wor-ship un-to ser-vice, Forth in thy dear name we go
Who didst on the cross, for-sak-en, Work thy mer-cy's per-fect deed:
Still the cap-tives long for free-dom; Still in grief men mourn their dead.
In its height and depth and great-ness Dawns up-on our quick-ened sight,
To the child, the youth, the a-ged, Love in liv-ing deeds to show.
We, thy ser-vants, bring the wor-ship Not of voice a-lone, but heart,
As, O Lord, thy deep com-pas-sion Healed the sick and freed the soul,
Mak-ing known the needs and bur-dens Thy com-pas-sion bids us bear,
Hope and health, good will and com-fort, Coun-sel, aid, and peace we give,
Con-se-crat-ing to thy pur-pose Ev-ery gift thou dost im-part.
Use the love thy spir-it kin-dles Still to save and make men whole.
Stir-ring us to tire-less striv-ing Thine a-bun-dant life to share.
That thy chil-dren, Lord, in free-dom May thy mer-cy know, and live. A-men.

Thou, Whose Almighty Word

GENESIS 1:1-4
JOHN MARRIOTT, 1780-1825

DORT 664.6664.
LOWELL MASON, 1792-1872

1. Thou, whose al - might - y Word Cha - os and dark - ness heard,
2. Thou who didst come to bring, On thy re - deem - ing wing,
3. Spir - it of truth and love, Life - giv - ing, ho - ly Dove,
4. Ho - ly and bless - ed Three, Glo - ri - ous Trin - i - ty,
And took their flight: Hear us, we hum - bly pray, And where the
Heal - ing and sight, Health to the sick in mind, Sight to the
Speed forth thy flight; Move o'er the wa - ters' face, Bear - ing the
Grace, Love, and Might! Bound-less as o-cean's tide Roll - ing in
Gos-pel's day Sheds not its glo-rious ray, Let there be light!
in - ly blind: O now, to all man-kind, Let there be light!
lamp of grace; And in earth's dark-est place, Let there be light!
full - est pride, Through the world far and wide, Let there be light! A-men.

KINGDOMTIDE

O Holy City, Seen of John

MORNING SONG 86.86.86.

REVELATION 22:1-5 — WYETH'S *Repository of Sacred Music, Part Second,* 1813

WALTER RUSSELL BOWIE, 1882- — Harm. by A. C. L.

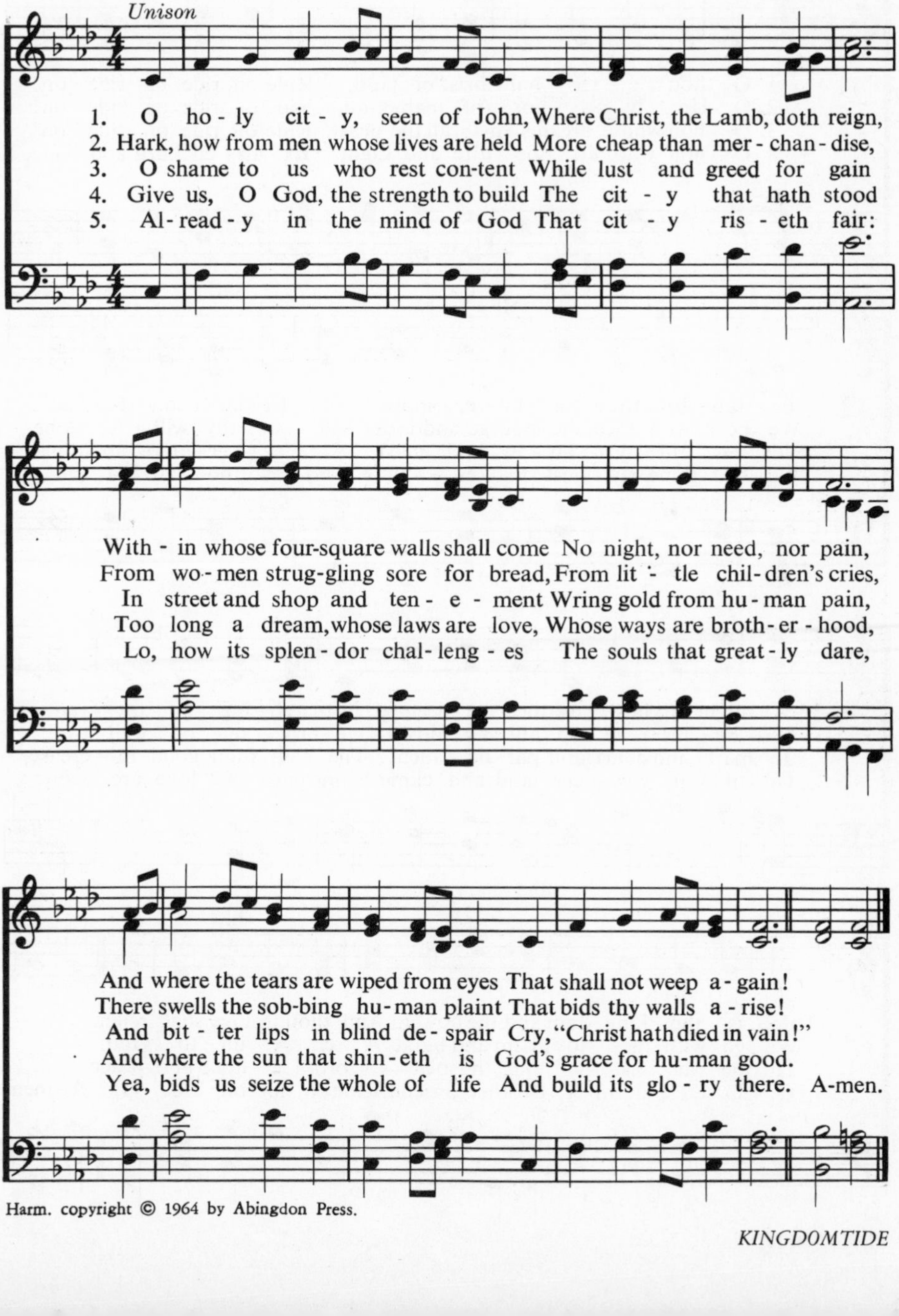
Unison
1. O ho-ly cit-y, seen of John, Where Christ, the Lamb, doth reign,
2. Hark, how from men whose lives are held More cheap than mer-chan-dise,
3. O shame to us who rest con-tent While lust and greed for gain
4. Give us, O God, the strength to build The cit-y that hath stood
5. Al-read-y in the mind of God That cit-y ris-eth fair:
With-in whose four-square walls shall come No night, nor need, nor pain,
From wo-men strug-gling sore for bread, From lit-tle chil-dren's cries,
In street and shop and ten-e-ment Wring gold from hu-man pain,
Too long a dream, whose laws are love, Whose ways are broth-er-hood,
Lo, how its splen-dor chal-leng-es The souls that great-ly dare,
And where the tears are wiped from eyes That shall not weep a-gain!
There swells the sob-bing hu-man plaint That bids thy walls a-rise!
And bit-ter lips in blind de-spair Cry, "Christ hath died in vain!"
And where the sun that shin-eth is God's grace for hu-man good.
Yea, bids us seize the whole of life And build its glo-ry there. A-men.

482

O Thou Eternal Christ of God

LLANGLOFFAN CMD
Trad. Welsh Melody
Hymnau a Thonau, 1865

CALVIN W. LAUFER, 1874-1938

1. O thou e - ter - nal Christ of God, Ride on, ride on, ride on!
2. O Ho - ly Sav - ior of man-kind, Ride on, ride on, ride on!
3. O Thou whose dreams en-thrall the heart, Ride on, ride on, ride on!
4. O Thou who art the Life and Light, Ex - alt - ed Lord and King,
Es - tab - lish thou for - ev - er - more The tri - umph now be - gun.
We bear with thee the scourge and cross If so thy will is done.
Ride on till tyr - an - ny and greed Are ev - er - more un - done.
We hail thine au - gust maj - es - ty And loud ho - san - na sing,
A might - y host, by thee re - deemed, Is march - ing in thy train;
And be the road up - hill or down, Un - bro - ken or well trod,
In mart and court and par - lia - ment The com - mon good in - crease,
Un - til in ev - ery land and clime Thine ends of love are won:
Thine is the king - dom and the power, And thou in love shalt reign.
We go with thee to claim and build A cit - y un - to God.
Till men at last shall ring the bells Of broth - er - hood and peace.
O Christ, Re - deem - er, Broth - er, Friend, Ride on, ride on, ride on! A - men.

KINGDOMTIDE

Rejoice, the Lord Is King

Philippians 4:4
Charles Wesley, 1707-1788

DARWALL'S 148th 66.66.88.
John Darwall, 1731-1789

1. Re-joice, the Lord is King! Your Lord and King a-dore!
2. Je-sus, the Sav-ior, reigns, The God of truth and love;
3. His king-dom can-not fail, He rules o'er earth and heaven;
4. Re-joice in glo-rious hope! Our Lord the judge shall come,
Re-joice, give thanks, and sing, And tri-umph
When he had purged our stains, He took his
The keys of death and hell Are to our
And take his ser-vants up To their e-
ev-er-more: Lift up your heart, lift up your voice!
seat a-bove: Lift up your heart, lift up your voice!
Je-sus given: Lift up your heart, lift up your voice!
ter-nal home: Lift up your heart, lift up your voice!
Re-joice, a-gain I say, re-joice!
Re-joice, a-gain I say, re-joice!
Re-joice, a-gain I say, re-joice!
Re-joice, a-gain I say, re-joice! A-men.

O God of Earth and Altar

KING'S LYNN 76.76.D.
Trad. English Melody

GILBERT K. CHESTERTON, 1874-1936

Arr. by R. VAUGHAN WILLIAMS, 1872-1958

Unison
1. O God of earth and al - tar, Bow down and hear our cry;
2. From all that ter - ror teach - es, From lies of tongue and pen,
3. Tie in a liv - ing teth - er The prince and priest and thrall;
Our earth - ly rul - ers fal - ter, Our peo - ple drift and die;
From all the eas - y speech - es That com - fort cru - el men,
Bind all our lives to - geth - er, Smite us and save us all;
The walls of gold en - tomb us, The swords of scorn di - vide;
From sale and prof - a - na - tion Of hon - or and the sword,
In ire and ex - ul - ta - tion A - flame with faith, and free,
Take not thy thun - der from us, But take a - way our pride.
From sleep and from dam - na - tion, De - liv - er us, good Lord!
Lift up a liv - ing na - tion, A sin - gle sword to thee. A-men.

Alternate tune: LLANGLOFFAN

KINGDOMTIDE

From Thee All Skill and Science Flow

CHARLES KINGSLEY, 1819-1875

MASSACHUSETTS CMD
KATHERINE K. DAVIS, 1892-

Unison
1. From thee all skill and sci-ence flow, All pit - y, care, and love,
2. And has-ten, Lord, that per-fect day When pain and death shall cease,
All calm and cour-age, faith and hope: O pour them from a - bove;
And thy just rule shall fill the earth With health and light and peace,
And part them, Lord, to each and all, As each and all shall need,
When-ev - er blue the sky shall gleam, And ev - er green the sod,
To rise like in-cense, each to thee, In no-ble thought and deed.
And man's rude work de-face no more The par - a - dise of God. A-men.

Alternate tune: GRÄFENBERG

O God, Before Whose Altar

LLANGLOFFAN 76.86.D.
Trad. Welsh Melody
Hymnau a Thonau, 1865

P. H. B. Lyon, 1893-

1. O God, be - fore whose al - tar The stars like ta - pers burn,
2. Those who give up life's boun - ty To serve a race to be,
3. All those op-pressed or lone - ly Or long at strife with pain,
4. O Lord, be ours the glo - ry Be - yond all earth-ly fame,
At whose in - scru - ta - ble de - cree The plan - ets wheel and turn:
Whose bones lie white a - long the trail Which leads the world to thee;
Who face the dark-ness un - dis - mayed And turn their loss to gain,
Like those to con - quer for thy sake De - spair and doubt and shame,
Though earth and sea and heav - en U - nite thy praise to sing,
Those who, when fears be - set them, Stand fast and fight and die:
Those who with love and meek - ness Out - last the years of wrong:
Till through a world made no - ble, Through lands from sin set free,
Man in his weak-ness yet may give A wor-thier of - fer - ing.
Their un - con - sid - ered lives go up Like in - cense to the sky.
Their si - lent cour-age pleads to heaven More el - o - quent than song.
The ar - mies of the liv - ing God Shall march to vic - to - ry. A-men.

Words used by permission of the Proprietors of Hymns Ancient and Modern.

Jesus, We Want to Meet

A. T. Olajida Olude, 1908-
Trans. by Biodun Adebesin, 1928-
Versed by A. C. L.

NIGERIA Irregular
A. T. Olajida Olude, 1908-
Harm. by M. O. Ajosè, 1912-

Unison

1. Je - sus, we want to meet On this thy ho - ly day; We gath - er
2. We kneel in awe and fear On this thy ho - ly day; Pray God to
3. Thy bless - ing, Lord, we seek On this thy ho - ly day; Give joy of
4. Our minds we ded - i - cate On this thy ho - ly day; Heart and soul
round thy throne On this thy ho - ly day. Thou art our
teach us here On this thy ho - ly day; Save us and
thy vic - to - ry On this thy ho - ly day. Through grace a - lone
con - se - crate On this thy ho - ly day. Ho - ly Spir - it,
heaven - ly Friend, Hear our prayers as they as - cend; Look in - to
cleanse our hearts, Lead and guide our acts of praise, And our faith
are we saved; In thy flock may we be found; Let the mind
make us whole; Bless the ser - mon in this place; And as
our hearts and minds to - day, On this thy ho - ly day.
from seed to flow - er raise, On this thy ho - ly day.
of Christ a - bide in us On this thy ho - ly day.
we go, lead us Lord; We shall be thine ev - er - more. A - men.

Optional drumbeat patterns 

O Day of Rest and Gladness

MENDEBRAS 76.76.D.

CHRISTOPHER WORDSWORTH, 1807-1885 Arr. by LOWELL MASON, 1792-1872

1. O day of rest and glad - ness, O day of joy and light,
2. On thee, at the cre - a - tion, The light first had its birth;
3. To - day on wea - ry na - tions The heaven - ly man - na falls;
4. New grac - es ev - er gain - ing From this our day of rest,
O balm of care and sad - ness, Most beau - ti - ful, most bright:
On thee for our sal - va - tion Christ rose from depths of earth;
To ho - ly con - vo - ca - tions The sil - ver trum - pet calls,
We reach the rest re - main - ing To spir - its of the blest.
On thee the high and low - ly, Through a - ges joined in tune,
On thee our Lord vic - to - rious The Spir - it sent from heaven,
Where Gos - pel light is glow - ing With pure and ra - diant beams,
To Ho - ly Ghost be prais - es, To Fa - ther, and to Son;
Sing ho - ly, ho - ly, ho - ly, To the great God Tri - une.
And thus on thee most glo - rious A tri - ple light was given.
And liv - ing wa - ter flow - ing With soul - re - fresh - ing streams.
The Church her voice up - rais - es To thee, blest Three in One. A - men.

Safely Through Another Week

JOHN NEWTON, 1725-1807

SABBATH 77.77.D.
Arr. by LOWELL MASON, 1792-1872

1. Safe-ly through an-oth-er week God has brought us on our way;
2. While we pray for par-doning grace, Through the dear Re-deem-er's name,
3. Here we come thy name to praise; May we feel thy pres-ence near;
4. May thy Gos-pel's joy-ful sound Con-quer sin-ners, com-fort saints;
Let us now a bless-ing seek, Wait-ing in his courts to-day:
Show thy rec-on-cil-ed face, Take a-way our sin and shame;
May thy glo-ry meet our eyes, While we in thy house ap-pear;
Make the fruits of grace a-bound, Bring re-lief for all com-plaints;
Day of all the week the best, Em-blem of e-ter-nal rest;
From our world-ly cares set free, May we rest this day in thee;
Here af-ford us, Lord, a taste Of our ev-er-last-ing feast;
Thus may all our sab-baths prove, Till we join the Church a-bove;
Day of all the week the best, Em-blem of e-ter-nal rest.
From our world-ly cares set free, May we rest this day in thee.
Here af-ford us, Lord, a taste Of our ev-er-last-ing feast.
Thus may all our sab-baths prove, Till we join the Church a-bove. A-men.

Rise to Greet the Sun

LE P'ING 55.55.D.
Chinese Folk Melody
Adapt. by HU TE-NGAI, c. 1900-
Harm. by BLISS WIANT, 1895-

CHAO TZU-CH'EN, 1888-
Trans. by BLISS WIANT, 1895-

1. Rise to greet the sun, Red-dening in the sky,
2. Fa - ther, I im - plore, Safe - ly keep this child;
3. May this day be blest; Trust-ing Je - sus' love,
War-rior - like and strong, Come - ly as a groom;
Make my con - duct good, Ac - tions calm and mild:
My heart's freed from ill, Fair blue sky's a - bove.
Birds pass high in flight, Fra - grant flowers now bloom;
Ven - er - a - ting age, Hum - bly teach - ing youth,
Glad for cot - ton coat, Plain food sat - is - fies;
With the gra - cious light I my toil re - sume.
Al - ways serv - ing thee, Shar-ing thy rich truth.
All my count - less needs Thy kind hand sup-plies. A-men.

MORNING AND EVENING

The Day Is Past and Over

DU FRIEDENSFÜRST, HERR JESU CHRIST 76.76.88.

ANONYMOUS Greek, probably 6th Century
Trans. by JOHN M. NEALE, 1818-1866

BARTHOLOMÄUS GESIUS, 1555-c. 1613
Harm. by J. S. BACH, 1685-1750

1. The day is past and o - ver; All thanks, O Lord, to
2. The joys of day are o - ver; We lift our hearts to
3. The toils of day are o - ver; We raise our hymn to
4. Be thou our souls' pre - serv - er, O God, for thou dost
thee! We pray thee that of - fense - less The
thee, And call on thee that sin - less The
thee, And ask that free from per - il The
know How man - y are the per - ils Through
hours of dark may be. O Je - sus, keep us
hours of dark may be. O Je - sus, make their
hours of dark may be. O Je - sus, keep us
which we have to go. Lov - er of men, O
in thy sight, And guard us through the com - ing night!
dark-ness light, And guard us through the com - ing night!
in thy sight, And guard us through the com - ing night!
hear our call, And guard and save us from them all! A - men.

MORNING AND EVENING

492

We Lift Our Hearts to Thee

ST. THOMAS SM

JOHN WESLEY, 1703-1791 — AARON WILLIAMS, *The New Universal Psalmodist*, 1770

1. We lift our hearts to thee, O
2. O let thine o - rient beams The
3. How beau - teous na - ture now! How
4. May we this life im - prove, To
5. To God the Fa - ther, Son, And
Day - star from on high! The sun it - self is
night of sin dis - perse, The mists of er - ror
dark and sad be - fore! With joy we view the
mourn for er - rors past; And live this short, re -
Spir - it, One in Three, Be glo - ry, as it
but thy shade, Yet cheers both earth and sky.
and of vice Which shade the u - ni - verse!
pleas - ing change, And na - ture's God a - dore.
volv - ing day As if it were our last.
was, is now, And shall for - ev - er be. A - men.

Alternate tune: MORNINGTON

All Praise to Thee, My God, This Night

TALLIS' CANON LM

THOMAS KEN, 1637-1711 — THOMAS TALLIS, c. 1505-1585

1. All praise to thee, my God, this night, For
2. For - give me, Lord, for thy dear Son, The
3. Teach me to live, that I may dread The
4. O may my soul on thee re - pose, And
5. Praise God, from whom all bless - ings flow; Praise
all the bless - ings of the light! Keep me, O keep me,
ill that I this day have done, That with the world, my -
grave as lit - tle as my bed; Teach me to die, that
with sweet sleep mine eye - lids close, Sleep that may me more
him, all crea - tures here be - low; Praise him a - bove, ye
King of kings, Be - neath thine own al - might - y wings!
self, and thee, I, ere I sleep, at peace may be.
so I may Rise glo - rious at the Judg - ment Day.
vig - orous make To serve my God when I a - wake.
heav - enly host; Praise Fa - ther, Son, and Ho - ly Ghost. A - men.

494

Softly Now the Light of Day

MERCY 77.77.

Psalm 141:2
George W. Doane, 1799-1859

Arr. from Louis M. Gottschalk, 1829-1869
by Edwin P. Parker, 1836-1925

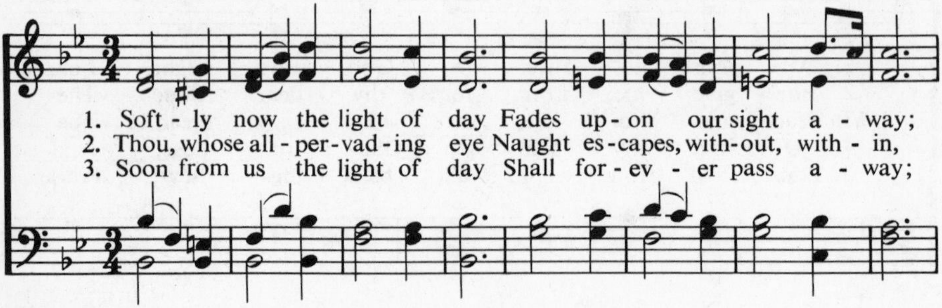
1. Soft - ly now the light of day Fades up - on our sight a - way;
2. Thou, whose all - per - vad - ing eye Naught es - capes, with - out, with - in,
3. Soon from us the light of day Shall for - ev - er pass a - way;

Free from care, from la - bor free, Lord, we would com - mune with thee.
Par - don each in - fir - mi - ty, O - pen fault, and se - cret sin.
Then, from sin and sor - row free, Take us, Lord, to dwell with thee. A - men.

495

Now the Day Is Over

MERRIAL 65.65.

Proverbs 3:24
Sabine Baring-Gould, 1834-1924

Joseph Barnby, 1838-1896

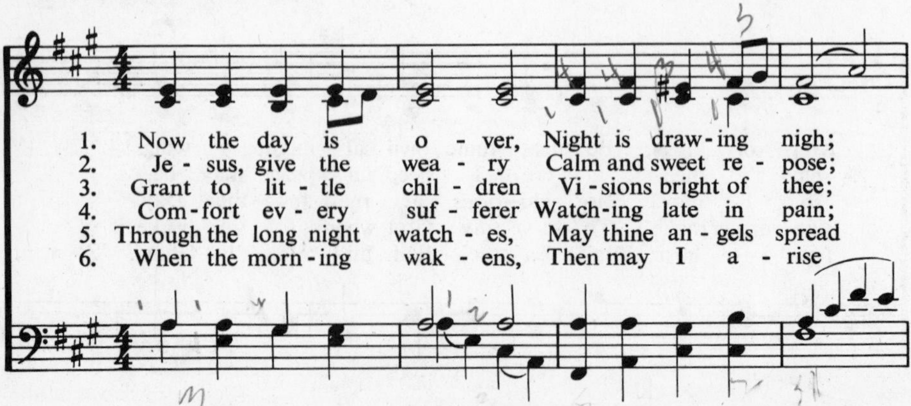
1. Now the day is o - ver, Night is draw - ing nigh;
2. Je - sus, give the wea - ry Calm and sweet re - pose;
3. Grant to lit - tle chil - dren Vi - sions bright of thee;
4. Com - fort ev - ery suf - ferer Watch - ing late in pain;
5. Through the long night watch - es, May thine an - gels spread
6. When the morn - ing wak - ens, Then may I a - rise

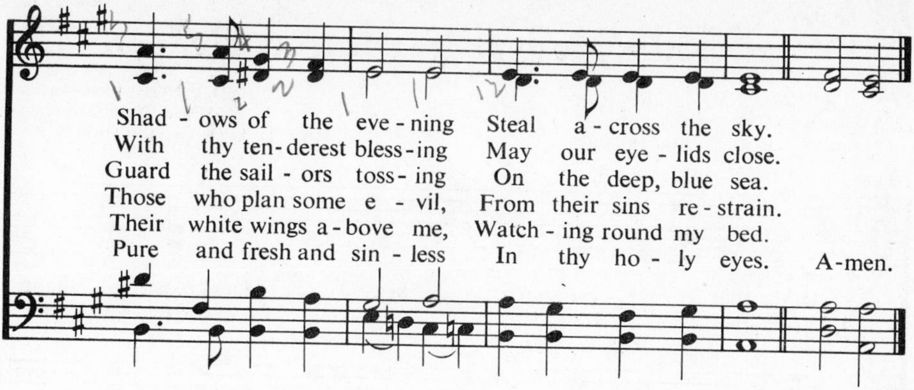
Shad - ows of the eve - ning Steal a - cross the sky.
With thy ten-derest bless - ing May our eye - lids close.
Guard the sail - ors toss - ing On the deep, blue sea.
Those who plan some e - vil, From their sins re - strain.
Their white wings a - bove me, Watch - ing round my bed.
Pure and fresh and sin - less In thy ho - ly eyes. A-men.

496

Savior, Breathe an Evening Blessing

STUTTGART 87.87.
Psalmodia Sacra, Gotha, 1715
JAMES EDMESTON, 1791-1867
Adapt. by HENRY J. GAUNTLETT, 1805-1876

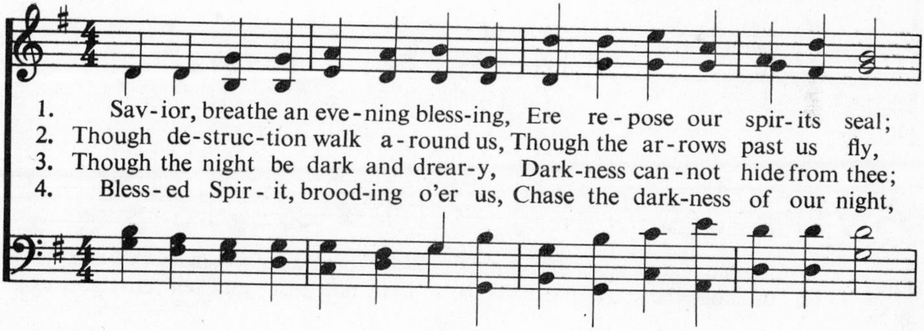
1. Sav - ior, breathe an eve - ning bless - ing, Ere re - pose our spir - its seal;
2. Though de - struc - tion walk a - round us, Though the ar - rows past us fly,
3. Though the night be dark and drear - y, Dark - ness can - not hide from thee;
4. Bless - ed Spir - it, brood - ing o'er us, Chase the dark - ness of our night,

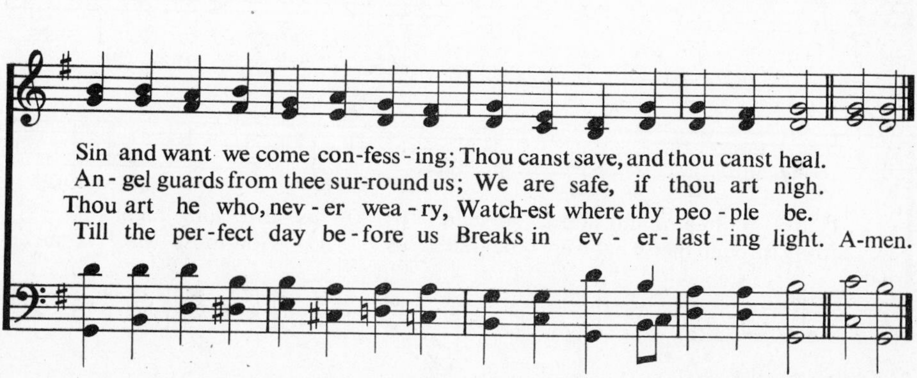
Sin and want we come con - fess - ing; Thou canst save, and thou canst heal.
An - gel guards from thee sur - round us; We are safe, if thou art nigh.
Thou art he who, nev - er wea - ry, Watch - est where thy peo - ple be.
Till the per - fect day be - fore us Breaks in ev - er - last - ing light. A-men.

497

God, That Madest Earth and Heaven

AR HYD Y NOS 84.84.888.4.

REGINALD HEBER, 1783-1826
FREDERICK LUCIAN HOSMER, 1840-1929

Trad. Welsh Melody
Harm. by L. O. EMERSON, 1820-1915

1. God, that mad - est earth and heav - en, Dark - ness and light,
2. When the con - stant sun re - turn - ing Un - seals our eyes,
Who the day for toil hast giv - en, For rest the night,
May we, born a - new like morn - ing, To la - bor rise;
May thine an - gel guards de - fend us, Slum - ber sweet thy mer - cy send us;
Gird us for the task that calls us, Let not ease and self en - thrall us,
Ho - ly dreams and hopes at - tend us, This live - long night.
Strong through thee what - e'er be - fall us, O God most wise! A - men.

At Thy Feet, Our God and Father

Psalm 65:2
James D. Burns, 1823-1864

St. Asaph 87.87.D.
William S. Bambridge, 1842-1923

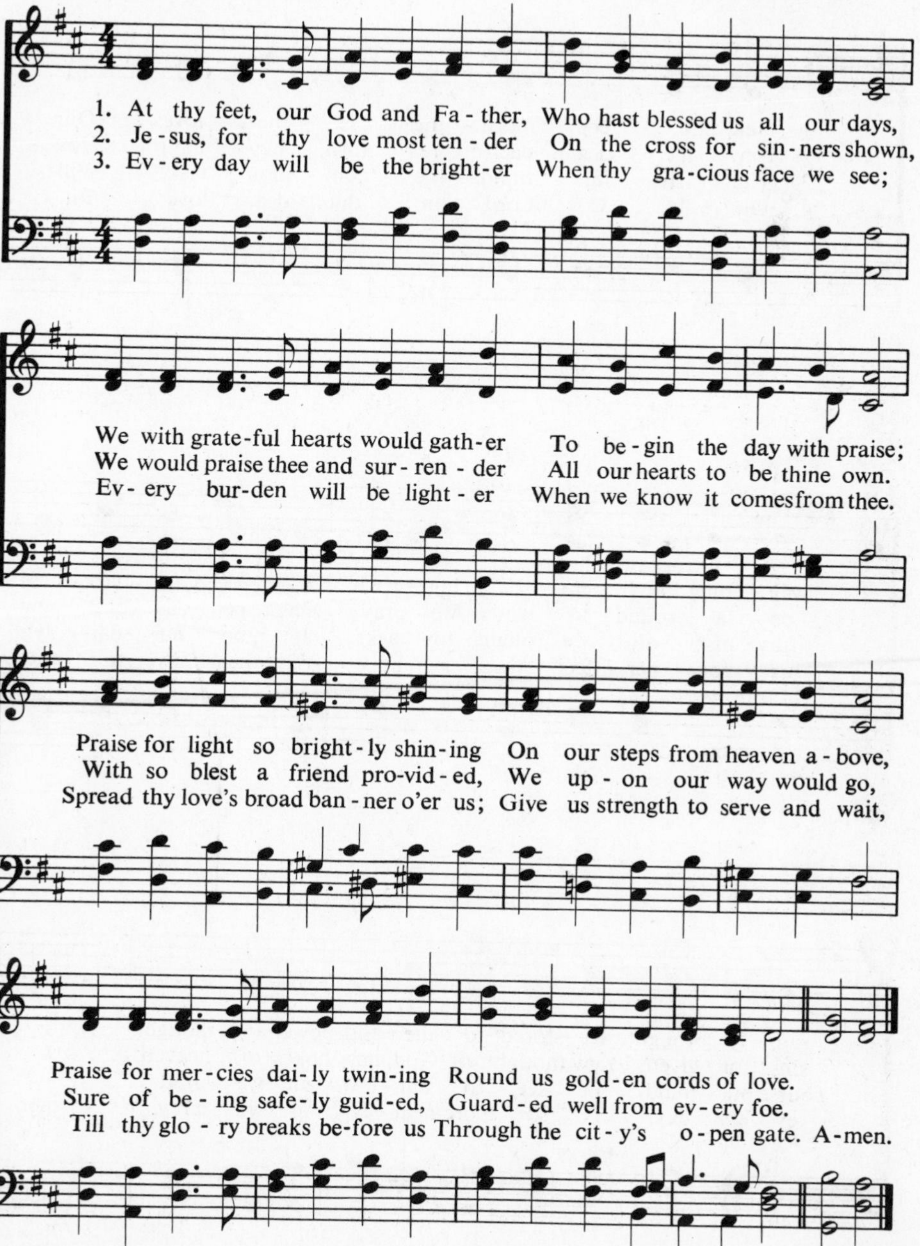
1. At thy feet, our God and Fa - ther, Who hast blessed us all our days,
2. Je - sus, for thy love most ten - der On the cross for sin - ners shown,
3. Ev - ery day will be the bright - er When thy gra - cious face we see;
We with grate - ful hearts would gath - er To be - gin the day with praise;
We would praise thee and sur - ren - der All our hearts to be thine own.
Ev - ery bur - den will be light - er When we know it comes from thee.
Praise for light so bright - ly shin - ing On our steps from heaven a - bove,
With so blest a friend pro - vid - ed, We up - on our way would go,
Spread thy love's broad ban - ner o'er us; Give us strength to serve and wait,
Praise for mer - cies dai - ly twin - ing Round us gold - en cords of love.
Sure of be - ing safe - ly guid - ed, Guard - ed well from ev - ery foe.
Till thy glo - ry breaks be - fore us Through the cit - y's o - pen gate. A - men.

MORNING AND EVENING

New Every Morning Is the Love

MELCOMBE LM
SAMUEL WEBBE, SR., 1740-1816
Rhythm alt. by A. C. L.

LAMENTATIONS 3:22-23
JOHN KEBLE, 1792-1866

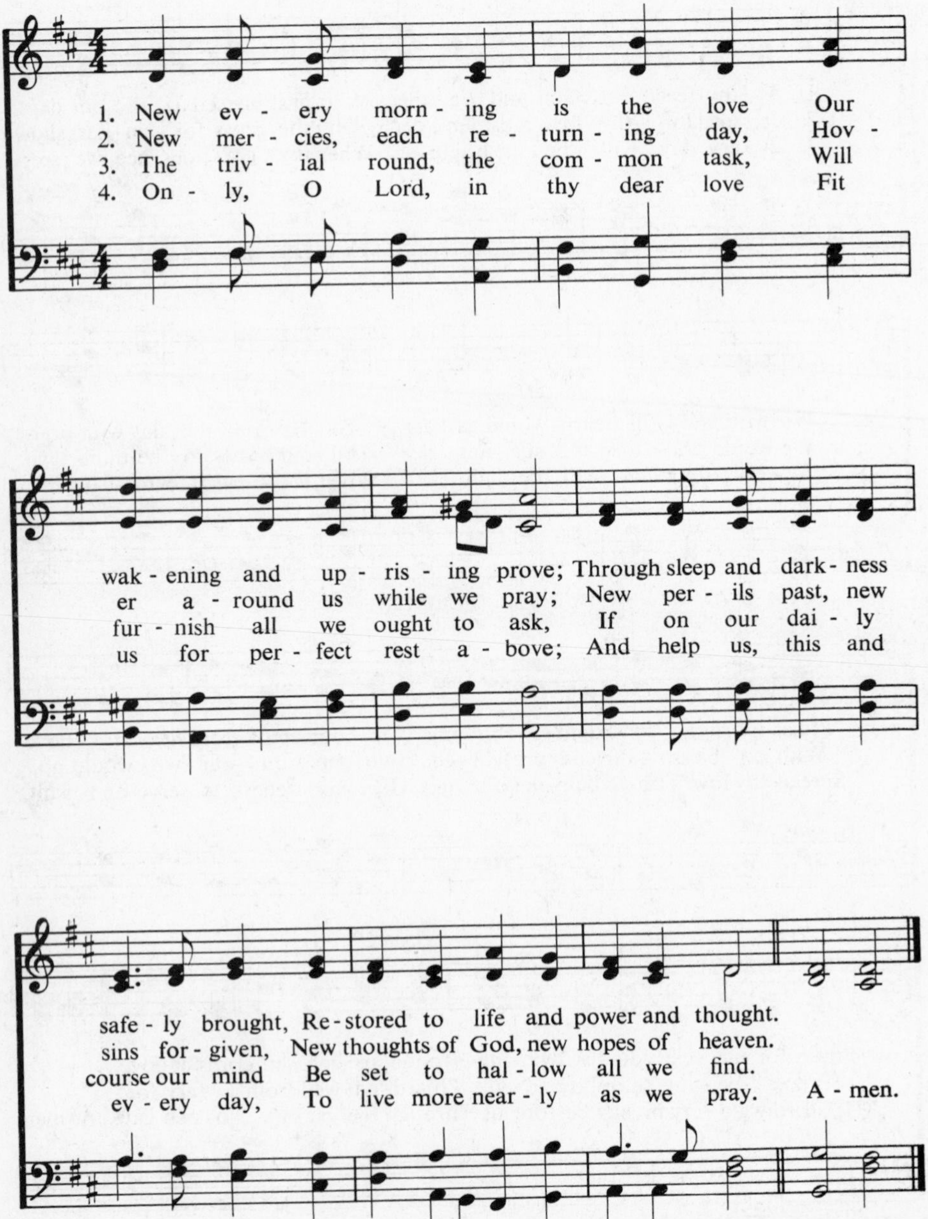
1. New ev - ery morn - ing is the love Our
2. New mer - cies, each re - turn - ing day, Hov -
3. The triv - ial round, the com - mon task, Will
4. On - ly, O Lord, in thy dear love Fit
wak - ening and up - ris - ing prove; Through sleep and dark - ness
er a - round us while we pray; New per - ils past, new
fur - nish all we ought to ask, If on our dai - ly
us for per - fect rest a - bove; And help us, this and
safe - ly brought, Re - stored to life and power and thought.
sins for - given, New thoughts of God, new hopes of heaven.
course our mind Be set to hal - low all we find.
ev - ery day, To live more near - ly as we pray. A - men.

The Day Thou Gavest, Lord, Is Ended

Psalm 113:2-3
John Ellerton, 1826-1893

COMMANDMENTS 98.98.
Genevan Psalter, 1547
Attr. to Louis Bourgeois, c. 1510-c. 1561

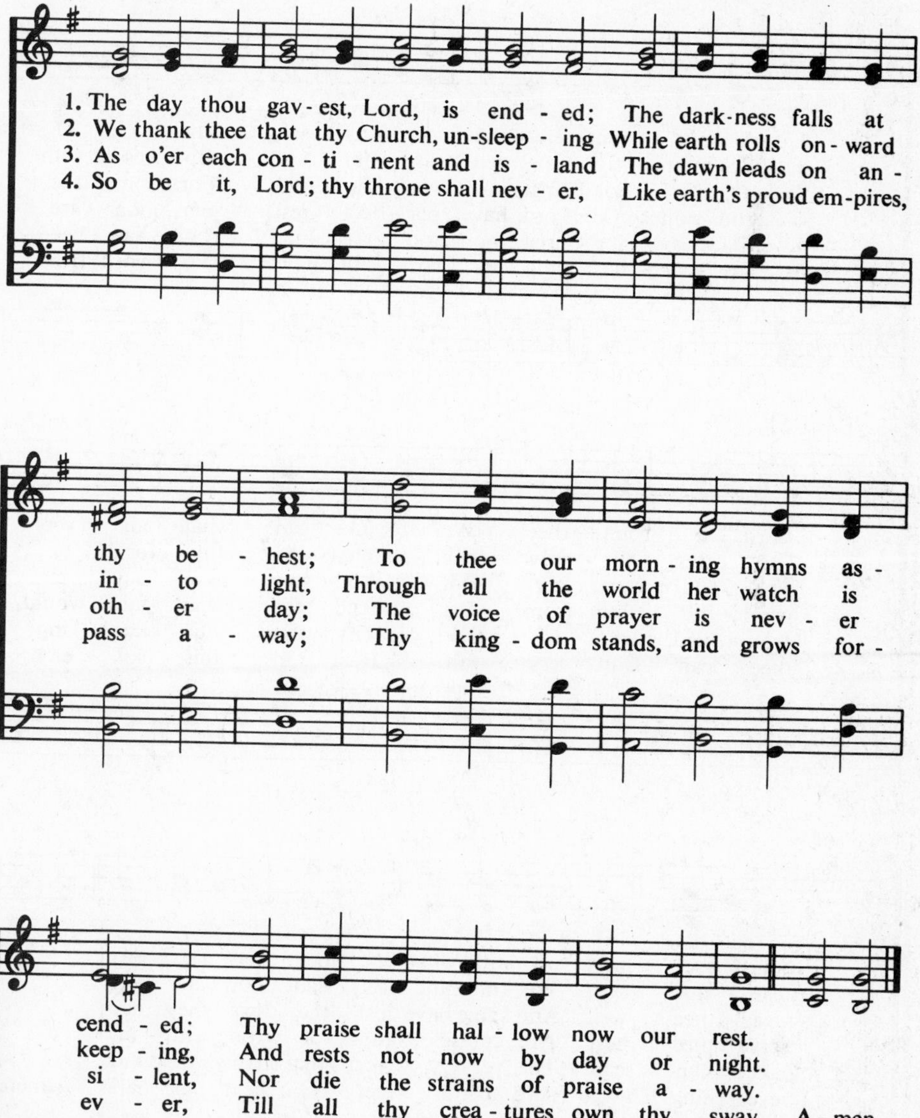
1. The day thou gav - est, Lord, is end - ed; The dark-ness falls at
2. We thank thee that thy Church, un-sleep - ing While earth rolls on - ward
3. As o'er each con - ti - nent and is - land The dawn leads on an -
4. So be it, Lord; thy throne shall nev - er, Like earth's proud em-pires,
thy be - hest; To thee our morn - ing hymns as -
in - to light, Through all the world her watch is
oth - er day; The voice of prayer is nev - er
pass a - way; Thy king - dom stands, and grows for -
cend - ed; Thy praise shall hal - low now our rest.
keep - ing, And rests not now by day or night.
si - lent, Nor die the strains of praise a - way.
ev - er, Till all thy crea - tures own thy sway. A - men.

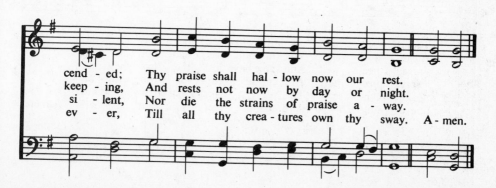

MORNING AND EVENING

At Even, ere the Sun Was Set

MARK 1:32
HENRY TWELLS, 1823-1900

ABENDS LM
HERBERT S. OAKELEY, 1830-1903

1. At e - ven, ere the sun was set, The sick, O
2. Once more 'tis e - ven - tide, and we, Op - pressed with
3. O Sav - ior Christ, our woes dis - pel; For some are
4. And none, O Lord, have per - fect rest, For none are
5. O Sav - ior Christ, thou too art man; Thou hast been
6. Thy touch has still its an - cient power; No word from
Lord, a - round thee lay; O in what di - vers
va - rious ills, draw near; What if thy form we
sick, and some are sad, And some have nev - er
whol - ly free from sin; And they who fain would
trou - bled, tempt - ed, tried; Thy kind but search - ing
thee can fruit - less fall; Hear, in this sol - emn
pains they met! O with what joy they went a - way!
can - not see? We know and feel that thou art here.
loved thee well, And some have lost the love they had;
serve thee best Are con-scious most of wrong with - in.
glance can scan The ver - y wounds that shame would hide.
eve - ning hour, And in thy mer - cy heal us all. A-men.

Sun of My Soul, Thou Savior Dear

LUKE 24:29 HURSLEY LM
JOHN KEBLE, 1792-1866 Adapt. from *Katholisches Gesangbuch*, Vienna, c. 1774

1. Sun of my soul, thou Sav - ior dear, It is not
2. When the soft dews of kind - ly sleep My wea - ried
3. A - bide with me from morn till eve, For with - out
4. If some poor wan - dering child of thine Have spurned, to -
5. Watch by the sick; en - rich the poor With bless - ings
6. Come near and bless us when we wake, Ere through the
night if thou be near; O may no earth - born cloud a -
eye - lids gent - ly steep, Be my last thought, how sweet to
thee I can - not live; A - bide with me when night is
day, the voice di - vine, Now, Lord, the gra - cious work be -
from thy bound - less store; Be ev - ery mourn - er's sleep to -
world our way we take, Till in the o - cean of thy
rise To hide thee from thy ser - vant's eyes.
rest For - ev - er on my Sav - ior's breast.
nigh, For with - out thee I dare not die.
gin; Let him no more lie down in sin.
night, Like in - fants' slum - bers, pure and light.
love We lose our - selves in heaven a - bove. A - men.

Day Is Dying in the West

ISAIAH 6:3
MARY A. LATHBURY, 1841-1913

CHAUTAUQUA 77.774. with Refrain
WILLIAM F. SHERWIN, 1826-1888

1. Day is dy-ing in the west; Heaven is touch-ing earth with rest; Wait and wor-ship while the night Sets her eve-ning lamps a-light Through all the sky.
2. Lord of life, be-neath the dome Of the u-ni-verse, thy home, Gath-er us who seek thy face To the fold of thy em-brace, For thou art nigh.
3. While the deep-ening shad-ows fall, Heart of love en-fold-ing all, Through the glo-ry and the grace Of the stars that veil thy face, Our hearts as-cend.
4. When for-ev-er from our sight Pass the stars, the day, the night, Lord of an-gels, on our eyes Let e-ter-nal morn-ing rise And shad-ows end.
Refrain
Ho-ly, ho-ly, ho-ly, Lord God of Hosts! Heaven and earth are

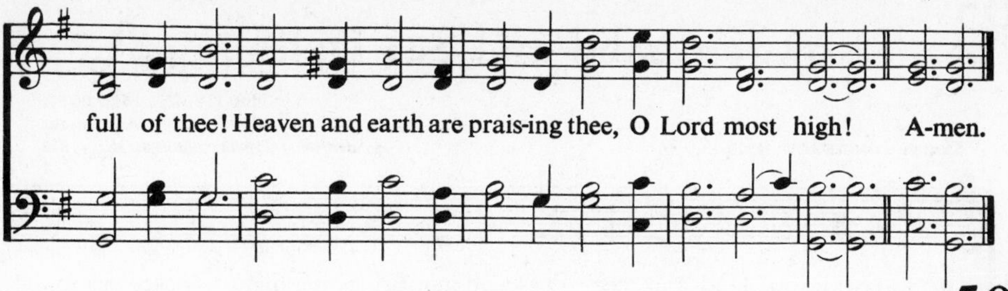
full of thee! Heaven and earth are prais-ing thee, O Lord most high! A-men.

504

Father, We Praise Thee

Attr. to GREGORY THE GREAT, 540-604
Trans. by PERCY DEARMER, 1867-1936

CHRISTE SANCTORUM 11 11 11.5.
French Church Melody
LA FEILLÉE'S *Méthode du Plain-chant*, 1782

Unison
1. Fa - ther, we praise thee, now the night is o - ver;
2. Mon - arch of all things, fit us for thy man - sions;
3. All ho - ly Fa - ther, Son, and e - qual Spir - it,
Ac - tive and watch-ful, stand we all be - fore thee; Sing - ing, we
Ban - ish our weak-ness, health and whole-ness send - ing; Bring us to
Trin - i - ty bless - ed, send us thy sal - va - tion; Thine is the
of - fer prayer and med - i - ta - tion; Thus we a - dore thee.
heav - en, where thy saints u - nit - ed Joy with-out end - ing.
glo - ry, gleam-ing and re - sound-ing Through all cre - a - tion. A-men.

Now, on Land and Sea Descending

VESPER HYMN 87.87.86.87.
Russian Air
A Selection of Popular National Airs, 1818

SAMUEL LONGFELLOW, 1819-1892

1. Now, on land and sea de-scend-ing, Brings the night its peace pro-found;
2. Soon as dies the sun-set glo-ry, Stars of heaven shine out a-bove,
3. Now, our wants and bur-dens leav-ing To his care who cares for all,
4. As the dark-ness deep-ens o'er us, Lo! e-ter-nal stars a-rise;
Let our ves-per hymn be blend-ing With the ho-ly calm a-round.
Tell-ing still the an-cient sto-ry, Their Cre-a-tor's change-less love.
Cease we fear-ing, cease we griev-ing; At his touch our bur-dens fall.
Hope and faith and love rise glo-rious, Shin-ing in the spir-it's skies.
Ju-bi-la-te! Ju-bi-la-te! Ju-bi-la-te! A-men!
Let our ves-per hymn be blend-ing With the ho-ly calm a-round.
Tell-ing still the an-cient sto-ry, Their Cre-a-tor's change-less love.
Cease we fear-ing, cease we griev-ing; At his touch our bur-dens fall.
Hope and faith and love rise glo-rious, Shin-ing in the spir-it's skies. A-men.

The Day Is Slowly Wending

VESPER HYMN (RENDLE) 77.77.64.

MAY ROWLAND, 1870-1959

LILY RENDLE, 1875-

1. The day is slow - ly wend - ing To - ward its si - lent end - ing, But mid the light de - clin - ing The eve - ning star is shin - ing:
2. Be - neath thy might - y car - ing The birds and beasts are shar - ing The love that sends the show - ers, The hand that gives the flow - ers:
3. Though long our day of test - ing, Now comes the hour of rest - ing, May wea - ri - ness and sad - ness Be lulled to peace and glad - ness:
4. The Sav - ior's cross is win - ning For - give - ness for the sin - ning, And while we kneel con - fess - ing, We hum - bly wait thy bless - ing:
5. All e - vil thoughts ex - pell - ing, Now make in us thy dwell - ing. O Spir - it, pure and ho - ly, Pos - sess these hearts so low - ly:
O Fa - ther, while we sleep, Thy chil - dren keep! A - men.

Come, Let Us Use the Grace Divine

JEREMIAH 50:5
CHARLES WESLEY, 1707-1788

ST. MARTIN'S CM
WILLIAM TANS'UR, 1706-1783

1. Come, let us use the grace di - vine, And
2. Give up our-selves, through Je - sus' power, His
3. The cov - enant we this mo - ment make Be
4. We nev - er will throw off his fear Who
all, with one ac-cord, In a per - pet - ual
name to glo - ri - fy; And prom - ise, in this
ev - er kept in mind; We will no more our
hears our sol - emn vow; And if thou art well
cov - enant join Our-selves to Christ the Lord;
sa - cred hour, For God to live and die.
God for - sake, Or cast his words be - hind.
pleased to hear, Come down and meet us now. A - men.

Come, Let Us Use the Grace Divine

JEREMIAH 50:5
CHARLES WESLEY, 1707-1788

COVENANT HYMN CM
THOMAS CANNING, 1911-

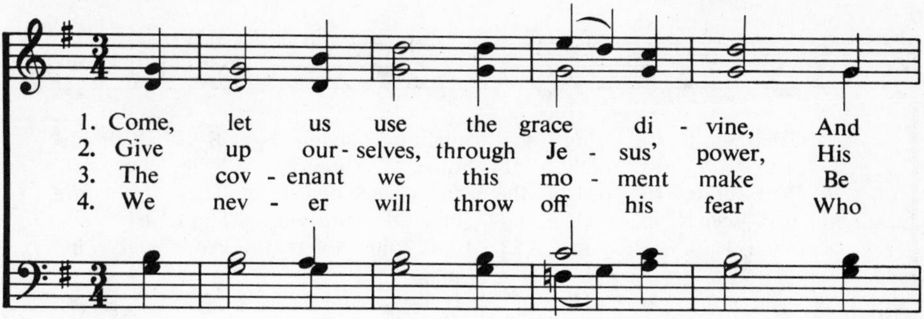
1. Come, let us use the grace di - vine, And
2. Give up our - selves, through Je - sus' power, His
3. The cov - enant we this mo - ment make Be
4. We nev - er will throw off his fear Who

all with one ac - cord, In a per - pet - ual
name to glo - ri - fy; And prom - ise, in this
ev - er kept in mind; We will no more our
hears our sol - emn vow; And if thou art well

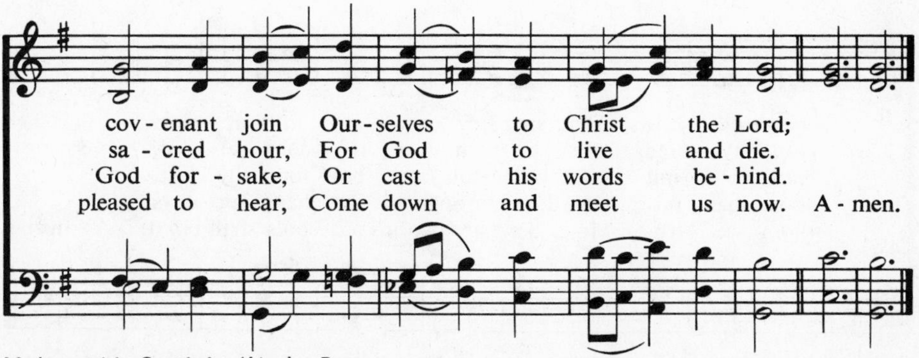
cov - enant join Our - selves to Christ the Lord;
sa - cred hour, For God to live and die.
God for - sake, Or cast his words be - hind.
pleased to hear, Come down and meet us now. A - men.

509

Great God, We Sing That Mighty Hand

Acts 26:22
Philip Doddridge, 1702-1751

WAREHAM LM
William Knapp, 1698-1768

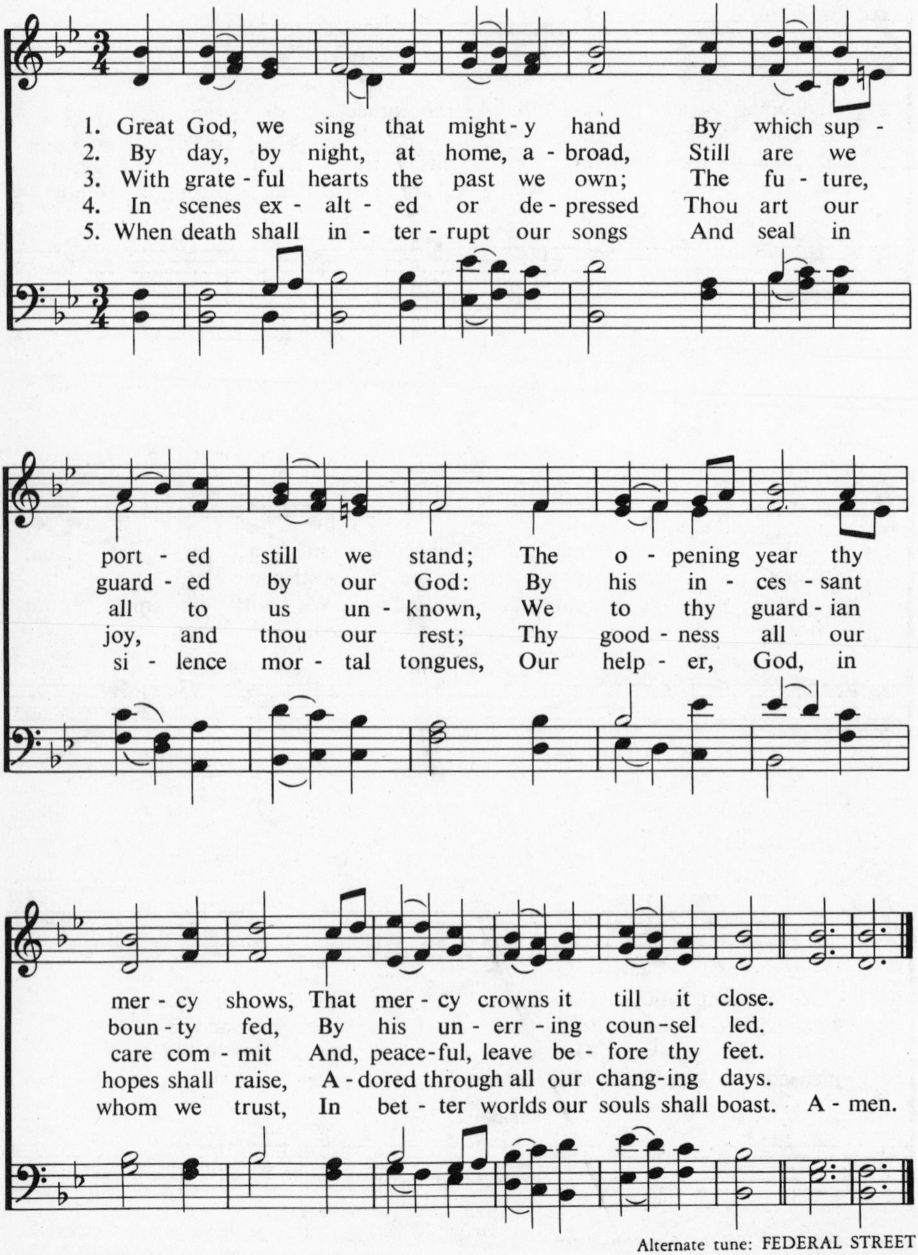

1. Great God, we sing that might-y hand By which sup -
2. By day, by night, at home, a - broad, Still are we
3. With grate - ful hearts the past we own; The fu - ture,
4. In scenes ex - alt - ed or de - pressed Thou art our
5. When death shall in - ter - rupt our songs And seal in
port - ed still we stand; The o - pening year thy
guard - ed by our God: By his in - ces - sant
all to us un - known, We to thy guard - ian
joy, and thou our rest; Thy good - ness all our
si - lence mor - tal tongues, Our help - er, God, in
mer - cy shows, That mer - cy crowns it till it close.
boun - ty fed, By his un - err - ing coun - sel led.
care com - mit And, peace - ful, leave be - fore thy feet.
hopes shall raise, A - dored through all our chang - ing days.
whom we trust, In bet - ter worlds our souls shall boast. A - men.

Alternate tune: FEDERAL STREET

Sing to the Great Jehovah's Praise

LOBT GOTT, IHR CHRISTEN CM
NICOLAUS HERMANN, c. 1485-1561
Harm. by A. C. L.

CHARLES WESLEY, 1707-1788

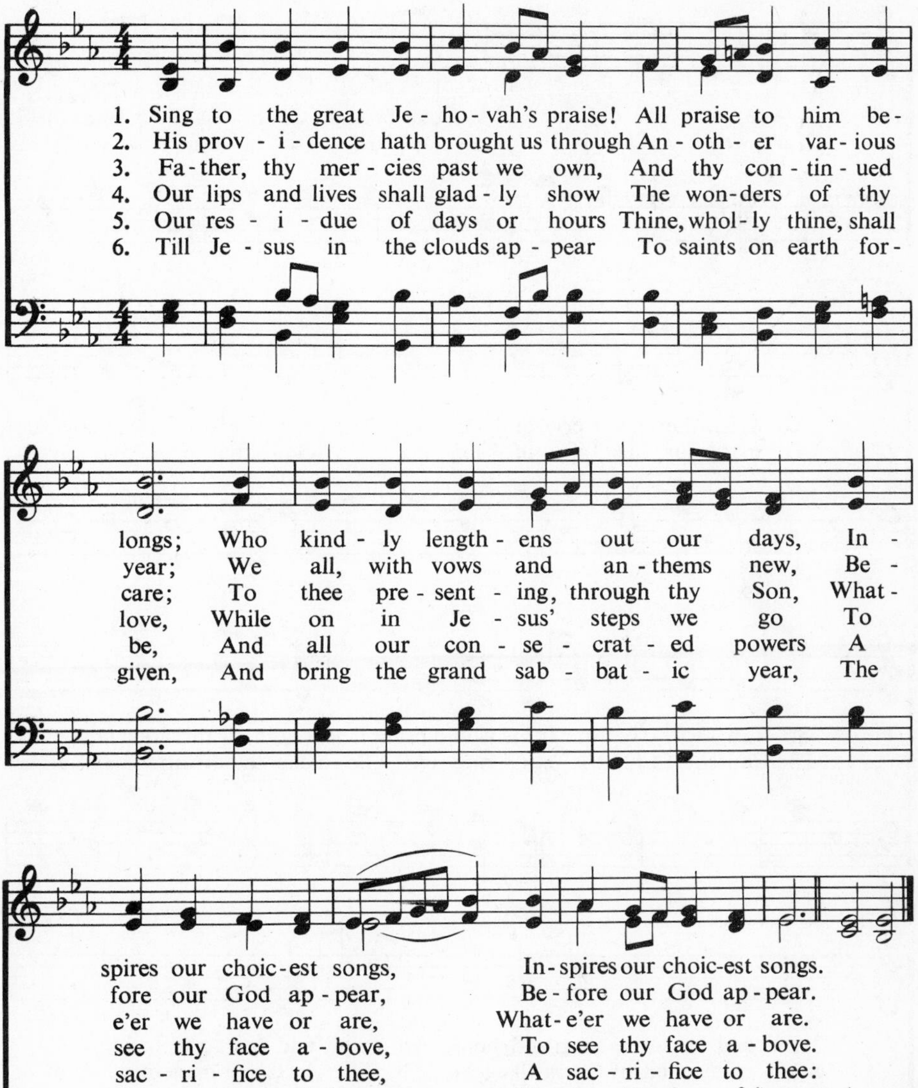
1. Sing to the great Je - ho - vah's praise! All praise to him be -
2. His prov - i - dence hath brought us through An - oth - er var- ious
3. Fa - ther, thy mer - cies past we own, And thy con - tin - ued
4. Our lips and lives shall glad - ly show The won- ders of thy
5. Our res - i - due of days or hours Thine, whol - ly thine, shall
6. Till Je - sus in the clouds ap - pear To saints on earth for -
longs; Who kind - ly length - ens out our days, In -
year; We all, with vows and an - thems new, Be -
care; To thee pre - sent - ing, through thy Son, What -
love, While on in Je - sus' steps we go To
be, And all our con - se - crat - ed powers A
given, And bring the grand sab - bat - ic year, The
spires our choic - est songs, In - spires our choic - est songs.
fore our God ap - pear, Be - fore our God ap - pear.
e'er we have or are, What - e'er we have or are.
see thy face a - bove, To see thy face a - bove.
sac - ri - fice to thee, A sac - ri - fice to thee:
ju - bi - lee of heaven, The ju - bi - lee of heaven. A-men.

511

As Men of Old Their First Fruits Brought

FRANK VON CHRISTIERSON, 1900-

HIGH POPPLES CMD
SAMUEL WALTER, 1916-

1. As men of old their first fruits brought Of or-chard, flock and field
2. A world in need now sum-mons us To la-bor, love, and give;
To God, the giv-er of all good, The source of boun-teous yield;
To make our life an of-fer-ing To God, that man may live;
So we to-day first fruits would bring, The wealth of this good land, Of
The Church of Christ is stir-ring us To make the dream come true: A
farm and mar-ket, shop and home, Of mind and heart and hand.
world re-deemed by Christ-like love, All life in Christ made new. A-men.

To Bless the Earth, God Sendeth

Psalm 65:9-13
The Psalter, 1912

FAR-OFF LANDS 76.76.D.
Melody of the Bohemian Brethren
Arr. by C. Winfred Douglas, 1867-1944

Unison
1. To bless the earth, God send-eth From his a - bun-dant store
2. The year with good he crown-est, The earth his mer - cy fills,
The wa - ters of the spring-time, En - rich - ing it once more.
The wil - der - ness is fruit - ful, And joy - ful are the hills;
The seed by him pro - vid - ed Is sown o'er hill and plain, And
With corn the vales are cov-ered, The flocks in pas-tures graze; All
with the gen - tle show - ers Doth bless the spring - ing grain.
na - ture joins in sing - ing A joy - ful song of praise. A-men.

ROGATION

513

We Plow the Fields

MATTHIAS CLAUDIUS, 1740-1815
Trans. by JANE M. CAMPBELL, 1817-1878

WIR PFLÜGEN 76.76.D. with Refrain
JOHANN A. P. SCHULZ, 1747-1800

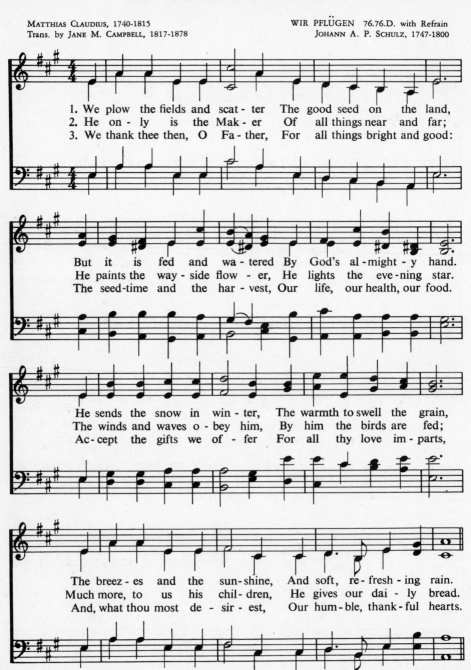

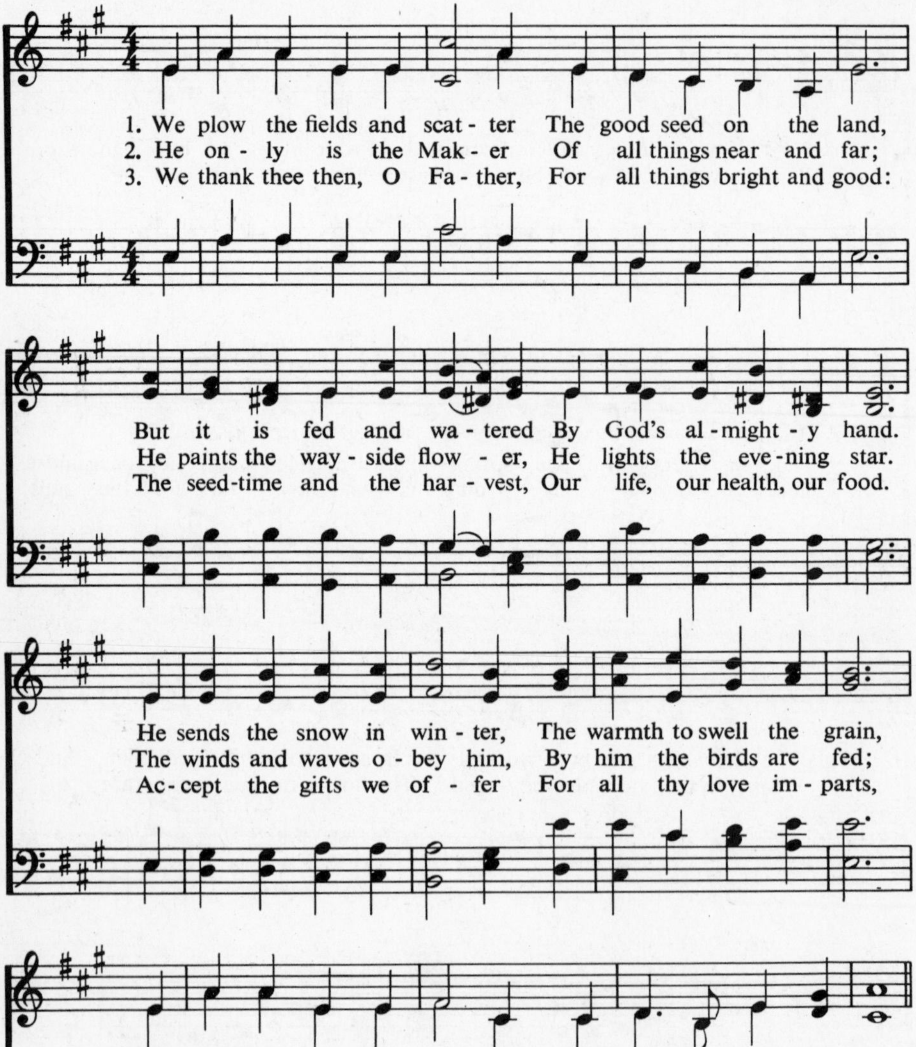

1. We plow the fields and scat - ter The good seed on the land,
2. He on - ly is the Mak - er Of all things near and far;
3. We thank thee then, O Fa - ther, For all things bright and good:
But it is fed and wa - tered By God's al - might - y hand.
He paints the way - side flow - er, He lights the eve - ning star.
The seed-time and the har - vest, Our life, our health, our food.
He sends the snow in win - ter, The warmth to swell the grain,
The winds and waves o - bey him, By him the birds are fed;
Ac - cept the gifts we of - fer For all thy love im - parts,
The breez - es and the sun - shine, And soft, re - fresh - ing rain.
Much more, to us his chil - dren, He gives our dai - ly bread.
And, what thou most de - sir - est, Our hum - ble, thank - ful hearts.

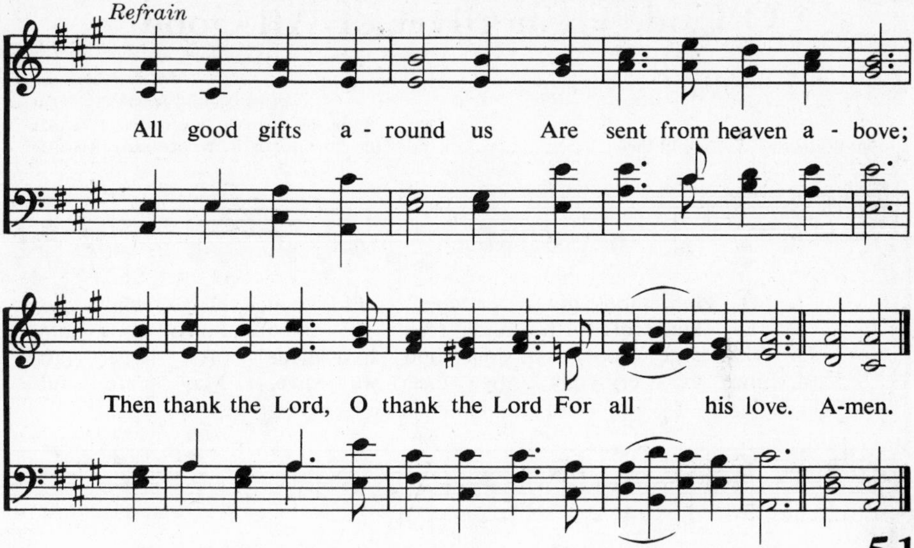
Refrain
All good gifts a - round us Are sent from heaven a - bove;
Then thank the Lord, O thank the Lord For all his love. A-men.

514

God, Whose Farm Is All Creation

SANKEY 87.87.
IRA D. SANKEY, 1840-1908
Harm. by A. C. L.

JOHN ARLOTT, 1914-

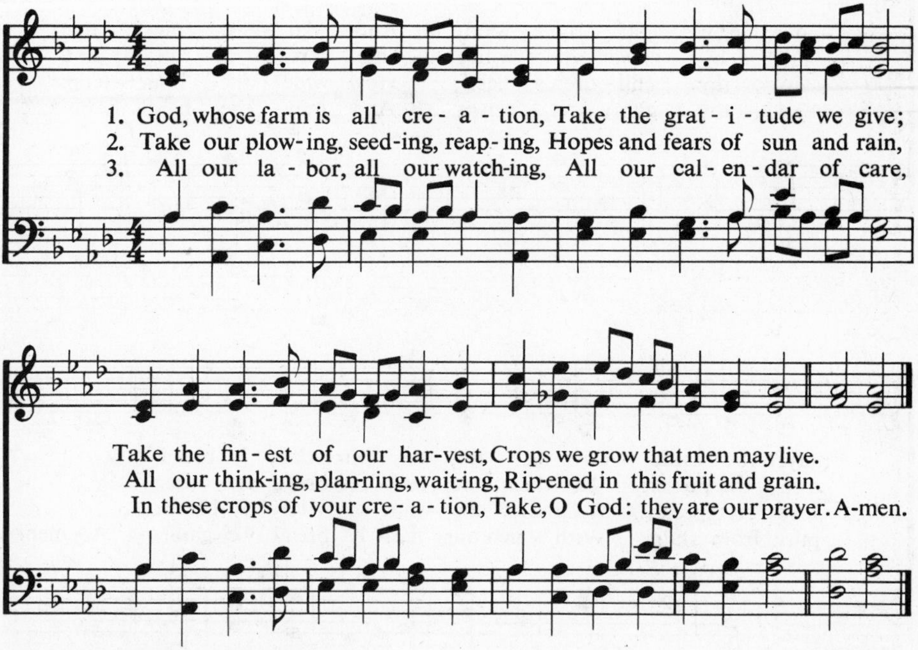
1. God, whose farm is all cre - a - tion, Take the grat - i - tude we give;
2. Take our plow-ing, seed-ing, reap-ing, Hopes and fears of sun and rain,
3. All our la - bor, all our watch-ing, All our cal - en - dar of care,
Take the fin - est of our har-vest, Crops we grow that men may live.
All our think-ing, plan-ning, wait-ing, Rip-ened in this fruit and grain.
In these crops of your cre - a - tion, Take, O God: they are our prayer. A-men.

515

O God, Thou Giver of All Good

PUER NOBIS NASCITUR LM
Adapt. by MICHAEL PRAETORIUS, 1571-1621
Harm. by GEORGE R. WOODWARD, 1848-1934

SAMUEL LONGFELLOW, 1819-1892

1. O God, thou giv - er of all good, Thy chil - dren
2. The life of earth and seed is thine; Suns glow, rains
3. What large pro - vi - sion thou hast made! As large as
4. Since ev - ery day by thee we live, May grate - ful
live by dai - ly food; And dai - ly must the
fall, by power di - vine; Thou art in all; not
is thy chil - dren's need; How wide the boun - teous
hearts thy gifts re - ceive; And may the hands be
prayer be said, "Give us this day our dai - ly bread."
e'en the powers By which we toil for bread are ours.
love is spread! Wide as the want of dai - ly bread.
pure from stain With which our dai - ly bread we gain. A - men.

Music used by permission of A. R. Mowbray & Co., Ltd.

Happy the Home When God Is There

ST. AGNES CM

HENRY WARE, JR., 1794-1843 — JOHN B. DYKES, 1823-1876

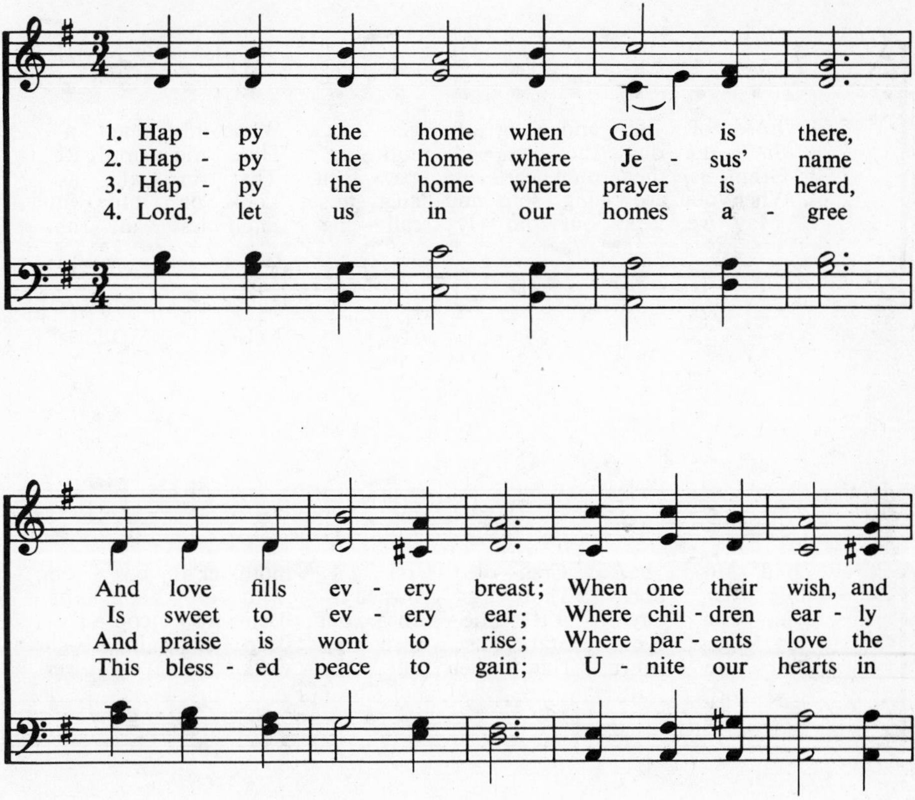
1. Hap - py the home when God is there,
2. Hap - py the home where Je - sus' name
3. Hap - py the home where prayer is heard,
4. Lord, let us in our homes a - gree
And love fills ev - ery breast; When one their wish, and
Is sweet to ev - ery ear; Where chil - dren ear - ly
And praise is wont to rise; Where par - ents love the
This bless - ed peace to gain; U - nite our hearts in
one their prayer, And one their heaven - ly rest.
lisp his fame, And par - ents hold him dear.
sa - cred Word And all its wis - dom prize.
love to thee, And love to all will reign. A - men.

517

Lord of Life and King of Glory

SICILIAN MARINERS 87.87.87.
TATTERSALL'S *Psalmody*, 1794

CHRISTIAN BURKE, 1857-1944

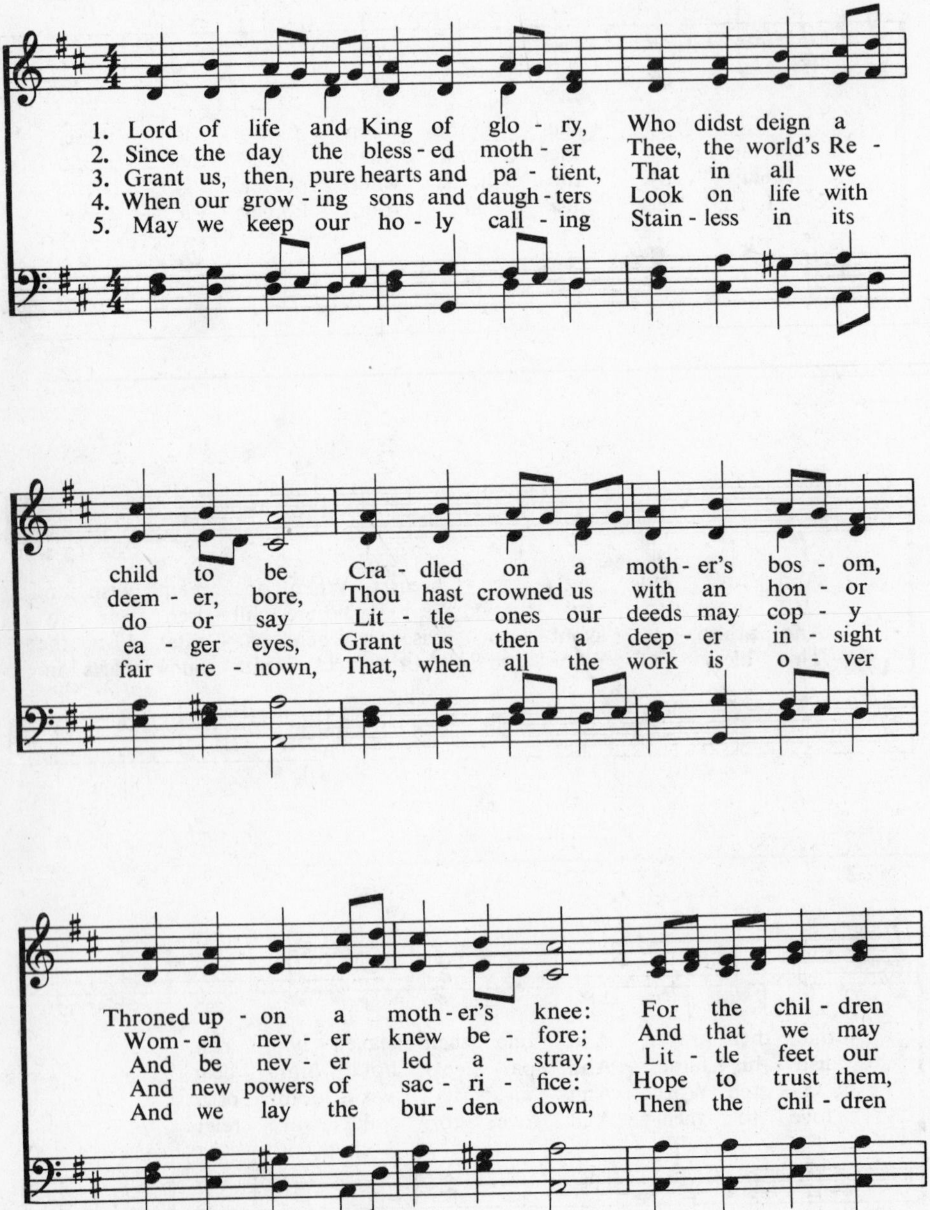
1. Lord of life and King of glo - ry, Who didst deign a
2. Since the day the bless - ed moth - er Thee, the world's Re -
3. Grant us, then, pure hearts and pa - tient, That in all we
4. When our grow - ing sons and daugh - ters Look on life with
5. May we keep our ho - ly call - ing Stain - less in its
child to be Cra - dled on a moth - er's bos - om,
deem - er, bore, Thou hast crowned us with an hon - or
do or say Lit - tle ones our deeds may cop - y
ea - ger eyes, Grant us then a deep - er in - sight
fair re - nown, That, when all the work is o - ver
Throned up - on a moth - er's knee: For the chil - dren
Wom - en nev - er knew be - fore; And that we may
And be nev - er led a - stray; Lit - tle feet our
And new powers of sac - ri - fice: Hope to trust them,
And we lay the bur - den down, Then the chil - dren

Words used by permission of the Mothers' Union.

thou hast giv - en We must an - swer un - to thee.
bear it meet - ly, We must seek thine aid the more.
steps may fol - low In a safe and nar - row way.
faith to guide them, Love that noth - ing good de - nies.
thou hast giv - en Still may be our joy and crown. A - men.

518 Be Present at Our Table, Lord

JOHN CENNICK, 1718-1755
Stanza 2, altered

OLD 100TH LM
Genevan Psalter, 1551
Attr. to LOUIS BOURGEOIS, c. 1510-c. 1561

1. Be pres - ent at our ta - ble, Lord; Be
2. We thank thee, Lord, for this our food, For
3. We thank thee, Lord, for this our food, But
here and ev - ery - where a - dored; Thy crea - tures bless, and
life and health and ev - ery good; By thine own hand may
more be - cause of Je - sus' blood; Let man - na to our
grant that we May feast in par - a - dise with thee.
we be fed; Give us each day our dai - ly bread.
souls be given, The bread of life sent down from heaven. A-men.

519

Ne'er Forget God's Daily Care

WIANT 77.77.
Chinese Melody
Arr. by BLISS WIANT, 1895-

CHAO TZU-CH'EN, 1888-
Trans. by BLISS WIANT, 1895-

Ne'er for- get God's dai - ly care: Health and food and clothes to wear.

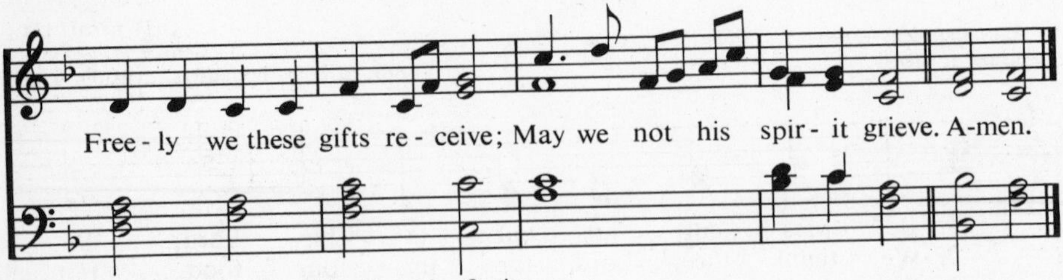
Free - ly we these gifts re - ceive; May we not his spir - it grieve. A-men.

520

O Lord, May Church and Home Combine

ST. PETER CM
ALEXANDER R. REINAGLE, 1799-1877

CARLTON C. BUCK, 1907-

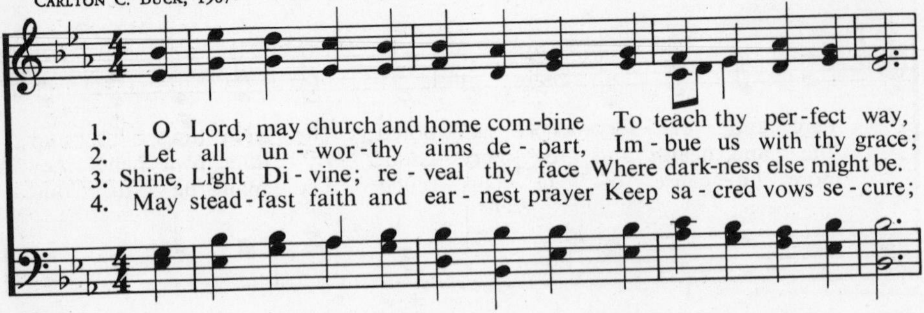
1. O Lord, may church and home com-bine To teach thy per-fect way,
2. Let all un - wor - thy aims de - part, Im - bue us with thy grace;
3. Shine, Light Di - vine; re - veal thy face Where dark-ness else might be.
4. May stead - fast faith and ear - nest prayer Keep sa - cred vows se - cure;

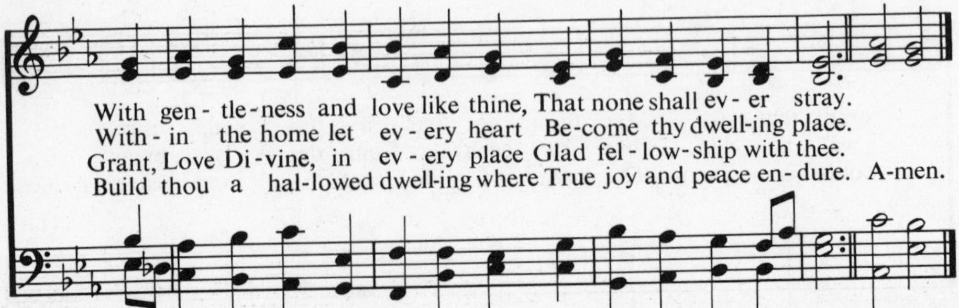
With gen - tle-ness and love like thine, That none shall ev - er stray.
With - in the home let ev - ery heart Be-come thy dwell-ing place.
Grant, Love Di - vine, in ev - ery place Glad fel - low-ship with thee.
Build thou a hal-lowed dwell-ing where True joy and peace en - dure. A-men.

Children of the Heavenly Father

Caroline V. Sandell-Berg, 1832-1903
Trans. by Ernest W. Olson, 1870-1958

TRYGGARE KAN INGEN VARA LM
Swedish Melody

1. Chil - dren of the heaven - ly Fa - ther Safe - ly
2. God his own doth tend and nour - ish; In his
3. Nei - ther life nor death shall ev - er From the
4. Though he giv - eth or he tak - eth, God his
in his bos - om gath - er; Nest - ling bird nor star in
ho - ly courts they flour - ish. From all e - vil things he
Lord his chil - dren sev - er; Un - to them his grace he
chil - dren ne'er for - sak - eth; His the lov - ing pur - pose
heav - en Such a ref - uge e'er was giv - en.
spares them; In his might - y arms he bears them.
show - eth, And their sor - rows all he know - eth.
sole - ly To pre - serve them pure and ho - ly. A - men.

522

Come, Ye Thankful People, Come

ST. GEORGE'S WINDSOR 77.77.D.

HENRY ALFORD, 1810-1871 GEORGE J. ELVEY, 1816-1893

1. Come, ye thank - ful peo - ple, come, Raise the song of har - vest home;
2. All the world is God's own field, Fruit un - to his praise to yield;
3. For the Lord our God shall come, And shall take his har - vest home;
4. E - ven so, Lord, quick - ly come, Bring thy fi - nal har - vest home;
All is safe - ly gath - ered in, Ere the win - ter storms be - gin;
Wheat and tares to - geth - er sown, Un - to joy or sor - row grown;
From his field shall in that day All of - fens - es purge a - way,
Gath - er thou thy peo - ple in, Free from sor - row, free from sin,
God, our Mak - er, doth pro - vide For our wants to be sup - plied;
First the blade, and then the ear, Then the full corn shall ap - pear;
Give his an - gels charge at last In the fire the tares to cast,
There, for - ev - er pu - ri - fied, In thy pres - ence to a - bide;
Come to God's own tem - ple, come, Raise the song of har - vest home.
Lord of har - vest, grant that we Whole - some grain and pure may be.
But the fruit - ful ears to store In his gar - ner ev - er - more.
Come, with all thine an - gels, come, Raise the glo - rious har - vest home. A - men.

O Lord of Heaven and Earth and Sea

OLDBRIDGE 888.4.

CHRISTOPHER WORDSWORTH, 1807-1885

ROBERT N. QUAILE, b. 1867

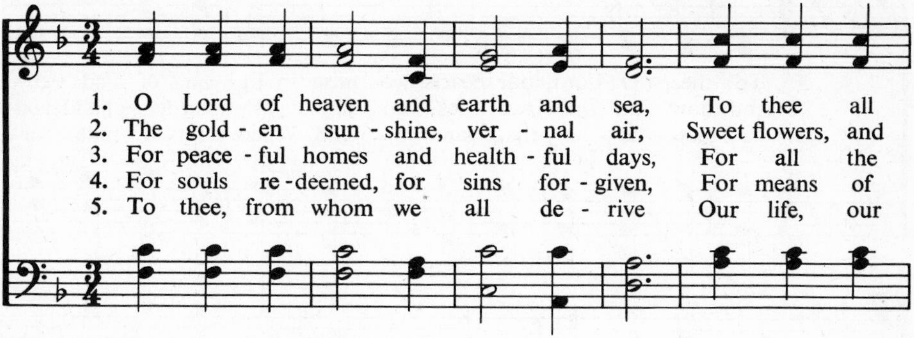
1. O Lord of heaven and earth and sea, To thee all
2. The gold - en sun - shine, ver - nal air, Sweet flowers, and
3. For peace - ful homes and health - ful days, For all the
4. For souls re - deemed, for sins for - given, For means of
5. To thee, from whom we all de - rive Our life, our

praise and glo - ry be! How shall we show our
fruit thy love de - clare; When har - vests rip - en,
bless - ings earth dis - plays, We owe thee thank - ful -
grace and hopes of heaven: What can to thee, O
gifts, our power to give: O may we ev - er

love to thee, Who giv - est all?
thou art there, Who giv - est all.
ness and praise, Who giv - est all.
Lord, be given, Who giv - est all?
with thee live, Who giv - est all! A - men.

524 To Thee, O Lord, Our Hearts We Raise

NORSE AIR 87.87.D.
Norse Folk Melody
Arr. by WILLIAM J. KIRKPATRICK, 1838-1921

PSALM 65:13
WILLIAM C. DIX, 1837-1898

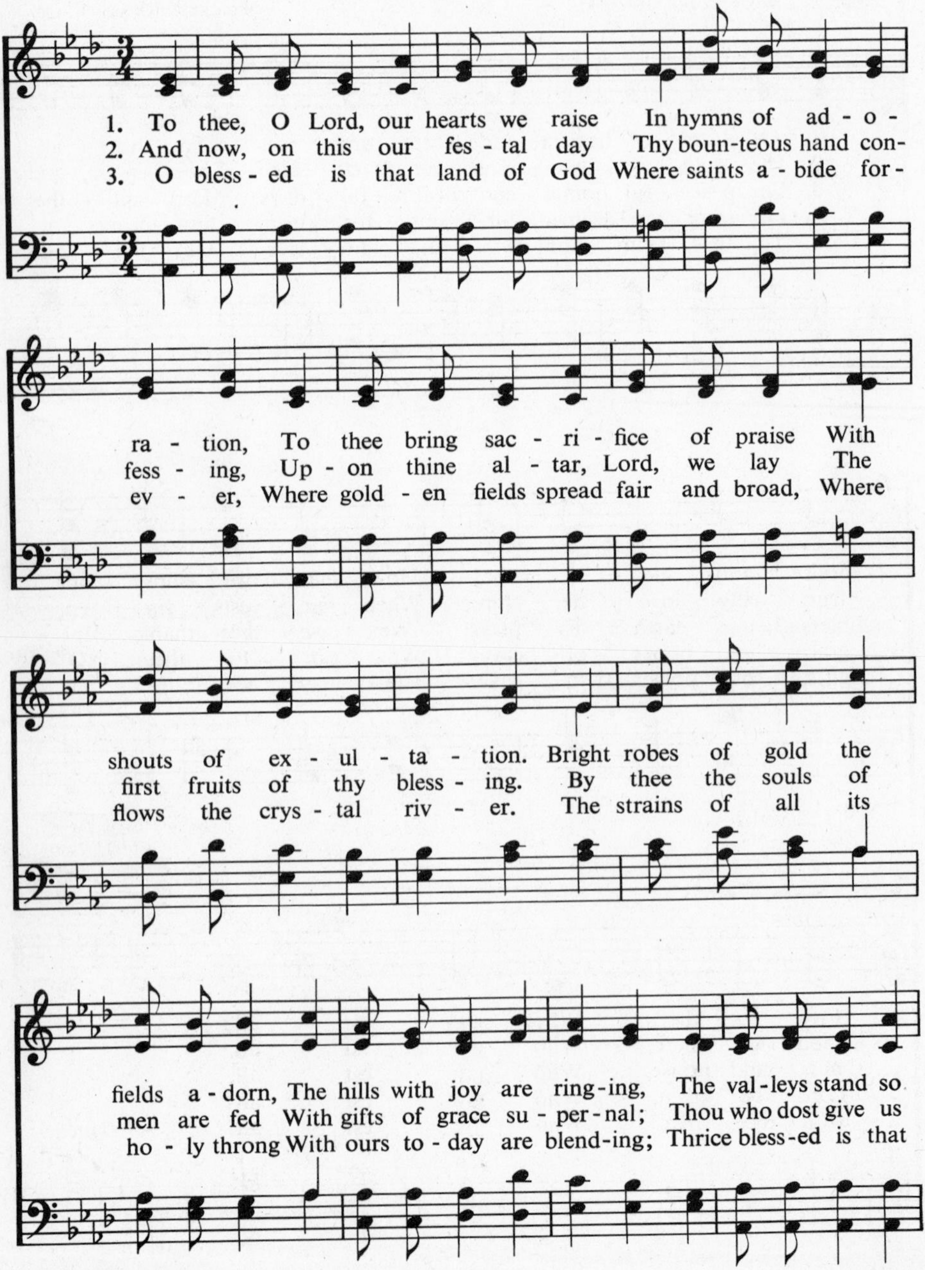
1. To thee, O Lord, our hearts we raise In hymns of ad - o -
2. And now, on this our fes - tal day Thy boun-teous hand con-
3. O bless - ed is that land of God Where saints a - bide for -
ra - tion, To thee bring sac - ri - fice of praise With
fess - ing, Up - on thine al - tar, Lord, we lay The
ev - er, Where gold - en fields spread fair and broad, Where
shouts of ex - ul - ta - tion. Bright robes of gold the
first fruits of thy bless - ing. By thee the souls of
flows the crys - tal riv - er. The strains of all its
fields a - dorn, The hills with joy are ring-ing, The val-leys stand so
men are fed With gifts of grace su - per - nal; Thou who dost give us
ho - ly throng With ours to - day are blend-ing; Thrice bless-ed is that

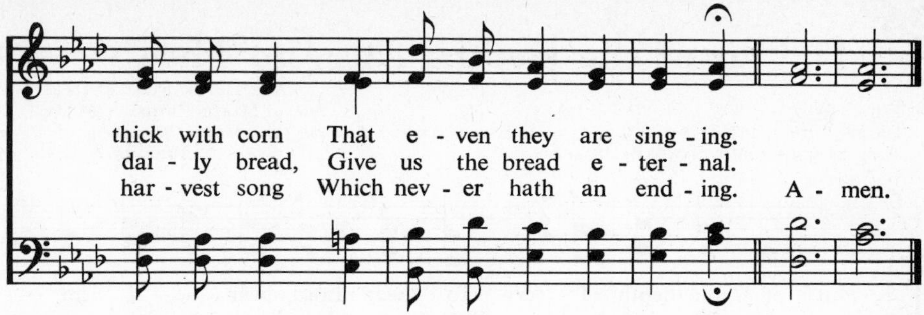
thick with corn That e - ven they are sing - ing.
dai - ly bread, Give us the bread e - ter - nal.
har - vest song Which nev - er hath an end - ing. A - men.

525

For All the Blessings of the Year

CHILDHOOD 888.5.

ALBERT H. HUTCHINSON

Henry Walford Davies, 1869-1941

1. For all the bless - ings of the year, For all the friends we hold so dear, For peace on earth, both far and near, We thank thee, O Lord.
2. For life and health, those com - mon things, Which ev - ery day and hour brings, For home, where our af - fec - tion clings, We thank thee, O Lord.
3. For love of thine, which nev - er tires, Which all our bet - ter thought in - spires, And warms our lives with heaven - ly fires, We thank thee, O Lord. A - men.

Music from *A Students' Hymnal* by permission of Oxford University Press.

Out of the Depths I Cry to Thee

AUS TIEFER NOT 87.87.887.

PSALM 130
MARTIN LUTHER, 1483-1546
Trans. by CATHERINE WINKWORTH, 1827-1878

Attr. to MARTIN LUTHER, 1483-1546
JOHANN WALTHER'S *Geistliches Gesangbüchlein*, Wittenberg, 1524
Harm. by A. C. L.

Unison
1. Out of the depths I cry to thee; Lord, hear me, I im -
2. Thou grant - est par - don through thy love; Thy grace a - lone a -
3. And thus my hope is in the Lord, And not in my own
plore thee! Bend down thy gra - cious ear to me; I lay my
vail - eth. Our works could ne'er our guilt re - move; Yea, e'en the
mer - it; I rest up - on his faith - ful word To them of
sins be - fore thee. If thou re - mem - berest each mis - deed, If each
best life fail - eth. For none may boast him - self of aught, But must
con - trite spir - it. That he is mer - ci - ful and just, Here is
should have its right - ful meed, Who may a - bide thy pres - ence?
con - fess thy grace hath wrought What - e'er in him is wor - thy.
my com - fort and my trust; His help I wait with pa - tience. A - men.

And Can It Be That I Should Gain

FILLMORE 88.88.88.

ACTS 16:26
CHARLES WESLEY, 1707-1788

Attr. to JEREMIAH INGALLS, 1764-1828
Harm. by A. C. L.

1. And can it be that I should gain An in - terest
2. 'Tis mys - tery all! th' Im - mor - tal dies! Who can ex -
3. Long my im - pris - oned spir - it lay, Fast bound in
4. No con - dem - na - tion now I dread; Je - sus, and
in the Sav - ior's blood? Died he for me, who caused his pain?
plore his strange de - sign? In vain the first - born ser - aph tries
sin and na - ture's night; Thine eye dif - fused a quick - ening ray;
all in him, is mine; A - live in him, my liv - ing Head,
For me, who him to death pur - sued? A - maz - ing love! how
To sound the depths of love di - vine. 'Tis mer - cy all! let
I woke, the dun - geon flamed with light; My chains fell off, my
And clothed in righ - teous - ness di - vine, Bold I ap - proach th'e -
can it be That thou, my Lord, shouldst die for me?
earth a - dore; Let an - gel minds in - quire no more.
heart was free, I rose, went forth, and fol - lowed thee.
ter - nal throne, And claim the crown, through Christ my own. A - men.

ALDERSGATE

528

Where Shall My Wondering Soul Begin

FILLMORE 88.88.88.
Attr. to JEREMIAH INGALLS, 1764-1828
Harm. by A. C. L.

CHARLES WESLEY, 1707-1788

Unison
1. Where shall my won - dering soul be - gin?
2. O how shall I the good - ness tell,
3. And shall I slight my Fa - ther's love,
4. Out - casts of men, to you I call:
5. Come, O my guil - ty bre - thren, come,

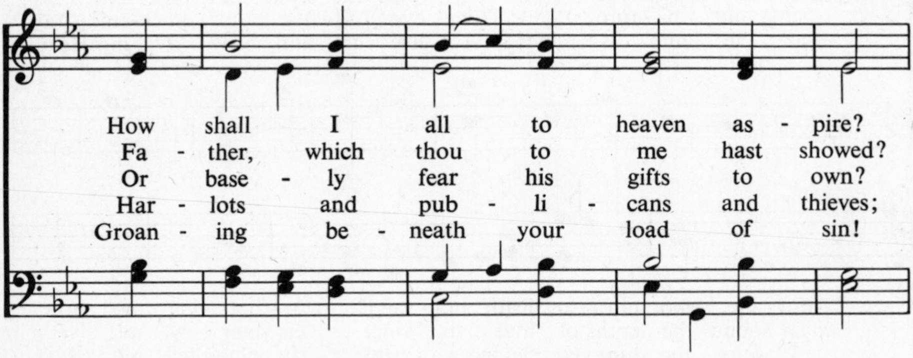
How shall I all to heaven as - pire?
Fa - ther, which thou to me hast showed?
Or base - ly fear his gifts to own?
Har - lots and pub - li - cans and thieves;
Groan - ing be - neath your load of sin!

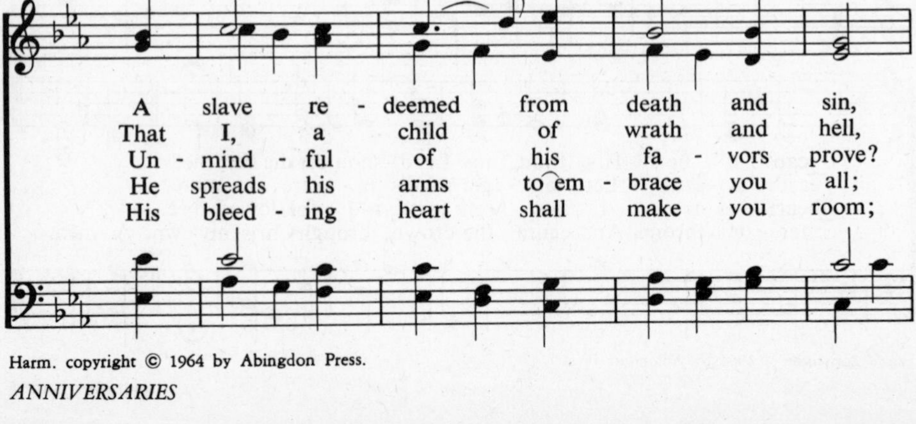
A slave re - deemed from death and sin,
That I, a child of wrath and hell,
Un - mind - ful of his fa - vors prove?
He spreads his arms to em - brace you all;
His bleed - ing heart shall make you room;

A brand plucked from e - ter - nal fire,
I should be called a child of God,
Shall I, the hal - lowed cross to shun,
Sin - ners a - lone his grace re - ceive.
His o - pen side shall take you in.
How shall I e - qual tri - umphs raise,
Should know, should feel my sins for - given,
Re - fuse his righ - teous - ness to im - part,
No need of him the righ - teous have;
He calls you now, in - vites you home:
Or sing my great de - liv - erer's praise?
Blest with this an - te - past of heaven.
By hid - ing it with - in my heart?
He came the lost to seek and save.
Come, O my guil - ty bre - thren, come! A - men.

ALDERSGATE

Come, O Thou Traveler Unknown

CANDLER LMD

GENESIS 32:22-30

CHARLES WESLEY, 1707-1788

Trad. Scottish Melody

Harm. by C. R. Y.

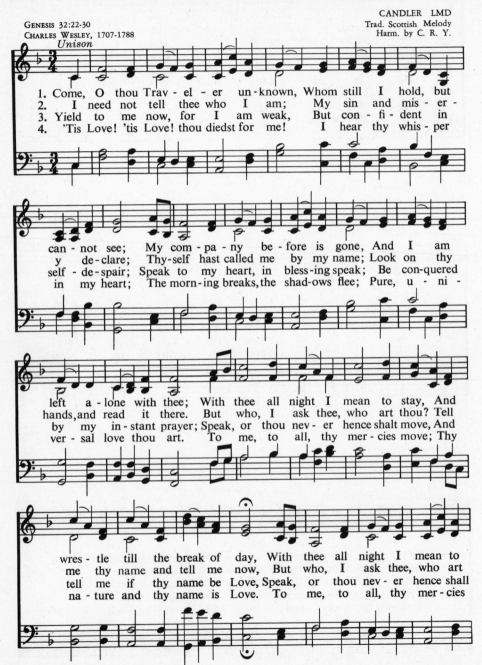

Unison
1. Come, O thou Trav - el - er un-known, Whom still I hold, but
2. I need not tell thee who I am; My sin and mis - er -
3. Yield to me now, for I am weak, But con - fi - dent in
4. 'Tis Love! 'tis Love! thou diedst for me! I hear thy whis - per
can - not see; My com - pa - ny be - fore is gone, And I am
y de - clare; Thy-self hast called me by my name; Look on thy
self - de - spair; Speak to my heart, in bless-ing speak; Be con-quered
in my heart; The morn-ing breaks, the shad-ows flee; Pure, u - ni -
left a - lone with thee; With thee all night I mean to stay, And
hands, and read it there. But who, I ask thee, who art thou? Tell
by my in - stant prayer; Speak, or thou nev - er hence shalt move, And
ver - sal love thou art. To me, to all, thy mer - cies move; Thy
wres - tle till the break of day, With thee all night I mean to
me thy name and tell me now, But who, I ask thee, who art
tell me if thy name be Love, Speak, or thou nev - er hence shall
na - ture and thy name is Love. To me, to all, thy mer - cies

ANNIVERSARIES

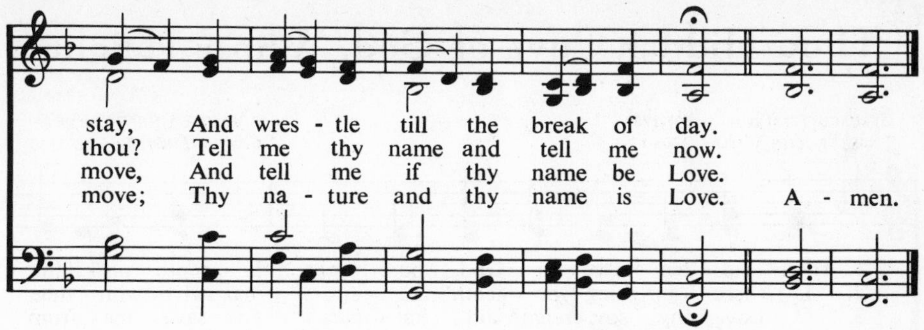
stay, And wres - tle till the break of day.
thou? Tell me thy name and tell me now.
move, And tell me if thy name be Love.
move; Thy na - ture and thy name is Love. A - men.

Alternate tunes: FILLMORE and ST. CATHERINE

530

Christ, from Whom All Blessings Flow

CANTERBURY 77.77.

CHARLES WESLEY, 1707-1788

Adapt. from ORLANDO GIBBONS, 1583-1625

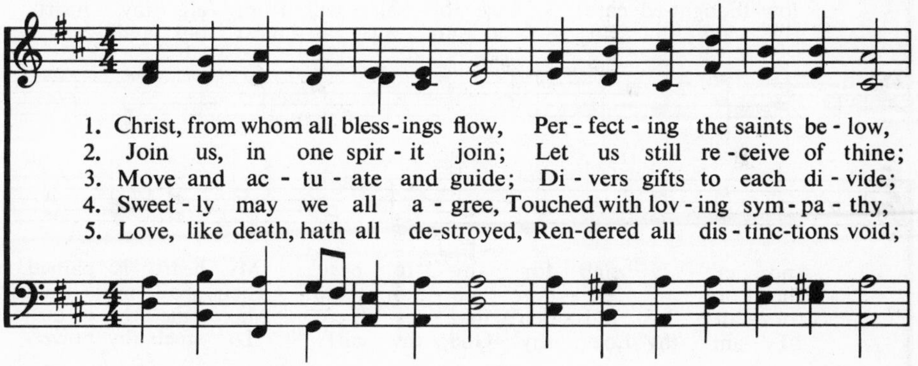
1. Christ, from whom all bless-ings flow, Per - fect - ing the saints be - low,
2. Join us, in one spir - it join; Let us still re - ceive of thine;
3. Move and ac - tu - ate and guide; Di - vers gifts to each di - vide;
4. Sweet - ly may we all a - gree, Touched with lov - ing sym - pa - thy,
5. Love, like death, hath all de-stroyed, Ren-dered all dis - tinc-tions void;

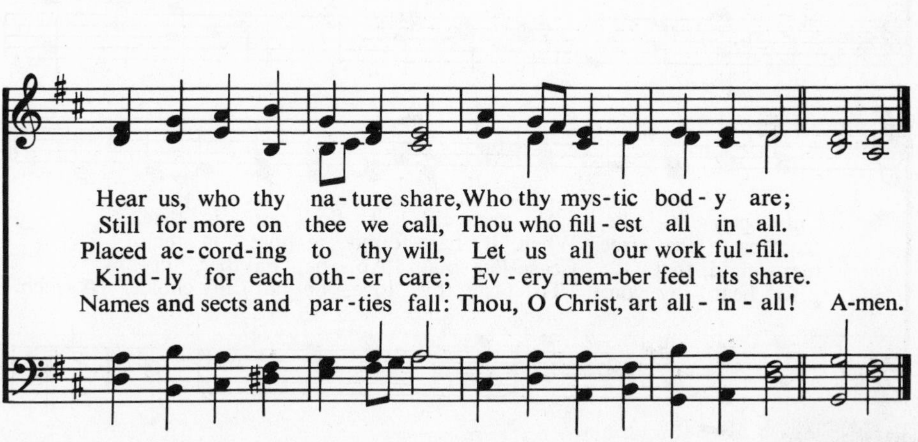
Hear us, who thy na - ture share, Who thy mys - tic bod - y are;
Still for more on thee we call, Thou who fill - est all in all.
Placed ac - cord - ing to thy will, Let us all our work ful - fill.
Kind - ly for each oth - er care; Ev - ery mem - ber feel its share.
Names and sects and par - ties fall: Thou, O Christ, art all - in - all! A-men.

ALDERSGATE

531 Thou Hidden Love of God, Whose Height

GERHARD TERSTEEGEN, 1697-1769
Trans. by JOHN WESLEY, 1703-1791

VATER UNSER 88.88.88.
Geistliche Lieder, Leipzig, 1539

1. Thou hid - den Love of God, whose height, Whose depth un - fath -
2. Is there a thing be - neath the sun That strives with thee
3. O Love, thy sov-ereign aid im - part To save me from
4. Each mo - ment draw from earth a - way My heart that low -
omed no man knows, I see from far thy beau - teous light
my heart to share? Ah, tear it thence and reign a - lone,
low-thought-ed care; Chase this self - will from all my heart,
ly waits thy call; Speak to my in - most soul and say,
And in - ly sigh for thy re - pose; My heart is pained,
The Lord of ev - ery mo - tion there! Then shall my heart
From all its hid - den maz - es there; Make me thy du -
"I am thy Love, thy God, thy all!" To feel thy power,
nor can it be At rest till it finds rest in thee.
from earth be free, When it hath found re-pose in thee.
teous child, that I Cease-less may, "Ab - ba, Fa-ther," cry.
to hear thy voice, To taste thy love, be all my choice. A - men.

Now Praise We Great and Famous Men

ECCLESIASTICUS 44:1-15
WILLIAM G. TARRANT, 1853-1928

ACH GOTT UND HERR 87.87.
As Hymnodus Sacer, Leipzig, 1625

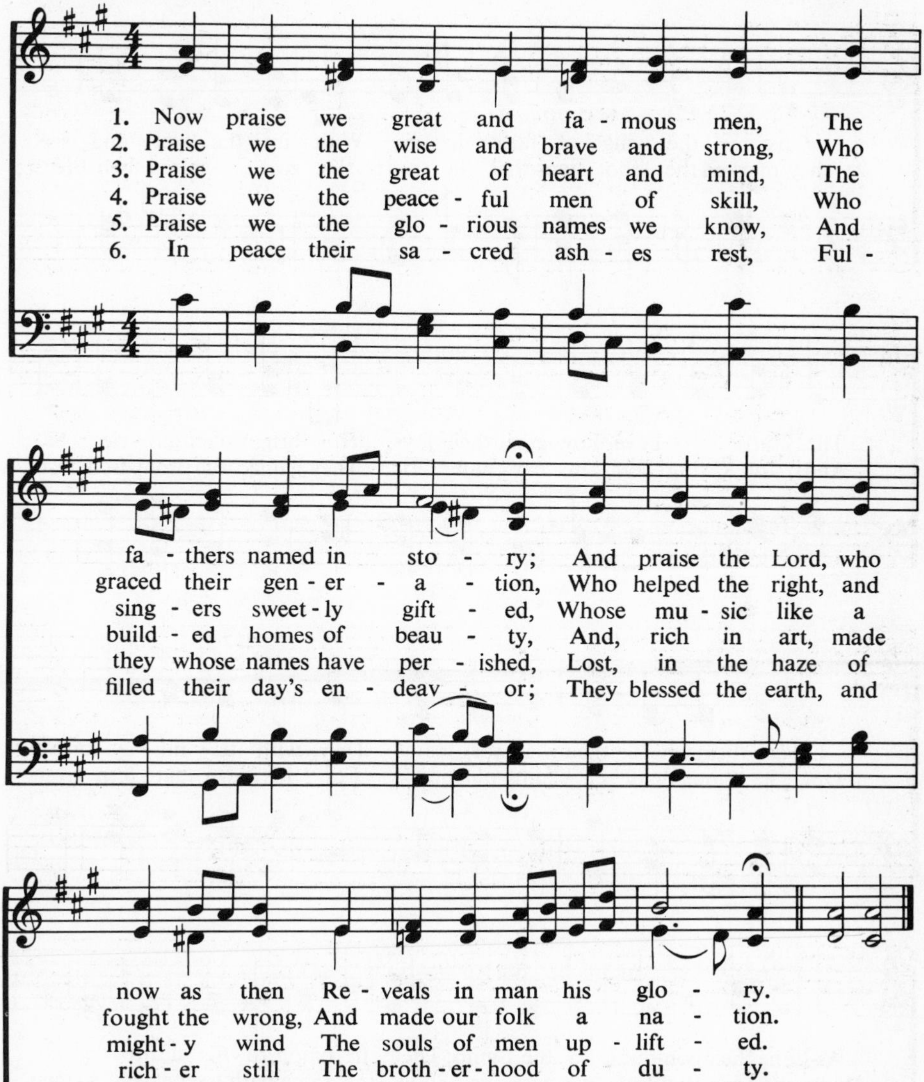
1. Now praise we great and fa - mous men, The
2. Praise we the wise and brave and strong, Who
3. Praise we the great of heart and mind, The
4. Praise we the peace - ful men of skill, Who
5. Praise we the glo - rious names we know, And
6. In peace their sa - cred ash - es rest, Ful -
fa - thers named in sto - ry; And praise the Lord, who
graced their gen - er - a - tion, Who helped the right, and
sing - ers sweet - ly gift - ed, Whose mu - sic like a
build - ed homes of beau - ty, And, rich in art, made
they whose names have per - ished, Lost, in the haze of
filled their day's en - deav - or; They blessed the earth, and
now as then Re - veals in man his glo - ry.
fought the wrong, And made our folk a na - tion.
might - y wind The souls of men up - lift - ed.
rich - er still The broth - er - hood of du - ty.
long a - go, In si - lent love be cher - ished.
they are blessed Of God and man for - ev - er. A - men.

533

Give Me the Wings of Faith

SIMS CMD

Isaac Watts, 1674-1748 | William J. Reynolds, 1920-

1. Give me the wings of faith to rise With-in the veil and see
2. They marked the foot-steps that he trod; His zeal in-spired their breast;
The saints a - bove, how great their joys, How bright their glo - ries be.
And, fol-lowing their in - car - nate God, They gained the prom-ised rest.
I ask them whence their vic - tory came: They, with u - nit - ed breath,
Our glo - rious lead - er claims our praise, For his own pat - tern given,
As-cribe their con-quest to the Lamb; Their tri-umph to his death.
While the long cloud of wit-ness - es Show the same path to heaven. A-men.

Alternate tune: TWENTY-FOURTH

534

For the Might of Thine Arm

CORMAC Irregular
Trad. Irish Melody
Harm. by A. C. L.

Charles Silvester Horne, 1865-1914

Unison
1. For the might of thine arm we bless thee, our God, our fa-thers' God;
2. May the shad-ow of thy pres-ence a-round our camp be spread;
Thou hast kept thy pil-grim peo-ple by the strength of thy staff and
Bap-tize us with the cour-age with which thou blessed our
rod; Thou hast called us to the jour-ney which faith-less feet ne'er trod;
dead; O keep us in the path-way their saint-ly feet have trod;
For the might of thine arm we bless thee, our God, our fa-thers' God.
For the might of thine arm we bless thee, our God, our fa-thers' God. A-men.

Alternate tune: HEREFORD

535

Happy the Souls to Jesus Joined

BALLERMA CM
FRANÇOIS H. BARTHÉLÉMON, 1741-1808
Adapt. by ROBERT SIMPSON, 1790-1832

CHARLES WESLEY, 1707-1788

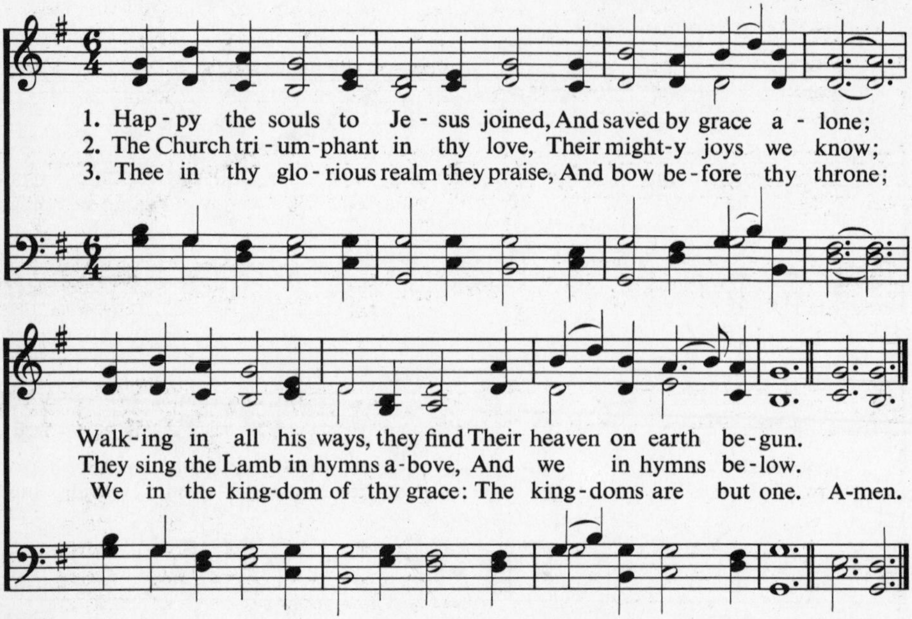

1. Hap-py the souls to Je-sus joined, And saved by grace a-lone;
2. The Church tri-um-phant in thy love, Their might-y joys we know;
3. Thee in thy glo-rious realm they praise, And bow be-fore thy throne;
Walk-ing in all his ways, they find Their heaven on earth be-gun.
They sing the Lamb in hymns a-bove, And we in hymns be-low.
We in the king-dom of thy grace: The king-doms are but one. A-men.

536

For All the Saints

SINE NOMINE 10 10 10. with Alleluias
R. VAUGHAN WILLIAMS, 1872-1958

WILLIAM W. HOW, 1823-1897

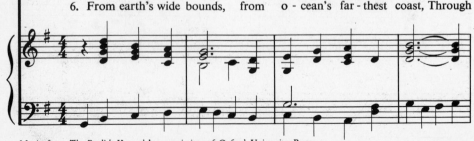

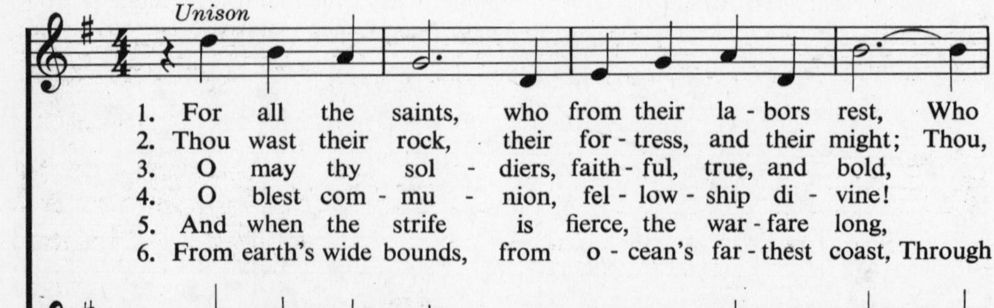

Unison
1. For all the saints, who from their la-bors rest, Who
2. Thou wast their rock, their for-tress, and their might; Thou,
3. O may thy sol-diers, faith-ful, true, and bold,
4. O blest com-mu-nion, fel-low-ship di-vine!
5. And when the strife is fierce, the war-fare long,
6. From earth's wide bounds, from o-cean's far-thest coast, Through

thee by faith be - fore the world con - fessed, Thy
Lord, their cap - tain in the well - fought fight;
Fight as the saints who no - bly fought of old, And
We fee - bly strug - gle, they in glo - ry shine; Yet
Steals on the ear the dis - tant tri - umph song, And
gates of pearl streams in the count - less host,
name, O Je - sus, be for - ev - er blest.
Thou, in the dark - ness drear, their one true light.
win with them the vic - tor's crown of gold.
all are one in thee, for all are thine.
hearts are brave a - gain, and arms are strong.
Sing - ing to Fa - ther, Son, and Ho - ly Ghost,
Al - le - lu - ia, Al - le - lu - ia! A-men.

For All the Saints

SARUM 10 10 10. with Alleluias

William W. How, 1823-1897 — Joseph Barnby, 1838-1896

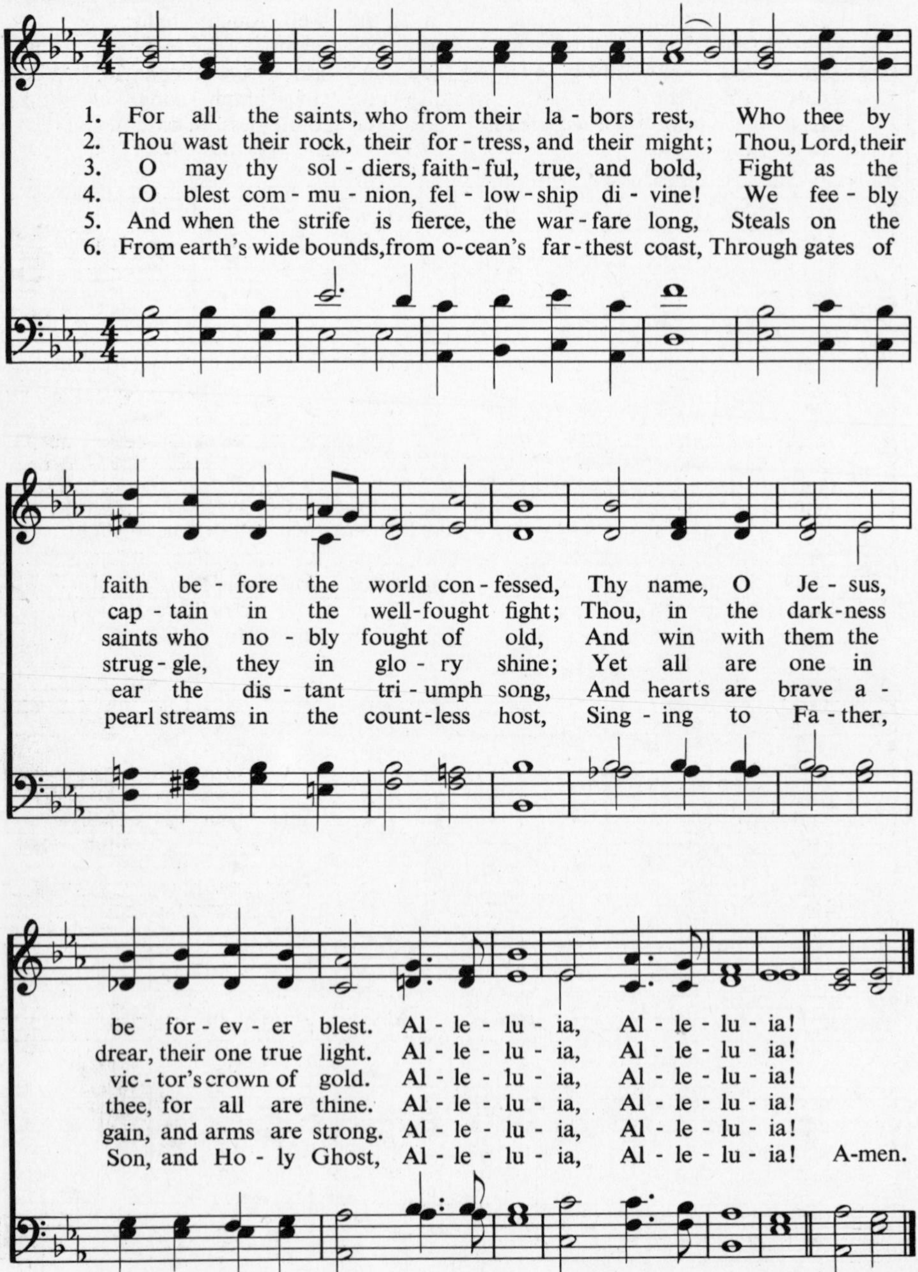
1. For all the saints, who from their la - bors rest, Who thee by
2. Thou wast their rock, their for - tress, and their might; Thou, Lord, their
3. O may thy sol - diers, faith - ful, true, and bold, Fight as the
4. O blest com - mu - nion, fel - low - ship di - vine! We fee - bly
5. And when the strife is fierce, the war - fare long, Steals on the
6. From earth's wide bounds, from o - cean's far - thest coast, Through gates of
faith be - fore the world con - fessed, Thy name, O Je - sus,
cap - tain in the well-fought fight; Thou, in the dark - ness
saints who no - bly fought of old, And win with them the
strug - gle, they in glo - ry shine; Yet all are one in
ear the dis - tant tri - umph song, And hearts are brave a -
pearl streams in the count - less host, Sing - ing to Fa - ther,
be for - ev - er blest. Al - le - lu - ia, Al - le - lu - ia!
drear, their one true light. Al - le - lu - ia, Al - le - lu - ia!
vic - tor's crown of gold. Al - le - lu - ia, Al - le - lu - ia!
thee, for all are thine. Al - le - lu - ia, Al - le - lu - ia!
gain, and arms are strong. Al - le - lu - ia, Al - le - lu - ia!
Son, and Ho - ly Ghost, Al - le - lu - ia, Al - le - lu - ia! A-men.

538

Eternal Father, Strong to Save

MELITA 88.88.88.

WILLIAM WHITING, 1825-1878 — JOHN B. DYKES, 1823-1876

1. E - ter - nal Fa - ther, strong to save, Whose arm hath bound the
2. O Christ, whose voice the wa - ters heard, And hushed their rag - ing
3. O Ho - ly Spir - it, who didst brood Up - on the wa - ters
4. O Trin - i - ty of love and power, Our bre - thren shield in
rest - less wave, Who bidst the might - y o - cean deep
at thy word, Who walk - edst on the foam - ing deep,
dark and rude, And bid their an - gry tu - mult cease,
dan - ger's hour; From rock and tem - pest, fire and foe,
Its own ap - point - ed lim - its keep: O hear us when we
And calm a - mid the storm didst sleep: O hear us when we
And give, for wild con - fu - sion, peace: O hear us when we
Pro - tect them where - so - e'er they go: Thus ev - er - more shall
cry to thee For those in per - il on the sea.
cry to thee For those in per - il on the sea.
cry to thee For those in per - il on the sea.
rise to thee Glad hymns of praise from land and sea. A-men.

539

God Be with You Till We Meet Again

Jeremiah E. Rankin, 1828-1904

GOD BE WITH YOU 98.89.
William G. Tomer, 1833-1896

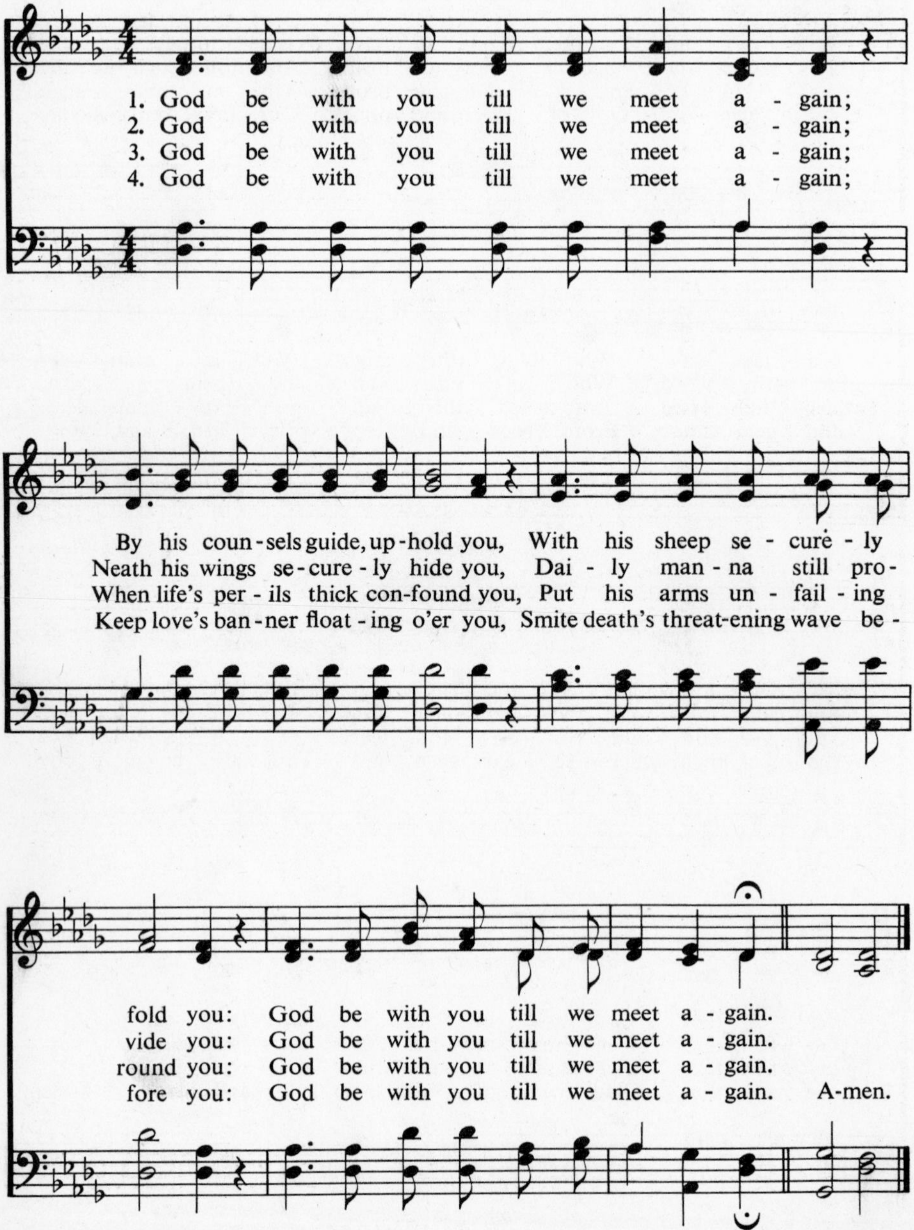
1. God be with you till we meet a - gain;
2. God be with you till we meet a - gain;
3. God be with you till we meet a - gain;
4. God be with you till we meet a - gain;
By his coun - sels guide, up - hold you, With his sheep se - cure - ly
Neath his wings se - cure - ly hide you, Dai - ly man - na still pro -
When life's per - ils thick con - found you, Put his arms un - fail - ing
Keep love's ban - ner float - ing o'er you, Smite death's threat-ening wave be -
fold you: God be with you till we meet a - gain.
vide you: God be with you till we meet a - gain.
round you: God be with you till we meet a - gain.
fore you: God be with you till we meet a - gain. A-men.

TRAVEL

God Be with You Till We Meet Again

RANDOLPH 98.89.

JEREMIAH E. RANKIN, 1828-1904

R. VAUGHAN WILLIAMS, 1872-1958

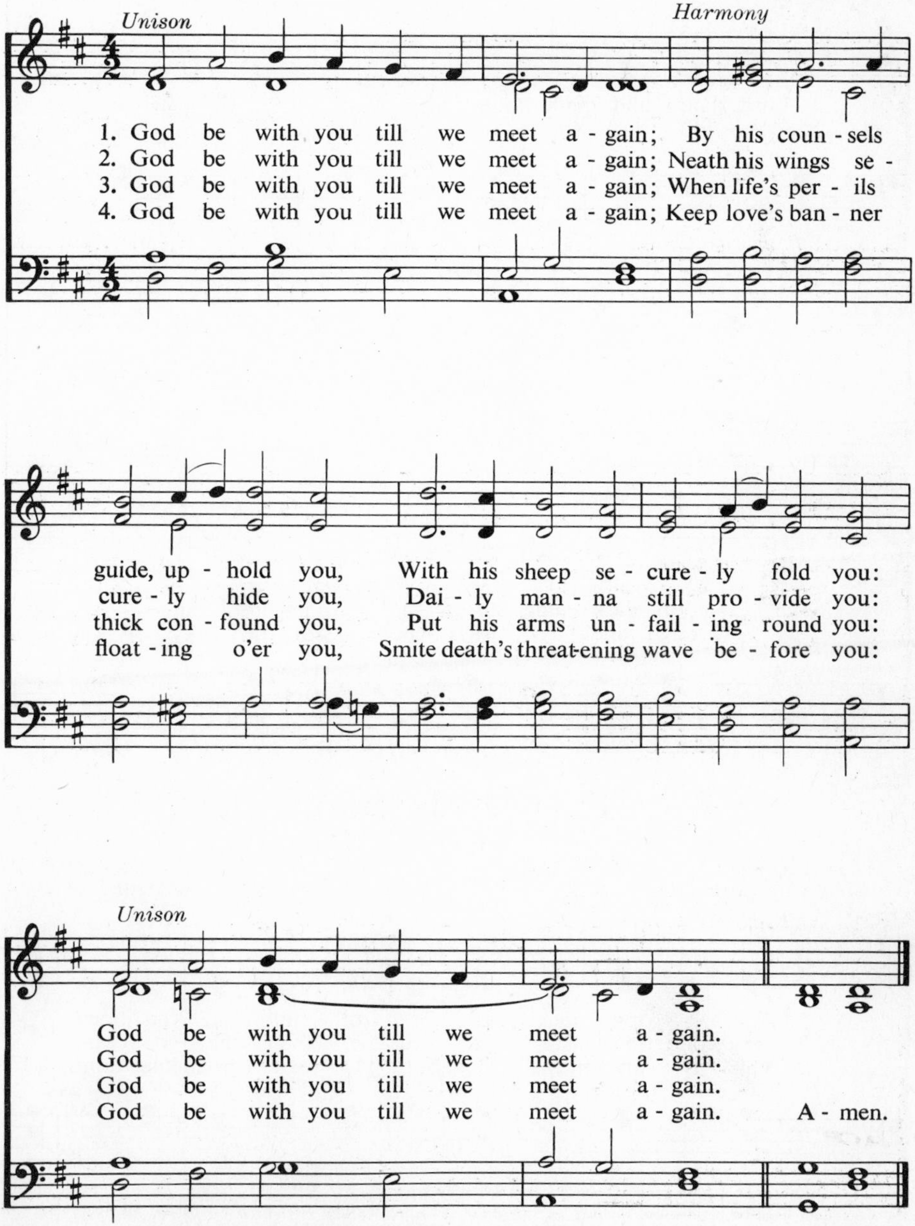
Unison
Harmony
1. God be with you till we meet a - gain; By his coun - sels guide, up - hold you, With his sheep se - cure - ly fold you: God be with you till we meet a - gain.
2. God be with you till we meet a - gain; Neath his wings se - cure - ly hide you, Dai - ly man - na still pro - vide you: God be with you till we meet a - gain.
3. God be with you till we meet a - gain; When life's per - ils thick con - found you, Put his arms un - fail - ing round you: God be with you till we meet a - gain.
4. God be with you till we meet a - gain; Keep love's ban - ner float - ing o'er you, Smite death's threat-ening wave be - fore you: God be with you till we meet a - gain.
Unison
A - men.

Music from *The English Hymnal* by permission of Oxford University Press.

TRAVEL

541

Lord, Guard and Guide the Men Who Fly

HESPERUS LM

Mary C. D. Hamilton, 1915- | Henry Baker, 1835-1910

1. Lord, guard and guide the men who fly Through the great
2. A - loft in sol - i - tudes of space, Up - hold them
spac - es of the sky; Be with them tra - vers - ing the
with thy sav - ing grace. O God, pro - tect the men who
air In dark - ening storms or sun - shine fair.
fly Through lone - ly ways be - neath the sky. A - men.

542

This Is My Song

FINLANDIA 11 10.11 10.11 10.

Lloyd Stone, 1912- | Jean Sibelius, 1865-1957

Stanza 3, Georgia Harkness, 1891- | Arr. for *The Hymnal*, 1933

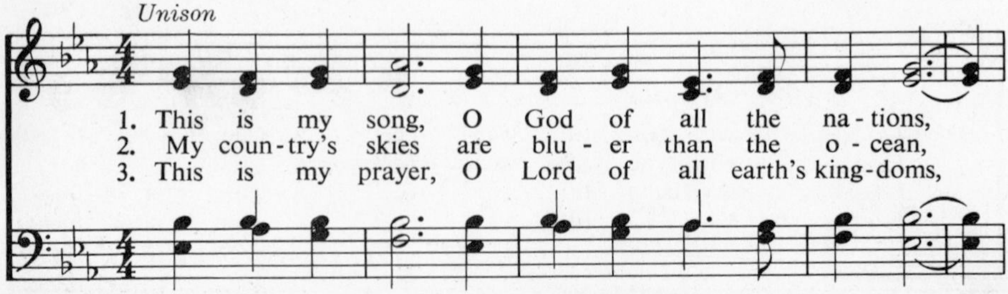

Unison
1. This is my song, O God of all the na - tions,
2. My coun - try's skies are blu - er than the o - cean,
3. This is my prayer, O Lord of all earth's king - doms,

A song of peace for lands a - far and mine. This is my
And sun - light beams on clo - ver - leaf and pine. But oth - er
Thy king - dom come; on earth thy will be done. Let Christ be
home, the coun - try where my heart is; Here are my hopes, my
lands have sun - light too, and clo - ver, And skies are ev - ery-
lift - ed up till all men serve him, And hearts u - nit - ed
dreams, my ho - ly shrine; But oth - er hearts in oth - er lands are
where as blue as mine. Oh, hear my song, thou God of all the
learn to live as one. Oh, hear my prayer, thou God of all the
beat - ing With hopes and dreams as true and high as mine.
na - tions, A song of peace for their land and for mine.
na - tions. My - self I give thee; let thy will be done. A - men.

O Beautiful for Spacious Skies

MATERNA CMD

KATHARINE LEE BATES, 1859-1929 | SAMUEL A. WARD, 1847-1903

1. O beau - ti - ful for spa-cious skies, For am - ber waves of grain,
2. O beau - ti - ful for pil - grim feet, Whose stern, im - pas - sioned stress
3. O beau - ti - ful for he - roes proved In lib - er - at - ing strife,
4. O beau - ti - ful for pa - triot dream That sees be - yond the years
For pur - ple moun - tain maj - es - ties A - bove the fruit - ed plain!
A thor - ough - fare for free - dom beat A - cross the wil - der - ness!
Who more than self their coun - try loved, And mer - cy more than life!
Thine al - a - bas - ter cit - ies gleam, Un - dimmed by hu - man tears!
A - mer - i - ca! A - mer - i - ca! God shed his grace on thee,
A - mer - i - ca! A - mer - i - ca! God mend thine ev - ery flaw,
A - mer - i - ca! A - mer - i - ca! May God thy gold re - fine,
A - mer - i - ca! A - mer - i - ca! God shed his grace on thee,
And crown thy good with broth - er - hood From sea to shin - ing sea.
Con - firm thy soul in self - con - trol, Thy lib - er - ty in law.
Till all suc - cess be no - ble - ness, And ev - ery gain di - vine.
And crown thy good with broth - er - hood From sea to shin - ing sea. A - men.

God the Omnipotent

HENRY F. CHORLEY, 1808-1872
JOHN ELLERTON, 1826-1893

RUSSIAN HYMN 11 10.11 9.
ALEXIS F. LVOV, 1798-1870

1. God the Om - nip - o - tent! King, who or - dain - est
2. God the All - mer - ci - ful! earth hath for - sak - en
3. God the all - righ - teous One! man hath de - fied thee;
4. So shall thy peo - ple, with thank - ful de - vo - tion,
Thun - der thy clar - ion, the light - ning thy sword;
Meek - ness and mer - cy, and slight - ed thy Word;
Yet to e - ter - ni - ty stand - eth thy Word;
Praise him who saved them from per - il and sword,
Show forth thy pit - y on high where thou reign - est;
Let not thy wrath in its ter - rors a - wak - en;
False-hood and wrong shall not tar - ry be - side thee;
Sing - ing in cho - rus from o - cean to o - cean,
Give to us peace in our time, O Lord.
Give to us peace in our time, O Lord.
Give to us peace in our time, O Lord.
Peace to the na - tions, and praise to the Lord. A - men.

CITY, NATION, WORLD

545

Mine Eyes Have Seen the Glory

BATTLE HYMN OF THE REPUBLIC 15 15 15.6.
with Refrain

Julia Ward Howe, 1819-1910

American Camp Meeting Tune

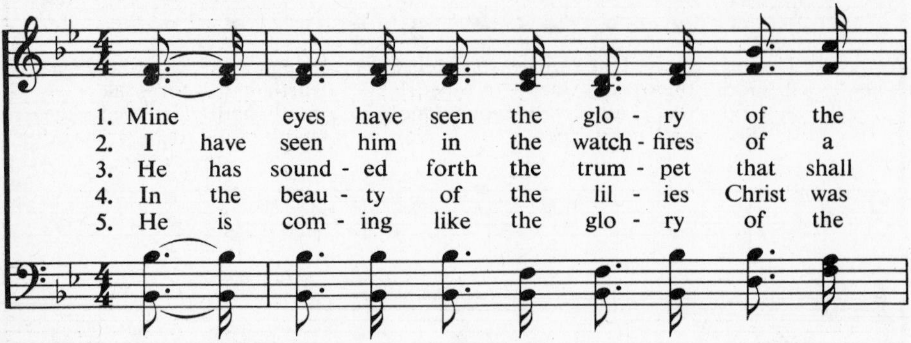
1. Mine eyes have seen the glo - ry of the
2. I have seen him in the watch - fires of a
3. He has sound - ed forth the trum - pet that shall
4. In the beau - ty of the lil - ies Christ was
5. He is com - ing like the glo - ry of the

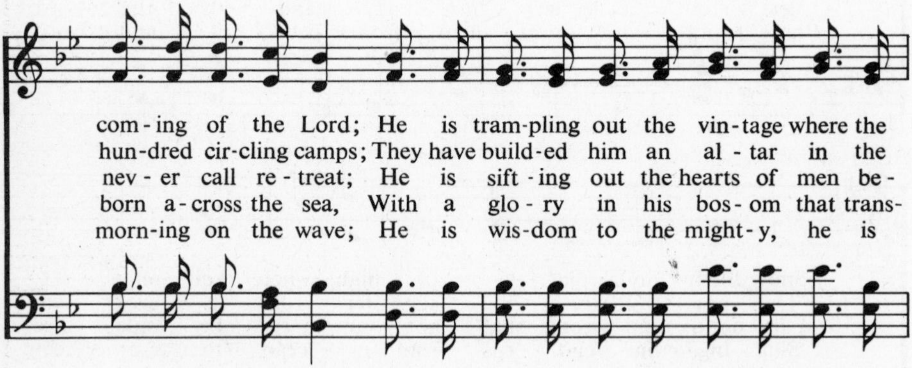
com - ing of the Lord; He is tram-pling out the vin - tage where the
hun-dred cir-cling camps; They have build-ed him an al - tar in the
nev - er call re - treat; He is sift - ing out the hearts of men be -
born a - cross the sea, With a glo - ry in his bos - om that trans-
morn-ing on the wave; He is wis-dom to the might - y, he is

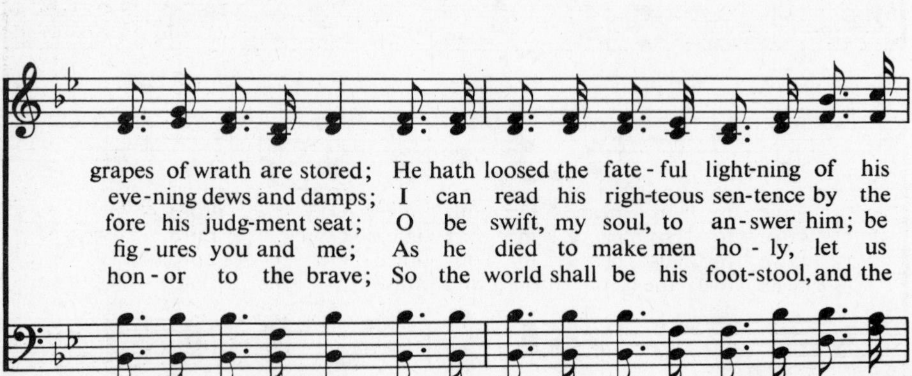
grapes of wrath are stored; He hath loosed the fate - ful light-ning of his
eve-ning dews and damps; I can read his righ-teous sen-tence by the
fore his judg-ment seat; O be swift, my soul, to an - swer him; be
fig - ures you and me; As he died to make men ho - ly, let us
hon - or to the brave; So the world shall be his foot-stool, and the

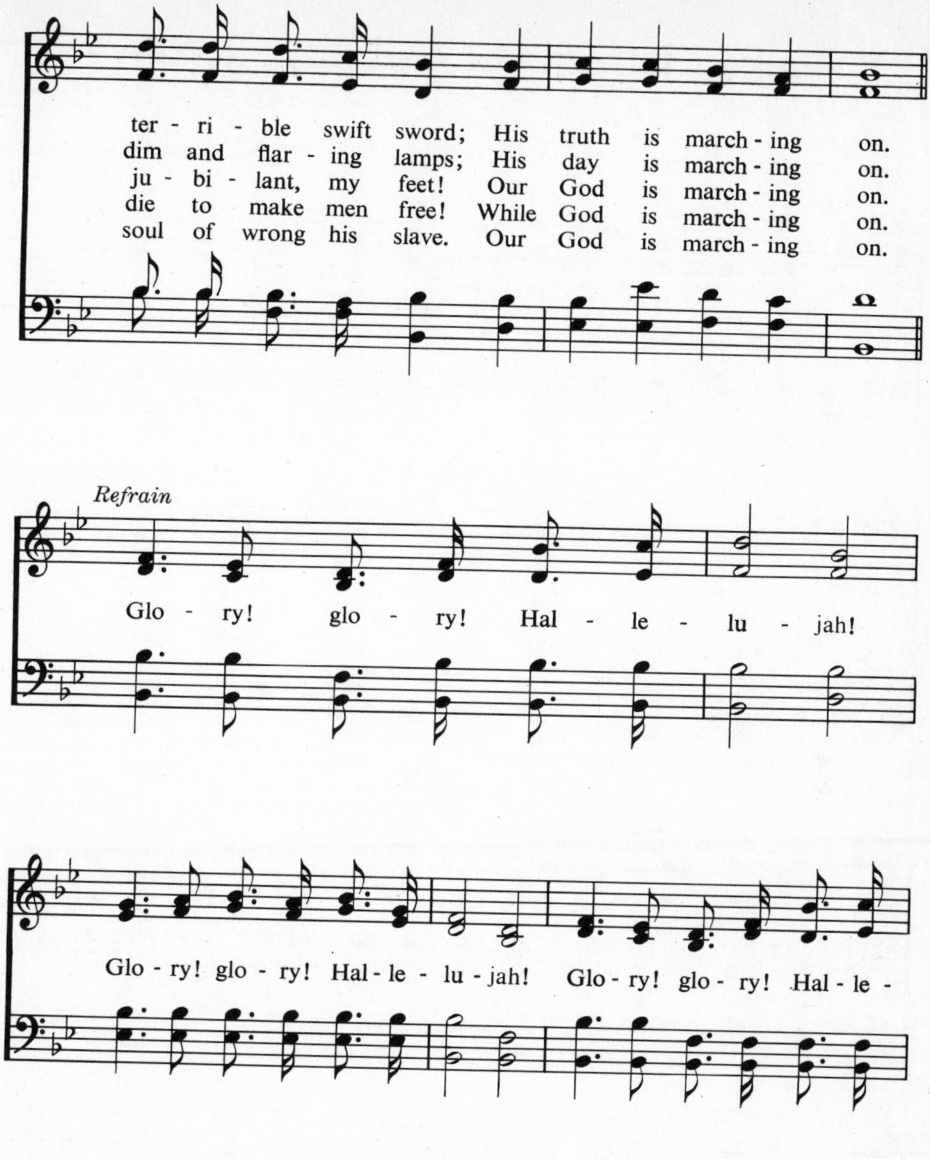
ter - ri - ble swift sword; His truth is march - ing on.
dim and flar - ing lamps; His day is march - ing on.
ju - bi - lant, my feet! Our God is march - ing on.
die to make men free! While God is march - ing on.
soul of wrong his slave. Our God is march - ing on.
Refrain
Glo - ry! glo - ry! Hal - le - lu - jah!
Glo - ry! glo - ry! Hal - le - lu - jah! Glo - ry! glo - ry! Hal - le -
lu - jah! His truth is march - ing on.

Judge Eternal, Throned in Splendor

TANTUM ERGO 87.87.87.

HENRY S. HOLLAND, 1847-1918

SAMUEL WEBBE, SR., 1740-1816

1. Judge e - ter - nal, throned in splen - dor, Lord of lords and
2. Crown, O God, thine own en - deav - or; Cleave our dark - ness
King of kings, With thy liv - ing fire of judg - ment
with thy sword; Feed thy faint and hun - gry peo - ples
Purge this land of bit - ter things; Sol - ace all its
With the rich - ness of thy Word; Cleanse the bod - y
wide do - min - ion With the heal - ing of thy wings.
of this na - tion Through the glo - ry of the Lord. A - men.

CITY, NATION, WORLD

My Country, 'Tis of Thee

AMERICA 664.6664.

SAMUEL F. SMITH, 1808-1895

ANONYMOUS in *Thesaurus Musicus*, 1744

1. My coun - try, 'tis of thee, Sweet land of lib - er - ty,
2. My na - tive coun - try, thee, Land of the no - ble, free;
3. Let mu - sic swell the breeze, And ring from all the trees
4. Our fa - thers' God, to thee, Au - thor of lib - er - ty,
Of thee I sing; Land where my fa - thers died, Land of the
Thy name I love; I love thy rocks and rills, Thy woods and
Sweet free - dom's song; Let mor - tal tongues a - wake; Let all that
To thee we sing; Long may our land be bright With free - dom's
pil - grims' pride, From ev - ery moun - tain - side Let free - dom ring!
tem - pled hills; My heart with rap - ture thrills, Like that a - bove.
breathe par - take; Let rocks their si - lence break, The sound pro - long.
ho - ly light; Pro - tect us by thy might, Great God, our King. A - men.

Not Alone for Mighty Empire

HYFRYDOL 87.87.D.

WILLIAM P. MERRILL, 1867-1954

ROWLAND H. PRICHARD, 1811-1887

1. Not a - lone for might - y em - pire, Stretch - ing far o'er
2. Not for bat - tle - ship and for - tress, Not for con - quests
3. For the ar - mies of the faith - ful, Souls that passed and
4. God of jus - tice, save the peo - ple From the clash of
land and sea, Not a - lone for boun - teous har - vests, Lift we
of the sword, But for con - quests of the spir - it Give we
left no name, For the glo - ry that il - lu - mines Pa - triot
race and creed, From the strife of class and fac - tion, Make our
up our hearts to thee: Stand - ing in the liv - ing pres - ent,
thanks to thee, O Lord; For the price - less gift of free - dom,
lives of death - less fame; For our proph - ets and a - pos - tles,
na - tion free in - deed; Keep her faith in sim - ple man - hood
Mem - o - ry and hope be - tween, Lord, we would with
For the home, the church, the school, For the o - pen
Loy - al to the liv - ing Word, For all he - roes
Strong as when her life be - gan, Till it find its

Words used by permission of the estate of William Pierson Merrill.

CITY, NATION, WORLD

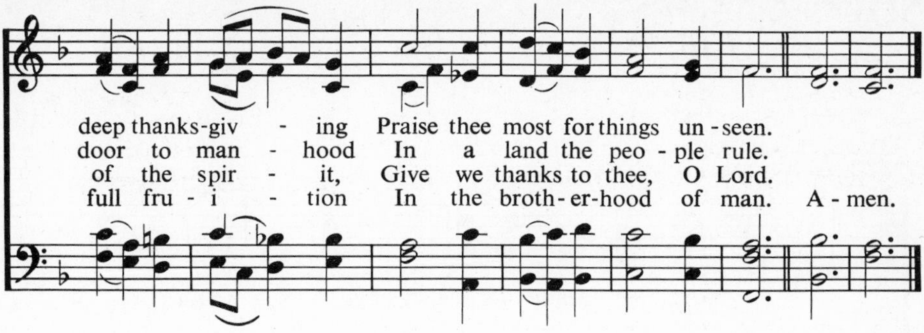
deep thanks-giv - ing Praise thee most for things un-seen.
door to man - hood In a land the peo-ple rule.
of the spir - it, Give we thanks to thee, O Lord.
full fru - i - tion In the broth-er-hood of man. A-men.

549

Behold Us, Lord, a Little Space

JOHN ELLERTON, 1826-1893

DUNFERMLINE CM
Scottish Psalter, 1615

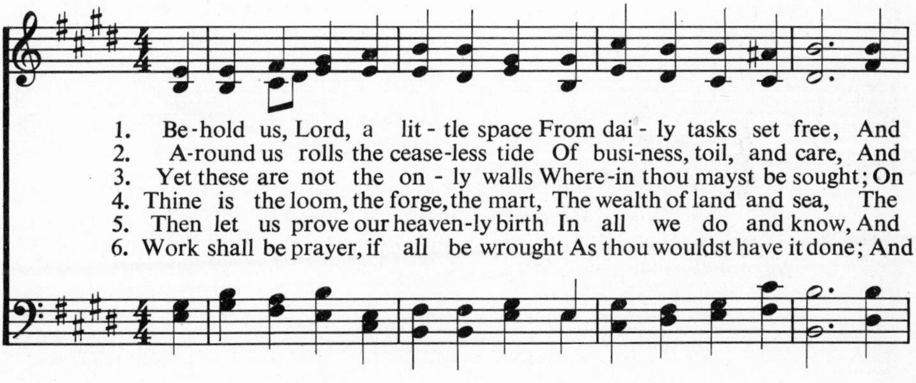
1. Be-hold us, Lord, a lit-tle space From dai-ly tasks set free, And
2. A-round us rolls the cease-less tide Of busi-ness, toil, and care, And
3. Yet these are not the on-ly walls Where-in thou mayst be sought; On
4. Thine is the loom, the forge, the mart, The wealth of land and sea, The
5. Then let us prove our heaven-ly birth In all we do and know, And
6. Work shall be prayer, if all be wrought As thou wouldst have it done; And

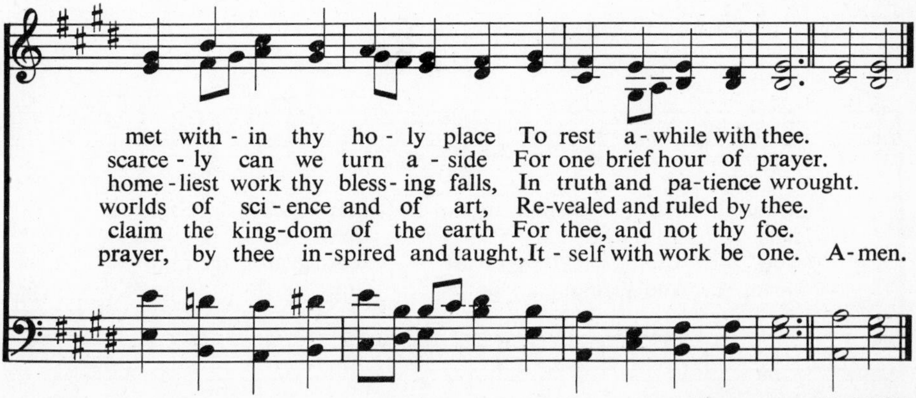
met with-in thy ho-ly place To rest a-while with thee.
scarce-ly can we turn a-side For one brief hour of prayer.
home-liest work thy bless-ing falls, In truth and pa-tience wrought.
worlds of sci-ence and of art, Re-vealed and ruled by thee.
claim the king-dom of the earth For thee, and not thy foe.
prayer, by thee in-spired and taught, It-self with work be one. A-men.

Alternate tune: ST. AGNES

CITY, NATION, WORLD

O God, Beneath Thy Guiding Hand

DUKE STREET LM

LEONARD BACON, 1802-1881 JOHN HATTON, d. 1793

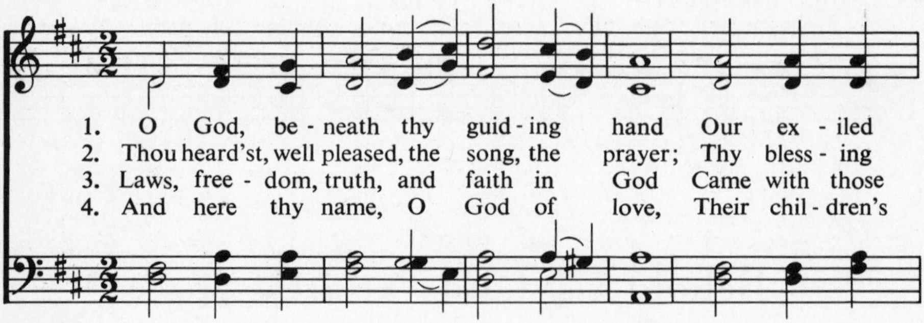
1. O God, be - neath thy guid - ing hand Our ex - iled
2. Thou heard'st, well pleased, the song, the prayer; Thy bless - ing
3. Laws, free - dom, truth, and faith in God Came with those
4. And here thy name, O God of love, Their chil - dren's

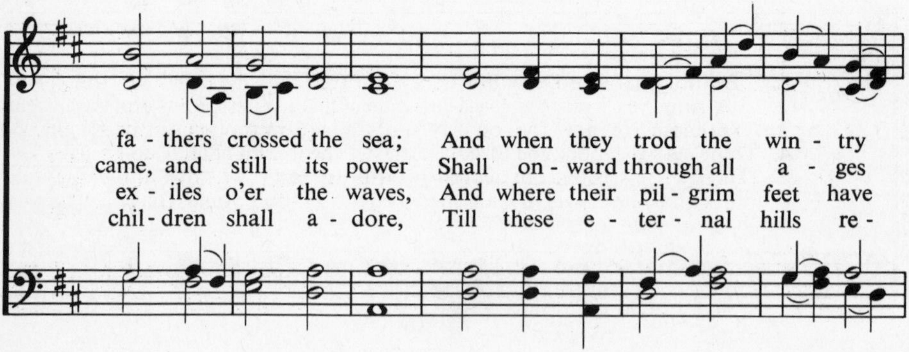
fa - thers crossed the sea; And when they trod the win - try
came, and still its power Shall on - ward through all a - ges
ex - iles o'er the waves, And where their pil - grim feet have
chil - dren shall a - dore, Till these e - ter - nal hills re -

strand, With prayer and psalm they wor - shiped thee.
bear The mem - ory of that ho - ly hour.
trod, The God they trust - ed guards their graves.
move, And spring a - dorns the earth no more. A - men.

Lord, While for All Mankind We Pray

JOHN R. WREFORD, 1800-1881

HARLECH CM
Trad. Welsh Melody

1. Lord, while for all man - kind we pray, Of
2. O guard our shores from ev - ery foe; With
3. U - nite us in the sa - cred love Of
4. Lord of the na - tions, thus to thee Our
ev - ery clime and coast, O hear us for our
peace our bor - ders bless, Our cit - ies with pros -
knowl - edge, truth, and thee; And let our hills and
coun - try we com - mend; Be thou her ref - uge
na - tive land, The land we love the most.
per - i - ty, Our fields with plen - teous - ness.
val - leys shout The songs of lib - er - ty.
and her trust, Her ev - er - last - ing friend. A - men.

552

God of Our Fathers

NATIONAL HYMN 10 10.10 10.

DANIEL C. ROBERTS, 1841-1907 — GEORGE W. WARREN, 1828-1902

Trumpets, before each stanza
1. God of our fa-thers, whose al-might-y hand
2. Thy love di - vine hath led us in the past;
3. From war's a - larms, from dead-ly pes - ti - lence,
4. Re-fresh thy peo - ple on their toil - some way;
Leads forth in beau - ty all the star - ry band
In this free land by thee our lot is cast;
Be thy strong arm our ev - er sure de - fense;
Lead us from night to nev - er - end - ing day;
Of shin - ing worlds in splen - dor through the skies,
Be thou our rul - er, guard - ian, guide, and stay,
Thy true re - li - gion in our hearts in - crease,
Fill all our lives with love and grace di - vine,
Our grate - ful songs be - fore thy throne a - rise.
Thy Word our law, thy paths our cho - sen way.
Thy boun - teous good - ness nour - ish us in peace.
And glo - ry, laud, and praise be ev - er thine. A - men.

ACTS OF PRAISE

553

Great art thou, O Lord, and greatly to be praised; great is thy power, and thy wisdom infinite. And thee would man praise: man, a part of thy creation; man, who bears about him his mortality, the witness of his sins, even the witness that thou dost resist the proud. Yet man would praise thee, he who is part of thy creation. Thou awakest us to delight in praising thee; for thou hast made us for thyself and our hearts are restless till they find rest in thee.

Grant, then, Lord, that I may know and understand whether first to call upon thee or to praise thee; whether first to know thee or to call upon thee. But who can call upon thee, not knowing thee? For he that knoweth thee not may call on thee as other than thou art. Or, is it rather, that we call on thee that we may know thee? But how shall they call on him in whom they have not believed? Or how shall they believe without a preacher?

Now, they shall praise the Lord who seek him, for those who seek shall find, and finding him shall praise him. Thee will I seek, O Lord, calling upon thee; and I will call upon thee believing in thee: for to us thou hast been preached. My faith, Lord, calls upon thee: that faith which thou hast given me, wherewith thou hast inspired me, through the incarnation of thy Son, through the ministry of thy preacher.

Augustine, The Confessions, *Book I, Chapter 1*

THE PSALTER

554

Blessed Is the Man

Blessed is the man who walks not in the counsel of the wicked,

nor stands in the way of sinners,
nor sits in the seat of scoffers;

but his delight is in the law of the Lord,

and on his law he meditates day and night.

He is like a tree planted by streams of water,

that yields its fruit in its season,

and its leaf does not wither.

In all that he does, he prospers.

The wicked are not so,

but are like chaff which the wind drives away.

Therefore the wicked will not stand in the judgment,

nor sinners in the congregation of the righteous;

for the Lord knows the way of the righteous,

but the way of the wicked will perish.

Psalm 1

555

O Lord, How Majestic Is Thy Name!

O Lord, our Lord, how majestic is thy name in all the earth!

Thou whose glory above the heavens is chanted by the mouth of babes and infants,

thou hast founded a bulwark because of thy foes,

to still the enemy and the avenger.

When I look at thy heavens, the work of thy fingers,

the moon and the stars which thou hast established;

what is man that thou art mindful of him,

and the son of man that thou dost care for him?

Yet thou hast made him little less than God,

and dost crown him with glory and honor.

Thou hast given him dominion over the works of thy hands;

thou hast put all things under his feet,

all sheep and oxen,

and also the beasts of the field,

the birds of the air, and the fish of the sea,

whatever passes along the paths of the sea.

O Lord, our Lord,

how majestic is thy name in all the earth!

Psalm 8

556

Who Shall Dwell on Thy Holy Hill?

O Lord, who shall dwell on thy holy hill?

He who walks blamelessly, and does what is right, and speaks truth from his heart;

who does not slander with his tongue, and does no evil to his friend,

nor takes up a reproach against his neighbor;

in whose eyes a reprobate is despised,

but who honors those who fear the Lord;

who swears to his own hurt and does not change;

and does not take a bribe against the innocent.

He who does these things

shall never be moved.

Psalm 15:1b-4, 5bc

557

Preserve Me, O God

Preserve me, O God,

for in thee I take refuge.

I say to the Lord,

"Thou art my Lord; I have no good apart from thee."

The Lord is my chosen portion and my cup;

thou holdest my lot.

The lines have fallen for me in pleasant places;

yea, I have a goodly heritage.

I bless the Lord who gives me counsel;

in the night also my heart instructs me.

I keep the Lord always before me;

because he is at my right hand, I shall not be moved.

Therefore my heart is glad, and my soul rejoices;

my body also dwells secure.

Thou dost show me the path of life; in thy presence there is fulness of joy,

in thy right hand are pleasures for evermore.

Psalm 16:1-2, 5-9, 11

558

The Glory of God

The heavens are telling the glory of God;

and the firmament proclaims his handiwork.

Day to day pours forth speech,

and night to night declares knowledge.

There is no speech, nor are there words;

their voice is not heard;

yet their voice goes out through all the earth,

and their words to the end of the world.

In them he has set a tent for the sun, which comes forth like a bridegroom leaving his chamber,

and like a strong man runs its course with joy.

Its rising is from the end of the heavens, and its circuit to the end of them;

and there is nothing hid from its heat.

The law of the Lord is perfect, reviving the soul;

the testimony of the Lord is sure, making wise the simple;

the precepts of the Lord are right, rejoicing the heart;

the commandment of the Lord is pure, enlightening the eyes;

the fear of the Lord is clean, enduring for ever;

the ordinances of the Lord are true, and righteous altogether.

More to be desired are they than gold, even much fine gold;

sweeter also than honey and drippings of the honeycomb.

Moreover by them is thy servant warned;

in keeping them there is great reward.

But who can discern his errors?

Clear thou me from hidden faults.

Keep back thy servant also from presumptuous sins;

let them not have dominion over me!

Then I shall be blameless,

and innocent of great transgression.

Let the words of my mouth and the meditation of my heart be acceptable in thy sight,

O Lord, my rock and my redeemer.

Psalm 19

559

My God, Why Hast Thou Forsaken Me?

My God, my God, why hast thou forsaken me?

Why art thou so far from helping me?

O my God, I cry by day, but thou dost not answer;

and by night, but find no rest.

Yet thou art holy,

enthroned on the praises of Israel.

In thee our fathers trusted;

they trusted, and thou didst deliver them.

To thee they cried, and were saved;

in thee they trusted, and were not disappointed.

All who see me mock at me,

they make mouths at me, they wag their heads;

"He committed his cause to the Lord; let him deliver him,

let him rescue him, for he delights in him!"

They divide my garments among them,

and for my raiment they cast lots.

But thou, O Lord, be not far off!

O thou my help, hasten to my aid!

I will tell of thy name to my brethren;

in the midst of the congregation I will praise thee:

You who fear the Lord, praise him!

all you sons of Jacob, glorify him,

for he has not despised or abhorred the affliction of the afflicted;

and he has not hid his face from him, but has heard, when he cried to him.

From thee comes my praise in the great congregation;

my vows I will pay before those who fear him.

All the ends of the earth shall remember and turn to the Lord;

and all the families of the nations shall worship before him.

For dominion belongs to the Lord,

and he rules over the nations.

Psalm 22:1ab, 2-5, 7-8, 18-19, 22-23ab, 24-25, 27-28

560

The Lord Is My Shepherd

The Lord is my shepherd;

I shall not want.

He maketh me to lie down in green pastures:

he leadeth me beside the still waters.

He restoreth my soul:

he leadeth me in the paths of righteousness for his name's sake.

Yea, though I walk through the valley of the shadow of death, I will fear no evil:

for thou art with me; thy rod and thy staff they comfort me.

Thou preparest a table before me in the presence of mine enemies:

thou anointest my head with oil; my cup runneth over.

Surely goodness and mercy shall follow me all the days of my life:

and I will dwell in the house of the Lord for ever.

Psalm 23 KJV

561

The Earth Is the Lord's

The earth is the Lord's and the fulness thereof,

the world and those who dwell therein;

for he has founded it upon the seas,

and established it upon the rivers.

Who shall ascend the hill of the Lord?

And who shall stand in his holy place?

He who has clean hands and a pure heart,

who does not lift up his soul to what is false, and does not swear deceitfully.

He will receive blessing from the Lord,

and vindication from the God of his salvation.

Such is the generation of those who seek him,

who seek the face of the God of Jacob.

Lift up your heads, O gates! and be lifted up, O ancient doors!

that the King of glory may come in.

Who is the King of glory?

The Lord, strong and mighty, the Lord, mighty in battle!

Lift up your heads, O gates! and be lifted up, O ancient doors!

that the King of glory may come in!

Who is this King of glory?

The Lord of hosts, he is the King of glory!

Psalm 24

562

In Thee I Trust

To thee, O Lord, I lift up my soul.

O my God, in thee I trust,

let me not be put to shame;

let not my enemies exult over me.

Make me to know thy ways, O Lord;

teach me thy paths.

Lead me in thy truth, and teach me,

for thou art the God of my salvation; for thee I wait all the day long.

Be mindful of thy mercy, O Lord, and of thy steadfast love,

for they have been from of old.

Remember not the sins of my youth, or my transgressions;

according to thy steadfast love remember me, for thy goodness' sake, O Lord!

Good and upright is the Lord;

therefore he instructs sinners in the way.

He leads the humble in what is right,

and teaches the humble his way.

All the paths of the Lord are steadfast love and faithfulness,

for those who keep his covenant and his testimonies.

For thy name's sake, O Lord,

pardon my guilt, for it is great.

Who is the man that fears the Lord?

Him will he instruct in the way that he should choose.

The friendship of the Lord is for those who fear him,

and he makes known to them his covenant.

May integrity and uprightness preserve me,

for I wait for thee.

Psalm 25:1-2, 4-12, 14, 21

563

The Lord Is My Light

The Lord is my light and my salvation;

whom shall I fear?

The Lord is the stronghold of my life;

of whom shall I be afraid?

When evildoers assail me, uttering slanders against me,

my adversaries and foes, they shall stumble and fall.

Though a host encamp against me,

my heart shall not fear;

though war arise against me,

yet I will be confident.

One thing have I asked of the Lord,

that will I seek after;

that I may dwell in the house of the Lord all the days of my life,

to behold the beauty of the Lord, and to inquire in his temple.

For he will hide me in his shelter in the day of trouble;

he will set me high upon a rock.

And now my head shall be lifted up above my enemies round about me;

I will sing and make melody to the Lord.

Hear, O Lord, when I cry aloud,

be gracious to me and answer me!

Thou hast said, "Seek ye my face."

My heart says to thee, "Thy face, Lord, do I seek."

I believe that I shall see the goodness of the Lord in the land of the living!

Wait for the Lord; be strong, and let your heart take courage; yea, wait for the Lord!

Psalm 27:1-5a, 5c-6a, 6c-8, 13-14

564

God's Forgiving Love

Blessed is he whose transgression is forgiven,

whose sin is covered.

Blessed is the man to whom the Lord imputes no iniquity,

and in whose spirit there is no deceit.

When I declared not my sin, my body wasted away

through my groaning all day long.

I acknowledged my sin to thee,

and I did not hide my iniquity;

I said, "I will confess my transgressions to the Lord";

then thou didst forgive the guilt of my sin.

Therefore let every one who is godly offer prayer to thee;

at a time of distress, in the rush of great waters, they shall not reach him.

Thou art a hiding place for me, thou preservest me from trouble;

thou dost encompass me with deliverance.

I will instruct you and teach you the way you should go;

I will counsel you with my eye upon you.

Many are the pangs of the wicked;

but steadfast love surrounds him who trusts in the Lord.

Be glad in the Lord, and rejoice, O righteous,

and shout for joy, all you upright in heart!

Psalm 32:1-3, 5-8, 10-11

565

Rejoice in the Lord!

Rejoice in the Lord, O you righteous!

Praise befits the upright.

For the word of the Lord is upright;

and all his work is done in faithfulness.

He loves righteousness and justice;

the earth is full of the steadfast love of the Lord.

By the word of the Lord the heavens were made,

and all their host by the breath of his mouth.

Let all the earth fear the Lord,

let all the inhabitants of the world stand in awe of him!

For he spoke, and it came to be;

he commanded, and it stood forth.

The Lord brings the counsel of the nations to nought;

he frustrates the plans of the peoples.

The counsel of the Lord stands for ever,

the thoughts of his heart to all generations.

Blessed is the nation whose God is the Lord,

the people whom he has chosen as his heritage!

The Lord looks down from heaven, he sees all the sons of men;

from where he sits enthroned he looks forth on all the inhabitants of the earth,

he who fashions the hearts of them all,

and observes all their deeds.

Our soul waits for the Lord;

he is our help and shield.

Yea, our heart is glad in him,

because we trust in his holy name.

Let thy steadfast love, O Lord, be upon us,

even as we hope in thee.

Psalm 33:1, 4-6, 8-15, 20-22

566

The Lord Is Good

I will bless the Lord at all times;

his praise shall continually be in my mouth.

My soul makes its boast in the Lord;

let the afflicted hear and be glad.

O magnify the Lord with me,

and let us exalt his name together!

I sought the Lord, and he answered me,

and delivered me from all my fears.

Look to him, and be radiant;

so your faces shall never be ashamed.

This poor man cried, and the Lord heard him,

and saved him out of all his troubles.

The angel of the Lord encamps around those who fear him,

and delivers them.

O taste and see that the Lord is good!

Happy is the man who takes refuge in him!

Come, O sons, listen to me,

I will teach you the fear of the Lord.

What man is there who desires life,

and covets many days, that he may enjoy good?

Keep your tongue from evil, and your lips from speaking deceit.

Depart from evil, and do good; seek peace, and pursue it.

When the righteous cry for help, the Lord hears,

and delivers them out of all their troubles.

The Lord is near to the brokenhearted,

and saves the crushed in spirit.

The Lord redeems the life of his servants;

none of those who take refuge in him will be condemned.

Psalm 34:1-8, 11-14, 17-18, 22

567

Trust in the Lord

Fret not yourself because of the wicked,

be not envious of the wrongdoers!

For they will soon fade like the grass,

and wither like the green herb.

Trust in the Lord, and do good;

so you will dwell in the land, and enjoy security.

Take delight in the Lord,

and he will give you the desires of your heart.

Commit your way to the Lord;

trust in him, and he will act.

He will bring forth your vindication as the light,

and your right as the noonday.

Fret not yourself over him who prospers in his way,

over the man who carries out evil devices!

For the wicked shall be cut off;

but those who wait for the Lord shall possess the land.

The steps of a man are from the Lord,

and he establishes him in whose way he delights;

though he fall, he shall not be cast headlong,

for the Lord is the stay of his hand.

Depart from evil, and do good;

so shall you abide for ever.

For the Lord loves justice; he will not forsake his saints.

The righteous shall be preserved for ever.

The salvation of the righteous is from the Lord;

he is their refuge in the time of trouble.

The Lord helps them and delivers them;

he delivers them from the wicked, and saves them, because they take refuge in him.

Psalm 37:1-6, 7bc, 9, 23-24, 27-28ab, 39-40

568

Praise to Our God

I waited patiently for the Lord;

he inclined to me and heard my cry.

He drew me up from the desolate pit, out of the miry bog,

and set my feet upon a rock, making my steps secure.

He put a new song in my mouth,

a song of praise to our God.

Many will see and fear,

and put their trust in the Lord.

Blessed is the man who makes the Lord his trust,

who does not turn to the proud, to those who go astray after false gods!

Thou hast multiplied, O Lord my God, thy wondrous deeds and thy thoughts toward us;

none can compare with thee!

Were I to proclaim and tell of them,

they would be more than can be numbered.

Sacrifice and offering thou dost not desire;

but thou hast given me an open ear.

Burnt offering and sin offering thou hast not required.

Then I said, "Lo, I come; in the roll of the book it is written of me;

I delight to do thy will, O my God;

thy law is within my heart."

I have told the glad news of deliverance in the great congregation;

lo, I have not restrained my lips, as thou knowest, O Lord.

I have not hid thy saving help within my heart,

I have spoken of thy faithfulness and thy salvation;

I have not concealed thy steadfast love

and thy faithfulness from the great congregation.

Do not thou, O Lord, withhold thy mercy from me,

let thy steadfast love and thy faithfulness ever preserve me!

Psalm 40:1-11

569

My Soul Thirsts for God

As a hart longs for flowing streams,

so longs my soul for thee, O God.

My soul thirsts for God, for the living God.

When shall I come and behold the face of God?

My tears have been my food day and night,

while men say to me continually, "Where is your God?"

These things I remember, as I pour out my soul:

how I went with the throng, and led them in procession to the house of God,

with glad shouts and songs of thanksgiving,

a multitude keeping festival.

Why are you cast down, O my soul,

and why are you disquieted within me?

Hope in God;

for I shall again praise him, my help and my God.

My soul is cast down within me,

therefore I remember thee from the land of Jordan and of Hermon, from Mount Mizar.

Deep calls to deep at the thunder of thy cataracts;

all thy waves and thy billows have gone over me.

By day the Lord commands his steadfast love;

and at night his song is with me, a prayer to the God of my life.

I say to God, my rock: "Why hast thou forgotten me?

Why go I mourning because of the oppression of the enemy?"

As with a deadly wound in my body, my adversaries taunt me,

while they say to me continually, "Where is thy God?"

Why are you cast down, O my soul,

and why are you disquieted within me?

Hope in God;

for I shall again praise him, my help and my God.

Psalm 42

570

God Is Our Refuge

God is our refuge and strength,

a very present help in trouble.

Therefore we will not fear though the earth should change,

though the mountains shake in the heart of the sea;

though its waters roar and foam,

though the mountains tremble with its tumult.

There is a river whose streams make glad the city of God,

the holy habitation of the Most High.

God is in the midst of her, she shall not be moved;

God will help her right early.

The nations rage, the kingdoms totter;

he utters his voice, the earth melts.

The Lord of hosts is with us;

the God of Jacob is our refuge.

Come, behold the works of the Lord,

how he has wrought desolations in the earth.

He makes wars cease to the end of the earth;

he breaks the bow, and shatters the spear, he burns the chariots with fire!

"Be still, and know that I am God.

I am exalted among the nations, I am exalted in the earth!"

The Lord of hosts is with us;

the God of Jacob is our refuge.

Psalm 46

571

A Clean Heart

Have mercy on me, O God, according to thy steadfast love;

according to thy abundant mercy blot out my transgressions.

Wash me thoroughly from my iniquity,

and cleanse me from my sin!

For I know my transgressions,

and my sin is ever before me.

Against thee, thee only, have I sinned,

and done that which is evil in thy sight,

so that thou art justified in thy sentence

and blameless in thy judgment.

Behold, thou desirest truth in the inward being;

therefore teach me wisdom in my secret heart.

Hide thy face from my sins,

and blot out all my iniquities.

Create in me a clean heart, O God,

and put a new and right spirit within me.

Cast me not away from thy presence,

and take not thy holy Spirit from me.

Restore to me the joy of thy salvation,

and uphold me with a willing spirit.

Then I will teach transgressors thy ways,

and sinners will return to thee.

Deliver me from bloodguiltiness, O God, thou God of my salvation,

and my tongue will sing aloud of thy deliverance.

O Lord, open thou my lips,

and my mouth shall show forth thy praise.

For thou hast no delight in sacrifice;

were I to give a burnt offering, thou wouldst not be pleased.

The sacrifice acceptable to God is a broken spirit;

a broken and contrite heart, O God, thou wilt not despise.

Psalm 51:1-4, 6, 9-17

572

God's Steadfast Love

Be merciful to me, O God, be merciful to me,

for in thee my soul takes refuge;

in the shadow of thy wings I will take refuge,

till the storms of destruction pass by.

I cry to God Most High,

to God who fulfills his purpose for me.

He will send from heaven and save me,

God will send forth his steadfast love and his faithfulness!

Be exalted, O God, above the heavens!

Let thy glory be over all the earth!

My heart is steadfast, O God, my heart is steadfast!

I will sing and make melody!

I will give thanks to thee, O Lord, among the peoples;

I will sing praises to thee among the nations.

For thy steadfast love is great to the heavens,

thy faithfulness to the clouds.

Be exalted, O God, above the heavens!

Let thy glory be over all the earth!

Psalm 57:1-3ac, 5, 7, 9-11

573

God Is My Rock and My Salvation

For God alone my soul waits in silence;

from him comes my salvation.

He only is my rock and my salvation, my fortress;

I shall not be greatly moved.

For God alone my soul waits in silence,

for my hope is from him.

He only is my rock and my salvation, my fortress;

I shall not be shaken.

On God rests my deliverance and my honor;

my mighty rock, my refuge is God.

Trust in him at all times, O people;

pour out your heart before him; God is a refuge for us.

Once God has spoken; twice have I heard this:

that power belongs to God;

and that to thee, O Lord, belongs steadfast love.

For thou dost requite a man according to his work.

Psalm 62:1-2, 5-8, 11-12

574

Thou Art My God

O God, thou art my God, I seek thee,

my soul thirsts for thee;

my flesh faints for thee,

as in a dry and weary land where no water is.

So I have looked upon thee in the sanctuary,

beholding thy power and glory.

Because thy steadfast love is better than life,

my lips will praise thee.

So I will bless thee as long as I live;

I will lift up my hands and call on thy name.

My soul is feasted as with marrow and fat,

and my mouth praises thee with joyful lips,

when I think of thee upon my bed,

and meditate on thee in the watches of the night;

for thou hast been my help,

and in the shadow of thy wings I sing for joy.

My soul clings to thee;

thy right hand upholds me.

Psalm 63:1-8

575

Praise Is Due to Thee, O God

Praise is due to thee, O God, in Zion;

and to thee shall vows be performed,

O thou who hearest prayer!

To thee shall all flesh come on account of sins.

When our transgressions prevail over us,

thou dost forgive them.

Blessed is he whom thou dost choose and bring near, to dwell in thy courts!

We shall be satisfied with the goodness of thy house, thy holy temple!

By dread deeds thou dost answer us with deliverance, O God of our salvation,

who art the hope of all the ends of the earth, and of the farthest seas;

who by thy strength hast established the mountains,

being girded with might;

who dost still the roaring of the seas,

the roaring of their waves, the tumult of the peoples;

so that those who dwell at earth's farthest bounds are afraid at thy signs;

thou makest the outgoings of the morning and the evening to shout for joy.

Thou visitest the earth and waterest it, thou greatly enrichest it;

thou providest their grain, for so thou hast prepared it.

Thou waterest its furrows abundantly, settling its ridges,

softening it with showers, and blessing its growth.

Thou crownest the year with thy bounty;

the hills gird themselves with joy,

the meadows clothe themselves with flocks,

the valleys deck themselves with grain, they shout and sing together for joy.

Psalm 65:1-9a, 9c-11a, 12b-13

576

May God Be Gracious

May God be gracious to us and bless us

and make his face to shine upon us,

that thy way may be known upon earth,

thy saving power among all nations.

Let the peoples praise thee, O God;

let all the peoples praise thee!

Let the nations be glad and sing for joy,

for thou dost judge the peoples with equity and guide the nations upon earth.

Let the peoples praise thee, O God;

let all the peoples praise thee!

The earth has yielded its increase;

God, our God, has blessed us.

God has blessed us;

let all the ends of the earth fear him!

Psalm 67

577

May Righteousness Flourish

Give the king thy justice, O God,

and thy righteousness to the royal son!

May he judge thy people with righteousness,

and thy poor with justice!

Let the mountains bear prosperity for the people,

and the hills, in righteousness!

May he defend the cause of the poor of the people,

give deliverance to the needy, and crush the oppressor!

May he live while the sun endures, and as long as the moon,

throughout all generations!

May he be like the rain that falls on the mown grass,

like showers that water the earth!

In his days may righteousness flourish,

and peace abound, till the moon be no more!

May he have dominion from sea to sea,

may all kings fall down before him, all nations serve him!

For he delivers the needy when he calls,

the poor and him who has no helper.

From oppression and violence he redeems their life;

and precious is their blood in his sight.

May his name endure for ever,

his fame continue as long as the sun!

Blessed be the Lord, the God of Israel,

who alone does wondrous things.

Blessed be his glorious name for ever;

may his glory fill the whole earth! Amen and Amen!

Psalm 72:1-8a, 11-12, 14, 17ab, 18-19

578

God Is Good

Truly God is good to the upright,

to those who are pure in heart.

But as for me, my feet had almost stumbled,

my steps had well nigh slipped.

For I was envious of the arrogant,

when I saw the prosperity of the wicked.

For they have no pangs;

their bodies are sound and sleek.

They are not in trouble as other men are;

they are not stricken like other men.

Therefore pride is their necklace;

violence covers them as a garment.

They set their mouths against the heavens,

and their tongue struts through the earth.

Therefore the people turn and praise them;

and find no fault in them.

And they say, "How can God know?

Is there knowledge in the Most High?"

Behold, these are the wicked;

always at ease, they increase in riches.

All in vain have I kept my heart clean

and washed my hands in innocence.

For all the day long I have been stricken,

and chastened every morning.

If I had said, "I will speak thus,"

I would have been untrue to the generation of thy children.

But when I thought how to understand this,

it seemed to me a wearisome task,

until I went into the sanctuary of God;

then I perceived their end.

Truly thou dost set them in slippery places;

thou dost make them fall to ruin.

How they are destroyed in a moment,

swept away utterly by terrors!

They are like a dream when one awakes,

on awaking you despise their phantoms.

When my soul was embittered,

when I was pricked in heart,

I was stupid and ignorant,

I was like a beast toward thee.

Nevertheless I am continually with thee;

thou dost hold my right hand.

Thou dost guide me with thy counsel,

and afterward thou wilt receive me to glory.

Whom have I in heaven but thee?

And there is nothing upon earth that I desire besides thee.

My flesh and my heart may fail,

but God is the strength of my heart and my portion for ever.

Psalm 73:1-6, 9-26

579

How Lovely Is Thy Dwelling Place

How lovely is thy dwelling place,

O Lord of hosts!

My soul longs, yea, faints for the courts of the Lord;

my heart and flesh sing for joy to the living God.

Even the sparrow finds a home, and the swallow a nest for herself, where she may lay her young,

at thy altars, O Lord of hosts, my king and my God.

Blessed are those who dwell in thy house,

ever singing thy praise!

Blessed are the men whose strength is in thee,

in whose heart are the highways to Zion.

O Lord God of hosts, hear my prayer;

give ear, O God of Jacob!

Behold our shield, O God;

look upon the face of thine anointed!

For a day in thy courts is better than a thousand elsewhere.

I would rather be a doorkeeper in the house of my God than dwell in the tents of wickedness.

For the Lord God is a sun and shield; he bestows favor and honor.

No good thing does the Lord withhold from those who walk uprightly.

O Lord of hosts,

blessed is the man who trusts in thee!

Psalm 84:1-5, 8-12

580

The Eternity of God

Lord, thou hast been our dwelling place

in all generations.

Before the mountains were brought forth, or ever thou hadst formed the earth and the world,

from everlasting to everlasting thou art God.

Thou turnest man back to the dust,

and sayest, "Turn back, O children of men!"

For a thousand years in thy sight are but as yesterday when it is past,

or as a watch in the night.

Thou dost sweep men away; they are like a dream,

like grass which is renewed in the morning:

in the morning it flourishes and is renewed;

in the evening it fades and withers.

For we are consumed by thy anger;

by thy wrath we are overwhelmed.

Thou hast set our iniquities before thee,

our secret sins in the light of thy countenance.

For all our days pass away under thy wrath,

our years come to an end like a sigh.

The years of our life are threescore and ten,

or even by reason of strength four-score;

yet their span is but toil and trouble;

they are soon gone, and we fly away.

Who considers the power of thy anger,

and thy wrath according to the fear of thee?

So teach us to number our days

that we may get a heart of wisdom.

Return, O Lord! how long?

Have pity on thy servants!

Satisfy us in the morning with thy steadfast love,

that we may rejoice and be glad all our days.

Make us glad as many days as thou hast afflicted us,

and as many years as we have seen evil.

Let thy work be manifest to thy servants,

and thy glorious power to their children.

Let the favor of the Lord our God be upon us,

and establish thou the work of our hands upon us, yea, the work of our hands establish thou it.

Psalm 90

581

The Shadow of the Almighty

He who dwells in the shelter of the Most High,

who abides in the shadow of the Almighty,

will say to the Lord, "My refuge and my fortress;

my God, in whom I trust."

For he will deliver you from the snare of the fowler

and from the deadly pestilence;

he will cover you with his pinions, and under his wings you will find refuge;

his faithfulness is a shield and buckler.

You will not fear the terror of the night,

nor the arrow that flies by day,

nor the pestilence that stalks in darkness,

nor the destruction that wastes at noonday.

A thousand may fall at your side, ten thousand at your right hand;

but it will not come near you.

You will only look with your eyes

and see the recompense of the wicked.

Because you have made the Lord your refuge,

the Most High your habitation,

no evil shall befall you,

no scourge come near your tent.

For he will give his angels charge of you

to guard you in all your ways.

On their hands they will bear you up,

lest you dash your foot against a stone.

When he calls to me, I will answer him;

I will be with him in trouble, I will rescue him and honor him.

With long life I will satisfy him,

and show him my salvation.

Psalm 91:1-12, 15-16

582

The Lord Reigns

The Lord reigns; he is robed in majesty;

the Lord is robed, he is girded with strength.

Yea, the world is established;

it shall never be moved;

thy throne is established from of old;

thou art from everlasting.

The floods have lifted up, O Lord, the floods have lifted up their voice,

the floods lift up their roaring.

Mightier than the thunders of many waters, mightier than the waves of the sea,

the Lord on high is mighty!

Thy decrees are very sure;

holiness befits thy house, O Lord, for evermore.

Psalm 93

583

Sing to the Lord a New Song

O sing to the Lord a new song;

sing to the Lord, all the earth!

Sing to the Lord, bless his name;

tell of his salvation from day to day.

Declare his glory among the nations,

his marvelous works among all the peoples!

For great is the Lord, and greatly to be praised;

he is to be feared above all gods.

For all the gods of the peoples are idols;

but the Lord made the heavens.

Honor and majesty are before him;

strength and beauty are in his sanctuary.

Ascribe to the Lord, O families of the peoples,

ascribe to the Lord glory and strength!

Ascribe to the Lord the glory due his name;

bring an offering, and come into his courts!

Worship the Lord in holy array;

tremble before him, all the earth!

Say among the nations, "The Lord reigns!

Yea, the world is established, it shall never be moved;

he will judge the peoples with equity."

Let the heavens be glad, and let the earth rejoice;

let the sea roar, and all that fills it;

let the field exult, and everything in it!

Then shall all the trees of the wood sing for joy before the Lord,

for he comes, for he comes to judge the earth.

He will judge the world with righteousness,

and the peoples with his truth.

Psalm 96

584

Light Dawns for the Righteous

The Lord reigns; let the earth rejoice;

let the many coastlands be glad!

Clouds and thick darkness are round about him;

righteousness and justice are the foundation of his throne.

His lightnings lighten the world;

the earth sees and trembles.

The mountains melt like wax before the Lord,

before the Lord of all the earth.

The heavens proclaim his righteousness;

and all the peoples behold his glory.

For thou, O Lord, art most high over all the earth;

thou art exalted far above all gods.

The Lord loves those who hate evil;

he preserves the lives of his saints; he delivers them from the hand of the wicked.

Light dawns for the righteous,

and joy for the upright in heart.

Rejoice in the Lord, O you righteous,

and give thanks to his holy name!

Psalm 97:1-2, 4-6, 9-12

585

The Victory of Our God

O sing to the Lord a new song, for he has done marvelous things!

His right hand and his holy arm have gotten him victory.

The Lord has made known his victory,

he has revealed his vindication in the sight of the nations.

He has remembered his steadfast love and faithfulness to the house of Israel.

All the ends of the earth have seen the victory of our God.

Make a joyful noise to the Lord, all the earth;

break forth into joyous song and sing praises!

Sing praises to the Lord with the lyre,

with the lyre and the sound of melody!

With trumpets and the sound of the horn

make a joyful noise before the King, the Lord!

Let the sea roar, and all that fills it;

the world and those who dwell in it!

Let the floods clap their hands;

let the hills sing for joy together before the Lord,

for he comes to judge the earth. He will judge the world with righteousness,

and the peoples with equity.

Psalm 98

586

Hear My Prayer, O Lord

Hear my prayer, O Lord;

let my cry come to thee!

Do not hide thy face from me in the day of my distress!

Incline thy ear to me; answer me speedily in the day when I call!

My days are like an evening shadow;

I wither away like grass.

But thou, O Lord, art enthroned for ever;

thy name endures to all generations.

Let this be recorded for a generation to come,

so that a people yet unborn may praise the Lord:

that he looked down from his holy height,

from heaven the Lord looked at the earth,

to hear the groans of the prisoners,

to set free those who were doomed to die;

that men may declare in Zion the name of the Lord, and in Jerusalem his praise,

when peoples gather together, and kingdoms, to worship the Lord.

Of old thou didst lay the foundation of the earth,

and the heavens are the work of thy hands.

They will perish, but thou dost endure;

they will all wear out like a garment.

Thou changest them like raiment, and they pass away;

but thou art the same, and thy years have no end.

Psalm 102:1-2, 11-12, 18-22, 25-27

587

Bless the Lord

Bless the Lord, O my soul;

and all that is within me, bless his holy name!

Bless the Lord, O my soul,

and forget not all his benefits,

who forgives all your iniquity,

who heals all your diseases,

who redeems your life from the Pit,

who crowns you with steadfast love and mercy,

who satisfies you with good as long as you live

so that your youth is renewed like the eagle's.

The Lord works vindication and justice

for all who are oppressed.

He made known his ways to Moses,

his acts to the people of Israel.

Psalm 103:1-7

588

The Lord Is Merciful

The Lord is merciful and gracious,

slow to anger and abounding in steadfast love.

He will not always chide,

nor will he keep his anger for ever.

He does not deal with us according to our sins,

nor requite us according to our iniquities.

For as the heavens are high above the earth,

so great is his steadfast love toward those who fear him;

as far as the east is from the west,

so far does he remove our transgressions from us.

As a father pities his children,

so the Lord pities those who fear him.

For he knows our frame;

he remembers that we are dust.

As for man, his days are like grass;

he flourishes like a flower of the field;

for the wind passes over it, and it is gone,

and its place knows it no more.

But the steadfast love of the Lord is from everlasting to everlasting upon those who fear him,

and his righteousness to children's children,

to those who keep his covenant

and remember to do his commandments.

Psalm 103:8-18

589

O Give Thanks

O give thanks to the Lord, for he is good;

for his steadfast love endures for ever!

Let the redeemed of the Lord say so,

whom he has redeemed from trouble

and gathered in from the lands, from the east and from the west,

from the north and from the south.

Some wandered in desert wastes,

finding no way to a city to dwell in;

hungry and thirsty,

their soul fainted within them.

Then they cried to the Lord in their trouble,

and he delivered them from their distress;

he led them by a straight way,

till they reached a city to dwell in.

Let them thank the Lord for his steadfast love,

for his wonderful works to the sons of men!

For he satisfies him who is thirsty,

and the hungry he fills with good things.

Let them thank the Lord for his steadfast love,

for his wonderful works to the sons of men!

And let them offer sacrifices of thanksgiving,

and tell of his deeds in songs of joy!

Psalm 107:1-9, 21-22

590

Praise the Lord

Praise the Lord. I will give thanks to the Lord with my whole heart,

in the company of the upright, in the congregation.

Great are the works of the Lord,

studied by all who have pleasure in them.

Full of honor and majesty is his work,

and his righteousness endures for ever.

He has caused his wonderful works to be remembered;

the Lord is gracious and merciful.

He provides food for those who fear him;

he is ever mindful of his covenant.

He has shown his people the power of his works,

in giving them the heritage of the nations.

The works of his hands are faithful and just;

all his precepts are trustworthy,

they are established for ever and ever,

to be performed with faithfulness and uprightness.

He sent redemption to his people;

he has commanded his covenant for ever.

Psalm 111:1-9a

591

I Love the Lord

I love the Lord,

because he has heard my voice and my supplications.

Because he inclined his ear to me,

therefore I will call on him as long as I live.

The snares of death encompassed me;

I suffered distress and anguish.

Then I called on the name of the Lord:

"O Lord, I beseech thee, save my life!"

Gracious is the Lord, and righteous;

our God is merciful.

The Lord preserves the simple;

when I was brought low, he saved me.

Return, O my soul, to your rest;

for the Lord has dealt bountifully with you.

For thou hast delivered my soul from death,

my eyes from tears, my feet from stumbling;

I walk before the Lord

in the land of the living.

What shall I render to the Lord

for all his bounty to me?

I will lift up the cup of salvation

and call on the name of the Lord,

I will pay my vows to the Lord

in the presence of all his people.

Precious in the sight of the Lord is the death of his saints.

O Lord, I am thy servant, the son of thy handmaid. Thou hast loosed my bonds.

I will offer to thee the sacrifice of thanksgiving

and call on the name of the Lord.

I will pay my vows to the Lord, in the presence of all his people,

in the courts of the house of the Lord, in your midst, O Jerusalem. Praise the Lord!

Psalm 116:1-3a, 3c-9, 12-19

592

Let Us Rejoice and Be Glad

O give thanks to the Lord, for he is good;

his steadfast love endures for ever!

Let those who fear the Lord say,

"His steadfast love endures for ever."

Out of my distress I called on the Lord;

the Lord answered me and set me free.

With the Lord on my side I do not fear.

What can man do to me?

It is better to take refuge in the Lord

than to put confidence in princes.

Open to me the gates of righteousness,

that I may enter through them and give thanks to the Lord.

This is the gate of the Lord;

the righteous shall enter through it.

I thank thee that thou hast answered me

and hast become my salvation.

The stone which the builders rejected

has become the chief cornerstone.

This is the Lord's doing;

it is marvelous in our eyes.

This is the day which the Lord has made;

let us rejoice and be glad in it.

Blessed be he who enters in the name of the Lord!

We bless you from the house of the Lord.

Thou art my God, and I will give thanks to thee;

thou art my God, I will extol thee.

O give thanks to the Lord, for he is good;

for his steadfast love endures for ever!

Psalm 118:1, 4-6, 8, 19-24, 26, 28-29

593

Teach Me Thy Statutes

Blessed are those whose way is blameless,

who walk in the law of the Lord!

Blessed are those who keep his testimonies,

who seek him with their whole heart,

who also do no wrong,

but walk in his ways!

Thou hast commanded thy precepts to be kept diligently.

O that my ways may be steadfast in keeping thy statutes!

Then I shall not be put to shame,

having my eyes fixed on all thy commandments.

I will praise thee with an upright heart,

when I learn thy righteous ordinances.

I will observe thy statutes;

O forsake me not utterly!

How can a young man keep his way pure?

By guarding it according to thy word.

With my whole heart I seek thee;

let me not wander from thy commandments!

I have laid up thy word in my heart,

that I might not sin against thee.

Blessed be thou, O Lord;

teach me thy statutes!

With my lips I declare all the ordinances of thy mouth.

In the way of thy testimonies I delight as much as in all riches.

I will meditate on thy precepts,

and fix my eyes on thy ways.

I will delight in thy statutes;

I will not forget thy word.

Psalm 119:1-16

594

Thy Law Is My Delight

Teach me, O Lord, the way of thy statutes;

and I will keep it to the end.

Give me understanding, that I may keep thy law

and observe it with my whole heart.

Lead me in the path of thy commandments, for I delight in it.

Incline my heart to thy testimonies, and not to gain!

Turn my eyes from looking at vanities;

and give me life in thy ways.

Confirm to thy servant thy promise,

which is for those who fear thee.

Turn away the reproach which I dread;

for thy ordinances are good.

Behold, I long for thy precepts;

in thy righteousness give me life!

Let thy steadfast love come to me, O Lord,

thy salvation according to thy promise;

then shall I have an answer for those who taunt me,

for I trust in thy word.

And take not the word of truth utterly out of my mouth,

for my hope is in thy ordinances.

I will keep thy law continually, for ever and ever;

and I shall walk at liberty, for I have sought thy precepts.

For I find my delight in thy commandments, which I love.

I revere thy commandments, and I will meditate on thy statutes.

I long for thy salvation, O Lord,

and thy law is my delight.

Psalm 119:33-45, 47-48, 174

595

The Lord Is Your Keeper

I lift up my eyes to the hills.

From whence does my help come?

My help comes from the Lord,

who made heaven and earth.

He will not let your foot be moved,

he who keeps you will not slumber.

Behold, he who keeps Israel

will neither slumber nor sleep.

The Lord is your keeper;

the Lord is your shade on your right hand.

The sun shall not smite you by day,

nor the moon by night.

The Lord will keep you from all evil;

he will keep your life.

The Lord will keep your going out and your coming in

from this time forth and for evermore.

Psalm 121

596

Peace Be Within You

I was glad when they said to me,

"Let us go to the house of the Lord!"

Our feet have been standing

within your gates, O Jerusalem!

Jerusalem, built as a city

which is bound firmly together,

to which the tribes go up, the tribes of the Lord,

as was decreed for Israel, to give thanks to the name of the Lord.

There thrones for judgment were set,

the thrones of the house of David.

Pray for the peace of Jerusalem!

"May they prosper who love you!

Peace be within your walls,

and security within your towers!"

For my brethren and companions' sake

I will say, "Peace be within you!"

For the sake of the house of the Lord our God,

I will seek your good.

Psalm 122

597

With Shouts of Joy

When the Lord restored the fortunes of Zion,

we were like those who dream.

Then our mouth was filled with laughter,

and our tongue with shouts of joy;

then they said among the nations, "The Lord has done great things for them."

The Lord has done great things for us; we are glad.

May those who sow in tears

reap with shouts of joy!

He that goes forth weeping, bearing the seed for sowing,

shall come home with shouts of joy, bringing his sheaves with him.

Psalm 126:1-3, 5-6

598

By the Waters of Babylon

By the waters of Babylon, there we sat down and wept, when we remembered Zion.

On the willows there we hung up our lyres.

For there our captors required of us songs, and our tormentors, mirth, saying,

"Sing us one of the songs of Zion!"

How shall we sing the Lord's song in a foreign land?

If I forget you, O Jerusalem, let my right hand wither!

Let my tongue cleave to the roof of my mouth, if I do not remember you,

if I do not set Jerusalem above my highest joy!

Psalm 137:1-6

599

The Glory of the Lord

I give thee thanks, O Lord, with my whole heart;

before the gods I sing thy praise;

I bow down toward thy holy temple and give thanks to thy name for thy steadfast love and thy faithfulness;

for thou hast exalted above everything thy name and thy word.

On the day I called, thou didst answer me,

my strength of soul thou didst increase.

All the kings of the earth shall praise thee, O Lord,

for they have heard the words of thy mouth;

and they shall sing of the ways of the Lord,

for great is the glory of the Lord.

For though the Lord is high, he regards the lowly;

but the haughty he knows from afar.

Though I walk in the midst of trouble, thou dost preserve my life;

thou dost stretch out thy hand against the wrath of my enemies, and thy right hand delivers me.

The Lord will fulfill his purpose for me;

thy steadfast love, O Lord, endures for ever.

Psalm 138:1-8b

600

Whither Shall I Go from Thy Spirit?

O Lord, thou hast searched me and known me!

Thou knowest when I sit down and when I rise up; thou discernest my thoughts from afar.

Thou searchest out my path and my lying down,

and art acquainted with all my ways.

Even before a word is on my tongue,

lo, O Lord, thou knowest it altogether.

Thou dost beset me behind and before,

and layest thy hand upon me.

Such knowledge is too wonderful for me;

it is high, I cannot attain it.

Whither shall I go from thy Spirit?

Or whither shall I flee from thy presence?

If I ascend to heaven, thou art there!

If I make my bed in Sheol, thou art there!

If I take the wings of the morning

and dwell in the uttermost parts of the sea,

even there thy hand shall lead me,

and thy right hand shall hold me.

If I say, "Let only darkness cover me,

and the light about me be night,"

even the darkness is not dark to thee, the night is bright as the day;

for darkness is as light with thee.

How precious to me are thy thoughts, O God!

How vast is the sum of them!

If I would count them, they are more than the sand.

When I awake, I am still with thee.

Search me, O God, and know my heart!

Try me and know my thoughts!

And see if there be any wicked way in me,

and lead me in the way everlasting!

Psalm 139:1-12, 17-18, 23-24

601

When My Spirit Is Faint

I cry with my voice to the Lord,

with my voice I make supplication to the Lord,

I pour out my complaint before him,

I tell my trouble before him.

When my spirit is faint, thou knowest my way!

In the path where I walk they have hidden a trap for me.

I look to the right and watch, but there is none who takes notice of me;

no refuge remains to me, no man cares for me.

I cry to thee, O Lord; I say, Thou art my refuge,

my portion in the land of the living.

Give heed to my cry;

for I am brought very low!

Deliver me from my persecutors;

for they are too strong for me!

Bring me out of prison,

that I may give thanks to thy name!

The righteous will surround me;

for thou wilt deal bountifully with me.

Psalm 142

602

Great Is the Lord

I will extol thee, my God and King,

and bless thy name for ever and ever.

Every day I will bless thee,

and praise thy name for ever and ever.

Great is the Lord, and greatly to be praised,

and his greatness is unsearchable.

One generation shall laud thy works to another,

and shall declare thy mighty acts.

On the glorious splendor of thy majesty,

and on thy wondrous works, I will meditate.

Men shall proclaim the might of thy terrible acts,

and I will declare thy greatness.

They shall pour forth the fame of thy abundant goodness,

and shall sing aloud of thy righteousness.

The Lord is gracious and merciful,

slow to anger and abounding in steadfast love.

The Lord is good to all,

and his compassion is over all that he has made.

All thy works shall give thanks to thee, O Lord,

and all thy saints shall bless thee!

They shall speak of the glory of thy kingdom, and tell of thy power,

to make known to the sons of men thy mighty deeds, and the glorious splendor of thy kingdom.

Thy kingdom is an everlasting kingdom,

and thy dominion endures throughout all generations.

Psalm 145:1-13b

603

The Lord Is Faithful

The Lord is faithful in all his words,

and gracious in all his deeds.

The Lord upholds all who are falling,

and raises up all who are bowed down.

The eyes of all look to thee,

and thou givest them their food in due season.

Thou openest thy hand,

thou satisfiest the desire of every living thing.

The Lord is just in all his ways,

and kind in all his doings.

The Lord is near to all who call upon him,

to all who call upon him in truth.

He fulfills the desire of all who fear him,

he also hears their cry, and saves them.

The Lord preserves all who love him;

but all the wicked he will destroy.

My mouth will speak the praise of the Lord,

and let all flesh bless his holy name for ever and ever.

Psalm 145:13c-21

604

Praise the Lord, O My Soul

Praise the Lord!

Praise the Lord, O my soul!

I will praise the Lord as long as I live;

I will sing praises to my God while I have being.

Put not your trust in princes,

in a son of man, in whom there is no help.

When his breath departs he returns to his earth;

on that very day his plans perish.

Happy is he whose help is the God of Jacob,

whose hope is in the Lord his God,

who made heaven and earth,

the sea, and all that is in them;

who keeps faith for ever;

who executes justice for the oppressed; who gives food to the hungry.

The Lord sets the prisoners free;

the Lord opens the eyes of the blind.

The Lord lifts up those who are bowed down;

the Lord loves the righteous.

The Lord watches over the sojourners, he upholds the widow and the fatherless;

but the way of the wicked he brings to ruin.

The Lord will reign for ever,

thy God, O Zion, to all generations. Praise the Lord!

Psalm 146

605

Praise the Lord from the Heavens

Praise the Lord! Praise the Lord from the heavens,

praise him in the heights!

Praise him, all his angels,

praise him, all his host!

Praise him, sun and moon,

praise him, you highest heavens!

Let them praise the name of the Lord!

For he commanded and they were created.

And he established them for ever and ever;

he fixed their bounds which cannot be passed.

Praise the Lord from the earth,

you sea monsters and all deeps,

fire and hail, snow and frost,

stormy wind fulfilling his command!

Mountains and all hills,

fruit trees and all cedars!

Beasts and all cattle,

creeping things and flying birds!

Kings of the earth and all peoples,

princes and all rulers of the earth!

Young men and maidens together,

old men and children!

Let them praise the name of the Lord,

for his name alone is exalted; his glory is above earth and heaven.

Psalm 148:1-3a, 4a, 5-13

606

Praise God in His Sanctuary

Praise the Lord! Praise God in his sanctuary;

praise him in his mighty firmament!

Praise him for his mighty deeds;

praise him according to his exceeding greatness!

Praise him with trumpet sound;

praise him with lute and harp!

Praise him with timbrel and dance;

praise him with strings and pipe!

Praise him with sounding cymbals;

praise him with loud clashing cymbals!

Let everything that breathes praise the Lord!

Praise the Lord!

Psalm 150

CANTICLES AND OTHER ACTS OF PRAISE

607

O Come, Let Us Sing

Venite, exultemus

O come, let us sing unto the Lord;

let us heartily rejoice in the strength of our salvation.

Let us come before his presence with thanksgiving;

and show ourselves glad in him with psalms.

For the Lord is a great God;

and a great King above all gods.

In his hand are all the corners of the earth;

and the strength of the hills is his also.

The sea is his, and he made it;

and his hands prepared the dry land.

O come, let us worship and fall down,

and kneel before the Lord our maker.

For he is the Lord our God;

and we are the people of his pasture, and the sheep of his hand.

O worship the Lord in the beauty of holiness;

let the whole earth stand in awe of him.

For he cometh, for he cometh to judge the earth;

and with righteousness to judge the world, and the people with his truth.

Psalm 95:1-7; 96:9, 13 Coverdale

608

We Praise Thee, O God

Te Deum laudamus

We praise thee, O God; we acknowledge thee to be the Lord.

All the earth doth worship thee, the Father everlasting.

To thee all angels cry aloud; the heavens, and all the powers therein;

to thee cherubim and seraphim continually do cry.

Holy, holy, holy, Lord God of Sabaoth;

heaven and earth are full of the majesty of thy glory.

The glorious company of the apostles praise thee.

The goodly fellowship of the prophets praise thee.

The noble army of martyrs praise thee.

The holy Church throughout all the world doth acknowledge thee;

the Father, of an infinite majesty;

thine adorable, true, and only Son; also the Holy Ghost, the Comforter.

Thou art the King of glory, O Christ.

Thou art the everlasting Son of the Father.

When thou tookest upon thee to deliver man,

thou didst humble thyself to be born of a virgin.

When thou hadst overcome the sharpness of death,

thou didst open the kingdom of heaven to all believers.

Thou sittest at the right hand of God,

in the glory of the Father.

We believe that thou shalt come to be our judge.

We therefore pray thee, help thy servants, whom thou hast redeemed with thy precious blood.

Make them to be numbered with thy saints,

in glory everlasting.

O Lord, save thy people, and bless thine heritage.

Govern them, and lift them up for ever.

Day by day we magnify thee;

and we worship thy name ever, world without end.

Vouchsafe, O Lord, to keep us this day without sin.

O Lord, have mercy upon us, have mercy upon us.

O Lord, let thy mercy be upon us, as our trust is in thee.

O Lord, in thee have I trusted; let me never be confounded.

609

Blessed Be the Lord God of Israel

Benedictus

Blessed be the Lord God of Israel;

for he hath visited and redeemed his people;

and hath raised up a mighty salvation for us,

in the house of his servant David;

as he spake by the mouth of his holy prophets,

which have been since the world began;

that we should be saved from our enemies,

and from the hand of all that hate us;

to perform the mercy promised to our forefathers,

and to remember his holy covenant;

to perform the oath which he sware to our forefather Abraham,

that he would give us;

that we being delivered out of the hand of our enemies

might serve him without fear;

in holiness and righteousness before him,

all the days of our life.

And thou, child, shalt be called the prophet of the Highest:

for thou shalt go before the face of the Lord, to prepare his ways;

to give knowledge of salvation unto his people

for the remission of their sins,

through the tender mercy of our God;

whereby the dayspring from on high hath visited us;

to give light to them that sit in darkness, and in the shadow of death,

and to guide our feet into the way of peace.

Luke 1:68-79 Coverdale

610

Blessed Art Thou, O Lord

Benedictus es, Domine

Blessed art thou, O Lord God of our fathers:

praised and exalted above all for ever.

Blessed art thou for the name of thy Majesty:

praised and exalted above all for ever.

Blessed art thou in the temple of thy holiness:

praised and exalted above all for ever.

Blessed art thou that beholdest the depths, and dwellest between the cherubim:

praised and exalted above all for ever.

Blessed art thou on the glorious throne of thy kingdom:

praised and exalted above all for ever.

Blessed art thou in the firmament of heaven:

praised and exalted above all for ever.

Song of the Three Young Men, 29-34 Coverdale

611

O Be Joyful in the Lord

Jubilate Deo

O be joyful in the Lord, all ye lands:

serve the Lord with gladness, and come before his presence with a song.

Be ye sure that the Lord he is God; it is he that hath made us, and not we ourselves;

we are his people, and the sheep of his pasture.

O go your way into his gates with thanksgiving, and into his courts with praise;

be thankful unto him, and speak good of his name.

For the Lord is gracious, his mercy is everlasting;

and his truth endureth from generation to generation.

Psalm 100 Coverdale

612

My Soul Doth Magnify the Lord

Magnificat

My soul doth magnify the Lord,

and my spirit hath rejoiced in God my Savior.

For he hath regarded

the lowliness of his handmaiden.

For behold, from henceforth

all generations shall call me blessed.

For he that is mighty hath magnified me;

and holy is his name.

And his mercy is on them that fear him

throughout all generations.

He hath showed strength with his arm;

he hath scattered the proud in the imagination of their hearts.

He hath put down the mighty from their seat,

and hath exalted the humble and meek.

He hath filled the hungry with good things;

and the rich he hath sent empty away.

He remembering his mercy hath helped his servant Israel;

as he promised to our forefathers, Abraham and his seed, for ever.

Luke 1:46-55 Coverdale

613

It Is a Good Thing to Give Thanks

Bonum est confiteri

It is a good thing to give thanks unto the Lord,

and to sing praises unto thy name, O Most Highest;

to tell of thy lovingkindness early in the morning,

and of thy truth in the night season;

upon an instrument of ten strings, and upon the lute;

upon a loud instrument, and upon the harp.

For thou, O Lord, hast made me glad through thy works;

and I will rejoice in giving praise for the operations of thy hands.

Psalm 92:1-4 Coverdale

614

Lord, Now Lettest Thou Thy Servant

Nunc Dimittis

Lord, now lettest thou thy servant depart in peace,

according to thy word.

For mine eyes have seen

thy salvation,

which thou hast prepared

before the face of all people;

to be a light to lighten the Gentiles,

and to be the glory of thy people Israel.

Luke 2:29-32 Coverdale

615

Out of the Depths

De Profundis

Out of the deep have I called unto thee, O Lord;

Lord, hear my voice.

O let thine ears consider well

the voice of my complaint.

If thou, Lord, wilt be extreme to mark what is done amiss,

O Lord, who may abide it?

For there is mercy with thee;

therefore shalt thou be feared.

I look for the Lord; my soul doth wait for him;

in his word is my trust.

My soul fleeth unto the Lord before the morning watch;

I say, before the morning watch.

O Israel, trust in the Lord, for with the Lord there is mercy,

and with him is plenteous redemption.

And he shall redeem Israel

from all his sins.

Psalm 130 Coverdale

616

Bless the Lord, All Works of the Lord

Benedicite, omnia opera Domini

Bless the Lord, all works of the Lord,

sing praise to him and highly exalt him for ever.

Bless the Lord, sun and moon,

bless the Lord, stars of heaven.

Bless the Lord, winter cold and summer heat,

bless the Lord, nights and days.

Bless the Lord, lightnings and clouds,

sing praise to him and highly exalt him for ever.

Bless the Lord, all things that grow on the earth,

bless the Lord, seas and rivers.

Bless the Lord, all creatures that move in the waters,

bless the Lord, all birds of the air.

Bless the Lord, you sons of men,

bless the Lord, you who are holy and humble in heart.

Bless him, all who worship the Lord, the God of gods,

sing praise to him and give thanks to him, for his mercy endures for ever.

The Song of the Three Young Men, 35, 40-41, 45, 47, 51, 54, 56-58, 60, 65, 68

617

Glory Be to the Father

Gloria Patri

Glory be to the Father, and to the Son, and to the Holy Ghost;

as it was in the beginning, is now, and ever shall be, world without end. Amen.

618

Glory Be to God on High

Gloria in Excelsis Deo

Glory be to God on high,

and on earth peace, good will toward men.

We praise thee, we bless thee, we worship thee,

we glorify thee, we give thanks to thee for thy great glory:

O Lord God, heavenly King,

God the Father Almighty.

O Lord, the only begotten Son, Jesus Christ:

O Lord God, Lamb of God, Son of the Father:

that takest away the sins of the world,

have mercy upon us.

Thou that takest away the sins of the world,

receive our prayer.

Thou that sittest at the right hand of God the Father,

have mercy upon us.

For thou only art holy; thou only art the Lord;

thou only, O Christ, with the Holy Ghost, art most high in the glory of God the Father. Amen.

619

Glory Be to God

Gloria Deo

God is spirit. They that worship him must worship him in spirit and in truth.

Glory be to God on high.

God is light. If we walk in the light, as he is in the light, we have fellowship one with another; and truly our fellowship is with the Father, and with his Son Jesus Christ.

Glory be to God on high.

God is power. They that wait upon the Lord shall renew their strength; they shall mount up with wings as eagles; they shall run and not be weary; and they shall walk and not faint.

Glory be to God on high.

God is love. Behold what manner of love the Father hath bestowed upon us, that we should be called the sons of God. Hereby perceive we the love of God, because he laid down his life for us.

Glory be to God on high.

From John 4:24; I John 1:7, 3b; Isaiah 40:31; I John 3:1a, 16a

620

The Beatitudes

Blessed are the poor in spirit,

for theirs is the kingdom of heaven.

Blessed are those who mourn,

for they shall be comforted.

Blessed are the meek,

for they shall inherit the earth.

Blessed are those who hunger and thirst for righteousness,

for they shall be satisfied.

Blessed are the merciful,

for they shall obtain mercy.

Blessed are the pure in heart,

for they shall see God.

Blessed are the peacemakers,

for they shall be called sons of God.

Blessed are those who are persecuted for righteousness' sake,

for theirs is the kingdom of heaven.

Blessed are you when men revile you and persecute you and utter all kinds of evil against you falsely on my account. Rejoice and be glad, for your reward is great in heaven, for so men persecuted the prophets who were before you.

Matthew 5:3-12

621

The Commandments

I

And God spoke all these words, saying,

"I am the Lord your God, who brought you out of the land of Egypt, out of the house of bondage.

"You shall have no other gods before me.

"You shall not make yourself a graven image, or any likeness of anything that is in heaven above, or that is in the earth beneath, or that is in the water under the earth; you shall not bow down to them or serve them; for I the Lord your God am a jealous God, visiting the iniquity of the fathers upon the children to the third and the fourth generation of those who hate me, but showing steadfast love to thousands of those who love me and keep my commandments."

Lord, have mercy upon us, and incline our hearts to keep thy law.

"You shall not take the name of the Lord your God in vain; for the Lord will not hold him guiltless who takes his name in vain.

"Remember the sabbath day, to keep it holy. Six days you shall labor, and do all your work; but the seventh day is a sabbath to the Lord your God; in it you shall not do any work, you, or your son, or your daughter, your manservant, or your maidservant, or your cattle, or the sojourner who is within your gates; for in six days the Lord made heaven and earth, the sea, and all that is in them, and rested the seventh day; therefore the Lord blessed the sabbath day and hallowed it."

Lord, have mercy upon us, and incline our hearts to keep thy law.

"Honor your father and your mother, that your days may be long in the land which the Lord your God gives you.

"You shall not kill.

"You shall not commit adultery.

"You shall not steal.

"You shall not bear false witness against your neighbor.

"You shall not covet your neighbor's house; you shall not covet your neighbor's wife, or his manservant, or his maidservant, or his ox, or his ass, or anything that is your neighbor's."

Lord, have mercy upon us, and write all these thy laws in our hearts, we beseech thee.

II

Hear what our Lord Jesus Christ says,

"Hear, O Israel: The Lord our God, the Lord is one; and you shall love the Lord your God with all your heart, and with all your soul, and with all your mind, and with all your strength. This is the great and first commandment. And a second is like it, You shall love your neighbor as yourself. On these two commandments depend all the law and the prophets."

Lord, have mercy upon us.

Christ, have mercy upon us.

Lord, have mercy upon us.

Exodus 20:1-17; Mark 12:29-30; Matthew 22:38-40

622

O Lord, Thou Art Great

O Lord, thou art great and glorious,

wonderful in strength, invincible.

Let all thy creatures serve thee,

for thou didst speak, and they were made,

thou didst send forth thy Spirit, and it formed them;

there is none that can resist thy voice.

For the mountains shall be shaken to their foundations with the waters;

at thy presence the rocks shall melt like wax.

But to those who fear thee, thou wilt continue to show mercy.

For every sacrifice as a fragrant offering is a small thing,

and all fat for burnt offerings to thee is a very little thing,

but he who fears the Lord shall be great for ever.

Judith 16:13b-16

623

The Lord Created Man

The Lord created man out of earth,

and turned him back to it again.

He gave to men a few days, a limited time,

but granted them authority over the things upon the earth.

He endowed them with strength like his own,

and made them in his own image.

He made for them tongue and eyes;

he gave them ears and a mind for thinking.

He filled them with knowledge and understanding,

and showed them good and evil.

He set his eye upon their hearts

to show them the majesty of his works.

And they will praise his holy name,

to proclaim the grandeur of his works.

He established with them an eternal covenant,

and showed them his judgments.

Their eyes saw his glorious majesty,

and their ears heard the glory of his voice.

And he said to them, "Beware of all unrighteousness."

And he gave commandment to each of them concerning his neighbor.

Their ways are always before him,

they will not be hid from his eyes.

Their iniquities are not hidden from him.

And all their sins are before the Lord.

Yet to those who repent he grants a return,

and he encourages those whose endurance is failing.

How great is the mercy of the Lord,

and his forgiveness for those who turn to him!

Ecclesiasticus 17:1-3, 6-10, 12-15, 20, 24, 29

624

Let Us Now Praise Famous Men

Let us now praise famous men,

and our fathers in their generations.

The Lord apportioned to them great glory,

his majesty from the beginning.

There were those who ruled in their kingdoms,

and were men renowned for their power,

giving counsel by their understanding,

and proclaiming prophecies;

leaders of the people in their deliberations,

wise in their words of instruction;

those who composed musical tunes,

and set forth verses in writing;

rich men furnished with resources,

living peaceably in their habitations—

all these were honored in their generations,

and were the glory of their times.

There are some of them who have left a name,

so that men declare their praise.

And there are some who have no memorial,

who have perished as though they had not lived.

But these were men of mercy,

whose righteous deeds have not been forgotten;

their prosperity will remain with their descendants,

and their inheritance to their children's children.

Their posterity will continue for ever.

And their glory will not be blotted out.

Their bodies were buried in peace.

And their name lives to all generations.

Peoples will declare their wisdom,

and the congregation proclaims their praise.

Ecclesiasticus 44:1-4ac, 5-9ab, 10-11, 13-15

625

The Souls of the Righteous

The souls of the righteous are in the hand of God,

and no torment will ever touch them.

In the eyes of the foolish they seem to have died,

and their departure was thought to be an affliction,

and their going from us to be their destruction;

but they are at peace.

God created man for incorruption,

and made him in the image of his own eternity.

The righteous live for ever, and their reward is with the Lord;

the Most High takes care of them.

With his right hand he will cover them,

and with his arm he will shield them.

Wisdom of Solomon 3:1-3; 2:23; 5:15; 5:16b

626

LISTEN, O KINGS

Listen, therefore, O kings, and understand;

learn, O judges of the ends of the earth.

Give ear, you that rule over multitudes,

and boast of many nations.

For your dominion was given you from the Lord.

And your sovereignty from the Most High,

who will search out your works

and inquire into your plans.

For the Lord of all will not stand in awe of any one,

nor show deference to greatness;

because he himself made both small and great,

and he takes thought for all alike.

To you then, O monarchs, my words are directed,

that you may learn wisdom and not transgress.

Therefore set your desire on my words;

long for them, and you will be instructed.

Wisdom is radiant and unfading,

and she is easily discerned by those who love her.

She hastens to make herself known to those who desire her,

she goes about seeking those worthy of her,

and she graciously appears to them in their paths,

and meets them in every thought.

The beginning of wisdom is the most sincere desire for instruction,

and concern for instruction is love of her,

and love of her is the keeping of her laws,

and giving heed to her laws is assurance of immortality.

Wisdom of Solomon 6:1-3, 7, 9, 11-12ab, 13, 16-18

627

THE SONG OF DAVID

Blessed art thou, O Lord, the God of Israel

our father, for ever and ever.

Thine, O Lord, is the greatness, and the power, and the glory, and the victory, and the majesty;

for all that is in the heavens and in the earth is thine;

thine is the kingdom, O Lord,

and thou art exalted as head above all.

Both riches and honor come from thee,

and thou rulest over all.

In thy hand are power and might;

and in thy hand it is to make great and to give strength to all.

And now we thank thee, our God,

and praise thy glorious name.

I Chronicles 29:10b-13

628

He Makes Nations Great

With God are wisdom and might;

he has counsel and understanding.

If he tears down, none can rebuild;

if he shuts a man in, none can open.

If he withholds the waters, they dry up;

if he sends them out, they overwhelm the land.

With him are strength and wisdom;

the deceived and the deceiver are his.

He leads counselors away stripped,

and judges he makes fools.

He looses the bonds of kings,

and binds a waistcloth on their loins.

He leads priests away stripped,

and overthrows the mighty.

He pours contempt on princes,

and looses the belt of the strong.

He makes nations great, and he destroys them:

he enlarges nations, and leads them away.

In his hand is the life of every living thing

and the breath of all mankind.

Job 12:13-19, 21, 23, 10

629

Where Shall Wisdom Be Found?

Surely there is a mine for silver,

and a place for gold which they refine.

But where shall wisdom be found?

And where is the place of understanding?

Man does not know the way to it,

and it is not found in the land of the living.

The deep says, "It is not in me,"

and the sea says, "It is not with me."

It cannot be gotten for gold,

and silver cannot be weighed as its price.

The topaz of Ethiopia cannot compare with it,

nor can it be valued in pure gold.

Whence then comes wisdom?

And where is the place of understanding?

God understands the way to it,

and he knows its place.

Behold, the fear of the Lord, that is wisdom;

and to depart from evil is understanding.

Job 28:1, 12-15, 19-20, 23, 28

630

The Goodness of Wisdom

Happy is the man who finds wisdom,

and the man who gets understanding,

for the gain from it is better than gain from silver

and its profit better than gold.

She is more precious than jewels,

and nothing you desire can compare with her.

Long life is in her right hand;

in her left hand are riches and honor.

Her ways are ways of pleasantness,

and all her paths are peace.

She is a tree of life to those who lay hold of her;

those who hold her fast are called happy.

The Lord by wisdom founded the earth;

by understanding he established the heavens.

Proverbs 3:13-19

631

The Lord Created Wisdom

Does not wisdom call?

Does not understanding raise her voice?

The Lord created me at the beginning of his work,

the first of his acts of old.

Ages ago I was set up, at the first,

before the beginning of the earth.

Before the mountains had been shaped,

before the hills, I was brought forth;

before he had made the earth with its fields,

or the first of the dust of the world.

When he established the heavens, I was there.

When he marked out the foundations of the earth, then I was beside him.

And I was daily his delight,

rejoicing before him always,

rejoicing in his inhabited world

and delighting in the sons of men.

For he who finds me finds life

and obtains favor from the Lord.

Proverbs 8:1, 22-23, 25-27a, 29c-31, 35

632

The Lord Shall Reign

It shall come to pass in the latter days

that the mountain of the house of the Lord

shall be established as the highest of the mountains,

and shall be raised above the hills;

and all the nations shall flow to it,

and many peoples shall come, and say:

"Come, let us go up to the mountain of the Lord,

to the house of the God of Jacob;

that he may teach us his ways

and that we may walk in his paths."

For out of Zion shall go forth the law,

and the word of the Lord from Jerusalem.

He shall judge between the nations,

and decide for many peoples;

and they shall beat their swords into plowshares,

and their spears into pruning hooks;

nation shall not lift up sword against nation,

neither shall they learn war any more.

Isaiah 2:2-4

633

The Lord My Righteousness

There shall come forth a shoot from the stump of Jesse,

and a branch shall grow out of his roots.

And the Spirit of the Lord shall rest upon him,

the spirit of wisdom and understanding,

the spirit of counsel and might,

the spirit of knowledge and the fear of the Lord.

He shall not judge by what his eyes see,

or decide by what his ears hear;

but with righteousness he shall judge the poor,

and decide with equity for the meek of the earth.

Righteousness shall be the girdle of his waist

and faithfulness the girdle of his loins.

The wolf shall dwell with the lamb,

and the leopard shall lie down with the kid,

and the calf and the lion and the fatling together,

and a little child shall lead them.

They shall not hurt or destroy in all my holy mountain;

for the earth shall be full of the knowledge of the Lord as the waters cover the sea.

Isaiah 11:1-2, 3b-4b, 5-6, 9

634

The Desert Shall Rejoice

The wilderness and the dry land shall be glad,

the desert shall rejoice and blossom;

like the crocus it shall blossom abundantly,

and rejoice with joy and singing.

The glory of Lebanon shall be given to it,

the majesty of Carmel and Sharon.

They shall see the glory of the Lord,

the majesty of our God.

Say to those who are of a fearful heart,

"Be strong, fear not! Behold, your God will come."

Then the eyes of the blind shall be opened,

and the ears of the deaf unstopped;

then shall the lame man leap like a hart,

and the tongue of the dumb sing for joy.

For waters shall break forth in the wilderness,

and streams in the desert;

the burning sand shall become a pool,

and the thirsty ground springs of water.

And a highway shall be there,

and it shall be called the Holy Way.

And the ransomed of the Lord shall return,

and come to Zion with singing;

they shall obtain joy and gladness,

and sorrow and sighing shall flee away.

Isaiah 35:1-2, 4ab, 5-7ab, 8ab, 10ab, de

635

COMFORT MY PEOPLE

Comfort, comfort my people, says your God.

Speak tenderly to Jerusalem, and cry to her that her warfare is ended,

that her iniquity is pardoned,

that she has received from the Lord's hand double for all her sins.

A voice cries, "In the wilderness prepare the way of the Lord,

make straight in the desert a highway for our God.

Every valley shall be lifted up,

and every mountain and hill be made low;

the uneven ground shall become level,

and the rough places a plain.

And the glory of the Lord shall be revealed,

and all flesh shall see it together."

Isaiah 40:1-5ab

636

BEHOLD YOUR GOD

Get you up to a high mountain, O Zion, herald of good tidings;

lift up your voice with strength, O Jerusalem.

Lift it up, fear not;

say to the cities of Judah, "Behold your God!"

Behold, the Lord God comes with might, and his arm rules for him;

behold, his reward is with him, and his recompense before him.

He will feed his flock like a shepherd,

he will gather the lambs in his arms,

he will carry them in his bosom,

and gently lead those that are with young.

Isaiah 40:9-11

637

The Sovereignty of God

Who has measured the waters in the hollow of his hand

and marked off the heavens with a span,

enclosed the dust of the earth in a measure

and weighed the mountains in scales?

Who has directed the Spirit of the Lord,

or as his counselor has instructed him?

Whom did he consult for his enlightenment,

and who showed him the way of understanding?

All the nations are as nothing before him,

they are accounted by him as less than nothing and emptiness.

Have you not known? Have you not heard? The Lord is the everlasting God,

the Creator of the ends of the earth.

He does not faint or grow weary,

his understanding is unsearchable.

He gives power to the faint,

and to him who has no might he increases strength.

Even youths shall faint and be weary,

and young men shall fall exhausted;

but they who wait for the Lord shall renew their strength,

they shall mount up with wings like eagles,

they shall run and not be weary,

they shall walk and not faint.

Isaiah 40:12-14ad, 17, 28-31

638

Behold My Servant

Behold my servant, whom I uphold,

my chosen, in whom my soul delights;

I have put my spirit upon him,

he will bring forth justice to the nations.

He will not cry or lift up his voice,

or make it heard in the street;

a bruised reed he will not break,

and a dimly burning wick he will not quench.

He will not fail or be discouraged

till he has established justice in the earth.

Thus says God, the Lord,

who created the heavens and stretched them out,

who spread forth the earth and what comes from it,

who gives breath to the people upon it and spirit to those who walk in it:

"I am the Lord, I have called you in righteousness,

I have taken you by the hand and kept you;

I have given you as a covenant to the people, a light to the nations,

to open the eyes that are blind,

to bring out the prisoners from the dungeon,

from the prison those who sit in darkness."

Isaiah 42:1-3ab, 4a, 5-7

639

Good Tidings

How beautiful upon the mountains

are the feet of him who brings good tidings,

who publishes peace, who brings good tidings of good,

who publishes salvation, who says to Zion, "Your God reigns."

Break forth together into singing,

you waste places of Jerusalem;

for the Lord has comforted his people,

he has redeemed Jerusalem.

The Lord has bared his holy arm

before the eyes of all the nations;

and all the ends of the earth shall see

the salvation of our God.

And you shall know that I, the Lord, am your Savior

and your Redeemer, the Mighty One of Jacob.

Violence shall no more be heard in your land,

devastation or destruction within your borders;

you shall call your walls Salvation,

and your gates Praise.

The sun shall be no more your light by day,

nor for brightness shall the moon give light to you by night;

but the Lord will be your everlasting light,

and your God will be your glory.

Isaiah 52:7, 9-10; 60:16b, 18-19

640

The Suffering Servant

I

Who has believed what we have heard?

And to whom has the arm of the Lord been revealed?

For he grew up before him like a young plant,

and like a root out of dry ground;

he had no form or comeliness that we should look at him,

and no beauty that we should desire him.

He was despised and rejected by men;

a man of sorrows, and acquainted with grief;

and as one from whom men hide their faces

he was despised, and we esteemed him not.

Surely he has borne our griefs and carried our sorrows;

yet we esteemed him stricken, smitten by God, and afflicted.

But he was wounded for our transgressions,

he was bruised for our iniquities;

upon him was the chastisement that made us whole,

and with his stripes we are healed.

II

All we like sheep have gone astray;

we have turned every one to his own way;

and the Lord has laid on him the iniquity of us all.

He was oppressed, and he was afflicted, yet he opened not his mouth;

like a lamb that is led to the slaughter,

and like a sheep that before its shearers is dumb, so he opened not his mouth.

By oppression and judgment he was taken away;

and as for his generation, who considered that he was cut off out of the land of the living, stricken for the transgression of my people?

And they made his grave with the wicked

and with a rich man in his death,

although he had done no violence,

and there was no deceit in his mouth.

Yet it was the will of the Lord to bruise him;

he has put him to grief;

when he makes himself an offering for sin,

he shall see his offspring, he shall prolong his days;

the will of the Lord shall prosper in his hand;

he shall see the fruit of the travail of his soul and be satisfied;

by his knowledge shall the righteous one, my servant, make many to be accounted righteous;

and he shall bear their iniquities.

Therefore I will divide him a portion with the great,

and he shall divide the spoil with the strong;

because he poured out his soul to death,

and was numbered with the transgressors;

yet he bore the sin of many,

and made intercession for the transgressors.

Isaiah 53:1-12

641

Seek the Lord

Seek the Lord while he may be found,

call upon him while he is near;

let the wicked forsake his way,

and the unrighteous man his thoughts;

let him return to the Lord, that he may have mercy on him,

and to our God, for he will abundantly pardon.

For my thoughts are not your thoughts,

neither are your ways my ways, says the Lord.

For as the heavens are higher than the earth,

so are my ways higher than your ways and my thoughts than your thoughts.

For as the rain and the snow come down from heaven,

and return not thither but water the earth,

making it bring forth and sprout,

giving seed to the sower and bread to the eater,

so shall my word be that goes forth from my mouth;

it shall not return to me empty,

but it shall accomplish that which I purpose,

and prosper in the thing for which I sent it.

Isaiah 55:6-13

642

I Will Greatly Rejoice

I will greatly rejoice in the Lord,

my soul shall exult in my God;

for he has clothed me with the garments of salvation,

he has covered me with the robe of righteousness,

as a bridegroom decks himself with a garland,

and as a bride adorns herself with her jewels.

For as the earth brings forth its shoots,

and as a garden causes what is sown in it to spring up,

so the Lord God will cause righteousness and praise

to spring forth before all the nations.

Isaiah 61:10-11

643

Behold, I Create

For behold, I create new heavens and a new earth;

and the former things shall not be remembered or come into mind.

But be glad and rejoice for ever in that which I create;

for behold, I create Jerusalem a rejoicing, and her people a joy.

I will rejoice in Jerusalem, and be glad in my people;

no more shall be heard in it the sound of weeping and the cry of distress.

They shall build houses and inhabit them;

they shall plant vineyards and eat their fruit.

They shall not build and another inhabit;

they shall not plant and another eat;

for like the days of a tree shall the days of my people be,

and my chosen shall long enjoy the work of their hands.

They shall not labor in vain,

or bear children for calamity;

for they shall be the offspring of the blessed of the Lord,

and their children with them.

Before they call I will answer,

while they are yet speaking I will hear.

The wolf and the lamb shall feed together,

the lion shall eat straw like the ox;

and dust shall be the serpent's food.

They shall not hurt or destroy in all my holy mountain, says the Lord.

Isaiah 65:17-19, 21-25

644

The New Covenant

Behold, the days are coming, says the Lord, when I will make a new covenant with the house of Israel and the house of Judah, not like the covenant which I made with their fathers when I took them by the hand to bring them out of the land of Egypt. But this is the covenant which I will make with the house of Israel after those days, says the Lord: I will put my law within them, and I will write it upon their hearts; and I will be their God, and they shall be my people. And no longer shall each man teach his neighbor and each his brother, saying, "Know the Lord," for they shall all know me, from the least of them to the greatest, says the Lord; for I will forgive their iniquity, and I will remember their sin no more.

Jeremiah 31:31-32a, 33-34

645

The Mercies of God

My soul is bereft of peace,

I have forgotten what happiness is;

so I say, "Gone is my glory,

and my expectation from the Lord."

Remember my affliction and my bitterness,

the wormwood and the gall!

My soul continually thinks of it,

and is bowed down within me.

But this I call to mind,

and therefore I have hope:

The steadfast love of the Lord never ceases,

his mercies never come to an end;

they are new every morning;

great is thy faithfulness.

"The Lord is my portion," says my soul,

"therefore I will hope in him!"

The Lord is good to those who wait for him,

to the soul that seeks him.

It is good that one should wait quietly

for the salvation of the Lord.

Lamentations 3:17-26

646

YET I WILL REJOICE

Though the fig tree do not blossom,
nor fruit be on the vines,
the produce of the olive fail
and the fields yield no food,
the flock be cut off from the fold
and there be no herd in the stalls,
yet I will rejoice in the Lord,
I will joy in the God of my salvation.

Habakkuk 3:17-18

647

IN THE BEGINNING WAS THE WORD

In the beginning was the Word, and the Word was with God, and the Word was God. He was in the beginning with God; all things were made through him, and without him was not anything made that was made. In him was life, and the life was the light of men. The light shines in the darkness, and the darkness has not overcome it.

The true light that enlightens every man was coming into the world. He was in the world, and the world was made through him, yet the world knew him not. He came to his own home, and his own people received him not. But to all who received him, who believed in his name, he gave power to become children of God; who were born, not of blood nor of the will of the flesh nor of the will of man, but of God.

And the Word became flesh and dwelt among us, full of grace and truth; we have beheld his glory, glory as of the only Son from the Father. And from his fulness have we all received, grace upon grace. For the law was given through Moses; grace and truth came through Jesus Christ. No one has ever seen God; the only Son, who is in the bosom of the Father, he has made him known.

John 1:1-5, 9-14, 16-18

648

GOD SO LOVED THE WORLD

God so loved the world that he gave his only Son, that whoever believes in him should not perish but have eternal life. For God sent the Son into the world, not to condemn the world, but that the world might be saved through him.

And this is the judgment, that the light has come into the world, and men loved darkness rather than light, because their deeds were evil. For every one who does evil hates the light, and does not come to the light, lest his deeds should be exposed. But he who does what is true comes to the light, that it may be clearly seen that his deeds have been wrought in God.

John 3:16-17, 19-21

649

The True Vine

Abide in me, and I in you. As the branch cannot bear fruit by itself, unless it abides in the vine, neither can you, unless you abide in me. I am the vine, you are the branches. He who abides in me, and I in him, he it is that bears much fruit, for apart from me you can do nothing. If a man does not abide in me, he is cast forth as a branch and withers; and the branches are gathered, thrown into the fire and burned. If you abide in me, and my words abide in you, ask whatever you will, and it shall be done for you. By this my Father is glorified, that you bear much fruit, and so prove to be my disciples. As the Father has loved me, so have I loved you; abide in my love. If you keep my commandments, you will abide in my love, just as I have kept my Father's commandments and abide in his love. These things I have spoken to you, that my joy may be in you, and that your joy may be full.

John 15:4-11

650

The Love of Christ

If God is for us, who is against us?

He who did not spare his own Son but gave him up for us all, will he not also give us all things with him?

Who shall separate us from the love of Christ?

Shall tribulation, or distress, or persecution, or famine, or nakedness, or peril, or sword?

No, in all these things we are more than conquerors through him who loved us.

For I am sure that neither death, nor life, nor angels, nor principalities, nor things present, nor things to come, nor powers, nor height, nor depth, nor anything else in all creation, will be able to separate us from the love of God in Christ Jesus our Lord.

Romans 8:31b-32, 35, 37-39

651

Spiritual Worship

I appeal to you therefore, brethren, by the mercies of God, to present your bodies as a living sacrifice, holy and acceptable to God, which is your spiritual worship. Do not be conformed to this world but be transformed by the renewal of your mind, that you may prove what is the will of God, what is good and acceptable and perfect.

Let love be genuine; hate what is evil, hold fast to what is good; love one another with brotherly affection; outdo one another in showing honor. Never flag in zeal, be aglow with the Spirit, serve the Lord. Rejoice in your hope, be patient in tribulation, be constant in prayer. Contribute to the needs of the saints, practice hospitality.

Bless those who persecute you; bless and do not curse them. Rejoice with those who rejoice, weep with those who weep. Live in harmony with one another; do not be haughty, but associate with the lowly; never be conceited. Repay no one evil for evil, but take thought for what is noble in the sight of all. Do not be overcome by evil, but overcome evil with good.

Romans 12:1-2, 9-17, 21

652

The Way of Love

If I speak in the tongues of men and of angels, but have not love, I am a noisy gong or a clanging cymbal. And if I have prophetic powers, and understand all mysteries and all knowledge, and if I have all faith, so as to remove mountains, but have not love, I am nothing. If I give away all I have, and if I deliver my body to be burned, but have not love, I gain nothing.

Love is patient and kind; love is not jealous or boastful; it is not arrogant or rude. Love does not insist on its own way; it is not irritable or resentful; it does not rejoice at wrong, but rejoices in the right. Love bears all things, believes all things, hopes all things, endures all things.

Love never ends; as for prophecy, it will pass away; as for tongues, they will cease; as for knowledge, it will pass away. For our knowledge is imperfect and our prophecy is imperfect; but when the perfect comes, the imperfect will pass away. When I was a child, I spoke like a child, I thought like a child, I reasoned like a child; when I became a man, I gave up childish ways. For now we see in a mirror dimly, but then face to face. Now I know in part; then I shall understand fully, even as I have been fully understood. So faith, hope, love abide, these three; but the greatest of these is love.

I Corinthians 13

653

The Ministry of Grace

Therefore, having this ministry by the mercy of God, we do not lose heart. We have renounced disgraceful, underhanded ways; we refuse to practice cunning or to tamper with God's word, but by the open statement of the truth we would commend ourselves to every man's conscience in the sight of God.

But we have this treasure in earthen vessels, to show that the transcendent power belongs to God and not to us. We are afflicted in every way, but not crushed; perplexed, but not driven to despair; persecuted, but not forsaken; struck down, but not destroyed; always carrying in the body the death of Jesus, so that the life of Jesus may also be manifested in our bodies. For while we live we are always being given up to death for Jesus' sake, so that the life of Jesus may be manifested in our mortal flesh. So death is at work in us, but life in you.

So we do not lose heart. Though our outer nature is wasting away, our inner nature is being renewed every day. For this slight momentary affliction is preparing for us an eternal weight of glory beyond all comparison, because we look not to the things that are seen but to the things that are unseen; for the things that are seen are transient, but the things that are unseen are eternal.

II Corinthians 4:1-2, 7-12, 16-18

654

By Grace You Have Been Saved

And you he made alive, when you were dead through the trespasses and sins in which you once walked, following the course of this world. But God, who is rich in mercy, out of the great love with which he loved us, even when we were dead through our trespasses, made us alive together with Christ, and raised us up with him, and made us sit with him in the heavenly places in Christ Jesus, that in the coming ages he might show the immeasurable riches of his grace.

For by grace you have been saved through faith; and this is not your own doing, it is the gift of God—not because of works, lest any man should boast. For we are his workmanship, created in Christ Jesus for good works, which God prepared beforehand, that we should walk in them.

From Ephesians 2:1-2a, 4-10

655

The Mind of Christ

So if there is any encouragement in Christ, any incentive of love, any participation in the Spirit, any affection and sympathy, complete my joy by being of the same mind, having the same love, being in full accord and of one mind. Do nothing from selfishness or conceit, but in humility count others better than yourselves. Let each of you look not only to his own interests, but also to the interest of others. Have this mind among yourselves, which you have in Christ Jesus, who, though he was in the form of God, did not count equality with God a thing to be grasped, but emptied himself, taking the form of a servant, being born in the likeness of men. And being found in human form he humbled himself and became obedient unto death, even death on a cross. Therefore God has highly exalted him and bestowed on him the name which is above every name, that at the name of Jesus every knee should bow, in heaven and on earth and under the earth, and every tongue confess that Jesus Christ is Lord, to the glory of God the Father.

Philippians 2:1-11

656

The New Life in Christ

He has delivered us from the dominion of darkness and transferred us to the kingdom of his beloved Son, in whom we have redemption, the forgiveness of sins.

He is the image of the invisible God, the first-born of all creation; for in him all things were created, in heaven and on earth, visible and invisible, whether thrones or dominions or principalities or authorities—all things were created through him and for him. He is before all things, and in him all things hold together. He is the head of the body, the church; he is the beginning, the first-born from the dead, that in everything he might be preeminent. For in him all the fulness of God was pleased to dwell, and through him to reconcile to himself all things, whether on earth or in heaven, making peace by the blood of his cross.

Colossians 1:13-20

657

We Have Been Born Anew

Blessed be the God and Father of our Lord Jesus Christ! By his great mercy we have been born anew to a living hope through the resurrection of Jesus Christ from the dead, and to an inheritance which is imperishable, undefiled, and unfading, kept in heaven for you, who by God's power are guarded through faith for a salvation ready to be revealed in the last time. In this you rejoice, though now for a little while you may have to suffer various trials, so that the genuineness of your faith, more precious than gold which though perishable is tested by fire, may redound to praise and glory and honor at the revelation of Jesus Christ. Without having seen him you love him; though you do not now see him you believe in him and rejoice with unutterable and exalted joy.

I Peter 1:3-8

658

God Is Love

Beloved, let us love one another; for love is of God, and he who loves is born of God and knows God. He who does not love does not know God; for God is love. In this the love of God was made manifest among us, that God sent his only Son into the world, so that we might live through him. In this is love, not that we loved God but that he loved us and sent his Son to be the expiation for our sins. Beloved, if God so loved us, we also ought to love one another. No man has ever seen God; if we love one another, God abides in us and his love is perfected in us.

We love, because he first loved us. If any one says, "I love God," and hates his brother, he is a liar; for he who does not love his brother whom he has seen, cannot love God whom he has not seen. And this commandment we have from him, that he who loves God should love his brother also.

I John 4:7-12, 19-21

659

Christ Our Passover

Christ, our paschal lamb, has been sacrificed. Let us, therefore, celebrate the festival,

not with the old leaven, the leaven of malice and evil, but with the unleavened bread of sincerity and truth.

For we know that Christ being raised from the dead will never die again; death no longer has dominion over him.

The death he died he died to sin, once for all, but the life he lives he lives to God.

So you also must consider yourselves dead to sin and alive to God in Christ Jesus.

Christ has been raised from the dead, the first fruits of those who have fallen asleep.

For as by a man came death, by a man has come also the resurrection of the dead.

For as in Adam all die, so also in Christ shall all be made alive.

I Corinthians 5:7b-8; Romans 6:9-11; I Corinthians 15:20-22

660

I Make All Things New

Then I saw a new heaven and a new earth; for the first heaven and the first earth had passed away, and the sea was no more. And I saw the holy city, new Jerusalem, coming down out of heaven from God, prepared as a bride adorned for her husband; and I heard a great voice from the throne saying, "Behold, the dwelling of God is with men. He will dwell with them, and they shall be his people, and God himself will be with them; he will wipe away every tear from their eyes, and death shall be no more, neither shall there be mourning nor crying nor pain any more, for the former things have passed away."

And he who sat upon the throne said, "Behold, I make all things new." Also he said, "Write this, for these words are trustworthy and true." And he said to me, "It is done! I am the Alpha and the Omega, the beginning and the end."

And I saw no temple in the city, for its temple is the Lord God the Almighty and the Lamb. And the city has no need of sun or moon to shine upon it, for the glory of God is its light, and its lamp is the Lamb. By its light shall the nations walk; and the kings of the earth shall bring their glory into it, and its gates shall never be shut by day—and there shall be no night there; they shall bring into it the glory and the honor of the nations.

Revelation 21:1-6a, 22-26

661

THE LORD GOD ALMIGHTY

Holy, holy, holy is the Lord God Almighty, who was and is and is to come!

Great and wonderful are thy deeds, O Lord God the Almighty!

Just and true are thy ways, O King of the ages!

Who shall not fear and glorify thy name, O Lord? For thou alone art holy.

Worthy art thou, our Lord and God, to receive glory and honor and power: for thou didst create all things, and by thy will they existed and were created.

Worthy is the Lamb who was slain, to receive power and wealth and wisdom and might and honor and glory and blessing!

Blessing and glory and wisdom and thanksgiving and honor and power and might be to our God for ever and ever!

To him who sits upon the throne and to the Lamb be blessing and honor and glory and might for ever and ever!

We give thanks to thee, Lord God Almighty, who art and who was, that thou hast taken thy great power and begun to reign.

Hallelujah! For the Lord our God the Almighty reigns. Let us rejoice and exult and give him the glory.

Revelation 4:8; 15:3-4a; 4:11; 5:12; 7:12; 5:13; 11:17; 19:6b-7a

CANTICLES WITH MUSIC

662

INSTRUCTIONS ON CHANTING

Chanting is essentially timed, tuned, and toned speech. Lying somewhere between the freedom of speech and the discipline of singing, chanting represents a compromise between the two. The natural flow and accentuation of the words take precedence over the notes of the chant, which in fact have no definite time values. A chant is merely a series of notes on which the words are recited.

Chanting must be rehearsed. With leadership and practice any congregation can learn to chant acceptably, but chants should not be attempted without adequate preparation and practice on the part of choir and congregation alike.

This hymnal contains two basic types of chant: plainsong (or psalm tones) and Anglican chant. Plainsong is intended for unison singing, preferably without accompaniment; Anglican chant is written to be sung in four parts and is more chorally conceived. Of the two, plainsong is easier to grasp quickly since all sing the same melody and the melodic formulas are usually simpler.

In plainsong (e.g., "O Come, Let Us Sing" no. 663) there are two halves to the chant. Most of the text is sung on a single chanting tone (called the "recitation") which is the same for both halves of the chant. The first is approached by an "intonation," giving the pitch and tonality, which is sung only on the first line of text; thereafter, it is omitted since the tonality has been set firmly. The third part of the chant is a closing formula ("inflection") which may consist of one or more notes to accommodate the number of syllables. The formula which closes the first half of the chant ("mediation") always gives the sense of being incomplete, while the formula closing the second half ("ending") gives the sense of a complete cadence.

In Anglican chant, there is no intonation, but rather a chord on which the major portion of text is chanted. In a "single chant" (e.g., "It Is a Good Thing to Give Thanks" no. 667) there are two parts: a chanting chord, two measures of semi-cadence, another chanting chord, and three measures of final cadence. In a "double chant" (e.g., "O Be Joyful in the Lord" no. 669) and in a "quadruple chant" (e.g., "Blessed Be the Lord God of Israel" no. 666) there is an alternating pattern of three and four measures throughout the chant. The longer the chant the more complex the musical development possible.

In plainsong only one tune is used; so, there is seldom a problem with an uneven number of verses; however, in the Anglican setting of "O Come, Let Us Sing" (no. 664), the ninth line must be sung to the second half of the chant before proceeding to the Gloria.

A few simple rules may help:

(1) Keep the rhythm of speech insofar as possible.

(2) All stresses and accents are those of good speech. Music accents are entirely secondary.

(3) If there is only one syllable for the recitation note, the time value is only as long as the unstressed syllable will read. The recitation always adjusts to the number of syllables to be sung and has no inherent time value.

(4) The bar line which breaks up the text is only a visual reminder of a musical change. Keep moving past bar lines as if they were not there. The pace of the recitation and inflection should be identical.

(5) At most commas dwell slightly on the syllable which precedes, then move ahead without taking a breath. Where a comma divides the thought into balanced or contrasting ideas a breath may be necessary.

(6) Syllables or words in **bold face type** are sung to two notes.

(7) A dash following the vertical line indicates that the preceding syllable is extended through the first note after the bar line (e.g., thy | —salvation).

(8) If there are more than two syllables to be sung to two notes, they should be sung freely in speech rhythm. For example, if there are three syllables as in "sheep of his" ("O Be Joyful in the Lord" no. 669), the first two words will be sung on the first note of the measure and the last to the second. The effect should be approximately that of a smooth triplet. Occasionally there will be four syllables as in "sing unto the" ("O Come, Let Us Sing" no. 664); these should be sung two syllables for each note but without hurrying.

(9) Words ending in "ed" are sung as normally pronounced. Occasionally the context of the chant will call for the pronounced "ed," as in "blessed."

(10) Chanting lends itself particularly well to antiphonal singing, with two different groups singing alternate verses.

The following procedure should be helpful in rehearsing chants:

(1) Read the words in unison until all speak with the same speed and inflection.

(2) Learn the chant music by humming or singing on a vowel sound (e.g., "Ah" or "Oh").

(3) Read the words again while the piano or organ provides the musical setting.

(4) Combine the words with the chant music.

O Come, Let Us Sing

Venite, exultemus

PSALMS 95:1-7; 96:9, 13

Tone V

*
**
**

1. O come, let us sing unto the | Lord;
 let us heartily rejoice in the strength of | our salvation.
2. Let us come before his presence with thanks- | giving,
 and show ourselves | glad in him with psalms.
3. For the Lord is a great | God;
 and a great | King above all gods.
4. In his hand are all the corners of the | earth;
 and the strength of the hills | is his also.
5. The sea is his, and he | made it;
 and his hands pre- | pared the dry land.
6. O come let us worship and fall | down;
 and kneel before the | Lord our Maker.
7. For he is the Lord our | God;
 and we are the people of his pasture, and the | sheep of his hand.
8. O worship the Lord in the beauty of | holiness;
 let the whole earth | stand in awe of him.
9. For he cometh, for he cometh to judge the | earth;
 and with righteousness to judge the world,
 and the | peoples with his truth.

Glory be to the Father, and to the | Son,
 and | to the Holy Ghost;
As it was in the beginning, is now, and ever | shall be,
 world | without end. Amen.

*
**
**

* The first two notes (Intonation) are sung only for the first verse.
** Used at any ending where there are extra syllables.
This setting is preferably sung in unison without accompaniment.

O Come, Let Us Sing

Venite, exultemus

PSALMS 95:1-7; 96:9,13 WILLIAM BOYCE, 1710-1799

1. O come, let us | sing unto the Lord;
   let us heartily rejoice in the | strength of our salvation.
2. Let us come before his presence with | **thanks**giving;
   and show ourselves | glad in him with psalms.
3. For the Lord is a | **great** God;
   and a great | King above all gods.
4. In his hand are all the | corners of the earth;
   and the strength of the | hills is **his** also.
5. The sea is | his, and he made it;
   and his hands pre- | pared the **dry** land.
6. O come let us worship and | **fall** down,
   and kneel before the | Lord our **Ma**ker.
7. For he is the | Lord our God;
   and we are the people of his pasture, and the | sheep of **his** hand.
8. O worship the Lord in the | beauty of holiness;
   let the whole earth | stand in awe of him.

*9. For he cometh, for he cometh to | judge the earth;
   and with righteousness to judge the world,
   and the | peoples with his truth.

Glory be to the Father and | to the Son,
   and | to the Holy Ghost;
As it was in the beginning, is now, and | ever shall be,
   world without | **end. Amen.**

* No. 9 sung to the second line of music.

We Praise Thee, O God
Te Deum laudamus

Vss. 1-6

Attr. to NICETA, BISHOP OF REMESIANA, 4th Century — EDWIN G. MONK, 1819-1900

Vss. 7-12

WILLIAM CROFT, 1678-1727

Vss. 13-16

EDWIN G. MONK, 1819-1900

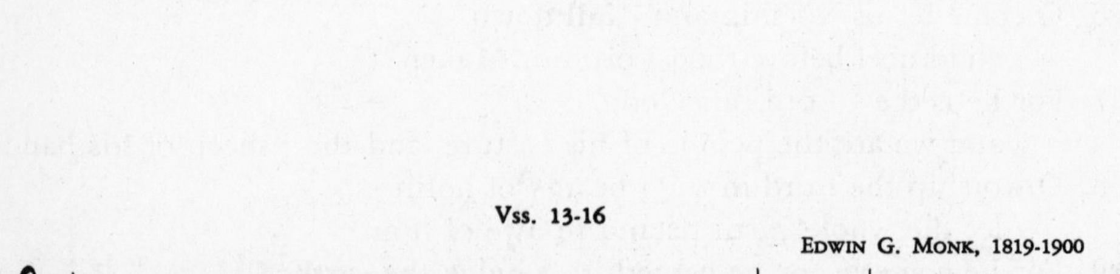

1. We praise thee, O God; we acknowledge thee to | be the Lord.
All the earth doth worship thee, the Father | ever**last**ing.
2. To thee all angels cry aloud; the heavens and all the | powers therein;
to thee cherubim and seraphim con- | tinually do cry,
3. Holy, holy, holy, Lord God of | Sabaoth;
heaven and earth are full of the majesty | of thy **glo**ry.
4. The glorious company of the apostles | **praise** thee.
The goodly fellowship of the | prophets **praise** thee.
5. The noble army of martyrs | **praise** thee.
The holy Church throughout all the world | doth acknowledge thee;
6. The Father, of an infinite majesty; thine adorable, true, and | only Son;
also the Holy | Ghost, the Comforter.

7. Thou art the King of | Glory, O Christ.
Thou art the everlasting | Son of the **Fa**ther.
8. When thou tookest upon thee to de- | liver man,
thou didst humble thyself to be | born of a **vir**gin.
9. When thou hadst overcome the | sharpness of death,
thou didst open the kingdom of heaven to | all be**liev**ers.
10. Thou sittest at the | right hand of God,
in the | glory of the **Fa**ther.
11. We believe that thou shalt come to | be our judge.
We therefore pray thee, help thy servants,
whom thou hast redeemed | with thy precious blood.
12. Make them to be numbered | with thy saints,
in glory | ever**last**ing.

13. O Lord, save thy people, and bless thine | heritage.
Govern them, and lift them | up for**ev**er.
14. Day by day we | magnify thee;
and we worship thy name ever, | world with**out** end.
15. Vouchsafe, O Lord, to keep us this day with- | **out** sin.
O Lord, have mercy upon us, have | mercy **up**on us.
16. O Lord, let thy mercy be upon us, as our | trust is in thee.
O Lord, in thee have I trusted; let me never | be con**found**ed.

For a hymn setting of this text, see hymn 8, Holy God, We Praise Thy Name.

666

Blessed Be the Lord God of Israel

Benedictus

LUKE 1:68-79 — WILLIAM CROTCH, 1775-1847

1. Blessed be the Lord God of | Israel;
   for he hath visited and re- | deemed his **people**;
2. And hath raised up a mighty sal- | vation for us,
   in the house of his | servant **David**;
3. As he spake by the mouth of his | holy prophets,
   which have | been since the world began;
4. That we should be saved | from our enemies,
   and from the hand of | all that **hate** us.
5. To perform the mercy promised to | our forefathers,
   and to remember his | holy covenant;
6. To perform the oath which he sware to our forefather | Abraham,
   that | he would **give** us;
7. That we being delivered out of the | hand of our enemies
   might | serve him without fear;
8. In holiness and righteous- | ness before him,
   all the | days of **our** life.
9. And thou, child, shalt be called the prophet | of the Highest:
   for thou shalt go before the face of the | Lord to prepare his ways;

10. To give knowledge of salvation | unto his people
for the re- | mission of their sins,
11. Through the tender mercy | of our God;
whereby the day-spring from on | high hath visited us;
12. To give light to them that sit in darkness,
and in the | shadow of death,
and to guide our feet in- | to the way of peace.
Glory be to the Father and | to the Son,
and | to the Holy Ghost;
As it was in the beginning, is now, and | ever shall be,
world without | **end.** Amen.

667

It Is a Good Thing to Give Thanks

Bonum est confiteri

PSALM 92:1-4

RICHARD FARRANT, c. 1530-1581

1. It is a good thing to give | thanks unto the Lord,
and to sing praises unto thy name, | O Most **High**est;
2. To tell of thy lovingkindness | early in the morning,
and of thy | truth in the **night** season;
3. Upon an instrument of ten strings, and up- | on the lute;
upon a loud instrument, | and upon the harp.
4. For thou Lord hast made me | glad through thy works;
and I will rejoice in giving praise for the oper- | ations of thy hands.
Glory be to the Father, and | to the Son,
and | to the Holy Ghost;
As it was in the beginning, is now, and | ever shall be,
world without | **end.** Amen.

668

Blessed Art Thou, O Lord

Benedictus es, Domine

SONG OF THE THREE YOUNG MEN, 29-34 — WILLIAM CROTCH, 1775-1847

1. Blessed art thou, O Lord | God of our fathers:
   praised and exalted above | all for**ev**er.
2. Blessed art thou for the | name of thy majesty:
   praised and exalted above | all for**ev**er.
3. Blessed art thou in the temple | of thy holiness:
   praised and exalted above | all for**ev**er.
4. Blessed art thou that beholdest the depths, and dwellest be- | tween the cherubim:
   praised and exalted above | all for**ev**er.
5. Blessed art thou on the glorious | throne of thy kingdom:
   praised and exalted above | all for**ev**er.
6. Blessed art thou in the firma- | ment of heaven:
   praised and exalted above | all for**ev**er.

Glory be to the Father, and | to the Son,
and | to the Holy Ghost;
As it was in the beginning, is now, and | ever shall be,
world without | **end. A**men.

O Be Joyful in the Lord

Jubilate Deo

Psalm 100 — Henry Aldrich, 1647-1710

1. O be joyful in the Lord | all ye lands:
   serve the Lord with gladness,
   and come before his | presence with a song.
2. Be ye sure that the Lord he is God; it is he that hath made us, and not | we ourselves;
   we are his people and the | sheep of his pasture.
3. O go your way into his gates with thanksgiving, and into his | courts with praise;
   be thankful unto him, and | speak good of his name.
4. For the Lord is gracious, his mercy is ever- | lasting,
   and his truth endureth from generation to | generation.

Glory be to the Father, and | to the Son,
and | to the Holy Ghost;
As it was in the beginning, is now, and | ever shall be,
world without | end. Amen.

For hymn settings of this text, see hymn 21, All People That on Earth Do Dwell, and hymn 22, Before Jehovah's Awful Throne.

670

My Soul Doth Magnify the Lord

Magnificat

LUKE 1:46-55

Tone VIII, 1

1. My soul doth magnify the | Lord,
   and my spirit hath rejoiced in | God my Savior.
2. For he hath re- | garded
   the lowliness of | his handmaiden.
3. For behold from hence- | forth
   all generations shall | call me blessed.
4. For he that is mighty hath magnified | me;
   and | holy is his name.
5. And his mercy is on them that | fear him
   throughout all | generations.
6. He hath showed strength with his | arm;
   he hath scattered the proud in the imagi- | nation of their hearts.
7. He hath put down the mighty from their | seat,
   and hath exalted the | humble and meek.
8. He hath filled the hungry with good | things;
   and the rich he hath sent | empty away.
9. He remembering his mercy hath holpen his servant | Israel;
   as he promised to our forefathers, Abraham and his | seed forever.

Glory be to the Father, and to the | Son,
   and | to the Holy Ghost;
As it was in the beginning, is now, and ever | shall be,
   world | without end. Amen.

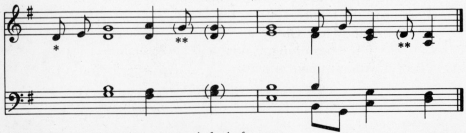

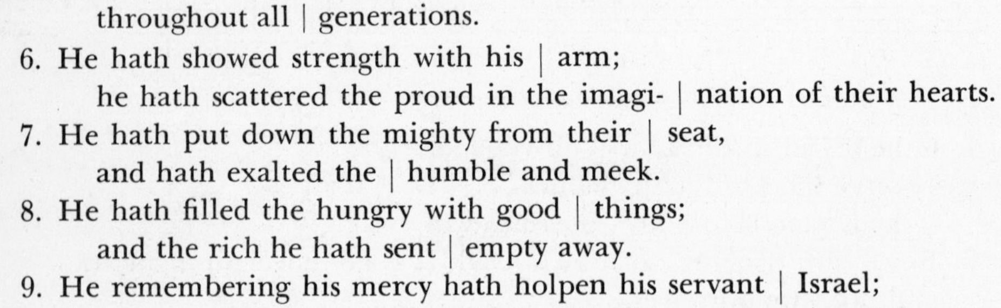

* The first two notes (Intonation) are sung only for the first verse.
** Used at any ending where there are extra syllables.
This setting is preferably sung in unison without accompaniment.

Out of the Deep

De Profundis

PSALM 130 — WILLIAM CROFT, 1678-1727

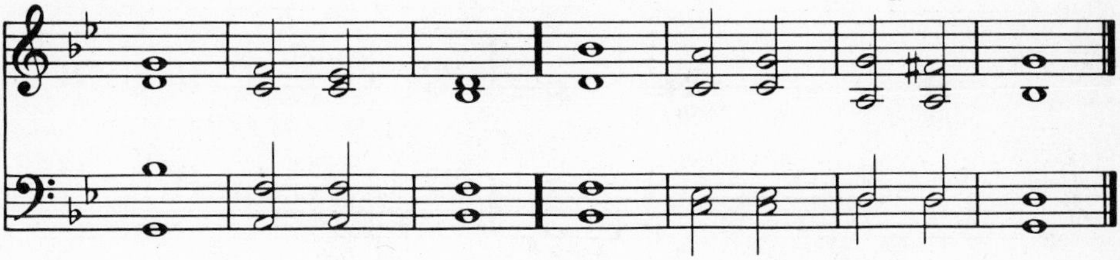

1. Out of the deep have I called unto | thee, O Lord;
   Lord, | **hear my** voice.
2. O let thine ears con- | sider well
   the | voice of my complaint.
3. If thou, Lord, wilt be extreme to mark what is | done amiss,
   O Lord, | who may a-**bide** it?
4. For there is | mercy with thee;
   therefore shalt | thou be **fear**ed.
5. I look for the Lord; my soul doth | wait for him;
   in his | word is **my** trust.
6. My soul fleeth unto the Lord before the | morning watch;
   I say, be- | fore the morning watch.
7. O Israel, trust in the Lord, for with the Lord there is | **mercy**,
   and with him is | plenteous re**demp**tion.
8. And he shall redeem | Israel
   from | **all his** sins.

Glory be to the Father, and | to the Son,
and | to the Holy Ghost;
As it was in the beginning, is now, and | ever shall be,
world without | **end**: **A**men.

For a hymn setting of this text, see hymn 526, Out of the Depths I Cry to Thee.

Out of the Deep

De Profundis

PSALM 130

Ancient Chant
Arr. by JAMES R. HOUGHTON, 1899 -

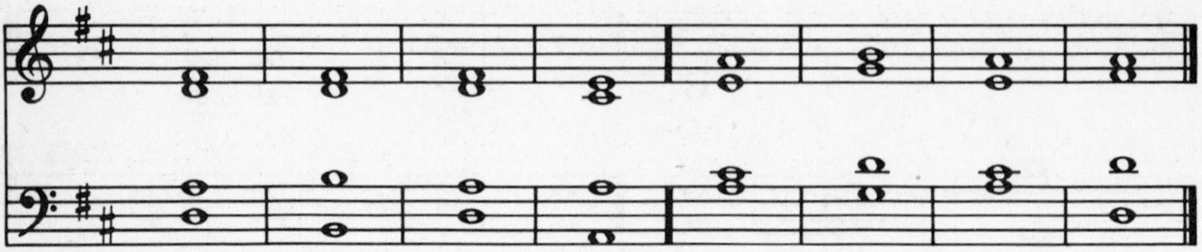

1. Out of the deep have I called unto thee O | Lord;
   Lord, hear my | voice.
   O let thine ears consider | well
   the voice of my com- | plaint.
2. If thou, Lord, wilt be extreme to mark what is done a- | miss,
   O Lord, who may a- | bide it?
   For there is mercy with | thee;
   therefore shalt thou be | feared.
3. I look for the Lord; my soul doth wait for | him;
   in his word is my | trust.
   My soul fleeth unto the | Lord
   before the morning watch; I say, before the morning | watch.
4. O Israel, trust in the Lord, for with the Lord there is | mercy,
   and with him is plenteous re- | demption.
   And he shall redeem | Israel
   from all his | sins.
   Glory be to the Father, and to the | Son,
   and to the Holy | Ghost;
   As it was in the beginning, is now, and ever | shall be,
   world without end. A- | men.

Lord, Now Lettest Thou Thy Servant

Nunc dimittis

LUKE 2:29-32

JOSEPH BARNBY, 1838-1896

1. Lord, now lettest thou thy servant de- | part in peace,
   ac- | cording to thy word.
2. For mine | eyes have seen
   thy |–sal-**vation**,
3. Which thou | hast prepared
   before the | face of **all** people;
4. To be a light to | lighten the Gentiles,
   and to be the glory of thy | people Israel.

Glory be to the Father, and | to the Son,
and | to the Holy Ghost;
As it was in the beginning, is now, and | ever shall be,
world without | **end**. **A**men.

AIDS FOR THE ORDERING OF WORSHIP

THE CHRISTIAN YEAR

674

A Lectionary for Public Worship

In addition to a psalm or other act of praise, two Scripture lessons may be read in each service of public worship: one from the Old Testament and one from the New, either Epistle or Gospel; but for the service of Holy Communion the two lessons are properly one from the Epistles and one from the Gospels, omitting an Old Testament lesson.

In the column headed "Acts of Praise," the first number refers to the Psalter, and the second number refers to a canticle or other act of praise.

The chapter and verse numbering of this Lectionary is that of the Revised Standard Version. The letter *a* after the number of a verse signifies the first major part of that verse; the letter *b,* the second major part; and the letter *c,* the third major part, etc.

Sundays are numbered as follows:

Advent Season: Four Sundays before Christmas Day, December 25, designated as Sundays *in* Advent.

Christmastide: Christmas Day, and one or two Sundays between December 25 and January 6, designated as Sundays *after* Christmas Day.

Epiphany Season: Four to nine Sundays between January 6, which is Epiphany Day, and the beginning of Lent, which depends upon the date of Easter Day, designated as Sundays *after* Epiphany Day.

Lenten Season: Six Sundays before Easter Day, designated as Sundays *in* Lent, of which the fifth may be called Passion Sunday and the sixth, Palm Sunday.

Eastertide: Easter Day and six other Sundays, designated as Sundays *after* Easter Day, of which the last may be called Ascension Sunday.

Pentecost Season: From eleven to sixteen Sundays beginning with Pentecost Sunday, the seventh Sunday after Easter Day, and continuing through the next to the last Sunday in August, designated as Sundays *after* Pentecost.

Kingdomtide: Thirteen or fourteen Sundays beginning the last Sunday in August and continuing until Advent, designated as Sundays *in* Kingdomtide.

	Acts of Praise[1]	Old Testament	Epistle	Gospel
		ADVENT SEASON		
1st Sunday	554, 660	Mal. 3:1-7*b*	Rom. 13:8-14	Mark 13:33-37
2nd Sunday	576, 647	Isa. 11:1-10	I Thess. 5:1-11	Luke 1:26-35
3rd Sunday	585, 612	Isa. 62:10-12	I Cor. 4:1-5	Luke 3:2*b*-6
4th Sunday	584, 609	Isa. 7:10-14	Titus 2:11–3:7	Matt. 1:18-25
		CHRISTMASTIDE		
Christmas Day	558, 655	Isa. 9:2, 6-7	Gal. 4:1-7	Luke 2:1-20
1st Sunday	555, 614	Isa. 42:1-9	I John 4:9-16	John 1:1-14
2nd Sunday	587, 620	Zech. 2:10-13	Heb. 1:1-12	Luke 2:21-32
		EPIPHANY SEASON		
1st Sunday	577, 636	Isa. 60:1-3, 6*b*	Eph. 3:1-12	Matt. 2:1-12
2nd Sunday	563, 642	Isa. 49:8-13	Eph. 2:11-18	Matt. 5:14-20
3rd Sunday	569, 631	I Sam. 1:19*c*-28	II Cor. 4:1-6	Luke 2:39-52
4th Sunday	574, 638	Jonah 3:1-5	I Cor. 1:18-31	John 12:20-36*a*
5th Sunday	602, 611	Hos. 6:1-3	Col. 1:21-29	John 1:19-30
6th Sunday	603, 648	Jer. 10:1-7	Acts 8:26-35	John 4:7-26
7th Sunday	605, 651	Hab. 2:18-20; 3:2-4	I Peter 2:4-10	John 1:35-51
8th Sunday	600, 653	Lev. 19:1-2, 15-18	Eph. 4:17-32	Luke 10:25-37
9th Sunday	556, 654	Prov. 4:10-18	I Cor. 2:1-16	Mark 1:14-22
		LENTEN SEASON		
Ash Wednesday	564, 615	Joel 2:12, 15-17	I Cor. 9:24-27	Matt. 6:16-21
1st Sunday	571, 641	Ezek. 33:7-16	I John 2:1-3, 15-17	Mark 1:9-12
2nd Sunday	593, 645	Exod. 33:18-23	Heb. 12:18-29	Matt. 17:1-9
3rd Sunday	594, 646	Amos 7:7-10, 14-16*a*	Rom. 6:15-23	Mark 10:17-27
4th Sunday	568, 635	Lamen. 3:22-26, 31-33	II Cor. 6:1-10	Luke 18:1-14
Passion Sunday	559, 640	Gen. 22:1-2, 9-13	Heb. 9:11-14	John 11:47-53
Palm Sunday	573, 634	Zech. 9:9-12	Phil. 2:5-11	Luke 19:29-40
Maundy Thursday	560, 649	Exod. 12:1, 3, 6-8, 11, 14, 25-27	I Cor. 11:23-26	Mark 14:17-25
Good Friday	559, 640	Isa. 52:13–53:12	Heb. 10:4-7, 10-23	Luke 23:33-38, 44-46
		EASTERTIDE		
Easter Day	557, 659	Isa. 25:1, 7-9	Acts 13:26-33	Mark 16:1-7
1st Sunday	596, 608	Job 19:1, 23-27	I Cor. 15:12-22	John 20:19-31
2nd Sunday	595, 643	Isa. 12:1-6	Rom. 6:3-11	John 6:37-40

[1] First number refers to the Psalter; second number refers to a canticle or other act of praise.

	Acts of Praise	Old Testament	Epistle	Gospel
3rd Sunday	597, 648	Ezek. 34:11-16, 30-31	I Peter 2:19-25	John 10:11-16
4th Sunday	602, 654	Deut. 7:6-11	II Cor. 5:1-10	John 16:16-22
5th Sunday	589, 656	Deut. 10:12-15, 20–11:1	I John 5:1-5, 11	John 17:1-5
Ascension Sunday	582, 657	Dan. 7:9-10, 13-14	Eph. 1:15-23	Luke 24:44-53

PENTECOST SEASON

Pentecost Sunday	583, 644	Jer. 31:31-34	Acts 2:1-8, 12-21	John 14:15-17, 25-27
1st Sunday	565, 642	Gen. 3:1-6, 22-23	Acts 3:1-7, 11-21	Matt. 11:2-6
2nd Sunday	555, 643	Gen. 9:8-15	Acts 4:8, 10-13, 18-20	Luke 10:1-11
3rd Sunday	556, 645	Gen. 28:10-22	Acts 9:22, 26-31	John 3:4-17
4th Sunday	558, 645	Gen. 45:4-11	Acts 15:1, 6-11	Matt. 16:13-19
5th Sunday	561, 649	Exod. 20:1-20	Acts 16:1-10	Luke 19:1-10
6th Sunday	562, 650	Num. 27:12-14*a*, 15-20, 22-23	Acts 18:24–19:6	John 10:1-10
7th Sunday	565, 651	Josh. 24:1-15, 24	Acts 17:21-31	Luke 8:4-15
8th Sunday	566, 652	Judges 7:2-7, 19-22	Acts 20:17-28, 32	Matt. 10:16-33
9th Sunday	567, 654	Ruth 1:1, 4-9, 16, 19*a*	Acts 28:16-20, 23-24, 30-31	Luke 15:1-10
10th Sunday	570, 655	I Sam. 9:15-17, 10:1	Romans 8:14-39	Luke 18:18-30
11th Sunday	573, 656	I Sam. 16:1-13	II Cor. 3:4-11, 17-18	Luke 11:1-4, 9-13
12th Sunday	572, 657	II Sam. 12:1-10, 13*a*	Eph. 3:13-21	Matthew 11:25-30
13th Sunday	574, 658	I Chron. 28:1-3, 5-10	Eph. 6:10-20	Matthew 20:20-28
14th Sunday	577, 660	II Chron. 6:1, 18-21	Eph. 4:1-8	John 2:1-11
15th Sunday	578, 661	II Kings 17:5-14, 18-23	Phil. 4:4-9, 19-20	Mark 14:3-9

KINGDOMTIDE

1st Sunday	580, 610	I Chron. 29:10-18	Rev. 19:1, 4, 6-8	Matt. 25:31-40
2nd Sunday	581, 616	I Kings 18:21-39	I Tim. 6:6-19	Luke 16:10-15
3rd Sunday	586, 620	Isaiah 6:1-8	II Cor. 5:17–6:2	Mark 10:28-31
4th Sunday	588, 622	Obadiah 1:1-4, 15-17*a*, 21	Col. 3:1-15	Matt. 7:15-23
5th Sunday	590, 623	Nahum 1:1-8	Heb. 13:1-6	Matt. 18:15-22
6th Sunday	597, 624	Micah 6:1-4, 5*d*-8	Heb. 11:1-3, 6	Matt. 8:23-27
7th Sunday	591, 625	Ezek. 18:23-32	James 1:17-27	Luke 21:1-4
8th Sunday	592, 626	Amos 5:18-24	II Timothy 2:1-13	Matt. 25:14-30
9th Sunday	598, 627	Isa. 55:1-7	Philem. 1:1-3, 10-16	Luke 15:11-32

	Acts of Praise	Old Testament	Epistle	Gospel
10th Sunday	601, 628	Ezek. 37:1-6, 11-14	II John 1:3-4, 6 & III John 1:11	John 8:1-11
11th Sunday	605, 629	Zeph. 3:8-13	I John 2:24-25, 28-29; 3:1-2	Mark 6:31-44
12th Sunday	602, 630	Haggai 1:3-9; 2:2-3	II Peter 3:8-14	Matt. 7:24-29
13th Sunday	604, 631	Ezra 1:2-4; 3:10-13	Jude 1:17-21, 24-25	Luke 13:22-24, 34-35
14th Sunday	606, 637	Isa. 40:1-5	II Thess. 1:3-5, 11-12; 2:1-2, 13-15	Luke 17:20-25

SPECIAL DAYS

Universal Bible Sunday	593, 621	Deut. 30:8-20	Romans 15:4-13	Luke 4:16-21
New Year's Day or Watch Night	580, 643	Eccl. 11:6-9; 12:13	Rev. 21:1-6*a*	Luke 9:57-62
Race Relations Sunday	573, 633	Gen. 1:1-3, 26-31	Acts 10:9-15, 34	Mark 3:31-35
Festival of the Christian Home	588, 658	Prov. 31:10-31	Eph. 5:25–6:4	Matt. 19:1-5, 10-14
Aldersgate Sunday	566, 615	Isa. 52:1-2, 7-12	Romans 5:1-11	Mark 12:28-34*a*
Ascension Day	561, 657	Dan. 7:9-10, 13-14	Eph. 1:15-23	Luke 24:44-53
Trinity Sunday	565, 661	Exod. 3:1-8*b*, 10-15	Romans 11:33-36	Matt. 28:16-20
Independence Day	595, 626	Deut. 1:5, 8-18	Gal. 5:13-15	John 8:31-36
Labor Day	555, 624	Amos 5:11-15	Col. 3:23-25	John 6:5-14, 26-27
Reformation Day	570, 654	Neh. 8:1-3, 5-8	Gal. 3:23-26	John 2:13-16
All Saints Day	556, 625	Isa. 51:11-16	Rev. 7:9-17	Matt. 5:1-12
World Order Sunday	596, 632	Micah 4:1-5	James 4:1-12	Matt. 5:43-48
Commitment Day	554, 651	Isa. 5:11-12, 20-24	I Cor. 3:16-17	Luke 21:23-26
Thanksgiving Day	575, 607	Deut. 8:7-18	II Cor. 9:6-12	Luke 12:16-31

675

A Table for Easter Day

A Table of the Days on Which Easter Day and Other Days Dependent on It Will Fall A.D. 1966-2000

Year of Our Lord	Sundays After Epiphany	Ash Wednesday	Easter	Pentecost	Sundays After Pentecost	Sundays in Kingdomtide	First Sunday in Advent
1966	7	Feb. 23	Apr. 10	May 29	12	13	Nov. 27
1967	5	Feb. 8	Mar. 26	May 14	14	14	Dec. 3
1968	8	Feb. 28	Apr. 14	June 2	11	14	Dec. 1
1969	6	Feb. 19	Apr. 6	May 25	13	13	Nov. 30
1970	5	Feb. 11	Mar. 29	May 17	14	13	Nov. 29
1971	7	Feb. 24	Apr. 11	May 30	12	13	Nov. 28
1972	6	Feb. 16	Apr. 2	May 21	13	14	Dec. 3
1973	9	Mar. 7	Apr. 22	June 10	10	14	Dec. 2
1974	7	Feb. 27	Apr. 14	June 2	11	14	Dec. 1
1975	5	Feb. 12	Mar. 30	May 18	14	13	Nov. 30
1976	8	Mar. 3	Apr. 18	June 6	11	13	Nov. 28
1977	7	Feb. 23	Apr. 10	May 29	12	13	Nov. 27
1978	5	Feb. 8	Mar. 26	May 14	14	14	Dec. 3
1979	8	Feb. 28	Apr. 15	June 3	11	14	Dec. 2
1980	6	Feb. 20	Apr. 6	May 25	13	13	Nov. 30
1981	8	Mar. 4	Apr. 19	June 7	11	13	Nov. 29
1982	7	Feb. 24	Apr. 11	May 30	12	13	Nov. 28
1983	6	Feb. 16	Apr. 3	May 22	13	13	Nov. 27
1984	9	Mar. 7	Apr. 22	June 10	10	14	Dec. 2
1985	6	Feb. 20	Apr. 7	May 26	12	14	Dec. 1
1986	5	Feb. 12	Mar. 30	May 18	14	13	Nov. 30
1987	8	Mar. 4	Apr. 19	June 7	11	13	Nov. 29
1988	6	Feb. 17	Apr. 3	May 22	13	13	Nov. 27
1989	5	Feb. 8	Mar. 26	May 14	14	14	Dec. 3
1990	8	Feb. 28	Apr. 15	June 3	11	14	Dec. 2
1991	5	Feb. 13	Mar. 31	May 19	13	14	Dec. 1
1992	8	Mar. 4	Apr. 19	June 7	11	13	Nov. 29
1993	7	Feb. 24	Apr. 11	May 30	12	13	Nov. 28
1994	6	Feb. 16	Apr. 3	May 22	13	13	Nov. 27
1995	5	Mar. 1	Apr. 16	June 4	11	14	Dec. 3
1996	6	Feb. 21	Apr. 7	May 26	12	14	Dec. 1
1997	5	Feb. 12	Mar. 30	May 18	14	13	Nov. 30
1998	7	Feb. 25	Apr. 12	May 31	12	13	Nov. 29
1999	6	Feb. 17	Apr. 4	May 23	13	13	Nov. 28
2000	9	Mar. 8	Apr. 23	June 11	10	14	Dec. 3

ADVENT SEASON

The four Sundays preceding Christmas Day

COLOR: Purple

For additional material appropriate to Advent see the section on the Christian Year in *The Book of Worship.*

Scripture Sentences or Calls to Worship

676

Lift up your heads, O gates! and be lifted up, O ancient doors! that the King of glory may come in. *Psalm 24:7*

677

The glory of the Lord shall be revealed, and all flesh shall see it together, for the mouth of the Lord has spoken. *Isaiah 40:5*

Collects

678

O almighty God, who hast taught us that the night is far spent and the day is at hand: Grant that we may ever be found watching for the coming of thy Son; save us from undue love of the world, that we may wait with patient hope for the day of the Lord, and so abide in him, that when he shall appear we may not be ashamed; through Jesus Christ our Lord. **Amen.**

679

Blessed Lord, who hast caused all holy Scriptures to be written for our learning: Grant that we may in such wise hear them, read, mark, learn, and inwardly digest them, that by patience, and comfort of thy holy Word, we may embrace and ever hold fast the blessed hope of everlasting life, which thou hast given us in our Savior Jesus Christ. **Amen.**

680

O God, who didst prepare of old the minds and hearts of men for the coming of thy Son, and whose Spirit ever worketh to illumine our darkened lives with the light of the Gospel: Prepare now our minds and hearts, we beseech thee, that Christ may dwell in us, and ever reign in our thoughts and affections as the King of love, and the very Prince of Peace. Grant this, we pray thee, for his sake. **Amen.**

681

O Lord, raise up, we pray thee, thy power, and come among us, and with great might succor us; that, whereas, through our sins and wickedness, we are sorely hindered in running the race that is set before us, thy bountiful grace and mercy may speedily help and deliver us; through Jesus Christ our Lord, to whom, with thee and the Holy Ghost, be honor and glory, world without end. **Amen.**

Christmastide

Usually two Sundays

Color: White

For additional materials appropriate to Christmastide see the section on the Christian Year in *The Book of Worship*.

Scripture Sentences or Calls to Worship

682

God so loved the world that he gave his only Son, that whoever believes in him should not perish but have eternal life. *John 3:16*

683

Behold, I bring you good news of a great joy which will come to all the people; for to you is born this day in the city of David a Savior, who is Christ the Lord. *Luke 2:10*

Collects

684

O God, who makest us glad with the yearly remembrance of the birth of thine only Son Jesus Christ: Grant that as we joyfully receive him for our Redeemer, so we may with sure confidence behold him when he shall come to be our judge, who liveth and reigneth with thee and the Holy Ghost, one God, world without end. **Amen.**

685

Eternal God, who by the birth of thy beloved Son Jesus Christ didst give thyself to mankind: Grant that, being born in our hearts, he may save us from all our sins, and restore within us the image and likeness of our creator, to whom be everlasting praise and glory, world without end. **Amen.**

Epiphany Season

Four to nine Sundays

COLOR: First Sunday, white; thereafter, green

For additional materials appropriate to Epiphany Season see the section on the Christian Year in *The Book of Worship.*

Scripture Sentences or Calls to Worship

686

Arise, shine; for your light has come, and the glory of the Lord has risen upon you. Nations shall come to your light, and kings to the brightness of your rising. *Isaiah 60:1, 3*

687

And I have other sheep, that are not of this fold; I must bring them also, and they will heed my voice. So there shall be one flock, one shepherd. *John 10:16*

Collects

688

Almighty and everlasting God, the radiance of faithful souls, who didst bring the nations to thy light and kings to the brightness of thy rising: Fill, we beseech thee, the world with thy glory, and show thyself unto all the nations; through him who is the true light and the bright and morning star, even Jesus Christ thy Son our Lord. **Amen.**

689

O God, who hast made of one blood all nations of men for to dwell on the face of the whole earth, and didst send thy blessed Son to preach peace to them that are afar off and to them that are nigh: Grant that all men everywhere may seek after thee and find thee. Bring the nations into thy fold, pour out thy Spirit upon all flesh, and hasten thy kingdom; through the same thy Son Jesus Christ our Lord. **Amen.**

690

O Lord, we beseech thee mercifully to receive the prayers of thy people who call upon thee; and grant that they may both perceive and know what things they ought to do, and also may have grace and power faithfully to fulfill the same; through Jesus Christ our Lord. **Amen.**

LENTEN SEASON

Six Sundays

COLOR: Purple

For additional materials appropriate to Lent see the section on the Christian Year in *The Book of Worship.*

Scripture Sentences or Calls to Worship

691

Come, let us walk in the light of the Lord, that he may teach us his ways and that we may walk in his paths. *Isaiah 2:5, 3c*

692

Seek the Lord while he may be found, call upon him while he is near; let the wicked forsake his way, and the unrighteous man his thoughts; let him return to the Lord. *Isaiah 55:6-7*

Collects

693

Almighty and everlasting God, who hatest nothing that thou hast made, and dost forgive the sins of those who are penitent: Create and make in us new and contrite hearts, that we, truly lamenting our sins and acknowledging our wickedness, may obtain of thee, the God of all mercy, perfect remission and forgiveness; through Jesus Christ our Lord. **Amen.**

694

Almighty God, who seest that we have no power of ourselves to help ourselves: Keep us, both outwardly in our bodies and inwardly in our souls, that we may be defended from all adversities which may happen to the body, and from all evil thoughts which may hurt the soul; through Jesus Christ our Lord. **Amen.**

Eastertide

Seven Sundays

Color: White

For additional materials appropriate to Eastertide see the section on the Christian Year in *The Book of Worship.*

Scripture Sentences or Calls to Worship

695

Minister: The Lord is risen!

People: **The Lord is risen indeed!**

696

Minister: Blessed be the God and Father of our Lord Jesus Christ! By his great mercy we have been born anew to a living hope through the resurrection of Jesus Christ from the dead.

People: **We have an inheritance which is imperishable, undefiled, and unfading.**

697

If then you have been raised with Christ, seek the things that are above, where Christ is, seated at the right hand of God. *Colossians 3:1*

Collects

698

O God, who for our redemption didst give thine only begotten Son to the death of the cross, and by his glorious resurrection hast delivered us from the power of our enemy: Grant us so to die daily to sin that we may evermore live with him in the joy of his resurrection; through Jesus Christ our Lord. **Amen.**

699

Almighty God, who through thine only Son hast overcome death, and opened unto us the gate of everlasting life: Grant, we beseech thee, that we who celebrate our Lord's resurrection may by the renewing of thy Spirit arise from the death of sin to the life of righteousness; through the same Jesus Christ our Lord. **Amen.**

700

O God, who through the resurrection of Jesus Christ hast freed us from the power of darkness and brought us into the kingdom of thy love: Grant, we beseech thee that, as by his death he has recalled us into life, so by his abiding presence he may bring us to the joys eternal; through him who for our sakes died and rose again, and is ever with us in power, the same thy Son Jesus Christ our Lord. **Amen.**

701

O almighty God, who alone canst order the unruly wills and affections of sinful men: Grant unto thy people, that they may love the thing which thou dost command, and desire that which thou dost promise; that so, among the sundry and manifold changes of the world, our hearts may surely there be fixed, where true joys are to be found; through Jesus Christ our Lord. **Amen.**

Pentecost Season

Eleven to Sixteen Sundays

Color: Red

For additional materials appropriate to Pentecost Season see the section on the Christian Year in *The Book of Worship.*

Scripture Sentences or Calls to Worship

702

But the hour is coming, and now is, when the true worshipers will worship the Father in spirit and truth, for such the Father seeks to wor-

ship him. God is spirit, and those who worship him must worship in spirit and truth. *John 4:23-24*

703

And it shall come to pass afterward, that I will pour out my spirit on all flesh; your sons and your daughters shall prophesy, your old men shall dream dreams, and your young men shall see visions. *Joel 2:28*

Collects

704

Grant, we beseech thee, merciful God, that thy Church being gathered together in unity by thy Holy Spirit, may manifest thy power among all peoples, to the glory of thy name; through Jesus Christ our Lord, who liveth and reigneth with thee and the same Spirit, one God, world without end. **Amen.**

705

O God, the protector of all that trust in thee, without whom nothing is strong, nothing is holy: Increase and multiply upon us thy mercy, that, thou being our ruler and guide, we may so pass through things temporal that we finally lose not the things eternal. Grant this, O heavenly Father, for the sake of Jesus Christ our Lord. **Amen.**

706

Almighty and everlasting God, who art always more ready to hear than we to pray, and art wont to give more than either we desire or deserve: Pour down upon us the abundance of thy mercy, forgiving us those things whereof our conscience is afraid, and giving us those good things which we are not worthy to ask, but through the merits and mediation of Jesus Christ thy Son our Lord. **Amen.**

707

Grant to us, Lord, we beseech thee, the spirit to think and do always such things as are right; that we, who cannot do anything that is good without thee, may by thee be enabled to live according to thy will; through Jesus Christ our Lord. **Amen.**

Kingdomtide

Thirteen or fourteen Sundays

Color: Green

For additional materials appropriate to Kingdomtide see the section on the Christian Year in *The Book of Worship.*

Scripture Sentences or Calls to Worship

708

O sing to the Lord a new song; sing to the Lord, all the earth: for he comes, for he comes to judge the earth. He will judge the world with righteousness, and the peoples with his truth. *Psalm 96:1, 13*

709

Thus says the Lord: "Let not the wise man glory in his wisdom, let not the mighty man glory in his might, let not the rich man glory in his riches; but let him who glories glory in this, that he understands and knows me, that I am the Lord who practice kindness, justice, and righteousness in the earth; for in these things I delight, says the Lord." *Jeremiah 9:23-24*

710

Minister: Make a joyful noise to the Lord, all the lands! Serve the Lord with gladness! Come into his presence with singing!

People: **Know that the Lord is God! It is he that made us, and we are his; we are his people, and the sheep of his pasture.**

Minister: Enter his gates with thanksgiving, and his courts with praise! Give thanks to him and bless his name!

People: **For the Lord is good; his steadfast love endures for ever, and his faithfulness to all generations.**

Collects

711

O God, who at this time didst teach the hearts of thy faithful people, by sending them the light of thy Holy Spirit: Grant us by the same Spirit to have a right judgment in all things, and evermore to rejoice in his holy comfort; through the merits of Jesus Christ our Savior, who liveth and reigneth with thee, in the unity of the same Spirit, one God, world without end. **Amen.**

712

Almighty God, our heavenly Father: Guide, we beseech thee, the nations of the world into the way of justice and truth, and establish among them that peace which is the fruit of righteousness, that they may become the kingdom of our Lord and Savior Jesus Christ. **Amen.**

713

O God, by whom the meek are guided in judgment, and light riseth up in darkness for the godly: Grant us, in all doubts and uncertainties, the grace to ask what thou wouldst have us to do, that the spirit of wisdom may save us from all false choices, and that in thy light we may see light and in thy straight path may not stumble; through Jesus Christ our Lord. **Amen.**

714

Almighty God, from whom all thoughts of truth and peace proceed: Kindle, we pray thee, in the hearts of all men the true love of peace, and guide with thy pure and peaceable wisdom those who take counsel for the nations of the earth, that in tranquillity thy kingdom may grow, till the earth is filled with the knowledge of thy love; through Jesus Christ our Lord. **Amen.**

GENERAL AIDS TO WORSHIP

Prayers for Use on Entering the Church

715

Almighty God, unto whom all hearts are open, all desires known, and from whom no secrets are hid: Cleanse the thoughts of our hearts by the inspiration of thy Holy Spirit, that we may perfectly love thee, and worthily magnify thy holy name; through Christ our Lord. **Amen.**

716

O God, who makest us glad with the weekly remembrance of the glorious resurrection of thy Son our Lord: Vouchsafe us this day such blessing through our worship of thee, that the days to come may be spent in thy service; through the same Jesus Christ our Lord. **Amen.**

717

O God, who hast taught us that in returning and rest we shall be saved, and that in quietness and confidence shall be our strength: Draw near to us now with thy mighty power and steadfast love, that in thy presence we may be still and know that thou art God; through Jesus Christ our Lord. **Amen.**

718

Let thy merciful ears, O Lord, be open to the prayers of thy humble servants; and, that they may obtain their petitions, make them to ask such things as shall please thee; through Jesus Christ our Lord. **Amen.**

Prayers with the Choir

Minister: The Lord be with you.

Choir: **And with thy spirit.**

Minister: Let us pray.

† *Then shall follow one of these prayers, or other prayer by the minister or member of the choir.*

719

O almighty God, who art worthy to be praised and to be held in reverence by all those who stand before thee: Pour out upon us, we pray thee, thy redeeming and sanctifying Spirit, that we, being cleansed from sin, may worship thee with unfeigned joy; grant that all our praises, begun and ended in thee, may make thy name glorious; through Jesus Christ our Lord. **Amen.**

720

Almighty God, at whose right hand are pleasures for evermore: We pray that as redeemed and forgiven children we may evermore rejoice in singing thy praises. Grant, we beseech thee, that what we sing with our lips we may believe in our hearts, and what we believe in our hearts, we may practice in our lives; so that being doers of the Word and not hearers only, we may obtain everlasting life; through Jesus Christ our Lord. **Amen.**

721

Most merciful and gracious God, who art the strength of all who put their trust in thee: Prepare us now to worship thee in spirit and in truth, with all reverence and godly fear. Quicken our devotion, that with holy gladness we may show forth thy most worthy praise, to the end that those who worship here may humbly receive thy Word, steadfastly cling to it, and obediently perform all such good works as thou dost appoint for us to do, that thereby we may manifest that thankfulness which we owe to thee for thy redeeming love; through Jesus Christ our Lord. **Amen.**

722

O God, before whose throne the whole family of heaven and earth bow down in ceaseless adoration: Accept, we pray thee, the praises which we offer thee this day. Make us to know the joy of thy salvation, that with glad hearts we may proclaim thy Word in such wise that the sorrowing may be comforted, the faint in heart made strong, the wayward restored to ways of life and peace, and thy saving health be made known to all nations; through Jesus Christ our Lord. **Amen.**

Prayers of Confession

723

Have mercy upon us, O God, according to thy lovingkindness; according to the multitude of thy tender mercies blot out our transgressions. Wash us thoroughly from our iniquities, and cleanse us from our sins. For we acknowledge our transgressions, and our sin is ever before us. Create in us clean hearts, O God, and renew a right spirit within us; through Jesus Christ our Lord. **Amen.**

724

Almighty and most merciful Father, we have erred and strayed from thy ways like lost sheep. We have followed too much the devices and desires of our own hearts. We have offended against thy holy laws. We have left undone those things which we ought to have done, and we have done those things which we ought not to have done. But thou, O Lord, have mercy upon us. Spare thou those, O God, who confess their faults. Restore thou those who are penitent, according to thy promises declared unto mankind in Christ Jesus our Lord. And grant, O most merciful Father, for his sake, that we may hereafter live a godly, righteous, and sober life; to the glory of thy holy name. **Amen.**

725

Our heavenly Father, who by thy love hast made us, and through thy love hast kept us, and in thy love wouldst make us perfect: We humbly confess that we have not loved thee with all our heart and soul and mind and strength, and that we have not loved one another as Christ hath loved us. Thy life is within our souls, but our selfishness hath hindered thee. We have not lived by faith. We have resisted thy Spirit. We have neglected thine inspirations.

Forgive what we have been; help us to amend what we are; and in thy Spirit direct what we shall be; that thou mayest come into the full glory of thy creation, in us and in all men; through Jesus Christ our Lord. **Amen.**

726

Almighty and most merciful God, who knowest the thoughts of our hearts: We confess that we have sinned against thee, and done evil in thy sight. We have transgressed thy holy laws; we have neglected thy Word and ordinances. Forgive us, O Lord, we beseech thee; and give us grace and power to put away all hurtful things, that, being delivered from the bondage of sin, we may bring forth fruit worthy of repentance, and henceforth may ever walk in thy holy ways; through Jesus Christ our Lord. **Amen.**

727

O almighty God, give us grace to approach thee at this time with penitent and believing hearts. We confess that we have sinned against thee and are not worthy to be called thy children; yet do thou in mercy keep us as thine own. Grant us true repentance, and forgive us all our sins; through Jesus Christ our Lord. **Amen.**

Words of Assurance

728

For as the heavens are high above the earth, so great is his steadfast love toward those who fear him; as far as the east is from the west, so far does he remove our transgressions from us. *Psalm 103:11-12*

729
As a father pities his children, so the Lord pities those who fear him.
Psalm 103:13

730
The Lord is gracious and merciful, slow to anger and abounding in steadfast love. *Psalm 145:8*

731
This is the message we have heard from him and proclaim to you, that God is light and in him is no darkness at all. If we walk in the light, as he is in the light, we have fellowship with one another, and the blood of Jesus his Son cleanses us from all sin. *I John 1:5, 7*

732
Jesus said: "Him who comes to me I will not cast out." *John 6:37b*

733
If we confess our sins, he is faithful and just, and will forgive our sins and cleanse us from all unrighteousness. *I John 1:9*

734
Your sins are forgiven for his sake. *I John 2:12b*

Prayers for Pardon and Forgiveness

735
May the almighty and merciful God grant us pardon, forgiveness, and remission of our sins; through Jesus Christ our Lord. **Amen.**

736
May almighty God, who caused light to shine out of darkness, shine in our hearts, cleansing us from all our sins, and restoring us to the light of the knowledge of his glory in the face of Jesus Christ our Lord. **Amen.**

737

O Lord, we beseech thee, absolve thy people from their offenses, that through thy bountiful goodness we may be delivered from the bonds of those sins which by our frailty we have committed. Grant this, O heavenly Father, for the sake of Jesus Christ, our blessed Lord and Savior. **Amen.**

Affirmations of Faith

738

THE APOSTLES' CREED

Minister: Let us unite in this historic confession of the Christian faith:
Minister and People: I believe in God the Father Almighty, maker of heaven and earth;

And in Jesus Christ his only Son our Lord: who was conceived by the Holy Spirit,[1] born of the Virgin Mary, suffered under Pontius Pilate, was crucified, dead, and buried;[2] the third day he rose from the dead; he ascended into heaven, and sitteth at the right hand of God the Father Almighty; from thence he shall come to judge the quick and the dead.

I believe in the Holy Spirit, the holy catholic Church, the communion of saints, the forgiveness of sins, the resurrection of the body, and the life everlasting. **Amen.**

739

THE NICENE CREED

Minister: Let us unite in this historic confession of the Christian faith:
Minister and People: I believe in one God: the Father Almighty, maker of heaven and earth, and of all things visible and invisible;

And in one Lord Jesus Christ, the only begotten Son of God: begotten of the Father before all worlds, God of God, Light of Light, very God of very God, begotten, not made, being of one substance with the Father, through whom all things were made; who for us men and for our salvation came down from heaven, and was incarnate by the Holy Ghost of the Virgin Mary, and was made man, and was crucified also for us under Pontius Pilate; he suffered and was buried, and the third day he rose again according to the Scriptures, and ascended into heaven, and sitteth

[1] Or Holy Ghost.
[2] Traditional use of this creed includes these words: "He descended into hell."

on the right hand of the Father; and he shall come again with glory, to judge both the quick and the dead; whose kingdom shall have no end.

And I believe in the Holy Ghost, the Lord, the giver of life, who proceedeth from the Father and the Son, who with the Father and the Son together is worshiped and glorified, who spake by the prophets. And I believe in one holy catholic and apostolic Church. I acknowledge one baptism for the remission of sins. And I look for the resurrection of the dead, and the life of the world to come. **Amen.**

740

A MODERN AFFIRMATION

Minister: Where the Spirit of the Lord is, there is the one true Church, apostolic and universal, whose holy faith let us now declare:

Minister and People: We believe in God the Father, infinite in wisdom, power, and love, whose mercy is over all his works, and whose will is ever directed to his children's good.

We believe in Jesus Christ, Son of God and Son of man, the gift of the Father's unfailing grace, the ground of our hope, and the promise of our deliverance from sin and death.

We believe in the Holy Spirit as the divine presence in our lives, whereby we are kept in perpetual remembrance of the truth of Christ, and find strength and help in time of need.

We believe that this faith should manifest itself in the service of love as set forth in the example of our blessed Lord, to the end that the kingdom of God may come upon the earth. **Amen.**

741

THE KOREAN CREED

Minister: Where the Spirit of the Lord is, there is the one true Church, apostolic and universal, whose holy faith let us now declare:

Minister and People: We believe in the one God, maker and ruler of all things, Father of all men, the source of all goodness and beauty, all truth and love.

We believe in Jesus Christ, God manifest in the flesh, our teacher, example, and Redeemer, the Savior of the world.

We believe in the Holy Spirit, God present with us for guidance, for comfort, and for strength.

We believe in the forgiveness of sins, in the life of love and prayer, and in grace equal to every need.

We believe in the Word of God contained in the Old and New Testaments as the sufficient rule both of faith and of practice.

We believe in the Church as the fellowship for worship and for service of all who are united to the living Lord.

We believe in the kingdom of God as the divine rule in human society, and in the brotherhood of man under the fatherhood of God.

We believe in the final triumph of righteousness, and in the life everlasting. **Amen.**

Prayers of Petition and Intercession

742

FOR ALL CONDITIONS OF MEN

O God, the creator and preserver of all mankind; we humbly beseech thee for all sorts and conditions of men; that thou wouldst be pleased to make thy ways known unto them, thy saving health unto all nations. More especially, we pray for thy holy Church universal, that it may be so guided and governed by thy good Spirit, that all who profess and call themselves Christians may be led into the way of truth, and hold the faith in unity of spirit, in the bond of peace, and in righteousness of life. Finally, we commend to thy fatherly goodness all those who are in any way afflicted or distressed in mind, body, or estate; that it may please thee to comfort and relieve them according to their several necessities, giving them patience under their suffering, and a happy issue out of all their afflictions. And this we ask for Jesus Christ's sake. **Amen.**

743

FOR THE CHURCH

O God our Father, we pray for thy Church, which is set today amid the perplexities of a changing order, and face to face with new tasks. Baptize her afresh in the life-giving spirit of Jesus! Bestow upon her a great responsiveness to duty, a swifter compassion with suffering, and an utter loyalty to the will of God. Help her to proclaim boldly the coming of the kingdom of God. Put upon her lips the ancient Gospel of her Lord. Fill her with the prophets' scorn of tyranny, and with a Christlike tenderness for the heavy-laden and downtrodden. Bid her cease from seeking her own life, lest she lose it. Make her valiant to give up her life to humanity, that, like her crucified Lord, she may mount by the path of the cross to a higher glory; through the same Jesus Christ our Lord. **Amen.**

744

FOR THE PRESIDENT AND OTHERS IN AUTHORITY

O Lord, our heavenly Father, whose glory is in all the world, and who dost from thy throne behold all the dwellers upon earth: Most heartily we beseech thee, with thy favor to behold and bless thy servants, *the President of the United States, the governor of this state,* and all others who bear rule throughout the world. Grant them wisdom and strength to know and to do thy will. Fill them with the love of truth and righteousness. So rule their hearts and prosper their endeavors, that law and order, justice and peace may everywhere prevail, to the honor of thy holy name; through Jesus Christ our Lord. **Amen.**

745

FOR THOSE WHO LABOR IN THE GOSPEL

Increase, O God, the faith and zeal of all thy people, that they may more earnestly desire, and more diligently seek, the salvation of their fellow men, through the message of thy love in Jesus Christ our Lord. Send forth a mighty call unto thy servants who labor in the Gospel, granting unto them a heart of love, sincerity of speech, and the power of the Holy Spirit, that they may persuade men to forsake sin and return unto thee. And so bless and favor the work of thine evangelists, that multitudes may be brought from the kingdom of evil into the kingdom of thy dear Son our Savior Jesus Christ. **Amen.**

746

FOR CHURCH, LAND, AND WORLD

Remember, O Lord, thy Church upon earth; deepen her influence and extend her power for good, till the kingdoms of this world become the kingdom of our Lord and of his Christ.

We pray for our beloved land: for our leaders and governors, and for all who have part in public service. Make them pure in motive, wise in counsel, and strong in action, doing right in the fear of thy holy name.

Father in heaven, look down in mercy upon our distraught and fevered world; forgive the mistaken ambitions, the selfish passions, and the presumptuous claims of men; remove all suspicion and bitterness from among the nations, and bring them to peace and concord by the redeeming love of Christ.

Have mercy, O Lord, upon those who are passing through sore trial: the poor, the sick, the anxious, the oppressed, those who are in danger from the fury of the elements or from the violence of men. Inspire in us and in our fellow men the will to help our suffering brethren. Heal, protect, and strengthen them according to their need. Comfort those in sorrow with the comfort which is in Christ Jesus our Lord.

We pray for our own dear ones, wheresoever they are, that, surrounded by thy love, they may be kept in health and joy, and abide in safety and peace; through Jesus Christ our Lord. **Amen.**

Offertory Sentences and Prayers

747

Remember the words of the Lord Jesus, how he said, "It is more blessed to give than to receive." *From Acts 20:35*

748

Let your light so shine before men, that they may see your good works and give glory to your Father who is in heaven. *Matthew 5:16*

749

Every man shall give as he is able, according to the blessing of the Lord your God which he has given you. *Deuteronomy 16:17*

750

Do not neglect to do good and to share what you have, for such sacrifices are pleasing to God. *Hebrews 13:16*

751

He who sows sparingly will also reap sparingly, and he who sows bountifully will also reap bountifully. Each one must do as he has made up his mind, not reluctantly or under compulsion, for God loves a cheerful giver. *II Corinthians 9:6-7*

752

Offer to God a sacrifice of thanksgiving, and pay your vows to the Most High. *Psalm 50:14*

753

Thine, O Lord, is the greatness, and the power, and the glory, and the victory, and the majesty; for all that is in the heavens and in the earth is thine; thine is the kingdom, O Lord, and thou art exalted as head above all. *I Chronicles 29:11*

754

O Lord, our God, send down upon us thy Holy Spirit, we beseech thee, to cleanse our hearts, to hallow our gifts, and to perfect the offering of ourselves to thee; through Jesus Christ our Lord. **Amen.**

755

Accept, O Lord, these offerings thy people make unto thee, and grant that the work to which they are devoted may prosper under thy guidance, to the glory of thy name; through Jesus Christ our Lord. **Amen.**

756

Accept these offerings, we beseech thee, O Lord, and mercifully direct and enable us by thy Holy Spirit, that all things which we do in thy name may be truly wrought in thee; through Jesus Christ our Lord. **Amen.**

757

O God, most merciful and gracious, of whose bounty we have all received: Accept this offering of thy people. Remember in thy love those who have brought it, and those for whom it is given, and so follow it with thy blessing that it may promote peace and good will among men, and advance the kingdom of our Lord and Savior Jesus Christ. **Amen.**

Ascriptions of Glory

758

Now unto the King eternal, immortal, invisible, the only wise God, be honor and glory for ever and ever. **Amen.** *I Timothy 1:17 KJV*

759

And now unto the blessed and only Sovereign, the King of kings and Lord of lords, who alone has immortality and dwells in unapproachable light, whom no man has ever seen or can see: to him be honor and eternal dominion. **Amen.** *I Timothy 6:15-16*

760

Now unto him that is able to do exceeding abundantly above all that we ask or think, according to the power that worketh in us, unto him be glory in the Church by Christ Jesus throughout all ages, world without end. **Amen.** *Ephesians 3:20-21 KJV*

761

The God of all grace, who has called you to his eternal glory by Christ, will himself restore, establish, and strengthen you. To him be the dominion for ever and ever. **Amen.** *I Peter 5:10-11*

762

Now unto him that is able to keep you from falling, and to present you faultless before the presence of his glory with exceeding joy: to the only wise God our Savior, be glory and majesty, dominion and power, both now and ever. **Amen.** *Jude 1:24-25 KJV*

Benedictions

763

The grace of the Lord Jesus Christ and the love of God and the fellowship of the Holy Spirit be with you all. **Amen.** *II Corinthians 13:14*

764

The Lord bless you and keep you: the Lord make his face to shine upon you, and be gracious to you: the Lord lift up his countenance upon you, and give you peace. **Amen.** *Numbers 6:24-26*

765

Now may the God of peace who brought again from the dead our Lord Jesus, the great shepherd of the sheep, by the blood of the eternal covenant, equip you with everything good that you may do his will, working in you that which is pleasing in his sight, through Jesus Christ: to whom be glory for ever and ever. **Amen.** *Hebrews 13:20-21*

766

And now may the blessing of God Almighty, Father, Son, and Holy Spirit, be among you and abide with you, now and evermore. **Amen.**

767

The peace of God, which passeth all understanding, keep your hearts and minds in the knowledge and love of God, and of his Son Jesus Christ our Lord; and the blessing of God Almighty, the Father, the Son, and the Holy Spirit, be among you, and remain with you always. **Amen.**

Prayers for Use Before Leaving the Church

768

Almighty God, who hast given us grace at this time with one accord to make our common supplications unto thee, and dost promise that, when two or three are gathered together in thy name, thou wilt grant their requests: Fulfill now, O Lord, the desires and petitions of thy servants, as may be most expedient for them, granting us in this world knowledge of thy truth, and in the world to come life everlasting. **Amen.**

769

Grant, we beseech thee, almighty God, that the words which we have heard this day with our outward ears may, through thy grace, be so grafted inwardly in our hearts, that they may bring forth in us the fruit of good living, to the honor and praise of thy name; through Jesus Christ our Lord. **Amen.**

770

O Lord God, Father Almighty, bless and sanctify this sacrifice of praise which has been offered unto thee to the honor and glory of thy name; through Jesus Christ our Lord. **Amen.**

771

O Lord, we beseech thee mercifully to receive the prayers of thy people who call upon thee; and grant that they may both perceive and know what things they ought to do, and also may have grace and power faithfully to fulfill the same; through Jesus Christ our Lord. **Amen.**

772

Direct us, O Lord, in all our doings, with thy most gracious favor, and further us with thy continual help, that in all our works, begun, continued, and ended in thee, we may glorify thy holy name, and finally, by thy mercy, obtain everlasting life; through Jesus Christ our Lord. **Amen.**

SERVICE MUSIC FOR THE ORDER OF WORSHIP

OPENING SENTENCES

(a) *Unison* Tone V

(b) *Unison* Tone V

(c) *Unison* Tone II

773

ADVENT SEASON (a) Our King and Savior draweth | nigh;
O come, let | us adore him.

774

CHRISTMASTIDE (b) Alleluia. Unto us a | child is born;
O come, let us adore him. | Alleluia.
(*Isaiah 9:6*)

775

CHRISTMASTIDE (b) The Word was made flesh and dwelt a- | mong us;
O come, let | us adore him.
(*John 1:14*)

776

EPIPHANY SEASON (b) The Lord hath manifested forth his | glory;
O come, let | us adore him.

777

LENTEN SEASON (c) Christ hath humbled himself, and become obedient unto | death:
even the death | of the cross.
(*Philippians 2:8*)

778

PALM SUNDAY (a) Blessed is he who cometh in the name of the | Lord;
Hosanna | in the highest.
(*Matthew 21:9*)

779

EASTERTIDE (a) Alleluia. The Lord is risen in- | deed;
O come, let us adore him. | Alleluia.
(*Luke 24:34*)

780

ASCENSION DAY (a) Alleluia. Christ the Lord ascendeth into | heaven;
O come, let us adore him. | Alleluia.

781

PENTECOST SEASON (a) Alleluia. The Spirit of the Lord ascendeth into | heaven;
O come, let us adore him. | Alleluia.

782

KINGDOMTIDE (b) I will bless the Lord at | all times;
His praise shall continually | be in my mouth.
(*Psalm 34:1*)

783

Come, Bless the Lord

PSALM 134:2 — AUSTIN C. LOVELACE, 1919-

Come, bless the Lord, all ye ser - vants of the Lord:
lift up your hands to the holy place, and bless the Lord.

784

Lord Jesus Christ, Be Present Now

HERR JESU CHRIST, DICH ZU LM

Attri. to WILHELM II, DUKE OF SAXE-WEIMAR, 1598-1662 — *Pensum Sacrum*, Görlitz, 1648

Trans. by CATHERINE WINKWORTH, 1827-1878 — Harm. from *Cantionale Sacrum*, Gotha, 1651

1. Lord Je - sus Christ, be pres - ent now, Our hearts in true de - vo - tion bow;
2. Un - seal our lips to sing thy praise, Our souls to thee in wor - ship raise;
Thy Spir - it send with grace di - vine, And let thy truth with - in us shine.
Make strong our faith, in - crease our light That we may know thy name a - right.

See also hymn 324, Let All Mortal Flesh Keep Silence and hymn 13, Open Now Thy Gates of Beauty.

785

Enter into His Gates

Psalm 100:4 Robert E. Scoggin, 1930-

En-ter in-to his gates with thanks-giv-ing, and in-to his courts with praise.

786

I Was Glad

Psalm 122:1 Austin C. Lovelace, 1919-

3
I was glad when they said un-to me, Let us go in-to the house of the Lord.
3

787

The Lord Is in His Holy Temple

Habakkuk 2:20 Carlton R. Young, 1926-

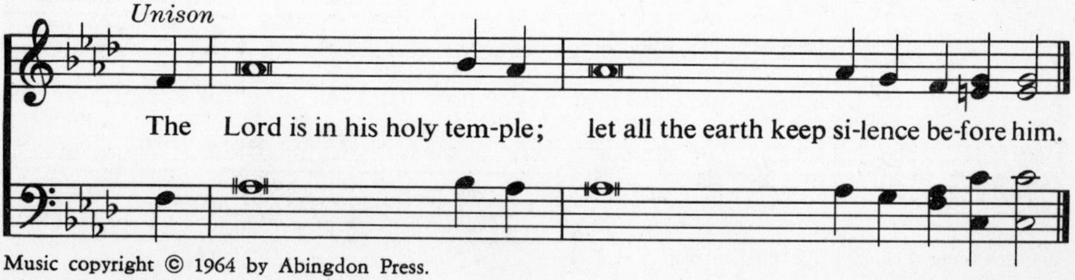
Unison
The Lord is in his holy tem-ple; let all the earth keep si-lence be-fore him.

788

God Himself Is with Us

GERHARD TERSTEEGEN, 1697-1769
Trans. COMPOSITE

ARNSBERG 668.668.33.66.
JOACHIM NEANDER, 1650-1680

God him-self is with us: Let us now a-dore him, And with awe ap-
pear be-fore him. God is in his tem - ple: All with-in keep
si - lence, And be-fore him bow with rev - erence. Him a-lone,
God we own; To our Lord and Sav - ior Prais-es sing for - ev - er.

789

This Is the Day the Lord Hath Made

TWENTY-FOURTH CM

ISAAC WATTS, 1674-1748

Probably by LUCIUS CHAPIN, 1760-1842

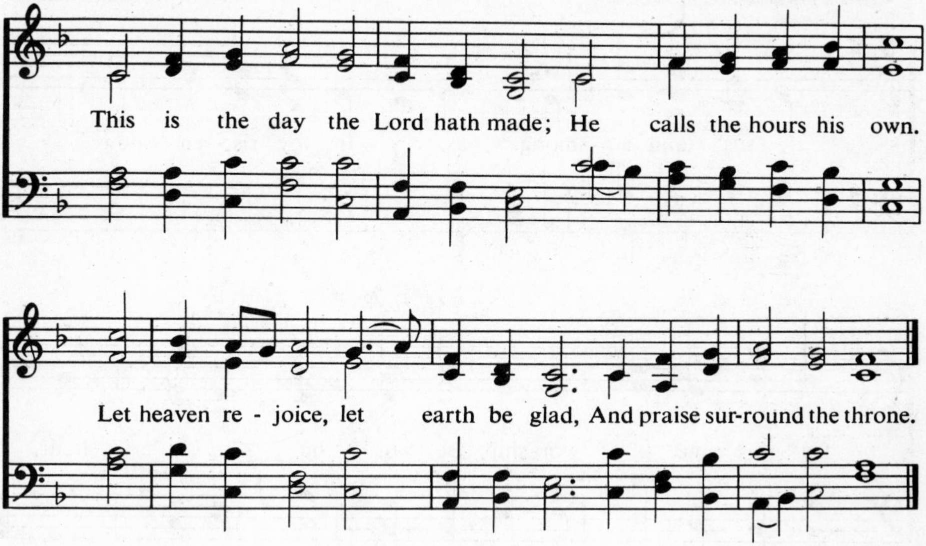
This is the day the Lord hath made; He calls the hours his own.
Let heaven re - joice, let earth be glad, And praise sur-round the throne.

790

Come, and Let Us Sweetly Join

SAVANNAH 77.77.

CHARLES WESLEY, 1707-1788

Foundery Collection, 1742

Come, and let us sweet-ly join Christ to praise, in hymns di - vine.
Give we all, with one ac - cord, Glo - ry to our com-mon Lord.

791

Jesus, Stand Among Us

GLENFINLAS 65.65.

WILLIAM PENNEFATHER, 1816-1873

KENNETH G. FINLAY, 1882-

Je - sus, stand a - mong us In thy ris - en power;

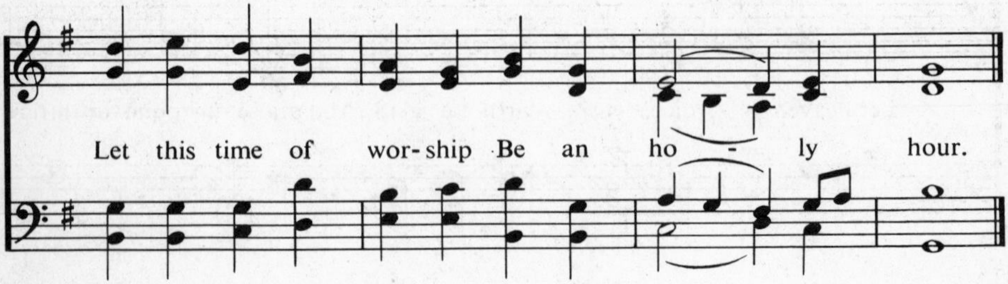
Let this time of wor - ship Be an ho - ly hour.

Music used by permission of Kenneth G. Finlay.

GLORY BE TO THE FATHER

792

Glory Be to the Father

Gloria Patri

HENRY W. GREATOREX, 1813-1858

Glo - ry be to the Fa - ther and to the Son and to the

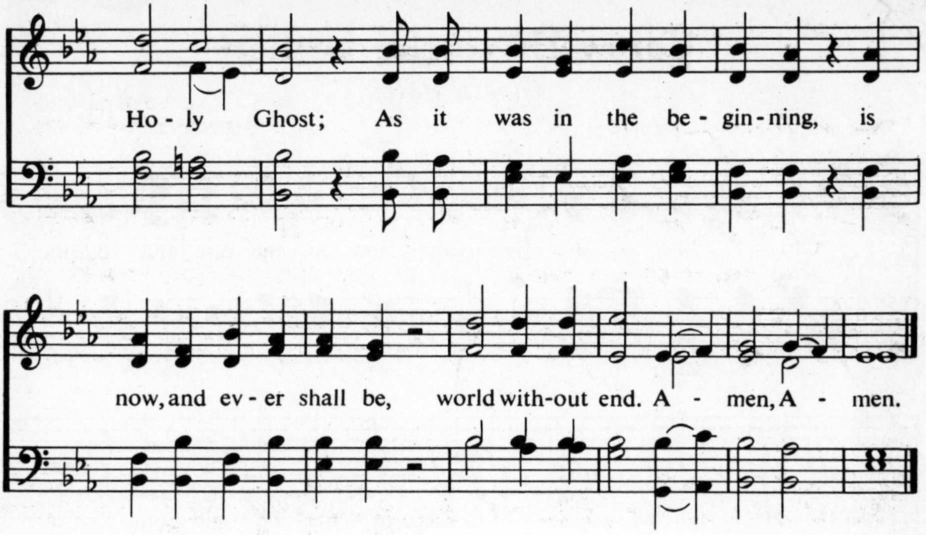
Ho - ly Ghost; As it was in the be - gin - ning, is
now, and ev - er shall be, world with-out end. A - men, A - men.

793

Glory Be to the Father

Gloria Patri

Mode VIII-1

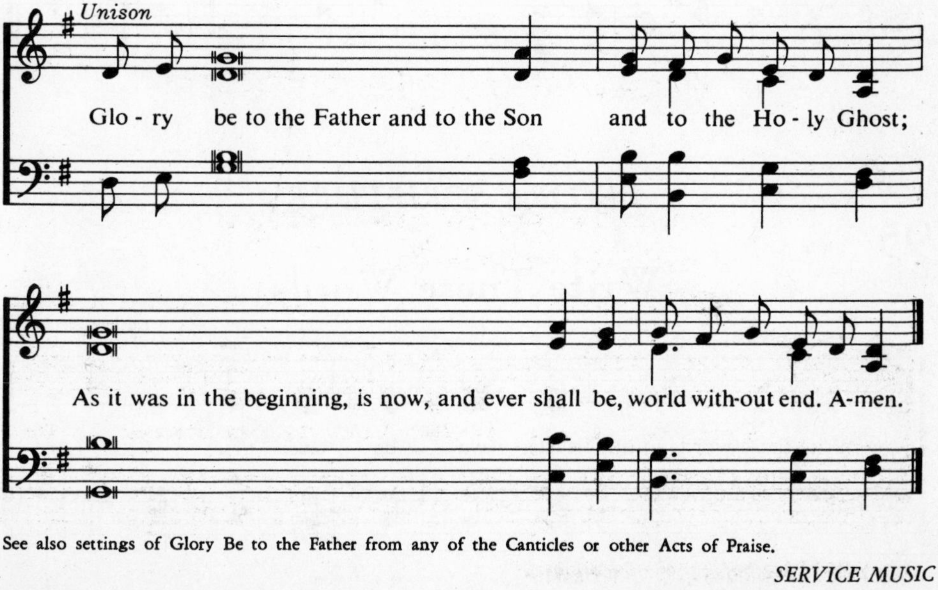
Unison
Glo - ry be to the Father and to the Son and to the Ho - ly Ghost;
As it was in the beginning, is now, and ever shall be, world with-out end. A-men.

See also settings of Glory Be to the Father from any of the Canticles or other Acts of Praise.

794

Glory Be to the Father

Gloria Patri

Charles Meineke, 1782-1850

Glo - ry be to the Fa - ther and to the Son and to the
Ho - ly Ghost; As it was in the be - gin - ning, is
now, and ev - er shall be, world with-out end. A - men, A - men.

BEFORE SCRIPTURE

795

Write These Words

Ancient Chant

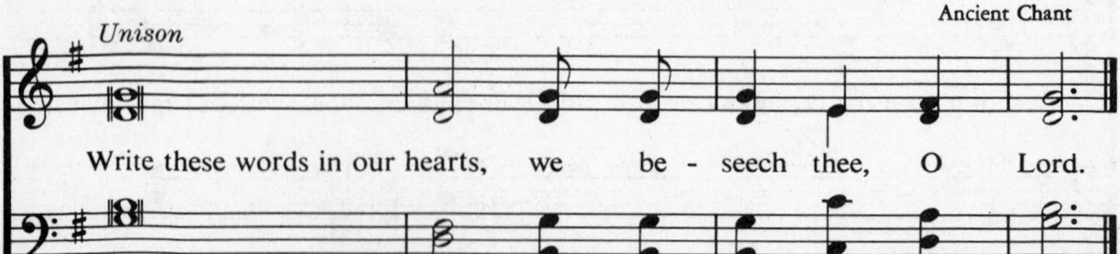

Unison
Write these words in our hearts, we be - seech thee, O Lord.

AFTER SCRIPTURE

799

Thanks Be to Thee

Gratia Tibi

THOMAS TALLIS, c. 1505-1585

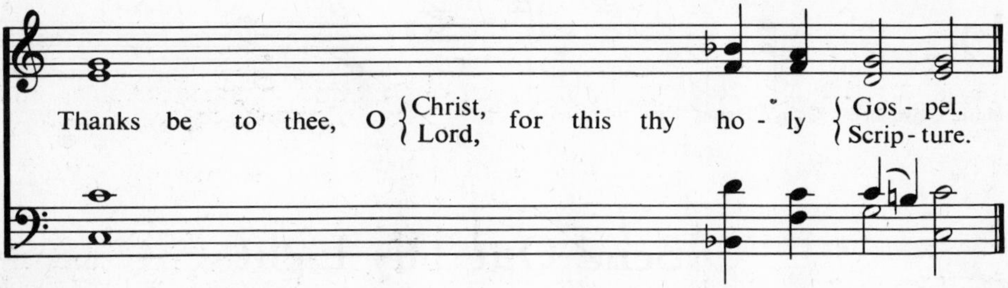
Thanks be to thee, O {Christ, / Lord,} for this thy ho - ly {Gos - pel. / Scrip - ture.}

800

Glory Be to God

Gloria Deo

JOHN MERBECKE, 1523-c. 1585

Glory be to God on high.

801

Praise Be to Thee

Laus Tibi

JOHN MERBECKE, 1523-c. 1585

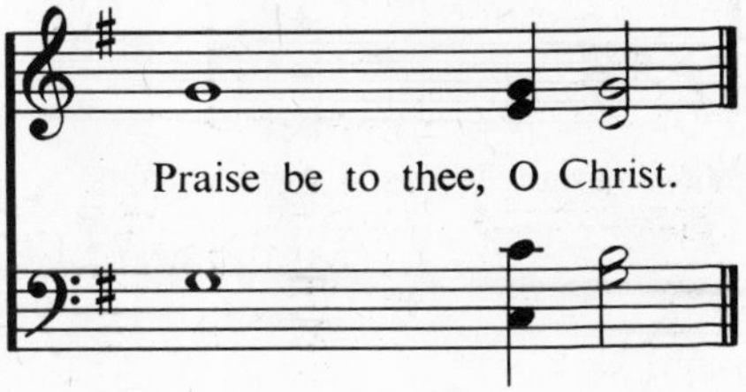
Praise be to thee, O Christ.

BEFORE PRAYER

802

Lead Me, Lord

PSALMS 5:8; 4:8

SAMUEL S. WESLEY, 1810-1876

Lead me, Lord, lead me in thy righ-teous-ness;

796

Let Thy Word Abide in Us

George Dyson, 1883-

Let thy word a - bide in us, O Lord.

797

O Send Out Thy Light

Psalm 43:3

Austin C. Lovelace, 1919-

O send out thy light and thy truth: let them lead me.
3
3

798

O Lord, Open Thou Our Eyes

Psalm 119:18

John Camidge, 1735-1803

V. O Lord, open thou our eyes R. That we may behold
won - drous things out of thy law.

Make thy way plain be - fore my face. For it is thou, Lord,
thou, Lord, on - ly That mak - est me dwell in safe - ty.

* Optional Ending.

803

Listen to Our Prayer

Text from India
Trans. by LEILA JACKSON BROWN, 1930-

BINTI HAMARI 65.55.65.
Melody from India

Lis - ten to our prayer, Lord; Hear our hum - ble plea.
Thy gra - cious ear, Lord, turn to us to - day;
1.
*
Lis - ten to our prayer, Lord; Hear our hum - ble plea.
2.
O give us peace, O give us peace. A - men.

*May end here with Amen.

804

God Be Merciful unto Us

PSALM 67:1 — RONALD A. NELSON, 1927-

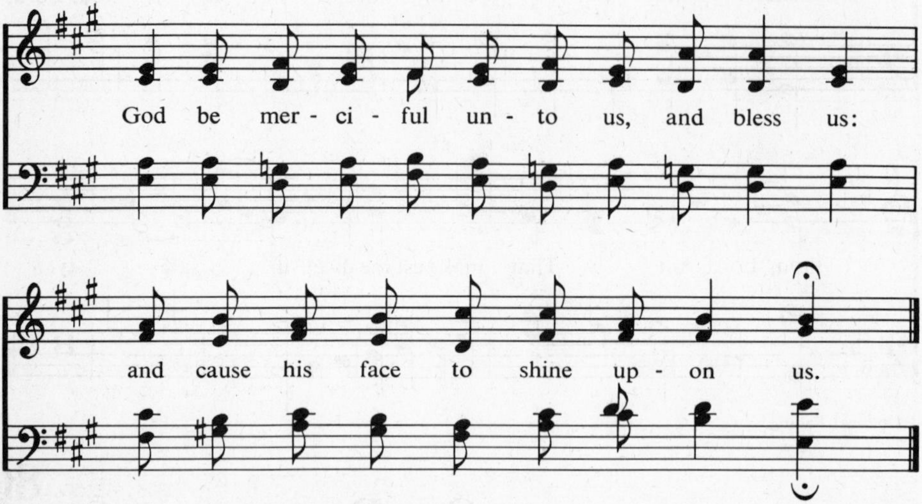
God be mer - ci - ful un - to us, and bless us:
and cause his face to shine up - on us.

VERSICLES BEFORE PRAYER

805

Ferial

THOMAS TALLIS, c. 1505-1585

V. O Lord, show thy mercy up-on us, R. And grant us thy sal-va - tion.
V. O God, make clean our hearts with-in us, R.And take not thy Holy Spirit from us.

806

Festal

Thomas Tallis, c. 1505-1585

V. O Lord, show thy mercy up-on us, R. And grant us thy sal - va - tion.

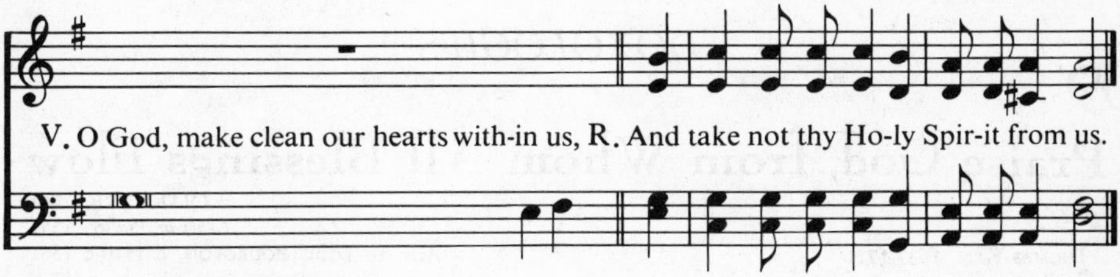
V. O God, make clean our hearts with-in us, R. And take not thy Ho-ly Spir-it from us.

See also hymn 262, Talk with Us, Lord.

OFFERING

807

All Things Come of Thee

I Chronicles 29:14*b*

Lloyd Morey, 1886-

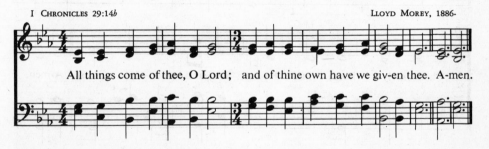

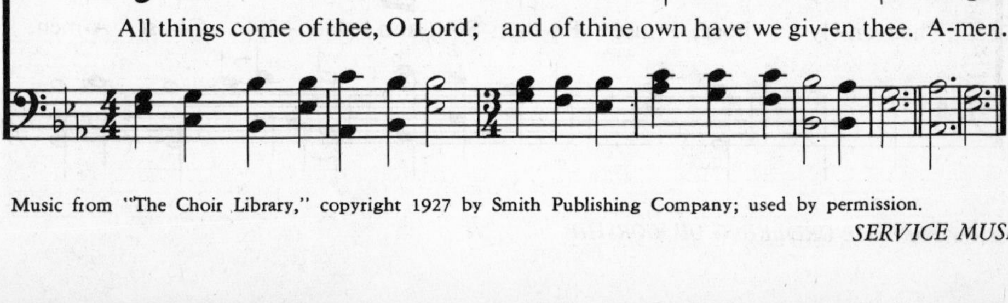
All things come of thee, O Lord; and of thine own have we giv-en thee. A-men.

808

All Things Come of Thee

I CHRONICLES 29:14*b* — Attr. to LUDWIG VAN BEETHOVEN, 1770-1827

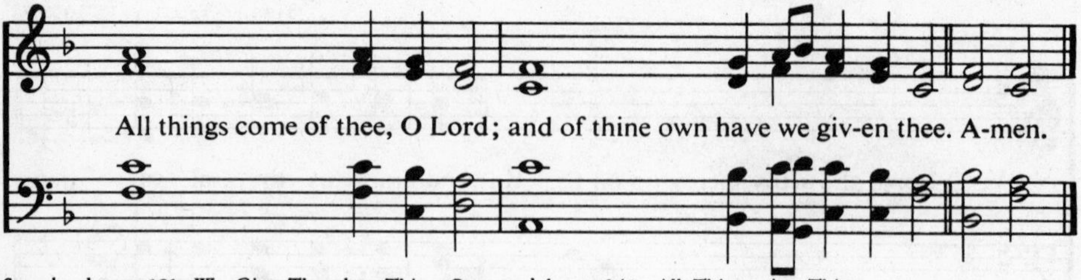
All things come of thee, O Lord; and of thine own have we giv-en thee. A-men.

See also hymn 181, We Give Thee but Thine Own and hymn 347, All Things Are Thine.

DOXOLOGIES

809

Praise God, from Whom All Blessings Flow

OLD 100TH LM
Genevan Psalter, 1551

THOMAS KEN, 1637-1711 — Attr. to LOUIS BOURGEOIS, c. 1510-c. 1561

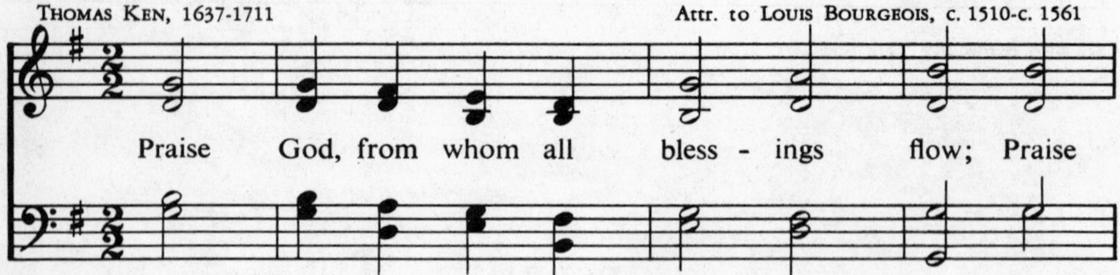
Praise God, from whom all bless - ings flow; Praise

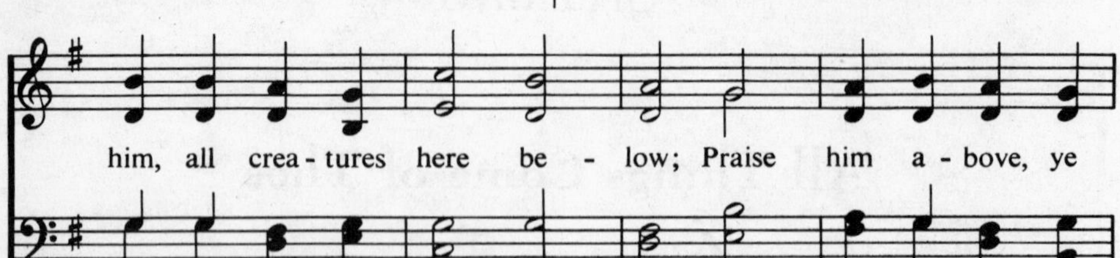
him, all crea - tures here be - low; Praise him a - bove, ye

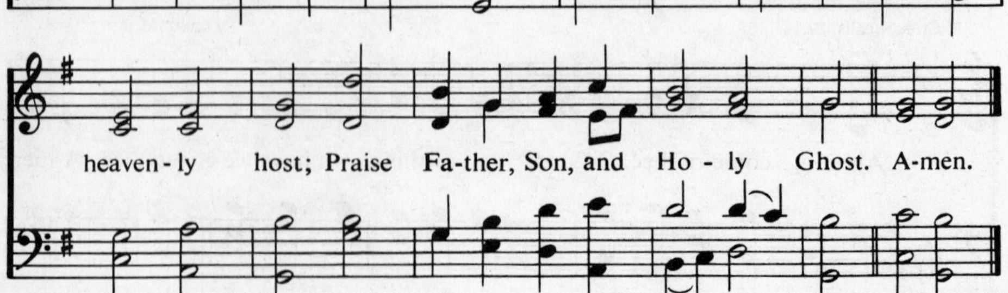
heaven - ly host; Praise Fa-ther, Son, and Ho - ly Ghost. A-men.

810

To God the Only Wise

ST. MICHAEL SM
Genevan Psalter, 1551

ISAAC WATTS, 1674-1748 — Adapt. by WILLIAM CROTCH, 1775-1847

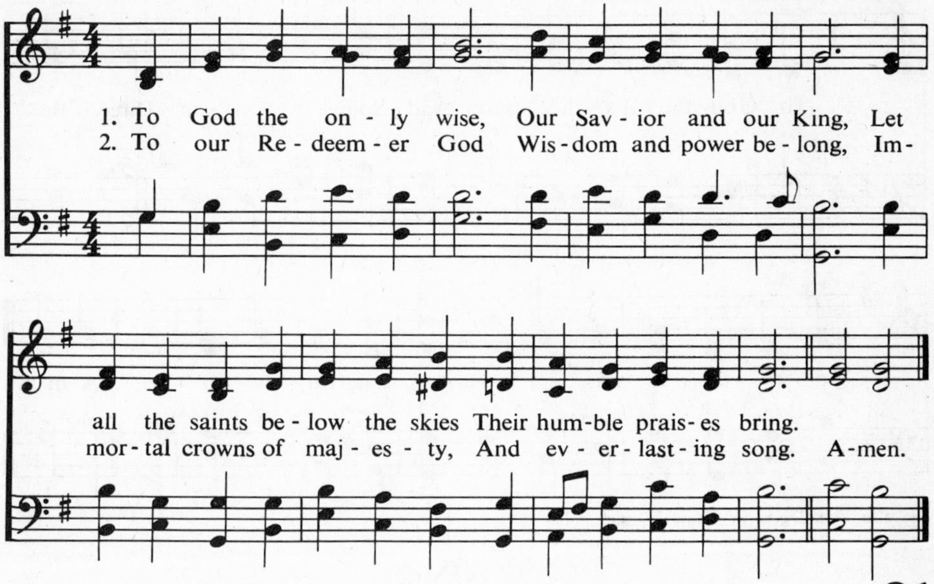
1. To God the on - ly wise, Our Sav - ior and our King, Let
2. To our Re - deem - er God Wis - dom and power be - long, Im-
all the saints be - low the skies Their hum - ble prais - es bring.
mor - tal crowns of maj - es - ty, And ev - er - last - ing song. A-men.

811

Sing We to Our God Above

SAVANNAH 77.77.

CHARLES WESLEY, 1707-1788 — *Foundery Collection*, 1742

Sing we to our God a - bove, Praise e - ter - nal as his love;
Praise him, all ye heaven - ly host, Fa - ther, Son, and Ho - ly Ghost. A-men.

812

To God the Father

ST. MICHAEL SM
Genevan Psalter, 1551
JOHN WESLEY, 1703-1791 — Adapt. by WILLIAM CROTCH, 1775-1847

To God the Fa - ther, Son, And Spir - it One in Three, Be
glo - ry as it was, is now, And shall for - ev - er be. A - men.

See also Doxologies in Topical Index, No. 851.

CLOSING

813

God Be in My Head

Sarum Primer, 1558 — HENRY WALFORD DAVIES, 1869-1941

God be in my head, and in my un - der-stand-ing;
God be in mine eyes, and in my look - ing; God be in my

mouth, and in my speak - ing; God be in my heart, and in my
think - ing; God be at mine end, and at my de - part - ing.

814

To Thee Before the Close of Day

Latin, c. 7th century
Trans. by JOHN M. NEALE, 1818-1866

JAM LUCIS LM
Plainsong, Mode VI

Unison
To Thee be - fore the close of day, Cre - a - tor of the
world, we pray That, with thy wont - ed fa - vor, thou
Would'st be our guard and keep - er now. A - men.

815

Father, Give Thy Benediction

ALTA TRINITA BEATA 87.87.

SAMUEL LONGFELLOW, 1819-1892

Laudi Spirituali, 14th Century

Fa - ther, give thy ben - e - dic - tion, Give thy peace be -
fore we part; Peace, which pass - eth un - der - stand - ing,
On our wait - ing spir - its send. A - men.

AMENS

816

A - men.

817

A - men.

818

Dresden

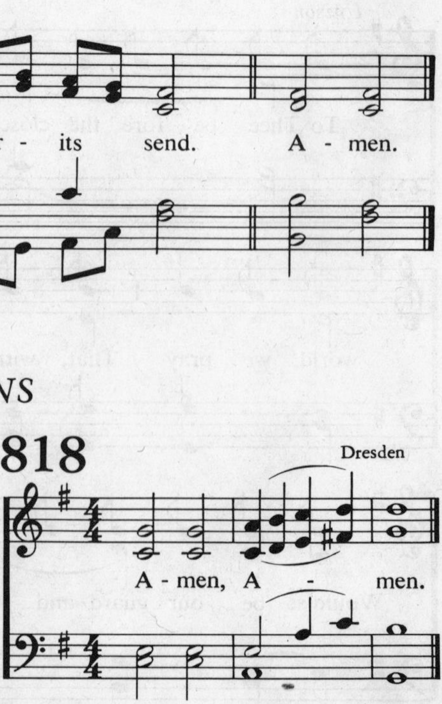
A - men, A - men.

819

Danish

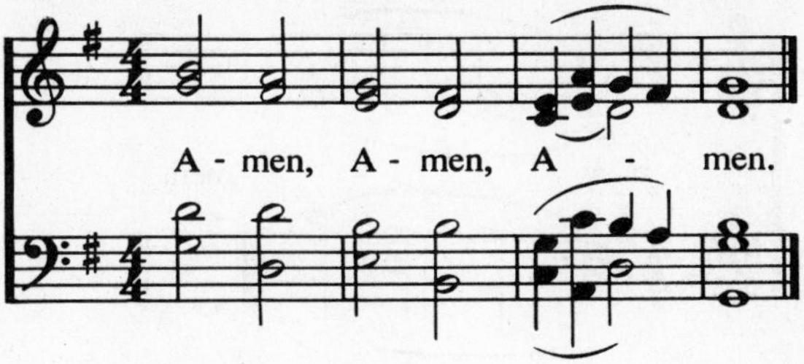
A - men, A - men, A - men.

820

Greek

A - men, A - men.

821

R. Evan Copley, 1930-

A - men.

822

Eric DeLamarter, 1880-1953

A - men, A - men.

823

George W. Briggs, 1875-1959

A - - men.

824

Louis Bourgeois, c. 1510-c. 1561

A - - men.

825

John Stainer, 1840-1901

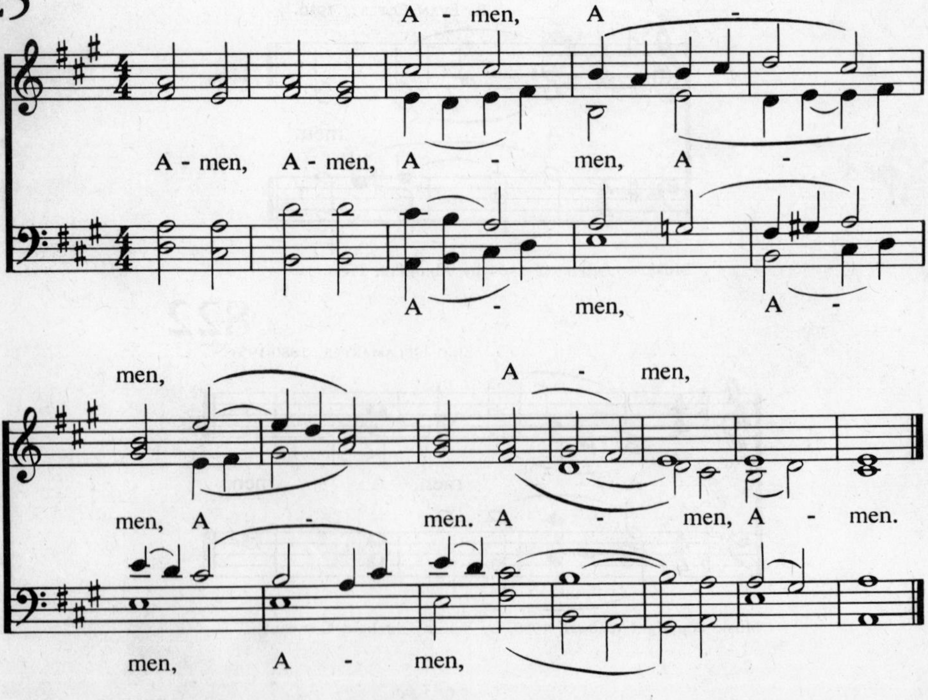
A - men, A -
A - men, A - men, A - men, A -
A - men, A -
men, A - men,
men, A - men. A - men, A - men.
men, A - men,

826

The Lord's Prayer

Ancient Chant

Unison
1. Our Father who art in heaven hal - lowed be thy name,
2. Give us this day our dai - ly bread;
3. And lead us not into temptation, but de - liv - er us from evil,
Thy kingdom come, thy will be done on earth as it is in heaven.
And forgive us our trespasses as we forgive those who tres-pass a-gainst us.
For thine is the kingdom, and the power,
and the glory for - ev - er. A - men.

827

Lord, Have Mercy upon Us

THOMAS TALLIS, c. 1505-1585

Lord, have mercy up - on us, and incline our
hearts to keep thy law.
Lord, have mercy up-on us, and write all these thy
laws in our hearts, we be - seech thee.

828

THE ORDER FOR THE ADMINISTRATION OF THE SACRAMENT OF BAPTISM

† *Our ministers are enjoined diligently to teach the people committed to their pastoral care the meaning and purpose of the Baptism of children and to urge them to present their children for Baptism at an early age.*

† *When youth and adults present themselves for Baptism, the minister shall take due care that they have been instructed in the meaning of Christian Baptism.*

† *This Sacrament should be administered in the church in the presence of the people in a stated hour of worship. But at the minister's discretion this Sacrament may be administered at another time and place.*

† *This Sacrament may be administered by sprinkling, pouring, or immersion.*

† *The minister shall see that the names of all baptized children are properly recorded as preparatory members on the permanent records of the church, and in each instance he shall deliver to the parents or sponsors a certificate of Baptism.*

† *Children baptized in infancy shall be reported annually in the number of preparatory members until they shall have been received into full membership in the church or shall have attained their adulthood.*

CHILDREN

† *Parents or sponsors presenting a child for Baptism should be members of Christ's holy Church.*

† *The parents or sponsors, with the child to be baptized, shall stand before the minister, who, addressing the people, shall say,*

Dearly beloved, Baptism is an outward and visible sign of the grace of the Lord Jesus Christ, through which grace we become partakers of his righteousness and heirs of life eternal. Those receiving the Sacrament are thereby marked as Christian disciples, and initiated into the fellowship of Christ's holy Church. Our Lord has expressly given to little children a place among the people of God, which holy privilege must not be denied them. Remember the words of the Lord Jesus Christ, how he said, "Let the children come to me, do not hinder them; for to such belongs the kingdom of God."

† *Then the minister shall address the parents or sponsors, saying,*

Beloved, do you in presenting *this child* for holy Baptism confess your faith in our Lord and Savior Jesus Christ?

We do.

Do you therefore accept as your bounden duty and privilege to live before *this child* a life that becomes the Gospel; to exercise all godly care that *he* be brought up in the Christian faith, that *he* be taught the Holy Scriptures, and that *he* learn to give reverent attendance upon the private and public worship of God?

We do.

Will you endeavor to keep *this child* under the ministry and guidance of the Church until *he* by the power of God shall accept for *himself* the gift of salvation, and be confirmed as a full and responsible member of Christ's holy Church?

We will.

† *Then the minister shall take the child in his arms, and shall say to the parents or sponsors,*

What name is given this child?

† *And then, repeating the name, though not including the surname, the minister shall baptize the child, saying,*

N., I baptize you in the name of the Father, and of the Son, and of the Holy Spirit. **Amen.**

† *Then the minister may have the people stand, and, addressing them, may say,*

Brethren of the household of faith, I commend to your love and care *this child,* whom we this day recognize as *a member* of the family of God. Will you endeavor so to live that *he* may grow in the knowledge and love of God the Father, through our Savior Jesus Christ?

† *Then the people shall say,*

With God's help we will so order our lives after the example of Christ, that *this child,* surrounded by steadfast love, may be established in the faith, and confirmed and strengthened in the way that leads to life eternal.

† *Then the minister shall say,*

Let us pray.

O God, our heavenly Father, grant that *this child,* as *he grows* in years, may also grow in grace and in the knowledge of the Lord Jesus Christ, and that by the restraining and renewing influence of the Holy Spirit *he* may ever be *a* true *child* of thine, serving thee faithfully all *his* days.

So guide and uphold the *parents* (*or sponsors*) of *this child* that, by loving care, wise counsel, and holy example, they may lead *him* into that life of faith whose strength is righteousness and whose fruit is everlasting joy and peace; through Jesus Christ our Lord. **Amen.**

† *Then the minister may give this or another blessing:*

God the Father, God the Son, and God the Holy Spirit bless, preserve, and keep you, now and for evermore. **Amen.**

YOUTH AND ADULTS

† *The person or persons to be baptized shall stand before the minister, who, addressing the people, shall say,*

Dearly beloved, forasmuch as all men have sinned and fallen short of the glory of God, and our Savior Christ said, "Unless one is born of water and the Spirit, he cannot enter the kingdom of God," I beseech you to call upon God the Father, through our Lord Jesus Christ, that of his bounteous goodness he will grant that *this person* may receive the forgiveness of sins, be baptized with water and the Holy Spirit, and may be received into Christ's holy Church, and be made a living *member* of the same.

Let us pray.

Almighty and everlasting God, the aid of all who need, the helper of all who call upon thee for comfort, the life of all who believe, and the resurrection of the dead: We call upon thee for *this* thy *servant,* that *he,* coming to thy holy Baptism, may receive remission of *his* sins and be filled with the Holy Spirit. Receive *him,* O Lord, as thou has promised by thy well-beloved Son, and grant that *he* may be faithful to thee all the days of *his life,* and finally come to the eternal kingdom which thou hast promised; through Jesus Christ our Lord. **Amen.**

† *Then, addressing the person or persons to be baptized, the minister shall say,*

Well beloved, you are come here desiring to receive holy Baptism. We have prayed that God, through our Lord Jesus Christ, would grant to receive you, release you from sin, sanctify you with the Holy Spirit, and give you the kingdom of heaven, and everlasting life.

Do you truly and earnestly repent of your sins and accept Jesus Christ as your Savior?

I do.

Do you believe in God, the Father Almighty, maker of heaven and earth; and in Jesus Christ his only Son our Lord; and in the Holy Spirit, the Lord, the giver of life?

I do.

Do you desire to be baptized in this faith?

I do.

Will you then obediently keep God's holy will and commandments and walk in the same all the days of your life?

I will, by God's help.

† *Then the minister shall say,*

Let us pray.

O merciful God, grant that all sinful affections may die in *this* thy *servant,* and that all things belonging to thy Spirit may live and grow in *him.* Grant that *he* may have the power and strength to triumph over evil, may receive the fulness of thy grace, and ever remain in the number of thy faithful and beloved children; through Jesus Christ our Lord. **Amen.**

† *The minister, asking the name of each person to be baptized, and then repeating the same, though not including the surname, shall baptize him, saying,*

N., I baptize you in the name of the Father, and of the Son, and of the Holy Spirit. **Amen.**

† *Then the minister may have the people stand, and addressing them, may say,*

Brethren of the household of faith, I commend to your love and care *this person,* whom we this day recognize as *a member* of the family of God. Will you endeavor so to live that *he* may grow in the knowledge and love of God the Father through our Savior Jesus Christ?

† *Then the people shall say,*

With God's help we will so order our lives after the example of Christ that, surrounded by steadfast love, you may be established in the faith, and confirmed and strengthened in the way that leads to life eternal.

† *Then the minister may give this or another blessing:*

God the Father, God the Son, and God the Holy Spirit bless, preserve, and keep you, now and for evermore. **Amen.**

829

THE ORDER FOR CONFIRMATION AND RECEPTION INTO THE CHURCH

† *This service shall be conducted in the church in the presence of the people at such a time in a stated hour of worship as the minister may determine.*

† *All who are to be confirmed as members of Christ's holy Church shall have been baptized, and instructed in the doctrines and duties of the Christian faith.*

† *Those to be confirmed shall stand before the minister, who, addressing the people, shall say,*

Dearly beloved, the Church is of God, and will be preserved to the end of time, for the conduct of worship and the due administration of his Word and Sacraments, the maintenance of Christian fellowship and discipline, the edification of believers, and the conversion of the world. All, of every age and station, stand in need of the means of grace which it alone supplies.

These persons who *are* to be confirmed *have* received the Sacrament of Baptism, *have* also been instructed in the teachings of the Church, and *are* now ready to profess publicly the faith into which *they were* baptized.

† *Then the minister, addressing those who are to be confirmed, shall say,*

Do you here, in the presence of God, and of this congregation, renew the solemn promise and vow that you made, or that was made in your name, at your Baptism?

I do.

Do you confess Jesus Christ as your Lord and Savior and pledge your allegiance to his kingdom?

I do.

Do you receive and profess the Christian faith as contained in the Scriptures of the Old and New Testaments?

I do.

Do you promise according to the grace given you to live a Christian life and always remain a faithful member of Christ's holy Church?

I do.

† *Then the candidates shall kneel, and the minister, laying his hands upon the head of each severally, shall say,*

N., the Lord defend you with his heavenly grace and by his Spirit confirm you in the faith and fellowship of all true disciples of Jesus Christ. **Amen.**

† *Those confirmed shall rise, and the minister, addressing the people, may say,*

Let those persons who are members of other communions in Christ's holy Church, and who now desire to enter into the fellowship of this congregation, present themselves to be received into the membership of The Methodist Church.

† *Then those confirmed and those to be received from other communions shall stand before the minister; and he, addressing them, shall say,*

Will you be loyal to The Methodist Church, and uphold it by your prayers, your presence, your gifts, and your service?

I will.

† *Then the minister may say,*

Let those who are members of other congregations of The Methodist Church, and who now desire to enter into the fellowship of this congregation, present themselves to be welcomed.

† *Here a lay member, selected by the Official Board, may join with the minister in offering the right hand of fellowship to all those received.*

† *Then the minister may have those received face the congregation, and, causing the people to stand, he shall address them, saying,*

Brethren, I commend to your love and care *these persons* whom we this day receive into the membership of this congregation. Do all in your power to increase *their* faith, confirm *their* hope, and perfect *them* in love.

† *Whereupon the people shall say,*

We rejoice to recognize you as *members* of Christ's holy Church, and bid you welcome to this congregation of The Methodist Church. With you we renew our vows to uphold it by our prayers, our presence, our gifts, and our service.

† *Then the minister may say,*

Go forth in peace, and be of good courage; hold fast that which is good, rejoicing in the power of the Holy Spirit. And the blessing of God, Father, Son, and Holy Spirit, be with you and remain with you for ever. **Amen.**

† *On any day when persons are to be received by transfer only, the minister will use only that part of the service which applies to them.*

830

THE ORDER FOR THE ADMINISTRATION OF THE SACRAMENT OF THE LORD'S SUPPER OR HOLY COMMUNION

† *It shall be the duty of the pastor to administer the Sacrament of the Lord's Supper at regularly appointed times to the people committed to his care, remembering the charge laid upon him at the time of his ordination: "Be thou a faithful dispenser of the Word of God, and of his holy Sacraments."*

† *The order for the administration of this Sacrament to the sick, to those confined to their homes, or to others in circumstances where the full*

service is impracticable, should include the Invitation, the General Confession, the Prayer for Pardon, the Comfortable Words, the Prayer of Consecration, the Prayer of Humble Access, the Words of Distribution, the Prayer of Thanksgiving, and the Benediction.

† *At the time of Holy Communion, the Lord's Table shall have upon it a fair white linen cloth. The elements of bread and wine shall be placed thereon. The pure, unfermented juice of the grape shall be used.*

† *It is our custom to deliver the elements into the hands of the people while they kneel before the Lord's Table. But at the discretion of the minister, the elements may be served to any or to all of the people while standing, or while seated in the pews.*

† *Upon entering the church, the people shall bow in prayer and shall remain until the entire service is concluded.*

† *All people who intend to lead a Christian life are invited to receive this holy Sacrament.*

† *The service may begin with a prelude.*

† *A hymn may be sung, the people standing.*

† *Or the minister may begin the service with one or more of the following or other suitable sentences from the Scriptures:*

Behold, I stand at the door and knock; if any one hears my voice and opens the door, I will come in to him and eat with him, and he with me.
Revelation 3:20

I am the living bread which came down from heaven; if any one eats of this bread, he will live forever; and the bread which I shall give for the life of the world is my flesh. *John 6:51*

The cup of blessing which we bless, is it not a participation in the blood of Christ? The bread which we break, is it not a participation in the body of Christ? Because there is one loaf, we who are many are one body, for we all partake of the same loaf. *I Corinthians 10:16-17*

Beloved, let us love one another; for love is of God, and he who loves is born of God and knows God. In this the love of God was made manifest among us, that God sent his only Son into the world, so that we might live through him. *I John 4:7, 9*

Christ our Paschal Lamb is offered up for us, once for all, when he bore our sins on his body upon the cross; for he is the very Lamb of God that taketh away the sins of the world: Wherefore let us keep a joyful and holy feast with the Lord.

From I Corinthians 5:7-8; I Peter 2:24; John 1:29

What no eye has seen, nor ear heard, nor the heart of man conceived, what God has prepared for those who love him, God has revealed to us through the Spirit. For the Spirit searches everything, even the depths of God. *I Corinthians 2:9-10*

† *Here the minister, facing the people, shall say,*

The Lord be with you.

People: **And with thy spirit.**

Minister: Let us pray.

† *Then, kneeling or bowed, the minister and people together shall say,*

Almighty God, unto whom all hearts are open, all desires known, and from whom no secrets are hid: Cleanse the thoughts of our hearts by the inspiration of thy Holy Spirit, that we may perfectly love thee, and worthily magnify thy holy name; through Christ our Lord. Amen.

Our Father, who art in heaven, hallowed be thy name. Thy kingdom come, thy will be done on earth as it is in heaven. Give us this day our daily bread. And forgive us our trespasses, as we forgive those who trespass against us. And lead us not into temptation, but deliver us from evil. For thine is the kingdom, and the power, and the glory, forever. Amen.

† *Then, standing, all shall sing or say,*

Glory be to God on high, and on earth peace, good will toward men. We praise thee, we bless thee, we worship thee, we glorify thee, we give thanks to thee for thy great glory: O Lord God, heavenly King, God the Father Almighty.

O Lord, the only begotten Son, Jesus Christ; O Lord God, Lamb of God, Son of the Father, that takest away the sins of the world: have mercy upon us. Thou that takest away the sins of the world, receive our prayer. Thou that sittest at the right hand of God the Father, have mercy upon us.

For thou only art holy; thou only art the Lord; thou only, O Christ, with the Holy Ghost, art most high in the glory of God the Father. Amen.

A. Glory Be to God on High

Gloria in Excelsis

Old Scottish Chant

Glory be to God on high, and on earth peace, good will toward men.
We praise thee, we bless thee, we wor - ship thee, we glorify thee, we give
thanks to thee for thy great glo - ry: O Lord God, heavenly King;
God the Fa - ther Al - might - y. O Lord, the only begotten Son,
Je - sus Christ; O Lord God, Lamb of God, Son of the Fa - ther:

That takest away the sins of the world, have mercy up-on us.
Thou that takest away the sins of the world, re - ceive our prayer.
Thou that sittest at the right hand of God the Father, have mercy up-on us.
For thou on - ly art holy; thou on - ly art the Lord; thou only, O Christ,
with the Ho - ly Ghost, art most high in the glory of God the Fa - ther. A-men.

† *The minister, facing the people while they remain standing, shall say,*

Ye that do truly and earnestly repent of your sins, and are in love and charity with your neighbors, and intend to lead a new life, following the commandments of God, and walking from henceforth in his holy ways: Draw near with faith, and take this holy Sacrament to your comfort, and make your humble confession to almighty God.

† *Then the minister, kneeling and facing the Lord's Table, and all the people, kneeling or bowed, shall make together this general confession:*

Almighty God, Father of our Lord Jesus Christ, maker of all things, judge of all men: We acknowledge and bewail our manifold sins and wickedness, which we from time to time most grievously have committed, by thought, word, and deed, against thy divine majesty. We do earnestly repent, and are heartily sorry for these our misdoings; the remembrance of them is grievous unto us. Have mercy upon us, have mercy upon us, most merciful Father. For thy Son our Lord Jesus Christ's sake, forgive us all that is past; and grant that we may ever hereafter serve and please thee in newness of life, to the honor and glory of thy name; through Jesus Christ our Lord. Amen.

† *Then the minister shall pray, saying,*

Almighty God, our heavenly Father, who of thy great mercy hast promised forgiveness of sins to all them that with hearty repentance and true faith turn to thee: Have mercy upon us; pardon and deliver us from all our sins; confirm and strengthen us in all goodness; and bring us to everlasting life; through Jesus Christ our Lord. **Amen.**

† *The minister, standing and facing the people, shall say,*

Hear what comfortable words the Scriptures say to all that truly turn to the Lord:

† *Then the minister shall say one or more of the following sentences:*

Come to me, all who labor and are heavy-laden, and I will give you rest. *Matthew 11:28*

God so loved the world that he gave his only Son, that whoever believes in him should not perish but have eternal life. *John 3:16*

The saying is sure and worthy of full acceptance, that Christ Jesus came into the world to save sinners. *I Timothy 1:15*

If we confess our sins, he is faithful and just, and will forgive our sins and cleanse us from all unrighteousness. *I John 1:9*

If any one sins, we have an advocate with the Father, Jesus Christ the righteous; and he is the expiation for our sins, and not for ours only but also for the sins of the whole world. *From I John 2:1-2*

† *Here the minister may offer a pastoral prayer, or he may say,*

Let us pray for the whole state of Christ's Church.

† *Then may follow this prayer, the minister beginning, the people responding:*

Most merciful Father, we humbly beseech thee to receive these our prayers for the universal Church, that thou wilt confirm it in the truth of thy holy faith, inspire it with unity and concord, and extend and prosper it throughout the world.

We beseech thee also, so to guide and strengthen the witness of the Church to those in authority in all nations, that they may maintain the justice and welfare of all mankind.

Hear us, we beseech thee, O Lord.

Give grace, O heavenly Father, to all ministers of thy Church, that both by their life and doctrine they may set forth thy true and lively Word, and faithfully administer thy holy Sacraments.

And to all thy people give thy heavenly grace, that with willing heart and due reverence, they may hear and receive thy holy Word, truly serving thee in holiness and righteousness all the days of their lives.

Hear us, we beseech thee, O Lord.

And we most humbly beseech thee, of thy goodness, O Lord, to support and strengthen all those who, in this transitory life, are in trouble, sorrow, need, sickness, or any other adversity.

Hear us, we beseech thee, O Lord.

We remember with thanksgiving those who have loved and served thee in thy Church on earth, who now rest from their labors (especially those most dear to us, whom we name in our hearts before thee). Keep us in fellowship with all thy saints, and bring us at length to the joy of thy heavenly kingdom.

Grant this, O Father, for the sake of Jesus Christ, our only mediator and advocate. Amen.

† *Then shall be read the lesson (s) from the Holy Scriptures. If two lessons are read, let one be the Epistle and the other the Gospel. An anthem or a hymn may be sung after the first lesson.*

† *Here the minister and people may say the Apostles' Creed or another of the Christian affirmations of faith, the people standing.*

14

† *Then shall follow the sermon.*

† *Here parish notices may be given.*

† *A hymn may be sung. The minister shall uncover the elements, and shall proceed to receive the offering from the people. When the offering is presented, the people shall stand, and a prayer of dedication shall be said or sung.*

† *Where custom prevails, an offering may be left by the people at the chancel when they come forward to receive the elements.*

† *The people shall remain standing, and the minister, facing the people, shall say,*

Lift up your hearts.

People: **We lift them up unto the Lord.**

Minister: Let us give thanks unto the Lord.

People: **It is meet and right so to do.**

† *Then the minister, facing the Lord's Table, shall say,*

It is very meet, right, and our bounden duty that we should at all times and in all places give thanks unto thee, O Lord, holy Father, almighty, everlasting God.

† *Here may follow the proper preface* (see No. 831)*, or else the minister immediately shall say,*

Therefore with angels and archangels, and with all the company of heaven, we laud and magnify thy glorious name, evermore praising thee, and saying:

† *Then shall all sing or say,*

Holy, holy, holy, Lord God of hosts: Heaven and earth are full of thy glory! Glory be to thee, O Lord most high! Amen.

B. Holy, Holy, Holy

Sanctus

John Merbecke, 1523-c. 1585

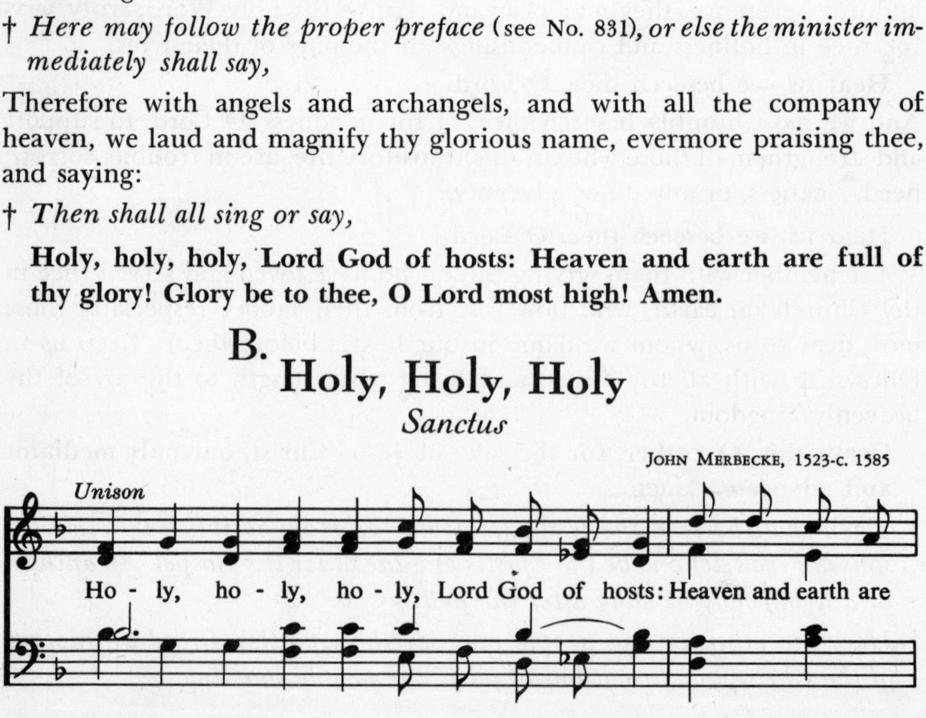
Unison
Ho - ly, ho - ly, ho - ly, Lord God of hosts: Heaven and earth are

full of thy glo - ry; Glo - ry be to thee, O Lord most high. A - men.

† *The people shall kneel or bow; the minister, facing the Lord's Table, shall offer the Prayer of Consecration:*

Almighty God, our heavenly Father, who of thy tender mercy didst give thine only Son Jesus Christ to suffer death upon the cross for our redemption; who made there, by the one offering of himself, a full, perfect, and sufficient sacrifice for the sins of the whole world; and did institute, and in his holy Gospel command us to continue, a perpetual memory of his precious death until his coming again:

Hear us, O merciful Father, we most humbly beseech thee, and grant that we, receiving these thy creatures of bread and wine, according to thy Son our Savior Jesus Christ's holy institution, in remembrance of his passion, death, and resurrection, may be partakers of the divine nature through him:

Who in the same night that he was betrayed, took bread [*here the minister may take the bread in his hands*]; and when he had given thanks, he broke it, and gave it to his disciples saying, Take, eat; this is my body which is given for you; do this in remembrance of me. Likewise after supper he took the cup [*here the minister may take the cup in his hands*]; and when he had given thanks, he gave it to them, saying, Drink ye all of this; for this is my blood of the New Covenant, which is shed for you and for many, for the forgiveness of sins; do this, as oft as ye shall drink it, in remembrance of me. **Amen.**

† *The minister shall kneel before the Lord's Table. After a brief silence, the minister and people together shall pray, saying,*

We do not presume to come to this thy table, O merciful Lord, trusting in our own righteousness, but in thy manifold and great mercies. We are not worthy so much as to gather up the crumbs under thy table. But thou art the same Lord, whose property is always to have mercy. Grant us therefore, gracious Lord, so to partake of this Sacrament of thy Son Jesus Christ, that we may walk in newness of life, may grow into his likeness, and may evermore dwell in him, and he in us. Amen.

† *Here may be sung or said:*

O Lamb of God, that takest away the sins of the world, have mercy upon us.

O Lamb of God, that takest away the sins of the world, have mercy upon us.

O Lamb of God, that takest away the sins of the world, grant us thy peace.

C.

O Lamb of God

Agnus Dei

Unison JOHN MERBECKE, 1523-c. 1585

O Lamb of God, that tak - est a - way the sins of the world,
have mer - cy up - on us. O Lamb of God, that tak - est a -
way the sins of the world, have mer-cy up - on us. O Lamb of
God, that tak - est a - way the sins of the world, grant us thy peace.

† *The minister shall first receive the Holy Communion in both kinds, and then shall deliver the same to any who are assisting him. Then the minister or those assisting him shall deliver the elements in both kinds to the people.*

† *During the distribution of the elements appropriate hymns may be sung or played.*

† *When the bread is given, one or both of the following sentences shall be said:*

The body of our Lord Jesus Christ, which was given for thee, preserve thy soul and body unto everlasting life.

Take and eat this in remembrance that Christ died for thee, and feed on him in thy heart by faith with thanksgiving.

† *When the cup is given, one or both of the following sentences shall be said:*

The blood of our Lord Jesus Christ, which was shed for thee, preserve thy soul and body unto everlasting life.

Drink this in remembrance that Christ's blood was shed for thee, and be thankful.

† *When all have communed, the minister shall place upon the Lord's Table all that remains of the elements, covering the same.*

† *Then the minister, standing and facing the people, shall say,*

The peace of the Lord be with you.

People: **And with thy spirit.**

Minister: Let us give thanks unto the Lord.

† *Then the minister, kneeling before the Lord's Table, and the people, kneeling or bowed, shall pray, saying,*

O Lord, our heavenly Father, we, thy humble servants, desire thy fatherly goodness mercifully to accept this our sacrifice of praise and thanksgiving; most humbly beseeching thee to grant, that, by the merits and death of thy Son Jesus Christ, and through faith in his blood, we and thy whole Church may obtain forgiveness of our sins, and all other benefits of his passion.

And here we offer and present unto thee, O Lord, ourselves, our souls and bodies, to be a reasonable, holy, and lively sacrifice unto thee; humbly beseeching thee that all we who are partakers of this

Holy Communion may be filled with thy grace and heavenly benediction. And although we be unworthy, through our manifold sins, to offer unto thee any sacrifice, yet we beseech thee to accept this our bounden duty and service, not weighing our merits, but pardoning our offenses;

Through Jesus Christ our Lord, by whom, and with whom, in the unity of the Holy Spirit, all honor and glory be unto thee, O Father Almighty, world without end. Amen.

† *Then a hymn may be sung.*

† *Then the minister shall let the people depart with this blessing:*

The peace of God, which passeth all understanding, keep your hearts and minds in the knowledge and love of God, and of his Son Jesus Christ our Lord; and the blessing of God Almighty, the Father, the Son, and the Holy Spirit, be among you, and remain with you always. **Amen.**

† *A postlude may follow.*

831

Proper Prefaces for Certain Days, to Precede the Sanctus in the Order for Holy Communion

Christmas

Because thou didst give Jesus Christ, thine only Son, to be born as at this time for us; who, by the operation of the Holy Ghost, was made very man, and that without spot of sin, to make us clean from all sin.

Therefore with angels, *etc.*

Epiphany

Through Jesus Christ our Lord; who, in substance of our mortal flesh, manifested forth his glory, that he might bring us out of darkness into his own glorious light.

Therefore with angels, *etc.*

Easter

But chiefly are we bound to praise thee for the glorious resurrection of thy Son Jesus Christ our Lord, who by his death hath destroyed death, and by his rising to life again hath restored to us everlasting life.

Therefore with angels, *etc.*

Pentecost

Through Jesus Christ our Lord; according to whose most true promise, the Holy Spirit came down as at this time from heaven, lighting upon the disciples, to teach them, and to lead them into all truth, whereby we have been brought out of darkness into the clear light and true knowledge of thee, and of thy Son Jesus Christ.

Therefore with angels, *etc.*

832

A BRIEF FORM OF THE ORDER FOR THE ADMINISTRATION OF THE SACRAMENT OF THE LORD'S SUPPER OR HOLY COMMUNION

† *This form for the administration of Holy Communion may be included in an order of worship, following the sermon.*

† *The minister shall uncover the elements, and shall proceed to receive the offering from the people. When the offering is presented, the people shall stand, and a prayer of dedication shall be said or sung.*

† *Where custom prevails, an offering may be left by the people at the chancel when they come forward to receive the elements.*

† *The people standing, the minister, facing the people, shall say,*

Ye that do truly and earnestly repent of your sins, and are in love and charity with your neighbors, and intend to lead a new life, following the commandments of God, and walking from henceforth in his holy ways: Draw near with faith, and take this holy Sacrament to your comfort, and make your humble confession to almighty God.

† *Then the minister, kneeling and facing the Lord's Table, and all the people, kneeling or bowed, shall make together this general confession:*

Almighty God, Father of our Lord Jesus Christ, maker of all things, judge of all men: We acknowledge and bewail our manifold sins and wickedness, which we from time to time most grievously have committed, by thought, word, and deed, against thy divine majesty. We do earnestly repent, and are heartily sorry for these our misdoings; the remembrance of them is grievous unto us. Have mercy upon us, have mercy upon us, most merciful Father. For thy Son our Lord Jesus

Christ's sake, forgive us all that is past; and grant that we may ever hereafter serve and please thee in newness of life, to the honor and glory of thy name; through Jesus Christ our Lord. Amen.

† *Then the minister shall pray, saying,*

Almighty God, our heavenly Father, who of thy great mercy hast promised forgiveness of sins to all them that with hearty repentance and true faith turn to thee: Have mercy upon us; pardon and deliver us from all our sins; confirm and strengthen us in all goodness; and bring us to everlasting life; through Jesus Christ our Lord. **Amen.**

† *The minister, standing and facing the people, shall say,*

Hear what comfortable words the Scriptures say to all that truly turn to the Lord:

† *Then the minister shall say one or more of the following sentences:*

Come to me, all who labor and are heavy-laden, and I will give you rest. *Matthew 11:28*

God so loved the world that he gave his only Son, that whoever believes in him should not perish but have eternal life. *John 3:16*

The saying is sure and worthy of full acceptance, that Christ Jesus came into the world to save sinners. *I Timothy 1:15*

If we confess our sins, he is faithful and just, and will forgive our sins and cleanse us from all unrighteousness. *I John 1:9*

If any one sins, we have an advocate with the Father, Jesus Christ the righteous; and he is the expiation for our sins, and not for ours only but also for the sins of the whole world. *From I John 2:1-2*

† *The people shall kneel or bow; the minister, facing the Lord's Table, shall offer the Prayer of Consecration:*

Almighty God, our heavenly Father, who of thy tender mercy didst give thine only Son Jesus Christ to suffer death upon the cross for our redemption; who made there, by the one offering of himself, a full, perfect, and sufficient sacrifice for the sins of the whole world; and did institute, and in his holy Gospel command us to continue, a perpetual memory of his precious death until his coming again:

Hear us, O merciful Father, we most humbly beseech thee, and grant that we, receiving these thy creatures of bread and wine, according to thy Son our Savior Jesus Christ's holy institution, in remembrance of his passion, death, and resurrection, may be partakers of the divine nature through him:

Who in the same night that he was betrayed, took bread [*here the minister may take the bread in his hands*]; and when he had given thanks, he broke it, and gave it to his disciples, saying, Take, eat; this is my body which is given for you; do this in remembrance of me. Likewise after supper he took the cup [*here the minister may take the cup in his hands*]; and when he had given thanks, he gave it to them, saying, Drink ye all of this; for this is my blood of the New Covenant which is shed for you and for many for the forgiveness of sins; do this, as oft as ye shall drink it, in remembrance of me. **Amen.**

† *The minister shall kneel before the Lord's Table. After a brief silence, the minister and people together shall pray, saying,*

We do not presume to come to this thy table, O merciful Lord, trusting in our own righteousness, but in thy manifold and great mercies. We are not worthy so much as to gather up the crumbs under thy table. But thou art the same Lord, whose property is always to have mercy. Grant us therefore, gracious Lord, so to partake of this Sacrament of thy Son Jesus Christ, that we may walk in newness of life, may grow into his likeness, and may evermore dwell in him, and he in us. Amen.

† *The minister shall first receive the Holy Communion in both kinds, and then shall deliver the same to any who are assisting him. Then the minister or those assisting him shall deliver the elements in both kinds to the people.*

† *During the distribution of the elements, appropriate hymns may be sung or played.*

† *When the bread is given, one or both of the following sentences shall be said:*

The body of our Lord Jesus Christ, which was given for thee, preserve thy soul and body unto everlasting life.
Take and eat this in remembrance that Christ died for thee, and feed on him in thy heart by faith with thanksgiving.

† *When the cup is given, one or both of the following sentences shall be said:*

The blood of our Lord Jesus Christ, which was shed for thee, preserve thy soul and body unto everlasting life.
Drink this in remembrance that Christ's blood was shed for thee, and be thankful.

† *When all have communed, the minister shall place upon the Lord's Table all that remains of the elements, covering the same.*

† *Then the minister, kneeling before the Lord's Table, and the people, kneeling or bowed, shall pray, saying,*

O Lord, our heavenly Father, we, thy humble servants, desire thy fatherly goodness mercifully to accept this our sacrifice of praise and thanksgiving; most humbly beseeching thee to grant, that, by the merits and death of thy Son Jesus Christ, and through faith in his blood, we and thy whole Church may obtain forgiveness of our sins, and all other benefits of his passion.

And here we offer and present unto thee, O Lord, ourselves, our souls and bodies, to be a reasonable, holy, and lively sacrifice unto thee; humbly beseeching thee that all we who are partakers of this Holy Communion may be filled with thy grace and heavenly benediction. And although we be unworthy, through our manifold sins, to offer unto thee any sacrifice, yet we beseech thee to accept this our bounden duty and service, not weighing our merits, but pardoning our offenses;

Through Jesus Christ our Lord, by whom and with whom, in the unity of the Holy Spirit, all honor and glory be unto thee, O Father Almighty, world without end. Amen.

† *Then a hymn may be sung.*

† *Then the minister shall let the people depart with this blessing:*

The peace of God, which passeth all understanding, keep your hearts and minds in the knowledge and love of God, and of his Son Jesus Christ our Lord; and the blessing of God Almighty, the Father, the Son, and the Holy Spirit, be among you, and remain with you always. **Amen.**

Communion Service in E Minor

PHILIP R. DIETTERICH, 1931-

833

Glory Be to God on High

Gloria in Excelsis

Unison
V. Glo - ry be to God on high, R. and on earth peace, good will toward men.
We praise thee, we bless thee, we wor-ship thee, we glorify thee, we give
thanks to thee for thy great glory: O Lord God, heavenly King;
God the Fa-ther Al-might-y. O Lord, the only begotten Son, Je-sus Christ;

O Lord God, Lamb of God, Son of the Fa-ther: That takest
away the sins of the world, have mer - cy up - on us.
Thou that takest away the sins of the world, re - ceive our prayer.
Thou that sittest at the right hand of God the Father, have mer-cy up-on us.

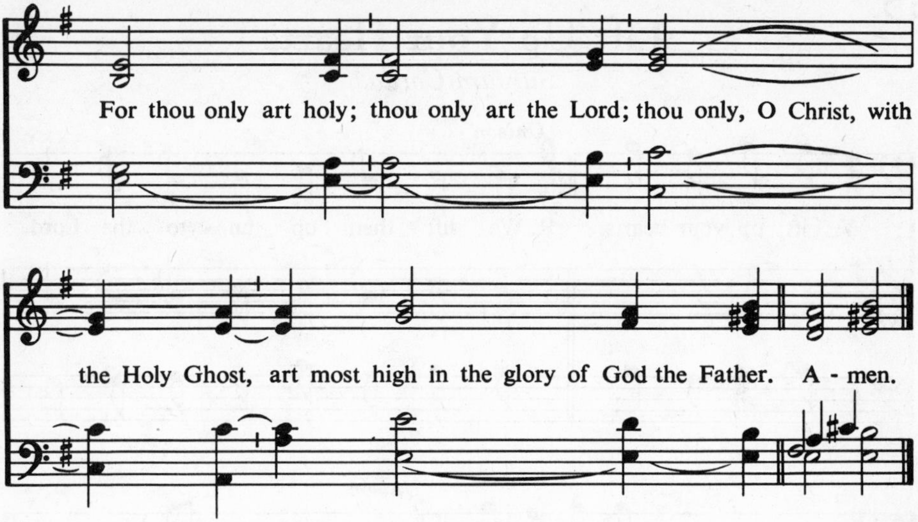
For thou only art holy; thou only art the Lord; thou only, O Christ, with
the Holy Ghost, art most high in the glory of God the Father. A - men.

834

Lord, Have Mercy upon Us

Kyrie Eleison

Lord, have mer - cy up - on us. Christ, have
mer - cy up - on us. Lord, have mer - cy up - on us.

835

Lift Up Your Hearts

Sursum Corda

Unison
V. Lift up your hearts. R. We lift them up un - to the Lord.

Unison
V. Let us give thanks un-to the Lord. R. It is meet and right so to do.

836

Holy, Holy, Holy

Sanctus

Unison
Ho - ly, ho - ly, ho - ly, Lord God of hosts:

Heav - en and earth are full of thy glo - ry;

Glo - ry be to thee, O Lord most high. A - men.

837

O Lamb of God

Agnus Dei

Unison
O Lamb of God, that tak - est a - way
the sins of the world, have mer - cy up - on us.
O Lamb of God, that tak - est a - way the

sins of the world, have mer - cy up - on us.
O Lamb of God, that tak - est a -
way the sins of the world, grant us thy peace.

838

Lord, Have Mercy upon Us

Kyrie Eleison

JOHN MERBECKE, 1523-c. 1585

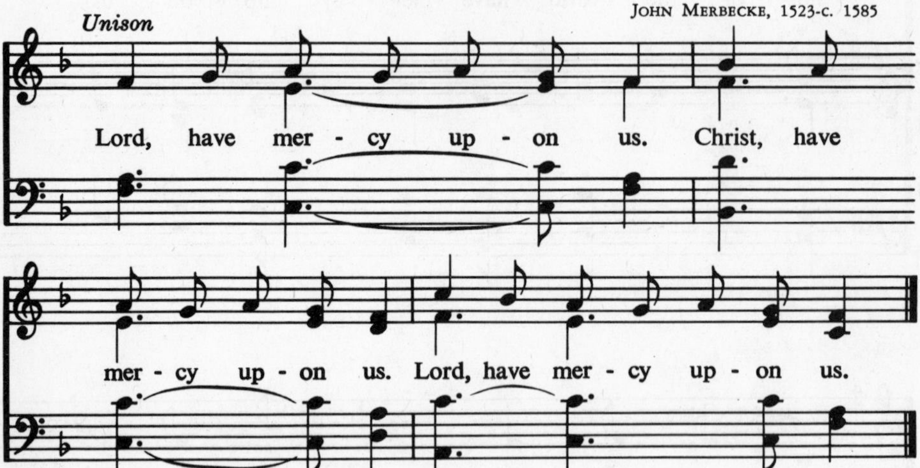
Unison
Lord, have mer - cy up - on us. Christ, have
mer - cy up - on us. Lord, have mer - cy up - on us.

839

Lord, Have Mercy upon Us

Kyrie Eleison

From a Lutheran Service of 1526

Unison
Lord, have mer - cy up - on us. Christ, have
mer - cy up - on us. Lord, have mer - cy up - on us.

Glory Be to God on High

Gloria in Excelsis

JOHN MERBECKE, 1523-c. 1585

Unison
V. Glo - ry be to God on high, R. and on earth peace, good will toward men.
We praise thee, we bless thee, we wor - ship thee, we glo - ri - fy thee,
we give thanks to thee for thy great glo - ry: O Lord God, heaven-ly King;
God the Fa - ther Al - might - y. O Lord, the on - ly be - got - ten Son,

Je - sus Christ; O Lord God, Lamb of God, Son of the Fa - ther:
that tak - est a - way the sins of the world, have mer - cy up - on us.
Thou that tak - est a - way the sins of the world, re - ceive our prayer.
Thou that sit - test at the right hand of God the Fa - ther,

have mer - cy up - on us. For thou on - ly art ho - ly;
thou on - ly art the Lord; thou on - ly, O Christ, with the Ho - ly Ghost,
art most high in the glo - ry of God the Fa - ther. A - men.

841

Lift Up Your Hearts

Sursum Corda

JOHN MERBECKE, 1523-c. 1585

Unison
V. Lift up your hearts. R. We lift them up un - to the Lord.
Unison
V. Let us give thanks unto the Lord our God. R. It is meet and right so to do.

842

Lift Up Your Hearts

Sursum Corda

JOHN CAMIDGE, 1735-1803

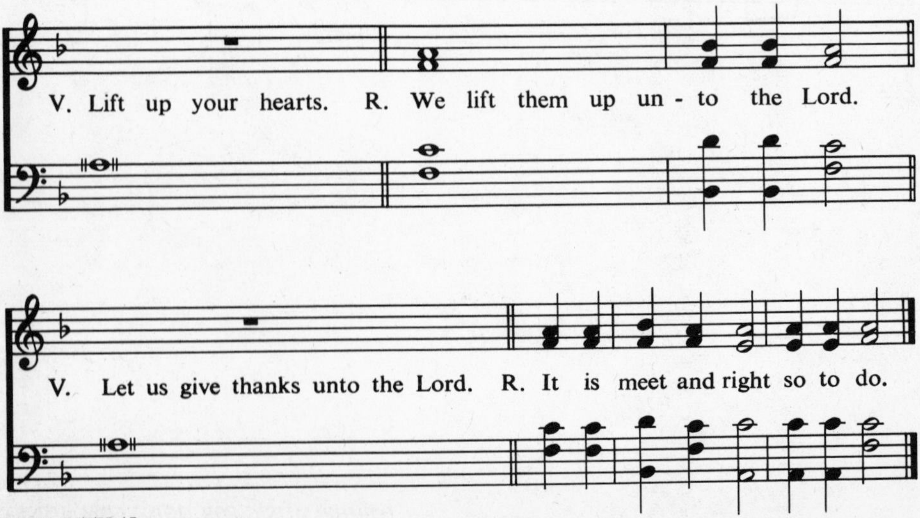
V. Lift up your hearts. R. We lift them up un - to the Lord.
V. Let us give thanks unto the Lord. R. It is meet and right so to do.

Holy, Holy, Holy

Sanctus

ANONYMOUS

Ho - ly, ho - ly, ho - ly, Lord God of Hosts:
Heaven and earth are full of thy glo - ry!
Glo - ry be to thee, O Lord most high! A - men.

Index of First Lines and Titles of Acts of Praise and Aids to Worship

(The Psalter and Canticles are indexed by Scripture, no. 846, and the musical settings of the Canticles appear in index no. 845.)

Accept, O Lord, these offerings thy people make unto thee 755
Accept these offerings, we beseech thee, O Lord 756
Almighty and everlasting God, the radiance of faithful souls 688
Almighty and everlasting God, who art always more ready to hear 706
Almighty and everlasting God, who hatest nothing 693
Almighty and most merciful Father, we have erred and strayed 724
Almighty and most merciful God, who knowest the thoughts 726
Almighty God, at whose right hand are pleasures for evermore 720
Almighty God, from whom all thoughts of truth and peace proceed 714
Almighty God, our heavenly Father: Guide, we beseech thee 712
Almighty God, unto whom all hearts are open 715
Almighty God, who hast given us grace at this time 768
Almighty God, who seest that we have no power of ourselves 694
Almighty God, who through thine only Son hast overcome death 699
And now may the blessing of God Almighty 766
Apostles' Creed 738

Benedicite, omnia opera Domini 616
Benedictus 609, 666
Benedictus es, Domine 610, 668
Blessed be the God and Father of our Lord Jesus Christ 696
Blessed Lord, who hast caused all holy Scriptures 679
Bonum est confiteri 613, 667

De Profundis 615, 671, 672
Direct us, O Lord, in all our doings 772

Eternal God, who by the birth of thy beloved Son Jesus Christ 685

Gloria Deo 619
Gloria in Excelsis Deo 618
Gloria Patri 617
Glory be to God on high 618
Glory be to the Father, and to the Son 617

Grant to us, Lord, we beseech thee, the spirit to think 707
Grant, we beseech thee, almighty God, that the words 769
Grant, we beseech thee, merciful God, that thy Church 704
Great art thou, O Lord, and greatly to be praised 553

Have mercy upon us, O God, according to thy lovingkindness 723

I believe in God the Father Almighty, maker of heaven and earth 738
I believe in one God: the Father Almighty, maker of heaven 739
Increase, O God, the faith and zeal of all thy people 745

Jubilate Deo 611, 669

Korean Creed 741

Let thy merciful ears, O Lord, be open to the prayers 718

Magnificat 612, 670
Make a joyful noise to the Lord, all the lands 710
May almighty God, who caused light to shine out of darkness 736
May the almighty and merciful God grant us pardon 735
Most merciful and gracious God, who art the strength of all 721

Nicene Creed 739
Nunc Dimittis 614, 673

O almighty God, give us grace to approach thee 727
O almighty God, who alone canst order the unruly wills 701
O almighty God, who art worthy to be praised 719
O almighty God, who hast taught us that the night 678
O God, before whose throne the whole family of heaven 722
O God, by whom the meek are guided in judgment 713
O God, most merciful and gracious, of whose bounty we have all 757
O God our Father, we pray for thy Church 743
O God, the creator and preserver of all mankind 742
O God, the protector of all that trust in thee 705
O God, who at this time didst teach the hearts of thy faithful people 711
O God, who didst prepare of old the minds and hearts of men 680
O God, who for our redemption didst give thine only begotten Son 698
O God, who hast made of one blood all nations of men 689
O God, who hast taught us that in returning and rest we shall be saved 717
O God, who makest us glad with the weekly remembrance 716
O God, who makest us glad with the yearly remembrance 684
O God, who through the resurrection of Jesus Christ 700
O Lord God, Father Almighty, bless and sanctify this sacrifice 770
O Lord, our God, send down upon us thy Holy Spirit 754
O Lord, our heavenly Father, whose glory is in all the world 744

O Lord, raise up, we pray thee, thy power 681
O Lord, we beseech thee, absolve thy people from their offenses 737
O Lord, we beseech thee mercifully to receive the prayers 690, 771
Our heavenly Father, who by thy love hast made us 725

Remember, O Lord, thy Church upon earth 746

Te Deum laudamus 608, 665
The peace of God, which passeth all understanding 767

Venite, exultemus 607, 663, 664

We believe in God the Father, infinite in wisdom 740
We believe in the one God, maker and ruler of all things 741
We praise thee, O God; we acknowledge thee to be the Lord 608

Index of Canticles with Music, Service Music, and Communion Music

All things come of thee
Beethoven . . . 808
Morey . . . 807
Amens
Bourgeois . . . 824
Briggs . . . 823
Copley . . . 821
Danish . . . 819
DeLamarter . . . 822
Dresden . . . 818
Greek . . . 820
Single . . . 816, 817
Stainer . . . 825

Blessed art thou, O Lord (*Benedictus es, Domine*) . . . 668
Blessed be the Lord God of Israel (*Benedictus*) . . . 666

Come, and let us sweetly join . . . 790
Come, bless the Lord . . . 783
Communion Service in E Minor . . . 833-837

Enter into his gates . . . 785

Father, give thy benediction . . . 815

Glory be to God on high (*Gloria Deo*) . . . 800
Glory be to God on high (*Gloria in Excelsis*)
Dietterich . . . 833
Merbecke . . . 840
Scottish chant . . . 830 (A)
Glory be to the Father (*Gloria Patri*)
Greatorex . . . 792
Meineke . . . 794
Mode VIII-1 . . . 793
God be in my head . . . 813
God be merciful unto us . . . 804
God himself is with us . . . 788

Holy, holy, holy (*Sanctus*)
- Anonymous 843
- Dietterich 836
- Merbecke .... 830 (B)

I was glad 786
It is a good thing to give thanks (*Bonum est confiteri*) 667

Jesus, stand among us 791

Lead me, Lord 802
Listen to our prayer 803
Let thy word abide in us 796
Lift up your hearts (*Sursum Corda*)
- Camidge 842
- Dietterich 835
- Merbecke 841

Lord, have mercy upon us (Response after commandments) 827
Lord, have mercy upon us (*Kyrie Eleison*)
- Dietterich 834
- Lutheran 839
- Merbecke 838

Lord Jesus Christ, be present now 784
Lord, now lettest thou thy servant (*Nunc dimittis*) 673

My soul doth magnify the Lord (*Magnificat*) 670

O be joyful in the Lord (*Jubilate Deo*) 669
O Come, let us sing (*Venite, exultemus*)
- Boyce 664
- Tone V 663

O Lamb of God (*Agnus Dei*)
- Dietterich 837
- Merbecke .... 830 (C)

O Lord, open thou our eyes 798
O send out thy light 797
Opening sentences for the Christian year
- Advent Season 773
- Christmastide 774, 775
- Epiphany Season 776
- Lenten Season 777
- Palm Sunday 778
- Eastertide 779
- Ascension Day 780
- Pentecost Season 781
- Kingdomtide 782

Our Father who art in heaven ... 826
Out of the deep (*De Profundis*)
Ancient chant (Houghton) ... 672
Croft ... 671

Praise be to thee (*Laus Tibi*) ... 801
Praise God, from whom all blessings flow ... 809

Sing we to our God above ... 811

Thanks be to thee (*Gratia Tibi*) ... 799
The Lord is in his holy temple ... 787
The Lord's Prayer ... 826
This is the day the Lord hath made ... 789
To God the Father ... 812
To God the only wise ... 810
To Thee before the close of day ... 814

Versicles before prayer
Ferial ... 805
Festal ... 806

We praise thee, O God (*Te Deum laudamus*) ... 665
Write these words ... 795

Index of Scripture of the Psalter, Canticles, and Other Aids to Worship

OLD TESTAMENT

Exodus

20:1-17 621

Numbers

6:24-26 764

Deuteronomy

16:17 749

I Chronicles

29:10-13 627
29:11 753
29:14 .... 807, 808

Job

12:13-19, 21, 23, 10 628
28:1, 12-15, 19-20, 23, 28 629

Psalms

1 554
4:8 802
5:8 802
8 555
15:1-4, 5 556
16:1-2, 5-9, 11 557
19 558
22:1, 2-5, 7-8, 18-19, 22-23, 24-25, 27-28 559
23 560
24 561
24:7 676
25:1-2, 4-12, 14, 21 562
27:1-5, 5-6, 6-8, 13-14 563
32:1-3, 5-8, 10-11 564
33:1, 4-6, 8-15, 20-22 565
34:1 782

Psalms (*continued*)

34:1-8, 11-14, 17-18, 22 566
37:1-6, 7, 9, 23-24, 27-28, 39-40 567
40:1-11 568
42 569
43:3 797
46 570
50:14 752
51:1-4, 6, 9-17 571
57:1-3, 5, 7, 9-11 572
62:1-2, 5-8, 11-12 573
63:1-8 574
65:1-9, 9-11, 12-13 575
67 576
67:1 804
72:1-8, 11-12, 14, 17, 18-19 577
73:1-6, 9-26 578
84:1-5, 8-12 579
90 580
91:1-12, 15-16 581
92:1-4 .... 613, 667
93 582
95:1-7 .... 607, 663, 664
96 583
96:1, 13 708
96:9, 13 .... 607, 663, 664
97:1-2, 4-6, 9-12 584
98 585
100 .... 611, 669
100:4 785
102:1-2, 11-12, 18-22, 25-27 586
103:1-7 587
103:8-18 588
103:11-12 728
103:13 729
107:1-9, 21-22 589

Psalms (*continued*)

111:1-9 590
116:1-3, 3-9, 12-19 591
118:1, 4-6, 8, 19-24, 26, 28-29 592
119:1-16 593
119:18 798
119:33-45, 47-48, 174 594
121 595
122 596
122:1 786
126:1-3, 5-6 597
130 .... 615, 671, 672
134:2 783
137:1-6 598
138:1-8 599
139:1-12, 17-18, 23-24 600
142 601
145:1-13 602
145:8 730
145:13-21 603
146 604
148:1-3, 4, 5-13 605
150 606

Proverbs

3:13-19 630
8:1, 22-23, 25-27, 29-31, 35 631

Isaiah

2:2-4 632
2:5, 3 691
9:6 774

Isaiah (*continued*)

11:1-2, 3-4, 5-6, 9 633
35:1-2, 4, 5-7, 8, 10 634
40:1-5 635
40:5 677
40:9-11 636
40:12-14, 17, 28-31 637
40:31 619
42:1-3, 4, 5-7 638
52:7, 9-10 639
53:1-12 640
55:6-7 692
55:6-13 641
60:1, 3 686
60:16, 18-19 639
61:10-11 642
65:17-19, 21-25 643

Jeremiah

9:23-24 709
31:31-32, 33-34 644

Lamentations

3:17-26 645

Joel

2:28 703

Habakkuk

2:20 787
3:17-18 646

NEW TESTAMENT

Matthew

5:3-12 620
5:16 748
21:9 778
22:38-40 621

Mark

12:29-30 621

Luke

1:46-55 .... 612, 670
1:68-79 .... 609, 666

Luke (*continued*)

2:10 683
2:29-32 .... 614, 673
24:34 779

John

1:1-5, 9-14, 16-18 647
1:14 775
3:16 682
3:16-17, 19-21 648
4:23-24 702
4:24 619

John (*continued*)

6:37 732
10:16 687
15:4-11 649

Acts

20:35 747

Romans

6:9-11 659
8:31-32, 35, 37-39 650
12:1-2, 9-17, 21 651

I Corinthians

5:7-8 659
13 652
15:20-22 659

II Corinthians

4:1-2, 7-12, 16-18 653
9:6-7 751
13:14 763

Ephesians

2:1-2, 4-10 654
3:20-21 760

Philippians

2:1-11 655
2:8 777

Colossians

1:13-20 656
3:1 697

I Timothy

1:17 758
6:15-16 759

Hebrews

13:16 750
13:20-21 765

I Peter

1:3-8 657
5:10-11 761

I John

1:5, 7 731
1:7, 3 619
1:9 733
2:12 734
3:1, 16 619
4:7-12, 19-21 658

Jude

1:24-25 762

Revelation

4:8 661
4:11 661
5:12 661
5:13 661
7:12 661
11:17 661
15:3-4 661
19:6-7 661
21:1-6, 22-26 660

APOCRYPHA

Judith

16:13-16 622

Wisdom of Solomon

3:1-3; 2:23; 5:15; 5:16 625
6:1-3, 7, 9, 11-12, 13, 16-18 626

Ecclesiasticus

17:1-3, 6-10, 12-15, 20, 24, 29 623

Ecclesiasticus (*continued*)

44:1-4, 5-9, 10-11, 13-15 624

Song of the Three Young Men

29-34 .... 610, 668
35, 40-41, 45, 47, 51, 54, 56-58,
60, 65, 68 616

Index of Scripture References of Hymns

OLD TESTAMENT

Genesis

1:1-4 480
1:31 34
5:24 268
28:10-17 287
28:10-22 263
32:22-30 529

Exodus

13:21 46
13:22 293
15 .... 446, 448

Leviticus

6:13 172
8:35 150
25:8-17 100

Deuteronomy

32:3 4

Judges

5:21 243

I Samuel

3:1-10 274

I Chronicles

17:16-17 92
29:5 182

Nehemiah

9:5 16

Job

19:25 445

Psalms

1 214
8 .... 41, 44
19 43
19:1-6 365
20:4 233
23 .... 67, 68, 217, 230
24 363
27:1-3 211
34 56
37:5 51
42 255
44 54
45 399
45:2 178
46 20
46:10 209
51:2 226
51:10 282
55:22 210
61:2 245
65:2 498
65:9-13 512
65:13 524
72 .... 359, 472
82 468
84 .... 25, 295
85 468
86 468
87:3 293
90 28
90:1 58
91 216
95 24
95:7-8 105
96 39
98 392

Psalms (*continued*)

100 .... 21, 22
103 .... 55, 65, 66
104 473
113:2-3 500
116:12-18 196
117 14
119:105 372
121 57
130 526
136 61
139:18 264
141:2 494
146 9
147:1 233
148 .... 31, 42
150 .... 15, 55

Proverbs

3:24 495
6:23 372

Song of Solomon

1:3 81
5:10-16 83

Isaiah

6:3 503
6:8 200
9:2-8 361
21:11-12 358
26:3 229
33:20-21 293
43:1-2 48

Jeremiah

8:22 212
50:5 .... 507, 508

Lamentations

3:22-23 499

Ezekiel

18:31-32 112

Daniel

7:9-10 459

Habakkuk

3:17-18 231

Zechariah

13:1 421

NEW TESTAMENT

Matthew

2:1-11 .... 397, 400, 402, 405
4:18-22 107
5:8 276
6:25-34 231
9:37-38 339
11:28 117
16:24-25 160
21:1-11 424
22:9 204
28:19-20 342

Mark

1:32 501
10:13-16 312
10:28 251

Mark (*continued*)

10:35-40 413
11:1-10 423
14:32-42 431
14:36 167

Luke

2:8-14 394
2:13-14 390
14:16-24 102
17:5 142
22:19 316
22:32 237
24:29 .... 289, 502
24:30-31 313

John

1:16 117
4:14 117
6:37 119
8:12 117
12:12-15 425
12:21 90
14:6 75
15:5 265
19:30 429
20:22 133

Acts

9:6 177
16:26 527
26:22 509

Romans

12:1 187
14:17 195

I Corinthians

2:2 124
15:20 440
16:13 239

II Corinthians

13:14 334

Galatians

3:22 118
5:25 138
6:14 .... 124, 416, 435

Ephesians

2:20-22 298
3:1 184
6:10-17 248
6:10-20 250

Philippians

1:21 218
2:5-11 .... 74, 76

Philippians (*continued*)

3:12-14 249
4:4 .... 233, 483

I Thessalonians

4:17 209

I Timothy

1:17 27
6:12 .... 240, 241

II Timothy

2:19 48

Hebrews

2:9-10 458
10:22 159
11 139
13:5 48
13:17 335

James

1:27 199

I Peter

1:16 266
5:7 53

I John

1:7 403
4:16 63
4:19 162

Revelation

1:7 364
3:20 108
4:8-11 26
7:9-12 409
11:15 453
19:12 455
22:1-5 481

APOCRYPHA

Ecclesiasticus

44:1-15 532
50:22-24 49

Index of Composers, Authors, and Sources

Abbey, Alonzo J. 290
Abelard, Peter 427
Adams, Sarah F. 263
Addison, Joseph 43, 52, 70
Adebesin, Biodun 487
Adkins, Leon M. 342
Ahle, Johann R. 257, 370
Ajosè, M. O. 487
Aldrich, Henry 669
Alexander, Cecil Frances 34, 107, 414
Alexander, James W. 418
Alford, Henry 522
Alington, Cyril A. 449
Allen, George N. 183
Ambrose of Milan 29
American Compiler of Sacred Harmony, No. 1 (1803) 426
American Folk Hymns 40, 212, 286, 287, 330, 404, 432, 436
American Melodies 48, 92, 93, 111, 115, 291, 421, 545
Amps, William 147
Ancient Chants 310, 435, 672, 795, 826, 830 (A)
Andrew of Crete 238
Anglican Chants 664, 665, 666, 667, 668, 669, 671, 672, 673, 830 (A)
Anonymous 3, 373, 384
  American 96
  English 14 (vss. 3-4), 547
  German 79, 91
  Greek 99, 353, 491
  Indian 803
  Irish 256
  Latin 78, 82, 298, 354, 386, 391, 418, 443, 447, 814
  Thai 214
Arlott, John 514
Arne, Thomas A. 239, 335
Arnold, John 443
As Hymnodus Sacer (1625), 127, 337, 532
Atkinson, Frederick C. 138

Babcock, Maltbie D. 45
Bach, J. S. 46, 172, 253, 373, 399, 418, 491
Bacon, Leonard 550
Baker, Henry 270, 541
Baker, Henry W. 67, 99, 357
Baker, Theodore 59
Bakewell, John 454
Bambridge, William S. 498
Baring-Gould, Sabine 305, 495
Barnby, Joseph 91, 169, 333, 495, 537, 673
Barthélémon, François H. 331, 461, 535
Barton, Bernard 368, 403
Bateman, Christian Henry 77
Bates, Katharine Lee 543
Bathurst, William H. 142
Bax, Clifford 475
Baxter, Lydia 87
Baxter, Richard 218
Bayly, Albert F. 479
Beach, Curtis 41
Beethoven, Ludwig van 38, 41, 440, 808
Bennard, George 228
Benson, Louis F. 314
Berggreen, Anton P. 274
Bernard of Clairvaux 329
Bernard of Cluny 303
Bickersteth, Edward H. 229
Blaisdell, James A. 321
Bliss, Philip P. 109, 148
Boberg, Carl 17
Bode, John E. 164
Bohemian Brethren Melody 85, 512
Bohemian Brethren's *Kirchengesänge* 4
Bonar, Horatius 117, 326, 327
Booke of Musicke (1591) 414, 428
Borthwick, Jane 105, 167, 209

Bortniansky, Dimitri S. 89
Bourgeois, Louis 21, 22, 307, 323, 500, 518, 809, 824
Bowie, Walter Russell 355, 481
Bowring, John 63, 358, 416
Boyce, William 664
Boyd, William 241
Bradbury, William B. 119, 121, 217, 222, 275, 431
Brady, Nicholas 54, 56, 255
Bridges, Matthew 455
Bridges, Robert S. 29, 412
Briggs, George W. 408, 460, 823
Brooks, Phillips 381
Brooks, R. T. 18
Brown, Leila Jackson 803
Brownlie, John 353
Bryant, William C. 345
Buck, Carlton C. 520
Buckoll, Henry J. 258
Budry, Edmond L. 450
Bullinger, Ethelbert W. 273
Bunyan, John 155
Burke, Christian 517
Burleigh, William H. 269
Burnap, Uzziah C. 243
Burns, James D. 498
Burrowes, Elisabeth 206
Burt, Bates G. 186, 252
Byrne, Mary E. 256

Camidge, John 798, 842
Campbell, Jane M. 513
Canaidau y Cyssegr (1839) 27
Canitz, Friedrich R. L. von 258
Canning, Thomas 508
Cantica Laudis (1850) 181
Cantionale Sacrum (1651) 347, 784
Carr, Benjamin 77
Carter, R. Kelso 221
Caswall, Edward 82, 91, 405
Cennick, John 300, 518
Challinor, Frederic A. 88
Chao Tzu-ch'en 490, 519
Chapin, Lucius 789
Charles, Elizabeth R. 430
Chatfield, Allen W. 284
Chesterton, Gilbert K. 484
Chinese Melodies 490, 519
Choral, The (1845) 43
Choralbuch (1815) 401, 463
Chorale Book for England, The (1864) 55
Chorister's Companion (c. 1782) 100, 122
Chorley, Henry F. 544
Christian Lyre, The (1831) 104, 251
Christierson, Frank von 356, 511
Clark, Alexander 95
Clark, Jeremiah 458
Claudius, Matthias 513
Clausnitzer, Tobias 257, 463
Clement of Alexandria 84, 86
Clephane, Elizabeth C. 417
Coffin, Henry S. 354
Collection of Church Music (1851) 403
Collection of Hymns and Sacred Poems, A (1749) 56, 282
Collection of Motetts or Antiphons, A (1792) 103
Compleat Psalmodist (1749) 443
Conkey, Ithamar 416
Converse, Charles C. 261
Cook, Joseph S. 395
Copenhaver, Laura S. 406
Copes, V. Earle (V. E. C.) 9, 34, 39, 94, 121, 161, 292, 295, 314, 319, 352, 391, 422, 459
Copley, R. Evan 821
Cosin, John 467
Coster, George T. 243
Cotterill, Thomas 113, 319
Cowper, William 98, 215, 231, 268, 421
Cox, Frances E. 4
Coxe, A. Cleveland 80, 308
Croft, William 28, 308, 409, 457, 665, 671
Croly, George 138
Crosby, Fanny J. 110, 145, 159, 175, 176, 205, 224, 226, 433
Crotch, William 16, 114, 277, 477, 666, 668, 810, 812
Crüger, Johann 49, 134, 220, 262, 318, 340, 341, 412
Crum, J. M. C. 441
Cummings, William H. 388

Cuninggim, Maud M. 349
Cutler, Henry S. 419
Cutts, Peter 62

Damon, William 284, 414, 428
Daniel ben Judah 30
Darwall, John 483
Davies, Henry Walford 525, 813
Davis, Katherine K. 96, 408, 485
Davis, Ozora S. 189, 202
Day's Psalter (1562) 313
Dearle, Edward 327
Dearmer, Percy 155, 370, 504
DeLamarter, Eric 822
Dexter, Henry M. 86
Didache (c. 110) 307
Dietterich, Philip R. 833-837
Dix, William C. 385, 397, 524
Doane, George W. 75, 494
Doane, William C. 459
Doane, William H. 87, 145, 159, 175, 185, 226, 433
Doddridge, Philip 53, 128, 249, 312, 325, 335, 509
Douglas, C. Winfred 78, 85, 155, 357, 512
Draper, William H. 60
Duffield, George, Jr. 248
Dutch Melody 69, 454
Dwight, Timothy 294
Dykes, John B. 26, 67, 82, 117, 146, 152, 173, 193, 272, 407, 516, 538
Dyson, George 796

Ebeling, Johann G. 379
Edgar, Mary S. 273
Edmeston, James 496
Edson, Lewis 100, 122
Ein schön geistlich Gesangbuch (1609) 44
Ellerton, John 236, 452, 500, 544, 549
Elliott, Charlotte 119, 144
Ellor, James 72
Elvey, George J. 184, 250, 288, 455, 522
Emerson, L. O. 497
English Carols 378, 383
English Melodies 33, 34, 37, 378, 383, 385, 484
Est, Thomas 54, 70, 131, 394
Evans, David 230, 443
Evans, William E. 352
Everest, Charles W. 160
Ewing, Alexander 303

Faber, Frederick W. 69, 151
Farrant, Richard 667
Farrington, Harry Webb 123
Fawcett, John 165, 306
Featherstone, William R. 166
Fink, Gottfried W. 343
Finnish Melody 230
Finlay, Kenneth G. 157, 255, 791
Fischer, William G. 116, 149, 245
Flemming, Friedrich F. 144
Folk Hymns
  American 40, 212, 286, 287, 330, 404, 432, 436
  Netherland 59
  Thailand 214
Folk Melodies. *See* Traditional Melodies
Fortunatus, Venantius 452
Fosdick, Harry Emerson 470
Foundery Collection (1742) 15, 309, 474, 790, 811
Foundling Hospital Collection, The (1796) 42
Francis of Assisi 60
Franck, Johann 220, 318
Franz, Ignaz 8
Frazier, Philip 40
French Carols 374, 441, 451
French Melodies 162, 324, 504
French Psalter (1561) 332

Gardiner, William 36, 160, 204, 351
Gauntlett, Henry J. 63, 65, 334, 405, 496
Gawler, William 171
Gay, Annabeth McClelland 202
Geistliche Kirchengesänge (1623) 19, 60
Geistliche Lieder (1539) 281, 531
Geistliches Gesangbüchlein (1524) 438, 526
Genevan Psalter (1547) 307, 468, 500
Genevan Psalter (1551) 16, 21, 22, 114, 277, 469, 475, 477, 518, 809, 810, 812
George, Graham 240, 425

Gerhardt, Paul 51, 132, 259, 379, 418
German Melodies 220, 391
Gesangbuch (Klug's, 1535) 58, 84
Gesangbuch (Leisentritt's, 1584) 448
Gesangbuch (Meiningen, 1693) 167, 201, 372
Gesangbuch der H. W. K. Hofkapelle (1784) 359, 423
Gesius, Bartholomäus 491
Giardini, Felice de 3, 292, 352
Gibbons, Orlando 135, 229, 311, 430, 530
Gill, Thomas H. 58
Gillman, Frederick J. 191
Gilmore, Joseph H. 217
Gladden, Washington 170
Gläser, Carl G. 1, 278
Gordon, Adoniram J. 166
Goss, John 18, 243
Gottschalk, Louis M. 494
Goudimel, Claude 468
Gould, John E. 247
Gower, John H. 312
Grant, Robert 113, 473
Greatorex, Henry W. 94, 403, 792
Gregory the Great 504
Greiter, Matthäus 9, 39
Grenoble Antiphoner (1868) 194
Grobel, Kendrick 84
Gruber, Franz 393
Gurney, Dorothy B. 333

Hamilton, Mary C. D. 541
Handel, George Frederick 249, 392, 450, 456, 476
Hankey, Katherine 149
Harding, James P. 400
Harkness, Georgia 161, 542
Harlow, S. Ralph 173
Harper, Earl E. 123
Harrell, Costen J. 351
Harrington, Karl P. 380
Harrison, Ralph 24
Hart, Joseph 104
Hassler, Hans L. 418
Hastings, Thomas 83, 103, 120, 232
Hatch, Edwin 133
Hatton, John 14, 23, 472, 550
Havergal, Frances R. 179, 187, 195, 274, 452
Havergal, William 68, 102, 141, 182, 276, 338, 368, 429
Haweis, Thomas 12, 130
Hawks, Annie S. 265
Haydn, Franz Joseph 6, 42, 43, 258, 293
Haydn, Johann Michael 295, 319, 473
Hearn, Marianne 169
Heath, George 246
Heber, Reginald 26, 320, 322, 323, 400, 419, 497
Hebrew Melodies 11, 30
Hedge, Frederick H. 20
Heermann, Johann 412
Heins, Francis D. 362
Helmore, Thomas 354
Hemy, Henri F. 151, 259, 344
Herbert, George 10
Herbst, Martin 95
Hermann, Nicolaus 389, 510
Herold, Louis J. F. 187
Hine, Stuart K. 17
Hirschberger Gesangbuch (1741) 219
Hodges, Edward 38, 41, 440
Hodges, John S. B. 320
Holden, Oliver 71
Holland, Henry S. 546
Holland, Josiah G. 380
Holmes, John Haynes 200
Holmes, Oliver W. 64, 270
Holst, Gustav 376
Hopkins, Edward J. 236
Hopkins, John H., Jr. 402
Hopper, Edward 247
Horne, Charles Silvester 534
Horsley, William 218, 225
Hosmer, Frederick Lucian 12, 497
Houghton, James R. 672
Housman, Laurence 469
How, William W. 108, 181, 372, 536, 537
Howard, Samuel 51, 339, 465
Howe, Julia Ward 545
Hoyle, R. Birch 450
Hu Te-ngai 490
Hughes, John 271, 470
Hull, Eleanor H. 256
Hunter, John 254
Husband, Edward 108
Hutchinson, Albert H. 525

Hutton, Frances A. 237
Hymnau a Thonau (1865) 260, 482, 486
Hymns and Psalms (c. 1788) 171
Hymns for the Young (1836) 121

Indian Melody 803
Ingalls, Jeremiah 527, 528
Irish Melodies 189, 256, 375, 534
Irons, William J. 440

Jackson, Robert 133
Jacobi, John C. 132
Jeffery, J. Albert 459
Jenks, Stephen 426
John of Damascus 437, 446, 448
Johnson, Erastus 245
Jones, William 296, 353, 356
Jude, William H. 107

"K" in Rippon's *A Selection of Hymns* (1787) 48
Katholisches Gesangbuch (c. 1774) 8, 254, 502
Keble, John 276, 499, 502
Kelly, Thomas 453, 458
Ken, Thomas 180, 493, 809
Kennedy, Benjamin H. 124
Kennedy, Gerald H. 153
Kentucky Harmony (1817) 142, 302
Supplement to (1820) 32
Kerr, Hugh T. 47
Kethe, William 21
Kingsley, Charles 485
Kingsley, George 187
Kirbye, George 54, 70, 394
Kirchengesänge (Bohemian Brethren's, 1566) 4
Kirkpatrick, William J. 208, 304, 524
Klug, Joseph 58, 84
Knapp, Phoebe P. 224
Knapp, William 29, 509
Knecht, Justin H. 108
Kocher, Conrad 35, 397
König, Johann B. 141, 182, 276
Kremser, Edward 59

La Feillée, François de 504
Lampe, John F. 56, 282, 350
Landsberg, Max 30
Lane, Spencer 237
Langran, James 269
Larcom, Lucy 188
Lathbury, Mary A. 304, 369, 503
Laudi Spirituali (14th century) 815
Laufer, Calvin W. 203, 482
Leeson, Jane E. 162
Leisentritt, Johann 448
Leoni (Meyer Lyon) 30
Lew, Timothy Tingfang 317
Lindeman, Ludwig M. 355
Littledale, Richard F. 466
Littlefield, Milton S. 197
Liturgy of St. James 324
Lloyd, William 200
Longfellow, Samuel 36, 135, 219, 296, 505, 515, 815
Longstaff, William D. 266
Lovelace, Austin C. (A. C. L.) 2, 32, 77, 86, 92, 123, 129, 137, 139, 142, 146, 152, 189, 190, 196, 206, 211, 213, 227, 251, 258, 301, 302, 329, 374, 375, 389, 396, 456, 476, 481, 487, 499, 510, 514, 526, 527, 528, 534, 783, 786, 797
Lowell, James Russell 242
Lowry, J. C. 142, 302
Lowry, Robert 177, 205, 265, 444
Luther, Martin 20, 281, 438, 526
Lvov, Alexis F. 544
Lyon, Meyer (Leoni) 30
Lyon, P. H. B. 486
Lyra Davidica (1708) 387, 439, 443
Lyte, Henry F. 66, 251, 255, 289

McCutchan, Robert G. 10, 111
McDonald, William 116
MacMillan, Ernest 395, 442
Madan, Martin 454
Mainzer, Joseph 139
Maker, Frederick C. 50, 235, 417
Malan, H. A. César 124
Mann, Arthur H. 164
Mann, Newton 30
Marlatt, Earl 413, 462
Marriott, John 480
Marsh, Simeon B. 126
Martin, Civilla D. 207

Martin, W. Stillman 207
Mason, Harry S. 413
Mason, Lowell 1, 53, 68, 98, 128, 140, 143, 150, 168, 206, 213, 246, 263, 278, 306, 329, 336, 338, 365, 368, 392, 435, 471, 480, 488, 489
Mason's Sacred Harp (1843) 137
Massie, Richard 438
Masterman, John H. B. 194
Matheson, George 184, 234
Maurus, Rhabanus 467
Medley, Samuel 168, 445
Meineke, Charles 794
Melodia Sacra (1815) 249
Mendelssohn, Felix 49, 167, 201, 264, 372, 388
Merbecke, John 800, 801, 830 (B), 830 (C), 838, 840, 841
Merrill, William P. 174, 548
Messiter, Arthur H. 233
Méthode du Plain-chant (1782) 504
Milligan, James L. 362
Milman, Henry H. 425
Milton, John 61, 468
Mohr, Joseph 393
Moment, John J. 11
Monk, Edwin G. 665
Monk, W. H. 35, 61, 99, 289, 397, 401, 447, 463
Monsell, John S. B. 62, 178, 240, 241, 398
Montgomery, James 16, 211, 237, 252, 313, 316, 337, 359, 382, 434
Moore, Thomas 103
Morey, Lloyd 807
Morison, John 361
Mote, Edward 222
Moultrie, Gerard 324
Münster Gesangbuch (1677) 79
Murray, James R. 384
Musikalisches Handbuch (1690) 102, 429

"Nachtstücke" (Robert Schumann) 195, 197
Nägeli, Johann G. 53, 140, 268, 306, 336
Neale, John M. 78, 99, 238, 298, 303, 354, 357, 391, 424, 437, 446, 448, 451, 491, 814
Neander, Joachim 7, 13, 55, 153, 788
Nederlandtsch Gedenckclanck (1626) 59
Nelson, Ronald A. 804
Netherlands Folk Hymn 59
Neumark, Georg 210
Newman, John Henry 272
Newton, John 81, 92, 293, 334, 489
New Version (Tate and Brady, 1696) 54, 56, 255
New Universal Psalmodist, The (1770) 5, 294, 492
Niceta, Bishop of Remesiana 665
Nichol, H. Ernest 410
Nicolai, Philipp 366, 399
Noel, Caroline M. 76
"Noël Nouvelet" 441
Norse Folk Melody 304, 524
North, Frank Mason 204, 407

Oakeley, Frederick 386
Oakeley, Herbert S. 501
Oliver, Henry K. 105, 118
Olson, Ernest W. 521
Olude, A. T. Olajida 487
Owen, William 364, 453
Oxenham, John 192, 225
Oxford Book of Carols, The (1928) 442

Page, Kate Stearns 6
Palestrina, Giovanni P. da 447
Palmer, Ray 143, 329, 340
Parish Choir, The (1850) 61
Park, J. Edgar 90
Park, Roswell 331
Parker, Edwin P. 494
Parker, William H. 88
Parkin, Charles 7
Parry, Joseph 125, 358
Peace, Albert L. 234
Peek, Joseph Y. 156
Pennefather, William 791
Pennewell, Almer T. 422
Pensum Sacrum (1648) 347, 784
Perronet, Edward 71, 72, 73
Pfautsch, Lloyd A. 238, 280
Phelps, Sylvanus D. 177
Piae Cantiones (1582) 395, 442
Pierpoint, Folliot S. 35
Pierpont, John 348
Pilgrim Hymnal, The (1904) 96

Pilsbury, Amos 191
Plainsong 78, 326, 354, 357, 467, 504, 663, 670, 773-782, 793, 814
Pleyel, Ignace J. 300, 348
Plumptre, Edward H. 233
Plymouth Collection (1855) 31
Polish Carol 396
Pollard, Adelaide A. 154
Pollock, Thomas B. 311
Pond, Sylvanus B. 196, 301
Pott, Francis 2, 447
Powell, Robert J. 315
Praetorius, Michael 515
Praxis Pietatis Melica (1653) 134, 262, 340, 341
Prentiss, Elizabeth P. 185
Prichard, Rowland H. 132, 360, 548
Procter, Adelaide A. 50
Prudentius, Aurelius Clemens 357, 405
Psalmes (Damon's, 1579) 284
Psalmodia Evangelica (1789) 198, 346, 363, 445
Psalmodia Sacra (1715) 63, 65, 334, 405, 496
Psalmody (Tattersall's, 1794) 165, 517
Psalter, The (1912) 44, 57, 512
Purday, Charles H. 47

Quaile, Robert N. 523

Rankin, Jeremiah E. 539, 540
Rawnsley, Hardwicke D. 411
Read, Daniel 80
Redhead, Richard 113, 162, 434
Redner, Lewis H. 381
Reed, Andrew 461
Reed, E. M. G. 396
Rees, Bryn Austin 141
Reinagle, Alexander R. 81, 192, 349, 520
Rendle, Lily 506
Repository of Sacred Music, Part Second (1813) 93, 129, 190, 481
Reynolds, William J. 533
Richardson, John 75
Ridout, Daniel L. 212, 244
Riley, Athelstan 19
Rinkart, Martin 49
Rippon, John 48, 71, 72, 73
Rist, Johann 373
Robbins, Howard Chandler 456
Roberts, Daniel C. 552
Roberts, John 27
Robinson, Robert 93
Röntgen, Julius 69, 454
Rossetti, Christina G. 375, 376
Rowland, May 506
Rumbaugh, Vida 214
Russell, Arthur Tozer 389
Russian Air 505
Ryden, Ernest E. 350

Sacred Harp, The (1844) 211
Sacred Melodies (1815) 36, 160, 204, 351
Sammis, John H. 223
Sandell-Berg, Caroline V. 521
Sankey, Ira D. 514
Sarum Primer (1558) 813
Schein, Johann H. 46, 172
Schlegel, Katharina von 209
Schlesische Volkslieder (1842) 79
Schmolck, Benjamin 13, 167
Schop, Johann 373
Schulz, Johann A. P. 513
Schumann, Robert 195, 197
Schütz, Johann J. 4
Schwedler, Johann C. 124
Scoggin, Robert E. 785
Scott, Clara H. 267
Scott, Robert B. Y. 477
Scott-Gatty, Alfred 199, 371
Scottish Melody 529
Scottish Paraphrases (1781) 361
Scottish Psalter (1615) 57, 215, 325, 345, 549
Scottish Psalter (1635) 52, 361
Scottish Psalter (1650) 68, 295
Scriven, Joseph M. 261
Seagrave, Robert 474
Sears, Edmund H. 390
Selection of Hymns, A (1787) 48
Selection of Popular National Airs, A (1818) 505
Shackford, John W. 201
Shaw, Martin 441
Shepherd, Thomas 183

Sheppard, Franklin L. 45
Sherwin, William F. 369, 503
Shrubsole, William 73
Shurtleff, Ernest W. 478
Sibelius, Jean 209, 542
Siena, Bianco da 466
Simpson, Robert 461, 535
Simpson, William J. S. 426
Small, James G. 163
Smart, Henry 66, 298, 342, 382, 437, 478
Smith, H. Percy 170, 462
Smith, Samuel F. 547
Smith, Walter Chalmers 27
Southern Harmony (1835) 227, 432
Sowerby, Leo 321
Spirituals: *See* Folk Hymns
Spohr, Louis 279
Stainer, John 825
Stead, Louisa M. R. 208
Stebbins, George C. 110, 154, 163, 179, 266
Steele, Anne 367
Stennett, Samuel 83, 291
Stocking, Jay T. 171
Stockton, John H. 101
Stone, Lloyd 542
Stone, Samuel J. 297
Stowe, Harriet B. 264
Stowell, Hugh 232
Stralsund Gesangbuch (1665) 55
Strassburger Kirchenamt (1525) 9, 39
Studdert-Kennedy, G. A. 190
Stutsman, Grace M. 377
Su Yin-lan 317
Sullivan, Arthur S. 2, 188, 305, 446
Supplement to Kentucky Harmony (1820) 32
Swain, Joseph 129
Swedish Melodies 17, 521
Symonds, J. Addington 198
Synesius of Cyrene 284

Tallis, Thomas 180, 216, 316, 367, 411, 493, 799, 805, 806, 827
Tans'ur, William 427, 507
Tappan, William B. 431
Tarrant, William G. 532
Tate, Nahum 54, 56, 255, 394
Tate, Nahum and Brady, Nicholas, *New Version* (1696) 54, 56, 255
Tattersall, William D. 165, 517
Taylor, Sarah E. 371
Taylor, Virgil C. 64
Taylor, Walter Reginald Oxenham 317
Tennyson, Alfred 146
Tersteegen, Gerhard 105, 531, 788
Teschner, Melchior 424
Thailand Folk Melody 214, 322
Theodulph of Orleans 424
Thesaurus Musicus (1744) 547
Thomas, Edith Lovell 6
Thompson, Mary A. 299
Thompson, Will L. 97
Threlfall, Jeannette 423
Thring, Godfrey 455
Thrupp, Dorothy A. 121
Tillett, Wilbur Fisk 85
Tindley, Charles A. 244
Tisserand, Jean 451
Tochter Sion (1741) 75
Tomer, William G. 539
Toplady, Augustus M. 120, 147
Towner, Daniel B. 223
Traditional Melodies
- American 48, 92, 93, 111, 115, 291, 421, 432
- Chinese 490
- Dutch 69, 454
- English 33, 34, 37, 378, 383, 385, 484
- Finnish 230
- French 324
- German 220, 391
- Hebrew 11
- Indian 803
- Irish 189, 256, 375, 534
- Norse 304, 524
- Russian 505
- Scottish 529
- Swedish 17
- Thailand 322
- Welsh 136, 231, 260, 482, 486, 497, 551

Tucker, F. Bland 74, 307, 427
Turner, Herbert B. 90
Tweedy, Henry H. 136, 260, 476
Twells, Henry 501

Union Harmony (1793) 71
United Presbyterian Book of Psalms (1871) 65, 216
United States Harmony (1799) 191

Vail, Silas J. 176
Van Dyke, Henry 38
Vaughan Williams, Ralph 33, 37, 60, 74, 76, 466, 484, 536, 540
Venua, Frederick M. A. 25
Vesperale Romanum (1848) 467
Virginia Harmony (1831) 92
Vulpius, Melchior 44, 178, 449

Wade, John F. 386
Walch, James 299
Walford, William 275
Walker, William 398
Wallace, William V. 158
Walter, Howard A. 156
Walter, Samuel 511
Walter, William H. 174
Walther, Johann 438, 526
Walton, James G. 151, 259, 344
Walworth, Clarence 8
Ward, Samuel A. 543
Ware, Henry, Jr. 343, 516
Waring, Anna L. 230
Warren, George W. 406, 552
Watts, Isaac 5, 9, 14, 22, 24, 25, 28, 31, 37, 39, 134, 239, 365, 392, 415, 435, 472, 533, 789, 810
Webb, George J. 248
Webbe, Samuel, Sr. 103, 499, 546
Weber, Carl M. von 94
Weimar, Georg Peter 285
Weissel, George 363
Wellesley, Garret 310
Wells, Marcus M. 106
Welsh Melodies 27, 112, 136, 231, 260, 464, 482, 486, 497, 551
Werner, J. G. 401, 463
Wesley, Charles 1, 15, 46, 89, 94, 100, 102, 111, 112, 114, 115, 118, 122, 125, 126, 130, 131, 137, 139, 140, 150, 152, 172, 182, 186, 193, 196, 227, 250, 253, 262, 277, 278, 279, 280, 281, 282, 283, 285, 288, 301, 302, 309, 310, 315, 328, 332, 336, 338, 339, 341, 344, 360, 364, 387, 388, 401, 409, 420, 429, 439, 443, 457, 464, 465, 471, 483, 507, 508, 510, 527, 528, 529, 530, 535, 790, 811
Wesley, John 9, 22, 51, 127, 213, 259, 492, 531, 812
Wesley, Samuel 428
Wesley, Samuel S. 24, 297, 802
West, Robert A. 23
Weyman, David 249
White, H. Kirke 32
Whitefield, George 387, 388
Whiting, William 538
Whittier, John Greenleaf 157, 158, 199, 235, 290, 347
Whole Booke of Psalmes, The (1592) 54, 70, 131, 394
Wiant, Bliss 317, 490, 519
Wile, Frances W. 33
Wilhelm II, Duke of Saxe-Weimar 784
Williams, Aaron 5, 294, 492
Williams, Peter 271
Williams, Robert 443
Williams, Thomas 198, 346, 363, 445
Williams, Thomas J. 242, 460
Williams, William 271
Willis, Richard Storrs 79, 390
Wilson, Hugh 328, 415
Winchester, Caleb T. 346
Winkworth, Catherine 13, 49, 55, 210, 220, 257, 318, 363, 366, 379, 399, 463, 526, 784
Wolcott, Samuel 292
Woodbury, Isaac B. 420
Woodward, George R. 515
Wordsworth, Christopher 488, 523
Work, John W. 404
Wreford, John R. 551
Wyeth, John 93, 129, 190, 481

Yigdal of Daniel Ben Judah 30
Young, Carlton R. (C. R. Y.) 19, 48, 140, 256, 268, 330, 364, 398, 426, 432, 453, 464, 529, 787
Young, John F. 393

Zinzendorf, Nicolaus von 127, 213
Zundel, John 283, 479

Index of Tune Names

Abends 501
Aberystwyth 125, 358
Ach Gott und Herr 532
Adelaide 154
Adeste fideles 48 (alt.)
with Refrain 386
Adoro te 326
Allgütiger, mein Preisgesang 285
All Saints New 419
All the Way 205
All the World 10
Alta Trinita beata 815
Amazing Grace 92
Amen, Jesus han skal raade 274
America 547
Amsterdam 15, 474
Ancient of Days 161 (alt.), 459
Angel's Story 164
Angel Voices 2
Antioch 392
Ar hyd y nos 497
Arfon 112, 463 (alt.)
Arfon (Major) 464
Ariel 168, 285 (alt.)
Arlington 142 (alt.), 239, 335, 349 (alt.)
Armenia 196, 301
Arnsberg 788
Arthur's Seat 243
Assurance, with Refrain 224
Aurelia 211 (alt.), 231 (alt.), 297
Aus der Tiefe 95
Aus tiefer Not 526
Austria 42, 293, 460 (alt.)
Author of Life 315
Autumn 331, 454 (alt.)
Ave virgo virginum 448
Away in a Manger 384
Ayrshire 157, 255
Azmon 1, 202 (alt.), 278

Ballerma 461, 535
Balm in Gilead 212
Bangor 427
Barnabas 332
Battle Hymn of the Republic, with Refrain 545
Beacon Hill 413
Bealoth 137
Beecher 283, 479
Bethany 263
Bethlehem 343
Binti Hamari 803
Blairgowrie 173
Boylston 150
Bradbury 121
Bread of Life 369
Bryn Calfaria 364, 453
Bullinger 273

Caithness 52, 361
Cambridge 24
Campmeeting 111
Candler 529
Canonbury 80 (alt.), 195, 197
Canterbury 135, 311, 430, 530
Carol 390
Charlestown 426
Chautauqua, with Refrain 503
Childhood 525
Christ Arose, with Refrain 444
Christe sanctorum 504
Christ lag in Todesbanden 438
Christmas 249, 394 (alt.)
Christmas Song 380
Christus, der ist mein Leben 44, 178
Cleansing Fountain 115, 421
Clonmel 189
Close to Thee 176
Coming to the Cross 116
Commandments 307, 500
Complainer 398
Conditor alme 78
Consolation 264
Consolator 103
Converse 261
Cooling 290
Cormac 534
Coronation 71
Covenant Hymn 508
Cranham 376
Creation 43
Cushman 90
Cwm Rhondda 271, 470

Darwall's 148th 31 (alt.), 483
Davis 129
Dennis 53, 306, 336
Detroit 32
Deus tuorum militum 194
Diadem 72
Diademata 184, 250, 253 (alt.), 288, 455
Divinum mysterium 357
Dix 35, 397
Dominus regit me 67
Dort 480
Down Ampney 466

Du Friedensfürst, Herr Jesu Christ 491
Duke Street 14, 23, 351 (alt.), 472, 550
Dundee (French) 215, 302 (alt.), 313 (alt.), 325, 345
Dunfermline 57, 549

Easter Hymn 387
with Alleluias 439
Ebenezer 242, 460
Ein' feste Burg 20
Eisenach 46, 172
Elizabeth 97
Ellacombe 359, 423
Ellers 236
Ellesdie 251
Epworth Church 422
Ermuntre dich 373
Eucharistic Hymn 320
Euclid 280
Evan 68, 338, 368
Eventide 289
Every Day and Hour, with Refrain 226
Ewing 303

Faithful Guide 106
Far-Off Lands 85, 512
Federal Street 105, 118, 509 (alt.)
Festal Song 174
Field 203
Fillmore 527, 528, 529 (alt.)
Finlandia 209, 542
Flemming 144
Forest Green 33, 37, 381 (alt.), 456 (alt.), 476 (alt.)
Foundation 48
Franconia 141, 182, 276
French Carol 441
Friend 163

Galilee 107
Garton 375
Gelobt sei Gott, with Alleluias 449
Geneva 124 469, 475
Gerald 279
Germany 36, 160, 204, 351
Glenfinlas 791
Gloria, with Refrain 374
God Be with You 539
God Rest You Merry, with Refrain 378
Go Tell It on the Mountain 404
Gordon 166
Grace Church, Gananoque 240
Gräfenberg 134, 262, 340, 341, 367 (alt.), 461 (alt.), 485 (alt.)
Greensleeves, with Refrain 385
Grosser Gott 8

Halifax 456, 476
Hamburg, 435
Hankey, with Refrain 149
Hanover 409
Harlech 551
Haydn 258
He Leadeth Me, with Refrain 217
Hebron 128, 365, 471
Hendon 124
Hereford 362, 534 (alt.)
Hermas 452
Herr Jesu Christ, dich zu 347, 784
Herr Jesu Christ, mein's Lebens Licht 127, 337
Herzliebster Jesu 412
Hesperus 270, 541
High Popples 511
Hinman 86
Holiness 266
Horsley 218, 225
Hursley 254, 502
Hyfrydol 42 (alt.), 132, 283 (alt.), 331 (alt.), 360, 548
Hymn to Joy 38, 41, 440

I Am Thine, with Refrain 159
I Want to Be a Christian 286
Ich halte treulich still 253
In Babilone 69, 454
In dulci jubilo 391
Innocents 61
Irish 56, 282
Italian Hymn 3, 86 (alt.), 292, 352

Jacob's Ladder 287
Jam lucis 814
Jesu, meine Freude 220
Jesus Is Calling, with Refrain 110
Judas Maccabeus, with Refrain 450
Just as I Am 169

Keble 146, 152
Kedron 191
Kent 350
Kingdom 314
King's Lynn 484
Kings of Orient, with Refrain 402
King's Weston 76
Kirken den er et gammelt Hus 4 (alt.), 355
Kremser 59

Laban 246
Lacquiparle 40
Lancashire 342, 437, 478
Langran 269
Lasst uns erfreuen, with Alleluias 19, 60
Lauda anima 18, 66 (alt.)
Laudes Domini 91
Le p'ing 490
Lenox 100, 122
Leoni 30
Let Us Break Bread, with Refrain 330
Liebster Jesu 257, 370
Llanfair, with Alleluias 443
Llanfyllin 136, 231
Llangloffan 260, 419 (alt.), 482, 484 (alt.), 486
Lobe den Herren 55
Lobt Gott, ihr Christen 389, 510
Louvan 64
Lower Lights, with Refrain 148

Lux benigna 272
Lyons 473

Mainzer 139
Maitland 183
Malvern 98
Manoah 70 (alt.), 403
Marion, with Refrain 233
Martin, with Refrain 207
Martyn 126
Martyrdom 68 (alt.), 328, 415
Maryton 170, 462
Massachusetts 485
Materna 543
Meditation (Gower) 312
Meirionydd 200
Melcombe 499
Melita 407, 538
Mendebras 488
Mendelssohn, with Refrain 388
Mercy 135 (alt.), 494
Merrial 495
Message, with Refrain 410
Messiah 187
Miles' Lane 73
Millennium 31
Mit Freuden zart 4, 355 (alt.)
Morecambe 138
More Love to Thee 185
Morning Song 190, 481
Morning Star 400
Mornington 310, 492 (alt.)
Munich 167, 201, 372

Naomi 140, 268
National Hymn 406, 552
Near the Cross, with Refrain 433
Need, with Refrain 265
Nettleton 93
Nicaea 26
Nigeria 487
Norse Air 304, 524
Nun danket 49
Nun freut euch 58, 84
Nyland 230

O filii et filiae, with Alleluias 451
O Jesu 219
O store Gud, with Refrain 17
Old 100th 21, 22, 518, 809
Old 107th 468
Old 113th 9, 39
Oldbridge 523
Olive's Brow 431
Olivet 143
Open My Eyes, with Refrain 267
Orientis partibus 162
Ortonville 83

Park Street 25
Pass Me Not, with Refrain 145
Passion Chorale 418
Peek 156
Penitence 237
Penitentia 327
Pentecost 241
Perfect Love 333
Perry 321
Picardy 324
Pilot 247
Pisgah 142, 302
Pleading Savior 104
Pleyel's Hymn 300, 348
Precious Name, with Refrain 87
Promised Land 291
Promises, with Refrain 221
Puer nobis nascitur 515

Randolph 540
Rathbun 416
Ratisbon 401, 463
Redhead 76 113, 120 (alt.), 434
Regent Square 18 (alt.), 66, 298, 382
Rendez à Dieu 323
Rescue 175
Rest 235
Retreat 232
Richmond 1 (alt.), 12, 130
Rockingham (Mason) 206, 213, 329
Rock of Ages, with Refrain 11
Royal Oak, with Refrain 34
Russian Hymn 544

Sabbath 489
St. Agnes 82, 193, 225 (alt.), 516, 549 (alt.)
St. Anne 28, 54 (alt.), 308
St. Anthony's Chorale 6
St. Asaph 498
St. Bernard 75
St. Bride 51, 339, 465
St. Catherine 151, 259, 344, 529 (alt.)
St. Christopher 417
St. Denio 27
St. Dunstan's 155
St. Edmund 188
St. Elizabeth 79
St. Flavian 313
St. George's Windsor 522
St. Gertrude 452 (alt.)
with Refrain 305
St. Hilda 108
St. Kevin 446
St. Louis 381
St. Magnus 458
St. Margaret 234
St. Martin's 507
St. Matthew 457
St. Michael 16, 114, 277, 477, 810, 812
St. Michel's 171, 189 (alt.), 260 (alt.)
St. Peter 81, 192, 349, 520
St. Petersburg 89
St. Stephen 296, 353, 356
St. Thomas 5, 16 (alt.), 294, 310 (alt.), 492
St. Theodulph 424
Salzburg 295, 319
Sandon 47, 272 (alt.)
Sankey 514
Sarum, with Alleluias 537

Savannah 309, 790, 811
Schmücke dich 318
Schumann 181
Selena 420
Serenity 158
Seymour 94, 95 (alt.)
Shaddick 186, 252
Sheng En 317
Shepherds' Pipes 202
Shirleyn 123
Sicilian Mariners 165, 517
Sims 533
Sine nomine, with Alleluias 74, 536
Slane 256
Something for Jesus 177
Song 46 229
Southwell 284
Spanish Hymn 77
Sri Lampang 214, 322
Stand by Me 244
Stephanos 99
Stille Nacht 393
Stockton, with Refrain 101
Stories of Jesus 88
Stuttgart 63, 65, 334, 360 (alt.), 405, 496
Surette 408
Sweet Hour 275

Tallis' Canon 180, 216, 493
Tallis' Ordinal 316, 367, 411
Tantum ergo 546
Tempus adest floridum 395, 442
Terra beata 45
The First Noel, with Refrain 383
The King's Majesty 425
The Old Rugged Cross, with Refrain 228
The Rock of Refuge, with Refrain 245
The Solid Rock, with Refrain 222
Tidings, with Refrain 299
Toplady 120
Trentham 133
True Happiness 227
Truehearted, with Refrain 179
Truro 198, 346, 363, 445
Trust and Obey, with Refrain 223
Trust in Jesus, with Refrain 208
Tryggare kan ingen vara 521
Twenty-Fourth 533 (alt.), 789

Unser Herrscher 7, 13, 153

Vater unser 531
Venice 147
Veni Creator 467
Veni Emmanuel, with Refrain 354
Vesper Hymn 505
Vesper Hymn (Rendle) 506
Vicar 161
Victory, with Alleluia 447
Vom Himmel hoch 281
Vox dilecti 117

W̦ zlobie lezy 396
Wachet auf 366
Wachusett 96
Waits' Carol, with Alleluias 377
Walda 238
Wareham 29, 509
Warum sollt ich mich denn grämen 379
Webb 248
Wedlock 211
Welwyn 199, 371
Wentworth 50
Were You There 436
Wer nur den lieben Gott 210, 420 (alt.)
Wiant 519
Wie schön leuchtet der Morgenstern 399
Winchester New 102, 429
Winchester Old 54, 70, 131, 394
Windham 80
Windsor 414, 427 (alt.), 428
Wir pflügen, with Refrain 513
Wondrous Love 432
Woodworth 119
Words of Life, with Refrain 109
Wylde Green 62

Metrical Index

SM
(Short Meter 66.86.)
Boylston 150
Cambridge 24
Dennis 53, 306, 336
Festal Song 174
Franconia 141, 182, 276
Laban 246
Mornington 310, 492 (alt.)
St. Bride 51, 339, 465
St. Michael 16, 114, 277, 477, 810, 812
St. Thomas 5, 16 (alt.), 294, 310, (alt.), 492
Schumann 181
Southwell 284
Trentham 133
Venice 147

SM with Refrain
Marion 233

SMD
(Short Meter Double)
Bealoth 137
Diademata 184, 250, 253 (alt.), 288, 455
Ich halte treulich still 253
Terra beata 45

CM
(Common Meter 86.86.)
Amazing Grace 92
Antioch 392
Arlington 142 (alt.), 239, 335, 349 (alt.)
Armenia 196, 301
Ayrshire 157, 255
Azmon 1, 202 (alt.), 278
Ballerma 461, 535
Bangor 427
Caithness 52, 361
Campmeeting 111
Christmas 249, 394 (alt.)
Christus, der ist mein Leben 44, 178
Cooling 290
Coronation 71
Covenant Hymn 508
Detroit 32
Diadem 72
Dundee (French) 215, 302 (alt.), 313 (alt.), 325, 345
Dunfermline 57, 549
Epworth Church 422
Evan 68, 338, 368
Gräfenberg 134, 262, 340, 341, 367 (alt.), 461 (alt.), 485 (alt.)
Harlech 551
Horsley 218, 225
Irish 56, 282
Lobt Gott, ihr Christen 389, 510
Maitland 183
Manoah 70 (alt.), 403
Martyrdom 68 (alt.), 328, 415
Meditation (Gower) 312
Miles' Lane 73
Naomi 140, 268
Ortonville 83
Perry 321
Pisgah 142, 302
Richmond 1 (alt), 12, 130
St. Agnes 82, 193, 225 (alt.), 516, 549 (alt.)
St. Anne 28, 54 (alt.), 308
St. Bernard 75
St. Flavian 313
St. Magnus 458
St. Martin's 507
St. Peter 81, 192, 349, 520
St. Stephen 296, 353, 356
Salzburg 295, 319
Serenity 158
Shaddick 186, 252
Shirleyn 123
Tallis' Ordinal 316, 367, 411
Twenty-Fourth 533 (alt.), 789
Winchester Old 54, 70, 131, 394
Windsor 414, 427 (alt.), 428

CMD
(Common Meter Double)
All Saints New 419
Bethlehem 343
Carol 390
Cleansing Fountain 115, 421
Clonmel 189
Euclid 280
Forest Green 33, 37, 381 (alt.), 456 (alt.), 476 (alt.)
Gerald 279
Halifax 456, 476
High Popples 511
Llanfyllin 136
Llangloffan 260, 419 (alt.), 482, 484 (alt.)
Massachusetts 485
Materna 543
Norse Air 304
Old 107th 468
Promised Land 291
St. Matthew 457
St. Michel's 171, 189 (alt.), 260 (alt.)
Shepherds' Pipes 202
Sims 533
Vox dilecti 117

LM
(Long Meter 88.88.)
Abends 501
Canonbury 80 (alt.), 195, 197
Conditor alme 78
Deus tuorum militum 194
Duke Street 14, 23, 351 (alt.), 472, 550
Eisenach 172
Federal Street 105, 118, 509 (alt.)
Germany 36, 160, 204, 351
Grace Church, Gananoque 240
Hamburg 435
Hebron 128, 365, 471
Herr Jesu Christ, dich zu 347, 784
Herr Jesu Christ, mein's Lebens Licht 127, 337
Hesperus 270, 541
Hursley 254, 502
Jam lucis 814
Keble 146, 152
Kedron 191
Kent 350
Louvan 64
Mainzer 139
Malvern 98
Maryton 170, 462
Melcombe 499
Old 100th 21, 22, 518, 809
Olive's Brow 431
Park Street 25
Pentecost 241
Puer nobis nascitur 515
Retreat 232
Rockingham (Mason) 206, 213, 329
Tallis' Canon 180, 216, 493
The King's Majesty 425
Truro 198, 346, 363, 445
Tryggare kan ingen vara 521
Veni Creator 467

Vom Himmel hoch 281
Wareham 29, 509
Winchester New 102, 429
Windham 80
Woodworth 119

LM with Refrain
He Leadeth Me 217
The Solid Rock 222
Veni Emmanuel 354

LMD (Long Meter Double)
Candler 529
Creation 43
Sweet Hour 275

447.447.44447.
W̧ zlobie lezy 396

54.54.D.
Adelaide 154

55.55.D.
Le p'ing 490

55.65.65.65. with Refrain
Judas Maccabeus 450

568.558.
St. Elizabeth 79

64.64. with Refrain
Need 265

64.64.D.
Bread of Life 369

64.64.664.
More Love to Thee 185

64.64.6664.
Bethany 263
St. Edmund 188
Something for Jesus 177

65.55.65.
Binti Hamari 803

65.64. with Refrain
Christ Arose 444

65.65.
Glenfinlas 791
Merrial 495

65.65.D.
Hermas 452
Holiness 266
King's Weston 76
Penitence 237
St. Gertrude 452 (alt.)
Walda 238

65.65.D. with Refrain
St. Gertrude 305

65.65.666.5.
St. Dunstan's 155

6 5 10.D.
Rescue 175

664.6664.
America 547
Dort 480
Hinman 86
Italian Hymn 3, 86 (alt.), 292, 352
Olivet 143

665.665.786.
Jesu, meine Freude 220

66.66.D.
Munich 167
Spanish Hymn 77

666.666.
Laudes Domini 91

66.66.88.
Arthur's Seat 243
Author of Life 315
Darwall's 148th 31 (alt.), 483
Lenox 100, 122
Millennium 31

66.66.12 12.
Christmas Song 380

66.77.78.55.
In dulci jubilo 391

66.84.D.
Leoni 30

668.668.33.66.
Arnsberg 788

669.D.
True Happiness 227

669.D. with Refrain
Trust and Obey 223

6 6 11.D.
Down Ampney 466

67.67.
Garton 375

67.67.66.66.
Nun danket 49
Surette 408

76.76. with Refrain
Near the Cross 433
Royal Oak 34

76.76.D., Iambic
Angel's Story 164
Aurelia 211 (alt.), 231 (alt.), 297
Complainer 398
Ellacombe 359, 423
Ewing 303
Far-Off Lands 85, 512
King's Lynn 484
Lancashire 342, 437, 478
Llanfyllin 231
Meirionydd 200
Mendebras 488
Munich 201, 372
Nyland 230
Passion Chorale 418
St. Hilda 108
St. Theodulph 424
Webb 248
Wedlock 211

76.76.D., Trochaic
Ave virgo virginum 448
St. Kevin 446
Tempus adest floridum 395, 442

76.76.D. with Refrain
Hankey 149
Wir pflügen 513

76.76.77.76.
Amsterdam 15, 474
Barnabas 332

76.76.88.
Du Friedensfürst, Herr Jesu Christ 491

76.86.D.
Llangloffan 486

76.86.86.86.
St. Christopher 417

777.6.
Canterbury 311

77.77.
Aus der Tiefe 95
Canterbury 135, 430, 530
Coming to the Cross 116
Innocents 61
Mercy 135 (alt.), 494
Orientis partibus 162
Pleyel's Hymn 300, 348
Savannah 309, 790, 811
Seymour 94, 95 (alt.)
Wiant 519

77.77. with Alleluias
Easter Hymn 439
Llanfair 443

77.77. with Refrain
Gloria 374

77.77.D.
Aberystwyth 125, 358
Arfon 112

Arfon (Major) 464
Easter Hymn 387
Faithful Guide 106
Martyn 126
Messiah 187
Sabbath 489
St. George's Windsor 522

77.77.D. with Refrain
Mendelssohn 388

77.774. with Refrain
Chautauqua 503

77.77.57. with Refrain
Rock of Ages 11

77.77.64.
Vesper Hymn (Rendle) 506

77.77.7.
Hendon 124

77.77.77.
Arfon 463 (alt.)
Dix 35, 397
Pilot 247
Ratisbon 401, 463
Redhead 76 113, 120 (alt.), 434
Toplady 120
Unser Herrscher 153

78.78.77.
Grosser Gott 8

78.78.88.
Liebster Jesu 257, 370

79.79. with Refrain
Every Day and Hour 226

8336.D.
Warum sollt ich mich denn grämen 379

83.83.77.83.
Stand by Me 244

847.847.
Haydn 258

84.84.54.54.
Stories of Jesus 88

84.84.84.
Wentworth 50

84.84.888.4.
Ar hyd y nos 497

85.83.
Stephanos 99

85.85.
Bullinger 273

85.85. with Refrain
Pass Me Not 145

85.85.843.
Angel Voices 2

86.86. with Refrain
Martin 207
Stockton 101

86.86.66. with Refrain
Words of Life 109

86.86.76.86.
St. Louis 381

86.86.86.
Morning Song 190, 481

86.86.88.
O Jesu 219

86.886.
Rest 235

87.87.
Ach Gott und Herr 532
Alta Trinita beata 815
Charlestown 426
Close to Thee 176
Dominus regit me 67
Galilee 107
Kingdom 314
Rathbun 416
Sankey 514
Stuttgart 63, 65, 334, 360 (alt.), 405, 496

87.87., Iambic, with Refrain
Greensleeves 385

87.87.D., Iambic
Friend 163
Norse Air 524

87.87., Trochaic, with Refrain
Lower Lights 148
Precious Name 87
Trust in Jesus 208

87.87.D., Trochaic
All the Way 205
Austria 42, 293, 460 (alt.)
Autumn 331, 454 (alt.)
Beecher 283, 479
Converse 261
Ebenezer 242, 460
Ellesdie 251
Hyfrydol 42 (alt.), 132, 283 (alt.), 331 (alt.), 360, 548
Hymn to Joy 38, 41, 440
In Babilone 69, 454
Nettleton 93
St. Asaph 498

87.87.47.
Bryn Calfaria 364, 453
Wylde Green 62

87.87.66.667.
Ein' feste Burg 20

87.87.77.
Amen, Jesus han skal raade 274
Unser Herrscher 13

87.87.78.74.
Christ lag in Todesbanden 438

87.87.86.87.
Vesper Hymn 505

87.87.87.
Bradbury 121
Cwm Rhondda 271, 470
Lauda anima 18, 66 (alt.)
Picardy 324
Pleading Savior 104
Regent Square 18 (alt.), 66, 298, 382
Sicilian Mariners 165, 517
Tantum ergo 546
Unser Herrscher 7

87.87.887.
Aus tiefer Not 526
Divinum Mysterium 357
Kirken den er et gammelt Hus 4 (alt.), 355
Mit Freuden zart 4, 355 (alt.)
Nun freut euch 58, 84

87.87.88.77.
Ermuntre dich 373

88.44.6. with Refrain
Kings of Orient 402

88.44.88. with Alleluias
Lasst uns erfreuen 19, 60

886.D.
Allgütiger, mein Preisgesang 285
Ariel 168, 285 (alt.)
Old 113th 39

887.887.4.84.8.
Wie schön leuchtet der Morgenstern 399

888. with Alleluias
Gelobt sei Gott 449
O filii et filiae 451
Victory 447

888.4.
Oldbridge 523

888.5.
Childhood 525
Jacob's Ladder 287

888.6.
Flemming 144
Just as I Am 169

88.88. with Refrain
The Rock of Refuge 245

88.886.
St. Margaret 234

88.888. with Alleluias
Waits' Carol 377

88.88.88.
Eisenach 46
Fillmore 527, 528, 529 (alt.)
Melita 407, 538
St. Catherine 151, 259, 344, 529 (alt.)
St. Petersburg 89
Selena 420
Vater unser 531

888.888.
Old 113th 9

88.88.88.88.
Schmücke dich 318

88.98. with Refrain
Open My Eyes 267

98.89.
God Be with You 539
Randolph 540

98.98.
Commandments 307, 500
Eucharistic Hymn 320
Sheng En 317
Sri Lampang 322

98.98.88.
Wer nur den lieben Gott 210, 420 (alt.)

98.98.D.
Rendez à Dieu 323

9 10.9 9. with Refrain
Assurance 224

10 4.66.66.10 4.
All the World 10

10 4.10 4.10 10.
Lux benigna 272
Sandon 47, 272 (alt.)

10 7.10 7. with Refrain
I Am Thine 159

10 8.87. with Refrain
Message 410

10 8.10 7. with Refrain
Jesus Is Calling 110

10 8.10 8.
Sri Lampang 214

10.10.
Song 46 229

10 10. with Refrain
Let Us Break Bread 330

10 10.9 10.
Slane 256

10 10 10. with Alleluias
Sarum 537
Sine nomine 74, 536

10 10.10 6.
Wachusett 96

10 10.10 10.
Adoro te 326
Ellers 236
Eventide 289
Field 203
Langran 269
Morecambe 138
National Hymn 406, 552
Penitentia 327

10 10.10 10.10.
Geneva 124 475

10 10.10 10.10 10.
Finlandia 209

10 10.11 11.
Hanover 409
Lyons 473

11 8.11 8.
Davis 129

11 10.10 11.
French Carol 441

11 10.11 9.
Russian Hymn 544

11 10.11 10.
Ancient of Days 161 (alt.) 459
Consolation 264
Consolator 103
Cushman 90
Morning Star 400
Peek 156
Perfect Love 333
Vicar 161
Welwyn 199, 371

11 10.11 10. with Refrain
Tidings 299
Truehearted 179

11 10.11 10.10.
Geneva 124 469

11 10.11 10.11 10.
Finlandia 542

11 11 11.5.
Christe sanctorum 504
Herzliebster Jesu 412

11 11.11 9. with Refrain
Promises 221

11 11.11 11.
Adeste fideles 48 (alt.)
Away in a Manger 384
Foundation 48
Gordon 166
St. Denio 27

11 12.12 10.
Nicaea 26

12 9.12 9.
Wondrous Love 432

13 13.13 13.
Blairgowrie 173

14 14.478.
Lobe den Herren 55

15 15 15.6. with Refrain
Battle Hymn of the Republic 545

Irregular
Balm in Gilead 212
Beacon Hill 413
Cormac 534
Cranham 376
Elizabeth 97
Go Tell It on the Mountain 404
Hereford 362, 534 (alt.)
I Want to Be a Christian 286
Kremser 59
Lacquiparle 40
Nigeria 487
St. Anthony's Choral 6
Stille Nacht 393
Wachet auf 366
Were You There 436

Irregular with Refrain
Adeste fideles 386
God Rest You Merry 378
O store Gud 17
The First Noel 383
The Old Rugged Cross 228

Topical Index

ALL SAINTS DAY
Best be the dear uniting love 338
Blest be the tie that binds 306
Captain of Israel's host 46
Children of the heavenly Father 521
Children of the heavenly King 300
Come, let us join our friends above 302
Faith of our fathers 151
For all the saints 536, 537
For the might of thine arm 534
Give me the wings of faith 533
God of our life 47
Happy the souls to Jesus joined 535
Holy God, we praise thy name 8
Look, ye saints! The sight is glorious 453
March on, O soul, with strength 243
Now praise we great and famous men 532
O God, before whose altar 486
One holy Church of God appears 296
The Son of God goes forth to war 419
We come unto our fathers' God 58
See also: REFORMATION DAY

ANNIVERSARIES: LOCAL CHURCH
All people that on earth do dwell 21
All praise to our redeeming Lord 301
All things are thine 347
And are we yet alive 336
At thy feet, our God and Father 498
Blessed Jesus, at thy word 257
Blest be the tie that binds 306
Children of the heavenly King 300
Christ is made the sure foundation 298
Come, Christians, join to sing 77
Come, let us, who in Christ believe 111
Faith of our fathers 151
From all that dwell below the skies 14
Glorious things of thee are spoken 293
God be with you till we meet again 539, 540
God of our life 47
How are thy servants blest, O Lord 52
How blessed is this place 350
How lovely is thy dwelling place 295
I love thy kingdom, Lord 294
Now thank we all our God 49
O God, our help in ages past 28
O Lord, may church and home combine 520
One holy Church of God appears 296
Sing to the great Jehovah's praise 510
The Church's one foundation 297
We come unto our fathers' God 58

ASCENSION. *See* ENTHRONEMENT OF CHRIST

BENEDICTION
Be not dismayed 207
Blest be the dear uniting love 338
Blest be the tie that binds 306
Forth in thy name 152
God be with you till we meet again 539, 540
Lord, dismiss us with thy blessing 165
May the grace of Christ our Savior 334
Pour out thy spirit from on high 337
Savior, again to thy dear name 236
See also: CLOSING, nos. 813-815, and AMENS, nos. 816-825

BEREAVEMENT. *See* CONSOLATION

CALL TO WORSHIP
All praise to our redeeming Lord 301
At thy feet, our God and Father 498
Behold us, Lord, a little space 549
Blessed Jesus, at thy word 257
Father, we praise thee 504
How blessed is this place 350
Jesus, we look to thee 310
Jesus, we want to meet 487
Open now thy gates of beauty 13
Spirit divine, attend our prayers 461
See also: OPENING SENTENCES, nos. 773-791

CALMNESS
Be not dismayed (*God Will Take Care of You*) 207
Be still, my soul 209
Blest are the pure in heart 276
Christ, from whom all blessings flow 530
Come down, O Love divine 466
Come, ye disconsolate 103
Dear Lord and Father of mankind 235
Give to the winds thy fears 51
God of our life 47
Have thine own way, Lord 154
How gentle God's commands 53
I know not what the future hath 290
I look to thee in every need 219
If, on a quiet sea 147
If thou but suffer God to guide thee 210
Immortal Love, forever full 157, 158
In heavenly love abiding 230
Jesus, priceless treasure 220
Lead us, O Father 269
Lord, it belongs not to my care 218
O come, and dwell in me 277
Open my eyes, that I may see 267
Peace, perfect peace 229
Still, still with thee 264
Take the name of Jesus with you 87
Take time to be holy 266
This is my Father's world 45
Thou hidden source of calm repose 89

CANTICLES
All people that on earth do dwell 21
Before Jehovah's awful throne 22

Out of the depths I cry to thee 526
See also: CANTICLES listed in index no. 845

CHANGING YEAR

All beautiful the march of days 33
All praise to our redeeming Lord 301
All the way my Savior leads me 205
And are we yet alive 336
Be not dismayed (*God Will Take Care of You*) 207
Blow ye the trumpet, blow 100
Come, let us use the grace divine 507, 508
For all the blessings of the year 525
Forth in thy name 152
God be with you till we meet again 539, 540
God is love; his mercy brightens 63
God moves in a mysterious way 215
God of all power and truth and grace 281
God of love and God of power 153
God of our life 47
God of the ages, by whose hand 206
Great God, we sing that mighty hand 509
He leadeth me: O blessed thought 217
I know not what the future hath 290
I need thee every hour 265
If thou but suffer God to guide thee 210
Lead, kindly Light 272
My Jesus, as thou wilt 167
Ne'er forget God's daily care 519
O for a closer walk with God 268
O God, our help in ages past 28
O God, thou giver of all good 515
Sing to the great Jehovah's praise 510
Through all the changing scenes of life 56
Turn back, O man 475
When all thy mercies, O my God 70
When the storms of life are raging (*Stand by Me*) 244
Watchman, tell us of the night 358

CITIZENSHIP

Book of books, our people's strength 370
Break forth, O living light of God 356
Eternal God, whose power upholds 476
For the might of thine arm 534
From thee all skill and science flow 485
God of the ages, by whose hand 206
God send us men 191
Lift up our hearts, O King of kings 194
Now praise we great and famous men 532
O holy city, seen of John 481
O Master Workman of the race 171
O young and fearless Prophet 173
Once to every man and nation 242
Rise up, O men of God 174
Servant of all, to toil for man 186
The Lord will come and not be slow 468
The righteous ones 214
The voice of God is calling 200
These things shall be 198
This is my song 542

COLLEGES. *See* SCHOOLS

COMFORT. *See* CONSOLATION

CONFLICT. *See* COURAGE

CONSOLATION

A mighty fortress is our God 20
Art thou weary, art thou languid 99
Be not dismayed (*God Will Take Care of You*) 207
Be still, my soul 209
Come, Holy Ghost, our souls inspire 467
Come, ye disconsolate 103
Come, ye sinners, poor and needy 104
Fairest Lord Jesus 79
From every stormy wind that blows 232
Go to dark Gethsemane 434
God is my strong salvation 211
Holy Ghost, dispel our sadness 132
I know that my Redeemer lives 445
If thou but suffer God to guide thee 210
Immortal Love, forever full 157, 158
Jesus is all the world to me 97
O Love divine, that stooped to share 270
O Love that wilt not let me go 234
Peace, perfect peace 229
There is a balm in Gilead 212
Thou hidden source of calm repose 89

CONVERSION. *See* DECISION FOR CHRIST

CORNERSTONE

Christ is made the sure foundation 298
Glorious things of thee are spoken 293
God of the ages, by whose hand 206
How firm a foundation 48
My hope is built 222
O God, our help in ages past 28
O living Christ, chief cornerstone 349
On this stone now laid with prayer 348
The Church's one foundation 297
Thou, whose unmeasured temple stands 345
See also: DEDICATIONS: BUILDINGS

COURAGE

A mighty fortress is our God 20
Am I a soldier of the cross 239
Are ye able 413
Awake, my soul, stretch every nerve 249
Captain of Israel's host 46
Children of the heavenly King 300
Christian, dost thou see them 238
Fight the good fight 240, 241
For the might of thine arm 534
Give to the winds thy fears 51
God is my strong salvation 211
God of grace and God of glory 470
Have faith in God, my heart 141
He who would valiant be 155
How firm a foundation 48
I look to thee in every need 219
Jesus, my strength, my hope 253
Lead on, O King eternal 478
Make me a captive, Lord 184
March on, O soul, with strength 243
O for a faith that will not shrink 142
Onward, Christian soldiers 305
Rise up, O men of God 174
Stand up, stand up for Jesus 248
The man who once has found abode 216

Truehearted, wholehearted 179
We come unto our fathers' God 58
When the storms of life are raging (*Stand by Me*) 244

DECISION FOR CHRIST

Come, every soul by sin oppressed 101
Come, let us use the grace divine 507, 508
Come, let us, who in Christ believe 111
Come, sinners, to the gospel feast 102
Come, ye disconsolate 103
Come, ye sinners, poor and needy 104
Dear Master, in whose life I see 254
Depth of mercy 94
Father, I stretch my hands to thee 140
God calling yet! shall I not hear 105
Have thine own way, Lord 154
Heavenly Father, bless me now 95
I am coming to the cross 116
I am thine, O Lord 159
Jesus is tenderly calling 110
Jesus, the sinner's friend, to thee 118
Just as I am, thine own to be 169
Just as I am, without one plea 119
More love to thee, O Christ 185
O happy day, that fixed my choice 128
O Jesus, thou art standing 108
O Master, let me walk with thee 170
Savior, teach me, day by day 162
Savior, thy dying love 177
Sinners, turn: why will you die 112
Take my life, and let it be consecrated 187
We are climbing Jacob's ladder 287
When we walk with the Lord (*Trust and Obey*) 223

DEDICATIONS: BUILDINGS

All nature's works his praise declare 343
All things are thine 347
Christ is made the sure foundation 298
Come, O thou God of grace 352
God of grace and God of glory 471
Happy the home when God is there 516
How blessed is this place 350
Now praise we great and famous men 532
The Lord our God alone is strong 346
To bless the earth, God sendeth 512

DEVOTION

All praise to our redeeming Lord 301
All praise to thee, my God, this night 493
Be thou my Vision 256
Behold us, Lord, a little space 549
Children of the heavenly Father 521
Come down, O Love divine 466
Come, Holy Spirit, heavenly Dove 134
Come, my soul, thou must be waking 258
Draw thou my soul, O Christ 188
God, who touchest earth with beauty 273
Have thine own way, Lord 154
Holy Spirit, faithful guide 106
Holy Spirit, Truth divine 135
Immortal Love, forever full 157, 158
Jesus, I my cross have taken 251
Jesus, lover of my soul 125, 126
Jesus, priceless treasure 220
Jesus, the very thought of thee 82
Jesus, thou joy of loving hearts 329
Jesus, thy boundless love to me 259
Lord, I want to be a Christian 286
Lord Jesus, I love thee 166
More love to thee, O Christ 185
O for a heart to praise my God 282
O Holy Savior, friend unseen 144
O Lord my God (*How Great Thou Art*) 17
O Thou who camest from above 172
Spirit of God, descend upon my heart 138
Take time to be holy 266
The Lord's my Shepherd, I'll not want 63
Thou my everlasting portion (*Close to Thee*) 176
What shall I do my God to love 130
What shall I render to my God 196
What wondrous love is this 432

DOXOLOGIES

All praise to thee, my God, this night 493
Awake, my soul, and with the sun 180
Praise God, from whom all blessings flow 809
Sing we to our God above 811
To God the only wise 810
To God the Father 812
See also final stanzas of hymns 2, 3, 8, 19, 26, 49, 60, 180, 298, 349, 352, 357, 370, 443, 446, 448, 467, 490, 488, 492, 493, 504

ENTHRONEMENT OF CHRIST

All hail the power of Jesus' name 71, 72, 73
And have the bright immensities 456
Angel voices, ever singing 2
At the name of Jesus 76
Come, let us rise with Christ 457
Crown him with many crowns 455
Eternal Son, eternal Love 471
Hail, thou once despised Jesus 454
Look, ye saints! The sight is glorious 453
Rejoice, the Lord is King 483
The head that once was crowned 458

FAITH

A mighty fortress is our God 20
All the way my Savior leads me 205
And can it be that I should gain 527
Arise, my soul, arise 122
Ask ye what great thing I know 124
Author of faith, eternal Word 139
Blessed assurance, Jesus is mine 224
Come, O thou Traveler unknown 529
Faith of our fathers 151
Father, I stretch my hands to thee 140
God of the ages, by whose hand 206
Have faith in God, my heart 141
Jesus, my strength, my hope 253
My faith looks up to thee 143
My hope is built 222
O for a faith that will not shrink 142
Spirit of faith, come down 137
Strong Son of God, immortal love 146
The Church's one foundation 297
We believe in one true God 463

FAMILY. *See* HOME: CHRISTIAN

FELLOWSHIP

All praise to our redeeming Lord 301
Blest be the dear uniting love 338
Blest be the tie that binds 306
For all the saints 536, 537
Happy the souls to Jesus joined 535
In Christ there is no east or west 192
Jesus, Lord, we look to thee 309
Jesus, united by thy grace 193
Let us break bread together 330
O brother man, fold to thy heart 199

FUNERAL

A mighty fortress is our God 20
Abide with me 289
Ask ye what great thing I know 124
Breathe on me, Breath of God 133
Captain of Israel's host 46
For all the saints 536, 537
Give me the wings of faith 533
Give to the winds thy fears 51
Guide me, O thou great Jehovah 271
Happy the souls to Jesus joined 535
Holy Ghost, dispel our sadness 132
I know not what the future hath 290
I'll praise my Maker while I've breath 9
Jesus, priceless treasure 220
Jesus, Savior, pilot me 247
Lord, it belongs not to my care 218
O God, our help in ages past 28
O Love that wilt not let me go 234
Servant of God, well done 288
The Lord's my Shepherd, I'll not want 68
Thou hidden source of calm repose 89
Thine is the glory 450
Through all the changing scenes of life 56

GRACE

Amazing grace, how sweet the sound 92
Come, let us use the grace divine 507, 508
Come, let us, who in Christ believe 111
Come, ye that love the Lord 5
How happy every child of grace 115
Jesus, lover of my soul 125, 126
Lord, in the strength of grace 182
Majestic sweetness sits enthroned 83
May the grace of Christ our Savior 334
What grace, O Lord, and beauty shone 178
What shall I do my God to love 130
What shall I render to my God 196
What wondrous love is this 432

GRATITUDE. *See* THANKSGIVING

GRIEF. *See* CONSOLATION

GUIDANCE

All the way my Savior leads me 205
Captain of Israel's host 46
God of our fathers 552
God of the ages, by whose hand 206
Guide me, O thou great Jehovah 271
He leadeth me: O blessed thought 217
Holy Spirit, faithful guide 106
If thou but suffer God to guide thee 210
Jesus, Savior, pilot me 247
Lamp of our feet 368
Lead, kindly Light 272
Lead on, O King eternal 478
Lead us, O Father 269
Lord, guard and guide the men who fly 541
O God, beneath thy guiding hand 550
O Guide to every child 84
Safely through another week 489
Savior, like a shepherd lead us 121
We come unto our fathers' God 58

HARVEST

All beautiful the march of days 33
All things bright and beautiful 34
As men of old their first fruits brought 511
Come, ye thankful people, come 522
For all the blessings of the year 525
God of the earth, the sky, the sea 36
God, whose farm is all creation 514
Lord of the harvest, hear 339
Not alone for mighty empire 548
To bless the earth, God sendeth 512
To thee, O Lord, our hearts we raise 524
We give thee but thine own 181
We plow the fields 513

HOLY WEEK

Ah, holy Jesus 412
Alas! and did my Savior bleed 415
Alone thou goest forth 427
Ask ye what great thing I know 124
Behold the Savior of mankind 428
Beneath the cross of Jesus 417
By thy birth and by thy tears 113
Christ Jesus lay in death's strong bands 438
Cross of Jesus, cross of sorrow 426
Dear Master, in whose life I see 254
Go to dark Gethsemane 434
He who would valiant be 155
Heavenly Father, bless me now 95
I am coming to the cross 116
In the cross of Christ I glory 416
In the hour of trial 237
Jesus, keep me near the cross 433
Jesus, priceless treasure 220
Lord Christ, when first thou cam'st 355
Lord, I want to be a Christian 286
Lord Jesus, I love thee 166
Lord, whose love through humble service 479
Make me a captive, Lord 184
Must Jesus bear the cross alone 183
My faith looks up to thee 143
Never further than thy cross 430
O Jesus, thou art standing 108
O Love divine, that stooped to share 270
O Love divine, what hast thou done 420
O Love that wilt not let me go 234
O sacred Head, now wounded 418
O Son of God incarnate 85
O young and fearless Prophet 173
On a hill far away (*The Old Rugged Cross*) 228
Rock of Ages, cleft for me 120
Savior, thy dying love 177
Take time to be holy 266
Take up thy cross 160

There is a balm in Gilead 212
There is a fountain filled with blood 421
There is a green hill far away 414
'Tis finished! The Messiah dies 429
'Tis midnight, and on Olive's brow 431
Were you there 436
What grace, O Lord, and beauty shone 178
What wondrous love is this 432
When I survey the wondrous cross 435
With thine own pity, Savior 340

HOME: CHRISTIAN

All people that on earth do dwell 21
Away in a manger 384
Be present at our table, Lord 518
Be thou my Vision 256
Blest be the dear uniting love 338
Blest be the tie that binds 306
Book of books, our people's strength 370
Children of the heavenly Father 521
Faith of our fathers 151
For the beauty of the earth 35
God be with you till we meet again 539, 540
God of our life 47
Happy the home when God is there 516
I would be true 156
In Christ there is no east or west 192
Jesus, united by thy grace 193
Lord of life and King of glory 517
Men and children everywhere 11
Now thank we all our God 49
O God, thou giver of all good 515
O Lord, may church and home combine 520
O Son of Man, thou madest known 197

HOPE

As pants the hart for cooling streams 255
Come, let us, who in Christ believe 111
Give to the winds thy fears 51
God of our life 47
God of the ages, by whose hand 206
Have faith in God, my heart 141
Hope of the world 161
Jesus, my strength, my hope 253
Jesus, the very thought of thee 82
My hope is built 222
O God, our help in ages past 28

HUMILITY

Dear Lord and Father of mankind 235
Dear Master, in whose life I see 254
Father eternal, Ruler of creation 469
Holy Spirit, Truth divine 135
How are thy servants blest, O Lord 52
How beauteous were the marks 80
Jesus, Lord, we look to thee 309
Jesus, the very thought of thee 82
Just as I am, without one plea 119
O for a heart to praise my God 282
O Thou who camest from above 172
Out of the depths I cry to thee 526
Spirit of God, descend upon my heart 138
Thou hidden Love of God 531
When I survey the wondrous cross 435

JOY

All people that on earth do dwell 21
Come, Christians, join to sing 77
Good Christian men, rejoice and sing 449
Good Christian men, rejoice 391
Joyful, joyful, we adore thee 38
Let us with a gladsome mind 61
O happy day, that fixed my choice 128
O how happy are they 227
Rejoice, the Lord is King 483
Rejoice, ye pure in heart 233
We, thy people, praise thee 6
Ye watchers and ye holy ones 19

LABOR

As men of old their first fruits brought 511
Awake, awake to love and work 190
Forth in thy name 152
From thee all skill and science flow 485
God, whose farm is all creation 514
I sing the almighty power of God 37
O God, thou giver of all good 515
O Master Workman of the race 171
O Son of Man, thou madest known 197
Servant of all, to toil for man 186
We bear the strain of earthly care 202

LIGHT

Break forth, O living light of God 356
Brightly beams our Father's mercy 148
Christ is the world's true light 408
Christ, whose glory fills the skies 401
God of the earth, the sky, the sea 36
Light of the world, we hail thee 398
O God of light, thy Word, a lamp 371
O Love that wilt not let me go 234
O Morning Star, how fair and bright 399
Thou, whose almighty Word 480
Walk in the light 403

LOVE

Awake, awake to love and work 190
Behold the Savior of mankind 428
Beneath the cross of Jesus 417
Blest be the dear uniting love 338
Blest be the tie that binds 306
Come down, O Love divine 466
Come, Holy Spirit, heavenly Dove 134
Draw thou my soul, O Christ 188
Eternal Son, eternal Love 471
God is love, by him upholden 62
God is love; his mercy brightens 63
God of love and God of power 153
Holy Spirit, Truth divine 135
How beauteous were the marks 80
I love to tell the story 149
Immortal Love, forever full 157, 158
In heavenly love abiding 230
I've found a Friend 163
Jesus, lover of my soul 125, 126
Jesus, priceless treasure 220
Jesus, thine all-victorious love 278
Jesus, thou joy of loving hearts 329
Jesus, thy boundless love to me 259
Lord Jesus, I love thee 166

Lord, whose love through humble service 479
Love came down at Christmas 375
Love divine, all loves excelling 283
More love to thee, O Christ 185
New every morning is the love 499
O Jesus, thou art standing 108
O Lord of heaven and earth and sea 523
O Love divine, how sweet thou art 285
O Love divine, that stooped to share 270
O Love divine, what hast thou done 420
O Love that wilt not let me go 234
O perfect Love 333
O sacred Head, now wounded 418
O Son of God incarnate 85
O Thou who camest from above 172
Of the Father's love begotten 357
Savior, like a shepherd lead us 121
Savior, thy dying love 177
Strong Son of God, immortal love 146
The King of love my Shepherd is 67
Thou hidden Love of God 531
What shall I do my God to love 130
What wondrous love is this 432

LOYALTY

A charge to keep I have 150
Are ye able 413
Awake, awake to love and work 190
Awake, my soul, and with the sun 180
Awake, my soul, stretch every nerve 249
Come, let us use the grace divine 507, 508
Come, my soul, thou must be waking 258
Dear Master, in whose life I see 254
Fight the good fight 240, 241
Forth in thy name 152
God of grace and God of glory 470
God send us men 191
I would be true 156
In the hour of trial 237
Jesus calls us o'er the tumult 107
Jesus, I my cross have taken 251
Jesus, my strength, my hope 253
Just as I am, thine own to be 169
Make me a captive, Lord 184
March on, O soul, with strength 243
Must Jesus bear the cross alone 183
My soul, be on thy guard 246
O for a faith that will not shrink 142
O God, beneath thy guiding hand 550
O God of earth and altar 484
O Jesus, I have promised 164
O young and fearless Prophet 173
Servant of God, well done 288
Soldiers of Christ, arise 250
Stand up, stand up for Jesus 248
Take my life, and let it be consecrated 187
Take up thy cross 160
The righteous ones 214
The Son of God goes forth to war 419
The voice of God is calling 200
Truehearted, wholehearted 179
When we walk with the Lord (*Trust and Obey*) 223
What shall I render to my God 130

MEMORIAL DAY

Eternal Father, strong to save 538
Father eternal, Ruler of creation 469
For the might of thine arm 534
God of grace and God of glory 470
God of our fathers 552
God, the Omnipotent 544
Judge eternal, throned in splendor 546
Lord, while for all mankind we pray 551
Mine eyes have seen the glory 545
My country, 'tis of thee 547
Not alone for mighty empire 548
Now praise we great and famous men 532
O God of earth and altar 484
O Lord, our fathers oft have told 54
These things shall be 198
This is my song 542
Turn back, O man 475

NEW YEAR. *See* CHANGING YEAR

OFFERTORY

All things are thine 347
All things come of thee 807, 808
We give thee but thine own 181

ORDINATION

All praise to our redeeming Lord 301
Be thou my Vision 256
Come, Holy Ghost, our souls inspire 467
God be in my head 813
How are thy servants blest, O Lord 52
Let Zion's watchmen all awake 335
Pour out thy spirit from on high 337

PEACE, INNER. *See* CALMNESS

PURITY

Blest are the pure in heart 276
Breathe on me, Breath of God 133
God of all power and truth and grace 281
God, who touchest earth with beauty 273
Jesus, lover of my soul 125, 126
I would be true 156
O for a heart to praise my God 282
Rejoice, ye pure in heart 233

REDEMPTION. *See* SALVATION

REFORMATION DAY

A mighty fortress is our God 20
Author of faith, eternal Word 139
Blessed Jesus, at thy word 257
Break forth, O living light of God 356
Faith of our fathers 151
For all the saints 536, 537
God hath spoken by his prophets 460
God send us men 191
He who would valiant be 155
How can a sinner know 114
How firm a foundation 48
March on, O soul, with strength 243
Now praise we great and famous men 532
One holy Church of God appears 296
Soldiers of Christ, arise 250
Thanks to God whose Word was spoken 18
See also: ALL SAINTS DAY

RESPONSES

Before Scripture
Let thy word abide in us 796
O send out thy light 797
O Lord, open thou our eyes 798
Write these words 795

After Scripture
Glory be to God 800
Praise be to thee 801
Thanks be to thee 779

Before Prayer
God be merciful unto us 804
Lead me, Lord 802
Listen to our prayer 803
O Lord, show thy mercy upon us 805, 806
Talk with us, Lord 262

Offering
All things come of thee 807, 808

Closing
Father, give thy benediction 815
God be in my head 813
To Thee before the close of day 814

Amens
Briggs 823
Bourgeois 824
Copley 821
Danish 819
DeLamarter 822
Dresden 818
Greek 820
Single Amen 816, 817
Stainer 825

After Commandments
Lord, have mercy upon us (Tallis) 827

See also Service Music Index, no. 845.

RURAL LIFE

All beautiful the march of days 33
All creatures of our God and King 60
All things bright and beautiful 34
As men of old their first fruits brought 511
Come, ye thankful people, come 522
Father, we thank thee who hast planted 307
For the beauty of the earth 35
God of the earth, the sky, the sea 36
God, whose farm is all creation 514
Lord of the harvest, hear 339
My country, 'tis of thee 547
Ne'er forget God's daily care 519
Now the green blade riseth 441
O beautiful for spacious skies 543
O God, thou giver of all good 515
O Lord of heaven and earth and sea 523
Spring has now unwrapped the flowers 442
This is my Father's world 45
To bless the earth, God sendeth 512
We plow the fields 513
We thank thee, Lord 203

SALVATION

All praise to our redeeming Lord 301
Amazing grace! how sweet the sound 92
Ask ye what great thing I know 124
Blessed assurance, Jesus is mine 224
Christ for the world we sing 292
Christ, whose glory fills the skies 401
Come, let us, who in Christ believe 111
Come, sinners, to the gospel feast 102
Depth of mercy 94
Father, I stretch my hands to thee 140
God is my strong salvation 211
Hail, thou once despised Jesus 454
How are thy servants blest, O Lord 52
How can a sinner know 114
I've found a Friend 163
Jesus, my strength, my hope 253
Jesus! the name high over all 341
Jesus, thy blood and righteousness 127
O could I speak the matchless worth 168
O for a thousand tongues to sing 1
O happy day, that fixed my choice 128
O Zion, haste 299
Pass me not, O gentle Savior 145
Praise, my soul, the King of heaven 66
Rescue the perishing 175
Sinners, turn: why will you die 112
Walk in the light 403
We've a story to tell to the nations 410
What wondrous love is this 432
Where shall my wondering soul begin 528
With thine own pity, Savior 340
Ye servants of God 409

SCHOOLS

Come, Father, Son, and Holy Ghost 344
From thee all skill and science flow 485
God of love and God of power 153
God of the ages, by whose hand 206
Lord, whose love through humble service 479
Not alone for mighty empire 548
O Guide to every child 84
The Lord our God alone is strong 346

SCIENCE

Behold us, Lord, a little space 549
Book of books, our people's strength 370
Eternal God, whose power upholds 476
From thee all skill and science flow 485
O how glorious, full of wonder 41
O God, before whose altar 486
The Lord our God alone is strong 346

SOCIAL ACTION

Behold us, Lord, a little space 549
Christ for the world we sing 292
God of grace and God of glory 470
Let us break bread together 330
Lift up our hearts, O King of kings 194
Lord, whose love through humble service 479
O God of earth and altar 484
O thou eternal Christ of God 482
O young and fearless Prophet 173
Rise up, O men of God 174
The voice of God is calling 200
There's a voice in the wilderness crying 362
Turn back, O man 475
Where cross the crowded ways of life 204
With thine own pity, Savior 340

TEACHERS

Dear Master, in whose life I see 254
Father of mercies, in thy Word 367
Go, make of all disciples 342
Lord, speak to me 195

TEMPERANCE

I want a principle within 279, 280
I would be true 156
Just as I am, thine own to be 169
O Jesus, I have promised 164
Take my life, and let it be consecrated 187

TEMPTATION

Christian, dost thou see them 238
From every stormy wind that blows 232
Go to dark Gethsemane 434
He who would valiant be 155
I look to thee in every need 219
I need thee every hour 265
I want a principle within 279, 280
In the hour of trial 237
Lord Jesus, think on me 284
O for a faith that will not shrink 142
Take the name of Jesus with you 87
What a friend we have in Jesus 261
When the storms of life are raging (*Stand by Me*) 244

THANKSGIVING

All people that on earth do dwell 21
As men of old their first fruits brought 511
Be present at our table, Lord 518
Come, ye thankful people, come 522
For all the blessings of the year 525
For the beauty of the earth 35
From all that dwell below the skies 14
God of our fathers 552
God, whose farm is all creation 514
Let us with a gladsome mind 61
Many and great, O God 40
Ne'er forget God's daily care 519
Not alone for mighty empire 548
Now thank we all our God 49
O God, beneath thy guiding hand 550
O God, thou giver of all good 515
O Lord my God (*How Great Thou Art*) 17
O Lord of heaven and earth and sea 523
Praise to the Lord, the Almighty 55
Sing to the great Jehovah's praise 510
Thanks to God whose Word was spoken 18
To bless the earth, God sendeth 512
We plow the fields 513
We, thy people, praise thee 6
When all thy mercies, O my God 70
See also: HARVEST

TRINITY

Ancient of Days 459
Christ is made the sure foundation 298
Come, Father, Son, and Holy Ghost 344
Come, thou almighty King 3
Eternal Father, strong to save 538
Father, in whom we live 465
Holy God, we praise thy name 8
Holy, Holy, Holy! Lord God Almighty 26
Now thank we all our God 49
Thou, whose almighty Word 480
We believe in one true God 463
See also: DOXOLOGIES

TRUTH

Break thou the bread of life 369
Dear Master, in whose life I see 254
God is my strong salvation 211
Holy Spirit, Truth divine 135
I would be true 156
Lead us, O Father 269
Once to every man and nation 242
Open my eyes, that I may see 267
Thou art the Way: to thee alone 75

UNITY

At length there dawns the glorious day 189
Blest be the dear uniting love 338
Blest be the tie that binds 306
Break forth, O living light of God 356
Christ is the world's true light 408
Happy the souls to Jesus joined 535
In Christ there is no east or west 192
Jesus, united by thy grace 193
Let us break bread together 330
O God of earth and altar 484
O Spirit of the living God 136
One holy Church of God appears 296
The Church's one foundation 297
These things shall be 198

WATCH NIGHT. *See* CHANGING YEAR

WITNESS

Brightly beams our Father's mercy 148
Go, make of all disciples 342
Heralds of Christ 406
I love to tell the story 149
O Master, let me walk with thee 170
O Master of the waking world 407
O Thou who art the Shepherd 201
O Zion, haste 299
Rescue the perishing 175
We've a story to tell to the nations 410
With thine own pity, Savior 340

ZEAL

Am I a soldier of the cross 239
Awake, my soul, stretch every nerve 249
Fight the good fight 240, 241
For the might of thine arm 534
God of grace and God of glory 470
God send us men 191
He who would valiant be 155
March on, O soul, with strength 243
My soul, be on thy guard 246
Sing praise to God, who reigns above 4
Soldiers of Christ, arise 250
Stand up, stand up for Jesus 248
Truehearted, wholehearted 179

Index of Hymns by Classification

THE GOSPEL AND CHRISTIAN EXPERIENCE

The Praise of God

Adoration

Angel voices, ever singing 2
Come, thou almighty King 3
Come, ye that love the Lord 5
From all that dwell below the skies 14
Holy God, we praise thy name 8
I'll praise my Maker while I've breath 9
Let all the world in every corner sing 10
Men and children everywhere 11
O for a thousand tongues to sing 1
O Lord, my God! When I in awesome wonder (*How Great Thou Art*) 17
O Thou in all thy might so far 12
Open now thy gates of beauty 13
Praise the Lord who reigns above 15
See the morning sun ascending 7
Sing praise to God who reigns above 4
Stand up and bless the Lord 16
Thanks to God whose Word was spoken 18
We, thy people, praise thee 6
Ye watchers and ye holy ones 19
see also
Father, we praise thee 504

Majesty and Power

A mighty fortress is our God 20
All people that on earth do dwell 21
Before Jehovah's awful throne 22
Come, let us tune our loftiest song 23
Come, sound his praise abroad 24
Great God, attend, while Zion sings 25
Holy, holy, holy! Lord God Almighty 26
Immortal, invisible, God only wise 27
O God, our help in ages past 28
O splendor of God's glory bright 29
Praise to the living God 30
The Lord Jehovah reigns 31
The Lord our God is clothed with might 32
see also
Ancient of days 459
Come, O thou God of grace 352
Come, thou almighty King 3
O worship the King 473

Creation

All beautiful the march of days 33
All things bright and beautiful 34
For the beauty of the earth 35
God of the earth, the sky, the sea 36
I sing the almighty power of God 37
Joyful, joyful, we adore thee 38
Let all on earth their voices raise 39
Many and great, O God 40
O how glorious, full of wonder 41
O Lord, our Lord, in all the earth 44
Praise the Lord! ye heavens adore him 42
The spacious firmament on high 43
This is my Father's world 45
see also
All creatures of our God and King 60
Now thank we all our God 49

Providence

Captain of Israel's host 46
Give to the winds thy fears 51
God of our life 47
How are thy servants blest, O Lord 52
How firm a foundation 48
How gentle God's commands 53
My God, I thank thee 50
Now thank we all our God 49
O Lord, our fathers oft have told 54
Praise to the Lord, the Almighty 55
Through all the changing scenes of life 56
Unto the hills I lift mine eyes 57
We come unto our fathers' God 58
We gather together 59
see also
And are we yet alive 336
God of our fathers 552
God moves in a mysterious way 215
Sing to the great Jehovah's praise 510
The Lord's my Shepherd, I'll not want 68
To bless the earth, God sendeth 512

Love and Mercy

All creatures of our God and King 60
God is love, by him upholden 62
God is love; his mercy brightens 63
Let us with a gladsome mind 61
Lord of all being 64
O my soul, bless God the Father 65
Praise, my soul, the King of heaven 66
The King of love my Shepherd is 67
The Lord's my Shepherd, I'll not want 68
There's a wideness in God's mercy 69
When all thy mercies, O my God 70
see also
Children of the heavenly Father 521
Immortal Love, forever full 157, 158
Now thank we all our God 49

The Gospel of Jesus Christ

His Name and Glory

All hail the power of Jesus' name 71, 72, 73
All praise to thee, for thou, O King divine 74
At the name of Jesus 76
Come, Christians, join to sing 77
Creator of the stars of night 78
Fairest Lord Jesus 79
How beauteous were the marks 80
How sweet the name of Jesus sounds 81
Jesus, the very thought of thee 82
Majestic sweetness sits enthroned 83
O Guide to every child 84
O Son of God incarnate 85
Shepherd of eager youth 86
Take the name of Jesus with you 87
Tell me the stories of Jesus 88
Thou art the Way: to thee alone 75
Thou hidden source of calm repose 89
We would see Jesus 90
When morning gilds the skies 91
see also
Christ, whose glory fills the skies 401
Crown him with many crowns 455
Hail, thou once despised Jesus 454
I know not how that Bethlehem's babe 123
Jesus! the name high over all 341
O for a thousand tongues to sing 1
Ye servants of God 409

Mercy and Grace

Amazing grace! how sweet the sound 92
Come, thou Fount of every blessing 93
Depth of mercy 94
Heavenly Father, bless me now 95
I sought the Lord 96
Jesus is all the world to me 97
Jesus, where'er thy people meet 98

Call

Art thou weary, art thou languid 99
Blow ye the trumpet, blow 100
Come, every soul by sin oppressed (*Only Trust Him*) 101
Come, let us, who in Christ believe 111
Come, sinners, to the gospel feast 102
Come, ye disconsolate 103
Come, ye sinners, poor and needy 104
God calling yet! Shall I not hear 105
Holy Spirit, faithful guide 106
Jesus calls us o'er the tumult 107
Jesus is tenderly calling 110
O Jesus, thou art standing 108
Sing them over again to me (*Wonderful Words of Life*) 109
Sinners, turn: why will you die 112

see also

O Love divine, what hast thou done 420

Repentance and Forgiveness

By thy birth and by thy tears 113
How can a sinner know 114
How happy every child of grace 115
I am coming to the cross 116
I heard the voice of Jesus say 117
Jesus, the sinner's friend, to thee 118
Just as I am, without one plea 119
Rock of Ages, cleft for me 120
Savior, like a shepherd lead us 121

see also

Out of the depths I cry to thee 526

Atonement and Salvation

Arise, my soul, arise 122
Ask ye what great thing I know 124
I know not how that Bethlehem's babe 123
Jesus, lover of my soul 125, 126
Jesus, thy blood and righteousness 127
O happy day, that fixed my choice 128
O Thou, in whose presence 129
What shall I do my God to love 130

see also

The people that in darkness sat 361
Thou hidden source of calm repose 89
all hymns under *Aldersgate Sunday* (526-531)
all hymns under *Lenten Season* (412-436)

The Holy Spirit

Breathe on me, Breath of God 133
Come, Holy Ghost, our hearts inspire 131
Come, Holy Spirit, heavenly Dove 134
Holy Ghost, dispel our sadness 132
Holy Spirit, Truth divine 135
O Spirit of the living God 136
Spirit of faith, come down 137
Spirit of God, descend upon my heart 138

see also

all hymns under *Pentecost Season* (459-467)

The Christian Life

Faith and Regeneration

Author of faith, eternal Word 139
Father, I stretch my hands to thee 140
Have faith in God, my heart 141
If, on a quiet sea 147
My faith looks up to thee 143
O for a faith that will not shrink 142
O Holy Savior, friend unseen 144
Pass me not, O gentle Savior 145
Strong Son of God, immortal love 146

see also

Come, O thou Traveler unknown 529

Discipleship and Witness

A charge to keep I have 150
Brightly beams our Father's mercy (*Let the Lower Lights Be Burning*) 148
Faith of our fathers 151
Forth in thy name 152

God of love and God of power 153
Have thine own way, Lord 154
He who would valiant be 155
Hope of the world 161
I am thine, O Lord 159
I love to tell the story 149
Immortal Love, forever full 157, 158
I would be true 156
I've found a Friend 163
Just as I am, thine own to be 169
Lord, dismiss us with thy blessing 165
Lord Jesus, I love thee 166
My Jesus, as thou wilt 167
O could I speak the matchless worth 168
O Jesus, I have promised 164
O Master, let me walk with thee 170
O Master Workman of the race 171
O Thou who camest from above 172
O young and fearless Prophet 173
Rescue the perishing 175
Rise up, O men of God 174
Savior, teach me, day by day 162
Savior, thy dying love 177
Take up thy cross 160
Thou my everlasting portion (*Close to Thee*) 176
Truehearted, wholehearted 179
What grace, O Lord, and beauty shone 178

see also

Come, ye that love the Lord 5
Go, make of all disciples 342
How can a sinner know 114
Jesus! the name high over all 341
Lead on, O King eternal 478
O for a thousand tongues to sing 1
We've a story to tell to the nations 410
With thine own pity, Savior 340
Ye servants of God 409

Consecration and Stewardship

Awake, my soul, and with the sun 180
Draw thou my soul, O Christ 188
Lord, in the strength of grace 182
Make me a captive, Lord 184
More love to thee, O Christ 185
Must Jesus bear the cross alone 183
Servant of all, to toil for man 186
Take my life, and let it be consecrated 187
We give thee but thine own 181

see also

As men of old their first fruits brought 511
Awake, awake to love and work 190
O gracious Father of mankind 260

Brotherhood and Service

At length there dawns the glorious day 189
Awake, awake to love and work 190
God send us men 191
In Christ there is no east or west 192
Jesus, united by thy grace 193
Lift up our hearts, O King of kings 194
Lord, speak to me 195
O brother man, fold to thy heart 199
O Son of Man, thou madest known 197
O Thou who art the Shepherd 201
The voice of God is calling 200
These things shall be 198
We bear the strain of earthly care 202
We thank thee, Lord 203
What shall I render to my God 196
Where cross the crowded ways of life 204

see also

All praise to our redeeming Lord 301
O Zion, haste 299
all hymns under *Kingdomtide* (468-486)

Trust and Assurance

All the way my Savior leads me 205
Be not dismayed (*God Will Take Care of You*) 207
Be still, my soul 209
Blessed assurance, Jesus is mine 224
God is my strong salvation 211
God moves in a mysterious way 215

God of the ages, by whose hand 206
He leadeth me: O blessed thought 217
I look to thee in every need 219
If thou but suffer God to guide thee 210
Jesus, priceless treasure 220
Lord, it belongs not to my care 218
Mid all the traffic of the ways 225
My hope is built 222
O Thou, to whose all-searching sight 213
Savior, more than life to me 226
Standing on the promises 221
The man who once has found abode 216
The righteous ones 214
There is a balm in Gilead 212
'Tis so sweet to trust in Jesus 208
When we walk with the Lord (*Trust and Obey*) 223

see also

Give to the winds thy fears 51
God of our life 47
How firm a foundation 48
I know that my Redeemer lives 445
Rock of Ages, cleft for me 120

Hope, Joy, and Peace

Dear Lord and Father of mankind 235
From every stormy wind that blows 232
In heavenly love abiding 230
O how happy are they 227
O Love that wilt not let me go 234
On a hill far away (*The Old Rugged Cross*) 228
Peace, perfect peace 229
Rejoice, ye pure in heart 233
Savior, again to thy dear name 236
Sometimes a light surprises 231

see also

Out of the depths I cry to thee 526
The King of love my Shepherd is 67

Courage in Conflict

Am I a soldier of the cross 239
Awake, my soul, stretch every nerve 249
Christian, dost thou see them 238
Fight the good fight 240, 241
In the hour of trial 237
Jesus, I my cross have taken 251
Jesus, Savior, pilot me 247
March on, O soul, with strength 243
My soul, be on thy guard 246
O sometimes the shadows are deep (*The Rock That Is Higher Than I*) 245
Once to every man and nation 242
Soldiers of Christ, arise 250
Stand up, stand up for Jesus 248
When the storms of life are raging (*Stand by Me*) 244

see also

God is my strong salvation 211
He who would valiant be 155
Holy Spirit, faithful guide 106
O for a faith that will not shrink 142
The Son of God goes forth to war 419

Prayer and Aspiration

As pants the hart for cooling streams 255
Be thou my Vision 256
Blessed Jesus, at thy word 257
Come, my soul, thou must be waking 258
Dear Master, in whose life I see 254
God, who touchest earth with beauty 273
Guide me, O thou great Jehovah 271
I need thee every hour 265
Jesus, my strength, my hope 253
Jesus, thy boundless love to me 259
Lead, kindly Light 272
Lead us, O Father 269
Master, speak! thy servant heareth 274
Nearer, my God, to thee 263
O for a closer walk with God 268
O gracious Father of mankind 260

O Love divine, that stooped to share 270
Open my eyes, that I may see 267
Prayer is the soul's sincere desire 252
Still, still with thee 264
Sweet hour of prayer 275
Take time to be holy 266
Talk with us, Lord 262
What a friend we have in Jesus 261

see also

Blest are the pure in heart 276
Breathe on me, Breath of God 133
Holy Spirit, Truth divine 135
Jesus, where'er thy people meet 98
Mid all the traffic of the ways 225
Spirit of God, descend upon my heart 138

Christian Perfection

Blest are the pure in heart 276
God of all power and truth and grace 281
I want a principle within 279, 280
Jesus, thine all-victorious love 278
Lord, I want to be a Christian 286
Lord Jesus, think on me 284
Love divine, all loves excelling 283
O come, and dwell in me 277
O for a heart to praise my God 282
O Love divine, how sweet thou art 285
We are climbing Jacob's ladder 287

see also

And are we yet alive 336
I am coming to the cross 116
Lord, it belongs not to my care 218
O Thou who camest from above 172
Thou hidden Love of God 531
Walk in the light 403

Death and Life Eternal

Abide with me 289
I know not what the future hath 290
On Jordan's stormy banks I stand 291
Servant of God, well done 288

see also

For all the saints 536, 537
How firm a foundation 48
I'll praise my Maker while I've breath 9
Jerusalem the golden 303
O God, our help in ages past 28
Rise, my soul 474
Sing with all the sons of glory 440

THE CHURCH

Nature and Mission

Christ for the world we sing 292
Christ is made the sure foundation 298
Glorious things of thee are spoken 293
How lovely is thy dwelling place 295
I love thy kingdom, Lord 294
O Zion, haste 299
One holy Church of God appears 296
The Church's one foundation 297

see also

Break forth, O living light of God 356
Eternal God, whose power upholds 476
God of grace and God of glory 470
How blessed is this place 350
O Master of the waking world 407
O Spirit of the living God 136
O Word of God incarnate 372
We've a story to tell to the nations 410

Unity and Fellowship

All praise to our redeeming Lord 301
Blest be the tie that binds 306
Children of the heavenly King 300
Come, let us join our friends above 302
Father, we thank thee who has planted 307

Jerusalem the golden 303
Jesus, Lord, we look to thee 309
Jesus, we look to thee 310
Jesus, with thy Church abide 311
O Shepherd of the nameless fold 304
O where are kings and empires now 308
Onward, Christian soldiers 305

see also

Christ, from whom all blessings flow 530
For all the saints 536, 537
For the might of thine arm 534
Give me the wings of faith 533
God be with you 539, 540
Happy the souls to Jesus joined 535
In Christ there is no east or west 192
The day thou gavest, Lord 500
The Son of God goes forth to war 419
We come unto our fathers' God 58

Baptism

See Israel's gentle Shepherd stand 312

see also

Glorious things of thee are spoken 293
I love thy kingdom, Lord 294
Now thank we all our God 49
The Church's one foundation 297

The Lord's Supper

According to thy gracious word 316
Author of life divine 315
Be known to us in breaking bread 313
Beneath the forms of outward rite 321
Bread of the world 320, 322, 323
Deck thyself, my soul, with gladness 318
For the bread, which thou hast broken 314
Here, O my Lord, I see thee 326, 327
How happy are thy servants, Lord 328
In memory of the Savior's love 319
Jesus spreads his banner o'er us 331
Jesus, thou joy of loving hearts 329
Let all mortal flesh keep silence 324
Let us break bread together 330
O the depth of love divine 332
The bread of life, for all men broken 317
The King of heaven his table spreads 325

see also

Come, let us, who in Christ believe 111
Happy the souls to Jesus joined 535

Marriage

May the grace of Christ our Savior 334
O perfect Love 333

see also

Be thou my Vision 256
Blessed Jesus, at thy word 257
Christ, from whom all blessings flow 530
Christ is made the sure foundation 298
Come, let us, who in Christ believe 111
God is love, by him upholden 62
God of our life 47
Now thank we all our God 49
O Lord, may church and home combine 520
We, thy people, praise thee 6
Father, give thy benediction 815
The Lord's Prayer 826

Processionals or Recessionals

For the beauty of the earth 35
God is love; his mercy brightens 63
Joyful, joyful, we adore thee 38
Love divine, all loves excelling 283
Now thank we all our God 49
Praise, my soul, the King of heaven 66
Praise the Lord! ye heavens adore him 42
Praise to the Lord, the Almighty 55

The Ministry

And are we yet alive 336
Blest be the dear uniting love 338

Go, make of all disciples 342
Jesus! the name high over all 341
Let Zion's watchmen all awake 335
Lord of the harvest, hear 339
Pour out thy spirit from on high 337
With thine own pity, Savior 340
see also
A mighty fortress is our God 20
All praise to our redeeming Lord 301
Come, Holy Ghost, our souls inspire 467
Faith of our fathers 151
God of grace and God of glory 470
God of love and God of power 153
Here, O my Lord, I see thee 326, 327
Master, speak! thy servant heareth 274
O Thou who art the Shepherd 201
O Word of God incarnate 372
O young and fearless Prophet 173

Dedications

All nature's works his praise declare 343
All things are thine 347
Come, Father, Son, and Holy Ghost 344
Come, O thou God of grace 352
Eternal God and sovereign Lord 351
How blessed is this place 350
O living Christ, chief cornerstone 349
On this stone now laid with prayer 348
The Lord our God alone is strong 346
Thou, whose unmeasured temple stands 345

THE CHRISTIAN YEAR

Advent Season

Break forth, O living light of God 356
Come, thou long-expected Jesus 360
Hail to the Lord's Anointed 359
Lift up your heads, ye mighty gates 363
Lo, he comes with clouds descending 364
Lord Christ, when first thou cam'st 355
O come, O come, Emmanuel 354
Of the Father's love begotten 357
The heavens declare thy glory 365
The King shall come 353
The people that in darkness sat 361
There's a voice in the wilderness 362
Wake, awake, for night is flying 366
Watchman, tell us of the night 358
see also
As pants the hart 255
Come, thou almighty King 3
Joy to the world 392
Let all mortal flesh keep silence 324
Love divine, all loves excelling 283
O Son of God incarnate 85
Thanks to God whose Word 18

Holy Scripture

Book of books, our people's strength 370
Break thou the bread of life 369
Father of mercies, in thy Word 367
Lamp of our feet 368
O God of light, thy Word, a lamp 371
O Word of God incarnate 372

Christmastide

All my heart this night rejoices 379
Angels, from the realms of glory 382
Angels we have heard on high 374
Away in a manger 384
Break forth, O beauteous heavenly light 373
Gentle Mary laid her child 395
God rest you merry, gentlemen 378
Good Christian men, rejoice 391
Hark! the herald angels sing 387, 388
In Bethlehem neath starlit skies 377
In the bleak midwinter 376

Infant holy, infant lowly 396
It came upon the midnight clear 390
Joy to the world 392
Let all together praise our God 389
Love came down at Christmas 375
O come, all ye faithful 386
O little town of Bethlehem 381
Silent night, holy night 393
The first Noel 383
There's a song in the air 380
What child is this 385
While shepherds watched their flocks 394

see also

I know not how that Bethlehem's babe 123

Epiphany Season

As with gladness men of old 397
Brightest and best 400
Christ, whose glory fills the skies 401
Earth has many a noble city 405
Go, tell it on the mountain 404
Light of the world, we hail thee 398
O Morning Star, how fair and bright 399
Walk in the light 403
We three kings 402

see also

Fairest Lord Jesus 79
How beauteous were the marks 80
The heavens declare thy glory 365

Hymns on Missions

Christ is the world's true light 408
Heralds of Christ 406
O God, whose will is life 411
O Master of the waking world 407
We've a story to tell 410
Ye servants of God 409

see also

All praise to thee, for thou 74
Christ for the world we sing 292
Eternal God, whose power upholds 476
Jesus shall reign 472
O God of light, thy Word, a lamp 371
O Thou who art the Shepherd 201
O Zion, haste 299
The Lord will come and not be slow 468
Thou, whose almighty Word 480

Lenten Season

The Passion

Ah, holy Jesus 412
Alas! and did my Savior bleed 415
Are ye able 413
Beneath the cross of Jesus 417
In the cross of Christ I glory 416
O Love divine, what hast thou done 420
O sacred Head, now wounded 418
The Son of God goes forth to war 419
There is a fountain filled with blood 421
There is a green hill far away 414

see also

Lord Christ, when first thou cam'st 355
Take up thy cross 160
What grace, O Lord, and beauty 178

Palm Sunday

All glory, laud, and honor 424
Hosanna, loud hosanna 423
Ride on, ride on in majesty 425
So lowly doth the Savior ride 422

see also

Lift up your heads 363
O thou eternal Christ of God 482
Tell me the stories of Jesus 88

Holy Week

Alone thou goest forth 427
Behold the Savior of mankind 428
Cross of Jesus, cross of sorrow 426
Go to dark Gethsemane 434
Jesus, keep me near the cross 433
Never further than thy cross 430
'Tis finished! The Messiah dies 429
'Tis midnight, and on Olive's brow 431

Were you there 436
What wondrous love is this 432
When I survey the wondrous cross 435

see also

I know not how that Bethlehem's babe 123
O Love divine, what hast thou done 420

Eastertide

Easter

Christ Jesus lay in death's strong bands 438
Christ the Lord is risen today 439
Come, ye faithful, raise the strain 446, 448
Good Christian men, rejoice and sing 449
I know that my Redeemer lives 445
Jesus Christ is risen today 443
Low in the grave he lay (*Christ Arose*) 444
Now the green blade riseth 441
O sons and daughters, let us sing 451
Sing with all the sons of glory 440
Spring has now unwrapped the flowers 442
The day of resurrection 437
The strife is o'er, the battle done 447
Thine is the glory 450
Welcome, happy morning 452

see also

Ask ye what great thing I know 124
God is love, by him upholden 62
I know not how that Bethlehem's babe 123

Ascension and Enthronement

And have the bright immensities 456
Come, let us rise with Christ 457
Crown him with many crowns 455
Hail, thou once despised Jesus 454
Look, ye saints! The sight is glorious 453
The head that once was crowned 458

see also

All hail the power of Jesus' name 71, 72, 73
Jesus shall reign 472
Rejoice, the Lord is King 483

Pentecost Season

Ancient of Days 459
Come down, O Love divine 466
Come, Holy Ghost, our souls inspire 467
Father, in whom we live 465
God hath spoken by his prophets 460
See how great a flame aspires 464
Spirit divine, attend our prayers 461
Spirit of life, in this new dawn 462
We believe in one true God 463

see also

Christ is made the sure foundation 298
Holy, holy, holy 26
all hymns under *The Holy Spirit* (131-138)
all hymns under *Aldersgate Sunday* (526-531)

Kingdomtide

Eternal God, whose power upholds 476
Eternal Son, eternal Love 471
Father eternal, Ruler of creation 469
From thee all skill and science flow 485
God of grace and God of glory 470
Jesus shall reign 472
Lead on, O King eternal 478
Lord, whose love through humble service 479
O day of God, draw nigh 477
O God, before whose altar 486
O God of earth and altar 484
O holy city, seen of John 481
O thou eternal Christ of God 482
O worship the King 473
Rejoice, the Lord is King 483

Rise, my soul 474
The Lord will come and not be slow 468
Thou, whose almighty Word 480
Turn back, O man 475
see also
Christ is the world's true light 408
Come, thou almighty King 3
Forth in thy name 152
Joyful, joyful, we adore thee 38
Judge eternal, throned in splendor 546
O how glorious, full of wonder 41
O young and fearless Prophet 173
Praise to the Lord, the Almighty 55
Thanks to God whose Word 18
all hymns under *Brotherhood and Service* (189-204)

TIMES, SEASONS, OCCASIONS

The Lord's Day

Jesus, we want to meet 487
O day of rest and gladness 488
Safely through another week 489
see also
Come, let us tune our loftiest song 23
Come, sound his praise abroad 24

Morning and Evening

All praise to thee, my God, this night 493
At even, ere the sun was set 501
At thy feet, our God and Father 498
Day is dying in the west 503
Father, we praise thee 504
God, that madest earth 497
New every morning is the love 499
Now, on land and sea descending 505
Now the day is over 495
Rise to greet the sun 490
Savior, breathe an evening blessing 496
Softly now the light of day 494
Sun of my soul, thou Savior dear 502
The day is past and over 491
The day is slowly wending 506
The day thou gavest, Lord 500
We lift our hearts to thee 492
see also
Awake, my soul, and with the sun 180
Christ, whose glory fills the skies 401
Come, my soul, thou must be waking 258
O splendor of God's glory bright 29
See the morning sun ascending 7
Still, still with thee 264
When morning gilds the skies 91

Seasonal Hymns

The Changing Year and Covenant

Come, let us use the grace divine 507, 508
Great God, we sing that mighty hand 509
Sing to the great Jehovah's praise 510
see also
All beautiful the march of days 33
Faith of our fathers 151
Forth in thy name 152
Lord, in the strength of grace 182
O God, our help in ages past 28
O happy day 128
Truehearted, wholehearted 179

Rogation

As men of old their first fruits brought 511
God, whose farm is all creation 514
O God, thou giver of all good 515
To bless the earth, God sendeth 512
We plow the fields 513
see also
O Lord, our Lord, in all the earth 44

The Christian Home

Be present at our table, Lord 518
Children of the heavenly Father 521

Happy the home when God is there 516
Lord of life and King of glory 517
Ne'er forget God's daily care 519
O Lord, may church and home 520

see also

all hymns under *Marriage* (333-334)

Harvest and Thanksgiving

Come, ye thankful people, come 522
For all the blessings of the year 525
O Lord of heaven and earth and sea 523
To thee, O Lord, our hearts we raise 524

see also

Not alone for mighty empire 548
Now thank we all our God 49
We gather together 59
We plow the fields 513

Anniversaries

Aldersgate Sunday

And can it be that I should gain 527
Christ, from whom all blessings flow 530
Come, O thou Traveler unknown 529
Out of the depths I cry to thee 526
Thou hidden Love of God 531
Where shall my wondering soul begin 528

see also

How can a sinner know 114
Thou hidden source of calm repose 89
all hymns under *Pentecost Season* (459-467)

Reformation and All Saints

For all the saints 536, 537
For the might of thine arm 534
Give me the wings of faith 533
Happy the souls to Jesus joined 535
Now praise we great and famous men 532

see also

A mighty fortress is our God 20
Come, Christians, join to sing 77
O God, before whose altar 486
all hymns under *Nature and Mission* (292-299) and *Unity and Fellowship* (300-311)

Travel

Eternal Father, strong to save 538
God be with you 539, 540
Lord, guard and guide the men who fly 541

City, Nation, World

Behold us, Lord, a little space 549
God of our fathers 552
God the Omnipotent 544
Judge eternal, throned in splendor 546
Lord, while for all mankind 551
Mine eyes have seen the glory 545
My country, 'tis of thee 547
Not alone for mighty empire 548
O beautiful for spacious skies 543
O God, beneath thy guiding hand 550
This is my song 542

see also

Father eternal, Ruler of creation 469
God send us men 191
Hope of the world 161
O day of God, draw nigh 477
O God of earth and altar 484
O holy city, seen of John 481
Once to every man and nation 242
Where cross the crowded ways 204

Index of First Lines and Common Titles of Hymns

A charge to keep I have 150
A mighty fortress is our God 20
Abide with me; fast falls the eventide 289
According to thy gracious word 316
Ah, holy Jesus, how hast thou offended 412
Alas! and did my Savior bleed 415
All beautiful the march of days 33
All creatures of our God and King 60
All glory, laud, and honor 424
All hail the power of Jesus' name (CORONATION) 71
All hail the power of Jesus' name (DIADEM) 72
All hail the power of Jesus' name (MILES' LANE) 73
All my heart this night rejoices 379
All nature's works his praise declare 343
All people that on earth do dwell 21
All praise to our redeeming Lord 301
All praise to thee, for thou, O King divine 74
All praise to thee, my God, this night 493
All the way my Savior leads me 205
All things are thine; no gift have we 347
All things bright and beautiful 34
Alone thou goest forth, O Lord 427
Am I a soldier of the cross 239
Amazing grace! how sweet the sound 92
Ancient of Days, who sittest throned in glory 459
And are we yet alive 336
And can it be that I should gain 527
And have the bright immensities 456
Angels, from the realms of glory 382
Angel voices, ever singing 2
Angels we have heard on high 374
Are ye able, said the Master 413
Arise, my soul, arise 122
Art thou weary, art thou languid 99
As men of old their first fruits brought 511
As pants the hart for cooling streams 255
As with gladness men of old 397
Ask ye what great thing I know 124
At even, ere the sun was set 501

At length there dawns the glorious day 189
At the name of Jesus every knee shall bow 76
At thy feet, our God and Father 498
Author of faith, eternal Word 139
Author of life divine 315
Awake, awake to love and work 190
Awake, my soul, and with the sun 180
Awake, my soul, stretch every nerve 249
Away in a manger 384

Be known to us in breaking bread 313
Be not dismayed whate'er betide 207
Be present at our table, Lord 518
Be still, my soul: the Lord is on thy side 209
Be thou my Vision, O Lord of my heart 256
Before Jehovah's awful throne 22
Behold the Savior of mankind 428
Behold us, Lord, a little space 549
Beneath the cross of Jesus 417
Beneath the forms of outward rite 321
Blessed assurance, Jesus is mine 224
Blessed Jesus, at thy word 257
Blest are the pure in heart 276
Blest be the dear uniting love 338
Blest be the tie that binds 306
Blow ye the trumpet, blow 100
Book of books, our people's strength 370
Bread of the world in mercy broken (EUCHARISTIC HYMN) 320
Bread of the world in mercy broken (RENDEZ À DIEU) 323
Bread of the world in mercy broken (SRI LAMPANG) 322
Break forth, O beauteous heavenly light 373
Break forth, O living light of God 356
Break thou the bread of life 369
Breathe on me, Breath of God 133
Brightest and best of the sons of the morning 400
Brightly beams our Father's mercy 148
By thy birth and by thy tears 113

Captain of Israel's host, and guide 46
Children of the heavenly Father 521
Children of the heavenly King 300
Christ Arose 444
Christ for the world we sing 292
Christ, from whom all blessings flow 530
Christ is made the sure foundation 298
Christ is the world's true light 408
Christ Jesus lay in death's strong bands 438

Christ the Lord is risen today 439
Christ, whose glory fills the skies 401
Christian, dost thou see them 238
Close to Thee 176
Come, Christians, join to sing 77
Come down, O Love divine 466
Come, every soul by sin oppressed 101
Come, Father, Son, and Holy Ghost 344
Come, Holy Ghost, our hearts inspire 131
Come, Holy Ghost, our souls inspire 467
Come, Holy Spirit, heavenly Dove 134
Come, let us join our friends above 302
Come, let us rise with Christ our Head 457
Come, let us tune our loftiest song 23
Come, let us use the grace divine (COVENANT HYMN) 508
Come, let us use the grace divine (ST. MARTIN'S) 507
Come, let us, who in Christ believe 111
Come, my soul, thou must be waking 258
Come, O thou God of grace 352
Come, O thou Traveler unknown 529
Come, sinners, to the gospel feast 102
Come, sound his praise abroad 24
Come, thou almighty King 3
Come, thou Fount of every blessing 93
Come, thou long-expected Jesus 360
Come, ye disconsolate, where'er ye languish 103
Come, ye faithful, raise the strain (AVE VIRGO VIRGINUM) 448
Come, ye faithful, raise the strain (ST. KEVIN) 446
Come, ye sinners, poor and needy 104
Come, ye thankful people, come 522
Come, ye that love the Lord 5
Creator of the stars of night 78
Cross of Jesus, cross of sorrow 426
Crown him with many crowns 455

Day is dying in the west 503
Dear Lord and Father of mankind 235
Dear Master, in whose life I see 254
Deck thyself, my soul, with gladness 318
Depth of mercy! can there be 94
Draw thou my soul, O Christ 188

Earth has many a noble city 405
Eternal Father, strong to save 538
Eternal God and sovereign Lord 351
Eternal God, whose power upholds 476
Eternal Son, eternal Love 471

Fairest Lord Jesus, Ruler of all nature 79
Faith of our fathers! living still 151
Father eternal, Ruler of creation 469
Father, in whom we live 465
Father, I stretch my hands to thee 140
Father of mercies, in thy Word 367
Father, we praise thee, now the night is over 504
Father, we thank thee who has planted 307
Fight the good fight with all thy might (GRACE CHURCH, GANANOQUE) 240
Fight the good fight with all thy might (PENTECOST) 241
For all the blessings of the year 525
For all the saints, who from their labors rest (SARUM) 537
For all the saints, who from their labors rest (SINE NOMINE) 536
For the beauty of the earth 35
For the bread, which thou hast broken 314
For the might of thine arm we bless thee 534
Forth in thy name, O Lord, I go 152
From all that dwell below the skies 14
From every stormy wind that blows 232
From thee all skill and science flow 485

Gentle Mary laid her child lowly in a manger 395
Give me the wings of faith 533
Give to the winds thy fears 51
Glorious things of thee are spoken 293
Go, make of all disciples 342
Go, tell it on the mountain 404
Go to dark Gethsemane 434
God be with you till we meet again (GOD BE WITH YOU) 539
God be with you till we meet again (RANDOLPH) 540
God calling yet! Shall I not hear 105
God hath spoken by his prophets 460
God is love, by him upholden 62
God is love; his mercy brightens 63
God is my strong salvation 211
God moves in a mysterious way 215
God of all power and truth and grace 281
God of grace and God of glory 470
God of love and God of power 153
God of our fathers, whose almighty hand 552
God of our life, through all the circling years 47
God of the ages, by whose hand 206
God of the earth, the sky, the sea 36
God rest you merry, gentlemen 378
God send us men, whose aim 'twill be 191
God, that madest earth and heaven 497
God the Omnipotent! King, who ordainest 544

God, who touchest earth with beauty 273
God, whose farm is all creation 514
God Will Take Care of You 207
Good Christian men, rejoice and sing 449
Good Christian men, rejoice, with heart 391
Great God, attend, while Zion sings 25
Great God, we sing that mighty hand 509
Guide me, O thou great Jehovah 271

Hail, thou once despised Jesus 454
Hail to the Lord's Anointed 359
Happy the home when God is there 516
Happy the souls to Jesus joined 535
Hark! the herald angels sing (EASTER HYMN) 387
Hark! the herald angels sing (MENDELSSOHN) 388
Have faith in God, my heart 141
Have thine own way, Lord 154
He leadeth me: O blessed thought 217
He who would valiant be 155
Heavenly Father, bless me now 95
Heralds of Christ, who bear the King's commands 406
Here, O my Lord, I see thee face to face (ADORO TE) 326
Here, O my Lord, I see thee face to face (PENITENTIA) 327
Holy Ghost, dispel our sadness 132
Holy God, we praise thy name 8
Holy, holy, holy! Lord God Almighty 26
Holy Spirit, faithful guide 106
Holy Spirit, Truth divine 135
Hope of the world 161
Hosanna, loud hosanna 423
How are thy servants blest, O Lord 52
How beauteous were the marks divine 80
How blessed is this place, O Lord 350
How can a sinner know 114
How firm a foundation, ye saints of the Lord 48
How gentle God's commands 53
How Great Thou Art 17
How happy are thy servants, Lord 328
How happy every child of grace 115
How lovely is thy dwelling place 295
How sweet the name of Jesus sounds 81

I am coming to the cross 116
I am thine, O Lord, I have heard thy voice 159
I heard the voice of Jesus say 117
I know not how that Bethlehem's babe 123
I know not what the future hath 290

I know that my Redeemer lives 445
I look to thee in every need 219
I love thy kingdom, Lord 294
I love to tell the story 149
I need thee every hour 265
I sing the almighty power of God 37
I sought the Lord, and afterward I knew 96
I want a principle within (EUCLID) 280
I want a principle within (GERALD) 279
I would be true 156
If, on a quiet sea 147
If thou but suffer God to guide thee 210
I'll praise my Maker while I've breath 9
Immortal, invisible, God only wise 27
Immortal Love, forever full (AYRSHIRE) 157
Immortal Love, forever full (SERENITY) 158
In Bethlehem neath starlit skies 377
In Christ there is no east or west 192
In heavenly love abiding 230
In memory of the Savior's love 319
In the bleak midwinter 376
In the cross of Christ I glory 416
In the hour of trial 237
Infant holy, infant lowly 396
It came upon the midnight clear 390
I've found a Friend, O such a Friend 163

Jerusalem the golden 303
Jesus calls us o'er the tumult 107
Jesus Christ is risen today 443
Jesus, I my cross have taken 251
Jesus is all the world to me 97
Jesus is tenderly calling thee home 110
Jesus, keep me near the cross 433
Jesus, Lord, we look to thee 309
Jesus, lover of my soul (ABERYSTWYTH) 125
Jesus, lover of my soul (MARTYN) 126
Jesus, my strength, my hope 253
Jesus, priceless treasure 220
Jesus, Savior, pilot me 247
Jesus shall reign where'er the sun 472
Jesus spreads his banner o'er us 331
Jesus! the name high over all 341
Jesus, the sinner's friend, to thee 118
Jesus, the very thought of thee 82
Jesus, thine all-victorious love 278
Jesus, thou joy of loving hearts 329

Jesus, thy blood and righteousness 127
Jesus, thy boundless love to me 259
Jesus, united by thy grace 193
Jesus, we look to thee 310
Jesus, we want to meet on this thy holy day 487
Jesus, where'er thy people meet 98
Jesus, with thy Church abide 311
Joy to the world! the Lord is come 392
Joyful, joyful, we adore thee 38
Judge eternal, throned in splendor 546
Just as I am, thine own to be 169
Just as I am, without one plea 119

Lamp of our feet, whereby we trace 368
Lead, kindly Light, amid th'encircling gloom 272
Lead on, O King eternal 478
Lead us, O Father, in the paths of peace 269
Let all mortal flesh keep silence 324
Let all on earth their voices raise 39
Let all the world in every corner sing 10
Let all together praise our God 389
Let the Lower Lights Be Burning 148
Let us break bread together on our knees 330
Let us with a gladsome mind 61
Let Zion's watchmen all awake 335
Lift up our hearts, O King of kings 194
Lift up your heads, ye mighty gates 363
Light of the world, we hail thee 398
Lo, he comes with clouds descending 364
Look, ye saints! The sight is glorious 453
Lord Christ, when first thou cam'st to men 355
Lord, dismiss us with thy blessing 165
Lord, guard and guide the men who fly 541
Lord, I want to be a Christian in my heart 286
Lord, in the strength of grace 182
Lord, it belongs not to my care 218
Lord Jesus, I love thee 166
Lord Jesus, think on me 284
Lord of all being, throned afar 64
Lord of life and King of glory 517
Lord of the harvest, hear 339
Lord, speak to me, that I may speak 195
Lord, while for all mankind we pray 551
Lord, whose love through humble service 479
Love came down at Christmas 375
Love divine, all loves excelling 283
Low in the grave he lay 444

Majestic sweetness sits enthroned 83
Make me a captive, Lord 184
Many and great, O God, are thy things 40
March on, O soul, with strength 243
Master, speak! thy servant heareth 274
May the grace of Christ our Savior 334
Men and children everywhere 11
Mid all the traffic of the ways 225
Mine eyes have seen the glory 545
More love to thee, O Christ 185
Must Jesus bear the cross alone 183
My country, 'tis of thee 547
My faith looks up to thee 143
My God, I thank thee, who hast made the earth 50
My hope is built on nothing less 222
My Jesus, as thou wilt 167
My soul, be on thy guard 246

Nearer, my God, to thee 263
Ne'er forget God's daily care 519
Never further than thy cross 430
New every morning is the love 499
Not alone for mighty empire 548
Now, on land and sea descending 505
Now praise we great and famous men 532
Now thank we all our God 49
Now the day is over 495
Now the green blade riseth from the buried grain 441

O beautiful for spacious skies 543
O brother man, fold to thy heart thy brother 199
O come, all ye faithful 386
O come, and dwell in me 277
O come, O come, Emmanuel 354
O could I speak the matchless worth 168
O day of God, draw nigh 477
O day of rest and gladness 488
O for a closer walk with God 268
O for a faith that will not shrink 142
O for a heart to praise my God 282
O for a thousand tongues to sing 1
O God, before whose altar 486
O God, beneath thy guiding hand 550
O God of earth and altar 484
O God of light, thy Word, a lamp unfailing 371
O God, our help in ages past 28
O God, thou giver of all good 515

O God, whose will is life and good ... 411
O gracious Father of mankind ... 260
O Guide to every child of thine ... 84
O happy day, that fixed my choice ... 128
O holy city, seen of John ... 481
O Holy Savior, friend unseen ... 144
O how glorious, full of wonder ... 41
O how happy are they who the Savior obey ... 227
O Jesus, I have promised ... 164
O Jesus, thou art standing ... 108
O little town of Bethlehem ... 381
O living Christ, chief cornerstone ... 349
O Lord, may church and home combine ... 520
O Lord my God! When I in awesome wonder ... 17
O Lord of heaven and earth and sea ... 523
O Lord, our fathers oft have told ... 54
O Lord, our Lord, in all the earth ... 44
O Love divine, how sweet thou art ... 285
O Love divine, that stooped to share ... 270
O Love divine, what hast thou done ... 420
O Love that wilt not let me go ... 234
O Master, let me walk with thee ... 170
O Master of the waking world ... 407
O Master Workman of the race ... 171
O Morning Star, how fair and bright ... 399
O my soul, bless God the Father ... 65
O perfect Love, all human thought transcending ... 333
O sacred Head, now wounded ... 418
O Shepherd of the nameless fold ... 304
O sometimes the shadows are deep ... 245
O Son of God incarnate ... 85
O Son of Man, thou madest known ... 197
O sons and daughters, let us sing ... 451
O Spirit of the living God ... 136
O splendor of God's glory bright ... 29
O the depth of love divine ... 332
O thou eternal Christ of God ... 482
O Thou in all thy might so far ... 12
O Thou, in whose presence my soul takes delight ... 129
O Thou, to whose all-searching sight ... 213
O Thou who art the Shepherd ... 201
O Thou who camest from above ... 172
O where are kings and empires now ... 308
O Word of God incarnate ... 372
O worship the King, all glorious above ... 473
O young and fearless Prophet of ancient Galilee ... 173
O Zion, haste, thy mission high fulfilling ... 299

Of the Father's love begotten 357
On a hill far away stood an old rugged cross 228
On Jordan's stormy banks I stand 291
On this stone now laid with prayer 348
Once to every man and nation 242
One holy Church of God appears 296
Only Trust Him 101
Onward, Christian soldiers 305
Open my eyes, that I may see 267
Open now thy gates of beauty 13
Out of the depths I cry to thee 526

Pass me not, O gentle Savior 145
Peace, perfect peace, in this dark world of sin 229
Pour out thy spirit from on high 337
Praise, my soul, the King of heaven 66
Praise the Lord who reigns above 15
Praise the Lord! ye heavens adore him 42
Praise to the living God 30
Praise to the Lord, the Almighty 55
Prayer is the soul's sincere desire 252

Rejoice, the Lord is King 483
Rejoice, ye pure in heart 233
Rescue the perishing, care for the dying 175
Ride on, ride on in majesty 425
Rise, my soul, and stretch thy wings 474
Rise to greet the sun 490
Rise up, O men of God 174
Rock of Ages, cleft for me 120

Safely through another week 489
Savior, again to thy dear name we raise 236
Savior, breathe an evening blessing 496
Savior, like a shepherd lead us 121
Savior, more than life to me 226
Savior, teach me, day by day 162
Savior, thy dying love 177
See how great a flame aspires 464
See Israel's gentle Shepherd stand 312
See the morning sun ascending 7
Servant of all, to toil for man 186
Servant of God, well done 288
Shepherd of eager youth 86
Silent night, holy night 393
Sing praise to God who reigns above 4
Sing them over again to me 109

Sing to the great Jehovah's praise 510
Sing with all the sons of glory 440
Sinners, turn: why will you die 112
So lowly doth the Savior ride 422
Softly now the light of day 494
Soldiers of Christ, arise 250
Sometimes a light surprises 231
Spirit divine, attend our prayers 461
Spirit of faith, come down 137
Spirit of God, descend upon my heart 138
Spirit of life, in this new dawn 462
Spring has now unwrapped the flowers 442
Stand by Me 244
Stand up and bless the Lord 16
Stand up, stand up for Jesus 248
Standing on the promises of Christ my King 221
Still, still with thee, when purple morning breaketh 264
Strong Son of God, immortal love 146
Sun of my soul, thou Savior dear 502
Sweet hour of prayer 275

Take my life, and let it be consecrated 187
Take the name of Jesus with you 87
Take time to be holy 266
Take up thy cross, the Savior said 160
Talk with us, Lord, thyself reveal 262
Tell me the stories of Jesus 88
Thanks to God whose Word was spoken 18
The bread of life, for all men broken 317
The Church's one foundation 297
The day is past and over 491
The day is slowly wending 506
The day of resurrection 437
The day thou gavest, Lord, is ended 500
The first Noel, the angel did say 383
The head that once was crowned with thorns 458
The heavens declare thy glory, Lord 365
The King of heaven his table spreads 325
The King of love my Shepherd is 67
The King shall come when morning dawns 353
The Lord Jehovah reigns 31
The Lord our God alone is strong 346
The Lord our God is clothed with might 32
The Lord will come and not be slow 468
The Lord's my Shepherd, I'll not want 68
The man who once has found abode 216
The Old Rugged Cross 228

The people that in darkness sat 361
The righteous ones shall be forever blest 214
The Rock That Is Higher Than I 245
The Son of God goes forth to war 419
The spacious firmament on high 43
The strife is o'er, the battle done 447
The voice of God is calling 200
There is a balm in Gilead 212
There is a fountain filled with blood 421
There is a green hill far away 414
There's a song in the air 380
There's a voice in the wilderness crying 362
There's a wideness in God's mercy 69
These things shall be: a loftier race 198
Thine is the glory 450
This is my Father's world 45
This is my song, O God of all the nations 542
Thou art the Way: to thee alone 75
Thou hidden Love of God, whose height 531
Thou hidden source of calm repose 89
Thou my everlasting portion 176
Thou, whose almighty Word 480
Thou, whose unmeasured temple stands 345
Through all the changing scenes of life 56
'Tis finished! The Messiah dies 429
'Tis midnight, and on Olive's brow 431
'Tis so sweet to trust in Jesus 208
To bless the earth, God sendeth 512
To thee, O Lord, our hearts we raise 524
Truehearted, wholehearted, faithful and loyal 179
Trust and Obey 223
Turn back, O man, forswear thy foolish ways 475

Unto the hills I lift mine eyes 57

Wake, awake, for night is flying 366
Walk in the light! so shalt thou know 403
Watchman, tell us of the night 358
We are climbing Jacob's ladder 287
We bear the strain of earthly care 202
We believe in one true God 463
We come unto our fathers' God 58
We gather together to ask the Lord's blessing 59
We give thee but thine own 181
We lift our hearts to thee 492
We May Not Climb the Heavenly Steeps .... 157 & 158
We plow the fields and scatter the good seed 513

We thank thee, Lord, thy paths of service 203
We three kings of Orient 402
We, thy people, praise thee 6
We would see Jesus; lo! his star is shining 90
Welcome, happy morning 452
Were you there when they crucified my Lord 436
We've a story to tell to the nations 410
What a friend we have in Jesus 261
What child is this, who laid to rest 385
What grace, O Lord, and beauty shone 178
What shall I do my God to love 130
What shall I render to my God 196
What wondrous love is this 432
When all thy mercies, O my God 70
When I survey the wondrous cross 435
When morning gilds the skies 91
When the storms of life are raging 244
When we walk with the Lord 223
Where cross the crowded ways of life 204
Where shall my wondering soul begin 528
While shepherds watched their flocks by night 394
With thine own pity, Savior, see 340
Wonderful Words of Life 109

Ye servants of God, your Master proclaim 409
Ye watchers and ye holy ones 19